Elijah B. Huntington

A Genealogical Memoir of the Huntington Family in this Country

Embracing all the known descendants of Simon and Margaret Huntington, who have retained the family name

Elijah B. Huntington

A Genealogical Memoir of the Huntington Family in this Country
Embracing all the known descendants of Simon and Margaret Huntington, who have retained the family name

ISBN/EAN: 9783337219840

Printed in Europe, USA, Canada, Australia, Japan

Cover: Foto ©ninafisch / pixelio.de

More available books at **www.hansebooks.com**

A

GENEALOGICAL MEMOIR

OF THE

HUNTINGTON FAMILY

IN THIS COUNTRY:

EMBRACING

ALL THE KNOWN DESCENDANTS

OF

SIMON AND MARGARET HUNTINGTON,

WHO HAVE RETAINED THE FAMILY NAME,

AND

THE FIRST GENERATION OF THE DESCENDANTS OF OTHER NAMES.

BY REV. E. B. HUNTINGTON, A. M.

STAMFORD, CONN.:
PUBLISHED BY THE AUTHOR.
1863.

Entered according to Act of Congress, in the year 1863,

BY ELIJAH B. HUNTINGTON,

In the Clerk's Office of the District Court for the District of Connecticut.

PRESS OF
JOHN W. STEDMAN,
NORWICH, CONN.

TO

JAMES MONROE HUNTINGTON,

FOR HIS GENEROUS INTEREST

IN THE SUBJECT OF THIS FAMILY MEMOIR, THIS TRIBUTE

TO THE MEMORY OF OUR DEAR DEPARTED, AND TO

THE WORTH OF OUR STILL SURVIVING KINSMEN, IS, WITH

THE AUTHOR'S GRATEFUL ACKNOWLEDGMENTS,

MOST AFFECTIONATELY DEDICATED.

ENGRAVINGS.

GOV. SAMUEL, LL. D. (FRONTISPIECE) ....No. 232
HON. BENJAMIN ....No. 92
HON. HENRY ....No. 313
GEN. JEDIDIAH ....No. 557
JEDEDIAH AND WIFE ....No. 784
EZRA A., D. D. ....No. 1184
RALPH ....No. 1407
JUDGE E. M. ....No. 1451
SARAH LANMAN ....No. 2140

CONTENTS.

INTRODUCTION .... ix.
FAMILY MEETING.. 9
   Collation and Addresses following it....................... 14
   Poem of Rev. Gurdon Huntington 27
   Historical Address of Rev. E. B. Huntington................ 35
THE PURITAN IMMIGRANT... 59
SECOND GENERATION 63
THIRD GENERATION 69
FOURTH GENERATION 77
FIFTH GENERATION 91
SIXTH GENERATION 139
SEVENTH GENERATION 205
EIGHTH GENERATION 289
NINTH GENERATION 351
TENTH GENERATION 367
APPENDIX 369
INDEX TO THE DESCENDANTS OF SIMON HUNTINGTON, IN THREE PARTS:
   I. Index to the Christian Names of the Huntingtons........ 379
   II. Index to the Family and Christian Names of the Children of Huntington Daughters................................ 405
   III. Index to the Intermarriages and Descendants not embraced by the two preceding Indexes 411
INDEX TO THE SURNAMES OF THOSE WHO HAVE MARRIED INTO THE HUNTINGTON FAMILY, IN TWO PARTS:
   IV. An Index to the Names of the Husbands of the Huntington Daughters 413
   V. An Index to the Names of the Wives of the Huntingtons..420
   VI. An Index to the Names of such as have aided in supplying Materials for this Work................. 425
CORRECTIONS AND ADDITIONS...................................... 428

INTRODUCTION.

While residing in Norwich, Conn., some twenty years since, at the solicitation of several of its older citizens, I commenced writing the history of that beautiful city. A few fragments from my manuscript found their way into one of the city papers and attracted the attention of Miss Caulkins of New London. As she had already collected ample materials for such a history, and, indeed, had her manuscript in readiness for the printer, at her request I cheerfully abandoned my attempt.

During my examination of the earlier records of the town I was struck with the frequency with which the Huntington name occurred, and especially with the honorable relation in which it stood. I had also preserved the names of my own immediate ancestors with the families in which they were found, so that I had already quite a list as a nucleus of a Huntington genealogy. I then formed the plan of which the following work is but a too poor execution.

In the Fall of 1855, I providentially met Dr Joshua Huntington (2444) of Brooklyn, N. Y., in whose possession I found a collection of names, with year dates, which proved a very great aid to me in locating the families and members whose names I already had; and also in introducing me into many families which I had not then found. This list had been made after extensive travel and correspondence among the families registered during a period of several years; and to its reliability, in the main, my own subsequent travel and correspondence, have furnished abundant testimony.

My friend and kinsman, Dr. Eliphalet Huntington (1386) of Windham, Conn., than whom there is no more reliable reporter of musty records, also interested himself in my enterprise and re-examined for me the earlier records of Windham, and thus corroborated or corrected my lists of the families of that town, so as to make the record doubly reliable—as nearly perfect as patient and discriminating labor can make it.

Then **Enoch Huntington** (1836) of Amesbury, cheerfully entered upon the task of reporting whatever the Amesbury records might testify respecting his ancestor, William, an honored pioneer in the settlement of that part of Massachusetts. **And his record,** with that copy which Dr. Joshua of Brooklyn had previously made, gave me a full account of the earlier generations in that branch of the family.

Besides these co-laborers in this work, I have received letters from more than three hundred persons, whose names appear on my lists, or who are by marriage connected with us, and so interested in our genealogy; and going still further, I have not hesitated to call upon men of experience and discernment of character for their impressions respecting several persons whose biographical sketches are briefly drawn.

Then, by travel, personally, or by throwing myself in the way of my kinsmen who have traveled, by visiting them at their homes or drawing them to my own, I have held personal conversations with nearly a thousand persons who are more or less clearly related to the name, and obtained from them many of the incidents and statistics found on these pages.

Besides, many an hour and week have I turned over the files of local newspapers, the pages of town and church records,—spelling out from the almost effaced and well-nigh undecipherable chronology of a rude age, the names and dates and deeds of the earlier generations of my work; while many an other hour and day have I spent among the still and oftentimes expressive monuments of the dead—to learn what I might of those whose forms I never saw.

Yet after all my pains taking, many omissions and errors no doubt will be found in the work,—errors, incidental, mainly, to the nature of the work itself. In justification, however, of my own fidelity and care, I may say, that where I could expect accuracy I have frequently found myself deceived. I have been obliged in many instances to correct the dates of birth, which parents have unhesitatingly given of their own children, by referring to the family bible or the town register; and in some instances persons have been in error regarding the dates affixed to their own names.

Yet I have felt myself at liberty, usually, to accept dates on the testimony of members of the family to which the dates belong, as that of parents respecting their children, and brothers and sisters respecting each other. Such authority I have freely received respecting the order in which the names occur; and in a few instances I have taken the testimony of still more distant relatives, when it had a sufficient air of credibility, either from what I knew of the family reported, or of the reporter.

But no one who has not attempted the thing itself, can ever realize the care needed to avoid mistakes, or the labor required for correcting them; and whoever has made trial of the task will, I am sure, grant all indulgence for the inaccuracies here found.

In regard to the arrangement of the families in the work I have followed what seems to me to be the most natural and on the whole the most easily understood method. Commencing with the common ancestor of the Huntingtons, I have, under the second generation given his children, arranged, as accurately as I could, according to ages. Commencing with the oldest of the second, I have in the third generation entered his children, then those of the next in order through the entire list, proceeding in the same order through all the generations. This makes a unit of the work—a single family in each of the generations, all of whose members sustain the same relationship to the common ancestor, though of very dissimilar relationships to one another.

The notation employed is also, as in spite of contrary reasons, I am obliged to think the most simple and expressive. It has none of the perplexing complexity of that in which the Roman letters indicate the number of each member in the family, while a small index marks his generation. If the generation is indicated at the top of the page, there surely is no need of repeating it ten or twenty, and even fifty times, as in some genealogies, by as many indices as there are new names. The families are made sufficiently distinct by the simple number and name and **chief residence of its parents at its head, in the middle of the page; and the dates of birth sufficiently attest the order in which they come.**

As to the scope of the work, I have been in this somewhat overruled by circumstances beyond my control. Originally intending to enroll all the descendants both in the male and female lines of our common ancestor, I found two reasons in my progress to dissuade me from the plan: first, the greatness of the work which would be required, and secondly, the compensation for its omission in the genealogies of other family names, of which the females in ours have been mothers. But while cutting off nearly one-half of my list by rejecting the female line of descent, I added to my original design what has cost me even more labor and care,—the changing of our family genealogy into a Family Memoir—the latter design embracing a much fuller account of the family than the other required. It is hoped that the biographical sketches in the work, necessitated by this change, will not prove either the least truthful or the least entertaining part of it. They have been mainly written under a great pressure of other labors, and though they can lay no claim to elegance of style, they may at least serve to clothe the else naked skeleton of our family frame with the healthy muscle of a real and vigorous life.

And now a word as to the reason for such an attempt. From first to last, the work has been to me both a duty and a delight. In its incipency the former feeling most urged, and as it has progressed the latter motive has furnished the most potent and steady stimulus to the endeavor. Our name, by common consent, has in all its generations been an honorable one. Of few could more good, or less harm, be said. It has been well represented in all the industrial, educational, civil and religious movements of a great people for two centuries, and the truth of history demanded the record of this representation. Several attempts had been made to trace the record. Dr. Joseph Huntington of Coventry, a member of the family as curious to learn of his kinsmen as he was to construct original theories in his sacred profession, made the attempt, yet scarcely entered before he abandoned the field. Several Family Trees have grown up under the constructive industry of other members of the family, yet have been left to the spoiling touch of the elements and time. Joseph C. Huntington of Norwich, later of New York city, had gathered a long list of names, yet did not pursue the classification of them. Dr. Joshua Huntington, now of Brooklyn, had gone still farther than any of these attempts. By extensive travel and correspondence he had gathered, years ago, nearly all that was essential to a pretty full genealogical list of the family for the first six or seven generations; yet other duties have been in the way of his completion of the work.

Such had been some of the heart-yearnings of the family towards some fitting family memorial, when my providential labors in Norwich commenced. The purpose then formed was delayed in its accomplishment by the urgency of professional demands upon my strength and time, until the fall of 1854. With a large school on my hands, requiring about eight hours of the day, I still found in the labor of collecting and arranging materials for the work, very pleasant though an expensive pastime for me. The weariness of my labor has, however, been more than compensated by the delight which its results have furnished, and if my labors shall prove acceptable to the large family in whose behalf they have been performed, I shall certainly never regret the weariness or the expense.

It has proved to be true in all these investigations, as was suggested during their progress by an honored name in another noble family, that I have found " coming out oftentimes with pleasant surprise, the light and the shade of many truly noble and lovely characters."

Besides these inducements to undertake and complete this work, I have been from the first sustained by the encouragement of those whose judgment I should feel proud to record, as ample justification of all the labor and expense I have incurred. Names, honored wherever known, and known wherever our tongue is spoken or read, have, with singular unanimity, testified to the excellence and eminence of the family whose record I have attempted to trace.

HUNTINGTON FAMILY MEETING.

The origin of this delightful meeting will be sufficiently exhibited in the following reprint of the Circular which convened it.

FAMILY CIRCULAR.

NORWICH CITY, December 30, 1856.

At a meeting of several gentlemen of the Huntington name, held at the Wauregan House, this 30th of December, 1856, for the purpose of considering the practicability of securing a meeting of the Huntington Family in this place ere long; the Hon. Jedediah Huntington was called to the Chair, and James M. Huntington appointed Secretary.

After a free expression of wishes and opinions, on motion of Wolcott Huntington, the following resolutions and vote were unanimously passed:

Resolved, That we regard with deep interest and gratitude the extensive diffusion of the Huntington name in this country; and that we look upon the widely scattered descendants of our fathers, as in some sort the members of our own families.

Resolved, That it would give us great pleasure to welcome back to the home of their ancestors and ours, so many of our name, with their descendants of their names, as may wish to unite with us in the enjoyment of such a reunion.

Resolved, That the third day of September, 1857, be set apart by us for that purpose; and that we hereby invite our kinsmen to meet with us on that day, in grateful celebration of the precious memory of our departed, and in joyous congratulation with each other, over the past history and the present honorable position of the family whose name we bear.

Voted, That the Rev. E. B. Huntington, of Stamford, be requested to prepare a Circular of invitation, embracing the action of this meeting, and forward to our kinsmen.

JEDEDIAH HUNTINGTON, Chairman.
JAMES M. HUNTINGTON, Secretary.

In accordance with the above action, the following letter was prepared and sent out.

STAMFORD, CONN., March 21, 1857.

MY DEAR KINSMEN—It gives me great pleasure to be able to transmit to you the preceding record. It expresses very distinctly the feelings and wishes of our Norwich cousins, and will, I am sure, plead its own claim. It deserves, what it will no doubt receive, a grateful response from very many of our family.

I am at liberty to promise you on the occasion of our meeting, an Historical Discourse, a Poem, and such devotional exercises as may be deemed appropriate. These exercises will be held in some suitable place in Norwich Town, commencing at 10 o'clock, on Thursday morning, September 3, 1857.

From pledges given by several members of our family, both of the Huntington and other names, I can also promise you a rich fund of reminiscence and sentiment, for your instruction and entertainment, during the hours of our afternoon festival; in which our Norwich cousins will see that ample provision is made for our physical refreshment.

To avoid disappointment from irregularities of trains, you will do well to reach the city as early, at least, as the evening of the day preceding our public exercises. A committee will be in readiness to provide for you on your arrival.

To avoid, also, needless delays and confusion, and to facilitate local arrangements for your entertainment and for our public exercises, please forward, at the earliest practicable date, to James M. Huntington, Norwich City, Conn., a list of such members of your family as may be expected to attend the meeting. That list will also secure for you a readier introduction to other members of the family.

Anxious to have the Genealogical Memoir upon which I am engaged, as nearly complete as possible before our meeting, I shall be greatly obliged to you for sending to me, if it has not already been done, a complete list of your family, with dates in full, of births, marriages and deaths.

May I ask of you the additional favor to extend this invitation to any members of our family in your vicinity, whom, through ignorance of their residence, I may have omitted.

Hoping to meet you and yours in our family circle at Norwich, and wishing for you a pleasant and profitable season of communion with your kindred there, on a spot hallowed equally by the affection and patriotism and piety of so many of our dear ones gone; and wishing, most of all, for you at length a glorious re-union with them in the communion above, I am, beloved kinsmen, in the bonds of a family whose study has only the more endeared to me its name,

Yours, most affectionately,

E. B. HUNTINGTON.

In acceptance of the above invitation a large number of the family came together in Norwich, on the third day of Sept. 1857. An organization of the meeting was effected by the appointment of the Hon. Jedediah, of Norwich, President, for the morning, and the Hon. Elisha, of Lowell, Mass., President for the afternoon. Vice-Presidents—Hon. Abel, of East Hampton, N. Y.; Felix A., Brooklyn, N. Y.; Judge Samuel H., Hartford, Conn.; Ralph, Boston, Mass.; Randolph G. H., New York City; Hon. Edward, of Rome, N. Y., and Edwin T., of Rochester, N. Y. James M., of Norwich, and Frank C., of New York City, were appointed Secretaries.

THE FAMILY MEETING. 11

At 10 o'clock, A. M., the family had assembled in the Rev. Mr. Arms' church in Norwich Town.

In the language of the Norwich papers of that date, from which the following record is mainly made: "It was indeed a memorable gathering of many members from many States and lands, and pleasant recollections of the day and of the re-union will long be cherished by those present. The number of the Huntington name, or blood, gathered on Thursday, was probably not far from 500. At all events it was great enough to fill the lower part of the Up Town Church full, while the galleries were crowded with citizens and strangers, attracted by sympathy in the occasion. Among the distinguished persons from abroad, we were pleased to notice Mrs. Sigourney, of Hartford, a deeply interested spectator of all that was said and done."

PROGRAMME OF EXERCISES.

VOLUNTARY ON ORGAN, ... By C. W. HUNTINGTON, HARTFORD.
A BRIEF BUT HEARTY WELCOME, ... By THE PRESIDENT.
INVOCATION . . . . . REV. MR. ARMS.
PROEM, Written by MISS CORNELIA HUNTINGTON, Authoress of Sea Spray, East Hampton, L. I., and recited by Mr. Geo. W. Huntington, Norwich City.

We come not here with pomp and plumed array,
   With blazoned banners or with trumpet's blare,
With martial music heralding our way,
   Or cannon booming on the startled air.
Nor yet on controversial errand bent,
   Old mooted, maddening questions to debate
With taunting tongue, and flashing eye, intent
   On wordy warfare waged for Church or State.
In stillness gathering, a kindred band
   Of peaceful pilgrims to one common shrine,
With cordial clasp in this our fatherland,
   And o'er ancestral dust, our hands to join.
We come, fresh scions from the honored stock
   Of good old Simon, pilgrim, sage and sire ;
Who, from a holier than old Plymouth's rock,
   But hailed this promised Canaan to expire.
We have come back to this, our early home,
   To seek loved friends, long severed from our side ;
And o'er our hearts thick-thronging memories come
   Of youth's proud hopes, and dreams of life untried.
Some have come back, in loneliness to tread
   The paths their feet have pressed in by gone years,
And in you silent city of the dead
   To trace loved names, 'mid blinding gush of tears,
And some are here, with earnest wish to see
   Scenes with life's holiest memories inwrought.
From legends learned beside the parent knee.

Or tales with home's heart music deeply fraught.
Kinsmen: well met! tho' meeting but to part;
  Like stranger ships, o'er trackless wastes that stray;
Each hails, "what cheer?" with genial warmth of heart,
  And prays, "God speed thee on thy landward way!"
So we, who meet to part, but part to meet
  Where wild "farewells" and partings never come,
Where each the cherished of his love shall greet
  In the soft light of an eternal home.

OPENING HYMN, Written by Rev. CYRUS HUNTINGTON, Ellicott's Mills, Md. The Music written by Chas. W. Huntington, Organist of the South Congregational Church, Hartford, Conn.

1.

They say we always love to roam
  O'er every land and sea,
And find at last some other home,
  New England, far from thee.
O yes! our own forefathers came
  Across the billows free;
And we who share their honored name,
  Share in their destiny.

2.

While some remain, where, crowned with snow,
  New England's hills are seen,
And crystal streams, with tuneful flow,
  Make all her valleys green;
Others have homes mid orange bowers,
  In constant verdure drest;
And others dwell where prairie flowers
  Invite the sun to rest.

3.

But who shall say, that we forget
  This dear ancestral home,
Where oft our memories have met,
  Our thoughts have often come?
When by this call our hearts were stirred
  As by some joyous chime,
Which long, long years ago, we heard,
  In blessed childhood's time.

4.

And now we meet, a kindred band,
  Here, where their ashes rest;
Who, wandering from their father-land,
  This better land possessed.

These are the hills on which they stood,
  Two hundred years ago:
Ours are the veins, in which their blood
  Courses with genial flow.

5.

Such as our fathers, in the days,
  The famous days of old,
Such be their children to their praise,
  Through ages yet untold.
To Heaven we swell this grateful song,
  Upon this sacred spot;
To us the past, the present belong—
  We ask no other lot.

PRAYER, ... REV. DANIEL HUNTINGTON, NEW LONDON.

This admirable prayer was promised, when written out, for publication with the other exercises. But after the decease of its author no copy of it could be found. This is to be regretted, as it would have added greatly to the value of our memorial of that pleasant meeting. It was well said, by a gifted clergyman who listened to it, that no word in it could have been changed for a better. No petition needed to be added, and none that was in it could be spared.

HISTORICAL ADDRESS, . . REV. E. B. HUNTINGTON, STAMFORD, CONN.

This address will appear after those at the Collation.

HYMN, Written by Mrs. John W. James, daughter of Ralph Huntington, of
  Boston.

We've met in love and gladness here,
  Upon this festal day;
'Tis hallowed ground, to all most dear,
  Though dwellers far away.

The spot where once our fathers dwelt,
  To us should sacred be;
At the same altars where they knelt,
  Let us, too, bend the knee.

From North, from South, from East and West,
  A kindred band we come,
With God's own favors richly blest,
  To our ancestral home.

Then let our grateful thanks ascend
  For all the mercies given;
And let our hearts and voices blend
  In joyous song to Heaven.

>   Do the blest spirits of our sires
>   Look down upon us now?
>   Then, with the strength such thought inspires,
>   We'll breathe a fervent vow,—
>
>   By the pure fame our fathers gained,
>   For honest deeds well done,
>   To future years we'll bear, unstained,
>   The name of HUNTINGTON.

POEM. . . . . . . REV. GURDON HUNTINGTON, SAG HARBOR, L. I.
This Poem will follow the addresses of the Collation.

Of the Collation we can speak in the highest terms. It was a model Collation, as from what we knew of the Norwich Cousins we had reason to expect. The Norwich papers said of it:

"The Old Court House never before witnessed so festive a scene. On the inner wall at the end of the hall fronting the entrance was displayed in conspicuous letters, the words, 'Kinsmen, well met!' The long tables which lined the Hall on either hand, were spread with a beauty and a bounty which vindicated at once the hospitality and the taste of those by whom the feast had been prepared. To enumerate the tempting viands, and other dishes, simple and compound, sweetened and seasoned, flavored and flecked and frosted, and fruits of every name and nature known to gastronomic palates or nomenclatures, were a work of supererogation. Such a feast of fat things might well inspire the 'flow of soul' which everywhere prevailed. When full justice had been done to all its nice things, the family repaired to the church, where at two o'clock, the chair was taken by the President, Dr. ELISHA HUNTINGTON of Lowell, Mass."

In a brief but very cousinly speech, he congratulated the cousins upon the felicities of this their first family meeting. After suggesting that the addresses be mainly autobiographical, and also brief, he called up as first speaker:

Rev. DAN. HUNTINGTON, of Hadley, Mass., now in his 84th year, the oldest member of the Huntington family then present. His remarks were listened to with great attention, being made up of historical reminiscences and anecdotes of much interest.

Rev. JOSEPH HUNTINGTON JONES, D.D., of Philadelphia, followed in a short speech, abounding in interesting facts.

Hon. ASAHEL HUNTINGTON, of Salem, next took the floor. He remarked that it gave him great pleasure to be present and to take part in the proceedings of the gathering. He approved of the suggestion which had been offered, of their becoming better acquainted. We are, he remarked, a pretty large family, and I don't know how we can better serve the purposes of such an occasion than by each telling his own story, and as the ladies cannot speak for themselves, we of the other side of the house must speak for them. My name is Asahel Huntington, of the Christopher branch. My ancestors settled in

Franklin six generations back, and the estate which they originally purchased has been in the family for the whole of these six generations.

Not an acre, not an inch has been alienated from the family—a good proof of their industrious, steady habits. The original estate had 96 acres, and was situated on the Lebanon road. Then it was a hard, rocky, sterile soil; now it is an excellent estate of 200 acres. Another remarkable fact is that this property has been in the possession of deacons up to the present generation. They were men who looked to the future world as their highest good, and satisfied themselves with a moderate portion of this world's goods. The family for several generations have been members of the church, and officers in it. The estate for many years was occupied by deacons who were innkeepers. The sign of the Seven Stars, which hung over that old house is still preserved in the attic of a house near by. I may remark here that no Huntingtons have ever been tories. We have no refugees among us. We have representatives from the Queen's dominions, but we have no tories. Well, as I was about to say, this old sign was to signify an invitation, cordial and hearty, to the soldier-wayfarer from generation to generation. This was before the days of the Maine Law, and, though I am a friend of the Maine Law, you will recollect that our ancestors had no such law. They kept a good article, and sold it with moderation and prudence.

My father was educated at Dartmouth, under the care then of Rev. Mr. Wheelock, who was by the way, a relative of ours by marriage.

He graduated in 1789, and was soon after made a minister at Topsfield, where he had five children. He died in 1813. After his death I went through Phillips Academy, at Andover, and entered Yale College in 1815, graduating in 1819. After graduation I studied law, and settled soon after in Salem, Mass., where I have been ever since.

I was riding in Andover one May morning last spring, along by the Merrimac—a river which has upon its banks as much associated capital as any on the continent—there is Lowell, and Lawrence, Nashua and Concord and Manchester,—a river rich in scenery, and remarkable for its picturesque beauty. Well, I was riding along the banks of this noble stream at 6 o'clock in the morning, and as I passed one house I noticed a man standing in the gateway. I was just then thinking of this meeting. The individual in question was a respectable looking man, and modest withal, and it immediately occurred to me that he was a Huntington. I rode on till I came to some men who were mending their nets, by the shore, and so strongly impressed was I with the conviction that the man was a Huntington, that I stopped and asked one of the fishermen, if any Huntingtons lived in that neighborhood. "This is one," he replied, turning to a young man standing near, "and you just passed one, up by that house," pointing to the very man whom I had passed. I went to see this man whom I knew by instinct, and found out his name was Moses Huntington. I told him of this meeting, and he promised to be here.

It has long been a question whether the Salisbury Huntingtons were from Simon or not; whether they were, as the doctors would say, sporadic or pure.

It seems that the Salisbury Huntingtons were there in 1643, and have been there ever since. This is the earliest settlement of any one of the name in the country. The banks of the Merrimac, then, was the site of the earliest settlement. I had some doubt on the point, as they were then Quakers. Now I believe they are about half and half. It is an authenticated fact that one of these Huntingtons had a license from the General Court to sell an article with a queer name, called, I believe, sturgin, always provided that he would give a bowl full to the judges at the beginning and end of each court.

I would state that my mother was a North, so that I am a Connecticut man on both sides. My great grandfather was Dr. Hezekiah Lord, a celebrated preacher of his time. He had in his congregation a certain woman who had been diseased for some twenty years or more. She conceived the idea that if she could hear a sermon from Dr. Lord it would cure her of her disease. The Doctor humored the old lady, and went to preach her the sermon. His text was in Isaiah xxxv. 3. "Strengthen ye weak hands, and confirm the feeble knees." While he was yet speaking, the woman rose up and walked, and the sinews and the flesh came upon her, and she was cured from that day. These facts are abundantly verified. The discourse has been published. The name of the woman was, I am just informed, Mercy Wheeler.

Permit me to say that I take great pleasure in being here, to sympathize in the objects of this meeting; to interchange greetings of affection, and more than all, to manifest my respect, reverence and love for the founders of this house. We come with great delight to this old homestead of our fathers, and as inheritors of a common blood and a common name, we would gather about the hearth stones of these old sturdy settlers, feast from the same board, and drink from the same fountain. We rejoice to come up to this beautiful and flourishing city, one of the chief ornaments of Connecticut, and here, Sir, standing as it were, by the graves of our fathers, to meet the descendants of this ancient blood and name. We are glad to come up here to Norwich—a city founded by our blood and name, and built up and increased by large infusions of the original stock. Those of us who have gone to other fields, may come up here and find the name of Huntington honored and respected. We are proud to find such a home of our fathers. I would say that we hail you all as kinsmen and cousins—all first cousins—and we are happy as one united family—a common brotherhood—to mingle our loves and friendships in one grand ovation of praise to Almighty God, for such faith and trust as have marked our blood and name.

Standing here to-day, let us remember that we have a present and a future, and it is required of us, as descendants of the Huntingtons, that we show the same faith, the same truth, the same integrity of character, the same Christian spirit as have marked the history of our race before.

Prof. FREDERIC D. HUNTINGTON, of Cambridge, Mass., was next called for. He said that the difficulties were real in the matter of his making a speech. It was not diffidence, for who could be diffident when speaking to one's own brothers and cousins in the bosom of one's own family. He could not say that he did not expect to be called on. Sundry letters and telegraphic despatches received at his house, expressed in perfectly intelligible English, had effectually dispelled any delusion of that sort. At the eleventh hour he had found it impossible *not* to come. As the time approached, the idea of being absent had made him more and more restless and uncomfortable, till at last his wife,—whom he had left that morning watching the movements of the very tenderest and freshest offshoot of his branch of the Huntington stock,—could no longer tolerate so uneasy a housemate, and begged him to be off. In fact he had felt a good deal like a boy away from home on Thanksgiving Day thinking what a merry time all the folks were having at dinner. But although he had come with an eager appetite and all possible speed, he was sorry he had not arrived till the *dinner*,—which was " Cousin E. B's" Oration,—was over. And now, in answering to the President's call, the real perplexity was not in saying something, but in deciding what *not* to say. To tell the truth, on the way down in the cars he had thought over two or three different speeches that *might* be made according to circumstances, but the circumstances were too good for the best of them. He remarked that on these historical and genealogical occasions, which are happily multiplying throughout the country, it was desirable that every speaker should have some knowledge of the records of the Past, so as to contribute something to the accumulating treasure. But here, said he, I must confess a sad deficiency. Nobody admires or respects that sort of accomplishment more than I do. Indeed, I probably honor it all the more, for the feeling of wonder and mystery connected with it. Nature has made me up on such a parsimonious plan, and has so utterly denied me the faculty for this sort of science, that a man like " E. B." here, who knows everything, root and branch, about a huge, ramified, complicated tribe spreading the network of its relationship over a continent, able to disentangle its twists and double-twists, affects me like some fabulous prodigy, with a touch of the supernatural upon him. In this most useful and mysterious learning I am utterly helpless. I never planted nor pruned a genealogical tree in my life. I never botanized upon one nor ate the fruit of one; I never planned nor copied one. I don't know the names of my grandfather's second cousins, nor what pleasant people their nephews courted, or their nieces were courted by and kindly consented to marry. I am shamefully behind these capitally-informed and richly-remembering kinsmen, who have spoken so surprisingly in your hearing. I cannot think up any such remarkable phenomenon among my ancestors as an honest lawyer,—like cousin Asahel, or any disinterested doctor like cousin Elisha; I can recollect no Christian deacon, on my father's side, who sold good liquor to his neighbors, and no uncle of his who grew genial over a golden punch-bowl. I am not even perfectly sure whether I am descended from the first Simon, the first Samuel, or the first Christopher. Enough for me to believe without misgiving that the Simon was a " Simon pure," the Samuel a son of many prayers, and the Christopher as worthy to be canonized as St. Christopher. Nor is all this ignorance to be excused on the plea of the absence of advantages. My father took untiring pains with me; there he sits now doubtless mortified with my stupidity; he has put the whole story into my hands and into my ears again and again; but I believe if he had used up a whole birch-tree on my body he would never have got the family-tree into my head. One fact, however, among other minutiæ, I do recollect, and never mean to forget. Tracing back the line through my father's father, a brother of one of my ancestors is found to have been a Captain of the Lifeguard of Charles the First. Going back on the line through my father's mother we come to Scrope, the Regicide! By that singular political divergence, I find I have in my veins blood intensely Tory and blood intensely Whig; by which mixture of the conservative and radical forces,—the extremes of loyalty and revolution,—I hope to keep myself a tolerably correct Republican,—reverential toward the old, in the Church and in the State, and yet not inhospitable in welcoming the new. But if any of you imagine that I have the least pride in a connection with a royal escort, or any disposition to cultivate aristocratic reminiscences, I shall take particular satisfaction in saying to you that my grandfather was a blacksmith as well as a farmer; and that he wore no coat-of-arms, but rather, when he was about his business, arms with no coat on them at all. Putting this with the fact that he lived honestly and died in the fear of God, and that he encouraged his son Dan, my beloved father, to become a preacher of the Gospel of Christ, have I not reason to be content with the "blood?"

Most cordially, Sir, do I join in this festival with you,—glad to grasp the hands of so many male cousins, and to offer to those of the other sex such affectionate and respectful salutations, as shall be most agreeable and proper! And by the way, let me just here mention an anecdote to illustrate the great value to all persons, whether Huntington or other, of cultivating in early life a legible hand-writing, an art to which I make, for the best of reasons, very humble pretensions indeed. Some weeks ago I was writing to a cousin by no means ill-favored or ill-tempered, and, alluding to this expected gathering, expressed a hope that she would be here, observing incidentally that it would be one of the advantages of so friendly and sympathetic a company that nobody, however tedious, would be much criticised, and certainly not *kissed*. Now, Sir, would you credit it, that in the awkwardness of my chirography, she found *two-lips* instead of one on the first letter of the word, made a *k* of the *h*, and so wrote back to me that, for her part, she did not see any great harm in it if near family relations *should* choose to kiss one another. I hope to find this cousin is present, and that by some means or other we can come to a full understanding and amicable agreement on that subject!

But, my kindred, there is a higher strain of thought than this; and the occasion is worthy of it. Wherever human hearts meet and kindle and warm as ours do now, the better elements in them must be moved. Nothing justifies this assembly but high purposes and hallowed feelings. We have come here, I am sure, to be made better men and women,—more faithful servants of that Most High "God of all the families of the earth," whose grace and goodness have brought us together,—more believing and diligent disciples of that Lord and Redeemer into whose name we have been baptized,—more active and effective members of that Church which we hope and pray may spread its benignant shelter over our children and our children's children,—more intelligent interpreters and generous friends of the stirring age that has favored our fraternal assembling. Every group of relatives, every domestic circle, is collected and classed in the mind and will of God to assist in the elevation and purifying of the whole great Household of the Race, as each constellation is set in the sky above us to bear a part in the majestic harmony of the Universe. Let us be made more conscious than ever before, then, of our wider relationship, and the sacred duties they bind upon us. Let not this meeting of our family narrow our sympathies, nor abridge our interest in those of all names, colors and conditions,—in Man,—but extend and strengthen them. We are more the children of our Heavenly Father than of our earthly ancestors. What is *human* in our blood is greater than what is *Huntington* in it. We have come here that we may go back with a heartier and more religious resolution to our several scenes of work. If they should be scenes of suffering, we will remember that "knowledge by suffering entereth," and follow on after him, our Master, who "thro' suffering" finished the mediatorial work given him to do, and is "made perfect" in his redemption and intercessory office in the Heavens. The whole nation is alive with interests and thoughts that are enough to arouse the sleepiest soul. We are not to be dreamers over dogmas, but workers among realities. We are to see to it, that in our public institutions, justice be wedded to love,—in our social life that we walk hand in hand with charity,—that thus may appear new ameliorations on earth, and new glories in heaven. The question at last will be not where this or that man was born, but to what end was he born; not of what name was he, but of what spirit; not what fortune did he lay up, but what treasure of holy living and righteous fruit does he leave behind him. Whether there be tongues they shall cease; whether there be knowledge it shall vanish away. But faith and hope and charity, after all our companies are scattered, and our places are empty, shall abide, clasping their immortal hands, and uttering the eternal praise of the Father, the Son, and the Holy Ghost. And let all the people say, "Amen."

Rev. A. HUNTINGTON CLAPP, of Providence, R. I., was then called up. He said that his mother was from the Simon-pure Huntington stock. He graduated at Yale, in 1842, and at Andover in 1845. Was settled for some time in Brattleboro. For the past two years had been pastor of a church in Providence. "I always revered," said the speaker, "the name of Huntington, and I hope to retain some degree of that reverence. My highest idea of a man was not taken from the scholar, the genius, or the commander. It was derived from my earliest childhood, from that same Simon Huntington, who lived in Hinsdale."

The speaker alluded in touching language to the early death of his mother and the noble integrity of his father.

A letter was read by Rev. E. B. Huntington, from the poetess, Mrs. L. H.

SIGOURNEY, giving many interesting incidents connected with the past history of the family.

MRS. L. H. SIGOURNEY'S REMINISCENCES.

The upper, or old town of Norwich. Conn., was, in ancient times, decidedly aristocratic. This aristocracy, not of wealth alone, but wealth combined with honorable ancestry, and high moral and religious example, was principally vested in two families: the Huntingtons and Lathrops. The former were the most numerous, and of those branches which were located around what was then called Huntington Square, my recollections are vivid, our own residence being in that neighborhood.

General Jabez Huntington, the father of this distinguished dynasty, I never saw, and presume he died before my birth. With the eldest son, Gen. Jedediah Huntington, a patriotic and saintly man, and the friend of Washington, I was not personally acquainted, he with his family being inhabitants of New London.

Judge Andrew Huntington, the second in succession, was a man of plain manners and incorruptible integrity. His few words were always those of good sense and truth, and the weight of his influence given to the best interests of society. His lady, a second wife, I believe, possessed an elegance of form and address, which would have been conspicuous at any foreign Court. She was especially fascinating to the children who visited her, by her liberal presentations of cake and other pleasant eatables, or which was equally alluring to some, a readiness to lend fine books with pictures.

Colonel Joshua Huntington had one of the most benign countenances I ever remember to have seen. His calm, beautiful brow, was an index of his temper and life. Let who would be disturbed or irritated, he was not the man. He regarded with such kindness as the gospel teaches, the whole human family. At his own fair fireside, surrounded by loving, congenial spirits, and in all his intercourse with the community, he was the same serene, and revered Christian philosopher.

General Ebenezer Huntington was a noble specimen of the soldier and patriot. I think I have been told that he left College at the age of sixteen, to join the army of our Revolution, and continued with it during the whole war of eight years. The elegant manner, and decision of character, that are wont to appertain to the higher grades of the military profession, were conspicuous in him, and unimpaired by age. He was the father of a numerous family, and a gentleman of extensive influence.

General Zachariah Huntington was a model of manly symmetry and beauty. He was tall, with noble features, a pure complexion, and a fresh color upon cheek and lip. Though more intimate in his family than in that of any of his other brothers, his daughter being my schoolmate and friend, I always felt afraid of him. To my childish fancy he seemed like one of the chieftains of the old Douglass blood, who ruled the Scottish kings.

With this remarkable brotherhood were two sisters, Elizabeth, the wife of

Col. John Chester, of Wethersfield, the mother of many children, richly gifted, both in person and mind; and Mary, the helpmeet of our excellent pastor, the Rev. Dr. Joseph Strong. A mistress was she of the minutiæ of that domestic science which promotes household comfort and happiness; plain in dress and manner, condescending to the lowliest, and of so easy and cheerful temperament that her words were always mingled with smiles. In those days a minister and his consort were expected to be patterns in all things to all people, and the closest critic perceived in her only those quiet, unambitious virtues that pertain to woman's true sphere, and a cloudless piety. Her husband had erected a handsome parsonage within the precints of *Huntington Square*, and they and their children formed an integral part of those weekly social gatherings, which kept bright the chain of affection, and the fountain of kindred sympathy. To be occasionally comprehended in these circles, and partake their "feast of reason and flow of soul," which comprised always a most liberal admixture of creature comforts, was accounted a rare privilege.

On such an occasion, I had more than once the pleasure of seeing the venerable mother of that noble race. To young eyes she seemed a person of extreme age, and probably surpassed fourscore.

It was beautiful to note how warmly she was welcomed, and what marked and sweet respect was paid her by all her descendents. Her presence seemed the center and crown of their enjoyments. Tenderly cared for and honored, she dwelt under the roof of her youngest son, General Zachariah Huntington, until her death, which I think was sudden, and from the effects of a severe influenza.

This son, who superintended a mercantile establishment, as well as the culture of his extensive grounds, took great delight in music. He possessed a scientific knowledge of it, with a voice of great power and melody. A desire to improve this important department of divine worship, induced him at one time to become the leader of our choir in church. This voluntary service was appreciated by the people, and the labor connected with it, felt to be on his part, both a condescension and a religious offering. When he gave out the name of the tune, which was then always done in a distinct enunciation, and we rose in our seats in the gallery, every eye turning to him for guidance, he seemed, with his commanding presence and dignified form, to our young minds, a superior being. One of his requisitions was imperative: that the female portion of the choir should sing without their bonnets. That article of apparel being then the antipodes of the present fashion, and formidable both for size and protrusion, he affirmed not only intercepted the sound but precluded striking the key tone with accuracy. None of us would gainsay his wishes, and the simplicity of the times counted it no indecorous exposure. Nevertheless, there was sometimes, as is wont to be in more modern days, among those who sustain the sacred harmony, a murmuring of discordant strings. One young lady, of the Huntington name, though not a relative of his own, chanced to take offence, and was seen on a Sunday morning, making her way to a seat in the body of the church.

"Come up to us, in the choir," said we.

"No: Zacheus may climb the tree alone for all me," was the reply.

It ought to be mentioned that this bad pun was by no means a fair exponent of her native wit.

The only daughter of this gentleman, Eliza Mary Huntington, my school associate and sisterly friend, returns to my heart, through the far lapse of years, as I gather these reminiscences, and claims a heart tribute. Full of life and spirit was that beautiful girl; earnest in her studies, and in the recesses for play, our leader. In the vigor of a fine constitution, she exulted in all graceful exercises, and the sensation of fatigue was unknown to her. Together we scaled the ledges of grey rock, with which our native region abounded, searching for hardy plants, where the wild honey suckle first threw out its bright, pink banner. In the evening we sometimes met and repeated to each other the lessons for the next day, knitting at the same time, with primitive simplicity, our own stockings. As the years of school fled away, and youth ripened, her beauty assumed a more tremulous delicacy, as though health might not be firmly rooted. Watched over like a fair rosebud was she, by the stately father, the doting mother, and two fond brothers, with the idolatry of affection. They would not that the winds of heaven should roughly visit her. She was early married, and removed to the city of New York. Early, too, was she transferred to that home, where they neither marry, nor are given in marriage, but are as the angels of God. It is doubtful whether the mother, whose life was especially garnered up in this daughter, ever surmounted the effects of her loss.

The following lines, in a description of the burial ground in that vicinity, have reference to this lovely lady:

>And is it so,
>That to my place of birth, where every germ
>Of hope was planted, I may never come
>But grief chastise the joy? When last the morn
>Spread forth her purple robe, I sought a friend,
>Who on my childhood and my youth would smile
>With affable regard, cheering a heart
>That often sighed in loneliness. Fair plants
>Still decked her garden, but she was not there
>To nurse their sweets. Her well-known mansion rose
>In wonted hospitality, but she
>Welcomed me not.
>   Ah! does that gentle head
>Rest with the ancient of thy noble house,
>In the tomb's silence? Many a falling tear
>Answers my question from the sons of need,
>Whom hungry, thou hast fed,—uncovered, clothed,
>And sorrowing, comforted.

        With silent course,
Unostentatious as the heaven-shed dew,
Thy bounties fell; nor did'st thou scatter gifts,
Or utter prayers with pharisaic zeal,
For man to note. Thy praise was with thy God.
In that domestic sphere where Nature rears
Woman's meek throne, thy work was eminent;
Nor breathed thy goodness o'er cold, stoic hearts.
What gentleness was thine—what kind regard
To him thou loved'st—what dove-like tenderness
In voice and deed. Almost disease might bear
Its lot without repining, wert thou near
Beside its pillow, or around its couch,
Like ministering angel.
      Scarce had Spring
Which shed its damp dews o'er thy daughter's grave,
Returned, ere thou wert waiting to ascend,
Like her, to that bright host, whose ceaseless harps
Hymn the Redeemer. She was as a rose
Gathered in loveliness, 'mid perfumed flowers,
And warbling birds of love, yet drooping still
For the pure breath of that celestial clime,
Where Summer hath no cloud. She with firm hand
Grasped the strong hope of everlasting life,
And thou, in trembling, yet confiding trust,
Did'st dare the waves of Death's tempestuous flood,
With the same anchor.
      So, ye are at rest,
Where sorrow comes not. Is there room for us,
In the same mansion, when the Master calls?

              L. H. S.

Hartford, Conn., May 1, 1857.

After the reading of the letter, the chairman called up,
Hon. JOSEPH T. BUCKINGHAM, for many years editor of the Boston Courier.

Mr. B. said—He was sorry that he had been called for to speak before the assembly, for he did not profess to be a public speaker; but his sorrow on this occasion was somewhat alleviated by what had been said by the gentleman who was first on the platform, namely, that the speeches ought to be short and to consist chiefly of personal history. He was relieved from much, even of this requirement, by having been silly enough, a few years ago, to publish his own personal memoirs, and he was now vain enough to suppose that some of the audience before him had seen the book. But to comply with the general requisition, he would state that he was born in the neighboring town of

Windham, that his father was a shoemaker, said to have been a pretty good one, and that his mother was Mary, the daughter of Solomon Huntington, who was, he believed, the third in descent from the original settler of the name of Huntington in that town. Mr. B. said his father, by a connexion with the commissary department in the war of the Revolution, was involved in losses, or in what was no better, the possession of some thousands of dollars in continental bills, which, at his death in 1783, were worth hardly enough to pay his funeral expenses. Of himself, Mr. B. said he had no personal history which it were not tedious to relate, and would be more tedious to the audience to hear. He was no scholar, had no college adventures to relate, was not a graduate of Harvard or Yale. His diploma came from an institution more ancient than either of them. All his learning except the simple elements of reading and writing, was obtained in a printing office, an institution originally contrived and established, as was generally supposed in the early period of its existence, by the Devil and Dr. Faustus. From one or both of them he must derive his claim, if he had a claim, to an honorary degree. And what further, said Mr. B., can I speak of here? I am not a doctor, Mr. Chairman, nor a clergyman, nor a lawyer. I have had, as an editor, something to do with politics; but that is here a prohibited topic, and my political sentiments are generally well known. Readers of political newspapers will not need to be reminded that I have often been reproached, and sometimes honored, for having said, some thirty years ago, that I was wishing to live and die in the faith of the Hartford Convention. I still subscribe to that declaration; and allow me to say, Mr. Chairman, that neither you nor I, nor any one present will ever see a convention of better men, or purer patriots, until we meet the "General Assembly of the Church of the first born," and mingle with the "spirits of the just made perfect." Since all the gentlemen who have preceded me in these desultory speeches have illustrated their ideas by the relation of anecdotes, permit me, Mr. Chairman, to relate one, and to leave the application of it where it justly belongs, to my own roving remarks. In one of the country villages of Massachusetts, at the commencement of the Revolutionary war, the minister of the parish was rather lukewarm in the cause of the Whigs, and went so far in justifying Tory principles that, to avoid a coat of tar and feathers, he deemed it expedient to leave his pulpit and make a temporary residence "in parts unknown." At the close of the war he returned and was desirous of renewing his clerical services, but he found that the people would not receive him. He remonstrated after this fashion: "Did I not preach the true doctrines of the Bible; did I not hold to original sin, total depravity, election, regeneration; didn't I hold to the perseverance of the saints, the everlasting punishment of the wicked and the eternal happiness of the righteous?" "Yes," said one of the deacons, "but there was one thing you didn't hold, and if you had held it you might have held your place as our minister till this time." "And pray what was that?" "You didn't hold your tongue."

Hon. SAMUEL HOWARD HUNTINGTON, of Washington, D. C., was next called for.

He thought that he should have been excused from speaking. While up, he would like to allude to a tradition of the family. We have a tradition that our ancestors were Puritans, and that there was among the brothers of our forefather Simon, one who was in the King's lifeguard. Now I would not make any comparison between roundhead and cavalier, between the Hartford Convention and any other political faith. The Huntingtons are always on one side or the other, and, furthermore, I believe they always act from their sober convictions of judgment. I have nothing to say of myself. My education was received at Yale College. My father was engaged in the Revolution, and was one of the unfortunate inmates of the Jersey prison ship. I have been gratified to learn that our venerable friend, Rev. Dan Huntington, began life in my father's family. The speaker returned thanks for the hospitality of the Norwich friends, and expressed an earnest desire to unite in some monument worthy of the Huntingtons.

Hon. ASAHEL HUNTINGTON, of Salem, wished to introduce a few resolutions. He remarked that a wish had been expressed to erect some memorial worthy of the Huntingtons. It became us, said he, to do something here which shall mark the event and be alike creditable to us. It is known to most of you that one of our name has been engaged for some time in writing the family history, and has been thus far successful. He has been at great expense in getting it up, and has it, I learn, nearly ready. We desire that it shall be forthcoming. The best way to mark the event we celebrate to-day is to resolve that this work be published, and that, as a part of it, there shall be prepared an account of this celebration. I would, therefore, Mr. Chairman, move the following resolution:

Resolved, That a committee of three be appointed who shall have charge of the publishing of the family history, together with a record of this day's proceedings, and that said committee have power to raise funds by subscription.

After being amended to read, "who shall co-operate with Rev. E. B. Huntington in the publishing of the family history," &c., it was adopted, and the following gentlemen were appointed such committee: Jedediah Huntington, of Norwich, Asahel Huntington, of Salem, Mass., and Ralph Huntington, of Boston, Mass.

The following resolutions were unanimously adopted:

Resolved, That we rejoice in this opportunity of coming up here to this early home of the founders of our house and family, and of uniting with our kinsmen and cousins inhabiting these homesteads of our fathers, in this great family party, where we may become acquainted with each other, draw closer the ties of affection and blood, and all join in testimonies of respect, veneration and love for the memory and character of a common ancestry.

Resolved, That we who have gone out from these ancient domains of our name and blood, and have now returned to join in this family festival, desire to express to our kinsmen and cousins here, our especial thanks and gratitude for their kind and generous reception, and their most grateful hospitalities, and to say to them, one and all, that we shall leave with them, on our departure, a record of our names and residences, and shall all be most happy, hereafter and always, to reciprocate their hospitalities, and to recognize at all times, the obligation of blood and kindred in our several homes and family circles.

Resolved, That for the able and most interesting Historical Discourse to which we have this day listened, our thanks are eminently due to the author, and are hereby rendered.

Resolved, That all of the name and blood are under especial obligation to the Rev. E. B. Huntington for his laborious researches in tracing out the descent and genealogy of our family; that we desire to express to him our thanks for his labors, and to manifest, by substantial tokens, our appreciation of his services in preparing the way for a pure and accurate family history.

After disposing of this business, short addresses were made by Rev. JONATHAN HUNTINGTON, of Nashville, Tenn., Hon. ABEL HUNTINGTON, of Long Island, and Rev. BENJAMIN S. HUNTINGTON, of Aston Ridge, Pa.

A vote of thanks was returned to the singers of the day, and a vote passed that the next meeting of the family be held in fifty years.

PARTING HYMN.—Authors of hymn and music, the same as those of opening hymn.

1.
'T was only this morning in gladness we met,
And the thrill of that meeting how can we forget!
'T was the coming of children, their portion to claim
In the measureless wealth of a long honored name.

2.
How swiftly have fled all the moments to-day,
And the shadows of evening forbid us to stay;
But a lifetime we 've lived in the scenes of the past,
As their far-shining glory around us they cast.

3.
Our hearts to this spot through the future will turn,
While thoughts of the past in our memories burn;
And then in the present we 'll strive for a name
Not wholly unworthy our ancestor's fame.

4.
The homes that now miss us are pleasant and fair,
And those who are dearest are waiting us there;
But kindred and friends! who are met with us here,—
Ye, also, for ever, for ever are dear.

5.
We knew when we met, that we met but to part,
Yet O, how that parting will sadden the heart;

But the links that have bound us together to-day,
Farewells can not sever, nor ages decay.

6.

Farewell! let us say, as we scatter again
To South, or to North, or the blue skirted main;
Each other in Friendship and Truth we will greet,
Whenever, wherever, however we meet.

BENEDICTION.—By Rev. DAN HUNTINGTON, of Hadley, Mass.

POEM, BY REV. GURDON HUNTINGTON, OF SAG HARBOR.

Wedlock! fond source of pure relationship,
The fountain-haunt of many a bliss, where throngs
Of tender dreams and shapes of happiness
Were by Creative Love designed to brood;
Wedlock! with mention of thy name, and thoughts
Of thy pure influences and concord fond,
Well may I ope this strain; so that my verse
Shall be, tho' graceless, like a stream that springs
Where sweet retirement is embowered 'mid blooms
Which breathe ambrosial odors. 'Round that bond
Which marriage ties with silken knot,
Heaven throws its sanction, interweaving it
As a thread of gold throughout the bond beloved.
Type of Messiah's union with His Church!
Comparison with holy lessons rife,
And teaching us how fond and pure should be
The union of the hearts which wedlock binds.
See'st thou yon river, that adown the vale
Flows on in majesty, wherein suffused
The soft and blushing glory of the morning rests,
'Till wave and sunshine-richness seem dissolved
Into one stream of light and power! So, in one tide
The affection and desires should flow,
Of those whom hymeneal bonds have joined,
Mingling and glowing in harmonious stream.
See'st thou yon stars that seem in Heaven to meet,
Blending their rays in soft, unquenching beams?
Across that azure sea above they float,
With even movement, keeping union e'er;
The zenith finds them still in commune rapt;
Their voice according and their light still blent.
When down the western hill they sink, and bid
The watchers, or the sky-charmed sage "good-night;"

So, like two voices, in some song of home,
Where music lavishes her tenderest heart,
Should flow harmoniously the wedded lives.
With awe-struck recognition of His laws,
And of that mystic union to God's Son,
In marriage stainless and love-lighted typed,
And with conviction of the holiness
Which unto wedlock's sweet alliance clings,
Our fathers, of the earlier days, did found
Our wide-spread, populous family,
And here th' eternal truths of virtue taught.
Here, doubtless, to the young, the parents sage,
The grand, ennobling doctrines of Heaven's word
Unfolded, telling to the listening soul
Of Him whose spirit everywhere doth brood,—
O'er the wild haunts and lonely rocky wastes,
As well as where bright civilization sheds
A flood of luxury and glory o'er
The populous realms of life; alike where flows
The murmuring chant of streams that ne'er
Mirrored the snowy sail; and where ships superb
In the crowded river's glassy depths ride deep,
By reason of the varied, glittering spoils,
Which commerce from far distant shores has won.
Here breathed they to the curious mind of youth,
The story of the holy men of old,
Who, in the childhood of our race, when yet
Narrow the river of corruption ran
Down Time's grave-margined stream, the turbid tide
Nobly resisted, and for Truth and God
Inscribed, and broad unfurled their vessel's flag.
The eventful course of years they told,
And marked their solemn lessons; then the tale
Most woeful, yet most triumphing, they breathed,
Of him who came to show how God and love
Could in a human heart reside; and how
The fearful gulf which shuts us out from Heaven,
Could, by a cross of wood, be safe bridged o'er;
Safe unto all who walk by faith's clear star,
And in the love-lit path of righteous life.
Thus in the ear of listening youth they poured,
Doubtless, their solemn lessons, and the stamp
Pressed kindly on the yet impressible heart,
That with the noble form of virtue e'er,
It might conspicuous prove. And so

In sacred virtue, and in industry,
The bases of our family renown and strength
They wisely, deeply laid.
                                I ween,
Like that mysterious tree Ezekiel saw
In fruity affluence and strength, that grew
Beside the sacred stream in Holy Land,—
So flourishes the tribe, or house, which strikes
The roots of its development in sound
And healthful virtues; while its veins
Are coursed by energy and living hope.
So swells rejoicingly the stream which springs
From broad-based hills that rise to seek the sky;
And 'neath the solemn and the mighty shade
Of ample ranges, takes its seaward course,
While beauty and prosperity smile bright
Upon the shore it laves.
                                Far o'er the seas,
From where the precious sunbeams light the marge
Of England's storied waters, mirroring
The crumbling pomp of feudal walls, and gleam
Of ivy-mantled towers and fanes: from scenes
Where still the genius of her power in strength
August and undecaying rules, they came,
The edifice of civilization here,
And Truth's fair form to rear. The ranks of war!
Dreadful and sad the mission which they haste
Upon the fields ensanguined to fulfill!
How sad the light which shines upon the folds
Of Victory's banners-light, which dying hopes,
And the faint, stifling flames of sinking life
Cast with their final flickerings; and which
The fires of ruin dart from crumbling seats,
Where power was throned, and from the ashy wrecks
Of art and beauty overwhelmed!
But fair, and wreathed with blessings is the brow
Of Christian civilization; and the end
Of her advance claims justly songs and praise.
Such were our father's aims.
                                Yet should again
The august genius of our Freedom sigh
O'er her immunities assailed, and call
For brave defenders, and for sacrifice.—
The martial genius of our slumbering sires

Would in their sons be seen to wake.
And as amid the incense flame of old,
Enkindled by Manoah, then sprang up
His manlike guest on angel wings. till then
Unseen; so, when the altar-fires are lit,
Of liberty again, shall those you've deemed
Of common earth spring up aloft and reach
The cloudless sky of freedom and of fame.
But to return:

      The angry waves,
—Storms of the desolate coast,—the snows
Burying the inclement shores in ice and gloom,
Quenched not their courage or their faith. The dream
Of southerly skies and climes might fair
Have gleamed and glowed in the mind's atmosphere;
But bleak and wintry was the scowl which gloomed
Above the shores where tempests drove their bark.
Yet in the cold, forbidding day of grief,
They sowed the seed which, smiled upon of Heaven,
When in the after glory of a summer-time
It sprouted, grew into flourishing beauty, bloomed,
And with a wealth of fruitage decked wide boughs.
As oaks that wrestle with September's gales,
As rocks and crags that battle with the surge,
How many were their struggles with the force
Of wild and wintry tempests. and the stern
And yet enchanting rudeness of the land,
O'er which a wierd and dim romance reposed,—
Romance of its untutored race—the tribes
Of plumed and painted. swarthy men!

      The charm
Which was breathed forth from those strange scenes,
And from the picturesque and novel life.
Which chronicled itself upon Time's chart,
In that wild realm of wood-girt hills and floods—
Solemn and mighty, and forest-shadowed plains,
Whose silence civilization scarce had broken,—
This charm was then but as a flickering light
On the dark cloud of their experience.
When want and war their feebly-guarded homes
Roughly assailed : They nerved themselves for strife ;
As from the marble crude the sculptor shapes
The form of grandeur and expressive grace;
As from the hideous belchings of the mouth,

Of flaming mountains, and from desolate mines
The builder hews in rock and scoria forms,
Wherewith he raises architectural grace,
The soaring pomp of beauty and of strength,—
So raised they a prosperity and name
Noble for virtue, energy and mind,—
Upraised it from amid their trials rough,
From elements in natural rudeness found.
The murky desolation of the sky
Grew bright; a fair-brow'd day was born;
Some still the plough drove in the rugged field;
Some in the ranks of war, upon the plains
Where streamed his banner like a meteor red,
Drew for their country and their homes their swords;
And lit with the bright flashing of their steel
A path 'mid dark and thorny fields,
To victory and renown. Theirs was a share
In glory's harvest; to the flowing stream
Of our prosperity and name, their sweat
And their life-currents added; blossoms fair
To the wreath of literary fame which binds
America's young brow, some added; light
And "orient pearls" of wisdom sowing thick
In the rude soil of the western world of mind.
Into the enchanted palace and the flowery fields
Of dreamy romance, some our footsteps led,
Lighting the scene with graphic charm;
While art, soft-hued, bewitching solace,
Of this our stirring, dusty life, sweet art
Wove the rich web of the entrancing dreams
Which spell-bound some; while science, too,
With mien august, and face symmetrical
As Grecian beauty, or a Doric fane,
Commanded reverence and love, and oped
Unto the awe struck, gladdened gaze of some,
Her gates magnificent, to the great world
Of God-stamped wisdom ushering.
But as the wheel of Time kept rolling,
 And our numbers were increased,
To the wide West, rich and glorious,
 A young band their footsteps pressed.
Some enchanted, where the Mohawk
 In blue luster seamed the mead,
Near the sparkle of its waters,
  Tarried, built and sowed the seed;

There they prospering were gladdened,
  With the joy of home and love,
Zoned with children as with flower-wreaths,
  Till Heaven called of these, above,
Not a few, fond, lovely spirits
  Which their gentle radiance cast
O'er the waves of life's swift river,
  Leaving thus a hallowed past.

When the cares of home were ended,
  When their toils in State were done,
On Religion's breast they languished,
  Life's light quenched, its courses run.

Others where Lake Erie's billows
  Bathed in diamond-light its shores;
Or amid New Jersey's green glades
  Found a home. Where ocean roars,

With "sea spray" gemming grassy meadows,
Others in a quiet shrine
  Their household happiness embowered,
To science given and art divine.

By the swift Missouri's waters;
  Where the Thames and Yantic glide;
'Mid New England's northern mountains,
  Widely spread our prospering tribe.

As bees unto the hive returning,
  Though fair flowers they leave for home,
So unto their olden homesteads
  Rich with memories sweet they come.

As in Spring the joyous swallows
  Thrilling with their early love,
Seek their peaceful, native valleys,
  So we come our hearts to prove.

As the waters brightly sparkling
  That from hill-sides course away,
Gliding on in creek and river
  Till they 're lost 'neath ocean spray;

From that mighty waste returning,
  Rising in the showery winds,
Fall in gladdening streams where erst they
  Gushed in fonts their course to find;

THE FAMILY MEETING.

So, from th' western world's wide ocean,
    From its heaving, restless tide,
Hither to their source our kindred
    Gather thick from every side.

Hither they've come, the aged, on whose sight
    These storied scenes burst with affecting power;
They gazed upon them in youth's rosy light;
    Now, in life's autumn and its soberer hour,
They greet the view again, and they are
Here by ancestral homes once more to rest.

Welcome! ye aged; in the name of those
    Whose lot and homes amid these scenes are fixed,
Welcome unto this spot where ceaseless flow
    The quenchless light and stream of memory's mixed
But clear associations blest; the same,
Though changed, this spot of olden name.

Death has been busy, as we have been told,
    Gathering the ripened sheaves to granaries full,
Those radiant in young bloom beside the old
    He has not shrunk with icy hand to cull;
Like miser antique, rich with ample store,
Whose pale and covetous clasp seeks more and more.

But here beside you, are the youthful throng
    Of sons and daughters, relatives of ours,
And those maturer; unto whom belong
    The features of the lost; as in the flowers
And fruitage of this year, we see the type
Of those that in your youth were fresh and ripe.

A welcome here our friends extend to all,
    To youth all glowing with its undimmed hopes,
And those who have responded to the call
    To active, thoughtful life of various scopes,
To all may Pleasure pure and sweet return
Proffer, full-flowing from her liberal urn.

Here may you feast, like bees among the flowers,
    Upon associations old, to memory dear,
Gladdened by visions of the vales and bowers
    And rushing streams you loved in childhood's years.
Beauteous and spotless to your fancy rise
The forms of lost ones in a heavenly guise!

Here may our contact strike ethereal sparks,
   Lighting the scene with wit and blameless glee.
Here in this ancient spot may care that carks,
   And all of bitterness and anguish flee;
May love and friendship smile like Eden's morn,
And sweet and holy visions here be born.

May sentiments of pure and sacred worth,
   Breathed forth from prayer from public thanks and praise;
Or having, mid our private converse birth,
   Like gems which 'mid its sand some stream displays;
May such now find impressible our hearts,
And rich and lasting values here impart.

Here at the ancient hive, may honey true,
   And gathered from th' eternal fields of Truth,
With its encloying sweets our souls imbue;
   Than an elixir true of life and youth
More gladdening and enduring in its power;
May sacred beams shine 'mid this festal hour!

So may this meeting favor our advance
   In the glad ways of peace, and turn the thoughts
As doves unto the ark where brightly glance
   The sunbeams of the love divine, and sought
Security of life and pleasure dwells,
And social joy forever freely wells.

In that communion noble opened here,
   Through its pure, glowing spirit, may our hearts
A foretaste drink of that commune so dear
   Which Heaven with its undying love imparts;
The silver bonds of kindred now renewed,
May they there then all of our own include.

As flocks of the like plumage, scattered far
   By harsh alarms, gather again on high,
Cutting with swift and eager wings the air
   Till their glad voices mingle in the sky,
So, tho' afar dispersed by life's shocks here,
May we in heaven's pure air unite fore'er!

The ocean shall give back its sunken pearls,
   And every deep the gems engulfed there:
The silenced notes of music wake: the world
   Of harmony their strains shall know once more;
The seed which, full of virtue fell to earth,
In a new growth to beauty shall have birth.

Yea: even those timid, youthful thoughts that rose,
    Rose and then fell, like fluttering, half-fledged birds,
Shall waken yet unto a life that knows
    No death-like darkness, if to holy words
And kindly they were joined; those thoughts in might
    Shall revel in th' unclouded realms of light.

But now 'tis fit this strain should know its close:
'Tis fit this stream of humble thought should cease:
And yet, perchance, oblivion's thirsty sands
May not at once drink up this current spent;
Since from a bosom stirred by love's pure breath
These parting words are voiced.

        Ancestral homes!
Tender and beautiful and fond the light
Which floats around ye! Here affections come,
Seeking the haunts and homes of buried worth,
As life's warm currents seek again the heart,
Or as the many echoes their one source.
Tombs of my sires, who in yon graveyard sleep!
There is a voice which in your silence speaks:
Amid your darkness and your dust there springs
A fresh and lovely light; and forms beloved
Start up and beckon with engaging smiles.

Scenes eloquent and solemn! ere I part,
Ere from my mind your picture floats to rest
Beneath a shadow for the while, may hopes
And strong resolves burn bright to meet
The sainted who have found the soul's sweet rest;
Whose spirits, purified and lighted up
With the image of "the Sun of righteousness,"
Have risen at His calling, as the drops
Of dew that image forth the Sun,
Rise at his summons to the glorious skies.

ADDRESS.

KINSMEN, COUSINS ALL:—

    You know how welcome you all are here to-day. The few words of our cousin President, so heartily spoken, assure us that we are not far from home; and those other hearty words from our poet cousins, to which you have listened with such delight, may well reconcile your hearts to this sacred place. You have "well met" on this pleasant day. This is for you a fitting place. These exercises, so well begun, are the appropriate exercises of such a convocation of cousins, as now assemble here. Children, with two exceptions, of the two pioneers of our name, who so largely aided in subduing the savage wildness of these old Indian haunts, and in training these hill-sides and plains to all their cultured beauty, as you see it now; children, with no exception, of that genial hearted puritan, whose spirit and faith still vitalize those more glorious structures of civil, social and religious life, which are, even now, the only stable support of your prosperity and joy; children, all, of such an ancestry, born alike to such an inheritance, living equally under the bonds, and to fulfill the sanctities of such co-heirship, it is well for us to meet, and here study together our mutual privileges and duties.

I shall make no attempt to win your atttention to the theme which you yourselves have assigned me. You expect to hear of the name which you are proud to bear, or with which you are not reluctantly allied. Already have I seen among you the glow of family affection, possibly of family pride; already have I felt the warm pulsations of a true Huntington sympathy here; and I know that you have called me to this service, because your love for the name, your veneration for its great and good, your affectionate interest in its extension, and your devotion to its present and future prosperity, have been a part of the noble inheritance which the fathers left. May this ennobling sentiment of our birthright never be less our characteristic, than it is to-day; and God grant that it may never be alienated from us, though ancestral halls and acres pass to other hands.

In treating of the Huntington family, in this country, I must touch, but lightly, the many themes which the subject suggests, leaving much more unsaid than spoken. And if, with all my clippings and omissions, I am still obliged to hold you a few moments beyond the length of ordinary discourse, I must charge the offense upon your ancestors or yourselves. Had my kinsmen been fewer or less successful, I could, in fewer moments, have read to you the story of their names and deeds. If the field they sowed were large and of fertile soil, 'twere meanness in us to garner but small crops.

Omitting all speculations about that invisible law which works out family character, preserving its identity even while so potently intermingling with others; and all comparisons of the Huntington name, with that of many another family which elsewhere we should equally honor, let us pass to the NAME itself, as the first point in our examination.

HUNTINGTON, like many of the modern family names in England, was originally conferred, as a title of honor, on a faithful servant of a grateful king. That tract of England lying between Cambridge on the East, and Northhampton and Bedfordshires on the West, from the earliest times of which we have any account, was celebrated for its extensive forests and marshes. These were filled with all kinds of English game; and for centuries after the old Iceni and the Romans held sway over the territory, it was the hunting ground of Saxon, Dane, and Norman, until disforested by the successive decrees of the second Henry and the first Edward. Collins tells us, that this hunting ground, called from its use, Huntington, was mainly noted for giving names to several honorable families.

I shall not attempt to rehearse the long story of **the** Huntington peerage in England, nor the repeated creations of nobles under this title; I will, however, indicate some points which may very likely lead **to a discovery of our ancestor's connexion.**

Before titles were hereditary in England, Siward, who had rendered important service in the restoration of Malcom Third, on the defeat of the famous Macbeth, in 1057, was honored with the officiary Earldom of Huntington—the first use, I think, of this name on record. He afterward became Duke of Northumberland. A son of his, Waldeof, married a niece of William the Conqueror, and the daughter of this Waldeof, marrying Simon St. Lys, brought him the Earldom of Huntington, and had by him a son, named also Simon. After his death she married David, brother of St. Maud, Queen of England, and he became King of Scotland. By this David she had a Henry, Earl of Huntington, who also had a son Simon St. Lys, the third of the name. Though this third Simon died without heirs, and so lost the title, we have gained this much from the record—the use of Huntington as a family name, and of Simon itself, which it is our more particular want to find.

But to pass by other families, made noble, technically, at least for a short time, we come to the Hastings family, in several of its branches, the bearers of this title. Hastings, a family name, from Hastings, the famous battle field between Harold and the Norman Conqueror, and so, in itself, a title of honor, was still further ennobled with the added Earldom of Huntington. This was first conferred by the Conqueror, upon Robert, portgreve of Hastings, one of his faithful dispensators, or stewards. In his family the title continued down to 1491, when, on the death of William Herbert, it became dormant.

In 1529, George Hastings, who had married Anne, **daughter of** Henry Stafford, second Duke of Buckingham, was created Earl **of** Huntington, and in this branch it descended through eleven earls, to Francis, **the twenty-third from the portgreve.** The ninth of this line was Theophilus, **whose wife was the eminent Lady** Huntington. On the death of Francis, in 1780, the Huntington estates and properties, now become quite extensive, passed over to Lord Rawdon, husband **of Mary Hastings.** But in 1819, Hans Francis, fourth son of Col. George **Hastings, was created Earl Huntington, and took his seat with his peers.**

Not to follow this re-creation of Huntington peers, further, it is not foreign here to say, that we have among us a family, whose resemblance to this last named Huntington, is sufficiently striking to suggest, if not indicate a common origin. It would not surprise me, if it shall be made clear, that the late Hon. Roger Huntington, **of this town, who you all know had no mean blood in his** veins, drew his form, and features, and manners, from the same common source, and that not many generations back, with this **Hans** Francis, the founder of the present line of Huntington nobility in the mother land. And if he had such relationship, then all of us also have it; for his great grandfather's great grandfather was the common ancestor of us all.

But whether one or another of **these noble names, or** some unknown descendant of some half dozen other belted earls, gave name to our ancestor; or, whether that name came from some still nobler origin, as that in which, by universal consent, that gifted scholar and industrious historian, Henry, was called the Henry de Huntington, from the city of his birth; this much is true, that noble blood must sometime have stirred in English veins, to have issued, in spite of all opposing forces, in such results in the Huntington line, as we are now enabled to collect.

Of our common ancestor, I can say but little. Indeed, I confess that my knowledge regarding him, is much less than I supposed I had, when I commenced my study of his family. That he was a good and true Englishman, and that his name was Simon, I have no reason to doubt. Tradition is positive and uniform respecting the latter, and both tradition and the character of the family which he founded, agree in attesting the former. But whether he, while in England, was a Norwich man; or, whether he had spent his life in amassing a fortune in the East Indies; or, whether he ever gloried in the outlawry, and reveled amid the gathered booty of a Robin Hood; or, whether his brother, more loyal than himself, to the powers that then were, was a special favorite of the first Charles, and the highest officer of his guard; these are questions which I shall not now be able to answer. That he was a religious man, and that his religious and political conscience was closely connected with his voluntary exile to this new world, seems more than probable; and when I shall succeed in deciphering the old records that may authenticate these positions, I will gladly lay the solution before you.

But of the time and place of the immigration of the family I can speak with more positiveness. It is not a matter of conjecture merely, nor yet of tradition alone. We have an authentic record, whose worst feature is that it so effectually contradicts our family tradition. We had been taught to believe, that about the year 1639, Simon Huntington, with his wife and three sons, came to the mouth of the Connecticut river; that the father having come within sight of the land died, and the family, burying him near the mouth of the river, for twenty years remained, as if to guard the sleeping dust, in the vicinity of his lonely grave.

This account, first stated distinctly, on the authority of the somewhat celebrated Joseph Huntington, D. D., of Coventry, and then published in several works, whose general accuracy gave credit to the report, came to be regarded as an authentic statement, and obtained, until recently, universal currency. But thanks to a reliable record of an earlier day, we can now antedate this immigration by several years.

Two hundred and twenty-four years ago, fifteen years before tradition supposes our ancestor came to this country, an English vessel freighted with a band of gifted and resolute English emigrants, might have been seen nearing the eastern coast of Massachusetts. On board that vessel was a family, consisting of a father, not far from forty years of age, his wife, some years his junior, and probably four sons. But from that family group the voice of mourning would have fallen upon your ear. The father is suddenly struck down and consigned to his ocean grave, leaving so prematurely his beloved wife and her helpless charge. A record of the Roxbury church, in the hand writing of its pastor, the Rev. John Elliot, informs us of the subsequent locality of that mother and her sons. It states that "Margaret Huntington, a widow, came to Roxbury in 1633; that she was a member of the church; that she had — sons with her; and that her husband had died on the passage, from the small pox.

This is, undoubtedly, the oldest record of the Huntington name in this country; and though brief, it answers for us, reliably, some questions, which, but for it, must have been forever unanswered.

It settles the time and place of the immigration of our family—the year 1633, at Boston. It shows that our common ancestor was not permitted to see this new world and aid in establishing and building up on New England soil his name. It shows that by maternal care, rather, the infancy of our name here was nurtured. It explains, in part at least, the absence of more satisfactory records respecting the family for the first few years after the immigration, the hand which should have penned the record having been cut off by that premature death. The surviving wife, amid the privations and perils of her early widowhood in the new and exposed settlement, with her dependent sons, the eldest yet several years below his majority and the youngest not yet five years of age, would find little time, even if in her earlier life she had been used to it, to make any continuous record of their progress. And so that early story of our feeble beginning here, its days of gloom and uncertainty, of exposures and weakness, of slow unfolding yet of steady progress, was never written, and we must ever regret the want of records, which the known condition of immigrant families most fully justifies.

A few words will suffice to state all that is now known, possibly all that can be known, of that mother and her family. Remaining about two and a half years in Roxbury under the pastoral care of Elliot, she married Thomas Stoughton, then of Dorchester, and with him, taking probably her youngest three sons, she removed to Windsor, Connecticut, then a new settlement, where she spent the rest of her life. It is no slight testimony to her position and ability as a woman, that she secured such an alliance. Her second husband stood very high among the noble pioneers of the Connecticut settlement; and was often honored with posts which called for the highest qualities to be found among the colonists. Under their united training, the three sons spent, probably, the last years of their majority. Whether the mother lived to see her sons settled in life, neither tradition nor record now shows.

Of two of those sons I can say but little. William the eldest of them, doubtless, was probably left by his mother in Massachusetts. As early as 1640, he is found among the landed proprietors of Salisbury, and from him have descended an unbroken line of the name, in the vicinity of Salisbury. My present list of those descendants, furnished almost entirely by our kinsman Enoch, of Amesbury, who is with us to-day, contains about two hundred and fifty names.

Of Thomas the youngest, probably still less can be said. In 1687, we find him in Branford, one of the company who in that year emigrated to Newark, New Jersey. He had married Hannah, daughter of the saintly Jasper Crane, and was a man not unworthy of the brotherhood to which he belonged, nor of the Puritan family into which he married. Of his descendants, I have been able to enroll only one son and daughter, two grandsons and one great grandson.

Of the remaining two sons, Christopher and Simon, and their descendants, we shall have more to say. The Huntington name in this land is, mainly, what they have made it. Not far from four thousand Huntingtons, in America, have been indebted to them for existence; and the story of that succession, from that day to ours, should furnish us, their children's children, many a lesson of devout thanksgiving and grateful joy. Some of the leading points of this family story, will now claim our attention.

Christopher, the elder of the two, having married Ruth, daughter of William Rockwell, of Windsor, after living several years in Saybrook, came with the first settlers of this town, in 1660, and was assigned his home lot on the corner, about a quarter of a mile east of where we now are. His family then consisted of his wife and two infant children, to which were afterwards added six others, making in all, four sons and four daughters. Three only of the sons had families. Of this Christopher, it is abundantly attested by the earliest records of the town, that he was a religious man, and that he enjoyed in a high degree the confidence and respect of the colonists. We find him equally employed, as a sort of pacificator, in those ecclesiastical, financial and civil disturbances to which the new colony was exposed, and his success evinces most desirable qualities, both of head and heart. He was the first town clerk whose election is on record; and, what is remarkable, he so well succeeded in training his descendants, that in a long line, even down to the year 1828, with but two short interruptions, they succeeded him in that office, the last of these Huntington town clerks being here with us to-day.

Simon, the other of these two sons, before coming to Norwich, had married in Saybrook, Sarah, daughter of Joseph Clark, of Windsor, and when they reached Norwich, in 1660, the family numbered five souls, and it was subsequently increased to twelve, making ten children, in all, of whom six were sons and four daughters. Of him, too, we find amplest testimonials in the early records of the town. As the first deacon chosen in Norwich, the preceding deacons having been chosen in Saybrook, he served with great fidelity and acceptance until his death; and it was doubtless felt to be a tribute to his success as well as one to the fitness of the son, that his son was chosen to succeed him. As first townsman, then the highest mayoralty known, and as deputy in the general Court of the State, he seems to have acted a prominent part in the civil and social movements of the day, ever deserving and receiving honor from his fellow townsmen. His house lot occupied a prominent position on the public square, a short distance this side of his brother Christopher's, and a portion of it is to-day in the possession of his worthy descendants of the same name. He was, also, for those days, a wealthy as well as honored man, transmitting his name, and not a little of his noble spirit through five of his sons and three of his daughters, to a numerous and widely scattered posterity.

Of the daughters of these two pioneers in the settlement of Norwich, I can only mention the names of the families with which they soon became allied by marriage; and the mention, itself, is no slight testimonial to their gifts and worth. Of Christopher's daughters, one married a Pratt, of Saybrook; another, a son of Lieut. Francis Griswold, both father and son being well known and influential men, but since represented among their descendants, by names still better known; and the third, a son of Thos. Bingham, of this town, the head of a numerous family, embracing many meritorious names, both of deceased and living representatives. Of Simon's daughters, one became the wife of Dr. Solomon, son of Lieut Thos. Tracy, and her descendants are among the first citizens of all the generations of this town; the second married a Forbes, of Saybrook; and the third took for husband, Joseph, son of the notable Lieut. William Backus, of this town, and became the mother of eight honored children, themselves the ancestors of worthy names.

Passing into the second generation of Huntingtons, born in this country, we find fifty-eight grand children of the two Norwich settlers. Their births, with only eight exceptions, are found on the records of the town. Of the eight families of the name, which this generation affords, five resided in Norwich, two in Windham, and one in Lebanon.

From these families spring twenty-nine families, of the name, in the next generation, who found their homes in eight different towns in this immediate vicinity; eleven in Norwich, seven in Windham, four in Lebanon, three in Mansfield, and one, each, in Franklin, Bozrah, Preston and Tolland. The sister families of this generation gifted with Huntington mothers, number among them noble names: the Wheelocks and Leffingwells, the Hydes and Lincolns, the Lathrops and Waleses, and Cranes, the Fitches and Clarks and Wrights, and the Carews and Adgates. Of course, my time will not suffice to tell you, here, even had I all the materials at command for doing it, of the many worthy things which might be said of so many, and so worthy names. Nor can I stop to tell you what I hope, at no very distant day, you may read, at your leisure, of the scattered routes which the seventy-three smart boys of these twenty-nine families took, where they stopped, and how they multiplied our name, until the Huntingtons in this land numbered over eight hundred souls, and were thriving in more than a hundred different towns. Those seventy-three patriarchs of our name have all gone, and but a few of their more than five hundred children still remain among us to testify to us of their great worth. Yet a few such remain and are here, to-day. Thank God, that in this place, and at this joyous hour, we may hail you—blessed, venerable fathers of our name. Ye are here to-day, the most eloquent prompters of our reverential love. Your names shall be dear to our hearts, as they will become household words in affectionate circles of your children's children, who shall glory in such a parentage, long after your departed feet shall have trod the immortal shore. We accept the lessons which your self-denying and heroic lives teach us, and will ever pray that we may transmit the priceless legacy to our children, and they to theirs.

I have spoken of the fourth generation as having nearly passed away, leaving, perhaps, the impression that all who are left of this generation, are now aged. But, as if to illustrate what is no uncommon freak in the growth of families, we can point to-day to our Rome cousins, and also to our gifted poet, from whom you are soon to hear, as a part of this same generation; enough still left of the youth and strength, the intellect and heart of the past generation, to suggest to us what their confreres, though so many years their elders, must have been.

Of this generation, numbering about five hundred souls, I have on record the families of about a hundred and thirty sons, scattered all over our country, and quite generously mingling with her Majesty's subjects in her provinces on the North; and of course I must not attempt here to locate for you their more than seven hundred children. Still less must I take you to the homes of the two hundred families springing from this fifth generation, and now numbering, though many of them still in the infancy of their growth, not many less than a thousand souls.

Of the next generation still, I can now report but about thirty families, and as these, with a single exception, are still young, their increase may be some less than two hundred. Here, too, we notice a freak of family growth, the opposite of that which appeared in our notice of the fourth generation. Among the infant families of this seventh generation, appears the mature circle of the late Joseph C. Huntington, of this town. The eldest son of this family, in the seventh generation, was born in the same year with our poet of this occasion, who is in the fifth. Though anticipating, by more than a generation, their own generation in the family, they are doubly welcome thus early to our inheritance. Their number and their position, give us noble promise of a good record to be made up when the last child of that seventh generation shall have been born. For, it must not be forgotten, that the last children of the fifth generation are yet to be born, and that but two families of the seventh, as far as we know, have yet in them the first fruits of the eighth.

Such is the Huntington Family, numerically. Extending to the tenth generation from SIMON, the puritan immigrant, embracing not far from four thousand of those still bearing the name, about one-third of whom are now living in the last four generations; you may find them scattered from the Atlantic to the Pacific, doing business from highest northern to furthest southern latitude on this continent, and also, quite extensively intermingling interests and forming matrimonial alliances with the old world.

Let me now indicate as briefly as I may, to what extent we have borne our part in the political, and social and educational movements of our country.

In five of our States we have furnished members for political conventions in which State Constitutions were made, or ratified, or amended. In Connecticut we were represented by three of the name in the Convention of 1788, for ratifying the Constitution of the United States—Samuel and Jedediah of Norwich, and Isaac of Bozrah. In the Convention of 1818, we had our Jonathan of Haddam. New York has had our Henry and Edward at work upon hers; Ohio, her second Governor, our Samuel, upon hers, and New Hampshire our George, of Walpole, upon hers. As representatives or senators, and they are about equally divided, we have furnished not less than thirty for State Legislatures, and a solid half-dozen for our national Congress, one of whom is with us to-day. Of Judges of County Courts, Superior Judges and Federal and Chief Justices, we can count at least fifteen; and of their right hand agents, at least four high sheriffs. Our Governors have been two, and one of them a President. Thus have we been represented in all the grades of office known both to our State and national constitutions.

Educationally we have also a creditable record. Nearly a hundred names on our list have taken collegiate honors; a number which, for its ratio to the entire list, is probably unequaled by any New England family. Our ministers have exceeded one third of our college list, and our lawyers and doctors have nearly equaled a third each. Of instructors and professors in colleges we have had several; and in all the grades both of private and public schools, we have not wanted successful and honored workers. In authorship, our State Historical Library will furnish several worthy specimens from deceased members of the family, and our later achievements are not without promise. There are living now several members, who, if true to the beginning of their course, will leave behind them no mean fruits of their scholarship and taste.

Nor have the Huntington daughters been behind their brothers in these contributions to the civil and educational movements of our land. They have been, eminently, the mothers of legislators, of divines, of doctors, of lawyers, and of teachers.

Leaving this table, thus spread out before you, let us pass now to a more particular notice of two of the most marked characteristics of the family. From the very beginning of our American history, our name has sustained an honorable rank for the PATRIOTISM and the PIETY of its representatives.

The old French war found in our family a readiness to dare and die, even, for the defense of their homes. Matthew, of Mansfield, at the call of his country, enlisted a company of the Mansfield boys numbering about sixty, and started for the seat of the war, on Lake George. You might have seen him defying flood and heat and that terrible foe, the camp distemper of that day, struggling to take his charge of boats and barges up the Hudson to Greenbush. One after another of his company yielded to the trial. Unhesitatingly he orders and leads the survivors on, hauling their boats against the current, wading often, until the weakness and failure of his men had made it necessary for himself to drag with his own strong and ready arm, the last boat around the last rapid in his course. He had accomplished his specific object, but you follow him no longer. That patriot heart ceased that night its beating, and our kinsman was next morning a lifeless victim to his excessive toil — self offered on the altar of his country's cause. Three years later in the same war, Elijah of this town, a son of that "justice Isaac, than whom no juster man then lived," engaged under Gen. Amherst in Col. Fitch's regiment, in his third campaign. He was more successful though he endured scarcely less toil and suffering, yet they were deemed of little account, when he could report to his father the surrender of the French, and the floating of "the flag of St. George in triumph on the gate of Montreal." "Let God," he adds, "have the praise of our success over the enemy, and may we never have occasion for another campaign in this country again." And so he proved himself to be the Christian patriot; in the day of his triumph pleading for the peace of his land. An incident, illustrative of the spirit with which that expedition was executed, is not without interest to us. That part of the army to which our kinsman belonged had, by a most fatiguing march of thirty-one days, traversed the distance from Schenectady to Fort Ontario, and had weathered in open boats and rude galleys, a most perilous crossing of the lake to its outlet into the St. Lawrence. Amherst determined to pass down the river and attack Oswegatchie and Isle Royal. Two armed vessels hindered the passage. Putnam put 1,000 men, including our kinsman, into fifty batteaux, and started to board the vessels. Ordering his men to strip to their waistcoats, taking his beetle and wedges with which to fasten the rudders of the vessels and so render them unmanageable, he entered the advanced boat with a chosen crew, and gave the signal. On they moved, so swiftly and resolutely, thus stripped for the encounter, that the French, panic-struck, abandoned the idea of resistance, one vessel being run aground, and the other striking her colors without a blow.

Our connexion with our revolutionary history is not deficient in interest or incident. In those days, when to cling to our country's cause was treason, patriotism was our family trait; and no threats of governmental vengeance, and no seductions of governmental favor, could for a moment weaken or repress it. American Independence had few warmer or truer friends than our name and family furnished. In this town was General Jabez, who cheerfully risked his extensive shipping interests, and voluntarily sacrificed his thousands in support of national resistance against foreign rule. His large property, his time, his counsels and his prayers were equally and efficiently consecrated to the successful issue of that memorable struggle; and when the aged patriot had by the cares and anxieties which that contest imposed upon him, been prematurely hurried to his grave, a whole community, and the whole country indeed, testified to their sorrow over what was felt to be a national loss. Nor less efficient in that struggle were the services and personal sacrifices of the five sons of the old patriot. All of them were ardent supporters of the revolution, and were then, or subsequently, honored with high military rank. It is no mean compliment, that the great Washington, whose discernment of character equaled, and indeed issued in, his abundant success, all through the war, made the elder brother, Jedediah, a counselor and confidant, and afterwards honored him with high testimonials of his regard. Nor less faithful to the obligations of that trying day, were other Huntingtons. Deacon Hezekiah, a christian and a judge, is at the head of a committee appointed in 1767, to bring in resolutions expressive of the feelings of the citizens. That committee headed by the two Hon's Hezekiah and Jabez, consisting of twelve other sturdy and brave patriots, had in it eight of the fourteen, who either had Huntington blood in them, or who were connected with the name by marriage. Capt. Simeon, the sturdy hammerer of iron, as sturdily resisted the enslavement of his native land, and with muscular arm and true patriot pluck, collared and shook too, to the satisfaction of both parties, the meddling tory, who had come down from Massachusetts to insult the patriots of Connecticut; and no tory thenceforward showed himself among the unflinching patriots of this locality. A letter of Gen. Jedediah may be seen in the American Archives recommending this Simeon for promotion, on the strength of his military bearing and courage.

I call up also from the stern realities of that trying day, an Amos, from Shaftesbury, doing valiant service at the head of his fearless band at Hubbardston, preferring a fearful risk in a spirited encounter with immense odds, under the generalship of Burgoyne, to an inglorious retreat. I follow his unquenched patriotism, under the trying ordeal of his tedious imprisonment, and rejoice to know, that when by exchange of prisoners he was again set free, he was ready to risk again the life which he had scarcely saved.

I see toiling, day after day, others of that generation; some in the march, some in the field of preparation and of contest, and more on their farms and in their shops at home, living and laboring, to a man, to aid their country in her desperate struggle for independence. And in this spirit, the daughters of our fathers shared. To a woman they were on the right side, and wo to the suitor who asked consent of maiden or mother, while yet undecided whether to hold on to the "flesh pots" of the good old English dame, or to strike boldly for a free home, for himself and her whom he sought for wife. Nor would it have been safe for a husband of one of those daughters to have showed the white feather in the fight. If no other resource had offered, you may know from what you have seen of some of them, when tried, how quietly she would have seated her timid lord by the cradle of their babe, while with a woman's pluck she would have shouldered his musket and knapsack for the field herself.

Great as were the sacrifices required of the patriots of that day, we are happy to believe that few families more cheerfully met them; and perilous as the struggle for independence was, few more heroically entered it, to encounter its dangers, and achieve its triumphs.

Still more marked has been the RELIGIOUS element of the family, as from its origin we had a right to expect. Probably all of the sons of the immigrant were religious men. Certainly the two who ultimately settled in Norwich were so, nor were their wives at all behind them, in this respect.

The one who settled at Newark, would hardly have been admitted into the family of that good old Jasper Crane, unless he had upon him the seal of orthodox puritanism; and, moreover, he signed before going from Connecticut, that memorable compact, in which he pledges the maintenance of the purity of religion professed in the Congregational churches.

William, of Salisbury, was at least a companion in that border settlement of men who feared and served God.

In the next generation we find three deacons, Simon and Christopher and Daniel, of this town, deacon Joseph and his cousin Thomas, two of the fathers of the Windham, and deacon Samuel, a strong pillar in the Lebanon church; and the religious influence of those six families, is to be measured only when we have comprehended the succeeding history of these three early churches, both on their original territory, and in the new churches for which they have supplied founders and colonists. Of this generation, embracing as far as is known, twenty souls, of whom six died in early life; nearly all were not only members of these three churches, but they were prominent among their membership. Perhaps few families can show a fairer religious record, in the first generation of its members born in this country. Passing into the next generation, we find in this town, the two deacons Ebenezer and Hezekiah, son of Christopher, a worthy successor of his father in the church, and Joseph of Windham, who also succeeded his father. Then there were Daniel, and Benjamin, and Jonathan, and Isaac, and Jabez, all men of religious principle, in Norwich, Jonathan, Nathaniel and Solomon of Windham, and Caleb and Samuel of Lebanon.

In the third generation we find no lack of the religious element. The good seed bears good fruit, rather, and we have no less than eight deacons, not to count the husbands of several of the Huntington daughters of that generation. And as if to fulfill the scriptural economy—first the blade, then the ear, and afterward the full corn in the ear, we find outgrowing from our deaconship, the higher ecclesiastical office of the ministry; and in this highest office of the church, we have no less than seven ministers of religion, no mean development of canonical orders: saintly men and one deacon in the first; good men and more deacons in the second, and both these, with the holy ministry in the third. Going on into the next generation we find fewer deacons, indeed, but then the old seed ripens here into the higher orders, and accordingly we find in the family ten who were thought worthy of ministerial vows. Five of this number are still living; one-half of the ministers in a generation, four-fifths of which are dead. Six of our daughters of this generation took, or were taken by as many ministers of the gospel, and the names of those husbands will best illustrate the character of these daughters: Rev. Dr. Lyman of Hadley; Rev. Dr. Strong of Norwich; Rev. Dr. Griffin of Boston; Rev. Samuel Perkins of Windham; Rev. Henry Smith, Camden, N. Y., and Dr. Thos. Baldwin of Boston.

In the next generation, many of whose sons are not yet old enough to have chosen, or at least to have entered upon a profession, we still find an encouraging assurance of more than a two fold increase. Already we number fifteen clergymen accredited, eleven of whom are alive, and nine of them should be, by promise, with us to-day; and several now in the course of preparation for the holy office. And even still later, in the next generation, we have two preachers, and three daughters the wives of preachers, and these are from the only families of the generation, which have reached the age for becoming ministers; yet, ample, as the first fruits of what will yet prove an abundant increase over all former generations. But we cannot linger upon this pleasant theme. I will not say that, as a family, our name has been especially marked for eminent piety. By very general consent we have been remarkably free from examples of extreme vice. There may have been rotten branches, that occasionally have disfigured the parent tree, but it has proved only the branch; we have found the limbs from which they cleaved off, as if not belonging to them, all sound, because the old trunk was sound to the core. I must not attempt to take you around among the homes of our family, where religion does her holiest work, and sheds her richest light, and achieves her heavenliest glory, to instance the many examples of every day piety among them. Least of all, can I carry you into that still more private sanctuary of the soul, where religion is born and nurtured, to show you how many of our name have there won the heavenly resident, and drawn to themselves the ministries of the heavenly grace. But, that many such home scenes and experiences have existed among us, we have no reason to doubt. The large number of members of the Christian churches of three evangelical denominations: Congregational, Episcopal, and Presbyterian, would suggest it. The large number of members holding official positions in these churches, would suggest, too, a higher than ordinary tone of piety.

Of the eighteen deacons of the church in this place, from its organization, seven have been of our name; and among its members are enrolled seventy-two of the name. The churches in this vicinity, embraced within the original territory of Norwich, have had an aggregate considerably greater than this; and for at least six of them, we have furnished one or more deacons.

But I cannot forbear mentioning a few personal illustrations of our kinsmen's faith. We owe it to the grace of God thus to make mention of its triumph. I must name, yet can hardly do more than name, our deacon Hezekiah, whose prayers and counsels, whose affability penetrated with the grace of his true piety, endeared his name to all who knew him. But one instance, I think, is on record, in which his piety is questioned. Dr. Benjamin Wheat had overheard two members of the Assembly in Hartford reporting evil of him, and made the report a ground of a sudden and grievous charge. But on examination the report was found groundless, and Dr. Wheat drew up a most humbling confession of having acted hastily and wickedly against the Christian character of one who was above reproach.

Need I more than name the Hon. Jedediah, honored most of all by a piety as philanthropic as it was Christian—a man whose consistency was proclaimed to be better and more effective than eloquence, yet whose counsels and prayers were so felicitous that none could forget them, and who won from the people among whom he lived, the application to himself of that divinest ascription—"the spirit of the Lord rested upon him."

I might speak of the truthful piety and warm-hearted benevolence of Rev. Asahel, for nearly a quarter of a century the "successful and useful minister of Topsfield," a man "in all social duties scrupulously exact;" whose moral and religious character was without a blot; whose "first object was to know the mind of the Lord, and whose decided purpose it was, then to declare it to his hearers." It is enough to repeat the record made of him by competent hands— "a faithful servant of Christ."

Nor should the name of our David, who won the title of the pious and devout minister—nor that of his son, Rev. Leverett Israel, the self-sacrificing and eminetly acceptable minister, be omitted.

Or, what more shall I say of that Christian pastor, the Rev. Nathaniel G., of Bethany, than that he drew the type of his religious experience from the deep wells of the original scriptures, dwelling much among the holiest and brighest example of religious faith; and that he was so persuaded of the realities of the religious life and the eventual consummation of religious hopes, that in the midst of deepest distress he could calmly and joyously exclaim, "it is all nothing compared to the glory before me."

Or, how shall I speak of the deep humility, the warmth of Christian love, the unswerving integrity, the disinterested devotion, and the burning zeal of the gifted Joshua, of Boston. If to preach the gospel to the poor was an evidence of his Master's commission from on high, few New-England pastors have given more abundant proofs of their divine appointment. I will not attempt to say how much he owed his eminent success to the true Christian sympathy, the rare Christian graces of that no less gifted wife whose memoir you may read.

But I must speak a word of the daughters in our Israel. There have been many polished stones among them. Their influence has been felt in the homes of many other names, and their memories are blessed in many other circles. But their names, their precious memories, their bright experiences are ours, too; and he who sent them to be the light and joy of our homes on earth, sent them no less to instruct and encourage our way to Heaven.

Ruth, daughter of the second Christopher, and wife of deacon Ralph, and mother of Rev. Dr. Eleazer Wheelock, was a woman as noticeable for her deep and humble piety, as for her intelligent use of religious influence; and among the fruits of both, we have the religious and literary history of Dartmouth College.

Nor less remarkable in both these qualities was that Lydia, daughter of our deacon Ebenezer, and wife of Dr. Jabez Fitch of Canterbury, the mother of President Ebenezer Fitch, through whom her maternal counsels contributed to the founding of another college, Williamstown, for the cause of learning and religion.

Let me instance, also, the character of Abigail, who married Azariah Lathrop, a woman who happily exemplified the meek and quiet spirit of the gospel. Her children blessed her, and their children also—that noble band of sisters—Mrs. Winslow, Hutchins, Perry and Cherry, who, yearning for the perishing heathen, lived for, and died among them.

Let me mention, also, Hannah, daughter of Col. Hezekiah and wife of Col. Joshua, of this town, "a memorial of whose virtues will live as long as any one remains who had the happiness to know her."

I may now speak, also, of Catherine, daughter of Henry of Rome, and wife of Col. William Williams of Utica, a woman in whose piety there was a completeness which best asserted its genuineness. Her faith was that which works. Her hands obeyed her heart; and blessed and comforted were they, who in the hour of their deep need and sadness, were found of her. It was a strong testimonial which her pastor bore to her character, but not fuller than the response of the mourning people, who knew her so well: "She was one of the rarest, choicest characters in the whole acquaintance of my life. To our partial vision she appeared to bear the perfections of heaven during the probation of earth."

I must also instance our Sarah Lanman, for one more illustration of Christian grace — a bright, a glorious triumph of Christian faith. Her name, her heroic life, her quenchless zeal, her hallowed death, are yours: and they plead as no form of human words can plead, with us all, to emulate the faith and works of her heaven-inspired life.

Nor can I forbear one other, and a still more pertinent illustration of this feature of our family history. The lambs of our fold have been the great and good shepherd's care. I hear the voices of departed babes taken from all our clasping arms, into the bright home above, sounding there sweeter praises than we who are left can learn to raise while on earth. Many of them began their sweet song below. Mary Hallam, whose memoir you may read, that sweet babe in Christ, began them here. She caught the spirit of heaven in her very infancy, and was drawn by it to the companionship and enjoyment of the heavenly company. Oh! how sweet, that earnest plea from that dear departing babe, longing to leave, even those whom she loved most, that she might be with Christ — "Give me to God." And so she passed away to join that large company of little ones that from all our fond circles have been taken into the safer, the heavenly home above. Beloved kinsmen, a review of the religious history of our family has left on my mind the pleasant impression that the number of those of our name who are now on the celestial heights, exceeds that of us who are still journeying through the vale below. May the great and good God bring us, each in his turn, safely up to their blessed companionship.

A third topic — biographical notices of several members of the family, for want of time, I must omit, with the single exception of a brief one of the most prominent name on our list.

SAMUEL, the second of a noble family of distinguished brothers, sons of Nathaniel, without the advantages of college, or even of private school instruction, attained a position the most honored and exalted which the world in his day could give. Perhaps he realized, more fully than any other member of our family, the ideal of a full and true Huntington — an actual impersonation of the form and spirit of the family.

Other pens, both American and European, have recorded his merits most appropriately. May not his kinsmen, whose name has borrowed from him no ephemeral luster, linger a moment over the story of his artless, yet honored and useful life.

The farmer's son became the cooper-boy; yet, while shaving staves and bending hoops, he was fast learning the art of shaping human conduct and bending human wills. He soon proved that the making of empty barrels did not necessitate the carrying of an empty head, and while he conscientiously made the one to hold, unleakingly, everything but sound, he filled, unceasingly, the other with good solid sense.

At his graduation from his apprenticeship, or very soon after it, he was thus self-taught admitted to the bar. At twenty-nine years of age he removed to Norwich, as a better field for his new profession; and rose rapidly to the front rank of jurists and civilians. At the opening of our Revolution, he had already been honored with many testimonials of public confidence. As representative of the town in the state legislature, as member of the state senate, as King's attorney, and judge of the superior court, he approved himself as every way worthy of higher trusts. And when the time came for calling the mother land to account for her unjust demands upon the resources of the hitherto filial daughter, now grown to a good degree of maturity, after reaching the period of her legitimate majority, who better than he could manage the case? Accordingly, he was in 1775, sent as delegate to the continental congress. The universal testimony respecting his position as a member of congress is, that during the whole period of his membership, nearly five years, he was one of its most prominent and influential members. You have seen his name among the signers of our Declaration. You have seen that placid gaze calmly comprehending the rising storm, yet serene in its quiet trust in the rectitude of every assertion and of every demand in that Declaration. You have followed him, steadily asserting its every claim; and so ably was it done, so uncompromisingly insisted on, so unimpeachably true to the great cause was the advocate, that the leaders of the age confided its consummation to his presidency; and midway in the fearful struggle to which it had led, our kinsman is chosen from among the master spirits of the age, which had made great souls, the President of the grandest movement of the age itself. How well he met the responsibilities of that new post for nearly two years, is best evinced in the reluctance with which congress accepted the resignation which his failing health compelled him to make. On returning to his native State, his services were again called for, in the council and on the bench. In 1786 he was chosen governor, and annually re-elected until his death, in 1796; and of the nine hundred votes cast in the town of his adoption, for the last term of his office, he received every vote. A noble and spontaneous tribute, of those who knew him best, to private, no less than public worth.

But the highest, or, more strictly, the deepest excellence of the man, is yet to be mentioned. Faith in God and loyalty only to His will, was the most vital spring in his life. He was a man true to every human obligation, because obedient to every divine law; and he who could never find it in his heart to deny his God, was found ready to acknowledge every claim of his country and his race.

Yet this truest man, this purest patriot, this sincerest Christian, was not above the reproach and hatred of his kind. So good a man was he, that a large price would have been any day paid for his head at the English Exchequer; and in an English political magazine for July, 1781, we find this tribute, the highest which such a journal could pay: "Samuel Huntington, the new President of the rebel congress, is the son of a farmer. He was bred to the law, and was poor at the breaking out of the rebellion, but being gifted with a smooth tongue, and being insinuating and deceitful, has become popular, and probably rich, by fleecing his deluded constituents." But no such defamation could reach the character of our incorruptible kinsman. Until the day of his departure he maintained his hold on the confidence and affection of all who knew him, and when he died it was no ordinary sorrow that paid its tribute to his great social, civil and religious worth.

For other names, worthy abundantly of a distinct notice here, I must refer you to the ready speakers who may this afternoon represent them; or to the record, when at length completed and published.

An honored list is that, composed of such names as Benjamin and Joshua and Isaac of the second generation; Gen. Jabez, Rev. Nathaniel, the three Rev. brothers, Jonathan, Enoch and Joseph, and Rev. Eliphalet, Hon's Henry, Gurdon, George and Benjamin, brothers, and Hon. Jabez, of Windham, of the third; Gen. Jedediah and brothers of whom you may hear, this afternoon, from the gifted pen of Mrs. Sigourney, and Samuel, governor of Ohio, Judge Samuel Gray, of Troy, and Hezekiah of Hartford, Hon. Jonathan of Haddam, and Hon. Ziba, of Lebanon, N. H., a list of which any family may be justly proud.

But I cannot dwell here.

I must not leave this summary of our history, without a more particular notice of the daughters of our name. They have fully equaled their brothers, in number, and in all those qualities of person and culture, which render either sex companionable. A few of them have loved the name so well that no other name could move them to drop it, and we Huntingtons cannot well blame them. Yet, where they have for reasons which overbear the strongest human resistances, consented to accept a change of names, they have quite uniformly, as I think, done still better. The honorable alliances thus formed have given to New England many and worthy names.

I have not time to run over the long list, and speak of the great personal merits of our fathers' daughters. Their names are embalmed in the holiest affections of fond and reverent household circles, of which their presence or their memory is the most sacred shrine.

To speak worthily of the families of the first generation of Huntington daughters, would be to write out a full genealogy of the Tracys, and Backuses, and Griswolds, and Binghams of New England. And in the next generation we should have to add those of the Lathrops, and Cranes, and Fitches, and Clarkes, and Adgates, and Turners, and Abels, and Hydes, and Wheelocks, and Leffingwells, and Lincolns; with all the honored names which have sprung from these. But I need not go into the next generation to recite, even, the family names, which only honored, to be more abundantly honored by our daughters.

Yet, that you may see what a theme of interest opens to every true Huntington in this branch of our family history, let me cite a few illustrative records.

Take that of Elizabeth, daughter of Samuel, in the first generation, of Lebanon. Born in 1689, she married, in 1710, Moses, a son of Daniel Clark and Hannah Pratt, first of Windsor, then of Hartford, and later of Colchester. She had six children, one of whom was Dr. John Clark, of Lebanon. Liking his mother's name so well, he took for wife, Jerusha, daughter of Col. Jabez Huntington of Windham, and their children were twelve. Of these, the oldest, the 2d Dr. John, of Lebanon, N. Y., marrying a daughter of Rev. Samuel Moseley of Hampton, had eight children; the Hon. Jabez, of Windham, marrying Amie Elderkin, had six children; Dr. Hezekiah, of Pompey, N. Y., marrying Lucy, daughter of the Hon. Moses Bliss of Springfield, had ten children; Dr. Diodatus, of Oswego, N. Y., had also ten; Hannah married the Hon. George Bliss, of Springfield, and had four children; Henry had six; Erastus, four; Thaddeus, eleven, of whom Grace Greenwood is a single specimen; and Elizabeth, wife of Rev. Ludovicus Weld of Hampton, had five. Thus, of the grand and great grandchildren of our Elizabeth, we have seventy-six souls; and among them, names not unknown, nor to be forgotten.

Of the next generation, Mr. Goodwin, whose list I have followed in this estimate, has registered forty-seven names. And what I think most note-worthy of this list is, that it takes its origin from a double Huntington source, all the descendants of the 2d John, having united the blood of the Lebanon Lieutenant, and the Windham Colonel. What Huntington will allow himself to wonder at the result?

For another illustration, take another Elizabeth of ours, the eldest daughter of Col. Jabez, of Windham. To name her husband is to praise herself. Abraham Davenport, son of Rev. John, of Stamford, and grandson of the New Haven divine, saw her, and the man who never before failed, triumphed here.

He is the man who, you may remember, called for lights for our legislative hall, on the 19th of May, 1780, affirming his preference, if the judgment day was approaching, of being found at the post of duty. One of the council of his native State, a judge of his native county, a man greatly beloved at home, he was worthy of her whom he gained. Their children were five; two of whom, James and John, were members of Congress. Their daughter Elizabeth married Dr. James Coggswell, whose daughter became the wife of the Rev. Dr. Samuel Fisher, of Greenbush, N. Y., and the mother of Rev. S. W. Fisher, of Cincinnati, Ohio.

Their grand children number, also, worthy names; and to do them full justice would lead us into many families whose worth the world acknowledges, and will ever bless. Among the names, I cannot forbear repeating such as Radcliff and Boorman, Lockwood, Apthorp, and Whelpley, the gifted pastor of the first Presbyterian church of New York; and Bruen, the still more apostolic pastor of the Bleecker street church; and Skinner, still honored with exalted post in the service of the Christian church; and Bushnell, whose name and praise have filled all Christian lands. All of these have found helps-meet among the daughters of our Elizabeth, and in doing so, they bring no reproach upon our name.

And now as we are upon the Elizabeths, I will mention that the daughter of Gen. Jabez, of Norwich, who married that truly Hon. John Chester, of revolutionary memory. It is no discredit to us to be thus brought into family relations with such names as Backus of Albany, Welles of Vermont, Chauncey and Ralston of Philadelphia, or to have furnished the mother of such sons as Dr. John, and Revs. William and Henry Chester of Philadelphia.

I might go on to speak of Mary, Solomon's daughter, and of the Buckinghams, who speak well of her share in their honorable career, but they can testify for themselves.

I might tell of the noble descendants of our Ruth, but the Wheelocks are historic characters, and have shaped the literary and moral history of other historic names. And are not also the Pomeroys and McClures, for whom her daughters were counted worthy to be the beloved companions and wives?

I might mention our Hannah, who won a Gideon Tomlinson, and gave Connecticut in her grandson a tried and faithful governor; and of our Lydia, who, giving herself to the Green Mountain youth, gave to Vermont her honored Gov. Galusha.

But the time will fail me, and I must pass on to one other illustration of our daughters' worth.

We are not without witnesses to the noblest traits and most heroic virtues of character among them. They have done and dared well and nobly; and in days when masculine nerves and man's endurance have been sorely tried, they have shown themselves ready for the test, nor have they been found wanting. I cannot stop to paint the patient and heroic endurance which many of our homes have witnessed from their faithful ministry, in days of trial. They have been the light which a merciful Heaven has sent to our else gloomy homes; and we should ever bless the boon which comes so timely to our help.

One instance, only, will my time enable me to exhibit, of this personal fortitude and achievement.

Susannah, daughter of deacon Caleb, of Lebanon, had married Anderson Dana, a lawyer of Ashford, and in 1772, went with her young family into the Wyoming settlement on the Susquehannah. She carried one child in her arms the whole distance, while an older one, only about three years of age, rode behind her, holding himself on. They reached that valley, and had rendered themselves comfortable, until the fatal summer of 1778. Nathan Denison and

Anderson Dana had been chosen to represent the valley in the next Assembly, to be held in Hartford. Alas! another fate was before them and their cherished homes. You have read the story of that terrible doom which so suddenly filled that peaceful valley with blood and deaths. Among the many husbands and fathers who went down, under the death shot, or the merciless tomahawk, or the consuming fire of that savage triumph, was the husband of Susannah, then the mother of seven children. And what could that helpless woman do? She had already gone through enough to have crushed to the earth, one would think, the mightiest frame. But her children were still alive, and must be saved. With a mother's presence, and with that unseen power which stays a mother's heart and hand, she shields and guides, and bears her pleading charge through bloody grounds and watched defiles, in maternal triumph, out of that valley of death; nor did she stop until her seven children had found in Ashford an asylum among their friends.

You will, I know, expect from me some notice, also, of the mothers of our family. They deserve such notice. They have come from the best families of the land. In nothing, I think, have the Huntington sons shown more discernment, or better taste, upon the whole, than in their selection of wives. We admit that they have been the better half of us; and our children have shared in the blessing. We cannot estimate their value to us. But we have not time to speak of their personal worth. Nor need we. Every record we have already made, is the best monument which we could rear to the precious memory, or the present excellence of our mothers and wives.

Our sons and daughters, their character and influence, the character and reputation of our family abroad, made what it is, more by maternal than paternal influence, these are the natural testimonials to the character and worth of our mothers; and the best wish we could offer for our sons is, that they may prove as discerning and as fortunate as their fathers before them.

Thus have I scattered before you, as my time has allowed, these disconnected pictures of the past,—too meager memorials of our honored and useful ancestry.

They have been thrown out, not so much as furnishing a true measure of their character and influence, but as indices, rather, of the leading spirit, the most spontaneous developments of their course; and they may serve as reliable exponents of a family portraiture of which we need not be ashamed.

Could we see rising before us, as a unit, the growth of these last two hundred years, springing from the germs of good old English sense, quickened by the vitalizing forces of Saxon resolution and English puritanism, as realized in the person of our eldest Simon—a growth uplifting its solid trunk with its massive limbs, and out-spreading branches and clustering foliage, studded all over its leafy arches, with freshest and sweetest blossoms of promise, or hanging low its outmost limbs, bending beneath their burdens of ripened fruits, we could not but rejoice in the sight, and bless the great husbandman for such seed, and such soil, and such care.

True, our tree may have had its faded leaf, its shriveled bud, its wasting twig, its decaying branch, its crooked limb, possibly, as what tree on mortal shore has not: yet the longer you look, and the more fully you comprehend the subject, the more you will see how much the freshness of its vigor exceeds the tokens of its decay, and how completely the symmetry of its proportions triumphs over the petty and occasional malformations in its less important members.

The old family tree never gave higher promise of fruitfulness than in 1857. It strikes out its roots deeper than ever into the soil of this great continent. Its branches wave over more numerous households than ever before. Blossoms thicken, and as sweet and fresh, gem its multiplied branches, and fruits never before surpassed in quality, never before equaled in amount, hang in promise all over its waving top. Heaven spare the old tree to a perpetual fruitfulness and growth.

GENEALOGICAL MEMOIR.

THE PURITAN IMMIGRANT.

SIMON, for so tradition has named him, was born in England, and married, probably, Margaret Baret, of Norwich, or its immediate vicinity, in England. He died, while on the voyage to this country, of small pox, in 1633, and his body was consigned to its ocean grave.

With the exception of those mentioned in the Appendix of this work, he was, undoubtedly, the ancestor of all the Huntingtons on this continent; and it is much to be regretted that no record can now be found, to tell us of his parentage, his character, or of his estate. What has been believed respecting him, and what is most probable, a few lines will trace.

Beyond doubt he was an Englishman. Tradition has quite uniformly made him a Norwich man; and as uniformly, has ascribed his removal to this country to the persecutions to which nonconformists were subjected, during the high handed administrations of Laud and the first Charles. The character of his immediate descendants is perhaps in proof of both statements; they were thoroughly English in their feelings, affinities, and language; and that they were as thoroughly religious, their names and official connexion with the early churches in this country abundantly attest.

Tradition has, also, with great uniformity, ascribed to him a family consisting of his wife Margaret and three sons, Christopher, Simon and Samuel; and has placed his leaving England in the year 1639 or 1640; and made the landing of his family at Saybrook, Ct., himself having died off the coast, though his body, it claims, was brought ashore and buried at the mouth of the Connecticut.

These traditions we have endeavored to verify and authenticate, but the attempt, after much endeavor, has not only utterly failed, but has resulted in an absolute disproval of nearly all which they claim. No record has ever been found of the immigration into Saybrook, in the years mentioned. No record exists to show that the Huntingtons were at Saybrook, before they are recorded as living in Massachusetts. The church records of Roxbury, Mass., contain the earliest record of the Huntington name known in New England;

and is in the handwriting of Rev. John Elliot himself, the pastor of that ancient church. It is a "record of such as adjoined themselves unto the fellowship of this church of Christ at Roxborough, as also of such children as were born unto them under the holy covenant of this church, who are most properly the seed of the church." This is the record of Margaret Huntington.

MARGARET HUNTINGTON, WIDOW, CAME IN 1633. HER HUSBAND DIED BY THE WAY OF THE SMALL POX. SHE BROUGHT ——— CHILDREN WITH HER.

The blank in this record, where the number of her children should be found, is much to be regretted. Positive certainty in regard to their number, we may not now be able to attain.

Margaret Huntington, as is supposed, though I have been able to find no record to attest it, married in 1635 or 6, Thomas Stoughton, then of Dorchester, Mass, and moved to Windsor, Conn. Her husband became a prominent man, being the deputy from that ancient town, several times, to the General Court. Whether she had any children by him does not appear, from the Roxbury or Windsor records, nor is her death to be found at Windsor. Her husband died in Windsor, March 25, 1661.

Of the birth place or residence of SIMON, it is not probable that anything can be learned. There is nothing existing among his descendants, which can be relied upon as conclusive, regarding his English home. The different coats of arms which have been shown, furnish no such evidence. They have been imported quite recently, or designed from the blazon of some dictionary of heraldry, and only show that the name Huntington had been honored in England. But until it can be shown that SIMON, whom we accredit as the ancestor of the American Huntingtons, was descended from one or the other of these titled families, the arms themselves are of no historic use. Nor is there any thing reliable in the tradition that Simon was from Norwich, in England. Having examined the minutest records of that city, found in our largest libraries in this country, including that well nigh exhaustive work, Bloomfield's Topographical History of Norwich, in which the name, even, appears but once, I am forced to relinquish this tradition as useless to us in determining the origin of the family in England.

———

Just as the first sheets of this work were in the printer's hand, my friend Chancellor Walworth informed me of the recent discovery of three long lost volumes of records, in the State Library in Hartford, which might shed some light upon this point of our family history. By the kindness of C. J. Hoadley, Esq., Librarian, the records were put into my hands for examination, and by an act of especial kindness the following letter was transcribed by his own careful pen, for such use as I might make of it in this work. I have thought best, as the letter has such authority, to print it entire, only modernizing its orthography, punctuation, and use of capitals.

"Cousin Christopher Huntington:

Your letter dated about the 20th September, 1649, from Saybrook, I received; and do perceive that you have and shall receive to the value of 140 pounds of my brother Stawton, (Stoughton,) which when you have received and security for what shall be behind unpaid, then give him and my sister an acquittance, as from me, in full discharge of all matters and demands that I can or may lay claim unto from them. So, (for) the dividing of this 140 pounds, it shall be thus done: whatever is lost, as a cow, or by reason the commodities may not be altogether worth so much as you took them for, shall be first deducted out of the 140 pounds; and then the rest shall be thus divided: you shall take out £5 pound parts, (apart) in the first place, and then divide the rest into five parts, whereof take two to yourself, one to Simon, one to Thomas, and one to Ann, which will be all the five parts, and then give to Simon the other five pounds, for my intent is he shall have five pounds more than one fifth part; and I suppose you now know my intent and meaning herein, and let it be done thus. I well remember I told you that my cousin Ann should have £20, because that (of) her preferment by way of marriage, but I gave you no commission to dispose of the money but by my order. Let Thomas his first part be put into some good hand and security taken for it, with allowance for the forbearance, that when he shall come to be capable to employ it, he may receive it with the increase. Let me know what you do herein, and send me you an acquittance under your hand for your 2 parts as a gift given you by me; and one under Simon's hand for his, as a gift given him by me; also, under Ann her hand or mark, as a gift given her by me. Yet (if) she cannot write do you witness it; and for Thomas, likewise, a receipt under his hand, as a gift given him also. Let me receive these four acquittances by the next letters. Let the security for Thomas his part be taken in his own name, and the yearly increase that shall be allowed him for it put into the security also.

My father it hath pleased God to take away out of this world in August last. I pray God fit us all for the like change. My mother is made executive, but I cannot hear that any of you are mentioned in his will. For Balding in the Barbadoes, my father hath nothing to show of any debt due to my brother Huntingtons, but the debt which he owes is £17, which is my debt made over to me under his hand and seal before he went away, and £12 more he owes me upon a bond to myself, so the whole debt is £20, which hath been my loss all this while.

The parliament hath taken all the king's officers' places away from them all England over, that I have hereupon lost 200 pounds a year by this act; that now I am removing myself towards London, and so cannot, by reason of these distractions, think of sending you any merchandizing commodities. Let this enclosed be conveyed to my brother Stawton. If I can have time and leisure, I will against the next Spring send you over some commodities. But for Dutch cloth, I cannot accommodate you with, for I shall not have any wages or means to get them upon good terms. I should think the North

Country cloth should sell better than these base coarse cloths which you send me a pattern of. You mention in your letter of shot, but not what sorts and for what use, for thereby we may guess at the sorts. You should have written the price of this kind of cloth and the breadth, and I should have thereby known the better what to have done therein. You must hereafter write more particularly yt thing. I shall not further enlarge myself; but my love to yourself and your brothers and sister remembered. Committing you to the protection of the Almighty, rest,   Your loving uncle,

Norwich, this 20th of April, 1650.   PETER BARET.

Send your letters to me by Mr. Edward French at his warehouse in the George yard in Lombard Street in London."

The above letter comes most opportunely for our record of Margaret the wife of SIMON. It is authoritative on several points of the family history, and has its suggestions upon still others. It is also, perhaps the first step towards the discovery of the English home and connexion of SIMON, himself. But it is provokingly late in its appearance, as it must be allowed to modify to some extent opinions elsewhere expressed in this work, which it is too late now, in any other way, to correct.

And, first, the letter is sufficient to establish the family name of Margaret. I have accordingly inserted Baret after her christian name, where, but for this letter, we must have found only a blank.

Secondly, it establishes the correctness of our record as to three of the children of Margaret, as far as the names are concerned.

Thirdly, it shows that there was one daughter in the family; and I have accordingly as the work was passing through the press, inserted her name as the second number five, on the list.

Fourthly, it fully corroborates our supposition of the marriage of Margaret to a Mr. Stoughton.

Fifthly, it shows that Christopher Huntington was at Saybrook in 1649.

The letter has also its suggestions, possibly, at variance with the record, which after the most patient investigation the author felt himself authorized to make. These suggestions are in season to aid the reader in forming an opinion upon the points to which they refer.

First, it suggests a transposition of the names in the second generation, making Thomas, instead of Simon, number five. Of course a corresponding change will run through the first five generations; but as no descendants of Thomas belong to the later generations, no further transpositions in our record will be needed.

Secondly, it suggests that William, No. 2, is more probably a brother, than son of Simon. If this suggestion be accepted, it will simply transfer my record of his descendants in each of the generations, to the generation preceding. In all other respects the record will remain as it stands in the text.

Thirdly, as Christopher Baret was mayor of Norwich in 1634, the letter suggests that Margaret, the wife of Simon, may have been a relative, perhaps a daughter of his, since she gives his Christian name to one of her sons.

Should additional information come to the author, from any further research to which this letter may lead, he will gladly take some early opportunity to make the results known to those for whom this work is designed.

SECOND GENERATION.

1. SIMON. England.

2. WILLIAM, conjecturally, the eldest son of Simon and Margaret. He appears in Salisbury, Mass., as early as 1640. At a general meeting of the freemen of this town, on the 26th of 10th month in 1642, it was ordered that thirty families should remove to the west side of the Powow river, the dividing line between Salisbury and Amesbury. William's was probably one of the families who then crossed the river and became one of the pioneers in the new settlement of Amesbury, then called "Salisbury New Towne." He, however, retained possession of his share in the old Salisbury, as he was recorded as "townsman and comoner," there, on the third of twelfth month, 1650. He also paid the tax for the support of the Rev. Wm. Worcester, who was pastor over the first church in Salisbury, down to his death, in 1662. He married Joanna Bayley, a daughter of John Bayley, who went from Salisbury to Newbury, in 1650, and who died there in 1651. This relationship is fully shown by the recorded names, and the will of John Bayley, sen.; in which he provides that his son John shall pay certain legacies. In compliance with this provision, in 1652, John Bayley, jr., of Newbury, made a deed, in which he gave to the above Joanna and her two children, a lot of land on the Merrimac. Tradition makes him a religious man, and that he was a man of enterprise, and of a thoroughly English spirit is evinced by his occupancy of that exposed outpost of the English settlements of that day—opposition to French encroachments being the mainspring to the settlement of that frontier town. The residence of Wm. Huntington, in 1685–6, is given in the "Hoyt Family," as next to Thomas Hoyt. This was in Pleasant Valley, on the banks of the Merrimac, where the river is a half mile wide, and altogether a beautiful place. A part of this family possession has never been alienated, being now in the possession of Mrs. Davis, (1843).

The following minutes were copied from the Salisbury Town Records, and help to indicate the character and position of William Huntington.

1653-4, 1st month. One acre and ninety-two rods, his share of the Beach Common. Being one of the sixty-two persons of the division of the meadow toward Merrimac river, and the great Creek toward Merrimac river's mouth and the Barberry Meadow, he drew lot No. 55.

1654, 1st month. He is enrolled as one of the present inhabitants and commoners of the New Town.

1658, Oct. 29. He is recorded as drawing land by lot, and he was one of the thirteen to whose children 500 acres of land were given. His son John is mentioned as the child to inherit his share.

1660, 10th month. "A towns shiep is grantied to Willi Howntinton for his son."

1661. He was one of the twenty-five to whom lots were laid out at the Lion's Mouth.

1662, April 1. He drew 120 acres of land; and in March, 1662-3, thirty acres, "West of pond near Children's Land."

New Town. 11th month 18th day, 1663. He drew lots, "between Hamptonshire and Powow river," and in 1667, 12th month 18th day, he drew lots in four places.

In 1664 Wm. Huntington bought of John Hoyt, sen., a lot of land adjoining his own on Merrimac river.

He died about the year 1689.

For my record of the descendants of this William, as well as for the minutes above, I am mainly indebted to the labors of Enoch, (1836) of Amesbury.

3. THOMAS, probably the second son of Simon and Margaret, though we have no record of the date of his birth. With nothing to oppose such an order, I have arranged the last three of this family in the order in which they were "made free" by the general Court of Connecticut; Thomas being made free in 1651, Christopher in 1658, and Simon in 1663.

He appears to have resided in Windsor, Conn., as he purchased land there in 1656, and in 1658 was employed to mend the boat, and in 1660 was a fence viewer. He next appears on the records of the town of Branford in 1663. He married, probably, for his first wife, a daughter of Wm. Swain, of Wethersfield, and later of Branford; and for his second wife, Hannah, a daughter of Jasper Crane, merchant, who had moved from New Haven to Branford in 1652, at the settlement of the latter town. It will, perhaps, indicate, not doubtfully, his character that he secured, in that day, an alliance with two such families. The fathers of both of his wives were leading men, both in religious and civil affairs; having been the first deputies to the general Court of Electors from Branford, in May, 1653, and for the next four years; Mr. Swain having been a delegate from Wethersfield, previously to his removal to Branford. That he was not unworthy of the alliance, the record also shows. In 1665, when, to avoid an unpleasant controversy which had arisen between the Branford people and their neighbors, on the union of the New Haven and Connecticut colonies, the Branford people decided to remove beyond the jurisdiction of these two colonies, we find his name among those who subscribed the new compact. In that instrument they bind themselves to provide "with care and diligence for the maintenance of the purity of religion professed in the Congregational churches of Connecticut." The subscribers had been alarmed by the admission into the civil offices of the union, of men not connected with the Christian church.

These new adventurers having the purity of religion, mainly in view, in 1767 located themselves on the banks of the Passaic, in New Jersey, and laid there the foundations of the thriving city of Newark.

Among the pioneers of that new settlement, Thomas was a prominent man. In 1677 he was appointed constable. In 1683 he was one of the townsmen; the first officer in the colony. In 1681 he was one of a committee appointed to treat with the Governor, in regard to a supposed infringement on the rights of the town. In 1685 he was one of the deputies from Newark to the general court of the province of New Jersey.

As Samuel, his son, was made in 1694 a proprietor, which office the father had held, it is probable that Thomas was not then living. The last record of him that appears on the book, being that of 1685; the absence of his name from the list of those who, in 1689, contributed to the support of preaching, is pretty good evidence that between these years he had died.

His widow, Hannah, married John Ward, first of Branford, and afterward of Newark. And there is on record, a deed of land, in which this Hannah is named his wife, in 1695.

For the records on which my list of the descendants of this Thomas is made out and verified, I am indebted to the copies so carefully made by S. H. Conger, of Newark, N. J.

4. CHRISTOPHER probably accompanied his mother to Windsor, Conn., where he must have spent his youth. He here married, Oct. 7, 1652, Ruth, daughter of Wm. Rockwell, "a prominent and highly respected member of the community." He removed, probably, in the spring of 1654, to Saybrook, as the birth of one child appeared in 1653, on the Windsor records, and the death of another in May, 1654, on those of Saybrook. Here he remained until the spring of 1660, when, with a company of the Saybrook colony who had organized themselves into a church, under the care of Rev. James Fitch, he removed to the valley of the Yantic, and with his brother Simon, aided in laying the foundations of the new town of Norwich.. He had now reached the prime of his manhood; and proved himself one of the most efficient and useful of the hardy pioneers. His name occurs often in the earlier records of this enterprising town, and always in honorable relations. His house lot was one of the prominent localities in the settlement. In 1668 the general court granted him 100 acres of land, not more than twenty acres of it to be meadow. In 1678 appointed town clerk. In 1685, he was one of the twelve patentees of the new town of Norwich. In 1686 his name occurs as one of the committee "to make provision for maintaining the reverend minister."

His death had occurred in 1691, as appears from the probate of his will.

No stone marks the resting place of this pioneer of the Norwich settlement. He sleeps, doubtless, not far from the banks of the pleasant Yantic, in the meadow where rest, unmarked, the mortal remains of so many of the pioneers of the early settlement of Norwich.

5. SIMON, like his brother Christopher, spent his youth, probably, with his mother in Windsor. If the Norwich records are authority, he was born in England, in the year 1629, and of course was not far from four years of age when the family came to this country.

He seems to have possessed the spirit, and to have shared the fortunes of his brother Christopher. With him he appears at Saybrook, where, in Oct. 1653, he married Sarah, daughter of Joseph Clark, of Windsor, and later of Saybrook. In 1660 he joins the colonists who settled Norwich, and thenceforward stands among the first of that important settlement, both in church and state.

Here his house lot was also in a central and commanding position, and the records show him to have been a large land-holder, and in worldly matters, an enterprising man.

He was chosen, soon after the removal to Norwich, deacon of Mr. Fitch's church, in which office he served with acceptance, until, in consequence of his infirmities, he was succeeded by his son, in 1696.

In 1674, he, with that other veteran and tried pioneer, Thos. Leffingwell, represented Norwich in the general court, and he again was a member of the body in 1685.

In 1686 the town grant him and his sons thirty acres of pasture, westward of Goodman Sluman.

In 1690, and again in 1696, he was the townsman. In 1694 he was appointed a committee to treat with Mr. Jabez Fitch, with respect to his helping and succeeding his father in the work of the ministry. In the same year he was also on a committee to search out and report on the deficiencies in the records.

In 1697 he was one of the committee to seat the meeting house. In 1700 he was appointed on a commission to deed anew, lands about whose titles disputes had arisen, or would be likely to arise.

In 1703, April 27, he and his son Simon deed away thirty acres of pasture land, west of the great plains, to John Gifford.

The following record is copied from the Windham probate records.

To all Christian people to whom these presents may come: Know ye that I, Simon Huntington, sen., of Norwich, in the county of New London, in the colony of Connecticut, in New-England, have of my free will, given, granted unto my son Joseph Huntington, of the same town, county, and colony aforesaid, and do by these presents, give, grant, alienate and pass over my whole right, title, interest in and unto our thousand acre interest, or one allotment, in the new plantation, above Norwich, that was willed by Joshua, Sachem, son of Uncas. I, the aforesaid Simon Huntington, have freely and absolutely given, alienated and passed over unto the aforesaid Joseph Huntington, my whole allotment, situated and being in the southeast quarter of the aforesaid plantation above Norwich.

March 2, 1691. } Deed acknowledged Jan. 24, 1692. Before JAMES FITCH, Assistant.

' Deacon Huntington died in Norwich, June 28, 1706, aged 77 years; and Sarah, his wife, died in 1721, aged 88 years. The place of his burial, like that of his brother Christopher, is marked by no monument. The beautiful town and city, which, all along our national history, have been eminent for their patriotism and piety and enterprise, are the best monuments to the worth of these two prominent names among the noble band of pioneers, who, in times of trouble and want, laid the foundations for such prosperity.

5.¹ ANN. All that is known of her is what is found in the letter of Peter Baret, which is printed in our account of the Puritan Immigrant. No record of her marriage or death has been found. The Baret letter would seem to locate her at Saybrook, Conn., when it was written.

THIRD GENERATION.

II. WILLIAM. Salisbury, Mass.

6. JOHN, born in Amesbury, on Sabbath, the last week in Aug. 1643; married, Oct. 25, 1665, Elizabeth Hunt, and died about 1727.

He had a seat assigned him in the first Congregational meeting house built in Amesbury; and the records show that he was on terms of good will and intimacy with the first pastor of that church.

He was at one time constable of the town, and appears to have been a man of character and influence.

7. JAMES, died on the fifth day of the twelfth month, 1646. He was probably the second son, and died in infancy.

8. MARY, born May 8, 1648, in Amesbury, and married on the 14th day of the 6th month, 1667, Joshua Goldsmith. They probably had no children.

A bond from Jeremiah Davis, son of Mary, (30) dated Dec. 3, 1720, and acknowledged May 22, 1723, now in possession of Enoch Huntington, of Amesbury, says: "Am holden and firmly bound unto my honored grandfather, John Huntington, and my Aunt Mary Gouldsmith, widow;" the bond pledging her maintenance during her natural life.

Joshua Goldsmith and his wife Mary, sold " for and in consideration of valuable satisfaction in hand, already received in land and other good pay, of John Huntington, and for other good and lawful motives us thereunto inducing, do sell, &c., unto the above-said John Huntington, one-third part of the housing and lands, being the contents of, specified in a deed of gift, under the hand and seal of Jno. Bailey, of Newbury, in the County of Essex, formerly given and granted by the said Bayley unto our mother, Johannah Huntington, and to John and Mary, her two children, bearing date the 4th of the eleventh month, 1652; as also all right, &c., to all lands, goods, &c., belonging to our father, William Huntington, now deceased; this dated 24 day March, one thousand six hundred eighty-nine or ninety, re-affirmed or acknowledged and yielded up the right of dower, March 1, 1692-93."

III. THOMAS. Newark, N. J.

9. SAMUEL, born probably in Branford, married Sarah ——. In 1702, he and Sarah Huntington convey land to Nathaniel Ward. He is recorded, as "son and heir-in-law of Thomas Huntington, deceased," in a conveyance of land to J. & D. Crane. In 1704, Samuel and Sarah are again recorded as selling land. His will, is dated Nov. 11, 1704, and proved Nov. 19, 1712; previously to which, his death probably occurred. This Samuel was made, in 1694, one of the proprietors of the land in Newark.

10. HANNAH. Her grandfather, Jasper Crane, mentions this daughter of Thomas Huntington, in his will, calling her his grand-daughter. No other record of her has been discovered by the author.

IV. CHRISTOPHER. Norwich.

The death of the first Christopher, and the births of all but the first two of this family, are on the Norwich records.

11. CHRISTOPHER, born in 1653, lived one year and four months, and died in Saybrook. The first fact appears on the Windsor records, and the second, was taken from the Saybrook records before they were burnt in the old fort.

12. RUTH, born April 13, 1653, and probably a twin with the above Christopher. She probably died in infancy.

13. RUTH, born in Saybrook, in April, 1658, married, March 26, 1681, Samuel Pratt of Saybrook, who came to Norwich with the early settlers. They had one child recorded in Norwich, Samuel Pratt, born Feb. 11, 1683; and she died Feb. 14, 1683.

14. CHRISTOPHER, born in Norwich, Nov. 1, 1660, being "the first born of males in the town." Born, thus, during the first year of the history of his native town, and destined to grow up in its infancy, and spend his manly vigor and mature age in its forming period, he was also designed and used by Providence, as a prominent contributor to the prosperity of its most vital secular interests, and a marked pillar of support to those of religion. His character, molded, mainly, by the very best of all influences, those of a quiet home, in which every day piety hallows every day toil, and over which a sense of duty rules as the deepest incentive to its labors and its pastimes alike, unfolded early with every element of consistency and strength. In a period of exposure and calling often for extreme adventure, he became resolute and fearless. In an age devoted to the revival of a simple and primitive piety, he became a humble, inflexible Christian; and with the best and amplest means at his disposal, trained himself to the most intelligent and effective discharge of every duty, either to God or the world.

He married, for his first wife, May 26, 1681, Sarah, born January, 1663, daughter of deacon Thomas Adgate, by his second wife, Mrs. Mary Bushnell, widow of Richard Bushnell, of Saybrook. She was the mother of his first eight children, and died in Norwich, in Feb. 1705–6, aged 42. He married for his second wife, in Oct. 1706, Mrs. Judith (Stevens) Brewster, widow of Jonathan Brewster, a great grandson of the venerable elder Brewster, the spiritual guide and teacher of the Mayflower pilgrims. She became the mother of four children.

In 1684 the town grant him a parcel of land on a small plain near the mouth of **Crane brook.**

In each of the years 1691, 1705 and 1709, he is on the record as the first townsman. He succeeded Richard Bushnell, as town clerk, which office he transmitted, in due time, to his son Isaac.

In 1695 or '96 he was appointed deacon, and in this office served with marked ability to the close of his life. He appears to have been a practical surveyor; and his decision on a dispute regarding land titles, was in those early days an end of all strife. He was, accordingly, on the commission with his uncle Simon, to re-deed the lands whose titles were in dispute.

He had become an extensive land holder, as the early records abundantly show. In 1705, July 21, he and his brother Thomas deed to John Elderkin, "all that our one hundred acres of upland and meadows, which we hold in partnership, as it was given to us by our honored father, Christopher Huntington, as by his last will and testament."

He died in Norwich, April 24, 1735, and his remains were interred, as his venerable headstone shows, on the brow of the hill in the southeast corner of the up-town burying lot in Norwich.

15. THOMAS, born in Norwich, March 18, 1664, must have attained some distinction, since he appears on the record toward the close of his life with that title, which in those days had highest significance. Thomas **Huntington, Esq.**

He married, Feb. 10, 1686-7, Elizabeth, second daughter of Lieut. William and Elizabeth (Pratt) Backus, one of the most enterprising of the Norwich settlers. He was a professed Christian, and as appears from contemporary records, an active and successful business man. In the fall after his marriage he removed with his cousin Joseph, (23) to aid in laying the foundations of the new town of Windham. Here his name occurs often in the early records, and always honorably. He received from his father, a tract of land, lying to the north of the town of Windham; now lying in the towns of Windham and Mansfield, his own house lot lying in the latter town. Accordingly, at the organization of the Mansfield church, Oct. 18, 1710, Thomas Huntington enters his name with ten others to constitute the new church. His wife's name is recorded among the members, on the 25th of the same month and year. He was ordained deacon, Feb. 20, 1714-15, and is in the record styled Capt. Thomas Huntington. In his will, dated Oct. 31, 1732, he divides his "lands and meadows, in and about the Nauchang Cedar Swamps," to his three sons, Thomas, Jedidiah and Eleazer. His tomb stone bears this inscription: "After he had served God and his people, Boath in Church and State, he fell asleep in Jesus, Nov. 7th, 1732."

His wife died, Dec. 29, 1728, and was also buried in the Windham burying ground.

Thos. Huntington, as appears from the Windham records, under date of

May 13, 1699. "grants to Mr. Samuel Whiting the one-half of a parcel of wilderness land, in the county of Hartford, bounded east by Nipmuc path, northerly, Windham bounds, southerly with Norwich town bounds, and westerly with Shetucket river, the above north bounds to begin at Windham southeast corner."

16. JOHN, born in Norwich, March 15, 1666, married, Dec. 9, 1686, Abigail, daughter of Samuel Lathrop, who was born in May, 1667. Her father had moved to Norwich from New London, to which place he had gone from Scituate, Mass., in 1648. He was the son of the Rev. John Lathrop, who, for nonconformity, being a preacher in the first congregational church organized in London, was imprisoned for two years, and who on being released in 1634, came to this country, and became the first minister of Scituate.

John was, also, as the records show, a man who commanded the respect and esteem of his fellow townsmen.

In 1691, Dec. 24, he was appointed constable in Norwich.

17. SUSANNAH, born in Norwich, in Aug. 1668. She married, Dec. 10, 1685, Capt. Samuel Griswold, born Sept. 16, 1665, and son of that Lieut. Francis Griswold, whom Miss Caulkins styles "one of the most active and enterprising men in the first company of settlers."

Her children were Francis, born Sept. 9, 1691; Samuel, born Feb. 8, 1693; Lydia, born May 28, 1696; Hannah, born April 13, 1699; Sarah, born Jan. 19, 1700–1; John, born Dec. 16, 1703; Joseph, born Oct. 17, 1706; and Daniel, born April 25, 1709 and died Dec. 22, 1724. She died in Norwich, March 6, 1727, and her husband having married again Hannah ———, died, Dec. 21, 1740. His second wife died Feb. 25, 1752. Twenty-three of her grandchildren, and sixty-four great grandchildren, and still later descendants, are to be found in Stiles' History of Windsor, under the Griswolds.

18. LYDIA, or as the records have chosen to enter the name, Lydyah, was born in Norwich, in Aug. 1672.

19. ANN, born in Norwich, Oct. 25, 1675, married, Oct. 28, 1697, Jonathan, son of Thomas and Mary (Rudd) Bingham. Her husband was born April 15, 1674, and was the third of eleven children. His father was afterwards deacon of the Windham church. He had a family and descendants respectable both in their numbers and for their characters.

V. SIMON, DEACON. Norwich.

20. SARAH, born in Saybrook in Aug. 1654. She married in Norwich, Nov. 23, 1676, Dr. Solomon, fourth son of Lieut Thomas Tracy, of whom Miss Caulkins says: "in the company of the Norwich proprietors he ranked high, having more education than most of them, and being in ability, enterprise and integrity equal to the first." Solomon was one of six sons, who were all of them active and leading men in the early history of the town. He was born in Aug. 1663. She is mentioned in the will of her uncle Jos. Clark of Saybrook, made Aug. 27, 1658, in Milford, and bequeathed five pounds. She died in 1683, and her husband married again, in 1689, Sarah, widow of Thomas

Shuuan, and died in 1732. Their children were: Lydia, born Oct. 11, 1677, and married March 31, 1698, Thomas, son of Lieut. Thomas and Mary (Bushnell) Leffingwell; and Simon, born Jan. 8, 1679, married, Jan. 11, 1708, Mary Leffingwell.

21. MARY, born in Saybrook, in Aug., 1657 and married a Forbes of Preston.

22. SIMON, born in Saybrook, Feb. 6, 1659, and taken by his parents to Norwich in the spring of the next year. Here he married Oct. 8, 1683, Lydia, born in Aug. 1663, daughter of John Gager, who in 1635 had gone from Charlestown, Mass. to Saybrook, and subsequently to New London, and thence in 1660 to Norwich. Her grandfather was that "right goodly man and skillful chyrurgeon," who had come to America in 1630 with Gov. Winthrop. And most worthy did she show herself to be of such an ancestry, falling behind them, neither in the depth of her piety, nor in her skill in ministering to all "aylements" both of the body and mind.

Like his cousin Christopher, Simon was destined to a most important service in the early history of the home chosen for him by his parents. Inheriting his father's piety and gifts, he was called by the church in 1696, to succeed him in the deaconship, and in this office he served with no less than the father's fidelity and acceptance, as long as he lived.

He was, also, engaged much upon the civil affairs of the town, serving in many of its most important offices, with marked ability. His house, occupying a central position, was honored as the magazine for the defensive weapons of the town, and as late as 1720, a report made to the town, states that it contained a half barrel of powder, 31 pounds of bullets and 400 flints.

In 1682 it was voted in town meeting, to grant "to Simon Huntington, jun., to take up one hundred akers of land on the Shawtoket, not prejudicing the highways nor former grants."

He died Nov. 2, 1736.

Lydia, his wife, as her gravestone attests, was born in Norwich, Aug. 8, 1663, lived with him fifty-five years, and survived him nine months, and died Aug. 8, in the 74th year of her age.

23. JOSEPH, born in Norwich, in Sept. 1661, the first of this family born in Norwich. Here he married, Nov. 28, 1687, Rebecca, third daughter of Dea. Thomas Adgate, by his second wife, Widow Bushnell, and born in June, 1666. In the same year of his marriage he went with its founders to the new town of Windham, and built his house on the very site, just east of the center of the town, where a portion of its materials are yet found in a house still occupied by his descendants of the fourth degree. Both himself and his cousin Thomas were prominent members of the first church founded here, of which he was chosen deacon in 1729, being the fourth deacon furnished by the two Norwich families of this name. He died in Windham, Dec. 29, 1747, and his wife followed him Nov. 28, 1748.

Joseph Huntington of Windham, under date of July 16, 1697, deeds to Richard Edgerton of Norwich, for £15 current pay, "all that my seventh lott called one thousand acre interest of upland and meadow lying and being at the place called Willimantuck, in the town of Windham aforesaid."

24. ELIZABETH, was born in Norwich in Feb. 1664 and died in infancy.

25. SAMUEL, born in Norwich, March 1, 1665. Here he married, Oct. 29, 1686, Mary, daughter, probably of Wm. Clark of Wethersfield. He removed to Lebanon in 1700, having sold his houselot and house in Norwich for a parsonage. Before his removal he had become a public man, having filled several offices, being as early as 1692 appointed constable, having already been one of the Townsmen. How well he was thought of in Norwich, appears from his appointment by the citizens of Norwich, ten years after his removal to Lebanon, on a Committee to locate the new meeting house about which a serious dispute had arisen. The site chosen by the committee was not approved by the town, and the church was erected upon another spot. But a few years vindicated the wisdom of the committee, as was abundantly testified by a second church, built upon the place selected by them.

He was a large landholder both in Norwich and Lebanon; and for his services as military manager, was entered on the records as Lieutenant, a title in those days won only by a true martial bearing, and intended as a most honorable distinction.

His wife's name appears on the list of the Lebanon church in 1701; but his own was not added until 1707.

In 1687, Feb. 13, the town of Norwich granted him a parcel of land at Trading Cove Brook, " by his father's, to be laid out by measure, 30 or 40 rods wide the length of his father's land.

He died in Lebanon, May 10, 1717 and his wife, Oct. 5, 1713.

26. ELIZABETH, born in Norwich. Oct. 6, 1669. She married, April 9, 1690, Joseph, the fourth child of Lieut. William and Elizabeth (Pratt) Backus, and born Sept 6, 1667. Her husband was one of the members of the congregational church in Norwich in 1707.

Her children were Joseph, born March, 1691; Samuel, Jan. 6, 1693; Ann, Jan. 27, 1695; Simon, Feb. 11, 1700-1; James, Aug. 14, 1703; Elizabeth, Oct. 27, 1705; Sarah, July, 1709, and Ebenezer, March 30, 1712. Joseph married Hannah, daughter of Richard and Mary (Talcott) Edwards and had a family of four children, in Hartford, Conn. Simon, afterwards pastor of the church in Newington parish in Wethersfield, married Eunice, daughter of Rev. Timothy and Esther (Stoddard) Edwards of East Windsor. He died Feb. 2, 1746 at Louisburg, Island of Cape Breton, being located there as Chaplain in the New England Army. He left eight children, of whom one was the Rev. Simon, pastor of the church in Granby, and later of the church in Guilford, and who died in Stratford, Aug. 7, 1823.

The descendants of this Elizabeth have been very numerous, and they include many eminent and honored names. Thirty-six of her great grandchildren, with others of her descendants, are found recorded in Goodwin's Genealogical Notes.

27. NATHANIEL, was born in Norwich in July, 1672, and died young.

28. DANIEL, born in Norwich, March 13, 1675–6, and married for his first wife, Jan. 31, 1705–6, Abigail, daughter of Thomas and Mary (Rudd) Bingham, who was born, Nov. 4, 1679, and died after becoming the mother of his first five children, Dec. 25, 1734. He married for his second wife, Rachel Wolcott of Windham. The name of the first wife is found on the Norwich first church records for the year 1707; and on her grave stone are inscribed these solemn warnings—"memento mori;" and "Mors vincet omnia." He does not appear to have taken a very active part in the public affairs of the town, yet was evidently a man of more than ordinary personal culture for those days, and seems to have entailed upon his descendants a large portion of his own native talent. His second, late, marriage will introduce a most marked anachronism into the family, making the fifth generation of his descendants nearly synchronize with the seventh generation of some of the descendants of his brother Simon. His name appears on the church records for the year 1724. He died in Norwich, Sept. 13, 1741. His widow married, Nov. 30, 1742, Joseph Bingham of Windham, who was born in 1687 and died, Sept. 4, 1765.

29. JAMES, born in Norwich, May 18, 1680. Here he married Feb. 3, 1702–3, Priscilla Miller. He was a man of more than ordinary energy, and was especially prominent in the more important business enterprises of the town in that early day. He was appointed with Lieut. Thomas Tracy, in 1722, " to go down to the Landing Place and lay out what may be needful for the town's use ;" and " the next year," as Miss Caulkins correctly reports, " Lieut. Simon Lathrop, Joshua, and James Huntington and Daniel Tracy, all spirited and enterprising men, then in the prime of life, each obtained a conveniency, and began improvements at the Landing-place."

Dec. 5, 1706, he deeded a 50 acre grant of land which was "granted me by the town of Norwich near the southwest corner of the town bounds" to Job Besstow.

He was the only one, in this generation, of that Huntington trio, of whom the same historian of Norwich says, " in the early part of the next (18th) century, there were, perhaps, no more distinguished men in the town."

He died, Sept. 3, 1727.

FOURTH GENERATION.

VI. JOHN. Amesbury, Mass.

29.[1] HANNAH, born in Amesbury, on the 16th day of the 6th month, 1666, and died next day.

30. MARY, born in Amesbury, on the 5th day of the 9th month, 1667, and married March 24, 1687, Abraham Joyce. She married again in 1689, Jeremiah Davis.

31. ELIZABETH, born in Amesbury, and married May 22, 1689, Lieutenant Thomas Hoyt, jr., son of Thomas and Mary (Brown) Hoyt, of Amesbury. He was a farmer and a man of note and influence. She died Jan. 29, 1721-2.

Their children were: John, born July 25, 1689, and married Sarah Barnard; Jacob, born June 19, 1691, and married Joanna Ring; Mary, born Aug. 15, 1693, and married John Lancaster; David, born March 12, 1695-6; Sarah, born May 4, 1698, and married Joseph Bartlett; Timothy, Lieut., born June 21, 1700, married Sarah Challis; Elizabeth, born March 11, 1701-2; Thomas, born Jan. 18, 1703-4, and married Ruth Barnard; Micah, Lieut., born Jan. 18, 1704; Daniel, born Jan. 23, 1707; and David, born Oct. 27, 1709, and married Mary Quimby.

Her grand children, as entered in the "Hoyt Family," are fifty-three in number, all of the name of Hoyt; and her great grand children of the same name, are 121; and her great great grand children, 142.

32. HANNAH, born in Amesbury, Nov. 19, 1671, and married a Chandler.

33. SARAH, born in Amesbury, Nov. 1, 1672, and died young, unmarried.

34. SUSANNAH, born in Amesbury, Feb. 4, 1674, and married a Downer.

35. WILLIAM, born in Amesbury, and "intended marriage," Dec. 11, 1708, and married Jan. 27, 1708-9, Mary Goodwin. He is probably the William who again "intended marriage," Oct. 23, 1725, and married the second time, Dec. 19, 1725, Mary Colby, widow. He was the executor of his father's will.

36. SAMUEL, born in Amesbury, where his intention of marriage is recorded, March 20, 1707-8, and his marriage, April 7, 1708, with Elizabeth Martin.

37. DEBORAH, born in Amesbury, Sept. 22, 1687, and married in 1713, Edmund Elliot.

IX. SAMUEL. Newark, N. J.

38. THOMAS, whose birth and marriage I have been unable to find.

39. SIMON, married Thankful ——, and had children. These two sons of Samuel Huntington are thus reported in Hinman's Genealogy of the First Puritan Settlers of the Colony of Connecticut. In 1724, Thomas and Simon Huntington, late of Newark, now of Whipanong, in the County of Hunterdon, "being equally interested in certain lands of our honored father, Samuel Huntington, late of Newark, deceased," sold land to Nathaniel Ward. Simon, above, died in Morris County, New Jersey, aged 74 years, and left to his brother Samuel, "my sermon book the ten virgins."

40. SAMUEL, gave his property to his nephew Samuel. This is the only record found against his name.

40.¹ HANNAH.

XIV. CHRISTOPHER, DEACON. Norwich.

41. RUTH, born in Norwich, Nov. 28, 1682, where she married, Jan. 8, 1707-8, Ralph Wheelock, of Windham, Conn., a son of Capt. Eleazer Wheelock, of Mendon, Mass., who was born in 1683.

She deserves especial notice in this memoir, both for her own great personal worth, and for the excellence and eminence of her descendants. Every tradition respecting her makes her a woman of unusual intelligence, and of rare piety. Her home, the main theater of her life, was blessed equally by her timely instructions, her holy example, and the administration of a gentle yet firm discipline. She died in Windham, Sept. 1, 1725. Her husband married for his second wife Mercy Standish, by whom he had but one child, Mary, born Nov. 28, 1728.

The children of Ruth were:

Elizabeth, born July 18, 1709.

Eleazer, born April 22, 1711, graduated at Yale College 1733, with much distinction, and ordained to the work of the ministry, in Lebanon, in 1735, where he labored in the ministry, and in the work of teaching, until 1770. While here he received the degree of Doctor of Divinity from the University of Edinburg. During these years he had been especially successful in teaching Indian youth; and the growth of the white population in that vicinity, led him to seek a more retired post, and Hanover, N. H., was chosen as the best place for establishing an Academy for the thorough training of such English and Indian youth as might be committed to his care. Hither he repaired, and here he had the satisfaction of laying the foundations of what has since become Dartmouth College, of which he was the first President. He married for his first wife Mrs. Sarah Maltby, a daughter of Rev. John Davenport, of Stamford, Conn., and for his second, Miss Mary Brismade, of Milford, Conn. Ruth, a daughter of his first wife, was the wife of Rev. Wm. Patten, D. D., of

Halifax, Mass., and mother of the Rev. Dr. Wm. Patten, of Hartford, Conn. She was a woman of marked accomplishments. Another daughter, Mary, married Prof. Woodward, of Dartmouth College; Abigail married Prof. Ripley, of the same college. John graduated in the first class of Dartmouth, in 1771, and succeeded his father in the Presidency of the college, which office he filled nearly forty years. His only child, a daughter, became the wife of the Rev. Dr. Allen, now of Northampton, and late President of Bowdoin College. Two other of his sons, Col. Eleazer, and James, graduated, also at Dartmouth College.

Ruth, born May 25, 1713.

Abigail, born March 3, 1717, married the Rev. Dr. Pomeroy of Hebron, Conn., and was the mother of seven children, who lived to honor their parentage.

John, born Jan. 24, 1720, and died on the 29th of same month.

Sarah, born July 7, 1725, married Dec. 21, 1742, Joseph Bingham, and had seven children, the first of whom was Jerusha, born Oct. 15, 1743, married, Sept. 19, 1769, Rev. Samuel Kirkland, the missionary to the Indians in Oneida, New York, and father of Dr. John Kirkland, the distinguished President of Harvard University, from 1810 to 1828.

Ralph Wheelock, the husband of Ruth, was chosen deacon of Windham church in 1729. He died in Windham, Oct. 15, 1718.

42. CHRISTOPHER, born in Norwich, Sept. 12, 1686, and married, first, Feb. 4, 1717-18, Abigail, widow of Barnabas Lathrop, who had died May 27, 1710. She became the mother of eight children, and died, June 2, 1730. He married, second, May 2, 1733, Elizabeth Ensworth, of Canterbury, Conn., who had one child, and died March 2, 1734-5. He married, third, June 4, 1740, Mary Brewster, who died without children, Dec. 24, 1749; when he married, fourth, Feb. 7, 1750-1, Mrs. Mary Gaylord, of Hebron, Conn., who died, March 14, 1761.

This Christopher removed to Norwich, West Farms, and here he lived, a useful man and consistent Christian, on the place now held by his descendant of the third degree, and died Feb. 11, 1759. His first wife was the fifth daughter of Caleb and Margaret (Post) Abel, and was born March 16, 1690.

43. ISAAC, born Feb. 5, 1688, and married Feb. 21, 1715-16, Rebecca, great grand daughter of Rev. John Lathrop, of England, and later of Scituate and Barnstable, Mass. He was early brought into the public service, in which he continued all his life. He was a professed Christian, having entered the church in 1731, on whose records his name often occurs, in relations which show he was regarded as a sound and safe ecclesiastical counselor. He was appointed, Oct. 21, 1746, on a committee, with Simon Tracy, his cousin Daniel, and Philip Turner, "to labor for the conviction and recovering of the Separates." These were the irregular and heterodox members of the church to which he belonged. He was as successor to his father, chosen town clerk, Dec. 6, 1726, yet had performed the duties of the office, from an apparently unknown date, commencing his services during the official period of his father,

and with the aid of his son Benjamin, continuing them down to his own death; the last entry, by his hand, being on the 9th of Jan. 1764, but a little more than a month previous to his death. This record was "examined" and attested by his son. He died, in the homestead built by his father, on soil taken from the Indians, Feb. 23, 1764, transmitting both his home and his office to his youngest son.

He was the first of that "distinguished" trio referred to in the sketch of No. 28.

44. JABEZ, born in Norwich, Jan. 26, 1691. He married for his first wife, June 30, 1724, Elizabeth, daughter of Rev. Timothy and Esther (Stoddard) Edwards, who was born in East Windsor, April 14, 1697, and who died in Windham, Conn., Sept. 21, 1733. After her death, he married for his second wife, May 21, 1735, widow Sarah Wetmore, who died in Norwich, March 21, 1783, in the 83d year of her age.

He removed to Windham, Conn., where he attained high rank among the distinguished men of that important town, both in civil and in military life, being, at his death, Sept. 26, 1752, a colonel of the Connecticut militia.

45. MATTHEW, born in Norwich, April 16, 1694. He married for his first wife, Sept. 3, 1719, Mary Morgan, who died March 20, 1720-1, the birthday of his first child. He married for his second wife, Dec. 12, 1721, Elizabeth Wheeler, who, after becoming the mother of one child, died Oct. 3, 1725. He married, the third time, May 17, 1726, Lydia Leonard. Receiving from his father his portion from that part of his estate which lies in what is now the town of Preston, he built upon it and lived, and, it is believed, died upon it, though the date of his death has not been found.

46. HEZEKIAH, born in Norwich, Dec. 16, 1696. He married for his first wife, July 9, 1719, Hannah Frink, who died Sept. 4, 1746. He married for his second wife, March 23, 1748-9, widow Dorothy Williams, of Bristol, and she died, Feb. 27, 1771, in her 67th year. In 1721 he and his wife united with the First Congregational Church of Norwich, of which they both became useful members, being himself appointed deacon in 1737. In the civil history of his town and state, he also became a prominent man. He showed himself ever ready to second and aid any enterprise, either in business, in civil or in religious affairs, which promised to promote the secular or religious interests of his native town. He was a member of the Connecticut Council from 1740 to 1743, and again from 1748 to 1773. He attained, also, the rank of lieutenant-colonel in the Connecticut Militia. As the crisis of our revolutionary history approached, he took a decided stand with the patriots of that day. His name is at the head of that committee of fourteen, of the prominent patriots of Norwich, who were called by their fellow-townsmen to direct the movement of the people, in the threatened conflict with the mother-land. He was prominent in the earnest controversy which ended in making Norwich half-shiretown of the county. He won the third place in that honored trio, consisting of James, (28) Isaac, his brother, and himself. Though above reproach, he was not beyond the reach of serious charges against his personal

character. This appears from the records of the Norwich church, as early as Feb. 12, 1747–8. Dr. Benj. Wheat had reported a slanderous charge, which he had overheard in Hartford, and had evidently aimed to make the most he could of it, by his own unfavorable construction. But, not so was the true and good man to be discredited. His own conscience moved the accuser publicly to recall the slander with a frank confession of having been moved thereto "by a want of brotherly love." It is believed that Hezekiah was not again attacked during his life.

He proved himself an intelligent and scholarly man; and we find his name among the subscribers to that work, so rare for its day, the Chronology of Thomas Prince. He was appointed Judge of the County Court, and served in this office, with no less success and distinction than in others he had filled. In the midst of his judicial duties he died very suddenly, in New London, Feb. 10, 1773. His gravestone in the old burying-ground, in Norwich Town, contains this well-earned tribute: "His piety, affability, prayers and example, wisdom and experience, endeared him to his friends and the State."

47. SARAH, born in Norwich, Jan. 5, 1699–1700. She married, as his second wife, April 23, 1724, Thomas, son of Thomas Bingham, of Windham. The record of their children's birth is on the Norwich books, as follows: Sarah, born March 7, 1730–1; Thomas, born Oct. 12, 1732; and Tryphena, born last day of September, 1735.

48. JEREMIAH, born in Norwich, Dec. 15, 1702, and died the next year.

49. JUDITH, born in Norwich, Sept. 10, 1707, and married, Nov. 10, 1725, Samuel, son of Samuel Leffingwell. Their children were: Hannah, born Sept. 22, 1726; Judith, born Jan. 28, 1728–9; Joanna, born Feb. 21, 1730–1; Samuel, born May 22, 1732; Cyrus, born Sept. 12, 1734; Jeremiah, born Jan. 17, 1736–7; Eunice, born June 20, 1739; Sarah, born June 26, 1742; Asa, born June 4, 1745; and Rufus, born April 16, 1750, and died Nov. 28, 1752.

Samuel Leffingwell died Aug. 6, 1753.

50. JOHN, born in Norwich, Nov. 14, 1709, and married, Nov. 5, 1735, Civil, daughter of Simon and Mary (Leffingwell) Tracy of Norwich. She was born Dec. 8, 1712, and died Feb. 13, 1748–9. He married, for his second wife, 1749, Mary, sister of his first wife, who died, March 7, 1786. His name occurs on the town records occasionally among its officers, though he does not seem to have been prominent, as his other brothers were. He united with the First Church in Norwich in 1742, his first wife, who on the record is called Sibil, in 1744, and his second wife in 1758. He was engaged in brewing a considerable portion of his life.

51. ELIZABETH, born in Norwich, May 6, 1712. She married, April 19, 1733, Capt. Matthew, son of John and Experience (Abel) Hyde, who was born in Norwich, April 27, 1711, and lived in that part of Norwich which has since become Franklin. She had a promising family of six sons and three daughters; and her descendants are very numerous. She died in Franklin, May 20, 1776, and her husband, who after her death married Hannah Pember, died in

Franklin in 1792, having had by his second wife six sons. The children of Elizabeth were: Ely, born Oct. 12, 1736; Matthew, born April 27, 1734; Christopher, born March 25, 1739, and died July 2, 1760; James, born April 6, 1741; Lorissa, born Oct. 11, 1743, and died June 4, 1762; Deborah, born April 5, 1746; Azraih, born Aug. 30, 1748; Uri, born Sept. 27, 1751, and died July 5, 1761; and Elizabeth, born Aug. 18, 1755.

52. JEREMIAH, born in Norwich, Dec. 20, 1715. He married, Nov. 11, 1744, Sarah Reynolds, who was born, Nov. 21, 1725, and died, April 5, 1747. He married for his second wife, Feb. 22, 1747–8, Hannah Watrous. At the close of the Revolution he went to Lebanon, N. H., where he died, June 18, 1794. His first wife was daughter of John Reynolds of Norwich and Lydia Lord of Lyme. His second wife was daughter of Ensign Isaac and Elizabeth (Brewster) Watrous of Lyme, and was born Dec. 2, 1725.

XV. THOMAS, DEACON. Mansfield, Conn.

53. THOMAS, born in Norwich, April 22, 1688, and married in Mansfield, Sept. 6, 1711, Elizabeth, daughter of John Arnold. She died in Mansfield, June 25, 1716, and he married, for his second wife, in April, 1733, Mehetabel, daughter of James Johnson, of Andover. He joined the Mansfield church, April 21, 1717, and seems to have been an active member. His name occurs on the Windham records, Dec. 11, 1744, as guardian for Dorcas, daughter of Wm. Huntington, and administrator on his estate. He died Jan. 8, 1755. His second wife took with her a letter to the church, July 1, 1733, and died in April, 1740.

54. JEDIDIAH, born in Norwich, March 14, 1692–3, where his and his older brother's births are recorded. The only other records found of him is that, noticed in the sketch of his father, his admission to the Mansfield church, May 18, 1712, and his death on the Mansfield second book of records, April 2, 1780, aged 87 years.

55. ELIZABETH, born, probably, in Windham, April 17, 1695, as her birth is found on the Windham records. The marriage of Caleb Chappel and Elizabeth Huntington, Dec. 6, 1722, is found on the Lebanon records. It is probably this Elizabeth.

56. ELEAZER, born in Windham, July 28, 1697. The Mansfield record has the same birth, dated the 7th instead of the 28th. He married, so the Mansfield record states, Feb. 25, 1718–19, Deborah, daughter of James Hovey. He was admitted to the Mansfield church, Sept. 19, 1734, and died March 7, 1748–9. His wife died Feb. 26, 1784.

57. RUTH, born in Windham, Aug. 8, 1699, united with the Mansfield church, Feb. 16, 1717–18, and married, Aug. 22, 1723, Samuel Lincoln. She had a family of seven sons: Samuel, born Dec. 27, 1724; John, born July 28, 1726; Nathaniel, born Nov. 18, 1728; Joseph, born April 19, 1730 and died same day; Jonathan, born April 18, 1731, and died same day; Eleazer, born March 7, 1732, and died Nov. 13, 1764; Daniel, born April 5, 1736, and died on the 20th of the same month.

Her grandchildren were numerous, and among her descendants are many respectable and enterprising names. She died Oct. 6, 1757.

58. LYDIA, born in Windham, in Feb. 1701-2. She married, Oct. 22, 1730, Dea. Nathaniel Wales of Windham, who died June 22, 1744.

59. WILLIAM, born in Mansfield and recorded there only, March 27, 1705. He married in Windham, March 12, 1734-5, Mary, daughter of Nathaniel Basset. She died, as appears from the Windham records, June 1, 1740. The date of his death is not on the record; yet he could not have lived many years after his wife, as the note of his brother Thomas' settlement of his estate shows. The list of his "effects personal" in the Windham probate records, exhibits £100, 13s., 11d., as the amount of their valuation. Dea. Ralph Wheelock, husband of (11) was appointed, Dec. 13, 1745, to complete the settlement of the estate.

60. CHRISTOPHER, born in Mansfield, Oct. 3, 1707, and died, May 29, 1714.

60. SIMON, born in Mansfield, July 6, 1710. He united with the church, Sept. 22, 1734, and married, Dec. 13, 1734, Ame, daughter of Israel Standish, of Preston, Conn. His name is entered on the Mansfield record as I have spelled it, twice, and his wife's twice. She is also called Ammi. On the Windham records the one is made Simeon and the other Amey. I have found nothing further respecting them than what is entered respecting their children.

Widow Ammi Huntington died, as appears from the Mansfield records, Feb. 24, 1798.

XVI. JOHN. Norwich, Conn.

62. ABIGAIL, born in Norwich, Feb. 19, 1687, and probably married, April 15, 1734, James Calkins of Lebanon, where the marriage is recorded.

63. JOHN, born in Norwich, April 20, 1688, and died Dec. 11, 1690.

64. JOHN, born in Norwich, July 4, 1691. He married, April 16, 1723, Thankful Warner of Windham, and early in the settlement of Tolland removed to that town, where he died June 2, 1737, as his grave stone attests. His wife died July 14, 1739.

65. HANNAH, born in Norwich, March 25, 1693-4, married April 4, 1725, in Lebanon, John Huit. Such a marriage is on record there; and this I suppose to be the Hannah named.

66. MARTHA, born in Norwich Dec. 9, 1696.

XXII. SIMON, DEACON. Norwich, Conn.

67. SIMON, born in Norwich, May 11, 1686, and died from the bite of a rattlesnake, July 29, 1707.

68. SARAH, born in Norwich, Feb. 3, 1687-8, and married, Dec. 18, 1712, William Lathrop, also of Norwich, who was born Sept. 20, 1688. He was a son of Israel and Rebecca (Bliss) Lathrop. Her descendants have been both numerous and eminent in character and position. She had William, born June 15, 1715; Joshua, born June 6, 1717 and died Dec. 16, 1717; Ezra, born

May 18, 1719; Jeremiah, born Feb. 16, 1721; James, born May 3, 1724 and died Dec. 29, 1726; Andrew, born April 29, 1728.

She died in Norwich, April 20, 1730.

69. EBENEZER, born in Norwich, May 1692. He married, June 20, 1717, Sarah, daughter of Dea. Thomas and Lydia (Tracy) Leffingwell, who was born in Norwich, Feb. 13, 1698–9. He was a member of the church in 1717, and was chosen deacon, Jan. 18, 1737, to succeed his father, in which office he served until 1764, on the appointment of his son. He died, Sept. 12, 1768 and his widow, April 1, 1770.

70. JOSHUA, born in Norwich, Dec. 30, 1698, and married, Oct. 16, 1718, Hannah, daughter of Jabez and Hannah (Lathrop) Perkins. He was admitted to the church in Norwich, at the same time with his wife, in 1727. He seems to have been a very active business man. As stated in the sketch of James, (28,) he was one of the most forward in commencing the new settlement at the Landing. He was allowed to take up "twenty feet square upon the water on the west side of Rocky Point, on the north side of Lieut. Lathrop's grant, if it be there to be had; not prejudicing the conveniency to be laid out by James Huntington and Daniel Tracy." He was highest on the list of subscribers to the bridge built in 1737, over the Shetucket to unite Norwich and Preston, an enterprise in which none but moneyed men in that day could engage. In his successful business career commenced that family distinction and wealth, which, at the opening of the Revolution, had placed his two surviving children at the head of the aristocracy, even of their own aristocratic town. He died Aug. 26, 1745. His wife who was born in 1701 died, also, in 1745.

XXIII. JOSEPH, DEACON. Windham, Conn.

71. JOSEPH, born in Norwich, Aug. 29, 1688, and was taken in infancy by his parents to Windham, where he married, July 6, 1719, Elizabeth Ripley of Windham. He was a member of the Windham church and chosen deacon in 1751. His wife died Jan. 4, 1774, and he, Dec. 5, 1783. He was a man remarkable for his great agility and strength, and, deacon though he was, he was a Nimrod among the hunters of his day.

72. NATHANIEL, born in Norwich, Sept. 1, 1691, and taken by his parents to Windham. Here he married, Feb. 28, 1723, Mehetabel Thurston of Bristol, R. I., who was born June 8, 1700, O. S. He was a farmer and clothier, and lived in Scotland Society, Windham, where he died Dec. 2, 1767. His widow died Oct. 4, 1781. They were both members of the Windham Congregational church.

73. JONATHAN, born in Windham, Oct. 7, 1695. He married for his first wife, Nov. 7, 1734, Elizabeth, daughter of Joseph and Elizabeth (Drake) Rockwell, who was born in Windsor, July 24, 1713 and died Sept. 24, 1751, aged 38 years and two months. Her grave stone records her virtues thus: "Faithful and dutiful wife, a kinder mother, charitable and beneficent neighbor, an understanding and exemplary Christian, her delight was in the

law of God and her life devoted to his glory. Christ Jesus, in whom she believed, was her all in prosperity, in adversity, in sickness and in death."

He married for his second wife, Aug. 7 1754, Mrs. Sarah Norton, who survived him, dying Feb. 19, 1788.

His grave stone contains this inscription, still legible: Hon. Jona. Huntington, Esq., died Sept. 15, 1773, Etat. 77. He was for several years a member of the Council of this colony and Judge of the Court for this county, which important offices he sustained with fidelity and reputation. He was, from early life to the time of his death, an ornament and a successful practitioner of physic. His life was a series of piety to God and benevolence to mankind, and the closing scene exhibited a striking picture of that fortitude and patience which Christ alone can inspire. Having endured the most exquisite pains, without a murmur or complaint, he at last meekly resigned his soul into the hands of Him who gave it, in well grounded hope of immortal glory."

The testimony of his grave stone is abundantly confirmed by contemporary history and by tradition.

He was an Assistant or member of the Upper House of the Connecticut Council from 1754 to 1758, where his associates, among whom he stood high, were among the ablest men Connecticut has yet produced: and the period of his membership was a trying period of our colonial history — that of the sanguinary French War. In May, 1749, he was appointed a Justice of Quorum, and as such had a seat on the bench from the June term 1749 to 1754, when he was appointed Chief Judge, and held this office until June 1757.

74. DAVID, born in Windham, Dec. 6, 1697, and married, June 30, 1725, Mary Mason, who was born Aug. 31, 1707. He died in Windham, in Sept. 1771. His wife was enrolled on the Windham church list of members in 1735.

75. SOLOMON, born in Windham, Feb. 6, 1700, and married, Oct. 31, 1727, Mary, daughter of Thomas and Margaret (Griswold) Buckingham, and granddaughter of Rev. Thomas and Esther (Hosmer) Buckingham of Milford, Conn. She was born, June 5, 1705 and died, Sept. 17, 1778. His name occurs frequently on the town records. He died, April 31, 1752.

76. REBECCA, born in Windham, Sept. 18, 1712, and married, Jan 24, 1734, John, son of John and Sarah (Spencer) Crane of Windham. He was born in Windham in 1709. She was a member of the Windham church.

77 SARAH, born in Windham, May 25, 1705. She married, March 28, 1728, Ebenezer Wright. Their children, born probably in Windham, were, Eliphalet, born Feb. 27, 1729; Elizabeth, born Nov. 30, 1730; Sarah, born Sept. 22, 1732; Elisha, born Sept. 26, 1734; Mary, born Jan. 15, 1737, and died, July 27, 1739; Amariah, born Feb. 11, 1739.

78. MARY, born in Windham, Aug 4, 1707, and married Theophilus Fitch of Canterbury, Conn. She joined the Windham church in 1729.

XXV. SAMUEL, LIEUT.
Lebanon, Conn.

79. ELIZABETH, born in Norwich, April 24, 1688-9. She married, Feb. 23, 1710, Moses, son of Daniel and Hannah (Pratt) Clark of Lebanon. He died Sept. 18, 1719, and she, Dec. 27, 1761. Their children, who were born in Lebanon, were: Mary, born Jan. 22, 1717; Moses, born Sept. 2, 1720; Anna, born Jan. 26, 1723; Elizabeth, born Jan. 25, 1725; John, born Jan. 7, 1728; and James, Sept. 15, 1730. This last son, Col. James Clark, was a Captain in the Revolution, and was in the engagement at Bunker Hill. He died in Lebanon, Dec. 29, 1826.

The Lebanon grave-yard contains these tributes to the memory of Mr. and Mrs. Clark: "Here lie interred the remains of Moses Clark, who was of a sober, charitable, virtuous disposition; who having served his generation faithfully, departed this life in hope of life eternal."

Of Elizabeth (Huntington) Clark, her gravestone thus speaks: "Here lies the body of Mrs. Elizabeth Clark, the wife of Mr. Moses Clark, who recommended herself and religion to the world by piety and good works: a mid wife who feared God, skillful and greatly useful in the art of healing, who, to the public loss and grief, was suddenly called to a better hope."

Of her descendants, we shall have occasion to speak again.

80. SAMUEL, born in Norwich, Aug. 28, 1691. He married, in Lebanon, Dec. 4, 1722, Hannah, daughter of Jonathan and Hannah (Avery) Metcalf, who was born Jan. 17, 1702. She was admitted to the Lebanon church, April 25, 1725. He was a Christian man, and elected deacon of the Lebanon church. He lived to his 94th year, and his wife died in Lebanon, Oct. 14, 1791.

Jonathan Metcalf, above, was son of Jonathan and Hannah (Kenric) Metcalf of Dedham, Mass.; grandson of Michael and Mary (Fairbanks) Metcalf; and great grandson of Michael and Sarah Metcalf, who were driven by the persecutions of Bishop Wren, of Norwich, England, to flee to New-England, in the spring of 1637. They settled in Dedham, Mass.

81. CALEB, born in Norwich, Feb. 8, 1693-4. He married, Jan. 28, 1720, Lydia Griswold, who was born May 28, 1696. They lived in Lebanon, Conn.

82. MARY, born in Norwich, Oct. 1, 1696, and died in Lebanon, July 30, 1712.

83. REBECCA, born in Norwich, Feb. 1698-9. She married, June 20, 1717, Joseph Clark, of Lebanon. Their children recorded in Lebanon, are: Mary, born July 11, 1720; Abigail, born Nov. 26, 1721; Joseph, born Dec. 8, 1723, and died 1748; Lydia, born Jan. 31, 1725-6, and died Jan. 3, 1728-9; Lydia, born Feb. 13, 1729-30; Rebecca, born Feb. 22, 1728; Asahel, born March 25, 1738.

Joseph Clark died in Lebanon, Sept. 10, 1769, almost 78 years old.

84. SARAH, born in Lebanon, Oct. 22, 1701.

85. JOHN, born in Lebanon, May 17, 1706. He married, in Lebanon, Mehitabel Metcalf, who was born July 26, 1706, and was a sister of his brother Samuel's wife.

86. SIMON, born in Lebanon, Aug. 15, 1708. He married, May 15, 1735, Sarah, (204) and resided in Lebanon, where he died, Aug. 22, 1753, of dysen-

tery; his will having been made Aug. 20th, and probated Oct. 2d, of 1753. His name occurs on the church records without date.

XXVIII. DANIEL.

87. ABIGAIL, born in Norwich, April 22, 1708, where she married, Sept. 10, 1724, Thomas Carew, who died Jan. 13, 1761. They lived in Norwich, and had children: Daniel, born May 7, 1726; Abigail, born Feb. 28, 1728-9; and Eliphalet, born July 30, 1740.

88. MARY, born in Norwich, Nov. 17, 1709, where she married, Feb. 9, 1730-1, Joseph Carew, brother of her sister Abigail's husband. They had: Simeon, born Dec. 7, 1731; Mary, born Sept. 2, 1734; Joseph, born April 13, 1738; Benjamin, born Jan. 28, 1739-40; Anne, born Dec. 7, 1741; Ebenezer, born Feb. 19, 1743-4, and died March 22, 1743-4; Ebenezer, born Sept. 12, 1745; Daniel, born June 22, 1747.

89. DANIEL, born in Norwich, March 24, 1711. He graduated at Yale, 1733, and married, Sept. 25, 1740, Sybil Bull, of Milford. She died, Oct. 12, 1744, when he married, for his second wife, July 24, 1746, Rebecca, (138). He died in Norwich, July 26, 1759, his widow living until April 15, 1798. He was a man of considerable prominence in the church, and in civil life. He was especially active in healing the serious difficulties occasioned by the erratic movements of the "Separates," in the middle of the last century, where his learning and piety were of signal use. His gravestone bears this memorial of his worth: "He had a liberal education, was an excellent scholar, sound reasoner, sagacious, just, and much esteemed in civil life, a plain Christian, kind hearted, tender, pious, faithful friend, a good neighbor, and an honest man."

90. ANNA, born in Norwich, March 20, 1715, and married, March 22, 1731, Thomas, son of deacon Thomas and Ruth (Brewster) Adgate, who was born Feb. 9, 1703, and died, Dec. 13, 1736. She married, for her second husband, April 21, 1739, Capt. Philip Turner, who died Jan. 13, 1755; and for her third husband, she married, June 7, 1757, Capt. Joshua Abel. Her children were: by her first husband, Thomas, born June 9, 1734; Jonathan, born May 10, 1736, and died March 5, 1760.

She had by her second husband, Philip, born Feb. 25, 1739-40, who became an eminent physician and surgeon, and married Lucy Tracy; Bela, born April 19, 1742; John, born Aug. 23, 1744; Anne, born Dec. 4, 1746; and Roger, who died May 7, 1751.

Her third husband was a son of Samuel and Elizabeth (Sluman) Abel, and was born Nov. 23, 1706. She died June 29, 1759.

91. JONATHAN, born in Norwich, Nov. 4, 1719, and married, Nov. 17, 1746, Eunice Lathrop. He was a religious man, and prominent in the organization of the sixth ecclesiastical society of Norwich, now the Rev. Dr. Bond's charge. He united with the infant church in 1760, and was for years very active in its affairs. The following certificate will show his spirit and position, in the church at the time of its date.

"The church of Christ at Chelsey, in Norwich, Conn., in New-England, to all the churches of Christ, and whomsoever it may concern, send greeting: Whereas, it has pleased God, in his providence, to call our reverend and worthy pastor, Mr. Nathaniel Whitaker, from us for a season, to go to Europe, to solicit charities for the Indian school, under the care of the Rev. Mr. Eleazer Wheelock, of Lebanon, and to promote Christian knowledge, among the Indians on this continent: We do unanimously recommend him, the said Mr. Whitaker, and his services, to all the churches and people of God, of whatever denomination, and wheresoever he may come, as a faithful minister of Jesus Christ, whose praise is in the gospel through the churches, earnestly requesting brotherly kindness and charity may be extended toward him as occasion may require, and that the grand and important cause in which he is engaged, may be forwarded and promoted by all the lovers of truth.

Wishing grace, mercy and truth, may be multiplied to you and the whole Israel of God, and desiring an interest in your prayers, we subscribe,

Yours in the faith and fellowship of the gospel.
JONATHAN HUNTINGTON,
ISAIAH TIFFANY.

By order, and in behalf of said church.
Norwich, Oct. 21, 1766."

He was the chairman of the building committee, for the first church built in the new society, in 1760. He died in Norwich, Aug. 9, 1801; and his wife, in May, 1803, in the 78th year of her age.

92. BENJAMIN, born in Norwich, April 19, 1736, graduated at Yale, in 1761. He married, May 5, 1765, Anne, (151) of Windham. He entered, soon after leaving college, upon the practice of law in his native town, and rose rapidly to the front rank of his profession. He seems to have been unusually devoted to his profession, being at once a severe student, and an active and successful advocate and business man. Though rather shunning than courting public life, he was not allowed to excuse himself from its claims; nor, when called to meet them, did he shrink either from public duties or dangers. In 1775 he was appointed, by the legislature of his native State, on the committee of safety, appointed to advise with the Governor of the State during the recess of the legislature. Only the ablest men and truest patriots of that trying day, would have been put upon that important committee. Again, in 1778, on the recommendation of Washington, he was appointed by the legislature, one of that convention to be held in New Haven, for the regulation of the army. From 1780 to '84, and again in '87 and '88, he was a member of the Continental Congress; and when the new government went into operation, in 1789, he was chosen to represent Connecticut in the First Congress of the United States.

From 1781 to 1790, and also from 1791 to '93 he was also a member of the upper house of the Connecticut Legislature. On the incorporation of Norwich city, in 1784, he was chosen, for an indefinite period, its first Mayor, in which office he served until his formal resignation, in 1796. He was also ap-

pointed in **1793**, a judge of the **superior** court of Connecticut, holding this **office until 1798**. Thus, for more than twenty years, during the most eventful period of **our** history, in which we had claimed and won our independence, and had commenced our most successful career in self-government, was he found continually called to serve his constituents in offices always onerous, and often hazardous. How well he discharged these trusts, their **own recurrence will** unequivocally evince. **A word on** this **point, however, is** due both to his memory and to the truth **of our revolutionary history.**

For some reason, never **explained, he was not in the** early stages of preparation **for the struggle, prominently identified with its measures.** Our explanation is that **he was not only a young man, and therefore** hesitated to put himself forward; **but, also, that he had formed such an** ideal for his professional course, that **all his** strength and **time were required in** attaining it. The stamp act dates with the **year of his marriage, just as he had laid the plans for his professional** studies, on which **his entire success was to depend.** And, with a nice discernment of what was most needed by **him, to prepare for the future call, which his country would make upon him, no less than to meet the high demands of his** profession, **he** gave himself **to an earnest pursuit of legal study and practice.**

And, for the time being, he could be spared from the **more public** discussions and services which the incipiency of our revolution required. His family were well represented in them by older members: Hezekiah, (16) **ripe in** years and counsel; Samuel, (232) already strong and facile for action; **Jabez,** (217) with means and a heart for the **work,** and **in** the work; and still others **of his own** family name, scarcely less ready and restive for the impending struggle, rendered it possible for him, without a breach of faith to the cause, **to await a maturer preparation for ampler service to be rendered at a later day.** And that future service fully justified his decision. **By the May of 1775, he was found ready for an** exigency which none but a strong **man** and true patriot could meet. He filled acceptably the post **to which the** patriot legislature **of his native State called him; and the fact of that appointment is, itself, no equivocal testimony respecting the** position **of their agent. They who** were called, in that crisis, **to** take the place of the legislature in **advising with their chief executive,** during **its period of adjournment, were known and tried men. Nor would Washington have recommended him for appointment by the legislature** to that **convention to be held in New Haven, in 1778, while the war was yet in progress, to arrange for its increased efficiency, unless he had already furnished ample proof, both of an interest not to be bribed, and a courage never to be intimidated.**

And that his family were thoroughly patriotic, and ready for any **sacrifice for which their country might call, is abundantly attested by this instance of their personal devotion.** On an occasion **of pressing want on the part of our revolutionary army, an earnest call was made upon the families of Norwich, for** supplies of clothing. **In the** absence **of Judge Huntington,** then **away in the service of the State, his wife, selecting a single blanket, in which to wrap**

her youngest child, forwarded all the rest to the army; and supplied their place on the beds at home, by blankets cut from the carpets on the floor, preferring, for the present, well sanded floors, without their accustomed covering, that so the noble patriotism of the needy army might be encouraged and rewarded.

Few men and few families of those trying days can show a purer and more patriotic record than he and his.

XXIX. JAMES. Norwich, Conn.

93. JERUSHA, born in Norwich, Jan. 15, 1704-5, and married, Oct. 16, 1729, Abner, son of Thomas Hyde, by whom she had two daughters: Phebe, born in Norwich, Feb. 28, 1731-2, who married, Nov. 8, 1750, Dr. John Barker, of Norwich, and had three sons and six daughters. She died at Norwich, West Farms, June 3, 1771; Jerusha, born Nov. 9, 1733, and died on the 19th same month.

After her death, Nov. 10, 1733, her husband married Mehetabel Smith, and by her had six sons and three daughters.

94. JAMES, born in Norwich, Feb. 2, 1706-7. He married, Dec. 3, 1735, Elizabeth Darby, who died June 12, 1790. They lived in that part of Norwich called the Great Plains, where he was a farmer. He died May 12, 1785.

95. PETER, born in Norwich, March 18, 1708-9, married, Aug. 8, 1734, Ruth Edgerton. He lived in Norwich, where he died, April 10, 1760, and his wife, Sept. 21, 1761, aged forty-six.

96. JACOB, born in Norwich, April 20, 1711, and died in 1726.

97. NATHANIEL, born in Norwich, Aug. 20, 1713. He married for his first wife, Nov. 5, 1735, Mary Brown, of Stonington; for his second, a Jones, and for his third, a Miss Pembroke.

98. ELIZABETH, born in Norwich, Aug. 14, 1716. She married, Nov. 9, 1732, Thomas, oldest son of Thomas and Elizabeth (Backus) Hyde, of Norwich, West Farms (Franklin). His grandfather was Samuel Hyde, who was one of the original proprietors of Norwich. He was a brother of Abner, husband of her sister Jerusha. Their children were: Thomas, born May 11, 1735, married Ednah Burleigh, and had three sons and four daughters; Vaniah, born Dec. 17, 1750, married Rebecca Barker, and had two sons and five daughters, one of the sons being the Rev. John Hyde, who married Lucretia, daughter of Rev. Dr. Nott, of Franklin; Jerusha, born June 14, 1737, married in 1763, Jonathan Bushnell, and had three sons and three daughters; Elizabeth, born Sept. 19, 1739, married, 1760, Joshua Edgerton, jr., and had one son and three daughters; Priscilla, born March 5, 1741-2, married Eliphalet Barker, of Lebanon, in 1764, and had five sons and three daughters; Zerviah, born Nov. 15, 1746, married, in 1765, Thomas Abel, of Norwich, and had two sons and seven daughters; Mary, born Nov. 2, 1754, married Joseph Knight, and second, Daniel Judd; Jane, born July 9, 1757, and is said to have married deacon Beckwith.

FIFTH GENERATION.

35. WILLIAM. Amesbury, Mass.

This family were all born in Amesbury.

99. JOHN, born Jan. 5, 1709-10 and married Abigail Jones. He resided on the homestead of his grandfather. His wife was a Friend and their children some of them married among the Friends.

100. LYDIA, born April 6, 1711.

101. MARY, born Jan. 13, 1712-13.

102. SARAH, born Nov. 3, 1716.

103. ELIZABETH, born Jan. 15, 1716-17, and married, Nov. 8, 1739, Andrew Whittier.

104. DEBORAH, born Jan. 1717-18, and married, June 23, 1739, Thomas Homan of Danvers, Mass.

105. WILLIAM, born Nov. 5, 1719, and married, Oct. 26, 1748, Mary Norton.

106. TIMOTHY, born Aug 3, 1721, and married Sarah ———. He married the second time. He died in 1811.

107. JUDITH, born April 9, 1727, and was the only child of the second wife.

36. SAMUEL. Amesbury, Mass.

This family were all born in Amesbury.

108. SAMUEL, born Jan. 13, 1709-10, and married Abigail Maxfield of Salisbury, Jan. 19, 1737.

109. ELIZABETH, born March 2, 1711-12.

110. JOHN, born Dec. 24, 1714.

111. ANNE, born March 16, 1716-17, and married, Dec. 25, 1746, Moses Ordway, and lived in Amesbury.

112. JONATHAN, born Feb. 20, 1719-20, and married Elizabeth ———.

113. DAVID, born Feb. 2, 1724-5, probably the David who was in an Amesbury company of militia at Bunker Hill. Is said to have deserted.

114. JACOB, born Dec. 29, 1726.

38. THOMAS. Newark, N. J.

115. SAMUEL, born in Newark in 1738, and married Margaret ———. He was a man of public spirit and of manly and generous impulse. His gravestone, standing in the rear of the first Presbyterian church of Newark, says that he died March 6, 1818, aged eighty years. The gravestone of Margaret, his wife, testifies that she died, Dec. 23, 1808, aged sixty-eight years.

116. A DAUGHTER, who married a Hedden, and had three sons, David, Job, and Simon, and one daughter, who married Daniel Ball of Newark, N. J.

39. SIMON. Whipanong, N. J.

117. SAMUEL, born, at least this seems most probably the one, in 1710, and died Sept. 7, 1784. He had married Elizabeth ———, who died June 4, 1775, aged seventy.

118. EUNICE OGDEN.
119. PHEBE GARD.
120. ELIZABETH PIERSON.
121. SARAH WINTER.
122. SIMON, jr., married "Lyba ———." He died in Morris County, July 17, 1770. A careful collation of names and dates has seemed to me to justify this record.

42. CHRISTOPHER. Franklin, Conn.

This family were all born in Norwich and recorded there.

123. CHRISTOPHER, born June 20, 1719. He married, Sept. 29, 1748, Sarah Bingham. They lived in Bozrah, Conn., where he died suddenly in March, 1800.

124. ELISHA, born Sept. 22, 1720. He married, Dec. 31, 1760, Dinah, daughter probably of Samuel and Dina (Hatch) Chapman. She was born in New London, July 20, 1731. He died, as appears from the Norwich records, Feb. 12, 1760.

125. RUTH, born Aug. 3, 1722, and married a Joshua Sherman in 1741. She died in 1742.

126. AZARIAH, born Nov. 26, 1723.

127. MARGARET, born in Norwich, Nov. 23, 1724, and married, Oct. 13, 1747, John, son of John and Margaret (Hyde) Tracy, and she was his first wife. She had four children, and her descendants have been both numerous and respectable. Her son John had eight children:—John, of Oxford, N. Y., a man of some eminence; Zebadiah L., Bela, Ulysses, Rachel, Harriet, Esther and Emily. Mary, her oldest daughter, married Andrew Hyde of Franklin, and had eight children: Andrew, Jude, George, Amasa, so long a hotel keeper in Franklin, Rodney, Lewis of Norwich, Lydia and Mary. Margaret, the second daughter, married Benjamin Storrs of Mansfield, and had four children: Lathrop, Huckins, Margaret and Oliver. Lydia the youngest daughter had no children.

FIFTH GENERATION.

128. THEOPHILUS, born Sept. 12, 1726. He married, Jan. 3, 1753, Lois, daughter of Samuel and Experience (Hyde) Gifford, who was born, also, in Norwich, Feb. 25, 1730-1. They lived in Norwich, New Concord Society, now Bozrah, where he was a deacon in the Congregational church, and its clerk from 1764 to 1778. In 1780 he went to Lebanon, N. H. and died in 1815.

129. BARNABAS, born May 29, 1728. He married, Dec. 11, 1751, Anne Wright, of Hebron, and lived in Franklin, Conn., where he was deacon in the Congregational church. He was a solid man, "an active and influential patriot, and highly respected for his moral worth." He was one of the selectmen of Norwich, who, on May 30, 1774, issued a call to the patriots of the town to meet on the sixth of the next month "to take into Consideration the Melancholly Situation of our Civil and Constitutional Liberties Rights and Privileges which are threatened with destruction, by the Enemies of his Majesty's Happy Reign and Government over the American Colonies."

His wife was born Oct. 18, 1725, and lived until July 21, 1821. Her character as a woman and a Christian was one of great excellence. He died in Franklin, April 14, 1787.

130. SARAH, born April 27, 1730, and married, May 12, 1756, Asa Kingsbury, who died Sept. 5, 1775. Their children recorded in Norwich are: Asa, born March 12, 1757; Sarah, born April 8, 1761; Eunice, born Nov. 9, 1767; and Lucy, born June 20, 1771.

131. ELIZABETH, born in Norwich, Feb. 3, 1734-5, and died Oct. 25, 1758.

13. ISAAC. Bozrah, Conn.

This family were all born and recorded in Norwich.

132. REBECCA, born Nov. 17, 1717, and died June 5, 1725.

133. ISAAC, born Aug. 25, 1719. He purchased land in the New Concord Society of Norwich, now Bozrah, in 1744, where he married, Jan. 24, 1749-50, Lucy Edgerton. He was a substantial farmer, and a prominent man in the town. He was a member of the Connecticut Convention in 1788, which ratified the Constitution of the United States. He died, having had no children, March 23, 1799, as his gravestone attests, "in hope of a glorious immortality." Lucy, his widow, died May 4, 1800, in her 77th year.

134. SARAH, born April 17, 1721. She married, Dec. 6, 1747, John Bliss of Norwich, who was born, May 16, 1717, and died April 15, 1809. Their children were: John, born March 14, 1748-9; Elizabeth, born Jan. 4, 1750-51; Zephaniah, born July 8, 1753; Sarah, born Feb. 9, 1757; and William, born Dec. 2, 1766. She died in Norwich, Jan. 25, 1806.

135. NEHEMIAH, born Jan. 2, 1722-3, and married, March 14, 1748-9, Lois Hinckly of Lebanon, Conn. She was daughter of Gershom and Mary (Bird) Hinckley, and was born in Lebanon, Sept. 24, 1727. They had no children. He was a man of property and enterprise, having established the Iron Works in the eastern part of Bozrah, which were subsequently improved by Nehemiah Huntington Fitch, who purchased the property. The Iron Works were removed many years since, and on the same ground now stands the beautiful

village, built and improved by the brothers Fitch. The following is the inscription on his gravestone in the Bozrah burying ground: "In memory of Nehemiah Huntington, Esq., a worthy officer both in church and state — beneficent, hospitable, and pious — a kind and tender husband, an indulgent master and a good neighbor. He died June 16, 1780."

His widow married in 1782, Dr. Elisha Tracy, the distinguished physician of Norwich. Her gravestone stands by the side of her first husband's in the Bozrah burying ground, and has the following inscription: "In memory of Lois Tracy, relict of Dr. Elisha Tracy, who died Oct. 3, 1790, in the 63rd year of her age, having been a few years separated from Nehemiah Huntington, Esq., her former husband."

136. DORCAS, born Feb. 23, 1724-5, and married, May 13, 1745, William Lathrop of Norwich. There is no other record connected with their names than that of his death, July 15, 1770.

137. REBECCA, born and died June 5, 1725.

138. REBECCA, born Dec. 4, 1726. She married, July 24, 1746, Daniel, (89) and died March 7, 1774.

139. MARY, born Nov. 26, 1728, and married, Sept. 3, 1750, Ebenezer Fitch, of Norwich, where he died, Feb. 13, 1797. Their children were: Eunice, born March 23, 1752, and died Aug. 31, 1753; Gerard, born July 14, 1753; Eunice, born April 17, 1755; Nabby, born Aug. 4, 1757; Ebenezer, born Oct. 29, 1759; Roger, born Sept. 13, 1761; Mary, born Jan. 3, 1764; Oliver, born July 23, 1766; Elizabeth, born Nov. 10, 1768; Sarah, born Aug. 10, 1771; and Charles, born Nov. 8, 1775.

140. SAMUEL, born March 23, 1731 and died in 1737.

141. JOSEPH, born Nov. 15, 1732 and died Jan. 29, 1813.

142. ELIJAH, born Dec. 21, 1734. Married, Dec. 19, 1764, Anna, daughter of Joseph and Mary (88) Carew, and went same year into Bozrah, where he lived and died, a useful and honored man. He was a member of the Connecticut legislature in 1791. Though early called into the service of his country, having served in three campaigns of the old French War, he preferred the less exposed and less noticed, yet none the less useful life of the farmer.

His first wife died April 9, 1770, and he married, the second time, March 21, 1771, Lydia, daughter of Thomas and Ann (Bingham) Baldwin, who was born, Oct. 19, 1740.

After a distressing confinement of eleven years, with an obstinate rheumatic complaint, induced at first by his exposures in his military campaigns, he died in Bozrah, March 20, 1814.

The following extracts from his correspondence, during his third and last campaign, are here inserted, as illustrative of the character of the man, and as containing authentic history of those days. From the camp at Fort Ontario, Aug. 8, 1760, he thus writes to his father in Norwich, Conn: "After a long and tedious march of thirty-one days from Schenectady, I arrived at this place in good health, the 29th of July. I call our passage from Schenectady to this place a march, though we came by water all the way, only at three carrying places, for we were obliged to wade a good part of the way up the Mohawk River to Fort Stanwix, at the head of the river. which is about 140 miles from Schenectady. In this distance there is one carrying place of about one mile. From Fort Stanwix, we carry about one mile again, and then take Wood Creek, which runs to the westward, and is a very small stream running into Oneida Lake. * * * Yesterday the two snows that we have in this (Ontario) Lake went down it, one of twenty and the other of eighteen guns, with a party of batteaux with them containing about 2,000 men. I expect the remainder of the army will go after them to-morrow or the next day, at furthest, to give the French a visit at Oswegochwe."

Camp at Montreal, 10th Sept., 1760.

Honored Father:

We landed on this Island, about eight miles above the city, last Sunday, and marched down within about two miles of the city, where we encamped without any opposition. Monday the French General capitulated. The inhabitants of Canada are to enjoy their habitations and become subjects of Great Britain. The regular troops are to be held as prisoners of war, and they are about four thousand. The Indians have never given us any trouble, but rather fallen in on our side.

Sir, you have doubtless heard of our success at Fort Levee, now William Augustus, on the 17th of August. We took a brig of fourteen guns and 120 men, within sight of the fort. There we landed on the two islands, on one side of the island that the French fort was on, and on the main on the other side of it; and began to entrench and build batteries — the French firing upon our men from their fort, but doing but little damage. The 23d we got our batteries open, and began to play upon them from the two islands and the main. The 25th, in the afternoon, the French surrendered and were all made prisoners of war. There were about 300 men in the fort, and they had thirty-five pieces of cannon, but no bombs. I cannot tell how many men we lost, but our loss is but small. Col. Fitch lost two men by the wounds on board our snows. The 31st we embarked at Fort William Augustus for this place, and we lost as many men in coming as we did at the siege, by reason of the falls in the river. Capt. Smith, from New London, had five men drowned. * * *

Sir, we have orders for all the Provincials to march to-morrow morning back to Oswego, which gives the regiments a great deal of uneasiness; for we are now 271 miles from Oswego, and one half of the way is a strong current, and it is not further, I suppose, from Albany by way of Crown Point, which way we always expected to go. The reason of our going by the way of Oswego, I cannot tell unless it be to work on the fort. * * * * *

Honored Sir, these lines leave me in good health, as I have been ever since I left home, for which I desire to be thankful. Let God have the praise of our success over the enemy; and may we never have occasion for another campaign in this country again.

Sir, your most obedient son,
ELIJAH HUNTINGTON.

P. S. The city of Montreal is about a mile in length and half a mile in breadth, within the walls. Gen. Amherst lies above the city, with about 10,000 men; Gen. Murray, from Quebec, below it, with about 4,000 soldiers and 3,000 marines; and Col. Haviland, from Crown Point, with about 6,000 men on the other side of the river."

143. BENJAMIN, born in Norwich, Feb. 22, 1736. He married, March 5, 1767, Mary, daughter of Joseph and Mary (88) Carew, and widow of James Noyes Brown. She died April 24, 1777. He was chosen to succeed his father in the office of town clerk, March 5, 1764, and resigned the post to his son Philip. He was one of the selectmen, with Barnabas (129), Samuel Tracy, and Elijah Brewster, who called together the first revolutionary meeting held in Norwich, June 6, 1774.

144. ABIGAIL, born in Norwich, July 29, 1739. She married, Dec. 20, 1764, Azariah Lathrop, of Franklin, who was born in 1728, and died Feb. 25, 1810. She was a most excellent woman, who "happily exemplified the meek and quiet spirit of the gospel." Her children were: Charles, born Jan. 11, 1770; Nabby, born March 24, 1772; Charlotte, born April 16, 1774, and died Nov. 3, 1777; Burrel, born May 25, 1776; Gerard, born Aug. 19, 1778; Charlotte, born Feb. 21, 1781; and Augustus, born Feb. 11, 1785.

Among her grand-children were the missionary sisters—the first Mrs. Myron Winslow, Mrs. Cherry, Mrs. Hutchins, and Mrs. Perry, three of whom were buried on heathen ground, at Ooolooville, Ceylon, and Rev. Dr. Daniel Lathrop, Mrs. Wm. A. Hallock, of New York, and C. L. Lathrop, who married (1027). She died March 9, 1820.

44. JABEZ, COLONEL. Windham, Conn.

145. ELIZABETH, born in Norwich, Nov. 1, 1725. She was married in Windham, by the Rev. Stephen White, Nov. 16, 1750, to the Hon. Abraham, son of Rev. John and Martha (Gould) Davenport, of Stamford, Conn. Her husband was born in Stamford, 1715, and graduated at Yale, 1732. He was a most worthy, and truly noble man, sustaining many offices, civil and military, with very marked ability. "Col. Davenport was possessed of a vigorous understanding and invincible firmness of mind, and of a weight of character which for many years decided, in this county, almost every question to which it was lent. He was early a professor of religion, and adorned its doctrines by an exemplary conformity to its precepts." He was for many years one of the council of the state, and at his death was judge of the Fairfield county court. "Of his country and all its great interests he was a pillar of granite." So testifies no lower authority than Dr. Dwight, to the character of Col. Davenport. His wife, who was quite infirm, for the last few years of her life, died Dec. 17, 1773. After her death he married again, Aug. 8, 1776, Mrs. Martha Fitch.

The following notice of the family of Elizabeth, is collected mainly from the genealogy of the Davenport family. Her children were:

Hon. John Davenport, born Jan. 16, 1752, graduated at Yale, 1770, married

FIFTH GENERATION.

May 7, 1780, Mary Silvester, daughter of the Rev. Dr. Noah Wells. He was chosen a member of congress to fill the vacancy made by the death of his brother James, and continued for eighteen years a member. He died Nov. 28, 1830, leaving a family of seven children: Elizabeth Huntington, who married the Hon. judge Peter W. Radcliffe, of Brooklyn, N. Y.; John Alfred, a graduate of Yale, who married Eliza M. Wheeler, and had six children, among whom are Rev. J. S. Davenport, an Episcopal minister at Oswego, N. Y., and Rev. James R., an Episcopal minister, also, in Albany; Mary Wells, who married James Boorman, of New York; Theodosia, who died unmarried; deacon Theodore, who married Harriet G. Cheesebrough, of New York, and has a family of seven children, and still lives, in honored usefulness, on the homestead of his ancestors for several generations; Rebecca Ann, who died unmarried; and Matilda, the wife of Rev. Peter Lockwood, of Binghampton, who has had a family of seven children.

Abraham, born Oct. 21, 1753, and died Oct. 25, 1754.

Elizabeth, born Sept. 16, 1756, married, Aug. 8, 1777, James Coggswell, M. D., of Preston. Her daughter, Alice, became the wife of the Rev. Dr. Samuel Fisher, of Greenbush, and mother of Rev. Samuel Ware Fisher, of Cincinnati, Ohio.

Hon. James, born Oct. 12, 1758, graduated at Yale, 1779, married Abigail Fitch, and after her death, Mehetabel Coggshall. He was a member of the Connecticut legislature, and judge of county court. In 1796 he was chosen member of congress, in which office he died suddenly, Aug. 3, 1797. His children are four: Betsey Coggshall, who married Chas. W. Aphthorp, of Boston; Abigail Fitch, the wife of that gifted preacher, Rev. Philip Melancthon Whelpley, of the first Presbyterian church of New York; Mary Ann, the wife of the no less eminent servant of God, Rev. Matthias Bruen, the first pastor of the Bleecker street church, in New York; and Frances Louisa, the wife of the Rev. Dr. Thomas Skinner, of the Union Theological Seminary.

Huntington, born April 18, 1761, and died Oct. 22, 1769.

146. SARAH, born in Norwich, June 20, 1727. She married, Aug. 22, 1748, Hezekiah Wetmore, of Middletown, and for her second husband, Feb. 19, 1758, Samuel Beers, of Stratford, where she died, Dec. 1, 1784. Her second husband died Oct. 17, 1798, aged seventy years, and four months. Her children were: Tryphena, baptized July 8, 1750; Hezekiah, baptized March 3, 1754, which were all her children by her first husband. By her second husband she had: Lucy, born Sept. 10, 1760, and married Geo. Smith, of Smithtown, L. I.; Sarah Ann, born June 6, 1762, married David Beers, of Fairfield, Conn.; William Pitt, born April 2, 1766, married Anna, daughter of Jonathan Sturgis, of Fairfield, and became an eminent lawyer, in Albany, N. Y.

147. TRYPHENA, born Aug. 27, 1729, and died at East Windsor, Aug. 19, 1745.

148. JERUSHA, born Aug. 24, 1731, and married, Nov. 7, 1751, Dr. John, son of Moses and Elizabeth (79) **Clark**, of Lebanon. Her husband was born in Lebanon, Jan. 7, 1728, graduated at Yale, 1749, and **died in** Utica, N. Y.,

Dec. 23, 1822. She died in Utica, Dec. 14, 1823. Their children and their families were as follows, collected from Goodwin's genealogical notes:

John, born June 13,1752, O. S., married Abigail, daughter of Rev. Samuel Moseley, of Hampton, Conn., was a physician, residing in Lebanon, N. Y., and had a family of eight children.

Jabez, born Nov. 2, 1753, married Annie, daughter of Jedidiah Elderkin, of Windham. He was a prominent man in civil life, and left a family of six children, of whom Elizabeth became the wife of Walter King, of Utica, N. Y.; Anna married Edward Vernon, of New York city; Jerusha married Jesse W. Doolittle, of Utica, N. Y.; Charlotte married the Hon. Samuel Huntington Perkins, of Philadelphia; and Edwards, the only son, married Hannah, daughter of Rev. Samuel and Anna (653) Perkins of Windham, is an attorney-at-law, has been judge of county court, and resides in Windham, Conn.

Israhiah, born May 16, 1755, and died June 1st of same year; Jerusha, born May 7, 1756, and died unmarried, in Utica, July 8 1840; Hezekiah, born Dec. 19, 1757, became a physician, married Lucy, daughter of Hon. Moses Bliss, of Springfield, Mass., and settled in Pompey, N. Y., where he had a family of ten children; Tryphena, born Feb. 19, 1760, married Ebenezer Bushnell of Lebanon, and had one son; Deodatus, born July 27, 1762, married Nancy, daughter of deacon Daniel Dunham, of Lebanon Crank, (Columbia,) Conn., was a physician, and resided last in Oswego, N. Y., and had a family of ten children; Hannah, born May 19, 1764, married Hon. Geo. Bliss, of Springfield, Mass., and had four children; Henry, born May 1, 1766, married Mary Ann, daughter of Capt. Vine Elderkin, of Windham, Conn., and had six children; Erastus, born May 11, 1768, married, first, Sophia Porter of Lebanon, Conn., and second, Sophia Flint, daughter of Royal Flint, and had four children; Thaddeus, born Feb. 12, 1770, a physician, married Deborah, daughter of Dr. Joseph Baker, of Brooklyn, and had eleven children, one of whom, Sarah Jane, has become widely known from her contributions to our popular literature, over the signature of Grace Greenwood; and Elizabeth, born Feb. 2, 1772, married Rev. Ludovicus Weld, of Hampton Conn., and had five children, one of whom, Lewis, was the distinguished successor of the Rev. Thomas H. Gallaudet, in the Am. Asylum, at Hartford, for the education of the deaf and dumb.

149. HANNAH, born in Windham, July 22, 1736. She married, Jan. 17, 1760, Gideon Tomlinson, of Stratford Conn., an officer in the army. They had only one child, Jabez Huntington, born Dec. 24, 1760. He married Rebecca Lewis, daughter of Joseph, of Stratford, and had four children, of whom, Gideon, was governor of Connecticut from 1827 to 1831.

She died in Stratford, Dec. 26, 1762, and her husband, Jan. 19, 1766.

150. JABEZ, born in Windham, April 15, 1738, graduated at Yale, 1758, and married, Aug. 6, 1760, Judith Elderkin, who was born in Norwich, March 2, 1743. He was early introduced into public life, and continued in it, meeting its various responsibilities acceptably, until his death. He was a member of the Connecticut council from 1764 to 1781, and was high sheriff of Windham county at his death, Nov. 24, 1782. His wife died Sept. 24, 1786.

151. ANNE, born in Windham, Jan. 29, 1740, and married, May 3, 1765, Benjamin, (92) of Norwich, where she died, Oct. 8, 1790.

152. SAMUEL, born in Windham, Oct. 19, 1742, and died Jan. 15, 1743.

153. LUCY, born in Windham, June 16, 1744. She married Col. Experience, a son of Huckins and Eunice (Porter) Storrs, of Mansfield, where she died, Feb. 6, 1801, and he died July 22, 1801. His birth was Sept. 18, 1734, being the second in a family of twelve children.

45. MATTHEW. Preston, Conn.

This family were all born in Norwich.

154. MATTHEW, born March 20, 1720–21, married, in 1742, Elizabeth Heath, of Preston, daughter of Richard Adams, of Massachusetts, and in 1745 removed to Mansfield, Conn. He was engaged in the French War of 1756–'60; for which he enlisted a company of about sixty soldiers from Mansfield and vicinity, and started with them for the seat of the war on Lake George. In attempting to take up the Hudson, a number of barges, the task proved more than a match for the strength of his company. One after another of his men gave out, and to supply the deficiency, as far as possible, he exerted himself all the more earnestly, aiding with his own muscular arms the tugging at the boats, until he succeeded in taking his entire charge over the last rapids in his way. But he had overtasked his mortal powers, and he fell suddenly, a victim to exertions which were deemed even in that day of prodigies, almost superhuman. He died at Greenbush. His widow subsequently married Capt. Peleg Heath. An old sword which he used, about four feet long, with an immense guard above the hilt nearly ten inches in diameter, was for several years in the family, but was subsequently worked up into butcher knives.

155. MARY, born July 17, 1723, and died May 6, 1745.

156. LYDIA, born April 25, 1728, and married, Sept. 10, 1745, Jacob Galusha, of Preston, who went, in 1775, to Shaftesbury, Vt. She died, May 6, 1764. Their children were: Mary, born Nov. 10 1746; David, born Oct. 30, 1748; Jacob, born Dec. 28, 1750; Jonah, born Feb. 11, 1753; Amos, born April 1, 1755; Elijah, born Oct. 23, 1757; Olive, born Dec. 4, 1759; Lydia, born June 1, 1762; and Anna, born May 6, 1764. From the third son, the late Gov. Galusha, of Vermont, is descended.

157. NATHAN, born Oct. 30, 1730, and married, in 1756, Amy, daughter of John Brown, of Preston. He owned and lived on a farm on the east side of the Quinebaug, about nine miles north of Norwich, and one and a half south of Jewett city, from which place he moved, in 1779, to Shaftesbury, Vt., where he died Nov. 14, 1794.

158. SARAH, born April 18, 1733, and died May 8, 1733.

159. ELIZABETH, born Nov. 14, 1734.

160. SAMUEL, born March 14, 1736.

161. AMOS, born Sept. 4, 1739. He married, 1767, Peace Clark. He went to Shaftesbury, Vt., where he became a man of some distinction in civil and military life. He had the charge, in our revolutionary war, of one of the two

companies, furnished by Shaftesbury for the service, and honored his captaincy. He was in the unequal fight of Hubbardston, on the 7th July, 1777, and of course was obliged to yield to the superior force, under Burgoyne's elated generals, Frazer and Riedesel. Yet not without the most determined resistance, did the company which he led, yield the ground, nor indeed would they consent to save themselves by flight. He, himself, was overborne by the sudden onset of Riedesel, after he had been successfully contesting the ground with the forces under Frazer, and was taken prisoner. He was kept for six months on board a prison ship, during which he was taken from Quebec to New York, where he was exchanged, with other prisoners, for those of the same rank in the hands of the Americans.

He subsequently devoted himself to the more peaceful pursuits of husbandry, and enjoyed the confidence, and shared in the honors awarded by his fellow-citizens. He was emphatically a peace maker. He died in Shaftesbury, July 2, 1822, a member of the Baptist church.

162. AME, born August 5, 1746.
163. ELIAS, born September 2, 1749.

16. HEZEKIAH, JUDGE. Norwich, Conn.

This family were all born in Norwich.

164. HANNAH, born July 1, 1720, and died, unmarried, March 23, 1744.
165. ANNE, born Aug. 9, 1722. She married, July 28, 1747, Prosper Wetmore, who was a prominent man in Norwich, being high sheriff of the county, when he died, in 1788.

They had one son, Andrew, born in Norwich, Oct. 30, 1751, and died next month. She died Aug. 12, 1754. He married for his second wife, Keturah Cheesebrough of Stonington, by whom he had six children.

166. EUNICE, born Dec. 1, 1724, and died Oct. 30, 1732.
167. HEZEKIAH, born Aug. 10, 1726. He graduated at Yale, 1744, and died a captive in Quebec, May 14, 1747, as Sylvester Judd states.
168. ELIAS, born Oct. 31, 1729, and died May 20, 1730.
169. ABIGAIL, born June 22, 1731. She married, first, Sept. 1, 1748, Thomas Frink, and for her second husband, Rev. Mr. Conant. She had one daughter whose birth is recorded in Norwich: Hannah, born July 29, 1749.
170. ELIJAH, born March 2, 1733-4, and died April 13, 1734.
171. EUNICE, born June 12, 1735, and married, March 24, 1757, John Williams. She died in 1766.
172. DOROTHY, born Sept. 27, 1737, and married, April 26, 1764, Rev. Abiel Leonard, S. T. D., of Woodstock. They had one daughter. After the death of his wife, Dr. Leonard married a Miss Green, of Bristol, R. I., by whom he had five children.

Dr. Leonard was born in Plymouth, Mass., Nov. 5, 1740, and was son of Rev. Nathaniel and Priscilla (Rogers) Leonard. He graduated at Harvard College, in 1740, and was settled in Woodstock, Conn., (Muddy Brook,) in 1763. In 1775 he was appointed chaplain in the revolutionary army, and con-

FIFTH GENERATION.   101

tinued in this service until 1778. The following extract from Rev. Mr. Learned's account of the churches and ministers in Windham County, Conn., will explain his mournful end. "Tradition says that in the summer of 1778, he was called home from the army by the sickness of a child; that having overstaid the period of his furlough, he was met on his return by the report that he had been superseded in office. This news so affected him, that he put an end to his life, in the western part of Connecticut, Aug. 14, 1778."

173. GURDON, born Aug. 14, 1739. He graduated at Yale, 1757. He married Nov. 8, 1764, Mrs. Lydia Lathrop, and died in Norwich, Dec. 28, 1767, leaving no children. His widow married Elisha Lathrop, Jan. 11, 1775, and had by him two sons and one daughter.

174. LUCY, born Dec. 18, 1741, and married Samuel Williams.

175. HANNAH, born Nov. 3, 1750. She married, Dec. 11, 1771, Joshua (559) and died April 23, 1815. "A memorial of her virtues will live as long as any one remains who had the happiness to know her."

50. JOHN.   Norwich, Conn.

176. JOHN, born in Norwich, Aug. 1736. He graduated at the New Jersey College 1759, joined the first church in Norwich in 1760, and received his Master's degree from Harvard in 1763. He entered the Christian ministry, being ordained and installed over the third Congregational church in Salem, Mass., Sept. 28, 1763. His early ministry gave much promise of future usefulness and eminence, but the hopes of his people and friends were soon disappointed. Quick consumption brought him to what all good people thought to be an untimely end. Though he had scarcely made proof of his fine talents, yet he had won a generous confidence in his great abilities and still more in his deep and fervent piety. He died, without marrying, in Salem, May 30, 1766.

177. SOLOMON, born in Norwich, Aug. 6, 1738. He married Dimis Fuller, and lived in Hebron, Conn., where he was a saddler. He died June 4, 1798, and his widow is believed to have died in East Haddam in 1800, to which place she is said to have moved from Hebron.

178. ANDREW, born July 8, 1740. He married, in 1764, Lucy Landphere. They lived in Griswold, Conn., where he was deacon in the Congregational church for fifty-one years, and where he died in 1830.

179. EZRA, born June 21, 1742. He married, Feb. 25, 1767, Elizabeth, (326) who died in Norwich, Oct. 19, 1796. He married the second time Oct. 8, 1797, widow Dean, whose maiden name was Mary Rudd of Franklin, Conn., and she died in Franklin, Nov. 12, 1804. He married, for his third wife, March 17, 1805, widow Lathrop, whose maiden name was Betsey Hyde, also, of Franklin. He spent the early portion of his life in his native town, where he was respected and honored. His fidelity as grand juror of the county, is evinced in a presentment which he made before Richard Hyde, one of his Majesty's Justices, in 1774, of five young persons—three of them specimens of the fast young men, and two, of the independent young women of that law-keeping day—for "meeting together and walking in the street in company,

upon no religious occasion, all which is contrary to the statute of this colony in such case made and provided."

He died in Franklin in 1820.

180. THOMAS, born Jan. 13, 1744–5. He graduated at Yale, 1768, and entered the medical profession, practicing first in Ashford, and afterwards in Canaan, Conn. He married Mary Ward of Attleborough, Mass., who was born, May 8, 1753, and died, March 31, 1828. He died in Canaan, Feb. 22, 1835. He was a man of a most genial disposition, making himself one of the most companionable of men. He was especially interested in the young, and for the age in which he lived, devoted himself, with no ordinary success, to their improvement. He was an early friend of common schools, and earnestly insisted upon the most efficient discipline and thorough instruction in them. He took great pains to secure good teachers and made himself their friend and helper. He left a volume of essays, which evince this interest in their increased intelligence and efficiency; and which show him to have been a man of an earnestly inquisitive mind. The preface to that volume, which was copyrighted Dec. 12, 1829, is a witness to his interest in the young, both as regards their intellectual and their moral culture.

"Having in years past attended to the duty of visitor of schools, I was pleased with the propriety and importance of a paragraph in the statutes of Connecticut, which directs to the appointment of the visitors of schools. The paragraph alluded to was in substance as follows: the visitors shall instruct the youth in letters, in religion, in morals and manners. I was convinced of the utility and importance of inculcating these things in early life; and the sciences of Natural Philosophy, Geography, and Astronomy, include many things which are very delightful, useful and ornamental, and which may be easily attained by all youths of common capacities. I have made some essays on these and other topics of literature, and have endeavored to exhibit some correct ideas on some very important theological subjects; and have made some observations upon the entire superiority of Christianity over all pretended schemes of religion, either ancient or modern, by fair comparison; and have just touched on some moral subjects. If I had viewed these subjects as being in any measure unimportant, I should have saved myself from much anxiety in attending to them. I hope that the infirmities of age may, in some measure, apologize for any inelegancies of diction which may have escaped for want of sufficient revisal."

The topics treated of in the essays, are: Letters; Geography; Attraction of Cohesion; Air; Light and Colors; Astronomy; Theology; God; Man; Saving Faith; Means of Grace; Decrees of God; Industry and Intemperance.

181. WILLIAM, born Dec. 30, 1746–7. He married, Feb. 15, 1770, Mary Cutler. He lived in Hampton, Conn., where he died in March, 1814.

182. CALEB, born in Norwich, Feb. 4, 1748–9. He married, June 17, 1795, Anne, (661) who died in Norwich, Sept. 16, 1851. He united with the first church of Norwich in 1788, and was chosen deacon of it in 1808. He was a most excellent man and devout christian. He lived to a very advanced age, preserving his faculties remarkably. He died March 1, 1842.

52. JEREMIAH.   Lebanon, N. H.

183. ASA, born in Norwich, Sept. 28, 1745, and died, Oct 28, 1746.

184. SARAH, born in Norwich, Dec. 15, 1748, and married, Feb. 2, 1775, Jonathan, son of Edmund Freeman of Mansfield, Conn. He was born March 21, 1745, O. S. They removed immediately to Hanover, N. H., where he had established himself, being with his father and some of his brothers and uncles of the same name, among the original proprietors of the township, under the charter granted by Gov. Wentworth in 1761. He was much engaged during the period of the Revolution in public service, civil and military, and subsequently he was much in public life. He was a member of the convention for forming the state constitution, and of that for ratifying the United States Constitution; and for many years was in one or the other branch of the state legislature; was one of the executive council of the state; was for two terms a representative in Congress; and for many years was a trustee and financial agent of Dartmouth College. He died Aug. 20, 1808. His widow survived him many years. She was an intelligent and devotedly pious woman. So thorough was she in ordering her household aright, that, during the frequent and often protracted absences of her husband, she seldom failed to conduct the usual morning and evening devotions, although the household was, at times, very large, embracing as it did several workmen and domestics. Nor did she allow the weakness and infirmities of age to interfere with the formal discharge of her religious duties. An incident is related in a biographical sketch of this interesting Christian, written for the Boston Recorder, worth preserving as eminently characteristic of her piety. A clergyman who visited her two or three years before her death, on kneeling to offer prayer "requested her in her infirmity to remain seated in her chair; but she rose and placed herself upon her knees at the age of 95, uttering these memorable words: 'It never yet hurt me to kneel in prayer.'"

She died, Sept. 8, 1846, wanting but three months and a single week of being 98 years old.

Her family consisted of: Peyton R., born Nov. 14, 1775, graduated at Dartmouth College, 1796, and is a lawyer in Portsmouth, N. H.; Jonathan, born May 28, 1777, married Mary Whitehouse of Pembroke, N. H., resides in Hanover, and has five children and twelve grandchildren; Christopher, born Feb. 3, 1779, left home on an Indian voyage, and has not been heard from since; Edward, born May 6, 1781, married first, Philura, daughter of Daniel Hough of Lebanon, N. H., and second, Elizabeth Duncan of Grantham, N. H., and had five children: Sarah, born Aug. 2, 1783; a pair of twins born Aug. 15, 1785; Asa, born Jan. 9, 1788, graduated at Dartmouth College, 1810, and entered the legal profession. He married Frances, daughter of Hon. Wm. King Atkinson, of Dover, N. H., and lives in Dover. He was a member of the convention of 1851 for revising the state constitution, has twice been a member of the state senate, and is now register of probate for Strafford County. He has had four children, Francis A., a graduate of Dartmouth, and a practicing lawyer in Calaveras County, California, Sarah Huntington, wife of the Rev. Dr. Marble, of Newtown, Conn., Abigail A., wife of Dr. Alfred W. Pike of Lawrence, Mass., and one that died in infancy; Samuel, born Feb. 21, 1790, a physician residing at Saratoga Springs, married Helen V. Rensellear Woodruff of Albany, N. Y., and has seven children.—Samuel, born May 2, 1818, and died at Metamoras, Mexico, in 1835, Peyton Randolph, born Oct. 14, 1821, and died May, 1841, Sarah Hannah, born Oct. 6, 1826, married Rev. James S. Bush of Orange, N. J., and died March 29, 1853, Hanlock Woodruff, born Jan. 14, 1829, and died June 2, 1849, while a member of Union College, Anna Elizabeth, born Oct. 2, 1832, and Charlotte Woodruff, born May 4, 1835, the last two dying young; and Hannah born March 23, 1792, and resides unmarried in Hanover.

185. JEREMIAH, born in Norwich, Feb. 8, 1751, married a Bates, and lived in Shaftesbury, Vt., where he was respected, and where he became a wealthy farmer. He died in 1831.

186. ASA, born in Norwich, Feb. 10, 1753. He married Mary Marsh. He resided for a while in Canaan, Conn., where he and his wife both died.

187. SAMUEL, born in Norwich, Feb. 24, 1755, and died in Virginia unmarried. He was in the army during a part of our revolution.

188. ELIAS, born in Norwich, Feb. 23, 1756–7. He removed with his father's family to Lebanon, N. H., where he lived and died on the homestead purchased by his father. He married Mary (Eaton), the widow of Seth West. They were both members of the Congregational church in Lebanon.

189. CHRISTOPHER, born in Norwich, May 24, 1759. He was some time in the army, and during the war of the revolution died at the South.

190. ANDREW, born in Norwich, Nov. 11, 1761, went also to Hanover, N. H., where he married in 1787, Lydia Davis, of Lebanon, N. H. She was born May 1, 1759. In 1830 he went to Pittsford, N. Y., where he died in 1845. He was in service in the war of the revolution, and was with Washington in his retreat from Long Island.

191. HANNAH, born in Norwich, March 24, 1764. She married, May 23, 1798, as his second wife, Rev. Noah Worcester, D. D., the minister of Thornton. They had no children. She died, much lamented, in 1832, and her husband, who was deservedly eminent as editor and as an acceptable Unitarian writer, died in Brighton, Oct. 31, 1837, aged 79 years.

192. HEZEKIAH, born in Norwich, Sept. 1, 1766, went to Hanover, N. H., where he married Esther, eldest daughter of Samuel Slade, of Hanover. Here he became a reed maker, and also an extensive farmer, but removed to Haverhill, N. H., where his wife died. He died in 1830, while on a journey to the West.

FIFTH GENERATION.

53. THOMAS. Mansfield, Conn.

193. MEHETABEL, born in Mansfield. May 31, 1712. baptized June 1, 1812 and married, in Mansfield, March 18, 1735-6, Nathaniel Basset, jr.

194. ANNE, born in Mansfield, Nov. 15, 1714, and married, in April 1747, Edmund Hovey.

195. ELIZABETH, born in Mansfield. May 19, 1735, and died May 24, 1735.

196. THOMAS, born in Mansfield, June 5, 1736, baptized on the 13th of the same month. He was married and lived at Fort Miller, N. Y. He died in 1805.

197. CHRISTOPHER, born in Mansfield. July 7, 1738, and baptized on the 9th of the same month. He married in Mansfield, May 7, 1761, Mary, daughter of Perez Dimock. She was born Oct. 9, 1739. In 1781 he went to Norwich, Vt., from which place he removed in 1789, to aid in the settlement of Roxbury, in the same state. He embraced the doctrine of universal salvation, and was an approved preacher of that denomination. He spent his last years in Compton, Canada East, where he died, Dec. 14, 1810, and his wife in 1833. From various sources of testimony, he seems to have been a man of unusual tenderness of feeling, kind and generous, and ever ready to do good. " His children, literally, call him blessed."

56. ELEAZER. Mansfield, Conn.

198. SAMUEL, born in Mansfield. Dec. 31, 1729, and baptized Jan. 11, 1729-30. He married, May 7, 1752, Abigail, daughter of Samuel Backus of Windham. After living in Mansfield some eight or nine years he went West.

199. ELEAZER, born in Mansfield, Sept. 19, 1734, and baptized on the 22d of same month. He married, Nov. 18, 1756, Phebe, daughter of David Hartshorn, of Norwich, Conn. He lived in Mansfield, and was most noted for his military bearing, being a famous captain of a noted military company. He died in Scotland parish, Windham, in 1808. In the record of his children's births, he is called ensign, at that of his seventh, and captain, at that of his ninth child.

59. WILLIAM. Windham, Conn.

200. MARY, born in Windham, as is inferred from the entry on the records there, Dec. 19, 1735.

201. DORCAS, born in Windham, Sept. 25, 1737.

202. ELIZABETH, born and died May 6, 1740. This record is found in Norwich.

61. SIMON. Mansfield, Conn.

203. ELIZABETH, born Dec. 5, 1735, as the Mansfield town records read, and baptized according to the South Mansfield church records, Dec. 4th of the same year,—one instance of many, in which an error has occurred in public records. She died Dec. 3, 1738.

204. RUTH, born in Mansfield, April 19, 1738, and baptized on the 28th of

same month. She married, March 25, 1773, Walter Trumbull, of Mansfield, by whom she had two sons, Walter and James.

205. SIMON, born in Mansfield, Dec. 2, 1740, and baptized Jan. 4, 1740–1.

206. ELIZABETH, born, as appears from the Windham records, June 12, 1743.

64. JOHN. Tolland, Conn.

207. JOHN, born in Tolland,(?) Feb. 22, 1726. He married, Mehetabel Steele, who was born June 6, 1733. He was a farmer, and lived in Tolland. He was accidentally killed by falling under a cart wheel, on the road from Hartford to Tolland, March 23, 1774.

The "Steele Family" says that John Huntington married Sarah Steele, who was born, as Mehetabel, above.

208. THANKFUL, born in Tolland, March 16, 1726, and died July 11, 1739.

209. SAMUEL, born in Tolland, July 14, 1728, and died during the French war. He was married, and had one child.

210. ANDREW, born in Tolland, Sept. 17, 1730, and died young.

211. ABIGAIL, born in Tolland, Oct. 1, 1732. She married, Jan. 24, 1754, James Steele, son of Rev. Stephen and Ruth (Porter) Steele, who was born Feb. 6, 1737. He was in the revolutionary war, and an officer. She died Jan. 6, 1769, and he married again, in September of the same year, Dorothy Converse. The children of Abigail above, were: Aaron, born Oct. 19, 1754, and died in New Jersey, while a member of the revolutionary army; James, born Oct. 30, 1756, married Jemima, daughter of Roger Wolcott, by whom he had twelve children. He was in the siege of Boston, and at the battle of Long Island; Zadoc, born Dec. 17, 1758, married Harriet Shurtleff, was taken prisoner by the Indians, who took Royalton, Vt., Oct. 17, 1780, and escaped from the prison on the island in the rapids above Montreal. He had ten children; Samuel, born May 10, 1761, married Sarah Shurtleff, was engaged with his brothers in the revolutionary struggle, and had nine children; Andrew, born Dec. 25, 1763, married Elizabeth Lathrop, of Tolland, and had eight children; Abigail born Aug. 16, 1765, and died March 12, 1772; and Deborah, born Dec. 31, 1768, married Dr. Philip Lyon, and died in October, 1800. (See Steele family.)

212. DEBORAH, born in Tolland, May 24, 1736.

69. EBENEZER, DEACON. Norwich, Conn.

213. SARAH, born in Norwich, April 28, 1718, and made profession of religion in 1742. She married, May 15, 1735, Simon (86). After his death, in 1753, she married Capt. Daniel Throop, of Lebanon. She died in Lebanon, Nov. 7, 1794.

214. SIMON, born in Norwich, Sept. 12, 1719, graduated at Yale, 1741, united with the church in 1742, studied theology and preached until his health failed. He married, for his first wife, Jan. 17, 1751, Hannah, only daughter of Daniel and Abigail Tracy, who was born Sept. 2, 1727, and died July 30,

1753. He married, for his second wife, Jan. 24, 1759, Zipporah, daughter of Capt. Ebenezer Lathrop. He was chosen deacon, to succeed his father, in 1764. He died Dec. 27, 1801, and his widow March 16, 1814, in the 81st year of her age.

215. LUCY, born in Norwich, May 28, 1722. She united with the church in 1742, and married, June 16, 1743, Dr. Elisha, son of Capt. Joseph and Mary (Abel) Tracy, a distinguished physician of Norwich, who was born May 16, 1712. Her children were: Lucy, born July 20, 1744, married, Dr. Philip Turner; Alice, born Oct. 11, 1745, married Elisha Leffingwell, and had a family of four sons and six daughters; Lucretia, born Sept. 5, 1747, and died, unmarried in 1825; Lydia, born Dec. 26, 1749, and married Alvan Fosdick, of Boston; Philura, born Sept. 30, 1751, who married (551). After her death, Oct. 12, 1751, her husband again married, April 16, 1754, Elizabeth Dorr, and had by her, Phinehas, Dr. Philemon, Elizabeth, Charlotte, Mary, Col. Elisha, Joseph Winslow, and Deborah Dorr.

216. LYDIA, born in Norwich, Oct. 27, 1735. She married, Aug. 22, 1754, Jabez Fitch, M. D., grand son of Major James, of Canterbury, and great grand son of Rev. James, the first pastor of the Norwich church. He was born May 23, 1728, in Newent parish, Norwich, became a physician of considerable eminence, and was chosen, Jan. 25, 1771, deacon of the Canterbury church. She united with the church in Canterbury in 1760. Her children were: Perez, born Sept. 5, 1755, and died next day; Ebenezer, born Sept. 26, 1756, the founder and first President of Williamstown College; Lydia, born Oct. 9, 1758, and lived ten months; Lydia born June 14, 1760, and married Dr. Elisha Perkins, of Lisbon; Abigail, born June 24, 1762, and lived nine months; Jabez Gale, born March 20, 1764, a colonel, and for twelve years United States Marshall, for the District of Vermont, under Washington and the elder Adams; Sarah, born April 28, 1766, married the Rev. Dr. Green; Anna, born Feb. 3, 1768, and married the Rev. Dr. Daniel C. Saunders, of Medfield, Mass.; Chauncy, born Jan. 17, 1771, a physician, of Sheldon, Vt.; Samuel, born March 3, 1773, a merchant in Burlington, Vt.; Lucy, born March 24, 1777; Alice, born June 2, 1781, married Rev. Dr. Coggswell, of Canterbury, and was the mother of Dr. Mason F. Coggswell, of Hartford, Dr. James, of New York, an eminent surgeon, and of Samuel, who was also a graduate of Yale. Her husband, though not a graduate, was a well read physician, and medical students, in large numbers, resorted to him for instruction. She died at Vergennes, Vt., April 4, 1803, and her husband, at his son's, Dr. Chauncy Fitch, in Sheldon, Vt., Dec. 19, 1806.

70. JOSHUA.

217. JABEZ, born Aug. 7, 1719, and graduated at Yale College, 1741. He married, first, Elizabeth, daughter of Samuel and Elizabeth (Tracy) Backus, Jan. 20, 1741-2. She was born Feb. 21, 1721, and died July 1, 1745, when he married, for his second wife, Hannah Williams, of Pomfret, July 10, 1746. She was born July 23, 1726, and died March 25, 1807. He was elected,

in 1750, a member of the general assembly of his native state, for many years represented his native town to the universal acceptance of his fellow citizens, presiding, often, over the deliberations of the lower house. Early after his graduation he entered into the West India trade, and by an honorable and efficient business career, laid the foundations of one of the amplest fortunes of that age. At the commencement of our revolution he was the owner of a large amount of shipping, which of course was very greatly endangered by the rupture with the mother land. But his patriotism prevailed over his commercial and pecuniary ambition. He cheerfully sacrificed his property and consecrated himself and his family to the cause of independence. He was one of the most active of the committee of safety during the war; and in the September session of the assembly for the year 1776, he was appointed one of the two major generals from Connecticut, for the militia of the state, David Wooster being the other; and on the death of Wooster, from a wound received in the skirmish with the British, retreating from Danbury, in April of the next year, he was appointed major general over the entire Connecticut militia.

His great exertions, made for his country's cause, during those trying years of our national history, together with the great pecuniary losses which, in such a struggle, were inevitable, were too much even for his strong mind and vigorous frame. As the pressure of the early excitement and indispensable action passed away, it was soon seen how greatly they had impaired his physical and mental powers. "On finding himself disabled from public service, he resigned all his offices, and spent the remainder of his life in retirement, at his seat in Norwich. He was seized with a fatal complaint, in Feb. 1779, and after a gradual decline of more than seven years, he died, Oct. 5, 1786."

Gen Huntington was a man of religious principle, having united with the church in 1741. It was very justly said in the funeral sermon delivered over his remains, "That a great man is fallen in this Israel, need not be mentioned for the information of this assembly." It is also stated in a note appended to the sermon, "he sustained an amiable and worthy character in the domestic relations and private walks of life." One other passage from that sermon, deserves transcribing for this notice: "As the train of melancholy distress which brought him to his end, probably originated from his painful and unremitted exertions for his country, in the time of danger; his country, surely, will not withhold the tear of grateful sorrow, but pay deserved respect to his memory, and teach succeeding generations to revere his dust; and as they pass his urn, to say, 'there lies the man who devoted his all to the public good; who sacrificed his ease, his health, and eventually his life, to serve and save his country.'"

But one incident in his life, almost too sacred for the page, even of family history, must here be sketched, as most distinctly and fully exhibiting his real character.

At the beginning of the revolution he was in the easiest and most prosperous worldly circumstances. His home was one of the most desirable, such as any family might be proud of, and wish to keep. Yet such were his business operations, that the threatened rupture must necessarily endanger them all. His family were now coming forward into mature manhood, with every promise of abundant wealth. This promise the rupture would probably for many years disappoint. Both the present condition and future prospects of his children, to whom he was attached, with no ordinary ties, no less than his own home were at stake. Should he run the risk? Should he court the danger? Should he deliberately invoke on such prosperity and such peace, so certain calamity? It was a trying question. It was well pondered by him. Himself and wife deliberated and prayed over it. They counted together the cost, and as the stern necessity approached they calmly and firmly decided to accept for themselves, personally, the peril of an open and final espousal of the cause of independence.

But, should their children be urged to unite with them in this perilous decision? On a bright morning, in the year 1774, when already the low mutterings of the coming storm were heard by the wakeful patriots of that day, Gen. H. and his noble wife had called together all the members of their beloved family to meet this issue. Five sons and two daughters—three of the sons with their youthful wives, are the thoughtful group in that mansion parlor. Even that little clear-eyed Zachariah, not yet in his tenth summer, must take his little seat and be one in that solemn act of patriotism, which they meet to perform. They are now ready. The father, tremulous with an emotion which even his own well schooled spirit could not entirely repress, as was fitting, leads them in an earnest supplication for divine guidance, and in some such words as these, broke the deep silence which follows.

"Children," said he, "your mother and I have been deciding for ourselves a question of duty to our country—a question which is to affect seriously our worldly circumstances and prospects. Before a final decision, which shall embrace you, personally, in the act of hostility to our dear mother land, we wish you also to count the cost. The risk must be great. Our homes, our stores, our ships, our lands may all be burned, or sunk, or ravaged, yet our country we may save. These colonies we may contribute to make independent and prosperous states. This land we may contribute to make a home for constitutional liberty, an asylum to which the abused and outraged of every other land may come for shelter—a land populous and prosperous, rich and happy. Believing this, and hoping this, we have solemnly decided that ours, henceforth, shall be the cause of the patriots. We have pledged ourselves, our property, our time and our lives, if need be, to this end. We shall now leave you to choose your lot with us, and assume its risks and dangers, or take your places with those who prefer still to cling to the mother land, to whose sway your parents can be no longer loyal!"

Then deliberately addressing each member of the family by name, he slowly asked the eventful question, solemnly repeating each name: "Jedidiah, Andrew, Joshua, Ebenezer, Elizabeth, Mary, Zachariah—my beloved boy,—are are you all ready to go with your parents, and share our risks and our reward?"

Not long did that beloved father await their reply. With one voice, they break the solemn silence, by a pledge of consecration to their parents' and their country's cause; nor did trial, or danger, or losses, ever find one of that devoted band, ready to recall the pledge so made. Their names were all identified with the protracted struggle which resulted in the independence of the United States; and so well did they perform the part assigned them in that memorable achievement that the faithful historian of those days has been obliged to leave this testimony to their success; "if the annals of the revolution record the name of any family which contributed more to that great struggle, I have yet to learn it." (See Gilman's oration at the Norwich Bicentennial celebration.

218. JEDIDIAH, born in Norwich, Feb. 1, 1721–2, and died, May 12, 1725.
219. ANDREW, born in Norwich, Oct. 2, 1724, and died Jan 14, 1739.
220. LYDIA, born in Norwich, March 15, 1727, and married, Nov. 3, 1746, Capt. Ephraim Bill, a prominent citizen of Norwich. She united with the Congregational church in Norwich City, 1786. Their children were: Sylvester, born June 15, 1747, and died, July 31, 1753; Lynde, born Sept. 3, 1749, and died, Aug. 11, 1753; Gordon, born, Sept. 29, 1751, and died, Aug. 6, 1753; Lydia, born July 7, 1753, and married Joseph Howland, whose descendants have been so prominent among the business men of New York; Hannah, born April 6, 1755, and died April 23, 1756; Gordon, born Aug. 26, 1757, Ephraim, born May 30, 1759, and died, Nov. 1780; Abigail, born June 18, 1761, and died, Oct. 2, 1775; Zachariah Huntington, born June 10, 1763, and died June 8, 1788; William, born April 19, 1765; and Hannah, born Sept. 21, 1769, married Thomas Lathrop of Norwich. Several of the descendants of this Lydia have been prominent in business and social position. She died Sept. 23, 1798, and her husband, Nov. 24, 1802, in the 84th year of his age.

221. ZACHARIAH, born Nov. 18, 1731. He never married. His death, which was lamented as a great loss both to his family circle and to the community, occurred in 1761. In a letter to his brother Jabez, his nephew Jedidiah, then a member of college in Cambridge, thus speaks of him: "When I reflect upon the pleasure and delight I took in his company and conversation, I cannot think of parting with him. My sorrow, alone, is not my only care, but, Sir, I am grieved for you, who have lost so loving a brother, as well as one so high in the esteem of all who were acquainted with him."

71. JOSEPH, DEACON. Windham, Conn

This family were all born in Windham.
222. JOHN, born Sept. 22, 1720, and died June 17, 1725.
223. JOSEPH, born Aug. 23, 1723, and died Dec. 23, 1726.
224. ELIPHALET, born May 15, 1725, and died Dec. 16, 1726.
225. ELIZABETH, born July 5, 1727, and died Dec. 22, 1788.
226. JOHN, born Dec. 22, 1729. He married for his first wife, March 11, 1756, Ann Wright, who died May 6, 1758. He married, for his second wife, April 15, 1770, Mrs. Mary, widow of Bartholomew Flint, and daughter of

Jeremiah and Margaret Welch of Windham. She lived until Sept. 2, 1829, to the age of 90 years. He died in Windham, Sept. 18, 1791.

227. MARY, born July 17, 1732, and married Jan. 5, 1758, Jabez Fitch of Windham. Their children were: Roswell, born Dec. 20, 1758; Anna, born June 15, 1764; Jabez, born Jan. 30, 1767, and is the ancestor of J. C. Fitch, the teacher of South Windham; Joseph, and Betsey.

228. JOSEPH, born Dec. 22, 1736, and died Oct. 12, 1760.

72. NATHANIEL. Windham, Conn.

This family were all born in Windham, Scotland Society.

229. NATHANIEL, born Nov. 25, 1724. He graduated at Yale in 1747. He prepared for the ministry, and was ordained and settled in Ellington, in 1749. He was accounted a young man of promise, but a pulmonary complaint set in soon after he commenced preaching, and prematurely ended his life, April 28, 1756. He had married Jerusha Ellsworth. "He was long," so Stiles' History of Windsor testifies, "remembered with unusual esteem and regret." His gravestone has this inscription: In memory of ye Rev. Mr. Nathaniel Huntington, A. M., 2d Pastor of the Church in Windsor six years and six months, who died Apr. ye 28, 1756, in the 32d year of his age.

230. ABIGAIL, born June 27, 1727. She married, Nov. 7, 1750, Richard Kimball, jr., of Scotland. Their children were: Mary, born Nov. 10, 1752, and married Aaron Mosher of Rochester; Elijah, born Sept. 19, 1754; Eunice, born Nov. 30, 1756, and married Henry Hebard; Jesse, born Feb. 5, 1759; Abigail, born Sept. 27, 1761; Lydia, born Aug. 6, 1763; Enoch, born Dec. 20, 1765; Richard, born July 16, 1768; Ebenezer, born June 24, 1771.

231. MEHETABEL, born Aug. 8, 1729, and married, probably, Nov. 24, 1748, Zebulon Webb of Windsor, Conn., and had children.

232. SAMUEL, born July 3, 1731. His early boyhood was spent upon the farm, in the shop, and in such common schools as the parish of Scotland in that day could afford. At sixteen years of age, he was, as was customary then, apprenticed to a cooper living near his father, to learn his trade. Here he spent the most of the time until he was of age. But, though an industrious boy, he was also noted very early for his serious and thoughtful air, and yet more for his studious habits. Whatever books he could get possession of, he seemed determined to make his own; and the usual pastime of ordinary boys became the most busily employed moments of his youth. "His mind," says the historian of Norwich, in a very truthful sketch of his life which appears in her Norwich History, " was naturally acute and investigating, and his thirst for mental improvement so great as to surmount all obstacles."

When ready to commence business for himself, as cooper, he found himself with a well stored head and an excited and working brain. Though contrary to his father's wishes, he gradually extended his reading, and even took his regular hours daily, for studying by himself the Latin language, which, without a teacher, he learned to read with facility and profit; and by the time he had entered on his twenty-second year he had deliberately laid hold of the legal profession as the calling into which he had grown. With few books, and those mainly borrowed, yet with a zeal and perseverance which no discouragement could repress, he urged his way to the bar, and before his thirtieth year had ended, he was not simply an established lawyer, but one who had already won distinction. As early as his twenty-eighth year, he had been drawn from his native town to Norwich, as a better field for his professional career. He found among the fair maidens of his native town, the daughter of his pastor, Rev. Ebenezer Devotion, one who for her comely looks and serious and intelligent ways had early won his regard, and moved his affections. She, too, inherited the same spirit which from his Puritan ancestors had descended upon himself. Her grandfather had taken for his wife, a daughter of that Edward Taylor who had been expatriated from Coventry, England, because, after the restoration of Charles he was found too good a man to endure so insufferable corruption; and her father drew his spirit and blood from the purest and most heroic of even Huguenot veins: so that Martha Devotion was fitted by birth and by training, to join her fortunes with that of the now aspiring civilian. Their marriage took place April 17, 1761.

Few marriages have brought together two more congenial spirits. Each was the other's helpmeet. Blessed with no children of their own, they were the more a care and joy to each other. Their home was felt to be a home to all who had the good fortune to enjoy its hospitalities. Nor did their cheerful fireside long or often want the joyous gladness, which a well filled quiver of happy children gives. Two of the gifted children of his brother, Joseph, knew no other home. They found this all ready for them. They were early in it, as if born to it; and to the last, they showed an affection and dutifulness towards their parents by adoption, which would do honor to any child, if witnessed towards his own parents. Their home was also the resort of a large circle of relatives and friends, made welcome with a cheer as bountiful as it was spontaneous. The following picture drawn by the pen of the historian of Norwich, is too truthful and too full of the very soul of that early day, to be omitted here.

"After the war, he built a new house and lived in quiet dignity. A lively and happy circle of young people used frequently to assemble in this house, as visitors to the Governor's adopted children, or attracted by the beautiful Betsey Devotion, Mrs. Huntington's niece, and the belle of Windham, who spent much of her time here. After the social chat and merry game of the parlor had taken their turn, they would frequently repair to the kitchen, and dance away till the oak floor shone under their feet, and the pewter quivered upon the dressers. These pastimes, however, had little in them of the nature of a ball; there were no expensive dresses, no collations, no late hours. They seldom lasted beyond nine o'clock. According to the good old custom of Norwich, the ring of the bell at that hour, broke up all meetings, dispersed all parties, put an end to all discussions, and sent all visitors quietly to their homes and their beds.

Mrs. Huntington was an affable but very plain lady. It is still remembered, that in a white short gown and stuff petticoat, and clean muslin apron, with a nicely starched cap on her head, she would take her knitting and go out by two o'clock in the afternoon, to take tea unceremoniously with some respectable neighbor, the butcher's or blacksmith's wife perhaps. But this was in earlier days, before Mr. Huntington was President of Congress or Governor of Connecticut."

But there was a still higher charm which adorned and hallowed that home: and one which is much nearer the secret of that great eminence to which it was so soon destined. Religion had set her holy seal upon its united head. Born of pious parents and descended from ancestors marked for their faith, they both had early yielded to the redeeming grace. Both had enrolled themselves among God's people—the husband before going to Norwich, and the wife soon after; and both were characterized for a piety, as unpretending as it was sincere, and as uniform as it was deep and fervent. For nothing was Mr. Huntington more marked through his entire public life than for his conscientious discharge of religious duties. In his family, in the prayer meeting, in the public services of the sanctuary, he was always found at his post and always ready for whatever duty the hour called him to perform. Old men who have died in our times, have recalled the fervor of his prayers and the unction of his exhortations in the social meeting; and the testimony of all who knew him, is uniform as to the steadfastness of his Christian principle, and the purity of his Christian character.

But, it is rather as a public man, and civilian, that Mr. Huntington is best known in history, and it is much to be regretted that for the truth of our history, no suitable biography of this eminent man has yet been written. It may have been in part owing to his excessive modesty, which led him to shrink from all public notice of his official career, during his life time; and it is doubtless also owing to the fact that he left no descendants to keep his memory before the generations that have lived since his day.

That he was an eminent actor during our revolutionary period, and a model statesman in those trying years, during which our government was in process of formation; that he was a wise and popular governor of his native state, where none but great and good men could hope for such a post; and that he made himself all this from a very humble station in his youth, without the aids of wealth and family fame, is the extent of our historic testimony to his memory. We have the statement without the exhibition of his greatness; a sort of involuntary admission of his claims to eminence, with no attempts to set it forth. And such testimony, it must be conceded, is no slight compliment to the man who has won it. It is even the noblest tribute to his worth. It makes him a character, above question, above reproach. He was so good and so prominent, and so fitted for all the exigencies of the day, that no one questioned his eminence, and no one needed to blazon it abroad; like the summer sun, or the gentle shower that all enjoy, yet of which little mention is made.

The public life of Mr. **Huntington, commenced** in 1764, when he represented

Norwich in the general assembly. It was certainly fortunate that such a man should have commenced his public service, at just such a crisis. The famous and odious stamp act had just been designed and laid before parliament : and the assembly, of which he was for the first time a member, would be called to meet the responsibility of yielding to the oppressive measure, or of opposing and resisting it. Grenville, now become prime minister, was urging forward the measure to its enactment, and men of clear heads and stout hearts were needed to confront him. Among these, Mr. Huntington soon became prominent. Both in the assembly and among his townsmen at home, he exposed the oppressive nature of the act, and gave his ready voice and vote against a recognition of its authority. When the town clerk of Norwich, his kinsman, Benjamin, (143) called a town meeting, April 7, 1765, to learn if the citizens wished him to use the stamps to be furnished by the crown, he was present to urge, what the meeting unanimously voted: " that the clerk shall proceed in his office as usual, and the town will save him harmless from all damage that he may sustain thereby."

The cause which he now espoused, and the governmental principles which he now advocated, were his pole star throughout his life. He was henceforth to be with the people, against all oppressive and unconstitutional acts of their rulers, even to the bitter but unavoidable end of revolution. The creed which was so soon to be immortalized in the declaration of a nation's independence, was already the most vital main-spring of his public acts. Yet, though opposed, with all his heart, to the stamp act, he was still a most loyal subject of the crown. He advised all moderation until better counsels should prevail in parliament, as he firmly believed would soon be the case. He was appointed, in 1765, the very year when the stamp act was to go into operation, the king's attorney for his state, and was of course expected to see that no disrespect should be shown the crown. This office he held until other official duties obliged him to resign it. In 1773, he was nominated a member of the council or upper house of the Connecticut assembly, and took his seat in 1775. In 1774 he was appointed associate judge of the superior court of Connecticut. In Oct., 1775, the general assembly of which he was now a member, appointed him with such men as Roger Sherman, Oliver Wolcott, Titus Hosmer and William Williams, a delegate to congress, in which body he took his seat on the sixteenth of Jan. 1776. Of this body he was a member until 1780; and it is due to the history of those years, the most eventful in our national existence, to say that no member of those busy congresses was more marked for his diligent and laborious working, or for his unselfish patriotism, or for his wise statesmanship than Mr. Huntington. None were consulted oftener or with more confidence than he; and none were readier to suggest or wiser to plan. The year on which he took his seat, finds him on many of the most important committees, such as were equally creditable to his head and his heart. With Jefferson and Livingston, we find him on the committee of Indian affairs, with Paine and Wilson and Lee and Morris, on that upon the manufacture of arms; with Wythe and Rutledge and Paine, on that on the capture and condemnation of prisoners; with the committee of one from each colony on supplies of ammunition; and on several committees raised to consider special cases of appeal, as that of Christopher Leffingwell, on the cargo of the brig Nancy; that of Henry Keppele, on sentence; and that of Hewes, a defrauded prisoner.

In March of this same year we find him appointed, also, a member of the marine court, constituted for the control of our navy. Nor was he less conspicuous on the memorable fourth of July of this memorable year. Four Connecticut names, of which his was not the least, are autographed on that Declaration of Independence, which was to witness to all coming generations, equally, the patriotism and the treason of its signers: "names," in the prophetic language of our last historian, "that will be household words in every family in the state, as long as the principles of 1776 shall survive in the hearts of the people."

How true to this hazardous declaration of his principles, Mr. Huntington subsequently proved: how intelligently and fearlessly he met all the responsibilities involved in it; how, step by step he showed himself more and more indispensable to its efficient maintenance; how he won for himself, from the leaders of that day, the place and honor of leadership over even themselves, is abundantly attested by their vote of Sept. 28, 1779, in which he is chosen their PRESIDENT, with a unanimity as honorable to them as to him. Nor did he fail in this trying office, an office which called for the highest qualities both of the jurist and statesman. From the date of his election, until his resignation, July 6, 1781, he was most incessantly and acceptably engaged in the engrossing cares of his office. Perhaps no one of those honored men who were called to that eminent post during the formative period of our government, occupied it with more credit than he. Certainly never did congress show sincerer reluctance than when, from utter exhaustion of his strength, he was forced to ask either for a temporary, or a final retirement from the office. For two months they delayed seeking for a successor, hoping that meanwhile he might so far recover as to justify his continuance. But such had been the tax upon his strength that he was compelled to insist upon his resignation, about a month before the close of his second year. The resignation was accepted, and a hearty vote of thanks testified to the confidence which congress reposed in him as the chief executive of the nation, and their gratitude for his impartial and able administration.

On retiring from the oppressive duties of his presidential career, he resumed, in August, his judicial post in the superior court of his native state, and also his seat in the council of the state.

In May of the next year, he was again elected to congress, but his health did not permit him to occupy his seat. Such service as he was able to render his country he still continued to perform in his official positions at home. Yet such was the impression among his fellow-citizens of the need of his counsel and statesmanship in congress, that he was again appointed in 1783; and in July of that year we find him once more a member of that body. In this office we find him unwearied and faithful as before, until his strength giving out, he was obliged to take his final leave of the national council, which he formally did on the fourth of November, 1783. No plea from his native state, which he had now so signally honored, could induce him again to accept a nomination for a post for which he felt he had not the requisite strength. He now retired to his beloved home, in Norwich, but not to the rest of private life. In 1784 he was appointed chief justice of the superior court of Connecticut. In 1785 he was chosen lieutenant-governor of the state; and the following year he was elected to succeed governor Griswold, as the chief magistrate. This office he continued to fill, being annually re-elected until his death.

As the chief justice of his state, he showed the same ability which had marked him in other official stations. Indeed, this seemed preeminently the place for which he was fitted. His studies had made him familiar with the history and science of jurisprudence. He had the patience needed for the complete mastery of whatever evidence or analysis was essential to the case. He was remarkable for his urbanity, his impartiality, and his inexorable demand for what was true and right. The following testimony on this point, from the Biography of the Signers to the Declaration of Independence, is fully authorized by all we have been able to gather regarding his judicial course. "Having at all times a perfect command over his passions, he presided on the bench with great ability and impartiality. No judge in Connecticut was more dignified in his deportment, more courteous and polite to the gentlemen of the bar, or more respected by the parties interested in the proceedings of the court. His name and his virtues are frequently mentioned by those who remember him in his judicial capacity, with respect and veneration."

As governor of his native state, he was exceeded in the confidence he inspired and in the esteem he won, by none of those great men who, at different times, have made that office illustrious. Perhaps the elder Trumbull, the right hand man of Washington in the most perilous days of our revolutionary period, exceeded him in popularity. But to stand second to such a man in popular admiration, and his peer in the popular confidence, is enough for the lasting fame of any man. Such, doubtless, was the true position of Mr. Huntington among the Connecticut governors.

The following testimonials to his personal characteristics will complete our too meager sketch of this truly eminent and estimable man. The same authority just quoted, says: "In his person, Mr. Huntington was of the common stature, his complexion dark, and his eye bright and penetrating; his manners were somewhat formal, and he possessed a peculiar faculty of repressing impertinence, and keeping aloof from the criticising observations of the multitude. Without inflicting upon others the consciousness of inferiority, he never descended from the dignity of his station. * * * Being a man of great simplicity and plainness of manners, he was averse to all pageantry and parade, and strictly economical in his expenditures. He maintained that it was a public duty to exhibit such an example as might, so far as his individual efforts could avail, counteract the spirit of extravagance which had begun to appear. His principal aim in his domestic arrangements was comfort and convenience without splendor; although not hostile to good living, he was simple, sparing and temperate in his diet. His conversation, studiously avoiding frivolous topics, was eminently instructive, and he delivered his sentiments in few, but weighty words. He inherited from nature a large share of that delicacy and sense of propriety which distinguish the man of honor and refinement. * * * It may be truly said that no man ever possessed greater mildness or equanimity than Mr. Huntington. A living witness can attest, that during a long residence of twenty-four years in his family, he never, in a single instance, exhibited the slightest symptoms of anger, nor spoke one word calculated to wound the feelings of another, or to injure an absent person."

Miss Caulkins, in her Norwich history, concludes her sketch of this eminent and good man, with this testimonial to his piety. " Mr. Huntington was always a constant attendant on public worship, and for many years a professor of religion. In conference meetings he usually took a part, and on the Sabbath, if no minister chanced to be present, he occasionally led the services, and his prayers and exhortations were always solemn and acceptable. During his last sickness, he was supported and animated by an unwavering faith in Christ and a joyful hope of eternal life. This sketch cannot be better concluded, than with the earnest wish breathed by a contemporary panegyrist: 'May Connecticut never want a man of equal worth to preside in her councils, guard her interests, and diffuse prosperity through her towns.'"

Though never a member of college he was honored equally by Yale and Dartmouth, from each of which he received, in 1787, the degree of LL. D.

The disease of which Mr. Huntington died, was dropsy of the chest, and his death occurred Jan. 5, 1796. His estimable wife had died eighteen months before, June 4, 1794, aged 56 years.

233. JONATHAN, born June 17, 1733. Without a collegiate education he became both a physician and a preacher, and in both professions maintained an honorable rank. He married in Lebanon, Oct. 26, 1757, Sarah, (291) who proved a true helpmeet for him, both in his care for the souls and the bodies of men. He was ordained and installed as the first pastor of the church in Worthington, Mass., June 26, 1771, where he continued to officiate acceptably to the close of his life, March 11, 1781. His wife died May 13, 1793. Mr. H. was a man of warm sympathies. He saw suffering only to pity and relieve it. He early became interested in the condition and labored for the improvement of the colored race in this country. He was one of the three pastors who encouraged the celebrated Lemuel Haynes to fit for the ministry, and cheerfully testified to the gifts and fitness of that wonderful man.

234. JOSEPH, born May 5, 1735. He graduated at Yale, 1762. His father had destined him to be a clothier, and kept him at this trade through his minority, much against his own wishes. But, moved like his older brother, Samuel, by a passionate love of books, and like him, though not to the same

remarkable degree, gifted with unusual inquisitiveness and capacity for mastering whatever study he attempted, and moreover, encouraged by the kindly aids furnished by his pastor, Mr. Devotion, he even at that late period commenced and completed successfully his preparation for college. He entered in his 23d year, 1758, and graduated honorably with the class. Within a year of his graduation, June 29, 1763, he was installed as pastor of the first church in Coventry, where he continued to labor in word and doctrine through his life.

Like his brother Samuel, he too had found in his pastor's family, the helpmeet he needed, and his marriage with Hannah, daughter of Rev. Ebenezer Devotion, was solemnized in 1764. She became the mother of his first three children and died Sept. 25, 1771, aged 26 years. He married, for his second wife, Elizabeth Hale of Glastenbury, Conn., who died in 1806, aged 58 years.

Dr. Sprague, in his Annals of the American Pulpit has given a most accurate estimate of his ministerial work in Coventry, from which I am happy to quote. He says that "his ministry commenced under some most unfavorable auspices. Though there had been two settled pastors there, and one of them, Mr. Meacham, had had a ministry of considerable length, yet the parish had become greatly reduced, the meeting house had been suffered to go to decay, and every thing else was in a state of corresponding depression. The services at his ordination were held in the open air; but whether this was because the meeting house was too small to accommodate the assemblage, or too much dilapidated to be safe or decent, does not appear. Immediately after he was settled, he began to urge upon the people with great zeal the project of building a new meeting house. They responded with unexpected cordiality and harmony to this proposal; and in a short time, they had the best house of public worship in the whole region, built at an expense of five thousand dollars. Mr. Huntington was exceedingly gratified by the success of this enterprise, and often recurred to it with pleasure in the later years of his ministry.

From the period of his settlement, the prosperity of his parish, at least in regard to temporal interests, began to revive; and they continued a united people during his whole ministry. The state of religion, however, was scarcely ever otherwise than depressed; but the same remark is equally applicable, with few exceptions, to the church at large. The period of his ministry embraced the old French war, the war that gave us our independence, and the French Revolution: and each of these events was fruitful of influences most adverse to a healthful and vigorous state of religion in this country.

After the death of the first Dr. Wheelock, President of Dartmouth college, Mr. Huntington was spoken of as the person most likely to succeed to the office; and communications were made to him on the subject, that gave him reason to expect that he would be elected. The result was different from what many had anticipated; but the college testified its respect for him, about the same time, (1780,) by conferring on him the degree of Doctor of Divinity. He was, also, the same year, elected a member of the board of overseers of the college and held the place till 1788.

In the spring of 1792, Dr. Huntington was invited to settle at Huntington, Long Island; and he actually made a journey thither before he declined the invitation. The fact that he should have even hesitated on the subject was an occasion of considerable disquietude in his own parish, and seems to have loosened, in some degree, the cord that bound him to his people.

Dr. Huntington continued his labors till near the close of life, though infirmities had, for some time, been increasing upon him, and his health was supposed to have suffered from repeated and severe domestic bereavements. His death, which seemed to be the result of a complication of diseases, took place on the 25th of December, 1794."

No portrait of Dr. Huntington it is believed is now in existence. But tradition has taken delight in representing him as a man of more than ordinary personal attractions. His finely proportioned form, his graceful movement, his genial spirit, beaming out from every feature and springing to greet and embrace all whom it could bless; his ready wit, ever keenest when most needed, and never at fault when wit had work to do; his immense stores of various fact and incident; and his marvelous felicity in anecdote; all contributed to make him, what all who knew him have agreed in styling him, a man of rare social gifts, a most agreeable companion, and a very dear friend.

Dr. Abbot of Peterborough, N. H., who succeeded Dr. Huntington in Coventry, and who had, therefore, a good opportunity of forming his opinion, in his letter to Dr. Sprague, bears this testimony to his personal appearance and character.

"Dr. Huntington was a man of fine personal appearance, and of popular, engaging manners. His intellectual endowments also were much above mediocrity. His perception was quick, his memory retentive, his wit ready, exuberant, and agreeable. He was much respected and beloved by his parishioners and friends, and exerted very considerable influence in the community at large. Dr. Huntington was undoubtedly one of the most popular preachers of the day. He spoke extemporaneously, seldom writing more than a skeleton of the principal topics of a discourse. During the greater part of his life, his reputation was very high; but as his health and strength of body and mind failed, his reputation seemed proportionably to decline. I remember hearing Dr. Backus of Somers, express the opinion at a meeting of ministers not long after Dr. Huntington's death, that he possessed superior talents; and that in the meridian of his life, the public estimate of him was fully up to his actual merits, but that, in his later days, it had fallen below it. He was not a laborious student. He had very few books, and depended chiefly on borrowing; but having an excellent memory, he retained a large part of what he read.

"He was favored with a good constitution, firm health, and a high flow of spirits, for many years; and as one of his parishioners remarked to me would easily ride over all difficulties."

The Rev. Daniel Waldo, in a letter found in the same work from which the above extract is taken, gives us this portraiture of Dr. Huntington.

"Dr. Huntington may be said to have been an accomplished gentleman. He was rather above the middle height, of a slender and graceful form, and remarkable for the urbanity of his manners. I remember that much of what he said to me, when I had the pleasure of passing a night with him, was a eulogy upon my grandfather, who was a somewhat distinguished teacher from Boston, and under whom he said he had received some part of his early education. He seemed to have an instinctive desire to make every body around him happy; and I should suppose that this, with his constitutional politeness, might have rendered it somewhat difficult for him to take the attitude of a reprover. He was, I think, eminently fitted to be popular in general society."

The reputation of Dr. Huntington since his death, has suffered from two causes—the extemporaneous manner of his preaching, and the posthumous work for which he will always be censured by those who deprecate its belief. He wrote so little, that he left no enduring memorial of his power as a preacher and orator. Scarcely a half dozen sermons or addresses of his, were ever written out and given to the press. And his printed sermons are probably less interesting and eloquent than the same when preached; the process of writing them, to which he was so little accustomed, really divesting them of their most striking excellences. I cannot refrain from quoting a gem from one of these sermons, that preached at Norwich in May, 1774, upon "The Vanity and Mischief of presuming on Things beyond our Measure." It will suggest what we might have had from his pen, had it been used more in his preparations for the pulpit. It occurs in the application of the discourse.

"Never, perhaps, was there any period of time; never, before, did the Christian people of this country, see the time, when the minds of the good, as well as others, were so much exercised about the non-essentials of religion, and so curious to know things that relate neither to saving faith, nor to an holy and virtuous life. * * * * * * * * * *

"All you need practice, all you can practice, all that God requires you either to believe or practice, all that is necessary for your usefulness or comfort in the world, and safe arrival at heaven, is so plain, that sincere, honest hearts may run as they read. Beloved, what you have to do is to follow God, even your own God, in the sincerity of your hearts and integrity of your hands; and the charming light of heaven shall break in upon your souls, bright and lovely as the morning, sweet and refreshing as the gentle rain."

But the work which has wrought most unfavorably upon Dr. Huntington's reputation among orthodox Christians since his death, is that famous posthumous production of his pen—Calvinism Improved. The mystery which overhangs this work has never been removed. When it was written, or with what aim, has never been shown. The work itself is a very distinct and able statement and defense of the doctrine of universal salvation.

I have heard old men who accepted the doctrines of the work, say that Dr. Huntington preached good Universalism for twenty years, but in such a way that he was not suspected, except by those who relished it. The letter of Mr. Waldo, above quoted, gives us this statement; "I remember to have heard Dr. Hart, with whom he was in intimate relations, say that, in a conversation with him, Dr Huntington raised objections against the doctrine of future punishment, professedly to see how he would answer them; and the same thing I was informed occurred in conversations with several others of his clerical brethren.

The letter of Dr. Abbot, also quoted above, has this additional fact: " Some time before his death, he wrote a Dialogue on Universal Salvation, and sent it to a brother minister, who resided at some distance, requesting his remarks upon it."

Dr. Sprague himself testifies that after the work was published to the astonishment of every body, "some of his," (Dr. Huntington's) "brethren recollected to have heard remarks from him, which, in the review, seemed of a dubious character."

It seems very clear, that for years the author had been persuaded of the incorrectness of the orthodox belief on this subject, and that he had been elaborating this exposition and defense as a justification of the position he would be called upon to take. That he would have given publicity to the work himself, had not a series of domestic bereavements and physical infirmities impaired his mental vigor, and prematurely brought him to his grave, the nice sense of honor which he uniformly showed, and the habitual freedom and independence of expression in which he indulged, are sufficient proofs.

The preface contains, also, his own explanation regarding his delay to publish the work. After stating that the work contained "a small part of a system of divinity, which the author has been meditating more than twenty years;" and also, that, "the author is quite beyond a doubt, in his own mind, with regard to the solid truth of his leading principles and arguments," he adds this explanation: "With respect to the due time of advancing this step forward, and so explicitly pouring in this additional light, he is not so positive. * * * I am in the same predicament, with regard to the due time of publication, that all men since the days of inspiration have been. Any author may misjudge, after his greatest possible exercise of judgment in the matter. Some have done it, as the great and learned Huss, who was one century before the due time, in attempting to pour in a flood of light upon the world. He offered nothing to the public but what was advanced in the next century by Luther and Calvin, and others, with glorious success." But the work itself, when published about a year after his death, was doomed to a very "limited circulation,—much the greater part of the edition having been consigned to the flames by one of his daughters." So effectual was the suppression of the work, that it is now almost impossible to find a copy.

The following are believed to be the only other published writings of Dr. Huntington. I copy the list from Dr. Sprague's work, having been unable to make any additions to it: A sermon on the vanity and mischief of presuming on things beyond our measure, delivered at Norwich, 1774; a plea before the ecclesiastical council at Stockbridge, in the case of Mrs. Fisk, excommunicated for marrying a profane man, 1779; an address to his Anabaptist brethren,

1783; an election sermon, 1784; a sermon at the instalment of the Rev. John Ellis, 1785, at Rehoboth, Mass.; a discourse at the interment of Capt. John Howard, of Hampton, 1789; thoughts on the atonement of Christ, 1791; and a sermon on the death of Mrs. Strong, 1793.

235. ELIPHALET, born April 24, 1737, and married, Nov. 11. 1762. Dinah Rudd. He was a farmer in Scotland Society, Windham, where he died June 15, 1799.

236. ENOCH, born Dec. 15, 1739, and graduated at Yale, 1759. He fitted for the ministry, and was ordained and installed over the first church of Middletown, Jan. 6, 1762, where he spent his life. He was considered, during his collegiate course, a youth of remarkable talents, and his classical and general scholarship, subsequently justified fully the decision. He was the Berkelyan scholar of his class. In the pulpit he was deservedly popular; his personal appearance, his easy and graceful manners, and his musical and well modulated voice, in the earlier part of his professional course, all contributing to such a result. He married, in Windham, Conn., July 17, 1764, Mary, daughter of Samuel Gray, who was born Oct. 14, 1744, and died Dec. 15, 1803. He was the teacher, for some months, of the gifted Dr. Dwight, who always remembered him with affection and respect. On the death of President Stiles, of Yale College, in 1795, Mr. Huntington was prominent as a candidate to succeed him, but his failing voice and health obliged him to decline the honor, and his pupil, Dr. Dwight was chosen. Mr. Huntington entered warmly into politics during our revolutionary period, taking sides with his brothers against England. Several of his sermons and addresses of that day, were printed, and have been preserved. They indicate the elements of a character scarcely inferior to that of his brother Samuel. I quote from a sermon preached on the occasion of a special fast, July 20, 1775, as illustrative, both of the spirit of the man, and the peculiar trials to which the patriots of that day were exposed: "To please the administration, and be what those who are seeking our hurt affect to style friends of government, neither our reason or religion, our voices or hands, must ever be used, but in perfect conformity to the pernicious, popish doctrines of implicit faith and passive obedience, and nonresistance. Any thing may be said, or written, or done in their favor and praise,—and pensions and promotion shall be the reward of their sycophants and tools; while any thing to the contrary, however supported by reason and the Christian religion, is misrepresented, falsified and punished, by every means in their power. Those ministers who exert themselves to support every tyrannical and arbitrary measure, are caressed as friends of government; while clergymen of different principles and conduct, of whatever church they be, who converse upon and preach up as occasion requires, the duties, the privileges and the liberty of the gospel; but who dare not attempt to press the religion taught by the Prince of Peace into the service of tyranny and oppression, are called fanatical courting preachers, incendiaries, independents, enemies of government and order, and are marked out as objects deserving severest chastisement."

In a sermon addressed to the freemen of Middletown, April 18, 1776, he thus meets his opponents: "And how **absurd** and inconsistent, and malicious is the conduct of those who **impute all the** exertions of our wisest and best **men** in the cause of **their country, to a spirit of faction and self interest, and wicked motives and designs.** This has been done by those who style themselves friends of **government on both sides of the water."**

In another sermon on political wisdom, preached in Middletown, April 10, 1786, he thus exhibits **the elements of his political creed.** "All intrigues **of deceit, all deviations from truth** and justice, are totally and equally opposed **to the public welfare and private bliss,** and where **indulged** they inevitably sap **the foundation of all their happy prospects; and the sure** destruction of every **corrupt and unreformed** people and individual, has been, and ever will be an attestation to this truth." In the same sermon he thus testifies to the wisdom and authority of the public measures of that infant period of our national government. "There was a time, methinks, when wise counsels in this country, in congress, and from them down through all **subordinate bodies, through** the whole country, were more readily followed, and thoroughly obeyed, **though** clothed with no formal, legal authority, than the commands of the most sovereign, powerful despot upon earth, ever were. Their recommendation carried **along with them a conviction of the equity and necessity** of them."

But no quotations **from these sermons and addresses would do justice to the learning and scholarship, or to the nervous eloquence of Mr. Huntington. Nor** did he, indeed, ever do full justice to himself. A nervous weakness afflicted **him almost from the beginning of his public life. His voice early** failed, **and so he was unable to achieve, in his later years, the full promise of** an **early maturity. His sermons, for years, were whispered from the pulpit,** yet so **great was his popularity that his people would not consent to his dismissal.**

The **only** published **writings of his, that I have found, are those from which I have already** quoted, and the following: **A sermon at the ordination of Isaac Parsons, in East Haddam, Oct. 28, 1772; a sermon at the ordination of Robert Hubbard, in Shelburn, Mass., Oct. 20, 1773; a sermon in Middletown, on a call of eighty-nine citizens, on the happy effect of union, and the fatal tendency of divisions, April 8, 1776; a sermon, Sept. 23, 1787, on occasion of the wreck of the schooner Unity, in which Joseph and John Henshaw, and James Cunningham, were lost; address at the house of Mr. Henshaw, Sept. 26, 1787; and a sermon, Sept. 30, 1787, from Rom. xiv: 9.**

Mr. Huntington was a Fellow of Yale College from 1780 to 1808. From the weakness mentioned above, he suffered more and more until his death, which **occurred in Middletown, June 12, 1809.**

237. SYBBEL, **born Oct. 22, 1742, and married, June 30, 1763, Rev.** John Eells, of Glastenbury, **who was** settled there in **1759, having** graduated at Yale in 1755. Their children **were:** Roger, born Sept. **22, 1764;** Mercy, born April 10, 1767, and married Daniel Wadsworth; Sybil, born Jan. 12, 1769; John, died May 1772; **and** John, born May 29, 1773. She died Nov 22, 1773, and

her husband subsequently married Sarah Wells, of Wethersfield, and had four children by her. He died May 17, 1791, aged 55 years.

238. ELIJAH, born Feb. 7, 1746, and died Oct. 22, 1753, of dysentery.

73. JONATHAN. Windham, Conn.

This family were all born in Windham.

239. JONATHAN, born Oct. 11, 1735, and died April 3, 1738.
240. ELIZABETH, born July 19, 1738, and died Oct. 4, 1741.
241. SYBBEL, born June 30, 1740, and died Jan. 20, 1741-2.
242. EUNICE, born Sept. 11, 1742, and married, 1764, Ebenezer Devotion, jr., son of the Rev. Ebenezer Devotion, as before, Nos. 232 and 234, making the third Huntington, who married into that family. Judge Eb. Devotion had by Eunice Huntington: Ebenezer, born Sept. 27, 1764; John, born Dec. 22, 1766; Jonathan, born Jan. 10, 1769; Eunice, born Sept. 6, 1770; Martha, born Jan. 25, 1773; Elizabeth, born Dec. 28, 1773, and died same day; and Louis, born Nov. 17, 1776.
243. JONATHAN, born Aug. 20, 1745, and died Feb. 15, 1754.
244. HORATIO, born June 28, 1755, and died Sept. 17, 1759.
245. ROGER, born Dec. 3, 1757. He married, for his first wife, Aug. 10, 1780, Susanna Elderkin, of Windham, who died Sept. 2, 1796, aged 35 years. He married, for his second wife, Nov. 29, 1798, Wealthan, (565) who died Jan. 20, 1835, and he died Nov. 29, 1855.

74. DAVID. Windham, Conn.

This family were all born in Windham.

246. NATHAN, born July 22, 1726. He married, Oct. 2, 1752, Mary Burley, who died Nov. 24, 1754; when he married, for his second wife, April 15, 1756, Mary Mason. He died in Windham, in 1818. He had joined the church in 1753.

247. HEZEKIAH, born Oct. 3, 1728, and married, Nov. 28, 1754, Submit Murdock. He was in service during the revolution, going to Boston with the first troops raised in Connecticut, with a major's commission. Seeing the miserable condition of the arms then in the hands of the soldiers, he went to Philadelphia and made a proposal to congress, to return to Windham and open a manufactory for repairing muskets, and other arms. On this condition, Washington returned his commission, and he served the government many years, in repairing and making arms. He claimed that he was the first man in America who made a gun. After exhausting his means in this service, he went to Philadelphia and effected a settlement with the government, receiving as his pay, 74,000 dollars of continental paper. The value of this suddenly depreciated, so that, to use his own language, a hundred dollars of it would not buy a breakfast. The entire package was kept many years, in hopes of its redemption by the government, and finally committed, by one of his sons, to the flames, after his death. He and his wife lived about ten years

FIFTH GENERATION. 125

in Walpole, N. H., but returned to Windham, Conn., about the year 1803, where he died, Sept. 17, 1897; and his wife, April 24, 1808, aged 74 years.

248. ANNE, born Nov. 14, 1730, and married, Dec. 23, 1755, Samuel, son of Robert Roundy, of Beverly, Mass., and Elizabeth Green, by whom she had six children: Asael, born Jan. 27, 1756; Amey, born March 30, 1759; Ede, born July 14, 1761; Alvin, born April 20, 1766; Samuel, born Dec. 19, 1768; and Anne, born May 15, 1771. She united with the Windham church in 1763.

249. DAVID, born Oct. 21, 1733, and died the next day.

250. MARY, born April 2, 1735, and married Richard Abby, of Windham. They had a son, Mexari, born Dec. 4, 1752.

251. LYDIA, born Aug. 29, 1738, and died next day.

252. DAVID, born Feb. 27, 1742-3, and married Tryphosa Bingham, and moved to Columbia, Conn.

75. SOLOMON. Windham, Conn.

This family were all born in Windham.

253. SOLOMON, born Nov. 24, 1728, and died Jan. 2, 1729.

254. MARGARET, born April 8, 1730, and married first a Mr. Tracy of Groton, who fell a sacrifice to a wound received in the attack on Fort Griswold, by the traitor Arnold in 1781. She had by him one son, Solomon, who lived in Middlebury, Vt. She married, second, a Mr. Williams, by whom she had several children, one of whom was Temperance, who married Gurdon (640).

255. ZERVIAH, born Feb. 24, 1732-3, and married Nov. 12, 1754, John Youngs. He was in the army. They had several children. One of the daughters married Frederick Manning, a stone cutter of Windham; a second, married Alfred Bingham of Windham. One of the sons, William, was father of the Hon. William Youngs of Pennsylvania.

256. REBECCA, born June 7, 1735, and married a Mr. Holbrook of Columbia, Conn. They had a daughter, Rebecca, and a son, Abel.

257. SOLOMON, born Oct. 19, 1737, and married, March 28, 1762, Anna Denison, who was born in 1742, and who through life sustained a most estimable character—"the emblem of true piety and love." She united with the Windham church in 1770, and died Sept. 6, 1807. He was somewhat prominent in his native town, where he died March 3, 1809.

258. TEMPERANCE, born Oct 6, 1739, married William Edwards of Coventry, and lived in Guilford, Vt. They had two sons and one daughter, who went west.

259. MARY, born Oct. 8, 1741. She married, Dec. 31, 1760, Capt. Nehemiah Tinker, who was born in 1740 in Mansfield, Conn., and died March 17, 1783. She died in the summer of 1798. Their children were: Sarah, born July 5, 1763; John, July 14, 1764; Nehemiah, May 11, 1766; Almarina, May 22, 1768; Lamson, June 24, 1770; Alexander, July 16, 1772; Joel, Sept. 2, 1774; Polly, July 12, 1776; Bela, Sept. 3, 1778; Joseph Buckingham, Dec. 21, 1779; and Lydia, July 27, 1782. Joseph B. Tinker in June, 1804, was

allowed to take the name Buckingham, instead of Tinker, and as Joseph T.
Buckingham he has been long and well known, especially as the Editor of the
Boston Courier. He married, July 28, 1805, Melinda, daughter of Caleb and
Mary (Murdock) Alvord, of Greenfield, Mass., by whom he has had a family
of thirteen children, among whom have been three lawyers, two ministers,
one physician, and one agent of the general government in western surveys.
He died in Cambridge, April 11, 1861.

The Personal Memoirs of Joseph T. Buckingham furnish ample testimony
to the personal worth of his mother. She must have been a woman of more
than ordinary intelligence and of sincere and true piety, poor in this world's
goods, but rich in faith. Her death was from consumption. Her son says of
her: "She was never happier than during the last six weeks of her life. She
well knew that life was near its close, and she looked for its end with entire
resignation and cheerfulness. If she expressed any impatience, it was that
the wheels of time moved so slowly. * * * In the intervals of
suffering, when strength revived, she labored to impress on my mind the necessity of faith in the Christian religion, according to the Calvinistic inter-
pretation; admonished me to be faithful to my employer; and charged me,
by all the love she bore me, to stay with him till I should be twenty-one years
old, whatever inconvenience and destitution I might endure, or whatever sacrifice it cost me."

260. LYDIA, born Nov. 2, 1744, and married, Nov. 13, 1762, Elihu Tinker,
brother of Nehemiah, husband of Mary, above. They lived in Worthington,
Mass. She had, born in Windham, before moving to Massachusetts, Abigail
Griswold, Aug. 20, 1761, and Elisha, born Oct. 30, 1766. After removing,
they had six sons: John resides in Worthington and is a wealthy farmer;
James, the youngest but one, lives in Hyde Park, Vt., and is a physician of
extensive practice; and Ralph, another son who is a physician in Tennessee.

50. SAMUEL, DEACON. Lebanon, Conn.

This family were all born in Lebanon.

261. SAMUEL, born Oct 16, 1723. He graduated at Yale in 1743, studied
theology and was a short time a preacher. He afterwards became a merchant,
and resided in Lebanon, Canterbury, and East Haddam. He married, first,
May 23, 1751, Rebecca Fairbanks, who died Sept. 15, 1754. He married for
his second wife, May 25, 1757, Dorothy Gates of East Haddam. She was
born May 5, 1729, and died Oct. 29, 1821. He was chosen deacon of the Canterbury church, while living there, March 26, 1753. About the year 1769 he
removed to East Haddam, where he continued to reside until his death, March
20, 1797. He probably went to Canterbury about the year 1752, as that is
the date of his own and his first wife's admission to the church there by letter.
His second wife was admitted to that church in 1759. He was chosen deacon
and clerk of the church in East Haddam in 1770. He was a justice of the
peace in East Haddam and a public man of considerable note.

262. MARY, born June 1, 1725, and married, Jan. 3, 1757, Rev. John Por-

ter of Bridgewater. She is called on the Lebanon church records, Mrs. Mary Huntington.

263. ZERVIAH, born July 23, 1727, and married, Dec. 28, 1753, Elisha Harvey of East Haddam. Their children as far as reported were: Elisha, born Jan. 8, 1755, and had a family, dying May 6, 1846; Asahel, died Aug. 26, 1783, aged twenty-five years; Huntington died aged twenty-five years, both he and his brother Asahel being prisoners in the Revolution; Samuel, died June 11, 1826, aged fifty-seven years; Sybil, died April 19, 1813, aged 47; and Olive died aged about fifty years.

264. OLIVER, born April 15, 1729, and married, June 24, 1761, Anna Lynde, who died March 23, 1811. He was a farmer and shoemaker and died in Lebanon, 1802.

265. WILLIAM, born Aug 12, 1731, and died Sept. 11, 1731.

266. WILLIAM, born Aug. 20, 1732. He married, Oct. 27, 1757, Bethia Throop, a lineal descendant of William Scrope, one of the judges who condemned Charles I., and whose name on coming to this country was changed to Throop. She was born in the year 1738. Her funeral sermon, preached by her pastor, Rev. Zebulon Ely, and afterwards published, bears this testimony to her piety. "The remains of a very worthy member of this church and society are before us. Early in life, in the sweet bloom of youth, she remembered her Creator. Her after life gave distinguished evidence that her supposed conversion was not a delusion but a glorious reality. Her acquaintance and friends can all testify that she adorned the Christian profession. She so appeared to love religion, and was so blessed in the family that she reared up, that she was entitled to the honorable appellation of a mother in Israel." Her death, which was from a cancer in the breast, occurred July 12, 1799. Capt. William Huntington was a farmer, a useful and Christian man. He died in Lebanon, May 31, 1816.

267. SYBIL, born in Feb. 1734-5, and married, Nov. 22, 1757, Rev. Eleazer May of Haddam. He graduated at Yale, 1752, and in 1756 was settled in Haddam, where he died June 30, 1803. She died in 1816. They had one son, Major Huntington May, who married Clarissa, daughter of Capt. John Brainard.

268. ELIPHALET, born April 14, 1737, and graduated at Yale, 1759. He was installed over the church in Killingworth, Jan. 11, 1764, where he preached until 1775. While here he married, April 24, 1766, Sarah, daughter of Joseph and Sarah (Walker) Elliot, and granddaughter of Rev. Dr. Jared Elliot of Killingworth, and the fourth generation removed from Dr. John Elliot of Roxbury, the great divine and apostle to the Indians. After his death, which occurred from small pox, Feb. 8, 1777, she married for her second husband, March 10, 1779, the Rev. Achilles Mansfield, who succeeded her first husband in the church at Killingworth.

269. JONATHAN, born March 19, 1741, and married Silence, daughter of Joseph Selden of East Haddam. He lived in East Haddam, in Hartford, Conn., engaged in mercantile business in Vermont, and later in Higganum, Conn.,

where he died in March. 1832. Valuable genealogical papers which he had collected of the family were destroyed by a fire.

270. ELEAZER, born May 9, 1744. He married Betsey Pitkin, and lived on a farm in Lebanon. He died in 1777.

271. JOSIAH, born Nov. 5, 1746. He married first, Sept. 13, 1770, Rhoda Loomis, who died, leaving a single daughter. He married for his second wife, Nov. 9, 1780, Abigail Gilbert, who was born May 16, 1748, and died Nov. 11, 1835. He was a merchant, " a respectable and pious man, and for many years a deacon of the Congregational church in Wethersfield, Rocky Hill parish, under the pastoral care of the Rev. Dr. Lewis. He died there March 29, 1835.

81. CALEB. Lebanon, Conn.

This family were all born in Lebanon, Conn.

272. CALEB, born Dec. 9, 1721. He married, Feb. 6, 1747, Zerviah Case, and moved to Ashford, probably after the birth of his children.

273. LYDIA, born June 3, 1722.

274. ELISHA, born April 25, 1724, and married, March 8, 1749–50, Elizabeth Denison, and lived some part of his life in Windham, and probably died in Mansfield. After the death of his first wife he married, probably June 12, 1777, in Ashford, where the births of his twin children are recorded.

275. ELIJAH, twin with Elisha, and married Abigail Dana. They lived in Mansfield and afterwards in Ashford, where he died in 1816.

276. ABNER, born March 6, 1726, and married, so the Lebanon records attest, Nov. 14, 1749, Mary Whitman from Norwich. They lived awhile in Windham and Mansfield, from which latter place they moved in 1801 to New Haven in Vermont, where he died in 1816.

277. JAMES, born April 25, 1728. He married Hannah, daughter of Jonathan Marsh. He was several summers the town shepherd. He was so conscientious that he refused taking care of the sheep on the Sabbath, and a boy was employed by the town for this service. He died Dec. 10, 1812, at the residence of his son Joseph, in Orange, Vt. His wife died in 1795, in Norwich, Vermont.

278. SUSANNA, born June 23, 1730, and married, June 5, 1757, Anderson Dana, a lawyer of Ashford, Conn. He was descended from Richard Dana, a French protestant who had fled from persecution, first to England, and about 1640 to America, settling at what is now the town of Brighton, Massachusetts. Their children, all born in Ashford, Conn., were: Evans, born May 10, 1758; Daniel, born Sept. 16, 1760; Susannah, born Jan. 16, 1762; Anderson, born Aug. 11, 1765; Ariel, born March 17, 1767; Sylvester, born July 1, 1769; and Eleazer, born Aug. 12, 1772.

In the fall of 1772 this family removed into the Wyoming valley, on the Susquehannah. With her seventh child in her arms, not yet two months old, and her sixth, a little boy of only three summers, holding on, as they journeyed on horseback, the mother rode that whole distance, some three hundred miles into the wilderness, the last fifty miles having only marked trees for her guide.

"Here," (I quote from the address of Rev. Mr. Bouton, at the funeral of Rev. Sylvester Dana, June 11, 1849, the latter being the little boy of three years alluded to above,) "for six years the Dana family prospered. In 1778 the father represented the town of Westmoreland in the general assembly of Connecticut. Returning home on the 28th of June, after an absence of eight weeks, he was an actor and a victim in that tragic scene which the very next week occurred in that beautiful valley. On the third of July a band of British troops and tories, led on by Col. John Butler, with seven hundred savage auxiliaries, attacked and utterly destroyed the settlement. Most of the men were slain, their homes burned, their property either destroyed or carried away, and women and children who escaped the massacre, fled through the wilderness to the nearest white settlement." Among those who thus fled, was Susannah Dana, who, "with seven children, in a state then of total destitution, commenced her flight on foot, amid the darkness of the night, through that dreary wilderness of fifty miles. Wolves howled on every side of them; but the terror of savages who might be on their track hastened their steps. Nor did they stop, except as necessity for rest and refreshment compelled, till the three hundred miles that separated them from their kindred in Ashford had been re-traced." Nor does this give the full measure of that mother's ability and courage. When it became apparent that their only safety was in flight, she set herself calmly to the work of collecting such food as would be most easily taken with them; and then, as though there was still something besides present salvation desirable, she collected a pillowcase of papers and public documents, as her husband had been much in public life for the colony, and determined if possible to take them with her. In this she succeeded, and Mr. Minor, the historian of that awful tragedy, acknowledges his obligations for that noble thoughtfulness. Few incidents in the lives of illustrious women exceed this, in all the elements of true greatness. Not till the family, eight in number, had reached Bullock's Mountain, ten miles from their late happy home, did they learn of the deaths of those two husbands, their needed protectors. Here they learned the horrible story, and alone, yet with unfaltering step, they urge on their unprotected flight.

279. EZEKIEL, born Aug. 2, 1732. He is said to have married twice. The records of his children's births are in two places on the town record.

280. DANIEL, born Feb. 3, 1737.

85. JOHN.   Lebanon, Conn.

This family were all born in Lebanon.

281. ANNA, born June 30, 1729, and married, June 18, 1752, Charles, son of Rev. Timothy and Elizabeth (Hyde) Collins, of Litchfield, South Farms. He was born at Litchfield, Aug. 5, 1727. Their children were all born in Litchfield, as follows: Lewis, born Oct. 29, 1753; Elizabeth, born Sept. 25, 1755, married James Perrepont, of Litchfield, and became the mother of the Rev. John Pierpont, the poet: Lois, born Oct. 11, 1757, married Robert Pierrepont, of Litchfield, one of whose daughters, married Governor Skinner, of

Vermont; Eunice, twin with Lois, married James Hococks, of Manchester, Vt.; Anna, born Oct. 10, 1759; Charles, born Aug. 14, 1761; Rhoda, born Oct. 5, 1764, and married Evelyn Pierrepont, and settled in New Haven, Conn.; Loraine, born May 1, 1767; Darius, born Nov. 8, 1769; David, born May 1, 1772, and lived in Branford.

282. ELIZABETH, born March 25, 1731, and died Dec. 1, 1736.

283. EUNICE, born April 25, 1733.

284. JOHN, born May 4, 1735, and died Dec. 14, 1736.

285. JOHN, born March 12, 1737, and married, June 22, 1769, Lucy, daughter of William Metcalf, and settled in East Haddam. She died April 13, 1818, aged 72, and he died March 5, 1830.

286. JOSEPH, born May 6, 1739. He married Rachel Preston, and lived in Harwinton many years. He died about 1820, and his wife about 1833, and were buried in the old grave yard of Harwinton.

287. ISRAEL, born April 6, 1741.

288. DANIEL, born March 16, 1743.

289. DAVID, born Nov. 24, 1745. He graduated at Dartmouth in 1773, and the same year received the honorary degree of M. A., at Yale. Having pursued the study of theology, acceptably under his pastor, Rev. Dr. Solomon Williams, of Lebanon, he was ordained to the work of the gospel ministry, and installed over the church in Marlborough, Conn., in 1776, and remained there until 1797, a laborious and successful minister of Christ. He married, Nov. 5, 1778, Elizabeth Foote, of Colchester, who proved to be to him a most excellent wife. She was as much distinguished for her fervent piety, and for her zeal in doing good, as for her remarkable intelligence, and her unusually complete personal culture.

After his dismission from his people in Marlborough, he preached a few Sabbaths in Salem, Conn., yet was never settled there. He was installed, Nov. 8, 1797, over what is now the South Church, in Middletown, Conn. This church had been seriously endangered by the Separatists; but by the judicious and successful labors of Mr. H., comparative harmony was restored, and the church again brought to accept more decidedly than ever, the orthodox Congregational platform. He removed from this field of labor in 1803, and was again installed over the Congregational church in North Lyme, on the 21st of December in that year. Here he remained a faithful preacher and pastor until his death, April 13, 1812. He was a man of eminent piety, and remarkable for a uniform and intense religious zeal. He preached twice on the day of his death, closing, most fittingly, his labors on earth by a sermon of great earnestness from the text, "Set thine house in order, for thou shalt die and not live." Before one o'clock, of the following morning, he was no more; yet though so suddenly called away, he left with all the composure of one about taking a pleasant walk. One who knew him well, testifies of him, that "he was a very serious minded man, and habitually sensible of the sacredness of his calling."

290. NATHANIEL, died soon after his birth.

86. SIMON.   Lebanon, Conn.

This family were all born in Lebanon.

291. SARAH, born March 5, 1738, and married Rev. Jonathan, (233) of Worthington, Mass., where she died, May 13, 1790.

292. EBENEZER, born Sept. 27, 1740, and married Sarah Edgerton. He died in the West Indies.

293. SIMON, born Feb. 8, 1742–3, and died Aug. 20, 1753.

294. EUNICE, born March 28, 1745, and married, Dec. 13, 1764, deacon Joshua Willes, of Franklin, the eighth child of Rev. Henry and Martha (Kirtland) Willes. Their children were: Jabez, born Sept. 10. 1765; Temperance, born March 4, 1768; Martha, born July 27, 1771; and Joseph Huntington, born June 15, 1781.

295. ANDREW, born May 9, 1747. He married, April 17, 1768, Ruth, daughter of Elijah Hyde, of Lebanon, and Ruth Tracy. She was born in Lebanon May 5, 1746. He was a military officer. He died July 16, 1811.

296. HANNAH, born Aug. 25, 1749, and married, Oct. 15, 1772, Rev. Joseph Lyman, D. D., of Hatfield. Her husband was the son of Jonathan and Bethia Lyman, and was born in Lebanon, April 14, 1749. He was graduated at Yale, in 1767, with high honor. After a popular tutorship there, he was ordained March 1, 1772, pastor of the Congregational church in Hatfield, Mass.; where, for over a half century he served the church and society with great ability, and wielded a marked influence among the ministry and churches of Western Massachusetts. He used to ascribe much of his pastoral success to his wife, whose ruling aim seemed to be to promote his usefulness. He was really one of the most commanding men in the ministry in his day; and in nothing of a worldly nature did he show more power over his contemporaries than in giving shape to pulpit influence during our revolutionary struggle. His colleague, Rev. Dr. Waterbury, late of Boston, speaking of him as he was, in the last two years of his life, makes this just estimate of his character; and this is said after he had passed into a state of bodily infirmity, which, to use his forcible language, "gave to him the aspect somewhat of a magnificent ruin." "The heavy column, and the broad span of the arch told, even in their dilapidation, the scale of grandeur on which the whole structure had been reared." * * * The Roman cast of his features, his expressive eye, his simplicity of language and manner, struck me very forcibly on my first introduction to him." This "great and good man" died March 27, 1828. He had seven children, only two of whom survived him. One of those was Jonathan Huntington, lawyer, of Northampton, Mass., one of whose daughters, is Martha, the wife of the Hon. LaFayette S. Foster, of Norwich.

297. JABEZ, born Feb. 16, 1752, and died Aug. 18, 1753.

89. DANIEL.   Norwich, Conn.

This family were all born in Norwich.

298. SYBIL, born Jan. 30, 1742. She lived single, and died in Stratford, April 11, 1820.

299. DANIEL, born Oct. 2, 1744. He studied medicine with Dr. Joseph Perry, of Woodbury, and commenced its practice in that town about the year 1767. He became a man of some distinction in his profession, and in the church, of which he was a deacon. He was also the first postmaster in Woodbury, which office he held from 1797 to 1814. He married a Tomlinson. "For several years before the close of his life," says Wm. Cothren, Esq., in his history of Woodbury, "he relinquished the active duties of his profession, and confined his attention to his drug store. He was a very celebrated chemical compounder." He died Feb. 19, 1819.

300. LEVI, born Aug. 5, 1747. He was one of the most active and successful of the enterprising men of Norwich, during the period following the revolution. He married Anna, daughter of Jabez and Anna (Lathrop) Perkins. In the great fire of Nov. 26, 1793, his own dwelling, and the store in which his business was done, were destroyed. His wife was born Oct. 4, 1754, and died Jan. 1, 1799, and he died Sept. 10, 1802.

301. FELIX, born Nov. 28, 1749, and married, March 10, 1773, Anna, daughter of Jacob and Mary (Brown) Perkins. His wife died in 1806, aged fifty years.

302. REBECCA, born Feb. 2, 1752, and died Aug. 4, 1753.

91. JONATHAN.   Norwich, Conn.

This family were all born in Norwich.

303. EUNICE, born Oct. 16, 1747, and married, March 24, 1771, Ebenezer Carew, of Norwich. Their children were: Anne, born Feb. 13, 1772; Charles, born July 1, 1774; Simon, born Oct. 2, 1776; Ebenezer, born June 24, 1778; and Elizabeth Lathrop, born Oct. 6, 1780, and died early. Mrs. Carew died Aug. 14, 1785.

304. LUCRETIA, born Oct. 6, 1749, and died unmarried, in 1826.

305. JONATHAN, born Oct. 16, 1751.

306. DANIEL, Sept. 26, 1753. He married widow Elizabeth Moore, who died June 5, 1811, aged fifty-three. He died April 28, 1811. They had no children.

307. LUCY, born June 1, 1755, and married Ebenezer Hyde, who was born in Lebanon, Conn., Nov. 26, 1755. He was brother of Ruth, wife of (295), and died at New York, in 1781, on board the "Jersey Prison Ship." They had two daughters: Elizabeth, born in Lebanon, March 15, 1778, and married a Capt. French; Eunice, born in Lebanon, Oct. 29, 1779, and married Jabez Kelley.

308. ELIPHALET, born April 8, 1757, and died June 13, 1759.

309. ABIGAIL, born April 25, 1761, and married John Pearce.

FIFTH GENERATION. 133

310. RUFUS, born July 28, 1763. He was a carver in wood, and died unmarried, Sept. 21, 1832.

311. HANNAH, born April 29, 1765. She married Dr. John, son of the eminent Dr. Philip Turner, (90) an eminent physician of Norwich. It is the testimony of one competent to bear witness, that he "seemed to inherit the strong qualities of his father's mind, and to surpass him in acuteness of perception and nicety of discernment." Their children were: Julia Frances Marionette, who married Rev. George Perkins; George F., who died at the age of 20 years; Betsey H., who became the second wife of Rev. Geo. Perkins; and Charles. Dr. Turner died May 7, 1837, aged 73, and his widow, May 7, 1845.

312. ELIPHALET, born March 2, 1768. He married a Daniels. He was a baker. He died in Oct., 1802, in Norwich.

92. BENJAMIN, LL. D. Norwich, Conn.

This family were all born in Norwich, and for my record of them, I am indebted, almost entirely, to Edward, (820).

313. HENRY, born May 23, 1766. He graduated at Dartmouth, in 1783, and entered upon the profession of law, but soon abandoned this for commercial pursuits. He established himself in business in New York city, and had also an interest in the partnership of Geo. Huntington & Co., of Rome, N. Y. Becoming largely interested in land speculation, he soon removed to Rome, where he spent the remainder of his life, in a most successful business career. He was chosen President of the Bank of Utica, and retained the post until his resignation, a short time before his death, when his failing health hindered his weekly visits to Utica. His business career, from its beginning to its close, was marked by a high tone of honor and integrity. Avoiding all the petty meannesses to which the ambitious man of business is tempted, he still won all the business ends which the most aspiring could wish. Nor was he without frequent testimonials to the confidence which his fellow-citizens reposed in his political character. In 1805, 1806, and 1807, he was a member of the New York senate; and in 1806, was also a member of the council of appointment. In 1816 and 1818, he was a member of the assembly. In 1821, he was a member of the convention for revising the state constitution. He was also one of the presidential electors, in the elections both of 1808 and 1812. Few men have stood fairer, for honor and integrity; and very few have won higher confidence and esteem for private and social worth. He married Catharine M. Havens. His death occurred at Rome, in 1846. The beautiful engraving which accompanies this sketch, is a perpetual and most faithful witness to some of the noblest traits of human character, which must have adorned the original.

314. GURDON, born March 16, 1768. He married, first, March 20, 1792, Susannah Tracy, who was born Aug. 8, 1770, and died, Aug. 21, 1793. He married for his second wife, July 6, 1794, Anna Perkins, who was born Feb. 1, 1768, and died April 21, 1802. He began life as a carriage maker at Norwich,

but after a few years removed to Rome where he became a merchant, and by his strict and unbending integrity and the genial kindliness of his heart, acquired the esteem and respect of all who knew him. He was successful in his business from which he retired some years before his death, which took place in 1840.

315. GEORGE, born June 5, 1770. He married, May 21, 1794, Hannah Thomas of Norwich. He was the first of the Huntington family who moved into Central New York. He first settled in Whitestown, in 1792, then the most important of all the New England settlements in that vicinity. He had little or no property, but opened a store as agent for Mr. Hyde of New London. In the succeeding year he removed to Fort Stanwix, near Rome, and by the assistance of his elder brother, Henry, established himself in business. A canal to connect the waters of the Mohawk with Wood Creek was then in contemplation, and was shortly afterwards constructed by the Western Inland Lock Navigation Company, thus forming the earliest connection of the waters flowing to the Hudson with those of the lakes. In this enterprise, the beginning of our system of internal improvements, he took a deep interest, and was, during the existence of the Company, its agent, giving his personal attention to the construction and support of the works. He represented, in part, the county of Oneida, in the Assembly in 1811, '12, '13 '19, '20, '21, and '22. He was a prominent and zealous member of the Congregational church for many years, and a liberal contributor, both of his substance and his energies, to every good work.

"The business connection of Henry and George Huntington, under the firm of George Huntington & Co., continued until his death. They gave up the mercantile business about the year 1817, and afterwards dealt largely in real estate, and interested themselves to a considerable extent in the manufacture of iron, cotton, &c. They were noted for their fair and honorable manner of doing business, never allowing themselves to be tempted by doubtful operations, or taking directly or indirectly more than strictly legal rates of interest. I have heard men who recollect occurrences of forty years since, speak of the firmness with which, during a season of great scarcity, 1816, when the crops were cut off and there was great and wide-spread distress for food, this company resisted all temptations to sell to speculators the large amount of grain in their possession, parting with it only in small quantities and at moderate prices, to those who needed it for their own sustenance. Their sagacity, probity and fair dealing, met with deserved success."

This prominent man, "the patriarch of the village," died in Rome, N. Y., Sept. 23, 1842.

316. LUCY, born Jan. 21, 1773. She married Dr. Matthew Brown, resided for a while at Rome, and afterwards at Rochester, N. Y. Their children were: Benjamin Huntington; Matthew, of Toledo; George H.; Henry H., Cashier of Peninsular Bank at Detroit; Mary Ann, and Elizabeth Radcliff.

317. NANCY, born March 30, 1775, and died unmarried in Rome in 1842.

318. BENJAMIN, born March 19, 1777. He was married in New London,

July 21, 1812, to Faith Trumbull, daughter of Gen. Jedidiah, (1362) a lady who inherited largely the virtues for which her father was so conspicuous. He engaged early in life in business in Detroit, but returned to New York City and became one of the most eminent of the New York exchange brokers. His first wife died in New York, April 5, 1838. He married for his second wife, Mrs. Mary Ann (Kempton) Wales of New York, who died April 8, 1850, aged fifty-five, and he died in New York, Aug. 3, 1850.

319. RACHEL, born April 4, 1779. She married at Rome, Jan. 19, 1800, William Gedney Tracy, a merchant of Whitestown, N. Y., who was born in Norwich, Conn., Nov. 15, 1768, and son of Jared and Margaret (Grant) Tracy. Their children were: Susannah, born Nov. 20, 1800, married Moses Bagg of Utica, N. Y., and died after a most useful and Christian life, July 17, 1859; Margaret, born Jan. 18, 1803, married Rev. Chauncey Goodrich of New Haven; William, born June 16, 1805, married Lucy Perkins of Lisbon, Conn., and is a lawyer in New York City; Ann Huntington, born Oct. 7, 1807, married William Curtis Noyes, an eminent lawyer of New York City; Charles, born Feb. 17, 1810, married Louisa Kirtland, and is a lawyer in New York city; Catherine, born July 10, 1812, married Milton D. Parker of Utica, N. Y., and was lost on board the Swallow, in April, 1845; Henry, born Feb. 10, 1815, and is a civil engineer; Edward Huntington, born March 31, 1817, and is a civil engineer; Frances, born Jan. 6, 1821, married William Henry Wells of Brattleborough.

320. DANIEL, born Dec. 27, 1781, and died on the 30th of the same month.

91. JAMES. Norwich, Conn.

This family, excepting the last member, have their names recorded in Norwich.

321. WILLIAM, born Feb. 1, 1736-7. He married, Dec. 11, 1763, Anne Pride, who died March 4, 1776. He married for his second wife, Feb. 11, 1777, Lois Durkee; and for his third wife, April 11, 1791, Elizabeth Waterman. He lived in Lebanon, Conn., for a few years, and thence went into Vermont, in which state he died, at Middlebury, July 4, 1816. He was at the battle of Bunker Hill, and was sent to Skeensboro to aid in building Arnold's fleet. He afterwards repaired to the frontier in New Hampshire, where he served as a minute man through the war. It was a great joy to him to recount in his old age the story of his exposures and hardships, and of his encounters with wild beasts and savages in that cold and snowy region.

322. MARY, born May 15, 1739, and married, Aug. 18, 1762, Eliphalet Carew. They had eight children; Eliphalet, born Jan. 30, 1764; Daniel and Azariah, twins, born Aug. 18, 1765, and died young; Azor, born Oct. 26, 1768; Nabby, born Nov. 27, 1770, and died May 12, 1779; Molly born June 6, 1772; Betsy, born July 18, 1777; Nabby, born Oct. 27, 1780.

323. JARED, born Jan. 20, 1740-1. He married, Dec. 26, 1776, Amy Gorton. He moved to Mansfield, Conn., in 1801, where he resided on a farm until his death, April 16, 1819. His wife died in Mansfield, Nov. 3, 1829.

324. JAMES, born Oct. 1, 1743, and married Hannah Curtiss. He went into Vermont and lived some time in Royalton, Vt.

325. JOHN, born Oct. 26, 1745, and married, Nov. 17, 1773, Abigail C., daughter of Capt. Joshua and Anne (Backus) Abel. She was born in Norwich, Jan. 19, 1752. He resided in Norwich, his wife dying in April 1814, and himself in 1815. He enlisted in 1777 in Capt. William Richards company of the first regiment for three years. He was at Reading in 1779, and on the first of January, 1780, he is on the muster roll of Col. Comfort Sagis' regiment, as sergeant.

326. ELIZABETH, born Nov. 22, 1748. She married Ezra (179) and died Oct. 19, 1796.

327. ABIGAIL, born Jan. 3, 1753, and married David Hough of Lebanon, N. H. He was a member of congress from his district from 1803 to 1807.

328. NANCY, born Nov. 2, 1755 and married, Dec. 2, 1772, Frederick Calkins of Chelsea, Vt., where she died in 1848.

329. ROGER, born in 1758. He married Polly Dyer. He was in the Revolution and for many years drew a pension. At the age of ninety-two he took great delight in the daily reading, in course, of his old family Bible. He died in Hartford, Vt. His name appears on the pension list of 1850.

330. SYBIL, born Dec. 3, 1760. She married Dudley Hammond, and lived in Chemung, N. Y., where she died in 1852.

331. EUNICE, born Dec. 20, 1766, and married Jabez Avery of Norwich.

95. PETER. Norwich, Conn.

This family were all born in Norwich.

332. RUTH, born Aug. 18, 1735, and married Benjamin Butler.

333. JERUSHA, born Oct. 20, 1737, and died unmarried, Oct. 18, 1777, in Norwich.

334. SIMEON, born April 2, 1740. He married first, Jan. 27, 1777, Freelove Chester, who died June 16, 1787. He married again at Wethersfield, Jan. 15, 1789, widow Keeney, who survived him and died Sept. 11, 1820. He was a blacksmith, and appears to have been an athletic and powerful man. He was in some repute as a military character, even before our Revolutionary war commenced. The fourth of July, 1774, gave him an occasion to display both his patriotism and his pluck. One Mr. Francis Green, a Boston tory and an eminent merchant, who for that reason thought he must be loyal, and so save, if possible, his craft, came into Norwich on that day to collect debts. The Norwichers had been notified of the approach of the tory some hours before his arrival, and the Green before Lathrop's tavern was covered with ardent liberty men, to give him what they deemed appropriate welcome. With few words, as it was now too late for speech making, the assembled patriots unanimously voted Mr. Green the use of fifteen minutes for his departure. He hesitated, his business was urgent, he wanted to collect some monies now due, he was in his king's dominions and should,—but his time for speeches in Norwich was now ended. Capt. Simeon Huntington, with no light hand.

gave the gentleman loyalist a sufficiently sensible demonstration of the presence and power, too, of another style of loyalty with which all Norwich men had become thoroughly possessed. Without further resistance, and without calling for his money, Mr. Green " entered his carriage and amid shouts and hissings drove off." Nor did it avail that on his return to Boston, he offered a reward for "any of the ruffians of Norwich, particularly for Capt. Simeon Huntington."

The estimate in which he was held by Gen. Jedidiah, during the war, is attested by one of the General's letters in the American Archives, directed to Gov. Trumbull of Conn., and dated Roxbury Camp, Sept. 9, 1775; in which he expresses his wish that Mr. Simeon Huntington would accept a second lieutenancy then vacant, and assigning as his reason; " I want officers of a military spirit."

This Simeon was one of the Common Council of Norwich City in 1785, as appears from a summons made by Jedidiah, then senior Alderman.

335. ZEPHANIAH, born Dec. 14, 1742. He was commissary of brigade in the war of the Revolution, being appointed in 1780. He died unmarried in 1820.

336. ELISHA, born June 6, 1745, and married Dec. 3, 1769, Mrs. Anna Ryan. He was a sea faring man and captain of his own vessel. He died in 1810.

337. PHEBE, born Jan. 18, 1747, and married, Nov. 22, 1787, Ebenezer, son of James and Sarah (Marshal) Hyde. She died July 5, 1799. She was a second wife, and her only child was Chloe, who was born Sept. 6, 1789, and married, Sept. 11, 1811, Samuel Webb of Windham.

338. FREDERICK, born Oct. 26, 1750. He married, Jan. 20, 1784, Sarah, daughter of John and Sarah (Huntington) (134) Bliss, who died Aug. 6, 1786, aged twenty-nine years. He afterwards married, July 28, 1787, Lydia Andrews, and lived in Hudson, N. Y. He was a sea captain. His first wife was a woman of marked excellency and strength of character. She and her two babes were buried in Norwich Town burying lot.

339. REUBEN, born Jan. 21, 1753. He was a blacksmith. He was married three times. His wives' names were Carey, Prevost, and Frazier. He died in 1804.

340. LEFFREY, or as the name was subsequently spelled, Eliphalet, born April 5, 1756. He married, June 15, 1784, Edna Clement, and lived in Plainfield, Vt.

97. NATHANIEL. Norwich, Conn.

341. JASPER.

342. ASA, born in Norwich, as his daughter, Mrs. Brainard, testifies.. He lived in Woodbridge, Conn., and still later in New Haven, Conn., where he died in 1825, aged 84 years, making his birth in the year 1741. He was a carpenter by trade, and was a man of more than ordinary refinement of manners, of kindly feelings, and of Christian principles. He married Polly Hine.

343. AMY, born 1746, married James Robertson.

344. PRISCILLA, married Benjamin Billings and Mark A. Dolph.
345. ELIZABETH. married Benjamin Hendricks and Dr. Graham.
346. HANNAH. married Jonathan Culver, whose son Roswell was father of Jonathan E. and Asa L. Culver, who for years were in business in Norwich city.
347. LYDIA, married, as the Lebanon church records testify, in 1788, Edward Lovegrove.
348. EPHRAIM JONES, born Dec. 10. 1763. and entered on the records as the entry states. Aug. 18, 1779. It is probable that the father of this family lived away from Norwich.

SIXTH GENERATION.

99. JOHN. Amesbury.

This family were all born in Amesbury.

349. JOHN, born Aug. 15, 1737, and married Hannah Weed. He occupied the homestead of his grandfather.

350. MARY, born Oct. 11, 1739, and married John Peaselee. They lived in Newtown, N. H.

351. MERRIAM, born Jan. 19, 1741, and married, first, Thomas Challis, and for her second husband, Stephen Brown. They lived in Newbury, where they had children.

352. SUSANNAH, born Nov. 11, 1743, and married John Peaselee, of Weare, New Hampshire.

353. WILLIAM, born May 18, 1747, and married Lydia Buxton. They lived in Amesbury, on a part of the original homestead, where his descendants still live.

354. SARAH, born May 8, 1750, and married Micah Sawyer of Newbury. They had children.

355. ELIJAH, born April 17, 1753, and married Elizabeth Rowell. He died in 1818, in Amesbury.

105. WILLIAM. Amesbury.

356. JUDITH, born in Salisbury, June 21, 1749, and married, in 1778, Wm. Brown, of Salisbury. They had children.

357. HANNAH, born Aug. 28, 1754, and married Moses Hoyt, Sept. 24, 1773. He was a son of Theodore and Hannah (Colby) Hoyt, and born Aug. 21, 1752. He was a shipwright, and received a pension for revolutionary service. She died Jan. 16, 1832, having had four children.

358. ISAAC, born in Amesbury, July 15, 1758, and married Hannah Gould, and lived in Amesbury.

359. WILLIAM, born in Amesbury, Oct. 18, 1762, and died without a family.

360. EPHRAIM, twin brother of the preceding, died also without a family. He had gone out with four others to take fish, off Newburyport bar, when a furious snow storm disabled them, near Ipswich, and they were picked up. One of them was already dead, and Ephraim lived but a short time.

106. TIMOTHY.   Amesbury.

361. WILLIAM, born in Southampton, N. H., April 30, 1755, and intended marriage, Jan. 16, 1782, with Sarah Goodwin. They lived in Amesbury, and he died in 1832. He was engaged in the revolution.

362. TIMOTHY, who was drowned, while young, though he was probably married, and had a family.

363. THOMAS, who lived in Boston, and never married.

364. MARY, who married a Mr. Elliot, and lived in Concord, N. H.

365. BENJAMIN, the son of a second wife, married, and lived in Kennebunk, Me. He died in 1845, aged 79, as his son testifies in his letter to Joshua ——.

365¹ JOHN, lived in Litchfield, and died in Vermont.

108. SAMUEL.   Amesbury.

366. JACOB, born June 16, 1741. He married Elizabeth ——, and lived in Amesbury.

367. JOHN, born Dec. 21, 1743. He married Betsey Hoyt, and lived in Weare, N. H. He served in the war of the revolution, five years under Gen. John Stark. He died in 1813.

368. JOSHUA, married Jane Quigley. They lived in Francistown, N. H.

369. JOSEPH, born in Amesbury, June 7, 1753, and married, March 3, 1775, Mary Colby. They lived in Francistown, N. H., where they united with the Congregational church, in 1779. She died Jan. 2, 1802. He married, again, Aug. 18, 1802, Persis Lovejoy, who also united with the Congregational church. He died Oct. 25, 1837, and his widow, May 26, 1842.

370. JOANNA, married Joseph Colby, of Weare, N. H.

112. JONATHAN.   Amesbury.

371. ELIZABETH, born in Amesbury, Sept. 16, 1763.

115. SAMUEL.   Newark, N. J.

My information regarding this family is mainly from Mrs. Rosenkrantz, daughter of Mrs. Lee, and from the venerable David Doremus, of Newark, who lived several years in the same house with Mr. Crane, who married Sarah (373).

372. PHEBE, who married William Lee, of Newark. She had only one child, a daughter, who married a Rosenkrantz, of Newark. Mrs Rosenkrantz is still (1858) living at the age of seventy-five. She has two sons, one living in Syracuse, N. Y., and the other in Newark, N. J.

373. SARAH, married Daniel Crane, of Newark, and had four children: a

SIXTH GENERATION. 141

daughter, who, at the age of ten years, was burned to death; and three sons, John Sargent, Joseph and William. Mrs. Crane was a most excellent woman.

374. MARY SARGENT, was born about the year 1777, and never married. She died about 1850, at the residence of her niece Mrs. Joseph W. Lee.

122. SIMON. Morris County, N. J.

375. SARAH, born March 6, 1744, and died March 13, 1785.

123. CHRISTOPHER. Bozrah, Conn.

This family were all born in Norwich, New Concord Society.

376. CHRISTOPHER, born July 14, 1749, and died in 1759.

377. SARAH, born Jan. 28, 1750–51, and died single, in Bozrah.

378. ABIGAIL, born June 13, 1753. She married, Nov. 17, 1778, Job Talcott, of Bolton, Conn.

379. RUTH, born Aug. 14, 1755. She married, Sept. 22, 1755, the distinguished divine, Dr. Thomas Baldwin, who was born in Bozrah, Conn., Dec. 23, 1753, and was settled, as pastor of the second Baptist church, of Boston, Nov. 11, 1779, and who died Aug. 29, 1825. She was an amiable woman, and an excellent wife. They had six children, the most of whom died young. Her death occurred Feb. 11, 1812.

380. THOMAS, born Oct. 28, 1757. He married, for his first wife, in Windham, Oct. 14, 1779, Nabby, daughter of Ebenezer and Sarah (Clark) Backus, and for his second wife, a Griswold. He lived at one time in or near Middletown, Vt., and was a justice of the peace for Rutland county. He was also a deacon of the Baptist church in Middletown, about the year 1820, after which he removed to Dresden, N. Y., as a letter to Dr. Joshua Huntington, in 1852, states.

381. CHRISTOPHER, born March 31, 1766. He married, May 20, 1794, Lucy, daughter of Jeremiah and Dorothy (Hills) Culver. He was a physician, and resided in Bozrah, where he died, July 17, 1821. His widow is now (1857) living in Manchester, at the age of 89, with her daughter, Mrs. Marble.

124. ELISHA. Norwich, Conn.

Both the children of this family have their births recorded in Norwich.

382. ELISHA, born April 23, 1762, in West Farms, Norwich. He married, May, 20, 1784, Nancy Rudd, who was born July 3, 1765, and who died Jan. 25, 1848. He died in Franklin, Feb. 3, 1833.

383. DINAH, born Feb. 13, 1765, and married, May 19, 1786, Samuel Judd. At least, such a marriage is on record, and this is the probable Dinah.

128. THEOPHILUS. Bozrah, Conn.

The births of all this family are recorded in Norwich, though they occurred in that part of it which is now the town of Bozrah.

384. THEOPHILUS, born Nov. 23, 1753. He married, first, Nov. 1, 1777, Ruth Talcott, of Bolton, and for his second wife, at Lebanon, N. H., Dec. 31, 1795,

Phebe, daughter of Capt. James Hall. He went to Western New York, and died at Clarence, Erie county, July 11, 1830. His first wife died at Chelsea, Vt., Feb. 10, 1793, and his second, Oct. 10, 1823.

385. SAMUEL, born July 29, 1756. He married Mary Bennet, 1783, and went to Buffalo, N. Y. He enlisted in the army of the revolution, April 23, 1777, for three years, and was enrolled as sergeant.

386. HIRAM, born Aug. 24, 1758. He married, in Chelsea, Vt., 1796, Lucy Perkins, and was a farmer. They lived in Chelsea, Vt. His wife was a daughter of Jacob and Martha Perkins, of Windham, Conn., and died Dec. 9, 1831. He died May 8, 1835. He also entered the army of the revolution in 1777.

387. LIBA, born Oct. 26, 1760. He married Sela Green, April 2, 1794. He was a wealthy farmer in Lebanon, N. H., and a man greatly respected. He was considerably in public life as justice of the peace, for more than twenty years deputy sheriff, and for two years a member of the state senate. His first wife died Nov. 29, 1818. He married for his second wife, in March, 1823, Hephzibah Hunton, who died May 9, 1836. He died Jan. 15, 1838.

388. ABEL, born Dec. 2, 1762, and died in Norwich, Sept. 9, 1778.

389. LOIS, born May 11, 1765, and married, May 15, 1786, Samuel Lathrop of Lebanon, N. H. She died in Lebanon, April 4, 1846.

390. MARGARET, born Nov. 2, 1768, and married Rufus Lathrop, and lived in Chelsea, Vt. Her descendants still live in Chelsea.

391. URIEL, born May 7, 1771, and married, in 1796, Betsy Hough. He was a member of Bowdoin College, and became a physician. He moved to Bowdoinham, Me., early in the settlement of that region, and continued to reside there until his death. "He was a man of respectable parts," and is spoken of by the old residents with a good deal of respect, as having been professionally kind and skillful, and a worthy and active member of the Baptist church in Bowdoinham.

392. NEHEMIAH, born April 20, 1776. He graduated at Dartmouth in 1803, and entered the legal profession in Peterboro, N. Y., in 1807. He married, in 1817, Hannah N. Lathop of Lebanon, N. H. He attained some distinction in his profession. He was a member of the state legislature in 1825 and '26, and died, much respected, March 26, 1855.

129. BARNABAS, DEACON. Franklin, Conn.

The births of this family are all recorded in Norwich, and they occurred in Franklin, then the West Farms parish of Norwich.

393. ANNA, born Oct. 19, 1752. She married, June 18, 1776, Silas Hartshorn of Franklin. She died Oct. 6, 1777.

394. BARNABAS, born July 5, 1754, and married, Nov. 13, 1788, Abigail, daughter of Joshua Perkins of Lisbon, Conn., where he was a successful farmer. He was a deacon of the Congregational church in Hanover Society, Lisbon. He died in Lisbon, Oct. 7, 1841, and his wife, May 7, 1843, in the 77th year of her age.

SIXTH GENERATION.

395. AZARIAH, born June 6, 1756. He married —— Parnell Champion. He was deacon of the Franklin church. He was a farmer and a worthy citizen. His wife died April 22, 1818-19, and he died Nov. 7, 1833.

396. MARY, born Sept. 12, 1758, and married, June 25, 1778, Jonathan, son of Samuel and Lurena (Fitch) Rudd, who was born May 20, 1756. They lived in Norwich, where she died in 1851. Their children were: Rev. Dr. John Churchill, born May 24, 1779, an Episcopal minister; Ricardo, born March 19, 1781, who married Lydia Ladd of Franklin and had one daughter; Charles, born Feb. 10, 1784, married and had a bookstore in Hudson, N. Y., and had two children, Edward Huntington of Kenosha, Wis., and Mrs. Mary Matthews of Buffalo, N. Y.

397. ASAHEL, born March 17, 1761. At an early age he became a Christian and resolved to devote himself to the work of the gospel ministry. Under the teaching of his pastor, the Rev. Dr. Nott, so lately the patriarch of the Connecticut ministry, he fitted for college and entered Dartmouth, where he was graduated in 1786, with the first honors of his class. His scholarship and talent are sufficiently evinced in thus standing first in a class which numbered on its lists such names as those of the Hon. Moses Fiske, Hon. Calvin Goddard, Norwich, Conn., Hon. Charles Marsh, LL. D., of Woodstock, Vt., and the Rev. Dr. Jonathan Strong, S. T. D., of Randolph, Mass.

His theological studies were pursued under those eminent teachers of the day, the Rev. Dr. Backus of Somers, and the Rev. Dr. Hart of Griswold, Conn., by both of whom he was commended, as one eminently worthy of the holy office on which he had set his heart.

At the earnest solicitation of the church and society in Topsfield, Mass., he was ordained there to the work of the gospel ministry, Nov. 12, 1789. While here, successfully engaged in his work, he married, June 2, 1791, Alethea, daughter of Dr. Elisha Lord, a celebrated physician of Abington, Conn., in whom he found a most timely and efficient helpmeet.

Of his labors in Topsfield, I am happy to quote the following testimonial from the interesting address given by the Hon. Nehemiah Cleveland, at the Topsfield Bi-centennial Celebration. In the address itself, he speaks of the most useful and acceptable ministry, of the plain good sense, of the unfailing discretion, of the mild benevolence and the blameless life, which made Mr. Huntington so safe a model and so sure a guide. In a note, in which he speaks more in detail of the life of Mr. Huntington, he says: "Here for nearly twenty-four years, flowed on the even and useful tenor of his way. With a people not particularly easy to please, he lived in unbroken harmony. He was orthodox in his opinions, but was too discreet to urge them with offensive pertinacity. His preaching was plain, sensible, and practical. His whole intercourse with his flock was so marked by social ease, by benevolent solicitude, and by judicious kindness, that he secured their warmest love, as well as esteem. His instructions were not confined to the pulpit. Compelled by the straitness of his income, and the wants of a growing family, he occasionally taught the town school. For several years before his death, he received into his family pupils from abroad. With what fidelity and ability he acquitted himself in this relation, many still remember. The language of affectionate veneration with which, at the late celebration, Judge Cummings and Mr. Benjamin A. Gould, recalled the name and virtues of their earliest teacher, will not soon be forgotten by the hundreds who listened to those glowing words of praise and gratitude."

" In the midst of his strength and usefulness, this truly good man was suddenly cut down. He died of the malignant sore throat, April 22, 1813, after an illness of four days. The funeral sermon was preached to a weeping audience by his intimate and long tried friend, Rev. Isaac Braman of New Rowley."

Of Mrs. Huntington, the widow thus bereaved, who spent her last years in the family of her eldest son, where she died, Aug. 31, 1850, in the eighty-fourth year of her age, we have this testimonial in an obituary notice taken from the Puritan Recorder:

"Mrs. Huntington was particularly happy in her relation to the church and people of Topsfield. There was a blending of dignity and gentleness in her person, that prepossessed every one in her favor. Her intercourse with the people was marked by prudence, kindness and condescension, by a lively sympathy in their joys and sorrows, and by many self-denying labors to do good among them. The writer knows not that she ever had an enemy; he is certain that she had many friends. Through all her earthly pilgrimage it was the aim of this excellent woman to live not unto herself. Her own comforts, and even wants, were forgotten in self-denying efforts for the good of others. It was her pleasure to nurse the sick and minister to the afflicted; and many living witnesses gratefully recall her fearless and faithful devotion to them in the hour of suffering and danger. In the closing scenes of her life, there were the calmness and peace, if not the triumphs of Christian faith. Her remains were deposited in the burying ground at Topsfield, by the side of that dust over which she had so many times shed, during her long widowhood, the tears of fond remembrance."

398. ELIZABETH, born July 17, 1763. She married, Dec. 13, 1781, Calvin Tracy of Coventry, and they removed west, and settled upon the Holland Purchase in New York. They had eight children: Anne Huntington, born January 12, 1783; Calvin, born March 16, 1784; Chester, born Nov. 1787; Elizabeth, born Nov. 4, 1789, and died June 28, 1795; Irene, born July 2, 1792, married Samuel Loomis of Coventry; Elizabeth, born June 17, 1796, married Arad Talcott; Gurdon Huntington, born July 13, 1798; and Mary, born June 8, 1800.

399. REBECCA, born Sept. 5, 1765, and married, Nov. 23, 1785, Stephen Ellis of Franklin, and removed with her sister, Mrs. Tracy, into the state of New York. Their children, whose births are on record in Franklin, are: Hezekiah H., born Oct. 5, 1791, and died May 18, 1795; Urania, born Nov. 28, 1786; Mary, born April 9, 1789; and Rebecca, born May 21, 1794, and died May 15, 1795.

SIXTH GENERATION.

399. LUCY, born Dec. 4, 1770, and died Dec. 21, 1773.

400. GURDON, born July 31, 1768, married first, Jan. 24, 1799, Esther, only daughter of Benjamin and Hannah (Atwood) Martin of Woodbury, Conn. She was a most excellent Christian woman and died in Cairo, N. Y., Nov. 16, 1819. He married, second, in Nov. 1821, Mary S. Prudden of Litchfield, South Farms. She survived him a few years and died in 1854 at Beloit, Wisconsin.

He pursued his early studies with his pastor, Rev. Dr Nott, and was a companion and fellow pupil with the no less venerable Dr. Eliphalet Nott of Union College. After pursuing his medical studies with Dr. Lord, about the year 1794, he removed to the banks of the Susquehanna, and located himself at Unadilla, New York.

Here he became a successful and deservedly popular physician. His rides extended often forty and fifty miles, and a more welcome visitor never entered those scattered homes. In this laborious field, journeying by day and by night, often winding his solitary way along almost untrodden paths, and fording unbridged streams, he was both a cheerful and happy man and a skillful and prosperous physician. He accumulated a handsome property, and attained the highest honors in the gift of his townsmen. He was a member of the New York assembly from Otsego County, from 1804 to 1810. In 1813 he removed to Cairo in Green County, N. Y., where he continued to reside until his death, July 13, 1847.

Dr. Huntington made a profession of religion in 1816, joining the Presbyterian church. He was ever a consistent member of the church, of which he was also an elder at the time of his death. He was a very retiring man, abounding much more in the good deeds of an excellent spirit, than in ostentatious professions. He was a most genial and companionable man, just such as every one hails as a friend. He had no enemy, and his memory is yet fragrant with the most precious savor of his generous and sanctified nature.

401. LUCY, born Dec. 4, 1770, and died Dec. 21, 1773.

402. HEZEKIAH, born Oct. 12, 1773, and died unmarried in 1838.

142. ELIJAH. Bozrah, Conn.

This family were all born in New Concord Society, Norwich, now Bozrah, and their births are all on the Norwich records.

403. ANNA, born June 4, 1767. She married, May 18, 1796, Capt. Oliver Fitch. She lived in Norwich, where she died, Jan. 7, 1808. She had one son, Edward Gould, who was born May 31, 1799, and a second son, Charles, born July 15, 1803, and died Jan. 7, 1808. Her husband died April 13, 1814, aged 47, having married, June 20, 1811, Miss Susan Finney.

404. ISAAC, born Oct. 21, 1769, and died June 12, 1770.

405. REBECCA, born Jan. 11, 1772. She married, Dec. 19, 1796, Ezra Lathrop. She lived in Bozrah, on the farm which her father had owned. She died in May, 1812, in Norwich, leaving three daughters: Mary, born June 21, 1803, (an earlier daughter of this name having died,) married Alanson Hough,

M. D., of Essex, Conn., where she died; Eunice, born Oct., 5, 1806, married, first, John, son of Capt. William Kelley, of Bozrah, who died, leaving one son, Henry, who is now (1862) living in Norwich city, second, Geo. Harrington, of Essex, where she died; and Rebecca Jane, born Dec. 17, 1811. She was early in life a devoted Christian, and went to India in 1839, as a missionary, where she became the second wife of Rev. Mr. Cherry. Besides the above daughters, they had two children who died in infancy. After the death of his wife, Mr. Lathrop married Miss Mary Pierce, of Plainfield, Conn., by whom he had two sons, one of whom is still living on the homestead of his grandfather Huntington.

406. EUNICE, born Dec. 28, 1773, and died single, in 1802.

407. ISAAC, born Nov. 7, 1775. He was a farmer and occupied, till his death, a part of the territory first taken up by his ancestor in Bozrah. He was a very retiring and unambitious, yet estimable man, and was always held in esteem in his neighborhood. He married, Nov. 27, 1807, Hannah, daughter of Joshua and Hannah (Dart) Maples, who was a most affectionate and excellent woman, and a member of the Baptist church. She died March 24, 1838, aged 52 years. He married again, April 30, 1839, Mrs. Esther, widow of Dr. Scott, of Bozrah. He died June 27, 1842, his widow surviving him several years.

408. ELIJAH, born Dec. 10, 1777. He married, in 1803, Lucretia, daughter of Elisha and Alice (Tracy) Leffingwell, of Norwich. She was born in Norwich, Nov. 14, 1782, and died in Bozrah, in 1816. He married, for his second wife, June 13, 1821, Olive, daughter of Joshua Stark, of Bozrah. He has always been esteemed and respected in his native town; where he has proved himself equally useful in promoting its secular and religious prosperity. His second wife, a most excellent woman, died in Bozrah, Sept. 26, 1862. He is still living, and though lame, is a very hearty old man, confidently awaiting his early departure to a better life.

409. WEALTHY, born Jan. 8, 1780, and married, Sept. 21, 1807, Joseph W. Tracy, second son of Jared and Margaret (Grant) Tracy, of Norwich, Conn. They resided in Norwich. Her husband was born March 9, 1773, and died April 3, 1845. She united with the first Congregational church in Norwich, in 1842, and died in New York city, July 11, 1849. Their children were: Jared Winslow, born May 29, 1812, and has for years lived in New York city; James Joseph, born Dec. 3, 1814, and is a hardware merchant in New York city; Edward Huntington, born April 21, 1817, married, Jan. 10, 1856, Louisa H. Thomas, and is residing in New York city; Sarah Grant, born Aug. 21, 1819, and died in 1838; Cornelia Margaretta, born Oct. 15, 1822, and lives in New York city; and Lydia Huntington, born July 3, 1825, and is also living in New York city.

410. NEHEMIAH, born April 20, 1782. He was for many of his earlier years an invalid, so much so that he lost almost entirely the years usually devoted to education. But he was characterized through life for his sterling good sense and judgment, and still more for his gentle and kind heart. If

any thing else was needed to render him beloved and esteemed, and trusted by all who knew him, it was his strict conscientiousness. He seemed to feel no other motive than duty; and how faithful he was to every conviction of duty, they best knew who saw him most. He married, for his first wife, Sept. 8, 1814, Nancy, an older sister of his brother Elijah's wife; and he found in her all those qualities and attainments he most prized and needed. She had mental endowments of a high order, and a personal culture which fitted her to grace any circle in which she might move. She was no less gifted with the graces of the spirit; being characterized for a piety as uniform and earnest as it was unobtrusive. She was most happy and skillful in the social and religious training of the family; yet she was felt to be as well fitted to lead in the social gatherings of her sisters in the church.

How harmoniously two such kindred spirits would move along through life together, was foreshadowed by a little incident, which transpired soon after their marriage. The one had been accustomed to regard the evening of Saturday as a part of the Christian Sabbath, and the other observed that of Sunday. They engaged a perpetual regard for each other's convictions, by a systematic avoidance of all work and secular pastime on both evenings, though they taught their children to reverence the evening of Sunday as sacred time.

Mrs. H. died July 12, 1835, most deeply lamented, yet not to be forgotten by those who had enjoyed her acquaintance. "I know of no one, so well prepared to go, and of no one whom we shall miss so much," was the heartfelt testimony of one of her neighbors, who had known her long and well. And many years after her death, the gifted Mrs. Sigourney was pleased to give her testimonial to the personal worth of one "whose friendship I so much prized." Mr. H. married, for his second wife, Dec. 21, 1841, Mrs. Anne, widow of Jirah I. Hough, and daughter of Timothy and Sorloma (Strong) Hinckley, of Lebanon, a most amiable and excellent woman, who still survives, living in Bozrah. He was chosen deacon of the church in Bozrah, several years before his death. From the commencement of the sabbath school and temperance enterprises, in this country, he was in theory and practically, a warm friend of both. Indeed, in every work which promised to promote human comfort or salvation, he was ever ready to engage. He was as steadily at his place in the prayer meeting in the busiest season of the year, as in his seat on the sabbath, in the church. This good man was taken to his rest, June 2, 1852, leaving, it is believed, no enemy behind him.

143. BENJAMIN. Norwich, Conn.

This family were all born in Norwich.

411. MARY, born March 8, 1768. She married, Oct. 29, 1791, Gardner Carpenter, and lived in Norwich. Their children recorded, were: George, born July 27, 1795; Mary Elizabeth, born Oct. 12, 1797; Gardner, born March 29, 1802; Henry, born Nov. 10, 1804; John, born March 4, 1807; and Charles, born Oct. 21, 1810.

412. PHILIP, born Sept. 26, 1770. He married, Jan. 17, 1796, Phila Grist,

who died Nov. 30, 1806, aged 38. He was chosen town clerk, immediately on the death of his father, Sept. 11, 1801, and served in this office until his death, which took place Feb. 4, 1825.

413. ALICE, born March 21, 1773. She married, in 1802, William Baldwin, and died, having had no children.

414. DANIEL, born June 10, 1776. He married, in Nov. 1803, Sarah Potter, of New London, and died, without children, Oct. 12, 1805. His wife was born Dec. 23, 1780, and died, April 8, 1850, as her grave stone attests.

150. JABEZ. Windham Conn.

This family were born in Windham and six of the births are on the records.

415. AMANDA SARAH, born June 26, 1761, and married Benjamin Chaplin.

416. AMANDA ANNA, born April 21, 1764, and married Gurdon Backus. They had several children, one of whom, Gurdon Huntington, graduated in 1806, at Williamstown College, and became a lawyer.

417. HANNAH, born Aug 7, 1765. She married Horatio Waldo, and lived in Bingham, Vt.

418. JABEZ born Aug. 23, 1767. He married Elizabeth Champlin, and within two weeks of his marriage he was accidentally killed in Philadelphia, whither he had gone to purchase stock in his business, which was that of carriage making.

419. JEDIDIAH, born Aug. 11, 1769, and died at sea, on a whaling voyage, never having married.

420. HEZEKIAH, born July 24, 1771, and died single, in St. Croix.

421. PHILENA. The date of her birth is not on the Windham records. She is said to have married a Boardman.

422. JOSEPH SPENCER, born Sept. 6, 1775. He married, Nov. 16, 1797, Nancy Morgan, of Norwich, who was born June 15, 1778, and still lives with her daughter, Mrs. Ward. After their marriage they went to Vermont. He died of yellow fever, in Newburgh N. Y., Oct. 15, 1805.

423. HENRY, died young.

424. WILLIAM, who, also, probably died young.

151. MATTHEW. Mansfield, Conn.

This family were all born in Mansfield, where their births are recorded.

425. ASA, born Oct. 19, 1743. He married, in 1765, Martha Freeman, and died without children.

426. JONAS, born March 28, 1746, and died June 26, 1751.

427. ABEL, born Dec. 24, 1748. He married Sarah Tuttle, and died in Willington, in 1790.

428. MARY, born Oct. 26, 1751, and died unmarried.

429. JONAS, born Aug. 19, 1754. He married, March 26, 1778, Rhoda Baldwin, who was born Dec. 25, 1758. He was a farmer in Mansfield, where he deid, Nov. 26, 1830. His wife died Oct. 16, 1824.

157. NATHAN.
Griswold, Conn.

This family were all born in Norwich, and have their births recorded there, though the place of their birth was in the present town of Griswold.

430. LUCY, born Feb. 26, 1756. She married Asa Burnham, and resided in Bennington Vt.; where their children were born. She died in Aug. 1827. Their children were: Eleazer, born July. 15, 1780, is a lawyer, residing in Aurora. N. Y., and has twice been a presidential elector. He married, first, Caroline Matilda, daughter of Hon. Walter Wood, who died June 27, 1832, leaving two sons and one daughter. He is now living with his second wife, Urania Smith, who has no children. Rebecca, born Feb. 5, 1782, and married Abel Cole, in 1803. They are living in Hanover, Shelby county, Indiana, and have had ten children; Julia Ann, born March 20, 1784, and married, in 1805, Charles Mattoon, of Lenox, Mass. She is a widow, now living in Lenox, and has five children, one of whom is the Rev. Chas. N. Mattoon, President of Farmers' College, near Cincinnati, Ohio. Polly, born June 2, 1786, married, in 1804, Allen Draper, of Shaftesbury, and had ten children. Asa N., born Jan. 9, 1789, married Martha S. Hammond, in 1818. Lucy, born March 8, 1791, married Geo. Galusha, in 1810, and had eleven children, Sophia Adaline, born April 15, 1797, married Seneca Wood, of Aurora, N. Y., in 1816, and had two children. Charlotte Maria, born June 9, 1803, married Sherman Smith, of Aurora, N. Y., in 1825, where they now reside, and have three children.

431. ZERUIAH, born Sept. 29, 1757, married David Cole, of Kingsbury, N. Y. Her name is, as above, on the Norwich record, though the family have it Jerusha.

432. SAMUEL, born June 3, 1759. He was a physician in Greensboro, Vt., and married, Jan. 24, 1780, Bethiah Dogget. He died Dec. 7, 1823. The following statement is made by his grand-daughter, Mrs. Hatch. (1991) in a letter to Dr. Joshua, in 1851. "With high reputation as a physician and surgeon, which he retained to the close of his life, he removed to Shaftesbury, Vt., and subsequently to Greensboro. He was a surgeon in the army during the last war. He was also a custom-house officer in 1812."

433. ELIZABETH appears on the family record, as dying in infancy, though not on the town records, with the rest of the family.

434. JOHN, born Oct. 8, 1763, married Olive Clark, and was a merchant in Middlebury, Vt. He died in Shaftesbury, in 1840.

435. HENRY, born Sept. 23, 1765, married twice; first, Chloe Stanley, and second, widow Peggy Brown. He was a farmer in Shaftesbury, where he died, Aug. 19, 1846.

436. ELIZABETH, born May 28, 1767, married Simon Bottom, of Shaftesbury, Vt. Two of her sons were, Col. Lemuel, and Judge Nathan Huntington Bottom (1077). She died in March, 1848.

437. EUNICE, born Feb. 12, 1769, married the Hon. Timothy Stanley, of Greensboro, Vt. She had eleven children, all of whom died before her death, excepting her daughter Mary, Mrs. Asa H. Billings, of Rochester, N. Y., at

whose house she died, in Nov. 1850. "She was remarkable for her intelligence and great mental capacity."

161. AMOS. Shaftesbury, Vt.

438. AMOS, born Aug. 21, 1768, married Pamelia Hurd, March 9, 1794. He was many years a magistrate in his native town, and a member of the Baptist church. He died Sept. 24, 1818.

439. LYDIA, born May 16, 1770, and married, June 17, 1790, Russel Loomis, who was born in Litchfield, Conn., Aug. 30, 1764. She died April 3, 1835, and he died Feb. 22, 1842. Their children were: Lydia, born March 18, 1791, married, in 1809, Truman Galusha, grandson of Lydia, (156) and lives in Jericho, Vt.; Asa, born Nov. 3, 1793, married Oct. 16, 1816, Clarissa, daughter of Gen. Samuel Cross, and lives in Shaftesbury; Julia, born Oct. 23, 1796, and died in 1816; Daniel, born Oct. 29, 1798, married, 1822, Eliza Beach, and lived in Bennington, Vt., where he died in 1833; Russel, born Aug. 3, 1801, married Mary W., daughter of Stephen Avery, and lives in Saratoga, N. Y.; Warren, born July 9, 1806; and Alfred, born Oct. 11, 1810. There are eleven grand children in this family.

440. MATTHEW, born June 1, 1772, married, May 12, 1793, Mary Catlin, and resided in Rome, N. Y., where he died, Jan. 11, 1857. He was a farmer.

441. ELIAS, born in Shaftesbury, Vt., Oct. 31, 1774, married, Jan. 4, 1798, Aurelia Galusha, daughter of Jacob (119). He was a prosperous farmer in Shaftesbury, Vt., where he died Sept. 8, 1854. His widow died April 30, 1862, aged 84 years.

442. DANIEL, born Nov. 8, 1776, married for his first wife, Clarissa, daughter of Gov. Jonas Galusha of Vt. She died May 26, 1823, and he married for his second wife, Jan. 2, 1825, Mrs. Laura A. Goddard. For about forty years he practiced medicine in Shaftesbury, Vt., when he removed to Perry, N. Y., where he died May 15, 1862.

443. ASA, born in 1780, and died in 1788.

444. PEACE, born in 1782, and died in 1785.

177. SOLOMON. Hebron, Conn.

This family were all born in Hebron.

445. CIVIL, born in 1765, married Caleb Gillet of Colchester in 1790, and died in 1811. They had children.

446. DIMIS, born in 1767, married Samuel (658) of East Haddam.

447. MARY, born in 1769, married Benjamin Bissel of St. Johnsbury, Vt., where she died March 13, 1813.

448. SOLOMON, born in 1771, married, in 1797, Betsey Fowler and lived in East Haddam, and in Lenox, N. Y., and from 1837 in Milan, Ohio, where he died June 5, 1848.

449. JOHN, born in 1775, married Eleanor Townsend and lived in Syracuse, N. Y. He died Aug. 24, 1825.

SIXTH GENERATION. 151

450. OZIAS, born in 1777. He lived in Norwich, Conn., where he died July 20, 1810, having never married.

451. RALPH, born in 1779, married, 1806, Ruth Horr. He is now living in Memphis, Mich., in the practice of medicine. He was a deacon of the Baptist church. He received his medical diploma from the Black River Medical Society.

452. PHILOXENA, born in 1781, married Heman Phelps, a farmer of Syracuse, N. Y. in 1799, and died June 19, 1829.

453. JARED, born Dec. 22, 1784, married, Nov. 6, 1808, Elvira Bliss of Columbia, who was born 1782. After her death in 1809 in East Haddam, he married in 1818, Martha Draper. They live in Owego, N. Y., to which place he went in 1813.

454. LAURA, born in 1786, married, April 1817, William Silliman (657) of East Haddam, and died May 2, 1826.

178. ANDREW, DEACON. Griswold, Conn.

This family were all born in Griswold, Connecticut.

455. LUCY, born June 7, 1765, married Nov. 10, 1785, and died in Oct. 1848.

456. ANDREW, born Nov. 23, 1766. He studied medicine and was a practicing physician in Ashford, Conn., Westford Society. He married, Feb. 3, 1790, Zerviah B. Smith, who was born Oct 15, 1772. He died in Ashford, Feb. 1, 1837, and his wife, May 13, 1837. He was a man of some distinction in his profession.

457. JOHN, born Jan. 16, 1769, and died Dec. 21, 1772.

458. ENOCH, born June 4, 1771, and died Dec. 28, 1775.

459. JOHN, born June 22, 1773, and died, unmarried, Nov 3, 1805.

460. DANIEL, born Oct. 20, 1775, married, April 24, 1800, Elizabeth Lord. A substantial farmer in his native town. He was appointed deacon in the Congregational church, April 5, 1821, and has been often honored by his fellow citizens with testimonials of their confidence. He is now living, 1862, in Groton with his son Simon.

461. BETSEY, born Dec. 19, 1777, married, Jan. 18, 1815, John Prentice. After his death she married, Feb. 1, 1832. Since the death of her second husband, whose name I have been unable to get, she has lived with Andrew Prentice of Gilead, Conn., a son by her first husband.

462. ELISHA, born July 30, 1780, and died April 7, 1784.

179. EZRA. Franklin, Conn.

This family were all born in Norwich, where their births are recorded.

463. CHARLES, born Nov. 5, 1767, and died July 25, 1775.

464. ASHER, born Feb. 25, 1770. Studied medicine with Dr. Philemon Tracy of Norwich, and commenced the practice of his profession in Preston, Conn. He married Lucy Andrus and removed to Chenango, N. Y., where he died in 1833.

465. JOEL, born March 2, 1772, married, July 26, 1801, Mary S. Bingham,

who died; after which he married, July 1, 1813, Laura Cheeney. He lived in Manlius, N. Y., and died there Dec. 21, 1850.

466. SILAS, born Nov. 13, 1774, and died Feb. 21, 1799.

467. CHARLES, who died July 25, 1775.

468. ABEL, born Feb. 21, 1777. Pursued his medical studies with Dr. Philemon Tracy of Norwich, and received his diploma from the Connecticut Medical Convention, in April, 1797, which down to the present time he has abundantly honored. In May, 1797, he went to East Hampton, L. I., and entered upon the successful practice of his profession, in which he soon achieved most honorable distinction. In addition to a good medical reputation, he secured also reputation for qualities which fitted him for public service in civil life; and was called, for a while, from his professional career, for the more noisy and stirring duties of political life. In 1820 he was appointed by the legislature of New York a member of the Electoral College, in which he gave his vote for James Monroe. In 1821 he was elected a member of the New York senate. In 1833-7 he was a representative in the United States congress, from the first congressional district of New York, and through both the twenty-third and twenty-fourth congresses he both by vote and speech showed himself to be a consistent democrat of the Jackson school. In 1845 he was appointed by President Polk, collector of customs for the port of Sag Harbor, and served through the term for which he was appointed. In 1846 he was a member of the convention for revising the constitution of the State of New York. In 1853 the Regents of the New York University conferred on him the honorary degree of M. D. Among the venerable forms present at our pleasant family meeting in Norwich in 1857, none was more so than that of this hale and still youthfully humorous and much beloved and honored man. "Late may he ascend to heaven."

He married, in Norwich, Frances Lee, daughter of George Lee of Norwich. Since the above was written, Dr. Huntington has deceased. He died in East Hampton, May 18, 1858, after a three week's illness. His departure was in perfect peace.

469. CHARLES, born Sept. 15, 1779, married, Aug. 3, 1810, Margaret Hyde. She was born July 8, 1783, and was daughter of Abel and Margaret (Tracy) Hyde. She died March 10, 1830, in Columbus, N. Y., where the family were residing on a farm. He removed to Chittenango, N. Y., where he died. The following obituary notice of this good man is taken from the New York Observer of Feb. 3, 1859.

"In Chittenango, Jan. 20th, in the 80th year of his age, Elder Charles Huntington.

"Mr. Huntington was born in Norwich, Conn., and emigrated to Sullivan, Madison county, in the year 1822, where he has continued to reside, with the exception of a few years spent in Chenango County.

"For many years he has professed faith in Christ, and for several years past he has been an efficient and useful elder in the R. D. church in Chittenango. Uniformly consistent as a Christian, and ever having the welfare of

Zion at heart, his influence in the church and community was eminently happy. Remarkably unselfish and kind in all his intercourse with his fellow men, he enjoyed, in a large degree, their confidence and friendship.

"The last sickness and death of Mr. Huntington was characterized by a peaceful trust in Christ—a fitting end to a consistent Christian life."

470. BETSEY, born Nov. 17, 1781, married Wheelock Bingham.

471. ANNE, born May 9, 1784.

472. DAVID, born April 24, 1788, graduated at Union College in 1808. He studied theology and was ordained deacon of the Protestant Episcopal church, by the Rt. Rev. Bishop Hobart, in Trinity church, New York city, in 1812; and in 1815 was ordained priest in St. Paul's church, Charlton, N. Y. He married for his first wife, Ann Dows of Charlton, N. Y., in 1813. His second wife whom he married in Charlton, also, was Catherine Callegan; and he married for his third wife, Lydia Blakslee Allen of Harpersville, N. Y., who still survives in Harpersville.

He was a devoted Episcopalian, classing himself neither with the technical High church nor Low church party, maintaining that they who went beyond, or fell below the plain, simple doctrine of the church, were equally erroneous. They who knew him, are ready to bear testimony to his efficiency as a minister of the gospel, and to his virtues as a citizen and man. His family can attest his tenderness as a parent, and his great private and personal worth. "In every relation of life he maintained himself without reproach. At times, tried above measure by the cares of the world, and adversities which he could not control, he still preserved his Christian integrity and faith to the end, and ever labored to discharge his duty to the flock of which he was minister." For several years he resided in Harpersville without parochial charge, yet ministering in the name of Christ as he had calls among the neighboring parishes. His former parishioners have fittingly testified their regards for him in the monument they placed to his memory, bearing the noble tribute : "He watched for our souls, as one that must give account." He died in Harpersville, April 9, 1855.

180. THOMAS. M. D.   Ashford and Canaan.

This family were all born in Ashford, Connecticut.

473. THOMAS, born Sept. 29, 1773, graduated at Williamstown College, 1798. He entered on the legal profession in Hartford, Conn., where he married Mary Newport Burbridge, who was born in Hartford, June 15, 1783. He spent the latter part of his life in editing and adapting to American practice, several standard English law works. He died Nov. 9, 1833.

474. MARY, born Oct. 17, 1776, married, Feb. 7, 1820, Alvan Rose, a carriage maker in Geneva, New York.

475. ERASTUS, born Jan. 8, 1779. He was a merchant and died single in Havana, Sept. 17, 1807.

476. MATILDA, born Dec. 29, 1780, married, June 14, 1803, Salmon Pease of Canaan, and removed in the autumn of 1826 to Charlotte, Vt., where Mr.

Pease died July 23, 1857. She is now living with her son, P. E., in Charlotte, Vt. She has had ten children, all born in Canaan, Conn., as follows: Frederick Salmon, born May 21, 1804, married Julia Lawrence Sept. 18, 1832, and is bookkeeper in the Commercial Bank, Albany; Calvin died young; Erastus Huntington, born Sept. 10, 1807, married Lydia B. Fry of Albany in 1837, and was a paper manufacturer at Balston and Little Falls, residing (1862) in Brooklyn, N. Y; Aaron Gaylord, born Feb. 22, 1811, married Anne Page. He is a graduate of the University of Vermont, and was for years a Congregational minister in Norwich, Vt; Calvin, born Aug. 12, 1813, married Martha, daughter of Judge Howes of Montpelier, Vt., May 11, 1843; he graduated at the University of Vermont in 1838; professor of Latin and Greek languages in 1842, and in 1855 elected president of the University, but is now, 1862, pastor of the first Presbyterian church in Rochester, N. Y.; Thomas Huntington, born Oct. 24, 1815, married first, Catherine Nadine, daughter of Abraham Coon, of Brooklyn, N. Y., April 16, 1838, second, Elizabeth Graham of New York, April 17, 1848, and third, Eliza Morris of Bethel, Vt., June 2, 1851; for the last twenty years he has been a bookseller in New Haven, Conn.; Peter Edward, born May 11, 1818, married Cordelia Rich of Charlotte, Vt., June 14, 1841, where he is a farmer; Mary Matilda, born Aug. 22, 1820, married George, son of Gen. John Francis of Royalton, Vt., and is a merchant in Mattoon; Reuben Owen, born Aug. 23, 1823, and died Jan. 27, 1848; Roscius Milton, born March 7, 1825, and died in the fall of 1844.

This family had a very pleasant family meeting at the residence of Gen. Francis, in Bethel, Vt., June 2, 1851, on the occasion of the third marriage of Thomas Huntington Pease, from the records of which the above minutes have been mainly made.

477. CLARISSA, born June 17, 1784, and resides in Charlotte, Vt., with her sister, Mrs. Pease.

478. HORACE, born July 8, 1786, married Chloe Franklin, who was born in Canaan, Feb. 15, 1793, and died Feb. 23, 1843. He was a farmer in Canaan, Conn., where he died March 13, 1846.

479. MILES, born April 29, 1789, and died May 1, 1790, in Ashford.

480. OWEN, born May 15, 1792, married Eunice, daughter of Thomas Day of Canaan. He was an iron manufacturer. He died Nov. 21, 1849, in California. His widow is living (1858) in Birmingham, Conn., with his daughters.

181. WILLIAM. Hampton, Conn.

The only record of this family which I have been able to find is that of the births of the first two children, on the Windham records. An epidemic swept off four of the family in the same winter.

481. WILLIAM, born Dec. 6, 1770, and died in 1791.

482. MARY, born Feb. 10, 1772, married Samuel Fuller, jr., in 1799, and died in 1814.

483. EUNICE, born 1774, married Dr. R. Leonard of Ashford, Connecticut.

484. SARAH, born 1776, and died in 1790.

485. CLARISSA, born 1778, and died in 1790.
486. CALEB, born 1780, and died in 1790.
487. ALISTHENA, born 1783.
488. ELISHA, born 1784, and died in 1790.

182. DEACON CALEB. Norwich, Conn.

This family were all born in Norwich, and died in infancy.
489. A DAUGHTER, died Sept. 7, 1790.
490 and 491. A SON and DAUGHTER, died June 17, 1797.
492. A DAUGHTER, died May 12, 1798.

185. JEREMIAH. Shaftesbury, Vt.

493. JEREMIAH, born in 1781, married Lydia Wait, and resided in Onondaga, N. Y. He died in 1856.
494. LEVI, born 1784, married Lucy Mosher, and lived in Onondaga Hollow, N. Y.
495. BENJAMIN, born 1786, married, in 1811, Susan Smith, and is a farmer in Springfield, N. Y. His wife was born in 1791.
496. SARAH, born in 1790, married Stephen Niles. They lived in Cambridge, N. Y., where she died in 1827.
497. ASA, born 1792, and married, widow Newton. He lived at one time in Rochester, N. Y., and died by his own hand, in Pittsford, N. Y., Aug. 19, 1857.

186. ASA. Cannan, Conn.

498. FANNY, died in Thornton, N. H., unmarried.
499. JONAS, married Polly Blodget, and resides in Chelsea, Vt.
500. MARY, born May 30, 1785, married Feb. 1, 1807, David, son of the Rev. Noah Worcester, (191) of Thornton, N. H. She lived in Brighton, Mass., where she died, Nov. 27, 1815.

188. ELIAS. Lebanon, N. H.

501. ELIAS, born July 18, 1797, married Lucinda Putnam, Feb. 18, 1818. He resided in Lebanon, N. H., and died, Feb. 6, 1825. He and his wife were both members of the Congregational church.
502. MARY, born 1799, married Daniel Richardson, and lived in Lebanon, N. H., where she died, April 4, 1830. She lived on the old homestead, purchased by her grandfather, in Lebanon. Her children were: Daniel Augustus, who is married, and lives in Lebanon; Mary Huntington, married Daniel Hinckley, of Lebanon; Elias Huntington, a graduate of Dartmouth College, 1850, and of the Andover Theological School, 1853; married a Miss Stevens, and is the pastor of the First Congregational church in Dover, N. H. Two others of her children died in infancy.

190. ANDREW. Pittsford, N. Y.

503. ANDREW, born May 8, 1789, was a physician, at Pittsford, N. Y., where he had been in practice since 1816. He married for his first wife, Lydia Munroe, of Shaftesbury, Vt. where he entered upon the practice of his profession in company with Dr. Daniel (299). She died March 31, 1838, in Pittsford, N. Y. He married, for his second wife, Sarah Upjohn, an English lady, and for his third wife, widow Tooker, of Pittsford. He died in Pittsford, March 12, 1861. He received his medical education at Dartmouth College, and became wealthy from his practice.

504. ASA, born Nov. 12, 1791. He resides in Hanover, N. H., and is a farmer. He has been employed considerably in public life, having been a member of the state legislature. He married for his first wife, in Feb. 1816, Achsah, daughter of deacon Samuel Slade, who died Feb. 2, 1834. He married for his second wife, March 17, 1836, widow Mary Redington, of Lebanon, N. H., and daughter of Hon. Stephen Maine, of Hartland, Vt. She was born Nov. 28, 1794.

505. SAMUEL, born May 16, 1794, married Nov. 11, 1817, Eunice Slade, sister of Asa's wife, of Hanover, where he died, Jan. 17, 1825.

506. LYDIA, born Nov. 16, 1796, married, Sept. 6, 1824, Barzillai Bush, M. D., who was a practicing physician, of Brockport, N. Y. She died May 5, 1833.

192. HEZEKIAH. Hanover and Haverhill, N. H.

507. FANNY, married Hosea S. Baker, a farmer, of Haverhill.
508. ESTHER, married Ezra Niles, a farmer, of Haverhill.

196. THOMAS. Fort Miller, N. Y.

509. JAMES.

197. CHRISTOPHER. Roxbury, Vt.

This family were all born in Mansfield, Conn.

510. CHRISTOPHER, born Nov. 11, 1761. He married, in 1787, in Vermont, Eunice Chadwick, and was a blacksmith, in Randolph, of that state. He moved to Covington, Tioga county, Penn. about 1816.

511. ELIJAH, born Aug. 21, 1763. He married, for his first wife, 1792, Sally Field, of Tunbridge, Vt., who lived but about a year after the marriage, leaving one son. He married, for his second wife, June, 1801, Lydia Parmlee, born in Newtown, Ct., Aug. 6, 1779, a most estimable Christian lady, who died May 27, 1851, aged 71 years. He was a soldier, during the revolution, but a providential accident, **as his mother** read it, hindered his entering the field as early as his eager patriotism would lead him to do so. **He had enlisted and was, as he supposed, all ready to start for the scene of strife on the following day. But, in the afternoon,** while using his axe, an ill-timed blow struck his foot and disabled him, to his mother's gratitude, for several months. Yet on his recovery he entered the army, and was in **service nearly three years.** On

becoming pious, his Christian zeal, which was habitually ardent and strong, moved him to enter the ministry. He accordingly commenced preaching, and for more than twenty-eight years before his death, he was the useful and much-beloved pastor of the Baptist church in Braintree, Vt., where he died, among the bereaved people of his ministry, June 24, 1828.

512. JEDIDIAH, born Aug. 9, 1765, married in 1794, Sarah Richardson. He moved, early, to Compton, Canada East, where he lived twenty-five years, and then removed to Brighton, N. Y. He was a farmer, and a genial and kind hearted man. He died Feb. 25, 1852, at the residence of his son, H. J., in Brighton, N. Y.

513. THOMAS, born June 10, 1767, married, Sept. 1795, Submit (728). He moved to Compton, C. E., in the spring of 1802, where he lived respected, and died of spotted fever, being sick only thirty-six hours, May 6, 1811.

514. PEREZ, born June 26, 1769, married, Sept. 1802, Abigail Hatch, of Mansfield, Conn. He died in Sept. 1831, in Compton, C. E., where he had been engaged in farming. His widow died in Lowell, Mass., July 19, 1847.

515. BENJAMIN, born July 5, 1771, married in Roxbury, Vt., April 30, 1801, Catharine Gustin, who was born April 12, 1779, in Harlow, N. H., and died Aug. 6, 1854, in Compton, C. E., where he also died, Feb. 25, 1841.

516. MARY, born Nov. 21, 1774, married, about the year 1812, Japhet LeBaron, of Hatley, C. E., where she died July 6, 1850, leaving two sons, Elijah Huntington, and Japhet. They are both living in Hatley, and are respectable citizens.

517. LYDIA, a twin with Mary, died of consumption, in June, 1792, in Roxbury, Vt.

518. GIDEON, born April 25, 1777, married for his first wife, widow Day, and for his second wife, June 16, 1815, in Compton, Cornelia, daughter of Samuel Bliss, of Connecticut, who moved to Stratford, Vt. She was born in 1781, and died June 12, 1859. He resides in Pompanoosuc, Vt., and is a farmer.

519. MEHETABEL, born May 28, 1780, and died of consumption, in Jan. 1816, in Compton, C. E., having never married.

198. SAMUEL. Mansfield.

The births of the first four of this family are found on the Mansfield records.

520. ELIPHALET, born May 6, 1753, and married, in 1774, Eleanor Bugbee.

521. ROSWELL, born Dec. 28, 1754, and married, Oct. 29, 1777, in Windham, Sarah Read. After his death, his widow married Samuel Spencer, by whom she had several children.

522. EUNICE, born Dec. 26, 1756, and married a Hebard, of Windham.

523. JOHN, born Oct. 21, 1759.

524. OLIVE, born June 27, 1767.

525. SAMUEL, born Aug. 9, 1769.

199. ELEAZER. Mansfield, Conn.

All of this family were born in Mansfield, where their births are on record.

526. PHEBE, born Nov. 2, 1758. She died unmarried in Vermont, in 1850.

527. ELEAZER, born March 17, 1760. He and his sister Phebe were baptized Aug. 16, 1761. He was drowned accidentally, June 18, 1762.

528. DEBORAH, born Sept. 3, 1763, and baptized Oct. 16. She married, Nov. 15, 1781, Azariah Balcom. Their dismission from the South Mansfield church took place Sept. 8, 1783, when they removed to Windham.

529. ELEAZER, born Feb. 2, 1766, and baptized April 12. He married, Sept. 20, 1789, Sarah, daughter of Thomas Davis, who died July 17, 1792. He married, Jan. 15, 1798, Phebe Palmer. He was a farmer and miller in Windham.

530. ASENATH, born Oct. 31, 1767, baptized Feb. 13, 1768. She married Zebediah Tracy, of Windham, and died in 1851, at the residence of her son, John Tracy, of Willimantic.

531. SHUBAEL, born Aug. 11, 1770, and baptized Oct. 14. He married, Nov. 16, 1794, Patience Thatcher, in Columbia, Conn., who was born in 1767. He lived in New Boston, and Woodstock, Conn., and died in March, 1835. His wife died in Aug., 1851.

532. LYDIA, born Aug. 25, 1772. She lived in Vermont, and never married.

533. ZERVIAH, born March 15, 1774, baptized June 5. She married Benjamin Jones. She united with the Windham church in 1801. In the printed catalogue, her husband's name is written Janes.

534. ELIZABETH, born June 16, 1776, and died Sept. 22, 1793.

535. EBENEZER, born Nov. 22, 1780. He married, Sept. 10, 1810, Lydia Peck. She was born in Franklin July 21, 1786. He went in 1811 to Acton, Vt., now Townshend, where he engaged in farming, a business which he pursued down to the commencement of the present year (1857). He was town clerk, in Townshend, eleven years, and for forty-one years a justice of the peace. He represented the town in the state legislature three years, and for the same length of time, was associate judge of the Windham county court, having been admitted to the bar in that county in 1837. His wife died June 12, 1857, and since that time he has been with his children in Western New York.

207. JOHN. Tolland, Conn.

This family were all born in Tolland.

536. JOHN, born May 11, 1749, and married in 1783, Rebecca Newell, who died in Ellington, Conn. He was a farmer, and lived for several years in Mexico, N. Y., where he died. He was engaged in the war of the revolution. His widow is reported on the pension list of 1840, as then living, at the age of 79, in Stafford, Conn.

537. THANKFUL, born July 23, 1750, and died Oct. 29, 1750.

538. MEHETABEL, born Jan. 24, 1752, married Hezekiah Betts, and went into Upper Canada, where she died in 1829.

SIXTH GENERATION.   159

539 and 540. TWIN DAUGHTERS, born Nov. 15. 1753, who died on the day of their birth.

541. ELISHA, born Dec. 17, 1754, married, in 1785, Esther Ladd, and went from Tolland to Watertown, N. Y., in 1811; to Mexico in 1814, and to Rotterdam on Oneida Lake in 1836, where he died. Sept. 25, 1838. His first wife died Dec. 19, 1816, of consumption, aged 52 years. He was living with his second wife at the time of his death. She was a widow Wells, her maiden name being Sarah Marsden. He was a farmer.

542. WILLIAM, born Sept. 19, 1757, married, Feb. 13, 1783, Prescendia Lathrop, and was one of the first settlers in the Black River valley, in Northern New York. He resided at Watertown. He married for his second wife, Dec. 2, 1810, Elvira Dresser. His first wife was born in Tolland, Jan. 30, 1761, and died March 20, 1810. He died May 11, 1842. The following is an obituary notice found in one of the Watertown papers. "At his residence, on the 11th inst., William Huntington, in the 85th year of his age. Mr. Huntington was one of our oldest and most respected inhabitants. He was a native of Tolland, Conn., and for three or four years served in the army of the revolution. In the year 1784 he emigrated to New Hampshire, where he resided till the winter of 1804, when he removed to Watertown. He was for many years a member, and an officer of the Presbyterian church, and in the last years of his protracted life it was evident to his friends that the absorbing subject of his contemplation, was his departure from this world; and he cheerfully expressed a readiness to go whenever God in his goodness should see fit to summon him away. He gave pleasing evidence that he was waiting and watching for the coming of the Lord; so that the large circle of his relatives and friends are not left to mourn without hope, but rather to rejoice in the hope and belief that he was numbered among the children of God by adoption."

543. HEZEKIAH, born Dec. 30, 1759. He studied law with Gideon Granger, of Suffield, and with John Trumbull, afterward judge of the superior court, and was admitted to the bar at Hartford, in 1789. He established himself in the practice of law at Suffield, in 1790, and soon attained eminence in his profession. In 1806 he was appointed, by Jefferson, attorney for Connecticut, and held this office until 1829. While residing in Suffield he represented this town in the general assembly of the state, in several sessions of the legislature, from May, 1802, to Oct. 1805. In 1801 he had been appointed one of the commissioners under the bankrupt law of the United States, and held the office about two years. In 1813 he removed to Hartford, where he continued to reside until his death, which occurred in Middletown. Conn., May 27, 1842. Mr. Huntington was marked for his great affability, which made him deservedly popular. He married, while in Suffield, Oct. 5, 1788, Susan Kent, who was born. Sept. 29, 1768. For the most of the above facts, the author is indebted to a brief sketch, by Thomas Day. Esq., in the thirteenth volume Connecticut reports.

544. DEBORAH, born Nov. 21, 1762, married Gamaliel Kent, a brother of her brother Hezekiah's wife.

545. SAMUEL, born March 23, 1765, married, 1787, Sally Howard, of Coventry. He was a blacksmith. This Samuel, I presume was a private at Fort Trumbull in 1813, in Capt. Blanchard's company from Windsor.

546. ABIGAIL, born March 29, 1767, married Dr. H. Farnsworth, of Ohio. They lived in Windsor. She died March 11, 1805.

547. RUTH, born May 12, 1769, married Abraham Malvesey. They became Shakers and went to Enfield. She died Jan. 31, 1833.

548. THANKFUL, born Oct. 3, 1771, and married Jonathan Hartshorn, of Hartford, Connecticut.

549. MARA, born Oct. 27, 1774, and died Aug. 3, 1777.

209. SAMUEL. Tolland, Conn.

550. THANKFUL, married an Olmstead, of East Hartford.

214. SIMON, REV. Norwich, Conn.

551. SAMUEL, born Nov. 15, 1751, married Dec. 19, 1782, Philura Tracy, daughter of (215). He was a farmer in Norwich, where he and his wife were received into the church in 1793. He died in Norwich, June 23, 1812, and his wife, Aug. 30, 1816.

552. HANNAH, born April 28, 1753, married, in 1779, Rev. Eliphalet Lyman, who was born in Lebanon, March 5, 1754, was pastor of the Congregational church in Woodstock from 1780 to 1825, and who died Feb. 2, 1836, aged eighty-two years. She was a woman of unusual brilliancy of intellect, and retained her mental faculties remarkably in her advanced years. She died suddenly in Woodstock, April 19, 1836. Her children were Eliphalet, Daniel, Asa, Joseph, Hannah and Mary.

553. ROGER, born Dec. 7, 1759. He was a young man of promise and a student of medicine. He died single, Sept. 7, 1789, from a wound inflicted upon his limb by the point of a penknife, while attempting to kill a fly. Having "lived beloved," he "died lamented."

554. DANIEL, born March 8, 1762, married, Jan. 18, 1787, Polly Edgerton, who died June 5, 1811, aged fifty-three years. He died Dec. 3, 1805.

555. EBENEZER, born Aug. 26, 1764, married, in Lebanon, Sept. 25, 1806, Eunice (759). He was a farmer residing on Bean Hill, Norwich, where he died Feb. 27, 1853.

556. ERASTUS, born Dec. 7, 1769, married for his first wife, March 20, 1806, Nabby, daughter of Ariel Hyde, who was born Nov. 12, 1786, and died July 1, 1811. He married for his second wife, April 13, 1815, Sarah, daughter of Gen. Joseph Williams, of Norwich, who is still living. He graduated at Yale in 1791, and entered the legal profession, which he soon abandoned for manufacturing and trade. He resided on Bean Hill, Norwich, where he died, Feb. 10, 1846.

SIXTH GENERATION.

217. JABEZ, Gen.   Norwich, Conn.

The following sketch of **Gen.** Jedidiah, is contributed by a grandson of the subject, **Rev. Geo.** Richards, of Litchfield, Conn.

557. JEDIDIAH, born Aug. 4, 1743, "was graduated at Harvard College in 1763, with distinguished honor. The social rank of his family is evinced by the order of his name on the college catalogue, it being the second on the list of his class, above that of Josiah Quincy. The Master's degree was also conferred on him by Yale College in 1770. After the close of his academic course, he engaged with his father in commercial pursuits, and, with the approach of the struggle for independence, became noted as a Son of Liberty, and an active captain of the militia. Promoted to the command of a regiment, he joined the army at Cambridge, April 26, 1775, just a week after the battle of Lexington. His regiment was part of the force detailed for occupying Dorchester heights; and, after the evacuation of Boston by the British, marched with the army to New York. He entertained the commander-in chief, on the way, at Norwich. During the year 1776, he was at New York, Kingsbridge, Northcastle, Sidmun's bridge, and other posts. In April of that year, he helped repulse the British at Danbury, Conn., assailing the enemy's rear, and effecting a junction with his fellow townsman, Arnold. In March, 1777, Roger Sherman writes that Col. Huntington was recommended by Gen. Washington as a fit person for brigadier, but that Connecticut had more than her share. On May 12 of that year, he was promoted to that rank, as Mr. Sherman states, " at Gen. Washington's request." In July, he joined Gen. Putnam at Peekskill, with all the Continental troops which he could collect; whence, in September, he was ordered to join the main army near Philadelphia, where he remained at headquarters, at Worcester, Whippin, White Marsh, Gulph Hills, etc. In November, on the information of the enemy's movement upon Red Bank, he was detached with his brigade, among other troops, to its relief, but Cornwallis had anticipated them. Having shared the hardships of his companions in arms at Valley Forge, through the winter of 1777-8, he, together with Col. Wigglesworth, was, in March, appointed by the Commander in Chief, " to aid Gen. McDougall in inquiring into the loss of forts Montgomery and Clinton, in the State of New York; and into the conduct of the principal officers commanding those posts." In May, he was ordered with his brigade to the North River, and was stationed, successively, at Camp Reading, Highlands, Neilson's Point, Springfield, Shorthills, Totowa, Peekskill, West Point, etc. In July, he was a member of the court martial which tried Gen. Charles Lee for misconduct in the battle of Monmouth; and in September he sat upon the court of inquiry to whom was referred the case of Major Andre. In December of 1780, his was the only Connecticut Brigade that remained in the service. On the 10th of May, 1783, at a meeting of officers, he was appointed one of a committee of four to draft a plan of organization, which resulted in their reporting, on the 13th, the Constitution of the Society of Cincinnati. On the 24th of June, Washington writes that the army was " reduced to a competent garrison for West Point; Patterson, Hun-

tington, and Greaton being the only brigadiers now left with it, besides the adjutant general." At the close of the war he received the brevet rank of major general.

On retiring from the army he resumed business in his native town, and was successively chosen sheriff of the county, treasurer of the state, and delegate to the state convention which adopted the Constitution of the United States. In 1789, he was appointed by President Washington collector of the customs at New London, then the port of entry for eastern Connecticut and Connecticut river, which office he retained under four administrations, and resigned shortly before his death. He died in New London, Sept. 25, 1818, where his remains were first interred, though subsequently transferred to the family tomb at Norwich.

At the age of twenty-three, he made a public profession of religion, and was for many years, an officer and pillar of the church of which he was a member. "His munificence, for its profusion, its uniformity, its long continuance, and for the discretion by which it was directed," was pronounced, "without an example, or a parallel, in his native state."

His first wife was Faith, daughter of Gov. Trumbull. She died at Dedham, Mass., in December of 1775, on her way to the camp. Two of her brothers, one of them the distinguished painter, were associated with her husband in the war, of which her father was one of the main supports. She left a son.

His second wife was Ann, daughter of Thomas Moore, who was born in New York, received his education at Westminster school, London, engaged in commercial pursuits in his native city, at the approach of the Revolution retired with his family to West Point, and, driven thence by violence, returned to the city, where he occupied a place in the custom house through the war. He died at the house of his daughter, in Norwich. Her brother was the late venerable Bishop Moore, of Virginia. Her uncle Stephen was the proprietor of the spot now occupied by our national military academy, which Gen. Huntington advised should be established there. She survived her husband, and was the mother of seven children.

558. ANDREW, born June 21-2, 1745, married, Nov. 26, 1766, Lucy, daughter of Dr. Joseph and Lydia (Lathrop) Coit, of New London, who was born July 2, 1746, and died May 9, 1776. Of her, his brother Jedidiah, in a letter dated Camp at New York, May 21, 1776, thus speaks: "The death of our sister Lucy, has made one more breach in our late happy family, though it ought to check our grief, that she left such good evidences of her interest in a better world." He married for his second wife, May 1, 1777, Hannah Phelps, of Stonington, who was born Dec. 16, 1760. He and his first wife united with the first Congregational church of Norwich in 1775, and eminently honored their Christian profession. His second wife, who lived until July 30, 1838, was a noble woman in all personal and social qualities. Mrs. Sigourney says of her, "she possessed an elegance of form and address, which would have been conspicuous at any foreign court. She was especially fascinating to the children who visited her, by her liberal presentations of cake and other

pleasant eatables, or, what was to some equally alluring, a readiness to lend fine books with pictures."

Of Mr. Huntington the same authority says: he "was a man of plain manners and incorruptible integrity. His few words were always those of good sense and truth, and the weight of his influence given to the best interests of society." He was engaged in commercial pursuits, and in 1793 embarked in the manufacture of paper at the Falls in Norwich. He was a judge of probate in his district, as late as 1813. During the war of the revolution he was a commissary of brigade, and was untiring in his exertions to secure prompt supplies for the army. Upon his services, Gov. Trumbull put great reliance, and it is on record that such reliance was not misplaced. He died April 7, 1824.

559. JOSHUA, born Aug. 16, 1751, married, Dec. 11, 1771, Hannah (175) and commenced business with his father. But at the summons of the revolution, he threw himself with all the ardor of a young patriot into the cause of his country. The battle of Lexington roused the martial spirit of the Norwich boys, and a hundred of them hastened, under command of Joshua, then lieutenant, to the scene of action and were annexed to Putnam's brigade. Under date of June 22, 1775, "Prospect Hill in Cambridge," he thus writes to his father: "I am now encamped on Prospect Hill, about one mile from Charlestown ferry. We have entrenched so strong that 'tis thought we shall be able to keep our ground. We have been fired at a number of times from the ships and floating batteries, but they were not able to reach us. Several men have been killed since Monday last, by guns going off accidentally, although the officers take all possible care to prevent it. We have two men in our company wounded in the battle, but not mortally. We lost none. I received your letters per Major Rodgers and brother Jed. Should have written you last week from Dedham, but came from there in the alarm on Saturday last as to the battle."

Another of his letters to his father, dated Cambridge, Sept. 18, 1775, shows the risks to which his business was exposed, while he was thus on duty. "As to the schooner had much rather have her chartered on low terms if Capt. Harris will risk her, than to let him have her on shares. Freight, I suppose, is much higher at this time than it commonly is, and suppose that Capt. Harris can well afford to give me half the freight she makes if I risk her; but I am willing you or brother Andrew should do with her as if she was your own. As to news, we have nothing remarkable at camp. It is a general time of health with the army. Though there are numbers sick, very few die. It is said to be very sickly in Boston, with the inhabitants as well as with the soldiers."

In another of his letters to his father, dated Cambridge, Sept. 25, 1775, he having been suggested as captain of that company which he had, as lieutenant, led to the army, he throws himself upon the advice of his father, assuring him that he shall be "entirely satisfied with your doing as you think will be of the most advantage for the good of the army in giving your advice in the matter."

A letter of his to his father, dated Cambridge, Nov. 22, 1775, shows how much he felt the claims of business and home upon him. "I have determined not to engage in the new army, as I am sensible my business calls me at home, and I know our business is such that I shall be of service to assist you. It is with much reluctance I shall leave the army, as I am offered as good a berth as I should expect. I can't say when I shall be at home, as the Connecticut troops are desired to stay the month of December. I am afraid our soldiers will not stay any longer than they first engaged for, so shall stay as long as our company will tarry and then return. As to news, we have nothing special at camp. We expect to entrench on Cobble Hill this night which, I expect, will distress our enemy."

That he did not leave the service, as both his business and his inclination would call him to do, is apparent from the following letters of still later date. That he was regarded as an officer of unusual merit at this early period of his connexion with the army, is abundantly evident from contemporaneous records. I find this allusion to his popularity, in a family letter of his brother, Jedidiah, dated at Providence, June 13, 1775: "I do not know what credit brother Joshua is in camp, but I find at this place and all along the road, he has got himself much honor, from the good order and regularity of his company. He is much spoken of for his good behavior."

After the evacuation of Boston by the British, the company of which he had command went with Putnam's brigade to New York.

A letter from him, dated Camp near King's Bridge, Sept. 20, 1776, shows his position at that period: "You have most likely heard of our retreat from the city, before this, but I will give you some of the particulars. Sunday morning last, our regiment, with a number of other regiments, were ordered to the lines a little below Turtle Bay, where lay five or six ships within musket shot of our lines. About six o'clock a most furious cannonade began from the ships. At the same time the enemy landed a large body of men a little above where our men were posted, and marched directly for the main road in order to cut off our retreat, which they had like to have effected, as the greatest part of our army were from six to fourteen miles distant from the city. In this skirmish we lost some men, though I think not many. I have been unwell about a fortnight, with a slow fever and the camp disorder, which prevented my being in the skirmish. I had not passed the road but a little while before the enemy came up; and if I had been with the regiment at the lines, I was so weak and feeble, I should, without doubt, have fallen into their hands. I have now left the regiment for a few days, and am with brother Chester, about sixteen miles from the city, getting better.

"The enemy made an attack last Monday on our people, 'tis said, with 2,500 men. Our men engaged them with spirit, and after an engagement of about an hour, the enemy retreated with great confusion. In the attack we lost fifteen or twenty men. As the enemy carried off the most of their dead, I cannot tell their loss. Our army are in very high spirits.

"I understand that our family are concerned in a privateer from New Londom. I told brother Andrew I should be glad to be concerned £100. Should be glad to know whether he has engaged any part for me or not. Brother Chester and Ebenezer are in usual health. I inclose you a letter for brother Joel."

From another letter, dated North Castle, Dec. 4, 1776, we still are able to follow his course, and to find him unwavering in it. "I received yours of Nov. 17th, since which our army have been constantly on the move. As to their present situation, it is impossible to give it to you. Brother Jed is stationed about fifty miles distant from me, in the Jerseys. Brother Chester and Ebenezer are at Peck Kilns, about thirty miles. They were all well a few days ago. There is a body of the enemy in the Jerseys, as far as Hackenback, the remainder, I believe, are on York Island. We have a flying report, that there is a fleet of the enemy lying at Frog's Point. If so, I think it likely they intend a visit to some part of New England. I hope the people will be spirited to oppose them, wherever they go. I wish to hear that our three month's men engage fast, as I am afraid our army will soon be very thin."

At a later period he was employed in securing shipping for the use of the war. In the fall of 1777 he had charge of the building of a frigate, at Gale's Ferry, for the service, and in July 8, 1779, he thus writes to Thomas Mumford, Groton. "I wish you to inform me if you know of a small privateer of eight or ten guns, to be sold at New London or elsewhere, as I want to purchase one of that size. If I should purchase I should be glad to have you concerned."

560. HANNAH, born July 3, 1753, and died Sept. 27, 1761.

561. EBENEZER, born Dec. 26, 1754, and graduated at Yale College in 1775, and, like his elder brothers, enlisted all his energies at once in the service of the revolution. He married, first, Dec. 10, 1791, Sarah Isham, of Colchester, who died in 1793. He married again, Oct. 7, 1795, Lucretia Mary McClellan, who died Nov. 5, 1819.

In the obituary notice which follows, notice is made of the refusal of the faculty of Yale College to grant him an honorable dismissal before the end of his senior year, to enable him to enter the army then about Boston. The following extract from a letter to his father, will explain the method by which he secured his diploma. Its date is, Roxbury Camp, Sept. 25, 1775. "I should be glad if you would get me a certificate from president Daggett that I am in regular standing in college, and likewise a recommendation, as I imagine I can have a degree without going to Commencement for it: as Dr. Langdon has given me encouragement that he will give me one if the New Haven President refuses it—if I am denied it, only because of my tarry from college this summer, and my leaving it without liberty, in the alarm last April."

The following obituary notice is taken from the Norwich Courier of June 25, 1834.

"When the battle of Lexington was fought, he was a student at Yale College. Young, ardent and ambitious, he made application to be discharged from his duties there, declaring at the same time his intention of commencing a military life. The Faculty having refused his petition, he left New Haven and joined a company of volunteers to march to Boston. Soon after he was appointed first lieutenant in a regiment of Connecticut troops commanded by Col. Samuel Wyllis; and in June, 1776, he was promoted, receiving a captain's commission, and near the close of the campaign did the duties of brigade major under Gen. Parsons. Soon after this he was appointed deputy adjutant general to the troops stationed on the North River, under Maj. Gen. Heath, for the defense of the Highlands. He also received the appointment of deputy paymaster.

In 1777, Congress authorized Gen. Washington to raise sixteen regiments, in addition to those which were to be raised by the respective states. In one of these, commanded by Col. Samuel B. Webb, he received the commission of major; and in 1778, Col. Webb and the lieutenant colonel of the regiment having been made prisoners, the command devolved upon Major Huntington, who was ordered to march to Rhode Island to reinforce the troops which were directed to attack the British army then at Newport. Major Huntington continued in command till 1779, when the lieutenant having been exchanged, resigned, and Major Huntington was promoted to a lieutenant colonelcy, to take rank from June, 1778.

Soon after this he joined the main army, when he was appointed to the command of a battalion of light troops to reinforce the army then acting against Cornwallis at Yorktown, where he continued until near the close of the siege, when he joined Gen. Lincoln as a volunteer aid, acting in that capacity during the rest of the siege, and up to the time of the surrender of Cornwallis and his army.

At the close of the war in 1783, he retired to private life, and in 1792, congress having appointed a system for the militia of the states, his excellency, Gov. Huntington, appointed him a general for the State of Connecticut, which situation he held under the successive governors, Wolcott, Trumbull, Treadwell, Griswold, Smith, and Wolcott, enjoying their entire confidence.

In 1799, in consequence of our relations with France, congress deemed it expedient to raise a body of troops for discipline, in case of need, and having given the command to Washington, with a request on the part of the then president, John Adams, that he would designate such officers as he should consider best qualified for the service, Washington named Gen. Huntington, who received a commission as brigadier.

During the war of the Revolution, Gen. Huntington was considered one of the best disciplinarians of the army. He enjoyed the personal friendship of Knox, Humphries, Jackson, and Trumbull; and at its close, in private life, was deemed a gentleman of strict integrity of character, and was honored by the suffrages of the people with a seat both in the national and state legislatures.

Very few living men know any thing of the embarrassments attending the officers who served in the war of the revolution, much of which arose from the depreciated and finally worthless paper currency. The writer of this notice has heard Gen. Huntington say that he had given a month's pay for merely crossing a ferry.

Gen. Huntington was elected a member of the United States House of Representatives in 1810, and again in 1817. His death took place in Norwich, June 17, 1834.

562. ELIZABETH, born Feb. 9, 1757, married, Nov. 25, 1773, Col. John Chester, of Wethersfield, who was born Jan. 18, 1749. He was son of John and Sarah (Noyes) Chester of Wethersfield. He was a colonel in the army of the revolution, and especially distinguished himself at the battle of Bunker Hill. He was much in public life, and always in highest esteem, both for his signal public service, and for his great personal worth. In all the private relations of the man and friend, he was an example to be copied. As a Christian he was unaffectedly devout, an Israelite, indeed, in whom there was no guile. A compeer with the noblest of our Connecticut worthies of that day of noble names, he was also the humble and beneficent friend of the poor, and the readiest comforter of the sorrowing and afflicted, and in all of his generous philanthropy, he found a ready help-meet in his gifted and accomplished wife. He died Nov. 4, 1809, and his widow, July 1, 1834. Their children, were: Elizabeth, born Nov. 10, 1774, married, June 8, 1807, Eleazer F. Backus, of Albany N. Y., and became the mother of Jonathan T. Backus, D. D., of Schenectady, and Rev. John Backus, of Baltimore; Mary, born April 20, 1779, married, June 8, 1806, Ebenezer Welles, of Brattleboro, Vt.; Hannah, born Oct. 27, 1781, married Charles Chauncy, of Philadelphia; Sarah, born June 17, 1783; John, born Aug. 17, 1785, graduated at Yale, 1804, married Rebecca Ralston, of Philadelphia, and was settled in Hudson, N. Y., and still later in Albany. He died in Philadelphia, Jan. 12, 1829; Charlotte, born March 20, 1787; Henry, born Oct. 3, 1790, and died March 1, 1791; Julia, born March 15, 1792, married, April 2, 1816, Matthew C. Ralston, of Philadelphia; Henry, born Dec. 22, 1793, and was a lawyer in Philadelphia; William, born Nov. 20, 1795, and is a clergyman; and George, born June 14, 1798, and died early.

563. MARY, born March 21, 1760, married, in 1778, Rev. Joseph Strong, of Norwich, who subsequently received the degree of Doctor of Divinity, from the College of New Jersey. He became eminent in his profession, and remained for fifty-six years pastor of the same church, having been installed as colleague with Dr. Lord, March 18, 1778, and retaining his post, though with Rev. C. B. Everest as his colleague, from 1829 until his death, Dec. 18, 1834. She survived him a few years, dying May 14, 1840. That she was a woman of rare excellence of character, many, very many are now living, in the parish where her life was spent, to testify. Their children were: Joseph H., born Nov. 27, 1781, and lived in Norwich; Mary Huntington, born Feb. 5, 1786, married Aaron P. Cleveland, a merchant of Boston, Mass.; and Henry, born Aug. 23, 1788, who became so prominent among the jurists of his native state.

564. ZACHARIAH, born Nov. 2, 1764, married, March 23, 1786, Hannah

Mumford. He was a merchant, and a man of distinction. In military life he attained the rank of major general. For a beautiful tribute to his personal character see Mrs. Sigourney's reminiscences, pages 21 and 22. He died June 23, 1850.

226. JOHN.   Windham, Conn.

This family were all born in Windham, Conn.

565. WEALTHAN, born Jan. 6, 1757, married, Nov. 29, 1798, Roger (245).

566. ANNA, born Jan. 24, 1771, married March 28, 1802, Eleazer Ripley, of Windham, who died March 28, 1823, aged 55 years; and she died Dec. 14, 1856. They had six children: John H., William, Elizabeth Ann, Elbridge, Harriet and Justin.

567. JOHN, born March 16, 1773, married, Feb. 1, 1813, Olive Smith. He lived and died in Windham, on the spot first selected by his great grandfather, deacon Joseph, at the settlement of the town. He was in the drug business. He died Feb. 2, 1829. His widow still lives on the old homestead.

568. JOSEPH, born Jan. 14, 1775, married, July 3, 1808, Parthena Smith, daughter of (611). He always lived in Windham, where he died, July 21, 1853. His widow is still living in Windham.

569. ELIPHALET, born Jan. 18, 1777, married, for his first wife, in March, 1803, Phebe Robinson, who died May 18, 1804. He married, for his second wife, Dec. 18, 1806, Hannah Moore, of Norwich, daughter of David, who was born April 11, 1780, and died in Belvidere, Ill., Sept. 1, 1846. He died in Norwich, where he had lived for years, Sept. 29, 1815.

570. GURDON, born Dec. 21, 1778, married Dec. 19, 1802, Mary Brown, daughter of Dr. Samuel Brown, of New London, who was born Feb. 20, 1784. He was for years engaged in mercantile business in his native town, and moved to Tecumseh, Mich., where he died, May 12, 1855. His wife died in Huron, Ohio, Oct. 15, 1831.

571. LUCY, born Dec. 9, 1780, and died Sept. 7, 1782.

572. FANNY, born Sept. 3, 1783, and died same day.

229. REV. NATHANIEL.   Ellington.

573. NATHANIEL, born Sept. 20, 1751, graduated at Yale, 1772, and died of consumption in 1774.

574. JERUSHA, born April 30, 1753.

575. EUNICE, born Oct. 5, 1754, and died, probably, March 17, 1755.

233. REV. JONATHAN.   Worthington.

576. SARAH, born in East Haddam, Conn., Oct. 22, 1758, and died on the 24th of same month.

577. LUCY, born in East Haddam, Nov. 16, 1759, married, for her first husband, Benj. E. Greene, of Worthington, Mass., by whom she had seven children: Wealthy, born 1776; Polly, born 1778; John, Job, Sarah, Lucy H. and

William E. After his death she married Asa Strong, of Vergennes, Vt., where she died, in 1824, and her second husband in 1832.

578. SIMON, born in Windham, Conn., April 15, 1762. He married Priscilla Benjamin, in Worthington, and resided in Hinsdale, Mass., where he was a substantial farmer, and a useful and honored citizen. He was unaffectedly benevolent, and truly pious. He was called to represent his town in the state legislature. His wife was born July 17, 1761, and died Jan. 24, 1846. He died Aug. 31, 1836. The following tribute to his memory from his grandson, Rev. A. Huntington Clapp, of Providence, R. I., is too true and good to be lost. He says of him: "He was of manly proportions, considerably above the medium size, and with a blended dignity and grace that marked him as one of Nature's noblemen. A dignified, but not formal politeness was natural to him, and never forsook him, even in the most ordinary intercourse of life. And yet those clear bright eyes, which beamed so gently from under the long, overhanging brows that veiled them, could flash fiery indignation, when he heard of a mean, dishonest, irreligious act or speech.

"Though a man of strong convictions—his opinions intelligently formed were firmly held—he was eminently a gentle man. Kindness was the law of his nature. It was by this, if at all, that he brought others to agree with him; and I have been told that in matters affecting important interests of the neighborhood, or town, his sentiments, however unpopular at first, were pretty sure, in the end, to prevail. No wonder he built up such a reputation as a peacemaker, and that so many referred their disagreements to his arbitrament, rather than to that of the law, and with so much more satisfactory results.

"But it was as a Christian, that he most honored himself in life, and is most clearly remembered by his survivors. He was an intelligent believer; knowing not only what he believed, but why he believed it. Firm in his own conscientious convictions, he was liberal to those who honestly differed, acting on the motto: 'In essentials, unity; in non-essentials, liberty; in all things, charity.' He was an earnest, practical Christian, living the religion he professed, so that even unbelievers were constrained to say, that if there were such a thing as vital piety, it would produce such a character and life as his.

"Young as I was, the religious services at his family altar, made impressions on my mind which could hardly have been effaced, even had they not been deepened by my last visit to him shortly before his death.

"There was something truly patriarchal in his mien, as he gathered his family around him morning and evening and on the Sabbath, read and expounded to them the Bible, and led them in prayer; his manner that of the assured Christian, yet with no tinge of irreverent familiarity. Every child felt that his prayer was true heart communion with God, that the exercise was one the old man loved, and that it shed a blessing over the household through all the day. Next to the Bible, he seemed to prize many of Watts' versions of the Psalms. I shall never forget the manifest satisfaction he took, during my last visit, in singing, many times a day, that version of the 119th Psalm, commencing,

> 'Behold thy waiting servant, Lord,
> Devoted to thy fear,
> Remember and confirm thy word,
> For all my hopes are there.'

"I have no doubt that it was on his lips within a few moments of the time when he stepped from the door of his earthly home, and fell to the ground, to find the portals of his heavenly mansion suddenly unfolded before him. What words could more fitly prelude the good man's exchange of earth for Heaven?

"On the whole, I have never met the man who seemed to me now, as I remember him, to have combined in more just and beautiful proportions, the essential elements of a true Christian gentleman; dignity and affability, deep spirituality, and 'round about common-sense,' attention to his own affairs, and active interest in others' welfare, unswerving adherence to principle, and unfailing cheerfulness of temper, rational enjoyment of this world, and delightful anticipations of the next."

579. EBENEZER, born in Windham, Conn., May 1, 1761, married, for his first wife, in Cummington, Mass., Nov. 29, 1787, Sarah Ward, who was born April 23, 1768, and died in Cummington, July 12, 1791. She was daughter of William and Sarah (Trowbridge) Ward, of Cummington. He married, for his second wife, in Northampton, May 6, 1792, Sarah, daughter of Rev. Benjamin Mills, and sister of the Hon. Elijah Hunt Mills, U. S. senator from Massachusetts. She was born in Chesterfield. He was a physician of some prominence in his profession, residing in Chesterfield, Mass., until 1794, when he removed to Vergennes, Vt., where he died, Dec. 4, 1834. His widow died at Vergennes, Dec. 29, 1860, aged 87. The following obituary notice, from the Vermont Chronicle, has been furnished by Rev. Otto Hoyt, who married her daughter:

"She was distinguished for intelligence, vivacity, meekness, discretion, benevolence and hospitality. In the varied relations she sustained, she was very highly esteemed and greatly beloved. During the ministry of Rev. Dr. John Hough, she became hopefully pious, and united with the Congregational church, in Vergennes; ever after, while her active powers remained, laboring faithfully to promote its interests, and rejoicing in its prosperity. Few, it is believed, more conscientiously obeyed the important precept, 'speak evil of no man,' or more exemplified that charity which the great apostle enjoins upon all. As the wife of a prominent physician, she had peculiar responsibilities. Coming, as her husband did, to Vermont, at so early a period in its history, his practice was widely extended, and often accompanied by peculiar privations and hardships. But while he lived, he found at home a wise counsellor, and one who deeply and tenderly sympathized with him in all his labors and sacrifices. She also, in an eminent degree, even down to old age, had the power of winning the affections of the young."

SIXTH GENERATION. 171

580. SARAH, born in Windham. Conn., in May, 1766, and died June 7, 1766.
551. RALPH, born in Windham, May 6, 1767, and died Nov. 22, 1767.
582. SARAH, born in Windham, Oct. 26, 1768, married Elisha Brewster, and resided in Worthington, Mass. Her children were: Theodosia, Sarah, Zipporah, Eliza, Lucy, and Elisha. She died in 1841.
583. CHARLOTTE, born in Windham, Conn., Nov. 16, 1770, married. Feb. 19, 1792, Thomas Marsh, and had children as follows: Aurora, born May 10, 1794, and died Aug. 7, 1814; Aurilla, born Nov. 7, 1796; Rufus and Ruby, twins, born Oct. 30, 1801; and Sophia, born March 20, 1809.
584. ELIZABETH, born in Worthington, Mass., May 23, 1773, married Asa Porter, and had eight children: Elizabeth, Mary Ruth, Huntington, Jonathan, Enos, Nahum, and Sarah.
585. SYBBEL, born in Worthington, Mass., Aug. 5, 1775, and died May 6, 1776.
586. JONATHAN, born in Worthington, Mass., Aug. 24, 1778, married in Bridport, Vt., Dec. 22, 1799, Dytha, daughter of John N. and Phebe (Aiken) Bennet, who died Sept. 3, 1803. He married, second, in Addison, Vt., July 29, 1804, Sarah, eldest daughter of James and Eunice (Collins) Hickox, of Watertown, Conn., who was born. April 23, 1783. He went to Vergennes, Vt., in 1801, and died in St. Albans, Vt., Feb. 28, 1856. Yet he lived not in vain. He was called to the deaconship in the Congregational church of this place in 1811, and alone, for a quarter of a century, he served faithfully and well the cause of religion. "He was a good and a faithful man," and his children, who follow him in a like profession of the same faith, unite in calling him blessed.

234. JOSEPH, D. D.   Coventry, Conn.

This family were all born in Coventry, Connecticut.
587. JOSEPH, born Sept. 13, 1767, married in 1788, Mirza Dow, a sister of the eccentric Lorenzo Dow. He was admitted to the bar in Charleston, S. C., and while engaged in the practice of his profession here, he was the victim of a fatal encounter, demanded as he felt by the code of honor where he was living, and died Aug. 19, 1794. His wife died in Coventry, Jan. 30, 1855, aged eighty-four years.
588. SAMUEL, born Oct. 4, 1765. On the Norwich records his marriage entry calls him Samuel, 3d. He was educated by his uncle Samuel (232), graduated at Yale, 1785, and married, Dec. 20, 1791, Hannah (1368). The entry of this marriage was not made until Jan. 22, 1799. He was admitted to the bar while in Norwich, and continued with his uncle until his decease, after which, in May, 1801, he removed to Cleveland, and in 1805 to Painesville, Ohio.

Here he was immediately introduced into public life, to which the remainder of his days were devoted. Gov. St. Clair appointed him lieutenant colonel of the first regiment of militia of Trumbull County. In October, 1802, the delegates of Trumbull county elected him as one of their two delegates to the convention to be held in Chilicothe on the first of the following month, to form a state constitution. By the first assembly of the state, of which he was a senator from Trumbull county, he was appointed in 1803 one of the three judges of supreme court, and in Dec. 1804, he was appointed chief judge by the legislature, which office he held until he was elected governor of the state in 1808. In this office he served for one term, two years.

He was one of the original proprietors of Fairport, and aided in its founding in 1812. During the war of 1812-14, he was paymaster in the northwest army. He was tendered the office of receiver of public monies at Steubenville, by president Jefferson, and also that of judge in the territory of Michigan, both of which he declined.

The following anecdote is illustrative of the condition of the Western Reserve at the time he removed to Ohio. While going from the east to Cleveland, where he then resided, " he was one evening attacked, about two miles out of the town, by a pack of wolves, and such was their ferocity, that he broke his umbrella to pieces in keeping them off, to which, and the fleetness of his horse, he owed the preservation of his life."

He died June 8, 1817, and his widow, Nov. 29, 1818.

589. FRANCES, born Sept. 15, 1769. She was educated by her uncle Samuel, of Norwich, where she resided until she married, May 17, 1796, the Rev. E. D. Griffin, D. D., of the Park street church, Boston, and afterwards president of Williamstown College. "She was a lady of uncommon delicacy and excellence of character." She died July 25, 1837. They had two children: Frances Louisa, born in 1801, who married Lyndon A. Smith, M. D., of Newark, N. J., and had five children: Edward D. Griffin, a physician in Newark, N. J., Lyndon A., Sanford Huntington, now a minister, and Frances Louisa, the oldest daughter, having died at the age of seventeen. Mrs. Smith, who was a lady of the "finest intellectual and moral qualities," died in 1852. The second, Ellen Maria, born in 1810, was the first child baptized in the Park street church. She married, in 1840, the Rev. Robert Crawford, and settled in North Adams, Mass., and still later over a Presbyterian church near Philadelphia. They have buried three children, and have four still living: Frances Huntington, James Douglass, Lyndon Smith, and Ellen Margaret. Mr. Crawford is now settled in Westfield, Massachusetts.

590. SEPTIMUS, born June 17, 1773, and died Sept. 23, 1776.

591. ELIZABETH, born Aug. 22, 1774, married, Nov. 9, 1794, Amasa Jones of Coventry, by whom she had nine children, six of whom are still, 1858, living. Her husband was a son of Col. Joel Jones, of Hebron, Conn. They resided in Coventry until 1816, when they removed to Wilkesbarre, Penn., where he died, Nov. 5, 1842, and his widow, April 16, 1843. Their children are: Judge Joel Jones, of Philadelphia, who graduated at Yale, was the first president of Girard College, has been mayor of Philadelphia, and has had six children: Joseph Huntington, D. D., a graduate of Cambridge, and pastor of the Sixth Presbyterian church in Philadelphia, and has four children: **Fanny Huntington**; Margaret Emeline; Maria, who married William Allis, and lives in West-

SIXTH GENERATION. 173

field, N. Y., and has five children; Eliza, married Joseph J. Wright, a surgeon in the U. S. Army, and died in St. Louis in 1854, leaving two sons and three daughters; Samuel, who is a physician; Mary Joanna, married Rev. O. Harris, and died in 1857, leaving one daughter; and Matthew Hale, a lawyer living in Easton, Penn., who has three children.

592. GEORGE W., born April 18, 1776, and died Aug 10, 1777.

593. SEPTIMUS G., born April 14, 1778, married in Feb. 1810, Mary Tyler Morse, of Wrentham, Mass. He removed in 1819 to Shelby County, Indiana. He was a man honored by his fellow citizens with frequent testimonials of their confidence. He had spent some portion of his life on the sea. He died July 29, 1844, at his residence in Shelby county.

594. HANNAH, born Dec. 22, 1779, and died Dec. 15, 1794.

595. HENRY, born Aug. 20, 1781, and died 1806, unmarried.

596. LUCRETIA, born Sept. 29, 1783, married, Jan. 14, 1806, Joseph G. Norton, of Hebron, and went to Buffalo, N. Y., in 1823, where he died, Sept. 12, 1844, and where she is still living a hale and hearty woman, blessed with the presence and ministries of her children. She has had five children: Abiel Abbot, who was drowned young at Hartford, Conn.; Elizabeth Huntington, died in Buffalo in 1846; Fanny Rose; Mary Lucretia, now, 1858, in Europe; Charles D., a lawyer in Buffalo, married a daughter of Hon. Oliver Phelps, of Canandaigua, N. Y., and has one son, Porter Norton.

597. PENELOPE, born April 21, 1788, and died Dec. 12, 1794.

598. JAMES, born Nov. 9, 1790, and died Sept. 9, 1794.

235. ELIPHALET. Scotland, Conn.

The births of the first six of this family are on the Windham records.

599. NATHANIEL, born Aug. 3, 1763, married Mary Corning, of Hartford. He resided in Hartford until 1800, afterwards in Waterford, Conn., and finally removed to Butternuts, N. Y., where he died in 1815. His widow lived to a very advanced age, and was "held in most affectionate veneration for her extraordinary energy of mind, her active benevolence, her cheerful temper, and exemplary piety."

600. ELIJAH, born Nov. 27, 1764. He was taken prisoner and died on board a prison ship in 1782.

601. SYBIL, born Feb. 8, 1766, married Col. Samuel Morgan, of Vermont. She died in February, 1826. The had six children: Sybil, Samuel, Harriet, Hezekiah Rudd, William, and Alice.

602. JAMES, born Nov. 16, 1767, and died on board the ship Jersey at New York, in 1783.

603. EUNICE, born Sept. 17, 1769, married Increase Mather, of Scotland, Windham, and died in July, 1800. They had three children: Alathea, Harriet and Charles.

604. JONATHAN, born Nov. 17, 1771, married, Oct. 20, 1796, Ann Lathrop, who was born in Windham, (Scotland parish), Oct. 14, 1774, and died in Boston, Mass., May 3, 1826. He married for his second wife, in Newark, N. J.,

in 1827, Elizabeth Graham, widow of Oliver Lathrop, and she died in August, 1838. He was by nature possessed of a voice of fine tone and great strength, which, while living with his uncle Samuel, in Norwich, he had cultivated with much care. His life was devoted to the teaching of music in Boston, Albany, and afterwards at St. Louis, where he died July 29, 1838.

605. ABIGAIL, born Jan. 2, 1775, and died in infancy.

606. ABIGAIL, born July 25, 1777, married Elisha Mills, and lived in Canandaigua, N. Y., where they had two children, and where she died in 1816.

607. ENOCH, born June 29, 1779, and died in 1782.

608. MARTHA, born March 5, 1782, married Thomas Pier, of Cooperstown, N. Y., where she died in 1811, having a family of children, one of whom was Jonathan Huntington.

609. LUCY, born June 15, 1787, and died at one year of age.

236. ENOCH, Rev. Middletown, Conn.

This family were all born in Middletown, and the dates of births and baptisms are taken from the autograph record of the father, now in possession of his granddaughter, Mrs. Whitlock, of New London, Connecticut.

610. ENOCH, born Oct. 19, 1767, and baptized on the following sabbath. He was prepared for Yale College by his father, and graduated in 1785, with high honor, receiving the Berkeley premium, as his father before him had done. He studied law, and when admitted to the bar, established himself in Middletown, where he spent his life. He soon secured an extensive practice, and attained eminence in his profession. He had many qualities to fit him especially for an advocate; and his extensive legal acquirements, and manly eloquence, won him a high place at the bar.

He married, Nov. 6, 1791, Sarah Ward, daughter of Greve Ward, of Middletown. Her mother subsequently married the Hon. Asher Miller, of Middletown. He died in Middletown in 1826.

611. MARY, born Aug. 28, 1769, and baptized on the following sabbath. She married, Sept. 17, 1797, Matthew Talcott, son of Rev. Noadiah Russel, of Thompson, Conn., and grandson of Rev. William, of Middletown, whose father, Rev. Noadiah was, also, pastor of the church in Middletown, and his father, William, came from England to New Haven. She was a most excellent woman, and devoted Christian. She died, June 9, 1857, in Middletown. Their children now (1855) living, are as follows: Mary Huntington, residing in Middletown; Harriet, now Mrs. George Larned, of Wickford, R. I., who has five children: Maria, Julia, George and Catherine, Julia Anne and Charles Huntington, of Middletown, William Huntington, a graduate of Yale, and subsequently tutor, now Principal of the Collegiate and Commercial Institute, of New Haven, and major-general of the Connecticut militia, who married Mary E., daughter of Dr. Thos. Hubbard, of the medical school, Yale College, and has had nine children, six of them still living, Frances Harriet, Henrietta Lee, Talcot Huntington, Thos. Hubbard, Philip Grey, and Edward Hubbard; Abigail Talcott; Frances Huntington, now Mrs. P. R. Roach, of New

York, who has had eleven children, five of whom are living, Jane Throckmorton, Talcott Russel, Fanny Huntington, Samuel Grey Southmayd, and Mary Russel; and Sarah E., now Mrs. Samuel Grey Southmayd, of New York.

612. LYDIA, born Feb. 28, 1771, and baptized on the following sabbath. She married, in 1813, Col. Simeon North, who was born in Berlin, Conn., July 13, 1765, and died in Middletown, Conn., Aug. 25, 1852. He was the father, by a former marriage, of the Rev. Simeon North, D. D., now President of Hamilton College, and was extensively engaged in manufacturing arms for the United States, during and subsequent to our last war with England, and was also successful in introducing important improvements into the processes of the manufacture. On removing to Middletown he purchased the Huntington place, the parsonage, which had so long been occupied by (236), which the family still retain. The following tribute to her memory, is the testimony of her son-in-law, Dr. North. "Being the oldest of her unmarried sisters, at the time of her mother's death, it became necessary for her to take charge of her father's domestic establishment, and to occupy thus a highly important position, both in relation to the family, and the parish with which her father was connected. In these relations she fulfilled her duties in a most successful and exemplary manner. During the later years of her father's life she spent much time in traveling with him, and thus became intimately acquainted with many of the most prominent ministerial families of the state. To a vigorous mind, and one quick in its perceptions, she added the culture of a good early education, and that refinement which is the natural result of long continued intercourse with refined and cultivated society. Her disposition was mild and winning; her manners dignified and graceful; her character and life, those of the true woman in the highest and best sense of the word: and I may add, she was a true exemplification of that religion of the New Testament which she professed. She had one child, Lydia Huntington, now the wife of Rev. Dwight H. Seward, of Yonkers, N. Y. Her death occurred Sept. 7, 1840. My recollections of her are those of mingled love and reverence, for though not my own mother, she yet, with singular fidelity, performed for me the offices of a maternal guardian, when I most needed such a guardianship. I am sure that I owe to her influence much of what I have had occasion most to value in the experience of my subsequent life."

613. LUCY, born Dec. 8, 1773, married Dec. 31, 1796, Simon, son of Elijah House, of Hebron, and had two children: Simon and Lucy.

614. SAMUEL, born Aug. 23, 1775, and died Nov. 28, 1776.

615. ESTHER. This, and the next name have the following record in their father's hand writing against them. "Sat. May 10, 1777, just at evening, about six and seven o'clock, we had born twin daughters, and the next day, being Lord's day, they were baptized by the names of Esther and Martha." Esther died Oct. 7, 1777.

616. MARTHA. Martha, married, June 20, 1801, Edward, son of Hezekiah Hulbert, of Middletown, who was born Dec. 12, 1776.

617. ESTHER, born April 8, 1780, married, (Dec. 23, 1804—Oct. 12, 1805,) Benj. Rosekrantz, jr., of Waterford, who was born Dec. 23, 1781. Their children are: Sally Hubbard, born Dec. 25, 1806; Enoch Huntington, born Oct. 16, 1808, a judge of superior court of New York; Mary Johnson, born Feb. 15, 1810; Henry, born Jan. 31, 1812; Ann Eliza, born March 3, 1815, and Caroline.

618. SAMUEL GRAY, born May 21, 1782, graduated at Yale, in 1800, taking the Berkeley premium, and entered the legal profession. He married for his first wife, Mary Johnston, of Middletown. He married for his second wife, June 23, 1825, Mrs. Janette C. Cheever, who died Nov. 14, 1856. He died, after an illness of a few days, in Troy, July 5, 1854. The following notice from the Troy daily Whig, is ample testimonial to his ability and great worth.

"At a meeting of the Rensselaer county bar, held the day after his death, among the resolutions passed were the two following:

"*Resolved*, That the bar of this city, by the death of the Hon. Samuel G. Huntington, have lost their oldest member—a lawyer and a scholar; a man thoroughly bred to his profession, and ever ready to impart to others the knowledge which his careful training, advanced age, and varied experience had given him.

"*Resolved*, That the extent and variety of his classical and legal learning may well awaken the emulation of us, his survivors, who are thus suddenly called on to mourn his unexpected death.

"Hon. D. L. Seymour, in seconding the resolutions, spoke as follows: 'We are again assembled to take appropriate notice of the death of one of our members. The oldest member of the Rensselaer bar has fallen. Although past three score years and ten, yet such had been the vigor and animation of his declining years, that his sudden demise affected us almost as if he had been struck down in the full strength of manhood. We feel deeply, by this sudden providence, the feeble tenure by which we hold all sublunary things. But, beside these considerations, which will be more appropriately enforced from the sacred desk, we, as brethren of the legal profession, feel that the bar of our county has sustained a loss, and that we individually mourn the death of a friend. The occasion seems, therefore, to demand something more than ordinary note of its occurrence.

"'Samuel Gray Huntington was the son of Rev. Enoch Huntington, and like most of the youth of his native state, received the rudiments of a thorough education in the excellent common schools, then, and still liberally and carefully sustained by the able legislators of that state. After leaving the common school, he passed through the education preparatory to admission to a collegiate course, and was admitted to Yale College, where he graduated with the honors of that ancient University in the year 1800.

"'Judge Huntington left college with a thorough classical education, and at once entered upon the study of the law, in the office of his brother, Enoch Huntington, Jr., then a practicing lawyer of good standing in his native town. After the usual period of study, he was admitted to practice at the bar of

Middlesex county, where he commenced business, in connection with his brother.

"'It is profitable to dwell for a moment upon this period of his life. He had selected the law for his profession, and in making that choice he doubtless felt as the young men in that day, in New England, were taught to feel, that the legal profession yielded to no other in dignity or importance. That the first object of the young lawyer, whether he consulted his reputation or his purse, was to master, not only the forms, precedents and superficial structure of the science, but its first principles, its very fountains, opening up through the social and political condition of man, and disclosing the necessary rules regulating his rights of person and property. At that day, too, the great lights of the bar and bench of his native state beckoned him onward in a course of honorable distinction in his profession. Such men as Reeve and Swift, adorned the bench, while Pierpoint Edwards, Goddard, Daggett and Gould, shone at the bar.

"'Entering upon the practice of his profession with such an excellent preparation, and under such incentives, his success was almost certain. He had already attained a reputable standing among the younger members of the bar of his native state, when about the year 1806, he removed to the state of New York, and settled in practice, in the village of Waterford, Saratoga county. Here he soon rose to eminence as a lawyer, and ranked among the ablest of the many distinguished men who have graced the bar of that county. He removed to Troy in the year 1825. For many years his professional business here was among the largest and most lucrative. His counsel was sought in the most important causes, particularly in those relating to real estate. In this branch of the law he was a perfect master, as well from his intimate acquaintance with the decisions of the English courts, as from the fact, that the period of his practice, reaching to upwards of half a century, embraced that space in the history of our country during which not only the system of our law of real estate, but in fact almost the entire body of American common law, has been formed. When he commenced practice there was no American commentator on the law, and the reported cases, either in Connecticut or New York, did not exceed half a dozen volumes.

"'Under the administration of Gov. Clinton, he was appointed to the office of judge of the court of common pleas of this county, and discharged its duties with great ability and impartiality. His decisions always commanded respect, as they were felt to be the result of an honest conviction of the right of the case, in a mind guided by patient research, and stored with legal lore.

"'In the death of Judge Huntington, his brethren of the bar mourn the loss of one in whose counsels they have often confided—whose legal acquirements did honor to their profession—whose professional relations to them all, were kind, courteous, and honorable, and whose social intercourse so often helped to strip labor of its drudgery—relieve life of its tedium, and to strew our pathway with pleasant, harmless trifles and gay flowers.'"

619. MEHETABEL, born June 18, 1784, and died in Middletown, Conn.

245. ROGER. Windham, Conn.

This family were born in Windham.

620. JONATHAN, born May 11, 1781, and died July 14, 1782.

621. HULDAH, born Nov. 14, 1782, and married in 1808, Anson Johnson, of Plainfield, and has resided in Brunswick, Me., where she is still living.

622. EUNICE, born Nov. 8, 1784, and married George W. Abbe, in 1823. She died April 5, 1830, leaving no children.

623. JUDITH, born Oct. 5, 1786, and died Aug. 29, 1787.

624. HENRY, born May 6, 1789. He was a lawyer in Lebanon, in 1821, and afterward resided in Windham. He married, Feb. 23, 1823, Clarissa Bibbins, who is still living in Windham. He died Dec. 27, 1836.

625. ELIZABETH, born June 28, 1791. She married, 1815, Ebenezer M. Johnson, brother of Anson, above, and has resided in Maine with her sister Huldah.

626. JOSHUA, born June 27, 1793, and lived in Windham, where he died March 22, 1862. He never married.

627. EBENEZER, born July 15, 1795, and died Oct. 12, 1796.

246. NATHAN. Windham, Conn.

This family were all born in Windham.

628. OLIVE, born Nov. 8, 175-, and died July 29, 1755. The last figure in the year of her birth is omitted in the record.

629. OLIVE, born July 19, 1757. She married Asa Robinson, jr., of Hampton, Sept. 17, 1777. Their children were as follows: Thomas, born Aug. 7, 1779; Whitney, born Sept. 21, 1782; Oliver, born April 21, 1785; Olive, born March 19, 1788; Lewis, born Dec. 14, 1790; Betsy, born Dec. 26, 1793; Nathan, born Aug. 15, 1796; and Mary, born Feb. 25, 1800.

630. EDNEY, born Jan. 15, 1760, and married Uriel Edgerton, of Franklin, Conn.

631. ANNA, born Jan. 2, 1762, and married David Edgerton, of Munson, Mass.

632. DANIEL, born Dec. 13, 1764, married, April 19, 1786, Merial, daughter of Perez Tracy, of Preston, Conn. He died in Windham, Nov. 21, 1824. His widow, born Nov. 27, 1765, died in Norwich, Conn., March 7, 1857. She had united with the Congregational church in Windham, more than sixty years before her death, and found herself, to the last, sustained by the hopes and consolations of religion.

633. MARY, born Nov. 5, 1766, and married Jeduthun Symonds. She had a son, still living in Windham; a daughter, Jerusha, who married a Fitch; and Mary, who married a Wilbur, of Plainfield, with whom she herself was living.

634. NATHAN, born in 1776, married, in 1798, Sarah (1276). He died in Windham, in Sept., 1818, and his widow, Jan. 16, 1850, married Daniel Ashley, of Hampton. She died in New York, Jan. 26, 1850.

635. LOUISA, married William Butler, of Hampton.

636. BETSEY, born 1777, and died 1796.

SIXTH GENERATION. 179

217. HEZEKIAH.

Windham, Conn.

This family were all born in Windham.

637. EUNICE, born Jan. 3, 1756. She married, Dec. 8, 1774, Capt. Ralph Ripley, a grandson of the daughter of Gov. Bradford, of Mass. Their children were: Bradford, born March 18, 1776; Elizabeth, born Aug. 9, 1778, and married first, a Young, and second, the Hon. John Baldwin, of Windham; Christopher, born Dec. 12, 1781; Eliphalet, born Oct. 31, 1784, married, Nov. 16, 1817, Julia Larabee; Eunice, born Nov. 12, 1786, married Horace Lathrop, of Cherry Valley, N. Y.; Ralph Huntington, born Nov. 16, 1789; Laura, born July 4, 1792, married Earl Swift, M. D., of South Mansfield, Conn.; and James, born Dec. 10, 1794, a colonel in the U. S. Army, and late superintendent of the arsenal in Springfield, Mass., and now, 1862, chief of the ordnance department in the United States service.

638. SUBMIT, born March 29, 1758, and died Oct. 18, 1759.

639. GAMALIEL, born Nov. 28, 1760, married Keturah Armstrong, of Franklin, Conn., Feb. 13, 1782, moved to Walpole after the birth of his first two children, and died there, Feb. 2, 1813, and his wife, July 5, 1831.

640. GURDON, born April 30, 1763, married, in New London, Dec. 25, 1785, Temperance Williams, (254), and moved to Walpole, N. H., in Oct. 1789. He was a goldsmith, and died in Walpole, N. H., July 26, 1804, his widow removing to Bloomfield, Ohio, where she died at the age of sixty-three, May 25, 1823. She was born Sept. 5, 1760, in Groton, Conn.

641. SUBMIT, born Aug. 8, 1765, married, Sept. 1, 1783, Minor Smith, of Windham, who died Jan. 23, 1823, in the sixty-fourth year of his age. She died, Dec. 22, 1856. Their children were: Alathea, who died in 1802, aged eighteen years; Parthena, born June 27, 1786, married (568); Lucy, married, first, Luther D. Leach, of Hampton, Conn., and, second, Harry Fuller, of Hampton; Henry, married Jane Campbell, of Cherry Valley, N. Y.; Lucretia, married, first, Clark Burnett, of Canterbury, Conn., and second, Mr. Buckingham of Norwalk, Ohio; Hezekiah Huntington, who died in infancy; Hezekiah Huntington, second, married Diantha Hale, now residing at Two Rivers, Wisconsin; Edmund, married Harriet Coats, of Lyme, was a man of large wealth and excellence of character, and died July 18, 1862, in Salem, Mass.; Edwin, married Amanda Frink of Windham, now living in Cleveland, Ohio; Julia, married Joseph Hyde, of Lebanon, Conn., now of Friendsville, Pa.; and Sophia, who married Lorenzo A. Kelsey, of Cleveland, Ohio.

642. SYBBEL, born Nov. 22, 1768, married, Jan. 12, 1792, Nathaniel Ripley, of Windham, Conn., and removed to Middlebury, Vt., where she died March 8, 1813. Their children were: Samuel Paintor, born Dec. 18, 1792, and died in Charleston, S. C., April 10, 1857; Julia, born Oct. 18, 1794, married Jonas Rice, of Bridport, Nov. 29, 1837; William Young, born Dec. 13, 1797, and lives in Rutland, Vt.; Erastus, born Nov. 23, 1801, and died May 29, 1802; Laura, born July 9, 1804, married Rev. Nelson Barbour, and died in Dummerston, Vt., May 8, 1846; Elizabeth, born Aug. 10, 1806, married Rev. John Stocker, and died at Muscatine, Iowa, March 11, 1851; and George Huntington, born Oct. 27, 1808.

643. LYDIA, born Aug. 7, 1775, and married, 1794, James L. Houston, of Windham. They lived in Middlebury, Vt., where he died, May 8, 1831. She married, for her second husband, Jan. 26, 1832, Nathan Jackson, and died at Brandon, Vt., Jan. 23, 1843, having had three children: Henry A., born 1799, and lives in Wisconsin; Jerusha S., born Oct. 31, 1806, married Asahel Hubbard, and lives in Whiting, Vt.; and Mary Ann, born Jan. 15, 1810, married John F. Goodell, and lives in Sudbury, Vermont.

644. JERUSHA, born March 7, 1780, married in Middlebury, Vt., Jacob Sherrill, and lives in New Hartford, N. Y.

252. DAVID. Columbia, Conn.

645. MASON, died single.

646. JOSEPH B., married, Nov. 28, 1814, Lucy Lord Avery, in Norwich, Conn. She died, July 26, 1833, aged thirty-nine, I infer from a record on a gravestone in the old Norwich city burying lot.

647. FANNY, died single in Columbia, Conn.

648. TRYPHOSA, died in 1775, in her ninth year.

649. TRYPHOSA, died single.

257. SOLOMON. Windham, Conn.

This family were all born in Windham.

650. MINOR, born April 22, 1763. He went to Yarmouth, Nova Scotia, in 1784, and married, in 1785, Martha Walker. He is enrolled by Sabine, in his history of the loyalists. He died in 1839, in Yarmouth, and his wife died in the same town several years later. He was a man much respected and trusted in Nova Scotia.

651. ALATHEA, born Nov. 29, 1764, married Midad Taylor, of Windham. This, I think, must be the Celinda who united with the Windham church in 1793.

652. ELIZABETH, born Jan. 15, 1767, married, Oct. 15, 1809, Benjamin Brewster, of Windham, who died, March 23, 1825. She had no children.

653. ANNA, born April 7, 1770, married, Feb. 24, 1793, Rev. Samuel Perkins, A. M., and resided in Windham, where she died April 17, 1829, and her husband, Sept. 22, 1850, aged eighty-three years. Her name on the church record, date 1821, is Nancy. Their children were: Anna Huntington, who married Sherman Converse, of New Haven, and died May 27, 1821, aged twenty-seven years; Samuel Huntington, who graduated at Yale, 1818, and has been a successful lawyer in Philadelphia for many years, and who is well known for his efficient benevolence; Horatio Nelson, who died in infancy; and Harriet, the wife of Judge Edwards Clarke, of Windham.

654. SOLOMON, born April 7, 1770, married, Oct. 25, 1801, Anna Jones, of New Haven, and resided in Mexico, N. Y.

655. JOSEPH DENISON, born Oct. 28, 1778, married, May 4, 1806, Gratia Ann Weller, of Westfield, who died Dec. 19, 1833, aged fifty-three years. He resided several years in Lancaster, Mass., and afterwards in Westfield, Mass.,

where he lived with his son-in-law, Esquire Leonard. He is now. (1861). in West Springfield, Mass.

656. MARY, born Feb. 23, 1781, married, Dec. 14, 1798, the Hon. John Baldwin, of Windham, a lawyer, a judge of the county court, and a member of congress; and who died in Windham, March 27, 1850, aged seventy-eight years She died, April 20, 1814, having had two children: John, who still lives in Windham; and Julia Ann, who died June 14, 1806, at three years of age. After the death of his wife, Mr. Baldwin married widow Elizabeth (Ripley 637) Youngs, who still survives.

261. SAMUEL, DEACON. Canterbury and E. Haddam, Conn.

This family were all born, it is probable, in Canterbury.

657. DOROTHY, born March 29, 1762, married, March 28, 1782, William Silliman, of East Haddam, where she lived. She died April 9, 1834. Her husband died in 1805, aged fifty-two years. Their children were: William, born in East Haddam, Aug. 16, 1784, married, April, 1817, Laura (454) who died in East Haddam, May 2, 1826, and he married. Nov. 2, 1827, Eliza Gillet, daughter of Caleb, and Civil (145) Gillet, who was born April 30, 1805, in Colchester. He died, Jan. 6, 1851, and his widow married, March 31, 1852, Samuel (1525); Dorothy, born Aug. 9, 1786, married Horace Brainard; Jeremiah, born April 21, 1789, and died, Dec. 12, 1791; Joseph, born April 25, 1791, and died aged eighteen years; Eliphalet, born Aug. 7, 1793, married Nancy Brainard Fuller; Huntington, born June 9, 1795, married Statira Chapman Fuller; Oliver, who married Mary Lester; and Olive, his twin sister, who married John Milton Brainard.

The following names and dates are from the Canterbury records, copied by Dr. Joshua Huntington.

657^1 REBECCA, born May 17, 1752, and died June 11, 1759.

657^2 HANNAH, born April 25, 1758, and died June 11, 1759.

657^3 JEREMIAH GATES, born April 9, 1760, and died Jan. 27, 1762.

658. SAMUEL, born June 4, 1764; was married three times, first, Jan. 24, 1788, to Martha Sears, who was born in 1765, and died July 26, 1795; second, in 1796, to Dimis, (446), who died in 1800; and third, in 1802, to Elizabeth, daughter of Jonathan Wells. He removed in 1803 to Middlefield, N. Y., where he died, Oct. 8, 1826.

659. MARY, born in East Haddam, June 18, 1770, and died single, Nov. 24, 1828.

660. JEREMIAH, born April 18, 1773, and died June 6, 1783.

264. OLIVER. Lebanon, Conn.

This family were all born in Lebanon.

661. ANNA, born July 21, 1762, and married Dea. Caleb (182).

662. LOUISA, born Nov. 12, 1763, married Dr. Lewis, grandson of Charles Collins, of Litchfield. They resided in Wilkesbarre, Pa., where she died June 7, 1858. She had ten children; Oristus, born Sept. 22, 1792, a man much in

public life, having been president judge of the second judicial district of Pennsylvania, and having one son, Charles J. Collins, a minister in the Presbyterian church, settled at Danville, Pa.; Lorenzo, of Cherry Ridge, Pa., who has one son: Abner, of Salem, Pa., who has four children; Alonzo, of Jefferson, Pa., who has two sons: Philura, who married a Dr. Daboll and had a large family; Lucius, of Cherry Ridge, Pa., who has one son: Decius, of Salem, who has three daughters; Huntington Lynde, of Cherry Ridge, Pa.; and Aretas, and Theron, both residing at Cherry Ridge.

663. HANNAH, born Aug. 12, 1765, and died July 29, 1783, as the Lebanon records attest.

664. LYNDE, born March 22, 1767. He graduated at Yale, in 1788, and was ordained pastor of the Congregational church in Branford, Conn., Oct. 28, 1795. He married, June 15, 1796, Anna, widow of Rev. Jason Atwater, his predecessor, in Branford, and daughter of Rev. Warham and Ann Williams, her mother, being a daughter of Rev. Samuel Hall, of Cheshire. Her paternal grand parents were the Rev. Dr. Stephen and Abigail (Davenport) Williams, of Springfield, Mass. His early ministry was one of promise, but a lingering disease soon set in, and prematurely terminated his period of earthly labor; not, however, until this record of his character and usefulness could be truthfully drawn: "Possessing a sound mind, the spirit of love and the wisdom of the prudent, he preached Christian doctrines and duties in their connection with all fidelity, was incessant in pastoral labors and an example to the flock. Entirely resigned, under a lingering illness he died in faith, Sept. 19, 1804."

The venerable Daniel Waldo, late chaplain in Congress, his classmate in college, thus testifies: "His standing in college as a classical scholar was respectable, and his moral and religious character unstained. He and Moses Hallock were two of the most exemplary scholars in the class. That he made an able and successful minister was a fact, though he died in the morning of life."

665. OLIVER, born Dec. 22, 1771, married, May 4, 1794, Abigail, daughter of Gad Talcott, of Hebron, who was born May 26, 1772. He removed in 1805 to Owego, N. Y., where he became "a substantial freeholder," and a prominent man. He was commissioned by Gov. Tompkins, in 1812, as brigadier-general of the 41st brigade of New York infantry; and in 1815 was appointed high sheriff of Broome county, and re-appointed again the next year. His wife, nobly descended from the best blood of the Mayflower, which she nobly honored, died in Owego, June 18, 1815, and he died in the same place, Nov. 13, 1823.

666. SAMUEL, born in 1773, and died March 4, 1813, in Lebanon.

667. ELIPHALET, born Sept. 19, 1777, married, Dec. 24, 1805, Nancy, daughter of James Clark, who died Dec. 24, 1827, aged 24. He married, for his second wife, Nov. 19, 1828, Sarah, daughter of Dennison Allen, of Windham. He has always lived in Lebanon, and has been honored repeatedly with important offices and commissions by his fellow-citizens. He died of typhoid fever, on Sabbath morning, Oct. 20, 1861.

SIXTH GENERATION. 183

668. LABETH, born in 1770, and died June 2, 1811, in Norwich, the death being on the Lebanon records.

669. LUCY, born in 1773, and died Dec. 4, 1775.

266. WILLIAM. Lebanon, Conn.

This family were all born in Lebanon.

670. DAN, born Aug. 9, 1758, and died Sept. 6, 1758.

671. RHODA, born Dec. 14, 1759, and died Dec. 11, 1764.

672. MARY, born Aug. 18, 1761, married Rev. Walter Lyon, a graduate of Dartmouth, in 1777, and pastor of the church in Abington Society, Pomfret, from 1783 to 1826, the year of his death. They had one son, Samuel Huntington, who married Maria Warner. He had two children, Samuel and Eliza Fitch (1562).

673. WEALTHY, born April 18, 1763, married, Jan. 2, 1783, Simon Fitch, a descendant of Rev. James Fitch, of Norwich. They had five children: Wealthy, Elizabeth, Thomas, Marietta and Eleazor.

674. RHODA, married Rev. William Lyman, D. D., who graduated at Yale, in 1784, was pastor of the Congregational church in a parish of East Haddam, from 1786 to 1824, when he removed to China, N. Y., where he died in 1833. They had eight children, three sons and five daughters.

675. WILLIAM, born March 6, 1765, married, April 6, 1788, Mary Gray. He was a farmer in his native town, and held in esteem and honor. He represented his town in the state legislature, in 1810, and again in 1812. He died Dec. 18, 1834.

676. EUNICE, born Jan. 14, 1769, married, March 28, 1798, Daniel Mason, of the fifth generation in descent from the famous Capt. John Mason, of Norwich. He died March 26, 1828. They had children as follows: Bethia Huntington, born March 8, 1800; Emma Elizabeth, born March 4, 1801; Mary Lyon, born June 28, 1802; Rhoda Louisa, born in 1804, and now wife of Rev. N. S. Hunt, of Bozrah; Julia Ann, born Oct. 10, 1805; Wealthy Fitch, born March 10, 1817, and died Dec. 25, 1830; John G. H., born Aug. 9, 1808, and died July 28, 1829; Abby Jane, born Dec. 28, 1811.

677. DAN, born Oct. 11, 1774, graduated at Yale, 1794, was tutor in Williamstown College from 1794 to 1796, and the next two years tutor in Yale. He was the pastor of the Congregational church in Litchfield, from 1797 to 1809, and of that in Middletown, from 1809 to 1816. From Middletown he removed to Hadley, Mass., where he has resided ever since. Of his character and promise in early life, I am permitted to record the testimony of his classmate, the Hon. Judge Thos. S. Williams, of Hartford, Conn. "His amiable temper, his good sense, and his pleasant manners, made him an agreeable companion. But he was too much of a student to spend much time in indulging his social nature. As a scholar, his standing in his class was high, and he was soon appointed as tutor at Williamstown, and from thence transferred to New Haven."

After removing to Hadley, he refused to settle again as pastor, though he continued to preach. He supplied for awhile a Unitarian congregation, and his views of Christian doctrines undergoing a change, he at length avowed himself a Unitarian. Yet with this change in his creed, we have the testimony of his orthodox brethren, no change was observable in his Christian character. His prayers in the family, and indeed the entire religious culture of his eminently Christian home, were what they had been while holding and teaching the orthodoxy of Connecticut. What his character as preacher was, before vacating the pulpit, is abundantly shown by the following testimonial from the pen of Rev. Parsons Cook, in Dr. Sprague's Annals of the American Pulpit. He is speaking of the settlement of a colleague with Dr. Hopkins, of Hadley, for which place Mr. Huntington, then recently dismissed from his people in Litchfield, was a candidate. "He was enjoying a splendid popularity as a preacher, and but for a jealousy of family influence, the people would have called him unanimously to be their pastor. While this matter was in agitation, Dr. Hopkins expressed great interest to secure his settlement; and even said that he would be willing to bear his shoes if he could see him settled there. He had such a strong conviction that the interests of the people would be promoted by it, that he would make any sacrifices to secure it."

He married, Jan. 1, 1801, Elizabeth Whiting, only daughter of Charles and Elizabeth (Porter) Phelps, of Hadley, who was born Feb. 4, 1779. She was a most excellent Christian woman, as is abundantly testified, both by the affection of her family, and by the grateful recollections of a large circle of beloved neighbors and friends. She was early a subject of grace, and united with the orthodox church in Hadley. Though, from a change in her views on the subject of the Trinity, she did not continue through life a communicant in that church, it is still recorded of her, by her husband, that "this sacred covenant it was her practice to renew, in form, with the most thorough examination and fervent prayer at the recurrence of each anniversary of her first vow, until the day of her death, which, by a singular providence, was itself one of those anniversaries, April 6, 1847."

It was one of the most blessed experiences of her life, that "all the beloved children for whom she had watched and prayed, and whom she had consecrated in baptism, gave reasonable evidence of a distinct and personal adoption of the Christian faith." Her last sickness was a painful one, extorting from her the earnest entreaty "of the patriarch, 'let me go, for the day breaketh.' Reminded of the loved ones who had gone before her, she replied, 'O, yes, I shall look them all up.'" Thus, sustained by her confiding faith, this gifted woman fell asleep in Jesus. "On the same day that admitted her to the Body of Christ below, she entered the church of the First Born."

Mr. Huntington is still enjoying a tranquil old age in the home he has so long loved. For the occasion of the eightieth anniversary of his birth, Oct. 11, 1855, he prepared for his children and grandchildren a sermon, which is a very pleasant and fitting memorial of the venerable man. What his faith still is, and where his hopes still rest, may best be learned from the close of that discourse. He had quoted that inspiring verse:

> "Rise, my soul, and stretch thy wings,
> Thy better portion trace;
> Rise from transitory things
> Towards heaven, thy native place."

He repeats the last line of the verse and adds: "There God is, and the throne of His grace. There Christ is, with open arms, ready to receive every returning sinner; the Resurrection and the Life, the Light and hope of every true believer." This sermon, with another upon the word "LEBANON," in the eighth verse of the fourth Song of Solomon, and several notes of interest to the family for whom they were prepared, were printed.

In addition to the above sermons, Mr. Huntington has had two election sermons printed, one in Connecticut and one in Massachusetts, and also a sermon which was preached in Wethersfield.

268. ELIPHALET, REV.   Killingworth, Conn.

678. SARAH, born Sept 19, 1768, married, Dec. 26, 1804, John Wilcox, of Branford, where she died in 1840. She left one son, E. H. Wilcox, of Branford.

679. MARY, born Sept. 29, 1770, married, Dec. 23, 1805, Josiah Rutly. Her husband died, Dec. 29, 1819. She had one daughter, Mary, who married Asa M. Bolles, a lawyer of Killingworth, after whose death she married, for her second husband, Rev. Owen Street, pastor in Lowell, Mass. She had two children by her first husband, and two by her second. She died in 1853.

680. JOSEPH, born Jan. 11, 1776, and died single, May 20, 1817.

269. JONATHAN.   Higganum, Conn.

681. SILENCE, born in East Haddam, and died and was buried in Hartford.

682. JONATHAN, born in East Haddam, July 2, 1770. He graduated at Yale, 1789. He married, at Norwalk, Oct. 10, 1802, Sarah Comstock, who died Feb. 21, 1808. He married, Nov. 24, 1808, Elizabeth Leeds Comstock, a sister of his first wife. He always resided in that part of Haddam known as Higganum, where he was engaged in mercantile and commercial pursuits. That he had the esteem and confidence of the community in which he lived, is shown by his many appointments to responsible offices and commissions. He represented his town several times in the state legislature, and was a member of the convention of 1818 which formed the state constitution. He was elected deacon of the church in Haddam in 1806, and held the office until his death, although he did not officiate after the year 1811. He was a man strongly attached to the institutions and duties of religion. His neighbors bear full testimony to his consistency as a Christian, and to his fidelity to all the social duties of the neighbor and citizen.

683. CYNTHIA, born in East Haddam, and married, in Windsor, Sept., 1806, Daniel Sayre, of Canton.

684. REBECCA, born June 18, 1775, married Allen M. Mather, of Windsor, who is now living. She died leaving one daughter, who was born Nov. 4, 1798.

685. PARTHENIA, born Oct. 27, 1778, married Allen Mather, and died Sept. 16, 1838. Her children were: Edward Huntington, born Oct. 2. 1806, died June 11, 1834; Sarah H. Baldwin; Mary, born Feb. 28, 1809; Samuel, born May 16, 1811; Julia, born Dec. 12, 1813; Harriet, born Feb. 6, 1816; and Sarah, born July 6, 1818.

686. SELDEN, born in Higganum, March 24, 1786, married, in Lyme, June 17, 1819, Ann Lord Johnson, who died Oct. 7, 1823. He married for his second wife, Jan. 27, 1832, Jeannette, daughter of Alexander and Elizabeth (McCurdy) Stewart, of New York city, who now resides in New York city. He, like his brother Jonathan, was engaged in shipping and commercial pursuits. In military life he attained the rank of lieutenant colonel. He was also active in religion, and died in June, 1846, in Higganum.

270. ELEAZER. Lebanon, Conn.

687. ELEAZER, born in 1776, and died single in 1799.
688. FANNY, married Mr. Bull of Wethersfield.

271. JOSIAH, DEACON. Rocky Hill, Conn.

689. A DAUGHTER, who married Mr. Robins. She left two daughters, Mrs. West, of Alexandria, Va., and Mrs. Holmes, of Elmira, N. Y., both of them women of more than ordinary culture and refinement.

690. WEALTHY, born Aug. 13, 1782.

691. ABIGAIL, born July 14, 1784, and died single, May 12, 1835.

692. NATHANIEL GILBERT, born Oct. 30, 1785, in Wethersfield, Rocky Hill parish. Moved by a fondness for study, he commenced under the instructions of Dr. Nathan Perkins, of Hartford, his preparation for college, and entered Yale, 1802. During his junior year, he became a subject of grace and resolved upon a preparation for the ministry. He graduated in 1806, and was honored with a master's degree in 1833. He was licensed by the Hartford North Association in 1809. In the following year he received a call to settle over the congregational church in Bethany, Conn., where he was ordained, Aug. 22, 1810. He married, in 1812, Miss Betsey, daughter of Zephaniah Tucker, of Derby. In this place he labored with great acceptance, until obliged, by the progress of pulmonary complaints, to ask and insist upon a dismissal, which was granted, greatly to the regret of his parish, in 1822. He removed to Orange in 1840, where he died in the faith he had preached, Feb. 20, 1848. Of his labors in Bethany, the Rev. C. Brewster, of Orange, Conn., in his funeral sermon says: "the church were harmonious during the whole time he was their pastor. It was also blessed with revivals, and one, especially, of considerable power." Of his character, the same authority says: "His piety was of the contemplative cast. He exhibited the Christian graces of meekness and resignation in no ordinary degree. As a minister, he applied himself diligently and faithfully to his work. His scholarship was of a high order. He had a good knowledge of the Greek and Latin classics, had read the Hebrew Bible through, and was probably a better Hebraist than any other pastor in

SIXTH GENERATION. 187

the vicinity at the time. He left behind him quite an amount of poetical composition, mainly of the religious cast. He prepared, also, two elementary geographies for the use of schools, which were published in Hartford." He contributed also several lengthy articles for the columns of the Christian Spectator, which evince a scholarship of a high order. His widow still lives with her daughter, Mrs. Merwin, in Milford.

693. JOSIAH, born June 18, 1787, and lived in Le Roy, N. Y.
694. ELEAZER, born March 1789, and lived in Hartford, Conn.

272. CALEB. Ashford, Conn.

These births are found on the Lebanon records, excepting the last.

695. ZEBULON, born Dec. 9, 1747, and died the following April.
696. EZRA, born March 24, 1749, and went to Nova Scotia. He married a Hannah Fitch, and died in Cornwallis, N. S., in 1827.
697. BATHSHEBA, born Dec. 12, 1750.
698. LYDIA, born Sept. 9, 1753.
699. CALEB, born 1758, and died at Cape Breton, in 1815.

274. ELISHA. Windham and Mansfield, Conn.

700. ELISHA, born Sept. 17, 1750, as the Norwich records show, and died in Mansfield, April 10, 1770, as appears from the Mansfield records. The Norwich record calls him a son of Caleb, of Lebanon.
701. ELIZABETH, born Jan. 8, 1751-2, as appears on the Norwich records.
702. MOLLY, born March, 18, 1754. This, and the next two births of this family, are found on the Windham records.
703. PHILURA, born Jan. 15, 1756.
704. ROBERT DENISON, born Aug. 14, 1758.
705. ANDREW G., born, as the Mansfield records testify, July 16, 1769.
705¹. ELISHA, born April, 1770.
705². CALVIN, born June 14, 1778, as the Ashford record shows.
705³. LUTHER, born June 14, 1778.

275. ELIJAH. Ashford, Conn.

The first two births of this family and the baptism of the first four children, are on the Mansfield town and church records, the last being of the same date, Nov. 5, 1761. The birth of the last son is on the Ashford records.

706. BEULAH, born Dec. 11, 1751, and died single, in Ashford, in 1835.
707. BETTE, born May 26, 1754, married, 1779, Nathaniel Bowditch. They resided in Providence.
708. HANNAH, born Feb. 13, 1758, married Nathan Lilley, Nov. 25, 1800, and lived in Ashford.
709. SARAH, born April, 1761, and died single in Ashford in 1837.
710. ABIGAIL, born Dec. 5, 1764, married Emmaus Lilley, and lived in Mansfield.
711. NATHAN, born Nov. 5, 1767, married, May 31, 1798, Elethea Butler of Ashford, who died April 12, 1833. He died in Ashford, Dec. 1, 1845.

712. ELIJAH, born May 21. 1772. married Hannah Colburn in 1811. He lived in Ashford, where he died Feb. 6, 1843.

276. ABNER. Windham and Mansfield, Conn.

The birth of the first of this family is found both on the Lebanon and Windham records. The others, commencing with Silas, are recorded on the Windham records.

713. DAVID, born Nov. 17. 1750, and resided at Bethel, Vt.

714. ABNER, born in Norwich, Conn., as his sons testify, July 21, 1752, married in 1787, Abigail Leavens, and in 1800 moved to New Haven, Vt. In 1817 he moved to Perry N. Y., where he died Jan 8, 1819. He was a justice of the peace in Vermont. He was in the revolutionary war and was present at the battle of Bunker Hill. His wife died in Jan. 1795.

715. SILAS, born in April, 1754, and died in New Haven, Vt.

716. SUSANNAH, born Sept. 16, 1756, and lived in Cincinnati, Ohio.

717. NATHAN, born Sept. 16, 1758, and died, Dec. 17, 1767.

718. JAMES, born June 23, 1760, married Rebecca Densman, of Canaan, and removed to Woodstock, Vt., where he died in Nov., 1811. At the age of fourteen he enlisted in the revolutionary army, and served as drum major through the war.

719. WHITMAN, born July 12, 1763. married, in Mansfield, Feb. 16, 1787, Susan Clark, who was born in Mansfield, Conn., Aug. 24, 1768, and died in New Haven, Vt., March 1, 1847. He resided in the latter place, where he died, Nov. 3, 1847.

720. MARY, born Aug. 10, 1765, and married Erastus Chapman, probably son of Simon and Alice (Rouse) Chapman.

721. DANIEL, born May 13, 1769, and had no family. He died in Constable, N. Y.

722. SABRY, born Dec. 2, 1772, and married Erastus Fuller, and lived in St. Lawrence county, N. Y.

277. JAMES. Lebanon, Conn.

My information regarding this family is mainly from Seth, (1250), and from William, (726).

723. ASA, born March 29, 1758, married, in 1785, Martha Hibbard, who was born June 16, 1761. Under the impression that he was called to prophesy against Quebec, Canada, he went to that city, took the small pox and died. His widow is now, (1861), living in Enfield, N. H., and is a happy and hopeful old lady.

724. ZEBULON, born Nov. 25, 1766, married, June 24, 1804, Keziah Nichols, who was born, April 11 1776, and now lives in Enfield, N. H. He died Dec., 1851.

725. JONATHAN, lived several years in Canada, married and had a son who died of cholera, in Bloomington College in 1832. Becoming convinced of the infidelity of his wife, he left her and went to the West, where he married again and had twin sons.

SIXTH GENERATION.   189

726. WILLIAM, born in Lebanon, Conn., May 26, 1775, and married, March 22, 1795, Elizabeth Derby, who was born Oct. 22, 1778, and died Nov. 3, 1826. He lives in Washington, Vt. He has twice represented the town in the state legislature, and has been much in public life in the town. He is now, 1859, in the enjoyment of his mental faculties, and lives in joyful hope of heaven.

727. JOSEPH, born in 1778 in Connecticut, married, 1807, Harriet Converse, and lived in Orange, Vt. He died in Charleston, Vt., in 1857.

728. SUBMIT, born, as her son Seth supposes, in Hartford, Vt., in 1769, married Thomas, (513).

729. ALICE, married Solomon Wadhams, of Boston, Vt., and had one daughter who lived, named Jerusha Leland. She died in 1858.

730. LYDIA, was killed by the accidental discharge of a gun at the age of fourteen.

279. EZEKIEL.   Lebanon, Conn.

These births are all on the Lebanon records.

731. JOSEPH, born May 25, 1758.

732. BETSY, born Sept. 3, 1760, in Cornwallis, Nova Scotia, as the Lebanon record shows.

733. ESTHER, born July 5, 1763.

734. EZEKIEL, born Nov. 1764.

735. DANIEL, born Sept. 6, 1766.

285. JOHN.   Lebanon, Conn.

736. FRANCES, born Jan. 21, 1770, and never married.

737. LUCY, born Jan. 25, 1772.

738. JOHN, born March 25, 1773, married Sophia A. Foster, and lived in Sunderland, Mass.

739. ABIGAIL, born Nov. 21, 1776, and married first, John Bird, and second, Benjamin Keese. She resided in Keeseville, N. Y.

740. ISRAEL, born at East Haddam Landing, June 2, 1781, and married Mary W. Fitch, of Woodstock, Vt. He has been a member of the New York legislature twice, in 1844 and 1845. He has resided in Utica and in Syracuse, N. Y., where he is still (1858) living. He has been extensively engaged in business, and was also, for some time, a teacher of a private school.

741. WILLIAM, born Oct. 31, 1784. He never married. He lived in Alabama.

742. EUNICE, born Oct. 31, 1784.

286. JOSEPH.   Harwinton, Conn.

This family were all born in Harwinton.

743. JOSEPH, born in 1780, and was a farmer at River Raisin, C. W.

744. WILLIAM, born in 1784, married Elizabeth Vincent, and resided in Wolcottville.

745. LUCY, who married Paul Bluzo. She lived and died in Vermont.
746. RACHEL, who married Andrew Frank, of Starkboro, Vt.
747. RHODA, who married William Tryon, of New Hartford.

289. DAVID, REV.   Hamburg, (Lyme) Conn.

This family were all born in Marlborough, Conn.

748. BETSEY KIMBERLY, born Aug. 8, 1779. She married Allen Bunce, and resided in North Lyme. They had two children, Timothy D., who resided at Greenport, L. I., where he had a family, and Susan, who lived in Lyme. The son, Capt. Timothy D. Bunce, died at sea, Sept. 12, 1860, having lost from the same vessel, a short time before, a promising son. Both father and son were much lamented.

749. DAVID, born March 1, 1784, and married, Jan. 30, 1808, Ann Carly. He was a bookseller in New York city. He was a most estimable and worthy man, and died while away from home, on business, in Norfolk, Va., March 18, 1819, after an illness of ten days. "He manifested the most humble resignation to the divine will." He had just completed the business which had called him abroad, and was on his way to his family in New York, when he was arrested by death. His wife died in New York, Feb. 1838.

750. ANNA, born Sept. 1, 1785, and died in Hamburg, Conn., Nov. 19, 1861. She was a devoted Christian woman, and died beloved and lamented by all who knew her. She was known, also, as Nancy, as her obituary calls her.

751. LEVERET ISRAEL FOOTE, born Dec. 28, 1787, graduated at Yale, 1811, and studied theology at Princeton, N. J., ordained pastor of the Presbyterian church in New Brunswick, N. J., in 1815, where he remained, most unweariedly laboring in his profession, until his death, May 11, 1820. This "excellent man and eminent servant of Christ," resembled, in the general features of his character, his father. He had a warm heart and a ready hand. The poor, the afflicted, the wronged and oppressed, were drawn toward him by the power of his deep and tender sympathy for them. He could find time, while ministering to the spiritual wants of the most cultivated of his congregation, to meet, weekly, with the most ignorant and neglected in his parish, for their instruction. "Seldom has one descended to the tomb more respected and beloved." His congregation, the neighboring clergy and the press, agree in testifying to his high excellence as a man, a Christian, and a pastor. In the sermon preached at his funeral, by the Rev. Dr. Miller, of Princeton, a most worthy tribute was paid to his high character in these relations, and also to his signal ability as a preacher and ambassador for Christ. Few men more nearly realized Cowper's delineation of the ministerial character, and though it was doubtless gain for him to die, it was felt that the church of Christ on earth had lost one of its most needed guides and defenders. He married Phebe Marvin, of Lyme, Conn., who, twenty years after his death, married a Rev. Mr. Palmer, of Ohio, who also is dead. She has resided with her son, in New York city, and is now (1861) with her daughter, in Pittsburg, Pa.

752. LOUISA, born May 29, 1790, and still resides in Hamburg, Lyme.

SIXTH GENERATION.   191

292. EBENEZER.   West Indies.

753. ROSWELL, born in 1763, and lived in North Carolina.

295. ANDREW, CAPT.   Lebanon, Conn,

This family were all born in Lebanon.

754. SIMON, born Feb. 18, 1769, or March 22, 1767, and married, as his son's record says, Feb. 18, 1795, Sarah Fitch. He resided in Lebanon, where he died, Oct. 3, 1819.

755. AZEL, born Oct. 25, 1770, married, in Leicester, Mass., Nov. 30, 1797, Hannah Robinson. They lived in Spencer, Mass., where he died, Sept. 8, 1839, and his widow, Aug. 4, 1850.

756. ELIJAH, born Nov. 18, 1772, married Eunice Frink, and lived in Carlisle, N. Y. He died, July 14, 1843, having had no children. His widow is still (1859) living.

757. EBENEZER, born Feb. 14, 1775, and married, Oct. 11, 1802, Mehetabel Swift, of Mansfield. He was a clothier and farmer, living in Beckel, Mass., where he died, Jan. 31, 1835. His wife is still living, (1857,) in her 77th year.

758. SARAH, born June 19, 1777, and married, in April, 1800, Joseph Rockwell, a farmer of Lebanon. She was the mother of seven children, among whom is the Rev. Prof. E. F. Rockwell, of Davidson College, N. C. They are Azel, born May 5, 1808, married Laura Hill, and lives in Lebanon, having five children: Philura, died at 14 years of age; Emily, now living; Eunice Huntington, died single in 1840, aged 33 years; Elijah Frink, now professor of languages, as above, was born Oct. 6, 1809, and married M. K. McNeill, of Fayettville, N. C., June 18, 1839; Andrew Huntington, married Caroline R. Porter, of Columbia, and has three children: Ruth, born March 6, 1814, and died May 5, same year; and Sarah Ann, born Oct. 16, 1816, and died Sept. 20, 1835.

She was a most excellent woman. She died Sept. 8, 1849, and her husband followed her on the 28th of the same month.

759. EUNICE, born July 30, 1779, married Ebenezer (555).

760. ROGER, born March 4, 1782, and died Aug. 22, 1783.

761. JABEZ, born Aug. 6, 1784, and died single, Nov. 12, 1832.

762. ROSWELL, born Sept. 14, 1786, married, Sept. 7, 1813, Sophia Tracy, of Franklin, and resided in Colchester, from 1827 to 1832, when he removed to Carlisle, N. Y., where he died, Jan. 23, 1862. His wife was daughter of Peter and Abigail (Hartshorne) Tracy, and was born in Franklin, Conn., Nov. 17, 1793.

763. JOHN, born May 27, 1789, and died April 16, 1791.

764. ANDREW, born May 31, 1791, graduated at Yale, 1815. He married May 1, 1819, Mary Chipman, of Shoreham, Vt. He was licensed to preach, by the Presbytery of North River, in 1825. He had studied theology with a class of young men, under the instruction of several pastors, in New York city, and the class was the origin of the New York Theological Seminary. He has lived as teacher and preacher in several places, and now (1857) is en-

gaged as stated supply for a church in Guilford Center, N. Y., where he commenced preaching, May 1, 1856. Since the above was penned he has removed to the pastorate of the Presbyterian church in Smyrna, N. Y.

299. DANIEL, (M. D.)   Woodbury, Conn.

765. SYBILLA, born 1769, and married David Stiles, son of David and Sarah (Minor) Curtiss, of Woodbury, where they resided. She united with the Woodbury Congregational church in 1792, and died Dec. 30, 1837, and he, Jan. 22, 1846. Their children were as follows: Sybilla Cleora, baptized, Nov. 23, 1794, married Roderick Stiles, and died Nov. 27, 1852; David H., baptized April 3, 1796, married Maria Summers, and second, Anna Guernsey; Sarah, baptized Feb. 11, 1798, married Rufus Stiles, Nov. 9, 1822; Nathan, baptized March 19, 1799, and died young; Daniel, baptized Nov. 8, 1801, married Julia F. Strong, and is president of Woodbury bank; Elvira, died unmarried, Dec. 24, 1837; Mary Ann N., baptized, June 16, 1805, and married Oliver S. Weller; William, baptized Sept. 24, 1809, and married Elizabeth Stoddard. He died March 19, 1841, without issue. The grand-children of Mrs. Curtiss have been ten.

766. ABIGAIL, born in 1770, united with the Congregational church in 1811, and died single in 1835.

767. DANIEL, born in 1772, and lived in Onondaga, N. Y.

768. CYNTHIA, born in 1774, married Zethan Bunnell, and died, Feb. 1804.

769. ISAAC, born in 1775, and died single, in Woodbury, Dec. 21, 1848. He is reported by Dr. Joshua, (2146) to have perished in the woods at Woodbridge, Jan. 4, 1849.

770. RUSSEL, who died, aged sixteen years.

771. ELVIRA, born in 1786, and married James Manville, of Woodbury, where she died in 1834.

772. MARY ANN, born in 1788, and died single in Woodbury, in 1805.

773. ALZA, born Aug. 12, 1794, married April, 1823, Nathaniel L. Proctor, who died, March 1, 1851, aged 67. She has two children, Nathaniel L. and William H. For the above record of this family I am indebted to the correspondence of Wm. Cothren, of Woodbury, and to his excellent History of Ancient Woodbury.

300. LEVI.   Norwich, Conn.

774. NANCY, born May 17, 1772, married Joseph Otis, a successful merchant of New York and a retired gentleman in Norwich. He left an imperishable memorial to his name in the excellent Otis Library of Norwich city, which he endowed. He died, sincerely lamented, in 1854. His wife "was a lady of many estimable qualities," and best known for her sincere and cheerful piety. She died Aug. 27, 1844.

775. BETSEY, born Dec. 2, 1774, married in June, 1798, Guilford Young, who was killed in Mexico. She died June 17, 1845. Two of her children, Levi H. and Guilford D., are dead. Four of them are still, 1862, living: Mrs.

SIXTH GENERATION. 193

Jane Gray, wife of Edward Y. Thomas: Mrs. Cornelia Ann, wife of David Y. Thomas; Marcus B., of Providence; and C. Cassius, who lives in Norwich city and has a family.

776. LYDIA, born June 27, 1776, and still living unmarried in Norwich.

777. LEVI, born Dec. 29, 1777, married Oct. 23, 1802, Catherine M., daughter of Peter Richards, who was killed at the storming of Fort Griswold in 1781. He died in Norwich, July 1, 1838. His wife, born April 11, 1781, died Aug. 6, 1818. "a Christian whose death was deeply lamented."

778. ASHER, who died Dec. 15, 1780.

779. SYBEL, died Nov. 24, 1782, aged six months and eighteen days.

780. SYBEL, died aged six months and twenty-seven days.

781. ASHER P., born Sept. 30, 1784, and died, without family, Feb. 1, 1841.

782. JABEZ, died July 22, 1787, aged four months and five days.

783. HEZEKIAH, born Aug. 27, 1789, and died May 15, 1796.

784. JEDIDIAH, born Sept. 13, 1791, married June 15, 1819, Eliza, daughter of Marvin Wait, of New London, and is, after a successful business career in mercantile pursuits, a retired gentleman in his native town. He has been much respected and honored for his private and public worth. The two beautiful engravings which accompany this sketch will be a perpetual witness to much that is attractive and estimable in the honored couple whom they represent.

785. LEONARD, died Jan 8, 1796, aged two years and four months.

301. FELIX. Norwich, Conn.

786. LUCY, born Feb. 21, 1774, married Sept. 20, 1795, Augustus Perkins. They lived in Norwich, where she died in 1822. Their children were: John Augustus, born July 21, 1796; George Apollos, born Sept. 18, 1798; Mary Brown, born Jan. 6, 1801; Rebecca Huntington, born Dec. 9, 1803; Isaac Huntington, born Dec. 18, 1806; Edward Henry, born April 4, 1810, and Simeon Abijah, born July 7, 1812.

787. REBECCA, born May 12, 1776, married Augustus Perkins, the husband of her deceased sister. She died in 1838.

788. SARAH, born July 16, 1778, married Cyrus Williams, of Stockbridge, Mass. She died in 1838, leaving no children.

789. MARY B., born Feb. 20, 1781, and died unmarried in 1801.

790. JAMES, born June 4, 1783, married, March 2, 1809, Zerviah, daughter of Rev. John and Hannah Tyler, of Norwich city. He died in Norwich, May 18, 1822, having been extensively engaged in commercial business.

791. CHARLOTTE, born Aug. 28, 1785, and died May 3, 1786.

792. CHARLOTTE, born Oct. 28, 1787, and still lives unmarried in Norwich.

793. FELIX A., born Nov. 1, 1789, married, Dec. 11, 1811, Frances Snow. He commenced an early apprenticeship to commercial pursuits, and at the age of twenty engaged in trade with his brother James, and continued in business in Norwich until 1825, when he removed to New York. He here engaged in the dry goods business as an importer. Between the years 1832 and 1846 he

was called by business to make a dozen voyages to Europe, during which he formed an extensive and desirable acquaintanceship both in England and on the continent. In 1849 he retired from business, removing from New York to Brooklyn, N. Y. His wife died, Jan. 23, 1859, aged sixty-nine years.

Mr. Huntington, whose death occurred Feb. 18. 1862, had been a member and officer of the church of the Redeemer in Brooklyn, from the organization of the parish. After his death, the vestry of the church testified in the strongest terms to his faithfulness and efficiency as an officer; to his wisdom and prudence as a counselor; to the sincerity of his Christian profession; to his "earnest desire for the extension of the church of our blessed Redeemer on earth; and to his evident preparation for the heavenly inheritance."

794. WILLIAM, born Aug. 24, 1793. He has never married, and lives at Charlotte C. H., Va. He is a teacher.

312. ELIPHALET. Norwich, Conn.

This family were all born in Norwich.

795. EUNICE, born in 1800, and died in January, 1807.

796. ABIGAIL, born Oct. 4, 1801, and still lives unmarried in Norwich.

797. MARY ANN, who married John H. Grace, of Norwich. She has had two daughters, and is still living in Norwich.

313. HENRY. (HON.) Rome, N. Y.

798. CATHERINE, born Dec. 3, 1797, married, March 26, 1833, Col. William Williams, "one of the most benevolent and enterprising citizens of Utica," N. Y. "and one of the most exemplary members and valuable elders in" the First Presbyterian church of that city. She died in Utica, Sept. 10, 1856. Her funeral sermon, by her pastor, the Rev. P. H. Fowler, contains a well deserved eulogy of her singularly pure and lovely character. From this it appears that in early life she became hopefully a Christian. " Religion took the entire possession of her soul, and became both a master passion and a controlling principle. Especially did it inspire her with its compassionate and benevolent spirit. * * * No one was more enlisted in labors for the heathen, and yet she was quite as much engaged for her own country, and was a model to us all of devotedness to the particular church and congregation to which she belonged. * * * There was a remarkable completeness in the piety of our friend. It was leaven in her heart while it was motion in her life. She was eminently a friend of the poor, a sympathizer with them, a visitor among them, a generous benefactor to them. Yet notwithstanding all she was and the much she did, she was the humblest of Christians, instinctively shrinking from boasting and display. * * * She was one of the rarest, choicest characters in the whole acquaintance of my life. I never knew one in whom it was more difficult to detect a fault. To our partial vision she appeared to bear the perfections of heaven during the probation of earth."

799. FRANCES, born Sept. 16, 1799, married, June 6, 1826, Nicoll H. Dering, M. D., of New York city. She died Feb. 2, 1841.

SIXTH GENERATION. 195

800. ANNE, born Feb. 23, 1801, and died Oct. 2, 1823.
801. HENRIETTA DESIRE, born June 15, 1803, married, Dec. 9, 1828, Benjamin H. Wright, of Rome.
802. GLORIANA, born Feb. 1, 1806, and died Dec. 3, 1808.
803. LUCY, born Feb. 2, 1808, and died Feb. 28, ——.
804. GLORIANA, born June 7, 1809, and died single, June 3, 1837.
805. ELIZABETH, born Aug. 6, 1811, married, Aug. 4, 1836, Charles C. Young, of Rome. She died Jan. 19, 1838.
806. HENRY, born July 11, 1813, and died in Rome, March 31, 1854.
807. BENJAMIN NICOLL, born May 5, 1816, married, Jan. 24, 1855, Mabel L. Utley, and resides in Rome. He is an extensive land holder and a prominent man. He was chosen member of the New York state senate in 1851 to fill a vacancy, and returned to the Senate in 1852 and '53. He is now, (1860), one of the presidential electors on the republican ticket.

314. GURDON. Rome, N. Y.

808. EDWARD, born Dec. 5, 1792, graduated at Union College, 1810, and died single, Dec. 16, 1816, in New York city, having just entered upon the practice of law.
809. SUSANNAH, born April 8, 1795, married, Oct. 22, 1815, Major James S. Dalliber, U. S. A., and resided in Rome. She died March 19, 1837, her husband having died Oct. 9, 1832. Their children were: Anne Huntington, born in Rome, Aug. 29, 1816, married De Witt C. Bancroft, Nov. 1, 1837, and died in Rome, Oct. 21, 1844; Susan, born at Watervliet, Nov. 5, 1818, and died Nov. 29, 1818; Elizabeth Perkins, born Jan. 2, 1820, and died Oct. 13, 1820; James Edward, born Dec. 8, 1821, married Achsah D. Swift, of Utica, Sept. 4, 1844; Sarah Perkins, born March 25, 1824, married Eli Whitney, of New Haven, June 17, 1845; Mary Huntington, born at Rome, June 20, 1826, married Wm. H. Dutton, of Utica, Dec. 30, 1846; Susan Elizabeth, born in Moriah, N. Y., Oct. 11, 1828, married Theodore W. Thompson, Sept. 1851; and Katherine, born May 8, 1831, married Augustus H. Burley, of Chicago, Ill., Oct. 3, 1855, and now resides in Chicago.
810. ANNE, born Nov. 20, 1796, and died Aug. 23, 1809.
811. ROBERT, born Sept. 26, 1799, and died May 13, 1801.
812. MARY PERKINS, born Jan. 7, 1801, and died, unmarried, March 24, 1825.

315. GEORGE, HON. Rome, N. Y.

This family were all born in Rome.
813. HANNAH THOMAS, born May 25, 1798, married, Sept. 4, 1819, Rev. Henry Smith, and resided in Camden, N. Y., where she died Jan. 14, 1836. They had two children, Hannah Huntington, who married Henry W. Coe, of San Jose, California; and Henry Huntington, who graduated at Princeton College and studied theology. He traveled in Europe, and on his return settled in Caldwell, as Presbyterian pastor. While in college, his name was

changed, by the New Jersey legislature, from Henry Huntington Smith to Henry Smith Huntington. He will therefore reappear in the next generation.

814. MARY MUMFORD, born June 12, 1800, and died single, July 31, 1826.

815. LUCY, born July 17, 1803, and died Aug. 2, 1803.

816. LUCY, born April 25, 1805, and died Nov. 3, 1806.

817. GEORGE, born Aug. 27, 1807, and died March 25, 1828. He had graduated at Yale in 1827, and entered the Theological Seminary at Andover, intending to devote his life to the work of the ministry. He was taken sick and obliged to give up his studies. He left the seminary for home, and was found in his hotel in New York city, in a dying condition, by Mrs. Benjamin Waight, who had him taken to her hospitable home, where he died as above. He had lived long enough to give to his friends and teachers high promise of usefulness.

818. HENRY, born Dec. 1, 1810, and died the next day.

819. CHARLOTTE, born Aug. 14, 1812, married, April 17, 1833, Charles C. Young, of New York city, where she died May 12, 1855.

820. EDWARD, born June 23, 1817, married, Sept. 4, 1844, Antoinette Randall, and is a gentleman of wealth and of great personal worth. He was a member of the convention of 1846, for amending the constitution of New York. He was one of the presidential electors in 1860.

The author is under special obligation to him for the interest he has taken in this memoir of the Huntingtons, and for his aid in making out the record of the branch of the family to which he belongs.

318. BENJAMIN. New York.

821. JEDIDIAH VINCENT, born in New York city, Jan. 20, 1815, and married Mary (2117). He was educated at Yale College, and at the New York University, graduating in 1835. He received his medical diploma at the University of Pennsylvania, in 1838. Finding literature more attractive than his profession, he devoted himself mainly to its pursuit. He labored, also, in the educational field, and received an invitation to the professorship of mental philosophy, in St. Paul's College, near Flushing, L. I. In 1841 he was ordained in the Prot. Episcopal church, and after a period assumed parochial duty in Middlebury, Vt. Declining health induced him to visit the South, and to reside for a while in Europe, where he spent four years, returning in 1849. In 1842 he published a volume of poems, among which were, " The Northern Dawn," a descriptive piece; a threnodia, " To Emmeline;" " The Trysting-place," and translations from the Greek Anthology. Several sonnets completed the volume. Griswold speaks of these poems as meditative, and finished in a style of scholarly elegance. A thoughtful critic of the time discerned in them passages which recalled the tender beauty of Tennyson. The novel, "Lady Alice," appeared in 1849, and was a decided success. Its high artistic merits elicited the **applause of critics**, and 20,000 copies were promptly sold. Soon followed another novel, "**Alban;**" a poem, " America Discovered;" " The Forest;" " The Pretty **Plate;**" "**The Blonde** and Brunette;" and "Rosemary."

Dr. H., for a season, edited the "Metropolitan Magazine," at Baltimore, and still later, the "Leader," at St. Louis. He has also lectured in several of our large cities, before associations. He died at Pau, in Southern France, of consumption, March 10, 1862. A beautiful tribute to his memory and personal worth appeared in the "Tablet," a single passage from which, is due to his name, in this record:

"With all his rare mental gifts, Dr. Huntington had the meekness and humility of a child, and had, in a most uncommon degree, the art of endearing himself to all with whom he came in contact. In him we saw combined the finished gentleman and the accomplished scholar, the humble, sincere, practical Christian; as a husband, as a brother, as a friend, as a citizen, Dr. Huntington was all that man ought to be, whilst as an author he has left a distinguished name among American writers. His death leaves a void in the ranks of American literature that will be long and severely felt. Dr. Huntington's health failed rapidly after 'Rosemary' was finished; he traveled to the north-west with some benefit, and by the advice of his physician sailed for France in November, 1861, to pass the winter in Pau. In that balmy climate he failed to find permanent relief, but gradually sank, soothed by the tenderest care of wife and friends, and on the 10th of March last went to his rest as calmly as a sleeping infant."

822. DANIEL, born Oct. 14, 1816, and married, at St. Ann's Church, Brooklyn, June 16, 1842, Sophia Richards. His life has been given to the cultivation of the fine arts, for which nature designed him, and in which his success has been a triumph. As a portrait painter he stands at the head of his profession, having a continental reputation. The following criticism, found in the "Whig Review," for Aug. 1846, exhibits his position among our artists at that time, and his fame and relative position have advanced steadily ever since.

"Huntington, to whom we are inclined to give the highest place among our artists of the highest school, sent five pictures, exclusive of three portraits, any one of which would have asserted his pre-eminence in this department of his art. Of these, our favorite is the Sacred Lesson, which, although not so full of spirituality, and perhaps not so elevated in tone as his Italy, seems to us a more finished work. The subject, a beautiful girl listening to the story of the crucifixion from an aged man, gave opportunity for all the harmony of contrast, and the embodiment of that high physical and intellectual beauty, of which Huntington seems to have such an admirable conception. His female heads are remarkable for their graceful contour, their high foreheads, but broad, low and classical brows, and for their perfectly feminine expression, which, as well as their freedom from that exaggeration of points of beauty, such as large eyes and small mouths, into which modern painters are apt to fall, gives them a truthful air which some of hotbed taste mistake for materiality. In fact, his women do not look like sylphs, angels, nor goddesses, but like women, which is the grand reason that they are so beautiful. His heads of old men have equal excellence, and are full of character and vigorous drawing. He seems conscious of his abilities in this way, for three of his pictures for this year present the contrast of feminine youth with masculine age. Huntington's pictures bear the stamp of high cultivation and of great genius. Not only are his conceptions beautiful, just, and of a high poetic order, and his designs clear, but his work is almost always well done; the tone of his pictures is such that the eye rests upon them with delight and contentment; the heart sympathizes with the sentiment expressed, and the judgment approves almost without a but. His effects are always simple, direct, and forcible, for he never descends into the pettiness of his art. His coloring is singularly beautiful, and reminds us of that of Lucca Giordano, *fa presto Lucca* as he was called, but among American artists it is peculiarly his own. Who has given us such unobtrusive reds and yellows, and such rich, quiet greens? Nobody has ever tried to do it: the very conception of such colors seems to have been left to him, for such was the character of his coloring before he had studied in Italy. They alone are enough to make a reputation, and yet they are but secondary to, though admirably in keeping with, his high poetic conception, his admirable drawing, and exquisite flesh tints. Indeed, so beautiful are these colors in themselves, and so harmonious are the broad masses in which they are introduced, that the eye, after wandering around upon the walls, turns unwittingly upon his pictures to drink in their cool, refreshing tone."

The estimate in which Mr. Huntington is held by the members of his own profession, is evinced by his election, in 1861, to the presidency of the National Academy of Design, as their third president, the first two having been, Prof. Morse, and A. B. Durand.

823. GURDON, born Nov. 27, 1818, graduated at Hamilton College, 1838. Ordained deacon of the Prot. Episcopal church, July 2, 1848, and presbyter, April 14, 1851. He was invited to Simmonsville, and Spraguesville, R. I., in 1848, from which post he went to Pottersville, N. Y., May, 1850. Called to Christ's church, Sackett's Harbor, N. Y., April 6, 1852, and to Sag Harbor, June 11, 1856, where he is now engaged. He has devoted much of his time to literature, and from early in his course, as student, has used a ready and skillful pen. His contributions to our poetic literature have been quite numerous, among which are the "Shadowy Land," now in press; "The Guests of Brazil;" "The romance of the Indian Country and its Tribes;" "Washington at the Battle of Princeton;" "The Watery World;" "The Mohawk River;" "Tuxedo Lake;" "Genevieve;" "Musings at Evening Hours;" "Child of Immortality;" "The Steamship." Three of his poems, on public occasions, have also been printed: on "Confidence and Affection," &c.: "Dignity and Triumphs of Mental and Moral Culture;" "Providence;" and a prose essay on "The Conditions and Materials of Poetry." His poem at the Huntington meeting, Sept. 3, 1857, appears in this book. He was married, Jan. 22, 1852, to Sarah Gold Sill, who died in Sag Harbor, Jan. 31, 1858. He married, the second time, Oct. 25, 1859, Miss Charlotte Marsh Sill, of Rome, N. Y.

SIXTH GENERATION. 199

321. WILLIAM. Middlebury, Vt.

The first eight births in this family are on the Norwich records.

824. JOHN, born Oct. 21, 1764, married, in 1804, Laura Burbank. He was a farmer and lived in Orange, Vt. He died in Jan. 1817.

825. SUSANNAH, born July 25, or 28, 1766, married David Whitney, a farmer of Tunbridge, Vt. She died in 1812.

826. WILLIAM, born Sept. 21, 1768, married, April, 1793, Delia Cleveland, and resided in Whiting, Vt. He died May 18, 1814.

827. MILLER, born Aug. 15, 1770, married Betsey Miller, and lived in Randolph, Vt., where he died in 1857.

828. ELIZABETH, born Sept. 13, or 15, 1772, married James Wilson, a Baptist preacher, and lived in Adams. N. Y., and later, in Sackett's Harbor, N. Y.

829. ANDREW, born Aug. 29, 1783, married, Feb. 28, 1816, Mary Cobb, and lived in Middlebury, Vt., where he died, March 30, 1816.

830. ANNA P., born Jan. 27, 1776, married Comfort Barnes, and lived in Randolph and Chelsea. Vt. She died March 23, 1856.

831. FANNY, born Nov. 14, 1777, married Nathan Bicknell, and lived in Brighton, Vt., and Lebanon, N. H. She died in 1823.

832. LOIS, born Sept. 11, 1780, married Sylvanus Martin, M. D., and lived in Plainfield, N. H.

833. EUNICE, born May 29, 1786, married, Sept. 1816, William Wainwright, and lived in Salisbury. Vt. She died Dec. 25, 1857.

834. REBECCA, born Aug. 13, 1789, married, March, 1846, Samuel Lewis, and lived in Brandon, Vt.,

323. JARED. Mansfield, Conn.

This family were all born in Norwich.

835. LURA, born Thursday, July 24, 1777, married Enoch Freeman, of Mansfield, Jan. 7, 1808, and has lived on Spring Hill, in Mansfield. He died, Dec. 16, 1855. They had five sons and one daughter: Azariah; Philura, who married a Crosby; Lorenzo; Enoch Huntington; Truman; and Jared Gorton. The mother still lives (1859) in Mansfield.

836. AMEY, born Thursday, April 9, 1779, married, Sept. 22, 1805, John Clark, of Ashford.

837. WEALTHY, born Friday, Feb. 22, 1781, married Zephaniah Hatch. They resided awhile in Monticello, N. Y. She died in 1853.

838. JARED, born Friday, Jan. 31, 1783, married, March 2, 1806, Candace Clark. He went, many years ago, into New York state, and thence into Michigan, where he died, in Howell, Livingston county, May 31, 1855, and where his widow still lives.

839. JOSEPH, born Friday, June 3, 1785, married, Feb. 23, 1809, Ruth Royce, who died Dec. 15, 1819. He married, for his second wife, March 2, 1820, Mrs. Betsey Smith, who died Nov. 23, 1831, and he married, the third time, Oct. 20, 1832, Sarah Thomas, who **is still living**. Their residence is in Monticello, N. Y.

840. BENJAMIN, born Monday, May 14, 1787, married Harriet Post, and lives in Thompson, N. Y.

841. JAMES, born Sunday, April 19, 1789, married Sarah, daughter of Jonathan Storrs, of Mansfield, and has always lived in Mansfield.

842. CHARLOTTE, born Wednesday, Nov. 16, 1791, married, Dec. 31, 1815, Solomon Landphere, of Ashford, where she continued to live.

324. JAMES. Royalton, Vt.

This family were born in Norwich.

843. HANNAH, married a Cleveland.
844. POLLY.
845. JAMES.
846. SALLY.
847. JACOB.
848. CHANDLER.
849. JOSHUA.

325. JOHN. Norwich, Conn,

This family were born in Norwich.

850. JESSE, born April 17, 1774. He was a saddler, in Norwich, where he died single, Dec. 21, 1851.

851. ANNA, born Dec. 2, 1776, and died single.

852. RICHARD, born March 29, 1778, and died Feb. 11, 1784.

853. NABBE, born Feb. 9, 1780, and died single, Aug. 5, 1804.

854. LUCRETIA, born July 31, 1783, married, Aug. 7, 1806, Epaphras Porter, one of the publishers of the "True Republican." He was a bookseller and binder, in Norwich Town. She died Nov. 12, 1850. Their children were: Francis Olmsted, born March 24, 1807, commenced a mercantile career with his uncle, Charles Huntington, but preferring a student's life, fitted for college in Plainfield, Conn., graduated at Yale, in 1828, and took charge of an academy in Harrisburg, Pa., where he was attacked with typhus fever, and died Sept. 25, 1829; James Madison, born Nov. 28, 1808, and died next day; Charles Henry, born Aug. 8, 1811, and commenced a mercantile career, also with his uncle Charles, but with an earnest longing for preaching the gospel, he abandoned business, fitted for college at Westfield, Mass., and graduated at Yale, in 1841; studied theology, and was licensed to preach, but was suddenly arrested by an attack of dysentery, and died in New Haven, Sept. 26, 1841; George Epaphras, born Dec. 19, 1812, married Aug. 31, 1840, Eleanor Morris, of Utica, N. Y., and has six children, Susan Lucretia, Cornelia Morris, Charles Henry, Geo. Shephard, Jane Stuart, and Ellen Huntington; Abby Huntington, born June 1, 1817, married George T., son of Dea. James Stedman, of Norwich, resided in Cincinnati, Ohio, but returned to Norwich, Conn., where she died of consumption, Oct. 30, 1856, having had four children, Charles, Frank, George and Thomas; Mary Snow died in infancy; and Jane Stuart, born Sept. 13, 1823, married, Oct. 7, 1844, William Osborn Thomas,

SIXTH GENERATION. 201

of Norwich, and had three children, Edward Stanley, William and Martha. She died of yellow fever in New Orleans, Aug. 3, 1853.

855. RICHARD, born Oct. 15, 1786, married. Nov. 21, 1830, Ellen Owens, who was born Feb. 20, 1794, in North Wales, (Eng.) They lived in Utica, N. Y., where he died, May 12, 1855, and where his widow still (1858) resides.

856. JOHN, born Feb. 20, 1789. He lived at one time in Zanesville, Ohio.

857. WILLIAM HENRY, born Aug. 13, 1793, married a Miss Stuart. He resided in Sidney, Ohio, where he died, Feb. 25, 1846.

858. CHARLES, born Nov. 16, 1795, was a merchant in New York city. He died in Ohio, having never married.

334. SIMEON, Capt. Norwich, Conn.

This family were born in Norwich, where their births are all on record.

859. PETER CHESTER, born Dec. 31, 1777, married, in Athens, N. Y., in 1805, Rachel Waring, daughter of Jonathan Waring. They resided for some time in Hudson, N. Y., and returned again to Connecticut. He was a blacksmith, and resided in Lebanon at the time of his death, March 13, 1836. His widow, a most affectionate woman, resided in South Coventry for years, and died there, Feb. 13, 1862.

860. SIMEON, born Sept. 10, 1779, and died Oct. 6, 1787.

861. JERUSHA, born June 7, 1781, married in Norwich, Dec. 7, 1803, William Tilley. They lived in Hudson.

862. EDWARD, born June 5, 1783, and died June 7, 1792.

863. MARTHA, born June 4, 1785, and died Aug. 11, 1791.

864. FREELOVE, born June 2, 1787, married James Lathrop, of New York city.

336. ELISHA, (Capt.) Norwich, Conn.

The births of this family are on the Norwich records.

865. GEORGE, born July 6, 1775. He was a carpenter, and died single at Demerara, W. I., in 1796.

866. RUTH, born Dec. 9, 1776, and died in Hudson, N. Y., from being thrown out of a sleigh in 1798.

867. ELISHA, born Sept. 1, 1779, married, in Hudson, Dec. 25, 1808, Lydia, daughter of Ichabod and Priscilla Paddock, of Nantucket, who was born in Hudson, Feb. 25, 1788. They lived in Hudson, where he was engaged in business, and where he died March 25, 1821. His widow lived in New York city, where she died in 1860.

868. ZEPHANIAH, born July 31, 1781, married Anna Greene, of New London. He was a seafaring man and was a captain of a vessel. He died on Staten Island.

338. FREDERICK. Hudson, N. Y.

The first two births of this family are on the Norwich records.

869. JOHN BLISS, born Nov. 6, 1784, and died July 19, 1786.

870. FREDERIC, born April 1, 1786, and died Aug. 1, 1786.
871. SALLY B., born July 29, 1788, married a Mr. Frederic Utley.
872. JOHN B., born March 28, 1790, and died in New Orleans, Oct. 8, 1817.
873. EDWARD, born May 13, 1792, is a sea captain and lives near Middletown, N. J.
874. FREDERICK, born Sept. 9, 1794, and died Aug. 3, 1796.
875. FREDERICK, born in Hudson, N. Y., March 18, 1797, married, first, in 1819, Julia Maxwell, when he removed to Savannah, where his family lived. He was a sea captain. His wife died in 1842, and he married again in 1844. He was harbor and shipping master for the port of Savannah, Ga., for two years. In 1847 he again went to sea, sailing to New Orleans in the schooner Portia; and in the fall of 1848, when three days out of Savannah, his schooner was lost, and he and his son George, with the entire crew, perished. After his death, his widow married a Mr. Richardson, of New York city, where she has since resided.
876. LYDIA, born Feb. 1, 1800.
877. ANN MARIA, born March 11, 1802, married, June 19, 1825, John, son of Lieut Lebbeus Chapman and Jemima Grinnel, of West Brook. He is a merchant, and resides in Claverack, N. Y. Their children are: Maria Huntington, born June 22, 1826; Emily A., born Feb. 2, 1828; Edward H., born April 14, 1830; John G., born May 28, 1832; Ann J., born May 11, 1837; and Juliette, born June 5, 1842.
878. HENRY, born April 27, 1805, and was lost, as is supposed, at sea, some time in the year 1832.

339. REUBEN. Norwich, Conn.

879. REUBEN CAREY. He was a ship carpenter. He lived at Nippenan, New York.
880. SAMUEL, who died at the age of twenty.
881. RUTH, who married Abel Hasbrouck.
882. JOHN FRASIER, who died in 1804.
883. PETER C., born in 1801, married Ann Goetschins, and was a dealer in leather in New York city.
884. LYDIA, who married John Jerome, a farmer.
885. REUBEN, who married Magdalen Hendrick, and was a farmer in Courtland county, N. Y.
886. MARGARET, who married Maurice Snyder, a farmer.

340. ELIPHALET. Plainfield, Vt.

The first three births of this family are on the Norwich records.
887. CHARLOTTE, born April 25, 1785, and lived in Bloomfield, N. Y.
888. SIDNEY, born Oct. 19, 1786, and went to Ohio.
889. CHARLES MOSELEY, born Feb. 13, 1789, and kept a public house in Montpelier, Vt.
890. MASON, who died single in Rochester, N. Y.

891. WALTER, who was a cabinet maker in Barre, Vt.
892. LEONARD, who was also a cabinet maker.
893. MARTHA, who died single in Rochester, N. Y.
894. MARY.
895. ROBERT.
896. EDNA L.

342. ASA. New Haven, Conn.

897. POLLY, born in Woodbridge, Conn., Dec. 30, 1780, married, in 1800, Rev. Israel Brainard, of Guilford, Conn., where they resided six years after their marriage. He was then sent out by the Connecticut missionary society into New York State, and located at Verona, where, for about thirty-four years, he preached and labored successfully in that outpost of settlements and of Christian institutions. During all of the fifty-six years of his ministry, he was greatly indebted to the untiring industry and economy of his wife. She was a woman of rare qualities. " Friends who knew her in early life, describe her as delicate and beautiful. Her genial temperament and ready wit rendered her social qualities attractive, alike to the ignorant and the learned. Her warm sympathy with all classes was peculiarly endearing. None could be long with her without being convinced that she wished to do them good, both temporally and spiritually. Her quiet performance of household duties, her night-long watchings by the sick bed, her earnest prayers, and her meek submission in affliction, all indicated a cheerful and chastened spirit." She still lives, and spends her declining years alternately with her sons-in-law, A. Clark, of Clark's Mills, N. Y., and Rev. G. W. Thompson, of Syracuse. She had eleven children, six of whom lived to maturity: Israel Huntington, born Feb. 8, 1801, and died in Albany, N. Y., July 8, 1836; Mary, born March 4, 1810, married Ammi B. Clark, of Kirkland, N. Y., and has four children; Harriet, born March 28, 1812; Cornelia, born May 14, 1814; Elizabeth, born Sept. 4, 1816, married, in 1838, Rev. George W. Thompson, and lives in Syracuse, N. Y., having four children; and David Lewis, born Feb. 12, 1821. Mr. Brainard died in Kirkland in 1854, aged eighty-two.

898. EBENEZER, born 1782, married Margaret ——. He was a man of some literary attainments, and for a time was an actor. He had traveled quite extensively in America, Europe, and Asia. After leaving the stage, because of his unwillingness to stoop to the low practices upon which the profession so largely depends, he lectured for some time in the West, and became a sort of pioneer in the new profession which has since been so much honored. He retired from public life, married, and lived on a farm in Alton, Ill., where he died in 1857.

899. CAROLINE, married Samuel B. Woodward, of New Haven. They had four daughters: Elizabeth; Sarah, who married Edward Bradley, of Cornwall Hollow, Conn.; Harriet, who has recently married; and Maria, who married Levi Goodale, of Cherry Grove, Ill., with whom her mother is now living.

900. HARRIET, married Capt. Elias Trowbridge, of Oswego, N. Y. They

have three children: Lewis Beale, a prominent man living in Buffalo; Alfred C.; and Frederic E.

901. HANNAH MARIA, married, in 1822, John Beecher, of New Haven. They had six children, three of whom survive: George Huntington, born in 1824, and married a daughter of the late Rev. Mr. Garfield, of New Haven, and who lives in that city; Jane Maria, born in 1833, married, in 1854, John K. Post, a prominent business man in Oswego, N. Y., with whom her mother now, (1858), resides; and Fanny Harriet, born in 1840, and lives with Mr. Post.

SEVENTH GENERATION.

349. JOHN.   Amesbury, Mass.

901.[1] JACOB, born Sept. 28, 1758, and died single, about 1779.

902. BENJAMIN, born April 24, 1760, married Elizabeth Buxton, and lived in Weare, N. H.

903. MOSES, born May 25, 1763, married Hannah Page, and lived in Amesbury, where he died, Jan. 15, 1854.

904. JOHN, born Aug. 25, 1776, married Jemima Bunker, and lived in Lincoln, Vt., where he died, July 5, 1853.

905. HANNAH, born Aug. 23, 1768, and died without children, Sept. 10, 1841, in Amesbury.

906. MARY, lived in Amesbury, and died single about 1814.

907. ABIGAIL, married David Currier, and lived in Amesbury.

908. DAVID, born May 13, 1770, and married Lydia Currier, who was born Jan. 9, 1768, and died Oct. 14, 1835. He died in Amesbury, in March, 1841.

909. SARAH, married Daniel Page, and lived in Berwick. They had children and grand-children.

909.[1] JUDITH, born April 12, 1773, and died single, June 19, 1851, in Amesbury.

353. WILLIAM.   Amesbury, Mass.

910. AMOS, born Aug. 8, 1771, married Content Osborne, and lived in Amesbury, where his wife died, in 1860. He belonged to the Society of Friends, and was able, at ninety years of age, to do a good day's work. He lived on a part of the original Huntington homestead, and died there, in Sept. 1861.

911. SARAH, married James Buxton, and has a family.

912. MERRIAM, married Jedidiah Peasely, and has children.

913. ELIZABETH, married Samuel Osborne, and has children.

355. ELIJAH, *Amesbury, Mass.*

914. HANNAH, born in 1785, married James Herbert, and died in 1820, leaving no children.

915. JOHN, born Dec. 3, 1786, married Ruth Drowne, was a ship-master, and resided in Wilmington, N. C. He died in 1839.

916. MOSES, born 1789, married Betsey Hoyt, and resided in Amesbury, where he died, suddenly, Feb. 12, 1861.

917. ABIGAIL, born in 1791.

918. MARY, born in 1793.

919. WILLIAM, born in 1795, and died in 1818.

920. LYDIA, born in 1797, and married Reuben Evans, in 1816.

921. STEPHEN, born in 1799, married Betsey Horne, and died in 1841.

922. ELIJAH, born in 1801, and lives in Salisbury, Mass.

358. ISAAC. *Amesbury, Mass.*

923. JUDITH, born about 1797, married Joseph Follensbee, of Amesbury, Mass., where they have a family.

924. HANNAH, born in 1800, married, and had a family, in New Hampshire.

351. WILLIAM. *Amesbury, Mass.*

925. WILLIAM, born in 1780, married Hannah Hoyt, and died in 1823.

926. THOMAS, died without a family, in 1822, in Amesbury.

927. TIMOTHY, died without a family, in 1823, in Amesbury.

928. ISAAC, married —— Badger, and died in 1849, in Amesbury.

365. BENJAMIN.

A letter from Joseph Huntington, (928¹) to Dr. Joshua, of Brooklyn, dated Atkinson, Me., March 3, 1852, gives the following list of the children of this Benjamin, as his brothers and sisters. The rest of the information which I have secured about this list and their descendants, was given me by George K., (1873³⁰) while a disabled Union soldier, on a visit to my house, from the hospital on David's Island.

928.¹ SARAH, married and had a family.

928.² TIMOTHY, married a Hall, and lived and died in Litchfield, Me.

928.³ JOSEPH, lived at one time in Atkinson, Me.

928.⁴ WILLIAM, married a Cunningham, and lived in Pittston, Me., where he died.

928.⁵ ANN, died, unmarried, in Litchfield, in 1858.

928.⁶ ELIZABETH.

928.⁷ BENJAMIN, born in Topsham, Me., March 14, 1804, married Lydia Chick, April 23, 1830, in Litchfield, and died March 7, 1859, in Litchfield, where his family now reside.

928.⁸ DANIEL, married a Wilson, and lives in Litchfield, Me.

928.⁹ JUDITH, married a Wilson, and lives near Bangor, Me.

360. JACOB. Amesbury, Mass.

The births in this family are on the Amesbury records.
929. RHODA, born Nov. 25, 1766.
930. TABITHA, born April 24, 1768.
931. GIDEON, born Sept. 19, 1770. He went from Francistown to Marshfield, Vt., in 1802.

367. JOHN. Weare, N. H.

932. ABNER, born in 1782, married Deborah Boynton, and lived in Weare, N. H. She died in 1853.
933. SAMUEL, born in 1784, and died in 1797.
934. JOHN, born in 1786, married Mary Philbrick, and lived in Bennington.
935. MOSES, born in 1788, married Olive Peterson, and lived in Weare, N. H. He died in 1846, leaving no children.
936. BETSEY, born in 1790, married Jonathan G. Fifield of Weare, N. H.
937. HANNAH, born in 1794, married Solomon Holt, of Groton.
938. BENJAMIN, born in 1796, married Polly Wilkins, and lived in Weare.
939. SAMUEL, born in 1798, married Harriet M. Hoag, and lived in Concord, N. H. He died in 1838.
940. HARRIET, born in 1801, married Lewis Lull, and lives in Warner, N. H.

368. JOSHUA. Francistown, N. H.

941. THOMAS.
942. JANE, who married Nathan Sleeper.
943. SUSAN.
944. BETSEY, married David Cochran, and lived in New Boston.
945. JOHN, lived in Francistown.
946. SAMUEL, is said to have gone early to Marshfield, Vt.
947. DAVID, lived in Marshfield.
948. JOSHUA, lived at one time in Nashua.
949. HANNAH, lived in Francistown.
950. SALLY.
951. ABIGAIL.

369. JOSEPH. Francistown, N. H.

952. GEORGE, born Nov. 14, 1776, married, May, 1801, Mary Clark. He died, Feb. 2, 1816, in Bennington, N. H. After his death, his widow moved to the Black River valley, in New York, where she died.
953. JOSEPH, born in Bennington, then Society Land, N. H., July 31, 1779, married, Nov. 1809, Rebecca Pettee, who was born July 29, 1783. He is a wheelwright. He moved to Francistown in 1823, where he and his wife both united with the Congregational church.
954. MARY, born July 31, 1783, married Iddo Osgood, of Keene, N. Y., in Nov. 1832. She united with the Congregational church in Francistown, in 1813. She had no children.

955. JOHN C., born April 26, 1786, married, in July, 1809, Charlotte Austin. They live in Keene, N. Y.

956. ABIGAIL, born Dec. 30, 1788, married Ebenezer Burtt, in Nov. 1809. She died Jan. 28, 1836, and he died in 1841. Their children were, Ebenezer; Lydia, who is dead; Elbridge; Samuel, who is dead; George, who is dead; Orandal; Mary, and Francis, who are dead.

957. RUTH S., born Sept. 21, 1791, and united with the Second Congregational church in Nashua, N. H. She has never married.

957.¹ SARAH, born Jan. 30, 1793, and died Feb. 9, 1795.

958. SAMUEL, born July 9, 1796, married, Nov. 11, 1824, Hannah Stickney, of Bennington. They are both members of the Congregational church in Bennington.

380. THOMAS. Middletown, Vt.

The first five of this family were born in Bozrah, and last, probably, in Middletown, Vt. I have been unable to learn anything definite from any of them, though my venerable uncle Elijah, (108) visiting that part of Vermont, in 1810, found the family then residing there, and in very respectable circumstances.

959. BACKUS.
960. JOHN.
961. ERASTUS.
961.¹ NABBY.
961.² MINERVA.
961.³ NOEL.

381. CHRISTOPHER. (DR.) Bozrah, Conn.

This family were all born in Bozrah.

962. RUTH BALDWIN, born Oct. 17, 1795, married David Boutelle, in Dec. 1818. He was a merchant in Boston, Mass., where she died, in Dec. 1823.

963. NABBY, born Aug. 3, 1797, married, Feb. 27, 1813, Horace Bidwell, of South Manchester, where they still reside. He is a farmer. They have had children.

964. CHRISTOPHER, born July 22, 1799, and married, in 1823, Mary Webb, of Windham. He was a dealer in shoes, in Hartford, and died, June 8, 1834, in that city, his wife surviving him about a dozen years.

965. ELISHA HYDE, born Dec. 3, 1803. His early life was spent in his native town, in the family of a hard working farmer, where he acquired habits of industry and economy. But he was too ambitious to delve long among the stony fields of Bozrah, and tried his fortune at shoe making, with his elder brother, in Hartford. Again he made an attempt, in Schenectady, N. Y., and in a few months removed to Geneva, where he married, Sept. 19, 1825, Phebe White. Remaining here about three years, he went to **Canandaigua**, where he lived about the same time, when he removed to his permanent home in Penn Yan. He was a man of unusual activity and energy in business, knowing no such word as fail.

For the last three or four years of his life he was engaged in business in Chicago, Ill. He was, also, president of the Mercantile Bank, at Beaver Dam, Wisconsin. He was attacked with paralysis, on the 6th of Jan. 1857, in Chicago, where he died on the 15th of the same month. His remains were interred in Penn Yan, where his family had continued to reside.

966. LUCY, born Dec. 21, 1805, married the Hon. Wm. B. Spooner, merchant, of Boston, where they still reside.

967. SARAH, born May 2, 1810, married, April 30, 1828, Henry Marble, a paper manufacturer, of North Manchester. They have had three sons: Charles; Henry; and George; the last of whom is dead.

382. ELISHA. Franklin, Conn.

This family were all born in Franklin.

968. CHARLES, born June 8, 1785, married, Cynthia, daughter of Eleazor and Prudee (Rogers) Tracy, of Franklin, March 15, 1809. He died in Norwich, Oct. 1, 1816.

969. ANNA, born Jan. 31, 1787, married, Feb. 25, 1813, John Cook. They resided in Norwich, Conn. Their children are: Ruth Ann, born Dec. 16, 1817, married Wm. H. Buck, of Albany, N. Y.; Sarah Howard, born Nov. 18, 1819, married N. S. Wentworth, of Norwich city; Lucy Lathrop, born Nov. 13, 1822, married Wm. Clemshire, of Albany, N. Y.; Lydia Tracy, born Aug. 7, 1827. Mrs. Cook died, in Norwich, Feb. 5, 1860.

970. MERANE, born April 23, 1789, married, in Franklin, Jan. 29, 1816, Jonathan B. Bennet, of Canterbury. They have had seven children: Charles Turner, born Nov. 27, 1816; Pardon Huntington, born June 25, 1818; Martha, who is dead; Merane, born Nov. 16, 1819; Joseph B., born Nov. 27, 1822; Asahel Elisha, born July 1, 1826; and Palmer. This family lived in Nelson, N. Y., where she died, in Oct. 1852.

971. ASHER, born Aug. 14, 1791, married, Feb. 27, 1816, Lydia Hyde, daughter of Daniel and Lydia (Rogers) Hyde, and born in Franklin, Aug. 25, 1795. They lived in Vernon, Conn., until 1835, when they went into Pennsylvania, and in 1856 to Athens, Pa., where he died, June 15, 1860.

972. TALITHA, born Feb. 13, 1794, married, in Franklin, Dec. 2, 1821, Azariah, son of Andrew Lathrop, of Bozrah. They reside in Vernon, and have had five children: A. Willis, born April 24, 1826, a lawyer in Iowa; E. Huntington, born Aug. 17, 1827; Philena Maria, born April 25, 1829, and is dead; Eliza L., born Nov. 1831; and Nancy Huntington, born Oct. 3, 1835.

973. LYDIA, born Dec. 29, 1795, married, in Franklin, March 26, 1818, Asa Peck, of Franklin. Their children were: Lydia T., married Clement Smith, and lives in New Haven, Conn.; Maria, born Aug. 5, 1821, and is dead; Samuel Rudd, born March 17, 1825, and lives in Toledo, Ohio; Thomas Scott, born Nov. 19, 1829, is in the Union army; Geo. Whitfield, born Jan. 12, 1832, is in the Union army; Henry M., born June, 1839, is also in the Union army. She died in Norwich, Oct. 12, 1853.

974. JONATHAN RUDD, born Dec. 14, 1798, married, Sept. 4, 1823, Linda

Baker. They lived in Vernon, where he died, Oct. 15, 1856, and where she still lives.

975. ZIBA, born Sept 12. 1801, married. in Franklin, Dec. 23, 1824, Nabby Ellis. They lived in Franklin, where he died, Sept. 30. 1828.

384. THEOPHILUS.

The first birth in this family is the only one on the Norwich records.

976. RUTH, born Dec. 28, 1778. married Dr. Ainsworth, of Medina. Ohio, where she died in Feb., 1855.

977. ASENATH, born Nov. 2. 1783. in Lebanon, N. H., married Richard Andrus, of Chelsea. Vt., and now, 1860, resides in North Tunbridge, Vt.

978. ABEL HALL, born Oct. 2, 1796, married. in 1822. Lucy Ann Jones, who was born Sept. 26. 1807. He died Sept. 23, 1828, in Erie county, N. Y., and his widow in May. 1846.

979. THEODA. born Nov. 27, 1799, married a Mr. Leech.

980. LOIS GIFFORD, born April 2, 1801, married, Oct. 2, 1823, a Mr. Parker. Between Ruth and Asenath were two daughters and a son; and between Asenath and Abel Hall, were three sons and three daughters, all of whom died in infancy, making fourteen children in the family.

385. SAMUEL.   Western New York.

981. POLLY, born in 1784.
982. SAMUEL, had no children.
983. PHILURA, married a Baptist clergyman.

386. HIRAM.   Chelsea, Vt.

This family were all born in Chelsea, Vt.

984. LAURA, born Aug. 1798, married. in 1818, Bela Blodgett. They lived several years in Boston. Mass., where he died, March 1. 1857. She is still living in Boston. Their children are: Zeruah Huntington, born 1820, married Samuel A. Clifford, and has four children; Lucia Caroline, born 1827, married, 1847, Asa R. Brown, of Montpelier, Vt., and has two daughters; Hiram Wayne Huntington, born 1833, died in Para. Brazil, 1854; and Mary L., born 1837, married, 1856, Charles H. Collagher, of West Newton, and has one son.

985. JACOB PERKINS, born in April. 1800. married, 1828. Betsy Spear, and is a Baptist minister living in Londonderry, Vt. His wife was a daughter of Dr. Moses and Judith Spear, of Vershire, Vt., and died in Chelsea in 1848. He married for his second wife, in 1850, Asenath Stevens, of Dabney, N. H. He is now, (1861), pastor of the Baptist church in Guilford, Vt.

986. LUCIA, born Jan. 18, 1805, and lives unmarried in Boston, Mass.
987. HARRIET, born September, 1808, and died September, 1810.

SEVENTH GENERATION. 211

387. ZIBA. Lebanon, N. H.

This family were all born in Lebanon, N. H.

988. ZERUAH, born Dec. 27, 1794, married in January, 1823, Hezekiah Ford. She died May, 1825, in Lebanon, N. H.

989. ZIBA, born July 9, 1796, died Nov. 9, 1797.

990. FANNY, born Sept. 17, 1798, married John W. Peck, of Lebanon, N. H., Nov. 7, 1821. Their children are: Eli, born June 12, 1824; Alonzo, born Jan. 7, 1826; John Murry, born Jan. 26, 1830; and Parthenia Waters, born Dec. 13, 1832.

991. ZIBA, born Sept. 6, 1800, married, March 5, 1835, Sarah Sprague. He is still living in Lebanon, N. H.

992. ADNAH, born July 17, 1802, married Lucy Conaut, who died. He married, second, Sarah Miller. He is a carpenter and resides in Ohio.

993. HARRY, born June 22, 1804, and died single, Aug. 14, 1833, in Lebanon N. H.

994. ALVAN, born Nov. 25, 1806, married Emily Downer, and is a farmer living in Strongsville, Ohio.

995. JULIAN, born Oct. 4, 1809, married Feb. 10, 1836, John S. Pierce. They are now living in Boston.

996. MATILDA CAROLINE, born Jan. 18, 1811, married May 22, 1836, James H. Parker, of Boston. They have one child and reside in Boston.

997. EDWIN NEHEMIAH, born June 24, 1816, and married Jan. 16, 1844, Laura Pierce. They live in Lebanon, N. H.

391. URIEL, (M. D.) Bowdoinham, Me.

All of this family died of consumption.

998. DELIA, born in 1796, and died Oct. 2, 1827.

999. HANNAH, born in 1798, and died Jan. 18, 1835.

1000. MINERVA, born in 1800, and died March 14, 1826.

1001. SOLON, died Feb. 16, 1830, aged 23, in the West Indies.

1002. URIEL, married Sarah Moulton, and died, having had no children. His widow married, in Topsham, Me., Sept. 2, 1859, Colonel George Lyons, of New York city.

394. BARNABAS. Lisbon, Conn.

1003. CLARISSA, born May 3, 1791, married, in Lisbon, Feb. 20, 1810, Martin Bottom, who was a farmer, and who died. She married, for her second husband, in April, 1820, Rufus Smith, and they live in Griswold. Her children were: Martin H., born Dec. 2, 1810; Rufus, born Sept. 17, 1821; Mary, born Nov. 7, 1825; and John B., born Dec. 13, 1832; the last one, alone, being now, (1858), alive.

1004. LUCY, born 1793, married, March 16, 1815, Barzillai Bishop, and has lived in Lisbon. The husband died, April 11, 1831. Their children are: Barzillai H., born April 25, 1816, and died Oct. 15, 1838; Nathan Perkins, born Feb. 15, 1818; Samuel, born April 9, 1821, and died April 11, 1821; Roger Adams, born Aug. 12, 1822, and died Feb. 12, 1855; Lucy, born Sept. 1, 1824, and died Aug. 25, 1851; Mary and Elizabeth, born July 24, 1828; Abigail, born Aug. 28, 1830, and died Jan. 31, 1855.

1005. BARNABAS, born June 30, 1800, married, Oct. 13, 1823, Juliette Morgan, and died Oct. 29, 1825, having had no children.

395. AZARIAH. Franklin Conn.

This family were all born in Franklin.

1006. ANNA, born Sept. 2, 1792, married, Nov. 30, 1809, Stephen, son of Josiah and Mary Robinson, of Canterbury, and lives in Attleborough, Mass. He was a teacher and farmer, and still later a physician, practicing his profession in Providence, where he died, Sept. 27, 1833. She died Dec. 13, 1869, leaving three sons and one daughter. They are all engaged in farming.

1007. AZARIAH, born Sept. 11, 1793, married, November, 1815, Lavinia, daughter of Benjamin and Martha (Carey) Greenslit, of Franklin. He is a thrifty farmer, and occupies the old Huntington homestead, in Franklin, having added to the original territory laid out by the town of Norwich to his great grandfather, Christopher, not an acre of which has ever been alienated.

1008. ASAHEL, born Feb. 10, 1795, married Sarah Gaylord, of Utica, where he resided. He died Oct. 31, 1822. He was a goldsmith.

1009. HENRY, born Sept. 19, 1798, and died Oct. 3, 1817.

397. ASAHEL, REV. Topsfield, Mass.

This family were all born in Topsfield.

1010. ALETHEA, born Oct. 10, 1792, and lived but five days.

1011. ALETHEA, born Jan. 26, 1794, and died Aug. 26, 1814.

1012. ELISHA, born April 9, 1796, graduated at Dartmouth in 1815, and received his medical diploma. He commenced his professional life in Lowell, to which place he had removed in 1824, two years before the incorporation of that city. In the following year, May 31, 1825, he married Hannah, daughter of Joseph and Deborah Hinckley, of Marblehead, who was born Oct. 2, 1800. As a physician and as a citizen, he rapidly rose to a deserved eminence in the enterprising city in which he had located himself. Perhaps few of its citizens have been more esteemed for an intelligent and practical interest in every movement which has promised to promote the prosperity of his adopted city, or of his native state. His name is identified with their educational, social, and civil progress, during the last quarter of a century. Both as the mayor of Lowell for several years, and as an officer in the state government, of which he has been the lieutenant governor, he has discharged his public duties with very great acceptance. His inaugurals, as mayor, show him to be a man whose head and heart are right on all questions which pertain to the social welfare of the people. Government, in his creed, should protect the wealth of the rich, but it should as certainly encourage and elevate the poor. Municipal provisions should follow the "Christian law" which requires us to relieve the unfortunate poor, "to assist and encourage him to help himself." Huntington Hall, by order of the city government named from him, will long be a faithful witness to the public esteem in which he is held.

On the death of Dr. Elisha Bartlett, M. D., late professor in the College of Physicians and Surgeons, in New York, Dr. Huntington was appointed by the Middlesex North District Medical Society to prepare a suitable commemorative address. This excellent tribute was delivered before that body, Dec. 26, 1855, and published by them.

His wife died Sept. 19, 1859, how much lamented, the following obituary notice, from the Journal and Courier, of Lowell, attests: "It is seldom the grave closes over any one among us who has left so many holy, pleasant, and enduring recollections as cluster about the memory of Mrs. Huntington. Early a resident of our city, she had gathered about her a large circle of friends, who enjoyed her intelligence and cultivation, and who will never forget her kindness and hospitality, as well as her ready sympathy in all that interested them. In the death of Mrs. Huntington, the poor and suffering have indeed lost a friend, whose words of kindness and counsel as well as her unostentatious charities, have soothed and gladdened many a sorrowful heart.

"The consistent religious character of Mrs. Huntington was never more beautifully developed than during her long and distressing illness. With a cheerful and trusting spirit she moved in her family circle, doing, every day, 'life's daily duties,' almost to its close, and then calmly and quietly laying herself down to the long last sleep that knows no waking, save in that brighter world, where pain, and sickness, and sorrow can never enter, and where the 'pure in heart shall see God.'"

1013. ASAHEL, born July 23, 1798, fitted for college at Phillips' Academy, Andover, Mass., and entered Yale in 1815, where he graduated in 1819. The following notice is from the record of the class meeting, held July 27, 1859, of which he was the chairman: "After leaving college he commenced his legal studies at Newburyport, and, after some interruptions, completed them at Salem, Essex county, Mass., in 1824. In March of that year, he was admitted to the bar, and commenced the practice of law at Salem, and continued in practice with marked success and high reputation, until 1851. During this time, he was repeatedly a member of the legislature of Massachusetts. In 1853, he was a member of the constitutional convention in that state; and the same year was mayor of Salem. He has also been attorney for the county of Essex; attorney for the district, consisting of the counties of Essex and Middlesex, in the administration of criminal cases; and when the district was divided, held the same office for the district of Essex. In 1851, he was appointed clerk of all the courts in Essex county; when he retired from practice, and accepted the office which he still holds, amid all the fluctuations of popular elections. He has been for many years an active and efficient promoter of the temperance reform; in his official capacity, as well as in private life, he has devoted his time, talents, and services to the cause; and as a legislator, and advocate, he has been instrumental in advancing its interests and promoting its success."

Mr. Huntington married, Aug. 15, 1842, widow Tucker, of Salem, whose maiden name was Caroline Louisa Deblois. They have continued to live in Salem, Mass., where he is greatly esteemed and honored.

1014. HEZEKIAH, born June 30, 1800, and died, unmarried, June 8, 1828.
1015. MARY ANN, born Aug. 18, 1802, and died, unmarried, May 9, 1836.

400. GURDON, (DR.)   Cairo, N. Y.

This family which consisted of seven children, five of them dying in infancy, were all born at Unadilla, N. Y.

1016. HANNAH A., born May 26, 1800, married, Oct. 1825, Calvin Balis, of Oswego, N. Y. He resided many years in New York city, and was at one time an alderman of the first ward. They had two children: Gurdon Huntington, born in Aug. 1826; and Henrietta E., born March, 1829, both of them dying in New York city. Mr. Balis died in Oswego, in June, 1847, where his widow now resides with her sister, Mrs. Brewster.

1017. ANNA MINERVA, born March 14, 1802, married, Oct. 1826, the Hon. David P. Brewster, of Oswego. Mr. Brewster was a member of the U. S. Congress for two terms, and first judge of Oswego county court, from 1833 to 1841. They have one son, Lucius Huntington, who was born in Oswego, July 31, 1827, married, Oct. 9, 1851, Maria P. Baron, and has two children, Anna Huntington, and William Baron.

1018. A SON, who died in infancy.

407. ISAAC.   Bozrah, Conn.

This family were all born in Bozrah.

1019. WEALTHY ANN, born Oct. 8, 1807, married, Sept. 18, 1827, Austin, son of Capt. Samuel Gager, of Bozrah. He was a farmer. She died from consumption, "after a lingering illness, which she bore with Christian fortitude," July 15, 1844, and he died from an accident, in June, 1846. Their children were: John; Charles; Maria; and Eliza.

1020. CHARLES MAPLES, born July 13, 1809. Is a farmer, though an invalid for much of his earlier life. He married, Nov. 18, 1833, Clarissa, daughter of William Kelley, of Bozrah, who died, having had no children, Nov. 29, 1853. Until 1857 he had lived on a part of the farm which his ancestors took from the aboriginal inheritors of it. He is at present somewhere in the West.

1021. LYDIA BALDWIN, born Sept. 6, 1813. She was the subject of a revival of religion in Bozrah, in 1830 and '31, and was propounded for admission to the Congregational church, but the scarlet fever entered the family and suddenly withdrew her to the church above. She died, Sept. 2, 1831.

1022. HANNAH DART, born Sept. 3, 1815, married Henry W. Hough, M. D., son of William Hough, of Bozrah. He was located in the practice of medicine in North Killingly, and still later in Putnam, where he has continued to reside since. For many years she was the subject of a most afflictive physical disorder, in the progress of which she lost all power of locomotion, so that she became as helpless, physically, as a babe. Yet with unexampled patience, and with a serene and quiet smile, she would sit all day, and with the only motion of her arm left under her control, turn over the leaves of some book, which she was reading, or wave the fan, whose cool breath she could yet feel. She died, Jan. 7, 1855, a peaceful and hopeful death. Her husband married, again, Mary Tripp, of Putnam, and is now (1862) a surgeon in the Union army.

1023. ISAAC, born Nov. 2, 1817, and died, of consumption, in Bozrah, April 20, 1849, unmarried.

1024. EUNICE, born Nov. 17, 1820, and died of scarlet fever, Oct. 10, 1831, in Bozrah.

1025. MARY, born May 24, 1826, married, Oct. 7, 1847, E. W. Yerrington, son of Joseph Yerrington, of Norwich, where they are now living. They have five children: Marietta Taylor, born Nov. 23, 1849; Theodore Webster, born Aug. 17, 1851; Arthur Meech, born June 2, 1855, and died Jan. 4, 1859; Charles Arthur, born Nov. 11, 1858; and a daughter, born Oct. 22, 1862.

1026. JOSHUA HENRY, born June 28, 1833. He commenced, early, teaching school, and fitted himself for college. He entered Dartmouth College in 1854, and removed to Amherst at the commencement of his sophomore year, where he graduated in 1858. He was, when last heard from, teaching a private school in Mississippi.

408. ELIJAH. Bozrah, Conn.

This family were all born in Bozrah,

1027. PHILURA LEFFINGWELL, born March 23, 1803, married, March, 1832, Christopher Leffingwell Lathrop, son of Dea. Charles Lathrop, of Norwich, and brother of that noble band of missionary sisters, the grand-children of (137). They went to Cleveland, Ohio, where they resided at the time of her death, Aug. 13, 1843. She was a woman of sterling good sense, and of unusually earnest and uniform piety. She left but one child, a daughter, Elizabeth Hutchins, born in Cleveland, Feb. 8, 1836, and married, in 1860, Wm. Merriam, and lives in Cleveland, Ohio.

1028. WINSLOW TRACY, born Aug. 25, 1807, entered early on the study of medicine, and received his diploma from the Pittsfield medical school in 1829. He commenced almost immediately, after graduating, the practice of his profession, in East Haddam, Conn., where he made good proof of his skill, and won for himself the confidence and esteem of a large circle of patrons and friends. He married, June 1, 1830, Almira Carson, of Pittsfield, Mass. In the summer of 1834, Dr. H. went to Albany, where he was invited by a circle of friends, to establish himself in business. He remained there only a few months, and located himself in Brooklyn, now Ohio city, where he rapidly secured an extensive practice, and at the same time engaged in speculations in real estate. While here, his wife died, in Feb. 1838. He married, for his second wife, in Akron, Ohio, July 12, 1840, widow Julia (Swift) Babcock, daughter of chief justice Swift of Windham, Conn., author of the Digest of Connecticut Laws. He removed to Akron, Ohio, where he fell a victim to his professional duty, dying Dec. 23, 1849, from a wound received at a post mortem examination. He was a warm friend, generous to others rather than just to himself, an earnest inquirer after truth, both in reference to his profession and to religion, and as eager to propagate, as to embrace, whatever he felt convinced was true. His widow still survives, and resides in Cleveland, Ohio.

1029. CAROLINE MATILDA, born Sept. 29, 1809. She united, early, with the Congregational church, in Bozrah, and married, Sept. 16, 1835, Daniel R. Hamlin, a financier of Buffalo, N. Y. In this city she has resided ever since. She has had two children: Charles W., born in Cleveland, July 20, 1836, who graduated at Hamilton College, in 1858, is now a law student; and Harriet Cornelia, born in Buffalo, N. Y., Aug. 24, 1842.

1030. LUCRETIA LEFFINGWELL, born Sept. 18, 1822, married, March, 1853, Lemuel B. Stark, son of Joshua Stark, of Granville, Ohio. She died in 1856, leaving two children, Olive, and an infant son.

1031. ALBERT E., born Aug. 4, 1828, and has always lived with his father in Bozrah.

1032. ALFRED J., born June 11, 1834; is now (1862) in the Union army.

410. NEHEMIAH, (DEA.)   Bozrah, Conn.

This family were all born in Bozrah.

1033. NANCY LEFFINGWELL, born June 14, 1813, married, Oct. 25, 1841, Alba C. Thompson, a merchant in Norwich city, where they have resided ever since. They have five children: Elizabeth Huntington, born Aug. 19, 1842; Malvina Huntington, born May 11, 1845; Frank, born July 23, 1848, and died in infancy; Annie, born Aug. 30, 1849; and Caroline Hamlin, born March 5, 1855.

1034. ELIJAH BALDWIN, born Aug. 14, 1816, married, in Windham, March 6, 1843, Julia Maria, daughter of Dea. Thomas and Laura (Lathrop) Welch, of Windham. He was a member of Yale College, class of 1840, and received from that college an honorary master's degree in 1851. He was licensed to preach, by the New London association of Congregational ministers, in 1845, and ordained to the work of the ministry, in Putnam, Conn., in 1848. He was dismissed from this charge in 1850, from vocal weakness; since which time he has been engaged in teaching. He has given one sermon and several addresses to the press, and has devoted his leisure, for years, to the preparation of this genealogical memoir.

1035. ELISHA TRACY, born Dec. 28, 1817, and married in Norwich, Sept 2, 1844, Malvina, daughter of Dr. Thomas Boswell. He was a jeweler, and the character he bore, and the esteem he secured, are well set forth in the sermon preached by his pastor, Rev. Dr. Bond, on the sabbath following his death. His disease had been one inexpressibly trying and painful, and terminated his useful life, on Wednesday, Feb. 16, 1859. "The example of an esteemed member and brother of our church, who, since the last sabbath, has 'finished his course,' furnishes a fresh and convincing illustration of the power there is in the hope of salvation to sustain and cheer the soul amidst the pains of protracted disease, and in the hour of death. His connection with this church, which he joined by profession, nearly seventeen years since, has been sustained in a manner that has uniformly evinced sincerity and stedfastness of faith. His sensitive modesty, his shrinking diffidence, and self distust, prevented him from assuming such duties and responsibilities, as would give special prominence to his position as a fellow-laborer in the common vineyard. But the services he has performed in the noiseless tenor of his way—the consistency he has ever manifested—the kind, fraternal sympathies, expressed in a countenance radiant with the smile of Christian affection—his increasing interest in the prosperity of the church—his growing love to his Saviour, are facts, to which we may refer, as illustrating the strength of his piety, as an ever operative principle, and its steady though quiet growth from the tender blade of his early experience, up to the full corn in the ear. I need not speak of what he was in his family, and to his friends, for nothing can be said to enhance the preciousness of his memory, as it will be cherished by them. I will not speak of him as a citizen, so well known, and so highly esteemed in the walks of business. It will be conceded, that here integrity and uprightness have preserved him, as a Christian. I would like, did my limits permit, to dwell on some of the attractive traits which his life has developed, and in which my own feelings have been deeply interested. For many a month he has borne his life-wasting sufferings in the patience of hope. With cheerfulness and consideration he set his house in order, in prospect of death, and when the expected crisis came, it found him so peaceful, so cheerful, so hopeful, so full of love, that the scene was divested of those sad and painful sensations, so often awakened in the chamber of death. He looked at death with the eye of faith, and in the light of hope—looked at it as a sleep in Jesus—from which he fully expected to awake to a higher and purer life in that kingdom where he had laid up treasures for eternity."

1036. WILLIAM DYER, born Dec. 18, 1821, married, Nov. 16, 1847, Mary Ann, daughter of Thomas Kinne, of Norwich, who died July 27, 1848. He married again, May 19, 1852, Calista, daughter of James Reed, of Springfield, N. Y., who was born March 29, 1830. He has resided for the last few years in Providence, R. I., where he has been in a market for the most of the time.

112. PHILIP. Norwich, Conn.

1037. BENJAMIN, born in Norwich, April 24, 1798. He was for years engaged in business as merchant in Norwich town. He was elected town clerk, Feb. 14, 1825, to succeed his father, and held the office until it was removed to the city, in Oct. 1830. He married, Sept. 30, 1830, Margaretta Perrit. They reside in Norwich town.

429. JOSEPH SPENCER.

1038. BETSEY MORGAN, born July 15, 1799, married Elam Cheesbrough, of Lisbon. They have five children: Nancy; Sarah; Elam P. A.; Eunice P.; and Diah L.

1039. THOMAS JEFFERSON, born Sept. 29, 1801, and died single, in Norwich, Oct. 1, 1825.

1040. NANCY E., born Feb. 23, 1804, married, Feb. 11, 1822, Henry Ward, of Norwich city, where they reside, in West Chelsea. Their children are: Henry Huntington, deceased; Thomas Spencer; Ann Elizabeth; Kneeland Huntington; Henry; George W.; Elizabeth Huntington; Emma Victoria, deceased; Emma Victoria; and Nancy Backus.

427. ABEL.

1041. MATTHEW, was killed by lightning in the house of his uncle Jonas.

1042. GURDON, left Connecticut with a very small amount of money in 1802, and worked his way into what was then the Western wilderness, as far as Batavia, N. Y. He had a family, and acquired considerable wealth and influence.

429. JONAS. Mansfield, Conn.

This family were all born in Mansfield.

1043. SARAH, born Feb. 3, 1779, married, Dec. 28, 1800, Elisha Hanks, and lived in Bath, Steuben County, N. Y. She had five daughters, of whom three are living and have families: Eveline, who married John Ostrander; Rosilla, who married Job Goff; Mary, who married Jonathan Sayre; all of them now residing in Scanona, near Bath, N. Y.

1044. BETSEY, born Feb. 28, 1781, married, Sept. 6, 1795, Josephus Denham, and lives in Lebanon, Ohio, where her husband died. They had one daughter, Cordelia.

1045. ELEAZER, born Aug. 23, 1783, and died in Dec. 1790.

1046. ASA, born Aug. 25, 1785, was a teacher, and later, a weaver and dyer, and died single in Mansfield, in May, 1826.

1047. POLLY, born Jan. 10, 1788, married Stephen Brigham in 1832, and died in Mansfield, May 30, 1852. They are both dead, leaving no children.

1048. OLIVE, born Jan. 13, 1790, married Hazard Johnson, of North Mansfield. They have two children, Semantha, who married a Fenton; and John.

1049. JOHN, born May 10, 1792, was a teacher and farmer, and died single, in Bath, N. Y., in Aug., 1822.

1050. CLARISSA, born March 5, 1794, married, Sept. 26, 1813, Christopher Reynolds, a farmer of Mansfield. She died in Mansfield, Conn., Sept. 21, 1860. Their children were: Adeline, born May 2, 1814, and married Jacob S. Eaton; Melissa, born March 14, 1816, married Charles Shumway; Elizabeth, born March 14, 1818, married Asa Saunders; Sarah, born Jan. 31, 1820, married Fayette Barrows; Julia, born Oct. 8, 1821, married Leander Derby; Glenn W., born Nov. 25, 1823, married Elizabeth Eaton; Jane, born Jan. 9, 1826, and died Aug. 8, 1827; John, born July 28, 1827, married Martha Slater; George, born Feb. 8, 1829, married Abbe E. Brown; Edwin, born March 23, 1830, married Mary J. Spencer; Benj. Franklin, born Jan. 29, 1833, married Amanda Hawkins; and Albert W., born Dec. 11, 1835, and married Rebecca Runyon.

1051. GEORGE, born Aug. 24, 1796, married, May 15, 1819, Anna Neally, and went to Bath, Steuben county, N. Y., where he has since lived. He commenced his life as teacher and farmer, and still follows the latter avocation, "among the mountains of Steuben, on a tributary of the Cohocton river." He was early elected constable and collector of taxes, which offices he filled from 1826 to 1830, when he was appointed under sheriff; and in the next year he was elected high sheriff for Steuben county, for three years. In 1835, he was elected state senator for the senatorial district embracing Chenango, Courtland, Tioga, Tompkins, Chemung, Steuben, and Allegany counties, which office he held four years. He was appointed, in 1840, United States marshal to take the census in his county, and since then has been a justice of the peace in the town in which he lives. He has had no children.

1052. MARVIN, born Feb. 9, 1799, married, Jan. 13, 1822, Lois Thompson, who was born Feb. 24, 1799. He resided in McGrawville, N. Y., for thirty-two years. He has been a teacher and is now a farmer. He is now, (1861), living in Truxton, N. Y. His wife, who was daughter of John and Lois Thompson, was a native of Willington, Connecticut, and died March 5, 1860, and had been for forty-four years a consistent member of the Baptist church.

1053. DWIGHT, born May 15, 1801, married, Nov. 26, 1823, Lucretia Starkweather, of Mansfield, where they have continued to live, in the north part of the town. He has been engaged in a variety of pursuits.

432. SAMUEL. (M. D.) Greensboro, Vt.

1054. ROBERT, born Oct. 21, 1780, in Plainfield, Conn., died Feb. 14, 1781, in Shaftesbury, Vt.

1055. BETHIA, born Oct. 21, 1780, married Elisha Jones, and lived in Lansingburg, N. Y. She died Oct. 27, 1851, in Lansingburg.

1056. JOHN, born March 20, 1782, in Shaftesbury, Vt., married Martha Bayley, and lived in Greensboro. He died Oct. 8, 1840, and his wife in Sept., 1850, in Perry, N. Y. He was a man honored for his intelligence and social worth, and especially for his overflowing benevolence.

1057. HENRY, born March 20, 1782, married, Jan. 24, 1807, Elizabeth Parmale, and lived in Greensboro, where he died, May 22, 1852. His wife died April 7, 1830. He was a useful and honored man, and held offices of trust in the town where he resided. The dates of these two brothers are given as they are reported by Henry (2003).

1058. BETSEY, born Jan. 17, 1784, and died March 12, 1795, in Shaftesbury.

1059. MARY, born Nov. 3, 1785, and died March 17, 1809, in Greensboro, Vermont.

1060. ROBERT, born June 28, 1787, and was a student. He lived at one time in Koscisco, Miss. He was in the practice of law and became judge. Mrs. Hatch, (1991), reports him as having received a collegiate education.

1061. ROXANA, born Dec. 15, 1788, and died June 16, 1809, in Greensboro, Vermont.

1062. NATHAN, born April 25, 1792, and died March 30, 1796, in Shaftesbury, Vermont.

1063. SOPHIA, born May 15, 1794, married Dr. Thomas Wright, of Cincinnati, and lived in Carthage, Ohio.

1064. ELIZABETH, born Dec. 6, 1797, and died May 12, 1809, in Greensboro. There were two others in the family who died in infancy. The dates of this family were supplied by Mrs. Hatch, from the family record in Greensboro, though different dates were given for the families of 1056 and 1057, by Dr. Huntington (1057).

434. JOHN. Middlebury, Vt.

1067. OLIVE, married a Wadsworth, of Middlebury, Vt.

1068. AMY, died young.

1069. LAURA, married William H. Bottom, and lived in Oxford, Upper Canada.

1070. FANNY, born Aug. 29, 1793, married, Feb. 13, 1814, Gardner Barton, a lawyer of Shaftesbury, Vt., who was born Sept. 1, 1791. She died March 22, 1831, and her husband, Jan. 7, 1847, both of them in Shaftesbury, Vt. Their children were: Jane Eliza, born Oct. 22, 1814, and died Jan. 18, 1853; Edwin Huntington, born Aug. 1, 1816, and is a merchant in New York city; Lorenzo Milton, born June 14, 1818, and is with his brother Edwin in business; an infant son, born and died, Feb. 14, 1821; an infant son born and died, Feb. 22, 1822; Caroline Amy, born Feb. 7, 1823, and died Aug. 23 of the same year; an infant son, born and died Sept. 10, 1825; Fanny; Mary Ann, born July 8, 1827, and died Dec. 28 of the same year; Mary Angeline, born Oct. 7, 1828; and Gardner, born March 22, 1831.

435. HENRY. Shaftesbury, Vt.

1071. EUNICE, born June, 1792, and died Dec. 8, 1797.

1072. CHLOE, born April 12, 1794, married, January, 1814, George Douglass, of Shaftesbury, who died Sept. 6, 1852, leaving five sons and two daughters: Henry H.; Norman R.; Thomas, born Oct. 3, 1819; Chloe L.; Margaret A.; George S.; Charles, born May 14, 1829. Ten of her grandchildren are now living. Thomas and Charles are hardware merchants in New York city.

1073. RUTH, born June, 1796, and died, single, in Shaftesbury, Oct. 1, 1838.

1074. JULIA, born Oct. 17, 1800, and lives in Shaftesbury.

1075. MARY, born June, 1802, married, Feb., 1823, Asa H. Whipple, of Shaftesbury, where they lived. She died, Oct. 12, 1839, leaving one daughter.

1076. EMILY, born April 6, 1806, married, Oct. 1831, Charles Spencer, jr., of Shaftesbury. She died, March 8, 1853, leaving three children.

438. AMOS. Shaftesbury, Vt.

This family were all born in Shaftesbury.

1077. PEACE, born July 17, 1795, married, Nathan Huntington Bottom, son of (436). He was Judge of the county court, and died Aug. 4, 1855, leaving his widow and four children in Shaftesbury.

1078. AMOS CLARK, born Aug. 28, 1796. He entered Union College in

1816, and sustained a high character for scholarship, but died, after a two days illness, of inflammation of the bowels, Feb. 2. 1820.

1079. MYRON, born Sept. 13. 1798. He was a successful farmer, but died early in life from typhus fever, Aug. 30, 1825.

1080. NATHAN, born March 21, 1800, and is now residing in Rochester, N. Y., where he is a successful member of the bar of the Supreme Court of the state of New York.

1081. HARLOW, born Sept. 26, 1801, married, June 12, 1826, Margaret Ford, daughter of Timothy Hyde, who was born at Pittstown, N. Y., May 21, 1804. They have continued to reside in Shaftesbury, where he is a thrifty farmer and wool grower. He was elected deacon of the Baptist church of Shaftesbury, in Nov., 1836.

1082. PAMELA, born June 26, 1804. She was a most excellent woman, " a pattern of female worth, and of filial devotion to her aged parents." She died, single, in Rochester, N. Y., March 1. 1845.

1083. GEORGE, born Oct. 7. 1806, married Abigail, youngest daughter of Gov. Jonas Galusha, of Vt., a son of (156). He was appointed deacon in 1854.

1084. ELON, born Sept. 3. 1808, married, Nov., 1835, Anjenette Cole. They reside in Rochester, N. Y., where he is engaged in the nursery business, and is also connected with the iron-safe and hardware establishment of Duryee and Forsyth Manufacturing Co. He was appointed one of the trustees of Rochester University, in 1850.

1085. CALVIN, born Oct. 14, 1810. Has been successfully engaged in mercantile life. Spent the summer of 1856 in Europe, and is now located in New Orleans, La.

440. MATTHEW. Rome, N. Y.

1086. ASA CLARK, born May 22, 1794, married, Oct. 9, 1815, Laura Clark, and resides in Rome, and is a farmer.

1087. MARY, born March 5, 1798, married, July 18, 1822, George Stedman. They lived in Rome, where she died Sept. 2. 1826.

1088. SARAH, born Oct. 24, 1799, and died on the 26th of the same month.

1089. MATTHEW, born July 1. 1801, and died on the 10th of the same month.

1090. MATTHEW L., born May 25, 1803, married, for his first wife, Jan. 25, 1826, Mary Henry, who is dead. He married the second time, Oct. 18, 1850, Helen B. Livingston. They resided in Rome, N, Y., where he was a merchant, and where he died Jan. 6, 1859.

1091. JAMES, born March 25, 1805, married, first, May 25, 1828, Sophronia Henry, who died. He married, the second time, Ellanor McKee, and has always resided in Rome. N. Y., and is engaged in farming.

1092. AMANDA, born May 31. 1807, married, Nov. 10, 1827, David Burrows, of Rome, and continued to reside there until her death, Sept. 13, 1839.

1093. LYDIA, born Nov. 5, 1809, married, May 10, 1827, Thomas G. Wright. She died Feb. 8. 1834.

441. ELIAS. Shaftesbury, Vt.

This family were all born in Shaftesbury.

1094. GEORGE, born Feb. 27, 1799, and died July 29, 1801.

1095. JACOB GALUSHA, born Nov. 1, 1800, married Patience, daughter of Hon. John H. Olin, of Shaftesbury, and resided several years in Buffalo, N. Y., engaged in the stone cutting business. He is now living in Shaftesbury, Vt.

1096. TRUMAN CLARK, born July 25, 1802, graduated at Union College in 1824, and entered on the profession of law. He has been state's attorney several years. He married Caroline Munroe, and after practicing law a short time, retired to the old homestead, where he has resided ever since.

1097. HARRIET A., born July 20, 1804, and married in Shaftesbury, Oct. 24, 1836, George Stedman, of Rome, N. Y., whose first wife was Mary (1087). She resided in Rome, where she died Jan. 3, 1838.

1098. ALONZO, born Sept. 1, 1805, married Nov. 28, 1833, Patience Lorain Dyer, who was a daughter of Daniel Dyer, one of the early settlers of that part of the country, and granddaughter of the Hon. Gideon Olin, of Shaftesbury, Vt. She was born in Clarendon, Rutland Co., Vt., Aug. 6, 1801. He studied law in Buffalo with the Hon. J. T. Hatch, and commenced business in Wayne Co., N. Y., where he practiced about two years, and removing then to Chicago, where he opened his office in the autumn of 1836. He engaged extensively in the land speculation of the next few years, but was driven from the fruitless operation by the revulsions of 1837, and returned to the practice of law. He was elected in 1836-7 state's attorney for the seventh Indiana circuit for two years, and on the expiration of this term he was re-elected for the same period, during which he showed himself an energetic and efficient prosecuting officer. Mrs. Huntington died in Chicago, Oct. 23, 1861. She was held in much esteem, both for her superior mental and social qualities and for her sincere piety; and her sudden death was felt to be no common bereavement.

1099. NORMAN S., born March 6, 1808, married, in 1839, Semanthe Strong, and is a farmer in Illinois.

1100. JANE, born May 24, 1810, married, Jan. 2, 1840, Smith Harpending, of Shaftesbury. He died in 1843, in Virginia. He was a printer and editor. He left one son, Ogden G., now (1859) in the Burr Seminary, Manchester, fitting for college. She is now living with her mother, in North Bennington, Vermont.

1101. AURELIA MIRANDA, born July 4, 1813, married, Dec. 3, 1840, John M. Cole. They lived in Danville, Ill., where she died, in 1846, leaving one daughter, who was born in 1844, and now lives in Shaftesbury, Vt.

1102. DELOS, born Sept. 20, 1815, and resides in Minnesota.

1103. EVELINE, born May 24, 1821, and died single, in Buffalo, N. Y., May 15, 1849.

1104. JENNETTE, born Jan. 6, 1824, and died in Shaftesbury, Feb. 9, 1825.

412. DANIEL, (M. D.) Perry, N. Y.

This family were born in Shaftesbury, Vt.

1105. LYDIA, born Sept. 3, 1798, and died in Shaftesbury, Jan. 29, 1809.

1106. NANCY, born April 7, 1800, married, in 1826, Jeremiah Clark, of Shaftesbury, where they resided, and she died, Aug. 26, 1831.

1107. DANIEL GALUSHA, born Feb. 17, 1802, married, Sept. 30, 1822, Oretta Andrus, and lives in Carlisle, N. Y., where he is engaged in trade.

1108. JONAS, born Feb. 27, 1804, married, first, Feb. 26, 1828, Abby A. Goddard, daughter of his father's second wife, who died in Perry, Aug. 17, 1842. He married, the second time, Nov. 9, 1843, Parthena Galusha. He is a physician, and commenced the practice of medicine in Perry, N. Y., from which place he recently removed to Kalamazoo, Michigan, where he is now (1862) living.

1109. MARY MYRANDA, born Aug. 14, 1806, and died in Shaftesbury, Dec. 25, 1813.

1110. MARTIN, born Dec. 28, 1808, married, Jan. 2, 1845, Julia Blydenburg. They live in Rochester, N. Y. He is a merchant tailor, and has been in California.

1111. EDWIN, born July 15, 1811, and died in Shaftesbury, July 28, 1816.

1112. ELON, born June 3, 1814, married, Oct. 10, 1850, F. R. Galusha, and lives in Kalamazoo, Michigan, without children.

1113. CLARISSA, born April 6, 1817, married, Dec. 1834, Martin Andrus, brother of her brother Daniel's wife. She died Oct. 26, 1855.

1114. LYDIA MYRANDA, Oct. 20, 1827, married, Sept. 26, 1848, E. B. Galusha, and they are living in San Francisco, Cal.

418. SOLOMON. Milan, Ohio.

The first four of this family were born in East Haddam.

1115. JOSEPH FOWLER, born Oct. 25, 1799, and died single, in Aug. 1847, in Milan, Ohio.

1116. DIMIS FULLER, born Dec. 4, 1800, and died Nov. 4, 1814.

1117. ELIZABETH, born Aug. 22, 1802, and now resides in New Haven.

1118. MARGARET HURLBURT, born Sept. 8, 1804, and died single, March 1, 1843.

1119. SOLOMON THEODORE, born Feb. 6, 1807, married, 1832, Laura Hall, in Lee, Mass. They reside in Syracuse, N. Y.

1120. LAURA HARRIET, born Feb. 20, 1809, and died single, Oct. 10, 1840.

1121. WILLIAM OZIAS, born in Colchester, Conn., Jan. 31, 1811, married in Lynn, Mass., July 2, 1839, Elizabeth Oliver. They reside in Milan, Ohio, to which place they went, in 1845, from Lynn, Mass., where they had lived ten years.

All of this family except the last are dead.
1122. ALMOND F.
1123. ELEANOR.
1124. MINERVA.
1125. MARY.
1126. LAURA, married a Henderson.
1127. ANGELINE.
1128. OZIAS.
1129. JOHN, was at one time a carriage maker in Peterboro. N. Y.

451. RALPH. (M. D.)   Memphis, Mich.

1130. LEWIS, born in 1807, and married Matilda H. Hollister, in 1846. He was blind, and engaged in the grocery business in Canton, N. Y.

1131. CAROLINE M., born in 1809, married E. W. Mitchell, in 1830. He is a farmer, and resides in Morris, N. Y.

1132. OZIAS, born in 1812, married in 1837, Amarylla Hyde, a merchant of Ogdensburg, N. Y.

1133. CHARLES R., born in 1814, married, in 1841, Mary S. Jones, and is a farmer.

1134. FRANKLIN W., born in 1817, married, in 1841, Susan M. Kingsbury, and is a druggist.

1135. SARAH A., born in 1820, married, in 1838, Ayres White, a teacher, living in Ogdensburg.

1136. ELIZABETH B., born in 1823, married, in 1848, Rev. Allen McLean, a Baptist clergyman, and lives in Michigan.

1137. EDWIN G., born in 1827, married, in 1849, Catherine Partet, and is a mechanic in Canton, N. Y.

1138. LAURA H., born in 1830, and married, in 1851, Samuel Flint, a merchant, of Brockville, Canada West.

1139. SUSAN J., born in 1836.

The record of the above family is as reported by Dr. Joshua.

453. JARED.   Owego, N. Y.

The first of this family was born in East Haddam, and the rest in Owego, New York.

1140. JARED BLISS, born May 2, 1809, married, in 1835, Dinis, daughter of Heman and Philoxena Phelps, and was a saddler, in Syracuse, N. Y., where he died, Feb. 19, 1851.

1141. ELVIRA M., born July 19, 1819, married, in 1846, James M. Swift, a merchant, of New York city, and son of Thomas Swift, of Falmouth, Mass. She died in Brooklyn, N. Y., Feb. 27, 1854.

1142. ADELINE E., born Sept. 4, 1821, married, in 1850, Fred. E. Platt, son of William Platt. He is a banker in Owego.

SEVENTH GENERATION.

1143. EMILY CATHERINE, born Aug. 9, 1823, married, in 1842, Jared F. Phelps, brother to Jared B.'s wife. He is a dentist, in Syracuse, N. Y.

1144. MARTHA A., born Oct. 12. 1825, and married in 1848, Milton W., son of John Hanchett, of Syracuse, N. Y.

1145. WILLIAM SILLIMAN, born Dec. 14. 1827, and is in a dry goods store in Cleveland, Ohio. He married, in 1861, Cornelia W. (1962).

1146. HARRIET LAURA, born Jan. 30, 1830, married James M. Swift, husband of her sister, Elvira M.

1147. GEORGE M., born Aug. 8, 1832, married, Oct. 1, 1857, Louisa Denton, of Binghamton. They are living in Owego.

1148. CHARLES T., born Nov. 16, 1834, and lives in Owego, unmarried.

456. ANDREW, (M. D.) Ashford, Conn.

This family were all born in Ashford.

1149. SOPHIA, born March 4, 1791, married, in Ashford, Jan. 28, 1813, deacon Elisha Byles, a good farmer, and most acceptable citizen, and deacon in the Congregational church. She was a most excellent Christian woman, and died much lamented, Nov. 7, 1849. Their children were: Josias, born March 31, 1814; Abigail, born Nov. 15, 1816; Lucy, born Sept. 15, 1819; Andrew Huntington, born Oct. 3, 1820; and Zerviah, born Dec. 31, 1830.

1150. ANNA, born June 4, 1792, and died Jan. 11, 1795.

1151. ELISHA, born May 23, 1793, married, 1830, Maria E. Givens. He was a merchant, and died in Mobile, Ala., Oct. 1853.

1152. ANDREW, born Aug. 1, 1795, and died Aug. 18, 1800.

1153. HORATIO, born Nov. 27, 1797, and died Aug. 15, 1800.

1154. LUCY, born Aug. 28, 1800, and died Jan. 12, 1804.

1155. ZERVIAH, born March 29, 1803, and died May 23, 1804.

1156. ENOCH SMITH, born Sept. 30, 1804, graduated at Amherst College, in 1831. He married, first, Sept. 8, 1836, Lucy Cowles, of Amherst, Mass. daughter of Dr. Chester Cowles. She died June 14, 1843. He married, for his second wife, Oct. 29, 1843, in Clinton, Elizabeth M. Talcott, widow of Dr. Wm. Talcott, of Winsted, and daughter of Edward and Sarane Wilcox, of Clinton. She died Feb. 1, 1852, and he married, for his third wife, in Fairfield, April 13, 1853, Esther, daughter of Burr and Abigail Lyon, of that town. He was settled as pastor in Clinton, and afterward engaged in business in Danbury. He also preached, for the most of his time, though not settled over any parish. He died, at his residence in Danbury, April 7, 1862.

1157. DAN, born Feb. 19, 1806, and died single, in Mississippi, Aug. 1843.

1158. MATILDA CLARK, born Dec. 26, 1808, married Francis Clark, of Chaplin.

1159. NATHAN BELCHER, born Feb. 22, 1810, married, May 16, 1833, Matilda Whiton. They resided in Illinois, where he was a farmer, until 1857, when he removed to Elbrige, N. Y. His first wife died Oct. 1, 1841, and he married, for his second wife, Dec. 9, 1841, Rebecca Willard, who died May 3,

1819. He married, third, Oct. 6, 1819, Jane Charevoy, daughter of Francis and Betsey Charevoy, who was born Jan. 2, 1805.

1160. AMELIA, born Aug. 16, 1811, and died June 10, 1847.

1161. ANDREW, born Dec. 7, 1813, and died Jan. 4, 1827.

460. DANIEL, (DEA.)   Griswold, Conn.

This family were all born in Griswold.

1162. HENRY, born Feb. 25, 1801, and died Dec. 3, 1809.

1163. LUCY, born April 15, 1803, and died April 15, 1838.

1164. GEORGE, born March 30, 1805, and died June 14, 1838. He was lost in the ill-fated Pulaski. He had been married, and lived in Savannah, Geo.

1165. ABIGAIL, born Nov. 27, 1806, and died Aug. 10, 1855.

1166. ANDREW, born July 29, 1808, married, first, June 3, 1835, Lydia, daughter of George Loring, of Preston, Conn., who died Jan. 21, 1839. He married, for his second wife, Sept. 10, 1840, Louisa T., daughter of E. B. Downing, M. D., of Preston, who died April 12, 1846. He married, the third time, Jan. 2, 1848, Mary F., daughter of Roswell Downing of Lisbon, Conn. Mr. Huntington was for many years a successful merchant of Springfield, Mass., where he was a member of the firm of Huntington, Day & Co. He died in Springfield, Aug. 19, 1858.

1167. SIMON, born July 21, 1810, married, Sept. 1833, Sarah Worthington, of Colchester. He was in the hatting business, and is residing in Groton, opposite New London, where he was postmaster. They have no children. He is now (1862) a conductor on the New London and Palmer railroad.

1168. WILLIAM, born July 9, 1812, married, Nov. 1833, Elizabeth, daughter of Joseph Tyler, of Griswold, who died Nov. 24, 1846. He married, in 1847, Eunice Avery, of Preston; after his death she married A. E. Emmons. He was a farmer, and died in Griswold, March 3, 1850.

1169. OLIVE, born Jan. 19, 1817, married Rev. Wm. P. Avery, of Griswold, Conn., who is now preaching in Griswold. They have two children: William, and Elizabeth.

1170. SYBEL, born Sept. 22, 1818. She is dead.

461. ASHER, (DR.)   Chenango, N. Y.

1171. HARRIET, born in 1790, married, Dec. 19, 1824, P. Babcock, and lived at North East, in Pennsylvania.

1172. FRANCIS, born in 1792, married in 1815, Philena Gates, and lived in Lysander, N. Y.

1172.¹ ELIZA, born in 1794, married John Babcock, and lived in Preston, Wisconsin.

1173. JUSTINIAN, born June 14, 1798, married, Feb. 8, 1823, Ambrosia Crandall, who died, March 19, 1855. He married, again, Oct. 28, 1857, Mrs. Permelia Keeler. He is a harness maker and farmer, residing in South Brookfield, N. Y.

1173.¹ LUCY ANN, born in 1803, married, in 1820, A. Babcock, and lives in Milton, Wisconsin.

465. JOEL. Manlius, N. Y.

1174. RALPH BINGHAM, born Nov. 21, 1802, was a sailor and is probably dead.

1175. MARY SOPHIA, born May 15, 1814, and died Jan. 17, 1826.

1176. WILLIAM EZRA, born March 27, 1816, married, Nov. 30, 1853, Elizabeth Huntington Safford, and lives in Baldwinsville, N. Y.

1177. LAURA PHILENA, born April 11, 1819, married, June 6, 1839, Edward M. Robinson. They lived in Pulaski, N. Y., where she died June 2, 1853.

1178. JULIA MARIA, born Sept. 1, 1822, married, Dec. 27, 1843, Charles Smith, and lives in Manlius, N. Y.

1178[1] JOEL CHEENEY, born June 27, 1824, and died Sept. 22 of the same year.

1178[2] LEMUEL CHEENEY, born Dec. 27, 1826, married, May 10, 1849, Julia C. Sharpe, and lives in Baldwinsville, N. Y.

468. HON. ABEL, (M. D.) East Hampton, N. Y.

This family were all born in East Hampton.

1179. MARIETTE, born Oct. 9, 1800, married, Feb. 1820, David Gardiner, of Brooklyn, N. Y. He is a man of wealth. Their children are: John Lyon, a practicing physician at Bull Head, L. I.; Charles Huntington, who was rector of the Episcopal church in Ashfield, Mass.; and Frances Lee, who married, Oct., 1856, Rev. C. P. Maples, who was rector of Trinity church, Portland, Oregon, but who is now in Ohio.

1180. CORNELIA, born June 24, 1803, and has always lived with her father. She has made frequent contributions to our periodical literature, and the Sea Spray, published in 1857, will be a perpetual memorial of the grace and vigor of her style, as well as a living picture of the past in that old sea-exposed domain, on which its well told tales were once the verities of human life. It is believed that still other productions from the same pen will soon be given to the world.

1181. ABBY L., born Aug. 9, 1806, and resides in East Hampton.

1182. GEORGE LEE, born July 15, 1811, received his medical diploma from the New York University, and has been a practicing physician in East Hampton. He married, Oct. 24, 1833, Mary Hoogland. He is successful in his profession, and an honored member of the community in which he lives. He is a member of the Presbyterian church.

469. CHARLES. Chittenango, N. Y.

1183. MARGARET ELIZABETH, born in Columbus, N. Y., Aug. 17, 1811, married, Sept. 16, 1846, Charles C. West, and resides in Columbus, N. Y. They have no children.

1184. EZRA ABEL, born June 12, 1813, graduated at Union College in 1833, and studied theology under Dr. Nott of that institution. He was ordained and installed pastor of the third Presbyterian church in Albany, N. Y., Feb. 9,

1837. While occupying this field, he married, July 30, 1839, Anna E., daughter of Rev. Jacob Van Vechter, D. D., and a granddaughter of the Rev. John M. Mason, D. D. He continued to labor with increasing success until his dismissal, Jan. 10, 1855. He was inaugurated Professor of Biblical criticism in the theological seminary at Auburn, N. Y., in June, 1855, and here he has remained since. He has given several sermons, at the call of those to whom they were preached, to the public, and they sufficiently indicate the grace and power with which their author uses the pen.

1. "Man's work not finished in this life." A funeral sermon occasioned by the death of Thomas H. Cushman, and preached in Albany, Nov. 21, 1841. 2. "The House of God, and the Law of the House;" based on Ezekiel 43:12, and preached at the dedication of the third Presbyterian church, Albany, Dec. 3, 1845. 3. "Your Fathers where are they?" a funeral sermon occasioned by the death of William Gould, and preached in Albany, Jan. 25, 1846. 4. "And they that rejoice as though they rejoiced not;" a discourse delivered at the funeral of David Perkins Page, A. M., first principal of the New York state normal school, Albany, Jan. 9, 1848. 5. "The strife for supremacy in the church;" from Mark 9:33, 34, preached at the opening of the Synod of Albany, Oct. 12, 1852. 6 and 7. "Last words of a pastor to his people;" two discourses delivered to the third Presbyterian church in Albany, Dec. 31, 1854, and Jan. 7, 1855, the last two Sabbaths of the author's pastoral connection with that church. 8. "A history of the third Presbyterian church;" published with the two foregoing discourses. 9. "Blessings received, the sign of blessings in store;" a discourse delivered Thanksgiving day, Nov. 20, 1856, in the first Presbyterian church, Auburn. 10. The annual sermon before the Central American education society, delivered in the Madison Square Presbyterian church, New York, May 17, 1857.

1185. SARAH AUGUSTA, born in Columbus, N. Y., May 12, 1815, and died in Schenectady, N. Y., Dec. 8, 1856.

1186. SILAS HYDE, born in Hartsville, N. Y., March 18, 1818, and married in Lackawaxen, Penn., Sally Ann Cahill.

1187. CHARLES, born in Hartsville, N. Y., May 18, 1820, graduated at Union college, studied theology, and was ordained a minister in the Presbyterian church. He married, in Lackawaxen, Penn., Sept. 1, 1847, Eliza Ellen Ridgeway. He died at Hoverleyville, Pa., Sept. 17, 1855, after a short but useful ministerial life.

1188. JOEL, born in Chittenango, N. Y., Oct. 27, 1822, graduated at Union College in 1848, and was a tutor there in 1849 and '50. He studied theology and was ordained. He died Aug. 12, 1854, in Albany, N. Y., of cholera, one month after his settlement as preacher in Milwaukie, Wisconsin.

Professor Pearson, of Union College, thus testifies respecting his character: "He was a fine scholar, and bid fair for eminence in his profession. His untimely death, while on a visit to his brother Ezra, in Albany, occasioned great grief to his friends, both here and at Milwaukie."

1189. MARY SOPHIA, born in Chittenango, N. Y., June 16, 1826, married

Isaiah L. Williams, Sept. 20, 1848, and resides in Chittenango, N. Y. They have three children: Helen Blanch, born June 29, 1851; Mary Anna, born Aug. 23, 1854, and died Oct. 16, 1854; and Frances Anna, born April 11, 1856.

472. DAVID, Rev.   Harpersville, N. Y.

1190. ELIZUR, born April 14, 1814, and died single at sea, on the homeward passage from Spain in 1833.

1191. EZRA, born Aug., 1818, is living, unmarried, in New York city.

1192. JOSEPH V. KIRK, born in 1820, is also living single in New York city.

1193. ELIZABETH, married H. V. S. Sherman, and went, early in the California excitement, to that land of gold.

1194. SARAH MARIA, the only child of the third wife, was born in Harpersville, and married Henry P. Keyes, of Conneaut, Ohio.

473. THOMAS, (Esq.)   Hartford, Conn.

1195. ERASTUS, born at Hartford, June 9, 1808, married, June 14, 1855, Elizabeth Hecker Vanderhoff, who was born in Newfoundland, May 21, 1828. He was a member of Capt. Partridge's military school. He is at present, (1860), a proof reader in Harper's printing establishment, and resides in Brooklyn, N. Y.

478. HORACE.   Canaan, Conn.

1196. HORACE F., born Oct. 2, 1812, in Canaan, married, Oct. 1, 1835, Annelia Webb, daughter of Zimri and Anna (Munroe) Webb, of New Preston, Conn. He was for years in the book trade in Columbus, Ohio. In 1852 he removed to the city of New York, where he has since resided.

1197. MARY, born Feb. 2, 1815, in Litchfield, and married, Jan. 21, 1831, Lorenzo W. King, a carpenter and master builder, who died in Bridgeport, Feb. 3, 1854. She lived with one of her daughters, Mrs. Rodgers, in Stamford, in 1856.

1198. MILES THOMAS, born Sept. 8, 1817, in Hartford. He married, Nov. 20, 1839, Harriet E. Pierce, and lived in Albany. He died in Canaan, Sept. 5, 1845.

1199. JOHN, born May 22, 1820, in Canaan. He married, Dec. 18, 1845, Julia Adams, and is a farmer in Canaan.

1200. MARTHA, born July 10, 1825, married Willis C. Rood, a farmer living in Canaan. She died Aug. 16, 1846, and her infant child with her.

480. OWEN.   Canaan, Conn.

1201. CLARISSA DIANTHE, born Oct. 7, 1829, married John R. Hubbell, of Birmingham. They have one child, Rosa Huntington.

1202. ANNIE SELINDA, born June 5, 1834, and resides, (1862), in New York city.

495. BENJAMIN. Springfield, N. Y.

1203. SYLVIA, born 1808, married, in 1842, J. P. Keller, who was born in 1809, and resides in Minden N. Y., and has one child.

1204. BENJAMIN, born in 1810, married in 1839, Elenora Ross, and lives in Rochester, N. Y. His wife was born in 1820.

1205. MARY, born in 1812, married, in 1834, Hosea F. Antisdel, lives in Cooperstown, and has two children.

1206. LYDIA, born in 1812, twin with Mary, married, in 1835, Peter Hardy, and lives in Springfield. N. Y., and has two children.

1207. ISAIAH, born in 1818, married, in 1854, Mary Green, and was a farmer in Springfield, N. Y. His wife was born in 1834.

1208. JULIA, born in 1822, married, in 1840, Seth B. Payne, and lives in Mohawk, Montgomery county, N. Y., and has two children.

1209. CHARLES, born in 1828 and lives single in Georgia.

1210. SAMUEL, born in 1832, is a merchant, and farmer, unmarried, in Springfield, N. Y.

1211. AMELIA, born in 1824, and died aged twelve years.

501. ELIAS. Lebanon, N. H.

1212. FANNY M., born June 4, 1820, and died single, Dec. 9, 1851, in Hanover, N. H.

1213. STEPHEN NEWTON, born Aug. 9, 1822, married Mary Bridgman, in Hanover, April 30, 1844, where he is a merchant. He has represented his town in the state legislature the last two years. He and his wife are Baptists.

503. ANDREW, (M. D.) Pittsford, N. Y.

1214. WALES MUNROE, born in Pittsford, March 5, 1820, married, Dec. 9, 1845, Dorothy Ann, daughter of James Hopkins. He is a physician, and in practice with his father, with whom he studied, in Pittsford. He graduated at the Geneva Medical College in 1842. His wife was born Jan. 20, 1826.

1215. LYDIA, born August, 1822, married, July 26, 1843, William C. Rowley, a lawyer, and resides in Rochester, N. Y. They have four children: Andrew Huntington, born April 22, 1844; Sara Evelyn, born March, 1846; Helen, born July, 1849; Eliza Voorhees, born April 9, 1853.

1215[1]. JOSHUA MUNROE, born Nov. 12, 1825, and died one year and six months old.

504. ASA, (HON.) Hanover, N. H.

1216. HENRY SLADE, born Sept. 11, 1818. Received his medical diploma at Dartmouth College in 1846, married Jane Lovett, of Charlton, N. Y., and settled in the practice of his profession, in Penfield, N. Y. He died in Penfield, Feb. 23, 1861.

1217. SARAH, born Dec. 16, 1819, and died Nov. 17, 1852, unmarried.

1218. HANNAH WORCESTER, born Aug. 7, 1821, married, Sept. 16, 1853, O.

S. Ingalls, a lawyer residing in Hanover, N. H. They have one child, Asa Huntington, born Dec. 4, 1855.

1219. ALICE SWIFT, born Nov. 9, 1823, married, March 16, 1848, O. S. Ingalls, and had two children: Mary Alice, born Dec. 28, 1848, and Orville Huntington, born Oct. 6, 1851. She died Jan. 21, 1853, after which her husband married (1218) as above.

1220. FANNY, born Jan. 18, 1825, married, June 6, 1849, George E. Spencer, a physician, who took his diploma at Dartmouth College in 1846, and is settled in his profession at Laconia, N. H. They have had one child which died young, and the mother died Oct. 4, 1855.

1221. WILLIAM, born Nov. 11, 1828, and died single, June 6, 1853.

1222. EDWARD, born July 4, 1831, and died March 3, 1858.

505. SAMUEL. Hanover, N. H.

1223. ELIZA, born Jan. 20, 1818, married Loren Nye, a farmer of Pittsford, N. Y., and have had four children: Minerva E., born Dec. 29, 1845; Samuel H., born Sept., 1848; Ida Stella; and Silas, born in the spring of 1856.

1224. SAMUEL DAVIS, born Sept. 25, 1819, married Maria Robinson, and resides in Blue Island, Ill.

1225. LYDIA, born Aug. 3, 1821, married Thompson Slade, of Hanover, where they reside and have two children, William and Lydia.

1226. HARRIET ANN, born Oct. 26, 1823, married —— Gibson, of Rochester, N. Y., and has one child. They live in Dundas, C. W.

510. CHRISTOPHER. Roxbury, Vt.

This family were all born in Roxbury.

1227. HANNAH, born in 1789, married Gen. Thomas Putnam.

1228. SHUBAEL, born in 1791, married Mary Kefts, was a blacksmith, and lived in Coventry, Pa.

1229. EUNICE, born in 1793, married Simon Clinton.

1230. STEPHEN, born in 1795, died from the accidental discharge of a musket at a training, in 1812.

1231. SARAH, born in 1797, married Loren Clark.

1232. CYNTHIA, born in 1799, married Letsoner Loundsbury.

1233. SALLY, born in 1801, married Josiah Graves.

511. ELIJAH, (REV.) Braintree, Vt.

All of this family were born in Braintree, Vt.

1234. ELIJAH, born Nov. 5, 1793, married at about 30 years of age, Susan Gordon, and lived for a while in Delaware county, Ohio, but in 1825 went to Perrysburg, Ohio, where he spent the rest of his life. He died from cholera, July 26, 1854, and his wife in 1857. He commenced life as a teacher, and in this pursuit took much interest, and met marked success. In an obituary notice of him, taken from the "Toledo Blade," we find the following testimonial to his worth:

"A good citizen has fallen. We heard of his death with feelings of the most profound regret. For twenty years Mr. Huntington has been a resident of Perrysburg, and during that period he has enjoyed the confidence of the community in which he lived. He was the man perhaps of all others, that Perrysburg could not afford to lose. Much of the credit which Perrysburg has obtained for its fine system of local education, is doubtless attributable to the valuable services of Mr. Huntington; and the same may be said of almost every enterprise of a public character in that town. He was a far-seeing, sensible man, and well acquainted with the political character of this country. His memory was unbounded. We never knew a person who could more readily refer to events in the past history of parties, even from the commencement of the Government. He knew the character and principles of every public man of note in the nation, and formed his own opinions, from extensive reading and profound reflection. He held successively several of the most important county offices in Wood county, and was once a representative to the legislature from this district. His loss will be severely felt in Perrysburg, and not easily replaced, but while this is true, it will also be true that Perrysburg will long retain the evidence of his wisdom, sagacity and devotion to her interests, in her schools and other local improvements."

1235. CHRISTOPHER, born March 5, 1802, married, Aug. 9, 1836, Charlotte Tilson, and lives in Randolph, Vt.

1236. LEVI, born Dec. 31, 1803, and died Jan. 10, 1804.

1237. JEHIEL, born June 23, 1805, married, June 8, 1843, Hannah Holman, and resides in Braintree, Vt. They have no children.

1238. LYDIA, born April 14, 1808, and died July 2, 1808.

1239. SALLY, born Aug. 19, 1809, and died single, Sept. 25, 1851.

1240. JOSEPH, born July 27, 1811, graduated at Middlebury College in 1837, having sustained a very high character for scholarship, and been offered a tutorship in the institution. He studied theology at Newton, Mass., and was settled as pastor over the Baptist church in Williamstown, Vt. But after a lingering illness, consumption, he died April 26, 1843, lamented equally for his piety and his brilliant talents.

1241. LYDIA, born July 27, 1811, married, April 25, 1839, Jarvis Tilson, of Braintree, Vt. They have four children: Dwight, born Feb. 1842; Nancy J., born Dec. 1843; Joseph M., born Dec. 1847; and Jonathan E., born July, 1853.

1242. SAMUEL PEARCE, born June 4, 1814, and died single, Nov. 27, 1840.

1243. ADONIRAM JUDSON, born July 6, 1818, entered Brown University, and was obliged to leave his class in the junior year, on account of health. He went into Virginia and taught, and spent the senior year of his college course in Columbia College, Washington city, where he graduated in 1843, and entered upon a tutorship. In 1846 he was elected professor of the Latin and Greek languages, which post he filled three years. He spent the next three years as pastor of a church, somewhere in Virginia, when he was re-elected to the professorship he had vacated in Columbia College, and which he continued to fill, until the spring of 1859. He was married, June 6, 1844, in Urbanna, Middlesex county, Va., to Elizabeth G., daughter of Dr. Richard A. Christian, of that place. After preaching here a while, he went to take charge of a church in Augusta, Ga., where he was when last heard from.

1244. NANCY JUDSON, born Dec. 12, 1821, and died Aug. 10, 1843.

512. JEDIDIAH. Brighton, N. Y.

1245. LYDIA, born March 14, 1795, and died, in Compton, Canada East, in 1817.

1246. SAMUEL DIMMOCK, born Aug. 2, 1797, married, first, in 1823, in Palmyra, N. Y., Mary Jane Howell, who died. He married, for his second wife, in 1840, Philura Reeves, and lives in Adrian, Mich., where he is a manufacturer of woollen goods.

1247. HORACE JEDIDIAH, born May 7, 1803, married, in 1830, Betsey L. Griswold, and was a farmer in Brighton, N. Y. He removed to Rochester, where he died in 1854.

1248. MARSHAL, born June 26, 1805, married, in 1835, Ann Case. He is a carpenter, and lives in Adrian, Mich.

1249. JAMES, born Aug. 2, 1810, died in Compton, C. E., 1813.

513. THOMAS. Compton, C. E.

1250. SETH, born in Roxbury, Vt., June 13, 1796, married, April 3, 1825, Mary Hovey, whose parents were from Connecticut. He is a successful farmer, and is living in Hatley, Stanstead county, Canada East. The facts and hints in his letters have been of great service in making out the record of this branch of the family.

1251. ALICE, born in Roxbury, Vt., Oct. 16, 1797, married, in 1813, Ebenezer Crosby. They have twelve children: Eliza, Abigail, Mary Ann, Susan, Thos. Huntington, Alonzo, Edwin, Charles, Olive, Levi, Albert, and Joel.

1252. JOEL, born July 6, 1799, in Roxbury, Vt. Went early into Mississippi, and after an absence of 17 years returned to visit the family, and married, before returning, in 1838, Mary Richardson. He returned South, and lost his wife, after the birth of her second son. He died at the South, after sending his two orphan children back to Canada, to be brought up by his wife's friends.

1253. OLIVE, born in Roxbury, Dec. 21, 1801, married Daniel C. Richardson, who died in 1845, leaving four children: Chauncy, Frederic Douglass, Emma; and Louisa.

1254. HULDA, born in Compton, C. E., July 11, 1806, married Alanson Harvey, and died in Eaton, C. E., leaving no children.

1255. LEVI, born in Compton, Aug. 16, 1808, married, in Northern New York, Mary Johnson, and lives in Wisconsin.

1256. LYDIA, born in Compton, May 27, 1810, married Samuel Fuller. They reside in Compton, where they have two children living: Albert, and Malvina, having lost two with consumption.

514. PEREZ.
Compton, C. E.

1257. HEMAN, born in Roxbury, Vt., May 18, 1803, married, in Peperell, Mass., Feb. 7, 1832, Sybil Boynton, who was born in that town, April 8, 1808. They are now residing in Lowell, Mass., he being engaged in one of the mills.

1258. ANSON, born in Compton, C. E., Dec. 11, 1805, married, June 4, 1828, Lois Patterson, of Hartland, Vt. She was born Sept. 12, 1805. He is an engineer, and has had superintendence of canal construction, and is now residing in Wauseon, Ohio.

1259. RUBY, born Aug. 1807, and died in 1810.

1260. JAMES, born in Compton, C. E., May 29, 1813, married, in Lowell, Mass., May 2, 1846, Rachel C. Burbank, who was born in Barnet, Vt., June 16, 1818. They settled in Green Lake, Marquette county, Wis., where he is a thriving farmer. He and his wife are members of the Baptist church.

515. BENJAMIN.
Compton, C. E.

The first two of this family were born in Roxbury, Vt., and the rest in Compton.

1261. THOMAS, born April 17, 1802, married, Feb. 5, 1827, Emily Hicks of Eaton, C. E., who was born Feb. 14, 1802. They have continued to live in Compton, where he is a farmer.

1262. CYNTHIA, born April 19, 1804, married Daniel Parker, and lived in Compton, where she died, Oct. 3, 1856.

1263. CATHERINE, born Nov. 24, 1806.

1264. JOSIAH G., born Feb. 24, 1809, married, June 1833, Lucinda Heath, and lives in Compton, where he is a carpenter.

1265. BENJAMIN, born April 16, 1811, married, Jan. 1832, Mehetabel Heath, and was a farmer, in Compton, where he died, Dec. 31, 1846.

1266. ALMIRA, born July 14, 1813, and lived, unmarried, in Compton. She died Dec. 31, 1857, " in the western country."

1267. PHILIP, born March 19, 1816, in Compton, where he died, in Oct. 1820.

518. GIDEON.
Pompanoosuc, Vt.

1268. SAMUEL BLISS, born in Compton, C. E., Sept. 10, 1816, married, in 1847, Jane Babcock, and is now engaged in manufacturing in Newburyport, Massachusetts.

1269. ELIZABETH MEHITABEL, born in Compton, C. E., July 17, 1818, married, at the age of sixteen, Charles Henry Larned, an officer in the United States army, who was stationed in Arkansas, where she died of consumption, Aug. 30, 1840, six months after the birth of her third daughter.

1270. JEDIDIAH PINNOCK, born in Compton, C. E., Feb. 16, 1820, and is a farmer, still single, and living with his parents in Pompanoosuc.

1271. STEPHEN DIMOCK, born in Compton, C. E., Jan. 15, 1822. He lived, unmarried, with his parents on the farm. He recently died in the Union army.

1272. WILLIAM AVERY, born in Hartland, Vt., Aug. 9, 1824, married, Feb. 11, 1846, Lydia H., daughter of Charles and Matilda Rogers, of Newburyport, and is now manufacturing in Lawrence, Mass.

520. ELIPHALET.

1273. REUBEN, born in 1775.
1274. ELEAZER, born in 1777.
1275. ROSWELL, born in 1779.
1275.¹ ARIEL, born in 1781.

521. ROSWELL. Windham, Conn.

1276. SARAH, born in 1778, married, in 1797, Nathan (634).

529. ELEAZER. Windham, Conn.

The first six of these births are on the Mansfield records.

1277. FANNY, born June 13 or 18, 1790, married Samuel K. Dodge, and lived in Berlin, Pa., having no children.

1278. MELANY, June 9, 1792, married in 1812, John Lincoln, of New Boston, Windham. They went to Lebanon, Penn., where they had five children: John, Lucy, Emily, Steadman, and Giles.

1279. HARRIET, born May 24, 1798, and has lived single, in Greenville, Norwich.

1280. ELIZA, born March 13, 1800, married Andrew Davison, and has five children.

1281. CHARLES, born May 20, 1802, married, in 1829, Nancy B. Strong of Coventry. He was engaged many years, as teamster, in Willimantic. Went to California and returned, moving his family to New Market, Ohio.

1282. MARCIA, born May 15, 1804, married James Bingham, and lived in Norwich, where she died, in 1850, leaving three daughters: Eliza A., Antoinette, and Mary, now Mrs. H. C. Albro, all of them living in Norwich.

1283. MINERVA, born in Windham, 1808, married Nathan Justin, and went to Manchester, in Penn.

1284. ERASTUS, born in Windham, March 18, 1810, married April 16, 1844, Ruth, daughter of John Sly of Norwich, who was born May 30, 1809. They lived in Greenville, Norwich, where he was successful in business, being employed in one of the manufactories. He died in Greenville, May 1, 1857. His family are now (1862) living in Norwich city.

1285. EDWIN, born March 3, 1813, in Windham, married, May 23, 1839, Emily, daughter of Samuel and Polly Price, and is a farmer in Osage, Iowa. His wife was born in Manchester, Wayne county, Penn., Oct. 23, 1819. He and his wife are Universalists.

1286. HORATIO, born Feb. 5, 1816, married, Nov. 12, 1840, Julia Horton. He is a millwright and resides in Osage, Iowa. He and his wife belong to the Universalist denomination.

531. SHUBAEL. Windham and Woodstock, Conn.

1287. ASA H., born Nov., 1795, and died single, in Aug. 1827.
1288. BETSEY, born Oct. 1797, married Alfred Carpenter, of Ashford.
1289. CLARISSA, born Sept., 1799, and died single, in April, 1832.
1290. ABNER, born March 1802, married, Nov. 1834, Almira Bartlett, of Auburn, Mass. He resided in Worcester, Mass.
1291. EUNICE, born Sept., 1804.
1292. WALDO, born Nov. 1806, married, Nov., 1837, Maria Ingraham, in Dudley, Mass., and died, leaving no child, in Nov., 1838, in Auburn.
1293. PHEBE, born July, 1809, and died in May, 1813.
1294. ALBERT, born Dec., 1812, married, at Auburn, Mass., Oct., 1838, Lavinia Stone, and was engaged in teaching.

535. EBENEZER, HON. Townshend, Vt.

This family were born in Townshend, Vt.

1295. DIANA, born June 14, 1811, married, April 22, 1835, Horace Cobb. They are now living in Spring Mills, N. Y. They have had seven children: Lucy Miranda, born Feb. 6, 1837; Daniel Horace, born Dec. 27, 1838; Henry Huntington, born Oct. 22, 1841; Aurelius H., born Jan. 5, 1843; Lydia Peck, born Jan. 18, 1844; Lyman Howell, born May 15, 1848; and Geo. Hamilton, born March 21, 1850. Mr. Cobb is a man of means and influence, and has been honored with testimonials of public confidence. He is a farmer.

1296. LUCRETIA, born June 25, 1815, and died July 25, 1816.

1297. EBENEZER HARTSHORN, born Feb. 27, 1817, married, Sept. 21, 1843, Mary Caroline, daughter of William G. Raymond, and lives in Madison, Wis. He was a merchant some fifteen years, and is now using his funds in moneyed speculations. His first wife was born April 17, 1820, in Coraline, N. Y., and died Oct. 9, 1851, and was buried in Bingham, Penn. He married, for his second wife, in Independence, Sept. 13, 1854, Adeline, daughter of Wm. W. Reynolds, who was born April 7, 1831.

1298. ELEAZER PECK, born Feb. 27, 1817, married, Dec. 5, 1844, Maria Miller, and resides in Bingham, Penn. He was a number of years a lawyer, but is now a preacher in the Methodist denomination.

1299. JARED HYDE, born Feb. 18, 1820, married, Jan. 10, 1842, Adaline Wait, and lives in Townshend, Vt., where he is a farmer.

1300. OLIVE, born March 31, 1822, married, Aug 26, 1847, Paul B. Lewis. They are now living in Independence, N. Y. They have one child, Clinton Huntington, born April 8, 1851. Mr. Lewis is a farmer in good circumstances.

1301. LUCRETIA, born April 15, 1827, married, Sept. 28, 1852, Joseph Powers, who was born May 10, 1809. They are living in Hebron, Wis., where he is engaged in an extensive cabinet manufactory, and owns also a flouring establishment. They have three children, Edward Clinton and Ellen Minerva, twins, born Oct. 26, 1853, and a daughter.

1302. DE WITT CLINTON, born April 27, 1831, married, May 25, 1853, Mary

E. Moore. He is a minister of the Methodist Episcopal denomination, and is now (1862) pastor of the Asbury church in Rochester, N. Y.

1303. MINERVA, born March 4, 1833, married, March 4, 1857, Miles Osgood, who is a mechanic, and owns and improves the farm which her father left in Townshend, Vt.

536. JOHN. Mexico, N. Y.

1304. JOHN, born in 1784, and died.

1305. REBECCA, born in 1786, and died.

1306. JOHN, born March 10, 1792, married, first, Ann Rodgers, of New London, who was born May 20, 1792, and died in 1822. He married, for his second wife, in New London, Feb. 12, 1824, Eliza Ann Kinner, who was born July 25, 1801, and who died in New London, where the family lived, Oct. 4, 1852, aged fifty-one years. He was drafted during the last war and served at fort Griswold. He was engaged in farming, and afterwards he moved into New London, and for several years was in the employ of the I. Wilson hardware manufacturing company, until his health failed. He died Oct. 13, 1855.

1307. FREDERIC A., born Feb. 14, 1790, married, Nov. 23, 1822, Mary Witter, and resides in Mexico, Oswego Co., N. Y., engaged in farming. His wife was born June 8, 1801.

1308. EPHRAIM, born 1792, and died in 1793.

1309. REBECCA, born in 1793, married Thomas Prentice, of Waterford, Ct. He was a farmer. She died in 1837, leaving four sons and two daughters.

1310. ANDREW, born in 1798, married, in 1828, Betsey Winter, sister of Mary, and is a preacher in Mexico, N. Y.

1311. MARY, born in 1796, married Roswell Richardson, and lives in Salem, New Hampshire.

1312. ROBERT G. H., born in 1800, married, Nov. 12, 1826, Lectania Hatch, and has resided many years in New York city, where he has been engaged in the insurance business. His wife died Sept. 24, 1851, and he married, for his second wife, June 19, 1856, Phebe Eliza Fuller.

1313. ALMIRA, born in 1802, married James Holden, of South Dansville, Steuben Co., N. Y., and has no children.

541. ELISHA. Mexico, N. Y.

This family were all born in Tolland.

1314. LUCIA, born in 1787, and died, without marrying, of consumption in 1812, in Watertown, N. Y.

1315. SAMUEL, born in 1789, married, but did not live long with his wife. He went to Kanzas to locate a land warrant last year, and is now, 1857, at Prairie City in that territory.

1316. AMBROSE W., born June 9, 1792, married, Oct. 17, 1817, Parmelia Keeler, who was born in 1797, and died of consumption in Mexico, N. Y., Jan. 14, 1832. He married again, Feb. 24, 1834, Jane McCymon, of Parish, N. Y. He is a farmer and lives in Union Square, Oswego Co., N. Y.

1317. ESTHER, born in 1793, and died of consumption, Aug. 25, 1814, aged twenty years and ten months and twenty-seven days.

1318. ELISHA, born June 6, 1790, married, Nov. 25, 1822, Nancy Fitch Hills, who was born Aug. 4, 1806. They reside in Wauseon, Fulton Co., Ohio. He is a farmer and has lived in Wauseon since 1836.

1319. APOLLOS, born Nov. 14, 1798, married in May, 1825, Eveline Tuttle, who was born Aug. 27, 1806, and died Dec. 2, 1833. He married, for his second wife, Nov. 3, 1836, Deborah Rowland, who was born May 24, 1802. He resides in Sandusky City, Ohio.

1320. NANCY, born in 1801, married John Whitney, and resided in Mexico, N. Y. They are both dead, she dying of consumption in 1832. She had two sons, Byron and Franklin, the latter of whom is still living and is a surveyor in Pulaski.

1321. LAURA, born in 1804, married Samuel Buckley, a merchant of Sacketts Harbor, N. Y. She died in 1828, having had two children, both of whom died soon after their mother.

1322. RUTH M., born in 1806 and died of consumption in 1834.

542. WILLIAM. Watertown, N. Y.

1323. WILLIAM, born March 28, 1784, married, in Plainfield, N. H., Nov. 28, 1805, Zina Baker, who was born May 2, 1786. He embraced the Mormon religion on its first promulgation, and removed, while his family were yet young, to Kirtland, Ohio, and, on the emigration of the sect to Nauvoo, Ill., he accompanied them with several of his family. Here he died, at Pisgah Grove, Iowa, Aug. 19, 1846.

1324. DYER, born Feb. 18, 1786, married, Sept. 14, 1820, Eliza A. Clark, who was born at Little Falls, N. Y., Dec. 25, 1800. He died in Watertown, N. Y., Aug. 8, 1851. He was a painter.

1325. JOHN LATHROP, born June 30, 1787, in New Grantham, N. H., married Rebecca, daughter of William Minor and Cynthia Hayes Lord, who was born in Woodstock, Vt., Jan. 14, 1796. They were married in Houndsfield, N. Y., Sept. 10, 1815. He now resides in Watertown, N. Y.

1326. HIRAM, born June 19, 1789, married Susan Blanchard, and died Aug. 30, 1826.

1327. AMBROSE WOODWARD, born Sept. 1, 1791, married, first, Oct. 11, 1818, Hannah Graves, who was born July 9, 1796, and died Nov. 27, 1827. He married again, Dec. 15, 1829, Prudence Cherry, who was born May 6, 1800. He is a farmer.

1328. PRECENDIA, born May 8, 1794, married, May 1, 1814, Joseph Kimball, who was born in Greenwich, R. I., May 25, 1788, and died in Watertown, N. Y., July 30, 1854. Their children were: George W. Kimball, born at Sacketts Harbor, March 30, 1822, and died at Sacramento, California, Nov. 2, 1850; Cornelia Ellis, born at Sacketts Harbor, Feb. 2, 1824, died July 11, 1825; Mary Precendia, born at Sacketts Harbor, Nov. 19, 1826, married Henry K. Kellogg, Sept. 12, 1848; Joseph C. and Josephine C., born at Watertown, N. Y., Feb. 27, 1832; Josephine C., married Charles F. Ives, March

12, 1852, and died April 21, 1852; Joseph C., married Mary M. McGiven, Nov. 10, 1852.

1329. CYRUS THOMPSON, born May 15, 1801, married, July 10, 1823, China Graves, who was born July 8, 1805.

1329¹ LUCIA, born Sept. 24, 1813, married a Mr. Clapp, and died May 2, 1833.

529. HEZEKIAH, Hon.   Hartford, Conn.

This family were all born in Suffield.

1330. HENRY WILLIAM, born Aug. 16, 1789, graduated at Yale in 1811, and was admitted to the bar. He married, April 21, 1817, Helen, daughter of William Dunbar, of Natchez, Miss. He went into Louisiana and became a planter, dying in Catahoula, of that State, Oct. 12, 1854.

1331. JULIA ANN, born Dec. 10, 1790, and married, Oct. 12, 1814, Leicester King, a merchant of Bloomfield, Ohio, where she died, Jan. 24, 1819. Their children were: Henry W., born Sept. 24, 1815, and died Nov. 21, 1857; Julia A., born Nov. 7, 1817; Susan H., born July 6, 1820, and died in 1837; Leicester, jr., born July 26, 1823; David, born Dec. 24, 1825; Helen D., born Nov. 19, 1827; Hezekiah Huntington, born Aug. 3, 1829; and Catherine B., born July 8, 1832.

1332. HORACE AUGUSTUS, born May 9, 1792, and married, in 1817, Maria Evans. He was a merchant in Natchez, Miss., where he died of yellow fever, Dec. 9, 1819, leaving no children.

1333. SAMUEL HOWARD, born Dec. 14, 1793, graduated at Yale in 1818, and after being admitted to the bar, entered upon the practice of law in the city of Hartford, where his father was then a successful lawyer and district attorney. He married, Oct. 25, 1825, Catherine H., daughter of George Brinley, of Boston. She died July 21, 1832, at the age of twenty-six years and five months. He married, for his second wife, Oct. 19, 1835, Sarah Blair, daughter of Robert Watkinson. He has always lived in Hartford, where he has been, from the commencement of his business life, a successful man and an honored citizen. In 1829, he was clerk of the state senate. He has been many years one of the trustees of Trinity College. He was judge of the county court, and on the establishment of the court of claims in Washington, D. C., he was selected as one worthy the trust to be reposed in its chief clerk. Though residing still in Hartford, he is still (1862) engaged in meeting the duties of this responsible office.

1334. HEZEKIAH, born Oct. 28, 1795, married, June 26, 1825, Sarah, daughter of William Morgan. She died, April 16, 1847. He married again, Sept. 25, 1856, Catherine B., daughter of George Sumner, M. D., of Hartford. He has continued to reside in Hartford, where he was a successful publisher. He is now president of the Hartford Fire Insurance Company. He has prospered in business, and is held in deserved esteem by his fellow citizens.

1335. SUSAN LYMAN, born Jan. 14, 1798, married, Oct. 21, 1833, Rev. J. B. Cook, of the Baptist denomination, who resides in Binghamton, N. Y.

They have one daughter, Susan Kent, born Dec. 26, 1837, now living with her parents.

1336. FRANCIS JUNIUS, born Dec. 3, 1802, married, Sept. 1, 1833, Stella Bradley, daughter of Michael Bull. He early engaged in publishing, and has continued to succeed in the business, first in Hartford and now in the city of New York. At present (1862) he is engaged in publishing musical books. His family, who have spent several years abroad, are now residing in Hartford, Conn.

551. SAMUEL. Norwich, Conn.

This family were all born in Norwich.

1337. ROGER, born Feb. 1, 1784, married, Jan. 30, 1814, Ann, daughter of Benadam Denison. She died, Sept. 15, 1819, aged 35 years. He married, for his second wife, Aug. 30, 1820, Amelia Matilda Lambert. He was engaged, early in life, in trade, and was a man of most unwearied industry, and a pattern for the nice method and accuracy with which he executed every trust. His moments, not employed in his business, were most actively devoted to reading and study. He rose to a high rank among the citizens of his native town, in all those qualities that secure public esteem, and confidence. He represented Norwich, and the senatorial district to which it belongs, in the state legislature, and was speaker of the house of representatives while in that branch. He was controller, also, of the state. He died at his residence in Bean Hill, Norwich, June 27, 1852. The general sentiment of the community, among which he had always lived, was well expressed in an obituary notice in one of the city papers. It says: "We are pained to record the unexpected death of our most respected friend and fellow-citizen, the Hon. Roger Huntington, of Norwich Town. Mr. Huntington was no ordinary man; and his high character and superior talents justly entitled him to the confidence and trust reposed in him by his fellow-citizens."

1338. HANNAH TRACY, born June 19, 1790, married, Nov. 19, 1810, Solomon Dickenson, a substantial farmer of Hatfield, Mass. Their children are: Abby Huntington, born Sept. 8, 1811; Samuel Huntington, Jan. 28, 1816; Philira Tracy, born Jan. 31, 1818, married March 8, 1843, George W. Hubbard, of Hatfield; Harriet Maria, born Sept. 21, 1825, married Dec. 19, 1849, David F. Wells, of Hatfield, and has one daughter. The family are still living in Hatfield.

1339. GILBERT, born May 26, 1796, married, June 5, 1836, Mary Ann M. Clement. He lived in Norwich, where he died, Aug. 21, 1841.

554. DANIEL. Norwich, Conn.

This family were all born in Norwich.

1340. BETSEY, born Aug. 24, 1793, married, Feb. 20, 1812, Asher Bennett, and lived in Norwich.

1341. LYDIA, born Aug. 20, 1796, married Joseph Bailey, a farmer, of Bozrah. She died in Jan. 1856, having had three daughters: Julia, married John

Barstow, of Bozrah, and has had two children; Mary, married **Oliver Fowler**; and Maria, married Lucius Brown.

1342. **Lucy Tracy**, born Feb. 14, 1799, married Cyrus Miner, of Norwich, and died, leaving children. Her husband died Dec. 14, 1848, aged 58 years.

1343. **Simon**, born Aug. 8, 1801, married **Sarah Smith**, soon after settling in Canada, where he was a preacher of the Methodist denomination. He died of inflammation of the lungs, after a brief illness, at Walsingham, Canada West, Aug. 25, 1856.

1344. **Daniel Lathrop**, born March 21, 1804, married, Nov. 26, 1829, Mary Ann, daughter of Simon Lathrop of Norwich. They reside at the Yantic, where he was for years engaged in manufacturing, and where he has a store.

555. EBENEZER. Norwich, Conn.

This family were all born in Norwich.

1345. **Mary Ann**, born Oct. 30, 1807, and still lives in the homestead in Norwich.

1346. **Cornelia Eliza**, born Feb. 8, 1809, and lives with her sister, above.

1347. **Edward Andrew**, born Oct. 23, 1811, married in Woodstock, June 26, 1850, Harriet A., daughter of Daniel Lyman, M. D., of South Woodstock, and grand-daughter of (552). They occupy the house left by their father, on Bean Hill. He was chosen deacon of the first Congregational church in Norwich, in 1857, and is the seventh of the name that have been called to the same office, in that ancient, and yet vigorous church.

1348. **William Lathrop**, born Feb. 3, 1817, and died Aug 11, 1825.

1349. **Samuel Tracy**, born Sept. 20, 1819, and died Aug. 10, 1825.

556. ERASTUS. Norwich, Conn.

This family were all born in Norwich.

1350. **George Cabot**, born July 20, 1807, married, for his first wife, at Cleveland, Ohio, Oct. 6, 1833, Angeline, daughter of Asahel Porter, of Waterbury, Conn. She died after the birth of her second child, and he married, for his second wife, Nov. 9, 1837, Emeline, eldest daughter of Datus Kelley, of Kelley's Island, Ohio. Here he resides, and is engaged, successfully, in the culture of the grape.

1351. **Charles Lyman**, born May 25, 1809, and died single, Feb. 3, 1832.

1352. **Joseph Hyde**, born June 11, 1811, married, in West Boxford, Mass., Eleanor, daughter of Jonathan Foster of that town. They are now (1862) residing in Norwich city, where he has a crockery store.

1353. **Albert Williams**, born Jan. 2, 1816, is still unmarried and engaged in business in Cincinnati, Ohio.

1354. **Henry Dwight**, born July 1, 1817, married, May 12, 1846, Sarah Hallam, daughter of Rev. Samuel Johnston, of Middletown, **Conn**. He is also in Cincinnati, Ohio, where the remaining four brothers are residing, and engaged in the successful importation and sale of crockery.

1355. JOHN CALDWELL, born Feb. 8, 1819, married, in Cincinnati, Ohio, Sept. 5, 1848, Mary, daughter of Jethro and Mercy Mitchell, of that city.

1356. WILLIAM COIT, born Sept. 8, 1821, married, in Cincinnati, Ohio, Sept. 2, 1851, Mary Elizabeth, sister of Sarah Hallam, above. She died, most deeply lamented, Jan. 26, 1857. He is in the jewelry business in Cincinnati. He married, Oct. 13, 1862, Mary Henderson, daughter of Joel Lindsley, D. D., of Greenwich, Conn.

1357. FREDERIC GILBERT, born Aug. 18, 1826, married in Cincinnati, in May, 1859, Mary, daughter of Lowell Fletcher.

1358. HORACE, born Aug. 2, 1828, is still unmarried, and in business with his brothers, in Cincinnati.

457. JEDIDIAH, GEN. Norwich & New London, Conn.

This family were all born in Norwich, excepting the eldest.

1359. JABEZ, born Sept. 17, 1767, in Lebanon, Conn. He graduated at Yale, 1784, having spent his boyhood and youth with his maternal grandfather, the elder Governor Trumbull, of Lebanon. He married, first, Dec. 12, 1792, Mary, daughter of Peter Lanman. She died, Sept. 29, 1809, aged 36. He married, for his second wife, Oct. 21, 1810, Sarah, an elder sister of his first wife, who was born Dec. 20, 1765, and died Feb. 19, 1850. She was remarkable for her intelligent and cheerful piety, during the twenty years of blindness, through which she was called to pass. He was a man of very marked qualities. Quick in reaching a conclusion, he was as positive and persistent in adhering to it, and as earnest in maintaining it. He was eminently conscientious also, so that, if he found himself at fault, he would acknowledge it as readily as detected. He was at one time connected with the Episcopal church or society in Norwich; yet, at length, he united with the Congregational church, of which Dr. Bond is now pastor, and of which he continued a useful member, and became an efficient deacon. He was induced to accept the office of major in the Connecticut regiment of the army raised by the elder Adams, but soon left the service. He was at one time president of the Norwich Bank, and treasurer of the Norwich Savings Society. He died in Norwich, Aug. 16, 1848.

1360. ELIZABETH MOORE, born Jan. 20, 1779, and died unmarried, March 21, 1823.

1361. ANN CHANNING, born Oct. 9, 1780, married, in 1800, Peter Richards, of New London. They resided, during his life-time in that city, where they had nine children: Henry Augustus, born Nov. 14, 1801, married Julia A. Haughton, of Montville, and had ten children; Wolcott, born June 15, 1803, now (1856) a physician in Cincinnati, Ohio, and has three children; Channing, born May 2, 1805, who is married, and has four children; Anne Huntington, born Sept. 2, 1807, now the wife of Rev. Dr. McLane, of Williamsburg, N. Y., and has six children; Eliza, born Oct. 18, 1809, now wife of James Haughton of Brookline, Mass., has seven children; Peter, born Oct. 28, 1811, married

Josephine, daughter of Gen. Swift, resides in Brooklyn, N. Y., and has six children; Hannah Dolbear, born Aug. 10, 1814, wife of Rev. Ephraim Lyman, of Washington, Conn., and has six children; George. born Nov. 2. 1816, is married, and has four children, and was several years pastor of the Winter street church, in Boston, Mass., but now is pastor of the first Congregational church in Litchfield, Conn.; and Jedidiah Huntington, born Sept. 20. 1822, is a physician in New York city. Mrs. Richards, a most excellent woman, died in Washington, Conn., Jan. 9. 1857.

1362. FAITH TRUMBULL, born Oct. 7. 1782. married Benjamin (318).

1363. HARRIET SMITH, born July 24. 1784, married, in New London, Sept. 18, 1806, John De Witt, who was a prominent citizen of Norwich, where the family lived. He died, April 2, 1848, at the age of 67, and his wife, Sept. 6, 1849. Their children, of whom the first three are recorded in Norwich, were: Harriet Richards, born July 31. 1808, and died young; Henry, born May 19, 1810; Martha, born June 29. 1812, married, first, Horatio Barstow, and second, a Mr. Converse; Mary, who married a Coggswell; Ann, who married a Hutchins; Joshua, who recently married in Cincinnati; Susan, who married a Butler; and Harriet, who married a Wild.

1364. JOSHUA, born Jan. 31, 1786, and graduated at Yale in 1804. He married, in 1809, Susan, daughter of Rev. Achilles Mansfield, of Killingworth, Conn. He was remarkable, during his college course, for his correct and gentlemanly deportment. His classmate and chum during the sophomore year, Dr. McEwen, late of New London, speaks of him as a young man of "very acceptable address, both private and public," as having "constitutional discretion," and "good common sense." A revival of religion occurred in college during his sophomore year, of which he became a subject. He very soon decided to devote himself to the work of the ministry, and this henceforth was the aim, or business of his life. A habit of stammering had been contracted, which threatened to interfere with this purpose; and at length his embarrassment was such as almost effectually to discourage his attempts. But so firm was his conviction of his duty, and so earnest his desire to do good in the work on which he had set his heart, that he set himself to the daily task of reading, and re-reading with steadiness, long passages, until he completely triumphed. After his graduation, he commenced with several young men the study of theology under the guidance of Dr. Dwight; and after leaving New Haven, as was customary in those days, he sought the instruction and training which were to be found in the study and pastoral duties of the private pastor. Such a school he enjoyed in the family of Rev. Asahel Hooker, of Goshen, Conn.; and here he laid a good foundation for the marked success which attended his brief but most useful ministry.

At the early age of twenty-one he commenced preaching. and from the first, though exceedingly youthful in appearance. both the manner and the matter of his discourses were such as to secure the approval of his hearers.

The memoir which appeared in the "Panoplist," for Dec. 1820, will exhibit the brief ministerial career and Christian character of Mr. Huntington, better than anything which can now be written. It is a tribute, penned by one who knew well, and who highly prized the subject of it. It is the worthy testimonial of a personal affection, which would forever embalm "those amiable and desirable qualities, on which the eye dwells with unmingled satisfaction."

The memoir says: "Few young men have been received with more decided marks of approbation on their first entering the pulpit; yet we never heard that it produced in him any indication of vanity. This we consider as a most remarkable triumph of good sense and piety over the love of distinction. During the year that Mr. Huntington preached as a candidate, the people in each of several vacant parishes were desirous of obtaining him for their minister. He received two formal invitations on the same day, one from the Old South church, Boston, and the other from the Congregational church in Middletown, Conn. About the same time he received an invitation from another church in a pleasant and populous town. The unanimity with which these calls were offered, by the most respectable congregations, in different parts of the country, is proof that the person to whom they were addressed was a youth of distinguished promise.

"After serious deliberation, and with the most judicious advice, he accepted the invitation from the Old South church, and was ordained as colleague pastor with the late Rev. Dr. Eckley, May 18, 1808.

"He had not quite completed the third year of his ministry, when the senior pastor was suddenly removed by death, and the weight of a large church and congregation rested upon him. Though deeply feeling his increased responsibility, he was not disheartened, but continued his faithful labors with alacrity and zeal. *   *   *   *   *   *   *

"In the steady, noiseless, conscientious discharge of his official functions, did this good man persevere, without any remarkable era in his life, till he was summoned to an early tomb. His progress was that of increasing usefulness, and extending reputation, and a most evident preparation for a better world."

His death occurred in Groton, Mass., at the residence of Rev. Dr. Chaplin, while he was returning homeward on a journey for his health, on Saturday, Sept. 11, 1819.

"On the succeeding Monday, the mortal remains were interred in Boston, with appropriate exercises and great solemnity. A sermon was delivered on the occasion by Rev. Mr. Dwight, in the Old South church, where an immense concourse was assembled to express their interest in this solemn event, and to pay a public tribute to distinguished worth. The clergy of Boston and the vicinity, the members of the church and congregation of which the deceased had been pastor, and a multitude of other acquaintances and friends united with the bereaved family and relatives in deploring their common loss, while they praised God for the bright example of Christian virtue which they had witnessed. The spacious house of worship, where the last sad offices were performed, was so crowded that many hundreds tried in vain to get admittance. The tokens of unaffected mourning were so numerous and so impressive that it could not be doubtful in what high and affectionate estimation the character of the departed minister and friend was held."

His widow survived him but a little more than four years. She was born in Killingworth, Conn., Jan. 27, 1791, and died in Boston, Thursday, Dec. 4, 1823. The "memoirs" of this gifted and beautiful woman was prepared by the Rev. Dr. B. B. Wisner, her pastor, and passed through several editions. It is a worthy memorial of a sainted and most lovely character, and occupies, as was predicted by the Rev. Dr. Gordon of Edinburg, in his commendations of the work, for the first Edinburg edition, "a high place among works of Christian biography."

1365. DANIEL, born Oct. 17, 1788, graduated at Yale in 1807, and studied theology. He married, first, July 21, 1812, Mary Hallam, daughter of Capt. Gurdon Salstonstall, and great granddaughter of the governor of that name. He was ordained in October of the same year, as the third minister of the Congregational church in North Bridgewater, Mass., in which office he continued until his health compelled him to abandon it in 1832. While there, his wife died in 1822. He married, for his second wife, Oct. 28, 1823, Alma, daughter of Benjamin French, of Boston, who died June 3, 1837; after which he married, for his third wife, Nov. 1, 1841, Sarah Sayr Rainey, of New London, who is still living.

The Connecticut Historical Society's Library contains four sermons or addresses written by Mr. Huntington; and a poem on religion delivered before the United Brother's Society, of Providence, R. I.; and "The Triumphs of Faith," before the Porter Rhetorical Society of Andover. He also prepared a very acceptable memorial of his own daughter, Mary Hallam, which was published by the American Sunday School Union. He delivered also one of the addresses at the anniversary of the Pilgrim Society in Plymouth. He died in New London, May 21, 1858. The following extracts from the tribute to the worth of this good man, found in the Congregational Year Book for 1859, deserves a place in this family memorial:

"His first settlement in the ministry continued twenty years, and was attended from time to time with the demonstration of the spirit and with power, so that great numbers were added to the Lord. * * * After a temporary respite from pastoral labors, he gained sufficient strength to gratify his fine literary taste in the instruction of successive classes of young ladies in the higher branches of an educational course, while residing in New London, the city of his birth and death. In this employment, combined with occasional preaching, as returning health permitted, seven years passed away usefully and pleasantly. But his heart yearned for a return to the labors of his love at his first entrance on public life; and receiving an earnest call from a portion of his original church and congregation, to take charge of them in the Lord, he cheerfully consented to the arrangement, and was received not only by them, but by the original church, and by all the churches and pastors who had known his going out and coming in in former years, with open arms. After passing thirteen years in this section of his former field, winning souls to

Christ, and making glad the hearts of all by his tender love and faithfulness, he obtained permission to retire to the home of his youth, and pass the evening of his days amid the scenes of his earliest aspirations. The separation occasioned many tears and much anguish of spirit to all concerned, though rendered imperative by the providence of God.

"From that day, for about six years, till near the time of his departure, he continued to preach the gospel, 'in season and out of season' as 'the open door was set before him,' all the while 'setting his house in order.' At the moment when his master called him, he was 'diligent in business, fervent in spirit, serving the Lord;' preaching his last sermon to the mission church in Mohegan, just four weeks before the messenger of death met him.

"The physical sufferings of his last days were very great, owing to the complicated disease which, with fierce strength, assailed his delicate frame; but his faith and patience failed not; no complaining or murmuring word fell from his lips; his mind was clear and unclouded to the last. * * * To the affectionate daughter who was trying to arrange the pillows for his aching head, he said: 'Let me go, for the day breaketh;' and to another, who asked if he would not lie down, he answered, 'Lay me down in Jesus' arms, other refuge have I none.' To a brother, according to the flesh, who said to him, 'I hope you can say with the Apostle, 'I know in whom I have believed,' he replied, after a moment's pause, 'I am persuaded that he is able to keep that which I have committed to him against that day.' * * * * *

"Far more delightful than easy would it be to portray the refined sensibilities, the generous sympathies, the self forgetting spirit of sacrifice and the heartfelt devotion to the world's welfare, that marked the life, and formed the elements of character in this departed servant of God; and but for his unfeigned humility, and the extreme modesty that imposed a constant restraint on the forth-putting of his native genius. * * * he had shone with far superior brilliancy in the starry firmament of earth's ambition, though less splendidly in that nobler firmament where stars never set, and the sun no more goes down."

1366. THOMAS, born Dec. 1, 1793, was educated for the medical profession. He married, first, Oct. 21, 1818, Elizabeth Colfax, who was born June 6, 1797, and died April 1, 1830. He married, for his second wife, April 19, 1831, Pauline Clark of Brooklyn, who was born July 12, 1798. Mr. Huntington was ordained as an evangelist of the Baptist denomination in Brooklyn, Conn., Sept. 3, 1834, where he is still residing.

558. ANDREW, JUDGE.   Norwich, Conn.

This family were all born in Norwich.

1367. JOSEPH, born Sept. 3, 1768, married, July 17, 1791, Eunice Carew, who was born Dec. 31, 1769, a daughter of Capt. Joseph and Eunice (Edgerton) Carew. He was a prominent man in Norwich Town and a merchant. He died June 16, 1837, and his wife Jan. 8, 1848.

1368. HANNAH, born July 20, 1770, married Samuel (588) and died Nov. 21, 1818.

1369. LUCY, born March 15, 1778, married, Oct. 31, 1796, Col. Elisha Tracy of Norwich Town. " She sought the interests of Zion with a true and zealous affection." Her husband was a son of Dr. Elisha Tracy, whose first wife was Lucy (215). He was a prominent citizen and much in public life. Their children were: William Swan, born Feb. 4, 1799; Winslow, born Jan. 13, 1801; Elizabeth Dorr, born July 22, 1803, married Erastus Williams of Norwich city; Lucy, born May 11, 1806, married Albert Smith of Norwich city; Hannah Phelps, born April 13, 1808; Elisha Dorr, born Jan. 4, 1811; and Stephen Decatur, born July 14, 1813. She died May 9, 1846, and her husband March 9, 1842, aged seventy-five years.

1370. CHARLES PHELPS, born Oct. 1, 1779, married, Dec. 19, 1802, Charlotte, daughter of Azariah Lathrop of Norwich. She was born Feb. 21, 1781, and died Jan. 8, 1805. He married for his second wife, April 28, 1806, Maria Perit, who was born Jan. 2, 1783, and died April 16, 1854. He was a man extensively engaged in mercantile business, both in Norwich and New York. He was also prominent in the civil affairs of his native town, which he represented in the state legislature. He died Sept. 28, 1850.

559. JOSHUA, COL. Norwich, Conn.

1371. ELIZABETH, born in Norwich, Nov. 8, 1774, married Hon. Ferdinand Wolcott of Litchfield, who was born Nov. 2, 1767, an honored member of an honored family. He was brother to the third Governor Wolcott of Connecticut, a son of the second, and grandson of the first governor of that name in the state, and a descendant of that noble man, the English Armiger, Henry Wolcott of Windsor, who succeeding a long line of titled ancestry in the mother land, came to establish in this a long line of nature's true nobility. The son of John Wolcott of Golden Manor, Tolland, England, has not yet wanted among his descendants worthy representatives of the spirit which the motto of the Wolcott Arms breathes and produces: " nullius addictus jurare in verba magistri;" " accustomed to swear in the words of no master."

Mr. Wolcott was much in public life, having been several years a member of the state senate, and clerk both of the county and superior courts. She died April 2, 1812. A letter written by Col. Benjamin Talmadge, then in Congress, dated Washington city, April 12, just after her death, speaks thus of this noble Christian woman: " In the death of Mrs. Wolcott, the religion of Jesus has received another glorious proof of its divine original. The account that we have received of the bright and unclouded prospects which broke in upon the mind of this dear disciple of Jesus, has so far cleared up the gloom of death, that we see much greater cause for gratitude and praise, than for mourning and sorrow. Far be it from us to suggest a single idea that should impress your minds with the belief that we can view this removal in any light than an irreparable loss, for we loved her when living and shall venerate her memory now that she is dead. * * * The circumstances attending this removal have been so merciful and gracious that we have felt constrained to make our acknowledgements to the great Author and finisher of our faith. * * * It becomes us to adore that wisdom and goodness which made the life of our deceased friend so useful and her death so triumphant, to admire and adore that glorious physician who could calm the troubled conscience, allay every fear, dispel every doubt, and so fortify the soul in the prospect of a solemn judgment, that it would even welcome death, as the messenger of peace. * * * That the triumphant death of your beloved daughter may be remembered with suitable marks of gratitude and praise, by the parents, by the bereaved consort and by us all, is the fervent prayer of your affectionate friends."

JOSHUA HUNTINGTON. BENJAMIN TALMADGE,
MARIA TALMADGE.

Their children were: Mary Ann Goodrich, born Aug. 9, 1801, married Asa Whitehead an eminent lawyer of Newark, N. J., and has one son, Frederic Wolcott; Hannah Huntington, born Jan. 14, 1803, married Rev. Frederic Freeman of Massachusetts, and had also one son, Huntington Wolcott; Joshua Huntington, born Aug. 29, 1804, married, first, Cornelia Frothingham, who had two children, and second, Harriet Frothingham, her sister; Elizabeth, born March 6, 1806, married J. P. Jackson, lawyer, of Newark, N. J., and has nine children: Laura Wolcott, who is married, Mary Elizabeth, Julia Huntington, Frederic Wolcott, Joseph Cook, John Peters, Hannah Wolcott, Huntington Wolcott, now (1858) in Princeton College, and Schuyler Brinkerhoff; Frederic Henry, born Aug. 19, 1808, married, first, Abby, daughter of Gardner Howland, and has four children: Elizabeth Huntington, Alice, Frederic Henry, and Gardner Howland, and second, Mrs. Sarah Chose; Laura Maria, born Aug. 14, 1811, married Robert G. Rankin, lawyer, of New York, and has: Frederic Wolcott, Anne, Laura, Charles, Robert, Fanny, Frank, Mary, and Cornelia. After her death, Mr. Wolcott married again Miss Sally W. (Goodrich) Cooke, and had four children: Charles Mohery, Chauncey Goodrich, Henry Griswold, and Mary Francis. He died in Litchfield, May 28, 1837.

561. EBENEZER, GEN. Norwich, Conn.

This family were all born in Norwich.

1372. ALFRED ISHAM, born June 2, 1793, married Caroline Sims, and was commission merchant at the South. He died in New Orleans, in June, 1854.

1373. WOLCOTT, born Aug. 20, 1796, married, in May, 1837, Jane Watkinson of Middletown, Conn. He was engaged in mercantile pursuits, in the earlier portion of his life, and later, in the insurance business. He lived, for several years before his death, on a portion of the territory first appropriated to Simon Huntington, (5) which has never been alienated from the family. He died suddenly in Norwich, from apoplexy, March 26, 1861. His widow is now residing in Middletown.

1374. LOUISA M., born Feb. 20, 1798, and is still in occupancy, with her sisters, of the old Huntington family mansion. May they long live to enjoy the precious memories of that distinguished and much honored home.

1375. GEORGE WASHINGTON, born Nov. 22, 1799, and is still unmarried and a merchant in New Orleans.

1376. EMILY, born July 6. 1801.

1377. NANCY L., born April 6. 1803.

1378. WALTER, born Nov. 1. 1804, is a merchant also in New Orleans.

1379. SARAH ISHAM, born May. 1, 1806.

1380. ELIZABETH, born Aug. 24. 1808, married. Nov. 19, 1839, Gabriel W. Denton of New Orleans, where she died July 17. 1845.

1381. MARIA H., born Dec. 13, 1810, married, Oct. 4. 1837. George Perkins, an attorney at law in Norwich city. They have two children: Sarah Huntington, born Feb. 11, 1839; and Elizabeth Denton, born May 7, 1848.

564. ZACHARIAH, GEN.   Norwich, Conn.

This family were all born in Norwich.

1382. THOMAS MUMFORD, born Dec. 28, 1786, married, in 1819, Mary Bowers Campbell, who was born June 27, 1802, and died in New York city. He lived in the house built by his father, and was engaged in mercantile pursuits. He died Sept. 11, 1851.

1383. JABEZ WILLIAMS, born Nov. 8, 1788, graduated at Yale, 1806, and read law at the celebrated Litchfield Law School, under those famous teachers, Judges Reeves and Gould, with the latter of whom he was himself subsequently associated in the instruction of the school. He commenced the practice of his profession in Litchfield, where he continued about thirty years. He represented Litchfield in the state legislature in 1829; and during his residence in Litchfield he won for himself the confidence and esteem of the community, and the reputation of a sound and able lawyer. He was elected a representative to congress in 1829, and continued in that branch of congress until 1834. He married, May 22, 1833, Sally Ann (2475) and returned to his native town, which he made his permanent home during the interim of his public duties at Washington. He was appointed judge of the superior court in 1834, and also of the supreme court of errors. On the death of the Hon. Thaddeus Betts, a senator in the United States Congress, from Connecticut, in 1840, Judge Huntington was appointed for the remainder of the unexpired term; and at the close of it, in 1845, he was re-appointed for another term; from which high trust he was removed, in the midst of his great labors, by his sudden death which occurred in Norwich, Nov. 1, 1847.

The following tribute appeared in the American Obituary of 1847: "A statesman of more unbending integrity, or more unwavering fidelity to the interests of the Union, never occupied a seat in the senate of the United States; and the records of that body, during the last eight years, bear ample testimony to the untiring industry, energy, and distinguished ability with which he discharged the responsible duties assigned him by his native state."

1384. ELIZABETH MARY, born Oct 5, 1793, married May 16, —, John Griswold of the firm of Griswold & Hull, New York city. For a fitting tribute to her personal worth see pages 22 and 23.

567. JOHN. Windham, Conn.

This family were all born in Windham, in a house containing now the timbers which were framed into the first house erected on the same spot by deacon Joseph Huntington, at the settlement of the town.

1385. JOHN, born in 1814, and died Feb. 20, 1819.

1386. ELIPHALET, born March 3, 1816, studied medicine, and received his diploma from Dartmouth, in 1848. Practiced some years in Chicopee, Mass., and since 1855 has been in Windham, and in Plainfield. He is the one mentioned in our introduction, as rendering important aid in collecting and verifying the lists of the Windham families. He is a member of the Congregational church, and was chosen deacon in 1862.

1387. RUFUS, born Feb. 14, 1818, married May 11, 1859, Mrs. Ellen Burnham, daughter of John Bass of Scotland, Windham. He has been in the drug business in Willimantic, but is now in Windham.

1388. ALATHEA C., born March 13, 1820, and is still living, unmarried, on the old homestead. She is a member of the Congregational church.

1389. CLARISSA P., born Sept. 24, 1826, and is living at home, unmarried, and is also a member of the Congregational church.

568. JOSEPH. Windham, Conn.

This family were all born in Windham.

1390. EDWARD, born June 18, 1809, and died single, Oct. 3, 1835.

1391. LAURA, born June 30, 1811, and still lives, single, at home.

1392. SAMUEL, born Dec. 3, 1812, and died Dec. 22, 1813.

1393. JAMES, born Oct. 23, 1814, married, at Newbury, Ohio, Oct. 13, 1846, Matilda Townshend, who was born in Withybrook, Eng. Nov. 30, 1825. They are now residing in Cleveland, where he is engaged in the shoe trade. They are both members of the Presbyterian church.

1394. LUCRETIA, born Sept. 5, 1816, and died Oct. 12, 1834.

1395. MARY JANE, born March 24, 1821, and died July 11, 1840. She was for years a consistent member of the Congregational church in Windham.

1396. JABEZ, born July 23, 1823, and died Jan. 7, 1824.

1397. CELIA, born Oct. 14, 1827, and died Dec. 10, 1834.

569. ELIPHALET. Norwich, Conn.

1398. MARY, born Oct. 8, 1807, married, June 11, 1855, Hezekiah Wells, formerly of Albany, N. Y., but now of Delavan, Wisconsin, a most exemplary and devoted Christian man, and possessed of a large estate. He was born Dec. 24, 1797. They have no children.

1399. FANNY, born March 11, 1809, married, July 23, 1829, William C. Carter, who was born Sept. 27, 1779. They reside in Delavan, Wisconsin. Their children are: Frances Laurette, born April 29, 1830; and Mary Frances, married, July 3, 1850, Dudley Corman, who was born March 10, 1827, an inde-

pendent farmer living near Delavan, Wisconsin. They have two children: Josephine, born Oct. 20, 1853, Mary Eliza, born Dec. 4, 1856. Frankey, their daughter, died Oct. 14, 1852.

570. GURDON. Windham, Conn.

1400. LUCY, born in Windham, Nov. 20, 1803, married, in Tecumseh, Mich., Feb. 20, 1845, Stillman, son of Bryant Blanchard, who was born in Rutland, Vt., Dec. 24, 1795. They have no children.

1401. SAMUEL BISHOP, born in Windham, Nov. 20, 1805, married Lucy W. daughter of David Young of Windham. They had no children. He died in Huron, Ohio, June 5, 1840, and she has since died.

1402. MARY, born April 1, 1808, in Windham, and died Oct. 22, 1820, in the same town.

1403. JOHN, born in Hampton, Oct. 7, 1811, and died in the same town, Feb. 21, 1812.

1404. GURDON, born in Windham, Jan. 9, 1815, and is now engaged in business as a provision merchant in Chicago, Ill. The author is under great obligations to him for the great interest he has taken in gathering materials for this work, among the Huntingtons of his acquaintance.

1405. EMILY BROWN, born in Windham, April 25, 1817, married in Sandusky City, Ohio, June 16, 1834, Daniel, son of John Williams, of Brooklyn. He was born March 3, 1809, and is now residing in Tecumseh, Mich. They have four children: Mary Huntington, born in Buffalo, N. Y., Aug. 29, 1836; John Lyon, born in Buffalo, July 9, 1838; Charles Gray, born in Tecumseh, Mich., Feb. 7, 1843; and Gurdon Huntington, born in Tecumseh, Sept. 11, 1851.

1406. HARRIET, born in Windham, April 23, 1819, married in Tecumseh, Mich., Aug. 14, 1843, Moses Wilson, son of John Gray of Claremorris, county Mayo, Ireland. He is an Irish barrister, and is now living in Dublin, Ireland, where they had one son, Wilson Huntington, born April 24, 1844.

578. SIMON. Hinsdale Mass.

This family were all born in Worthington, Mass., excepting Samuel and Jonathan.

1407. RALPH, born Nov. 23, 1784, married, Nov. 20, 1809, Judith Cooper, daughter of Perez and Lucy (Rand) Bradford. She was descended from the oldest son of Gov. William Bradford of Mayflower memory, and was possessed of great excellencies of person and of mind, but fell a victim to a pulmonary complaint at the early age of twenty-one years. She died in Boston, Nov. 8, 1812. Mr. Huntington enjoyed in youth only the ordinary advantages of the sons of our farmers of that period, in the common school. He fitted himself by such facilities, aided by the help of the village pastor, for teaching, and commenced his business career, alternating between the school-room in the winter, and the labors of the farm in the summer, equally industrious and successful in both. With the aid of his pastor's instruction, he pursued the higher branches of an English education, and at the age of twenty-one he was prepared to take charge of an academy in Hatfield, from which post he was called to a similar charge in Northampton, where he remained about two years. He now accepted a position as clerk in the Northampton Bank, and here, too, the same diligence which had before been characteristic of him was shown; employing his time, out of bank hours, in copying for the probate office, and register of deeds. In 1808, one of the directors of the bank sent him to Boston to transact for him some business, and after its successful execution, and a brief interim of travel he opened, in the fall of this year, an exchange office on State street, Boston, in which business he soon took his place among the first of the Boston exchangers and bankers. Relinquishing this business to his younger brother Benjamin, he entered on commercial life, establishing a house in connection with his brother Samuel, in St. Domingo, W. I., where for twenty years they prosecuted a large and lucrative trade. On the death of his brother he closed up his business in St. Domingo, and returned to Boston, where he has spent several years in connection with insurance companies, banks and other business corporations. As one of the original projectors and proprietors of the splendid Western Avenue connecting Brookline so closely with Boston, and promising so large an accession, for building purposes, to the territory of those cities, he deserves, and he will receive the grateful remembrance of both communities. At present he is president of the Boston and Roxbury Mill Corporation, and an extensive stockholder and director in the Boston Water Power Co.

1108. SAMUEL, born in Middlefield, Mass., Oct. 31, 1786, married in St. Domingo, Honorie Chanlatte, a French lady and a native of that island.

He commenced life as a lawyer, having pursued his legal studies with his kinsman, Judge Samuel Gray Huntington of Troy, N. Y. He opened an office first in Port Gibson, and soon in New Orleans, La., where he at once entered upon a career of marked popularity. He was possessed of many qualities which ensure success in that profession. His personal bearing, full of the graces of gentlemanly culture, his elocution, richly musical and skillfully varied, and his ready command of language felicitously adapted to his wants, all contributed to his early success. His reputation rapidly extended and he already held in promise a civic career, answerable to his native ambition, now excited by the stimulus of almost unbounded success. Suddenly a new turn is given to his impulsive course. The great South American Liberator, Bolivar, met him in one of his visits to New Orleans, and found it no difficult task to influence his youthful ambition with an ardent desire to share in the perils and glory of his own ambitious career. Quitting his business he eagerly engaged in the service of the chieftain. His heart, his hand, his means, were all consecrated to the cause; and but for the sudden loss of his health amid the excitements and diseases of his new life in a climate so enervating to one whose youth was fed on the bracing airs of a Berkshire home, his career would doubtless have run to its end parallel with that of Bolivar himself. Retiring from this adventurous field he entered into business with his brother Ralph, in St. Domingo, where to the end of his life he devoted himself with all his remaining vigor to its successful prosecution. His death occurred on a passage to the United States for his health, June 11, 1831.

1409. BENJAMIN, born June 1, 1789, married Caroline, daughter of Peter Dolliver of Boston, who survived her husband many years, and died in New York, Dec. 13, 1852. He commenced life in Boston as a broker, and continued in this business until his death, in June, 1852. His personal form and bearing were such as befits the military character, and he was easily introduced into the military corps, and attained the rank of colonel. An incident occurred during the visit of Lafayette to Boston, in 1824, which greatly pleased the colonel, as a tribute to the family of which he was justly proud. At one of the public occasions on which the citizens were introduced to Lafayette, as the name of Benjamin Huntington was announced, and the bearer presented, the illustrious and grateful Frenchman paused a moment to inquire if he was a relative of his old friend, Samuel Huntington, President of the Continental Congress. When the colonel answered in the affirmative, Lafayette again grasped his hand, and with much emotion exclaimed: "Young man, you have noble blood in your veins, see that you never dishonor it."

1410. SYBIL, born May 31, 1791, married Nathaniel Eager, son also of Nathaniel, a prominent citizen of Worthington, Mass., where she continues to reside. Their children have been: Samuel Huntington, deceased; Jennison, resided in Natchez with a family; James and Joseph, extensive wine dealers in New York city, the latter of whom has a family; Jonathan Huntington, with a family, in Worthington, Mass.; and Mary, who married Charles Starkweather, has seven children, and lives in Chicago, Ill.; Lucy, in Chicago, and Julia deceased. Mr. Eager died July 18, 1859.

1411. SARAH, born Nov. 4, 1793, married Levi Clapp of Worthington. She died in Worthington, leaving three children: Lewis, of Baltimore, Md.; Rev. Alexander Huntington, now pastor of the High street church in Providence, R. I.; and William Taylor of Conway, Mass.

1412. SOPHIA, born Aug. 24, 1796, married Oct. 31, 1820, Joseph White, a farmer of Hinsdale, Mass. Their children are: Sarah Huntington, born Nov. 30, 1821, married March 28, 1848, Charles T. (1717); Joseph H., born Jan. 28, 1824, is married and resides in Boston, where he is in the dry goods business; Sophia M., born March 6, 1826, married Stephen J. Wilcox, Dec. 29, 1851, and resides in Boston; James, born July 9, 1828, married Jan. 22, 1856, and is with his brothers in business in Boston; Jonathan Huntington, born July 25, 1836; Simon Huntington, born May 22, 1837; and Ralph Huntington, born July 11, 1841. The family, excepting Simon, are all living in Boston. Mr. White died Aug. 18, 1860.

1413. FRANCES, born Jan. 20, 1799, married Judge Elam Buel of Troy, N. Y. She died several years since, leaving one child, Lucy.

1414. LUCY, born Aug. 29, 1801, and died single, Aug. 16, 1828.

1415. JONATHAN, born in Hinsdale, Mass., Nov. 9, 1804, graduated at Williamstown College, 1827, and studied theology at Princeton, N. J. He married Rebecca Hamilton of Princeton, N. J., a sister of Prof. Hamilton of the

University at Nashville, Tenn. She died from the cholera which proved so fatal in Nashville. He is still (1858) living in Nashville, in business. He has acted as chaplain in the Union Army.

579. EBENEZER, (M. D.)   Chesterfield, Mass.

1416. FORDYCE, born Oct. 4, 1788, married, April 13, 1813, Eliza Smith. He is a merchant and has been considerably in public life. He was at one time judge of the county court. He resides in Vergennes, Vt., where he is engaged in trade.

1417. SARAH WARD, born Jan. 5, 1791, and died in Vergennes, June 30, 1813.

1418. LAURA JANE, born Aug. 18, 1793, married, May 11, 1819, Rev. Otto S. Hoyt, a congregational minister, who was lately settled in Hinsburg, Vt.

586. JONATHAN, DEA.   St. Albans, Vt.

1419. JOSEPH LYMAN, born at Hinsburg, Vt., Nov. 16, 1800, married, Jan. 1823, Minerva Bartow. He is a tanner and resides at Mason, Mich.

1420. ALFRED HENRY, born in Addison, Vt., April 25, 1805, married, at Highgate, Vt., Feb. 23, 1830, Minerva R. Hill. He still lives in St. Albans, Vt., where he is engaged in the jewelry business.

1421. COLLINS HICKOX, born in Addison, Vt., May 29, 1807, married, in Montreal, May 30, 1836, Caroline Cornelia Sterit, who died March 29, 1852. He married, for his second wife, July 6, 1853, Charlotte Maria Freligh. He is still living in St. Albans, Vt.

1422. CHARLOTTE BENNETT, born in Addison, Vt., Sept. 19, 1809, married, Feb. 4, 1850, Simon H. Kellogg of St. Albans, Vt., and lives in Farmersburg, Iowa.

1423. CHARLES ANDREW, born in Waltham, Vt., April 25, 1812, married, July 25, 1843, in Johnston, Vt., Lucretia Atwood, daughter of the Hon. Thomas Waterman of Johnston. They live in Rockford, Ill.

1424. SAMUEL, born at Vergennes, Vt., where also the remainder of the family were born, July 18, 1814, married, Oct. 1, 1832, in Bangor, N. Y., Eliza Hannah Walker, and is a bookseller in Burlington, Vt.

1425. SARAH, born May 28, 1817, and died single in St. Albans, Vt., June, 1846.

1426. LUCY, born Aug. 14, 1820, married Herman Benedict of Mt. Vernon, Ohio. They were married in St. Albans, Vt., in June, 1846, and have three children: Sarah; Charlotte Francis; born Aug. 1853, and Kate Flora, born Nov. 1856. They live in Cambridge, Mass.

1427. JAMES, born Dec. 10, 1822, graduated at Harvard University in 1852. Since graduating he has continued the jewelry business, by means of which he sustained himself, in part, while pursuing his collegiate course. He is settled in Cambridge, Mass. He married, in Cambridge, Mass., April 2, 1853, Hannah L. Stevens, a native of Gardiner, Me.

1428. SIMON, born Dec. 19, 1825, married, in St. Albans, Vt., Jan. 30, 1849,

Louisa Maria Kellogg, who was born in Swanton. Vt., June 25. 1826. They now live in Farmersburg. Iowa, where he is engaged in farming. He is also a manufacturer of writing fluid, quite extensively, and a dealer in drugs and patent medicines. They are congregationalists.

587. JOSEPH, Esq.   Charleston, S. C.

1429. FLAVIUS JOSEPHUS, born May 13, 1789, in Coventry. Conn., married Laura Beckwith, and is a farmer in Painesville, Ohio. His wife was from Dalton. Mass., and was born Nov. 6, 1801.

1430. EDWARD G., born in Washington. N. C. Oct. 22, 1792, married, for his first wife, Dec. 8, 1814. Nancy Loomis, who died in 1827. He married, second, Jan. 27, 1831. Eliza Clark, who is still living. He resided in South Coventry, where he was a farmer. He was a deacon in the first congregational church of South Coventry at the time of his death, Sept. 15, 1857.

588. SAMUEL, Gov.   Painesville, Ohio

This family were all born in Norwich.

1431. FRANCIS, born Jan. 19, 1793, married. May 4, 1821, Sally White, and lived in Painesville, Ohio, where he died March 3, 1822. He was a farmer.

1432. MARTHA DEVOTION, born March 31, 1795, married. Dec. 22, 1813, John H. Mathews, M. D., of Painesville, Ohio. Their children are: Samuel, born Nov. 1. 1816, graduated at Western Reserve College and entered the medical profession; Alfred, born Nov. 7, 1820, and is a farmer; Rodney, born Feb. 15, 1822, and is a practicing physician.

1433. JULIAN CLAUDE, born March 30, 1796, married. Oct. 12, 1823, Adeline Parkman. He is a farmer and substantial citizen of Painesville, Ohio. His wife died July 15, 1834, aged 29. He resides on the homestead of his father.

1434. COLBERT, born Oct. 17, 1797, married. May 8, 1833, Ellen Paine, who was born May 9, 1809. He also resides in Painesville, Ohio, where he is engaged in farming and surveying.

1435. SAMUEL, born Jan. 31, 1799, and died Jan. 11, 1804.

1436. ROBERT GILES, born June 15, 1800, married, Dec. 1, 1829, Mary L. Fitch. He was a physician, having graduated in medicine at New Haven, Conn., and settled in Ellsworth, Ohio, where he died, Jan. 13, 1839, of consumption. His obituary gives the following account of his last days, after mentioning the severe affliction which had visited his family, and their effect upon him, it says of him: " He forthwith commenced the duties of a christian; and during his lingering disease he was patient and happy, feeling no especial uneasiness, but regret, deep and often expressed, that his life had not been all spent in the service of God."

593. SEPTIMIUS G. Ind.

1437. MARY ELIZABETH, born Thursday, May 16, 1811, married, July 3, 1836, Jabez G. Bright, a respectable mechanic, by whom she had several children, only one of whom, a daughter, now married, lived to grow up. Mr. Bright died April 14, 1843, after which his widow married Seth T. Mitchell, by whom she has one son, Emerson. They reside in Franklin, Ind.

1438. LOUISA AUGUSTA, born July 16, 1813, married, Oct. 21, 1832, James Ritchey, M. D., a prominent citizen as well as successful physician of Franklin, Ind. They have had seven children, of whom their daughters only, four in number, are now living: Emily, born Nov. 1, 1833, married, Dec. 16, 1856, William P. Douthill, attorney at law; Angeline Elizabeth, born Aug. 19, 1837; Mary Louisa, born March 3, 1842; Clarinda, born June 16, 1846. Their mother died June 2, 1849.

1439. HENRY AUGUSTUS, born Monday, Aug. 26, 1816, married, Feb. 1850, Sarah Ann Edwards. He is a thrifty farmer, living in Sugar Creek township, Shelby county, Ind.

1440. JULIUS, born Sunday, Sept. 6, 1818, married, Nov. 10, 1846, Margaret Gainey, and is settled as a physician in Sugar Creek township, Shelby County, Ind.

1441. SEPTIMIUS GEORGE, born Feb. 26, 1823, married, May 15, 1851, Ruth Pherson. He is a well to do farmer, living in the same township with the two preceding brothers.

1442. WILLIAM CHARLES, born Saturday, Nov. 26, 1825, married, Oct. 11, 1851, Mary Ellen Moore of Danville, Ky. He is by profession, a teacher, having been several years successfully employed in this business. He had charge of the Plaquemine Female Seminary in Iberville Parish, La., which he left in 1856, to take the part of principal of the Pleasant Hill Male and Female Academies in De Soto Parish, La., where he is now (1858) engaged.

599. NATHANIEL. Butternuts, N. Y.

1443. MARY, died about 1800, aged 18 years.

1444. EMILY, born Nov. 23, 1787, married, Nov. 21, 1805, Eli Danielson, of Butternuts, N. Y. She died June 16, 1841, leaving three sons and three daughters: Lucius, the oldest son, is in South America, the other sons are dead. Fanny, the oldest daughter, married George Wells of Dover, Ill.

1445. FANNY, born Nov. 16, 1790, married, in 1806, Frederick Danielson, and died in Nov. 1833.

Their children were: Aborem S., born in Aug., 1807; Ashley Gaylord, **born** in April, 1809, and resides at Clifton Springs, N. Y.; Mary Huntington, born in March, 1811, and died in Dec., 1844; Fanny Rudd, born Jan., 1814; Emily Augusta, born Nov., 1818, and died Oct. 19, 1859; Amelia Adaline, born March, 1820; **Jenett** Scott, born Nov., 1822, **and** died Aug. 6, 1840; Frederick, born Jan., 1824, and died Aug., 1825; **and Susan** Alathea, born Sept., 1828.

1446. NATHANIEL, married Aula Markle in 1820, after whose death he mar-

ried Cynthia Tuttle of Watertown, N. J. He was a lawyer, having pursued his studies with the Hon. Isaac Bates of Northampton, Mass. He went to Indiana in 1816; and at the time of his death, which occurred in New Orleans in 1830, he was a member of the Indiana legislature.

1447. GEORGE P., was educated to mercantile life and was engaged in Penn Yan, and Ogdensburg, N. Y., and subsequently in Montreal, Canada. He died in 1835, in Longueil, C. W., having no family.

1448. JAMES, born Dec. 21, 1797, married Julia Holden of Penn Yan, N. Y. He was a merchant but is now a farmer, residing in Starkey, Yates county, N. Y. He has secured the confidence of his fellow citizens, who have honored him with proofs of their esteem. He has been a member of the New York State Senate.

1449. HALLAM, married Parmena Bennight, and is a farmer, living in Hudson, Laporte Co., Indiana. His military rank was that of colonel.

1450. ELIZA, born Nov. 3, 1803, married, March 17, 1825, Wallace Rea, clerk of the courts of Parke Co., Indiana. Their children were: John H., born March 27, 1826, and is now (1862) clerk of the district court of the United States for Indiana, and clerk of the circuit court of the United States; and William and Wallace, twins, who were born Oct. 27, 1830.

1451. ELISHA MILLS, born March 27, 1806, and married, Nov. 3, 1841, Susan Mary Rudd, daughter of Dr. Christopher Rudd of Springfield, Ky. She was born Jan. 8, 1820, and died Dec. 3, 1853. Her father's family were from Maryland, and were Catholics. Her mother was Nancy, daughter of Henry Palmer of Charleston, S. C. She was, on her father's side, related to Charles Carroll of Carrollton, and through her mother's mother, who was a Caldwell, she was related to John C. Calhoun of South Carolina. "She was distinguished for the graces both of her mind and person, for high intellectual cultivation, for the most refined and elegant tastes, as a charming pattern of wife and mother, and, as the crowning beauty of her character, for her pure and humble piety. No woman was more universally loved and admired, throughout the extensive circle in which she moved when living, and no one was ever more sincerely and deeply mourned at her death."

Mr. Huntington early devoted himself to the study of law, and was admitted to the bar at the early age of twenty-one. He had commenced preparing for college while living with his uncle, Elisha Mills of Canandaigua, N. Y.; but on the removal of his uncle, he entered, at the age of fourteen, the law office of the Hon. Mark H. Sibley, where, for a year, he won the confidence of his employer by his fidelity to the duties of the office, and for his persevering diligence out of office hours. In 1822, he went, with his older brother, Nathaniel, to Indiana, where he spent four years in varied exercise and travel, and reading, until he was admitted to the bar. He was soon appointed first prosecuting attorney, by the legislature. He then served four years in the legislature, when he was appointed president judge of his district, and held the office for four years. He was next appointed commissioner of the general land office at Washington City, D. C.; and subsequently, in 1842, he was nominated by President Tyler, and appointed United States district judge for Indiana. This office he held until his death, and its duties, in the words of the Hon O. H. Smith, in his history of Early Indiana, he "has discharged to the entire satisfaction of the bar." The same author gives this estimate of Mr. Huntington's ability: "His mind is of a high order, his judgment good, and his courtesy to the bar such as to make him highly esteemed by all. Long may he live, say the bar of Indiana, one and all, so far as I have ever heard."

The above estimate is fully sustained by a perusal of any of Judge Huntington's charges and decisions. They are eminently clear, sound, and practical. Their good common sense would give them weight, at once, with the court, the jury, and the people. They are such as only the clear-headed jurist, the inflexible judge, and the thoroughly loyal citizen would give.

Mr. Huntington was also eminently a social man, making just such a companion as any cultivated and highly gifted person would choose. His attainments, all made from the impulses of his own inquisitive mind, were very extensive and at ready command. He was a charming correspondent and conversationist. His interest in his family was exceedingly earnest, and it extended to the somewhat numerous family name in which he felt a true kinsmanly pride. He had counted much on being present with the family at their meeting in Norwich in 1857, but a sudden official engagement hindered him. In a letter to the author, apologizing for the disappointment, he said: "I have been hoping that I should be able to meet you and a thousand more of our blood, at Norwich on the 3d, according to intention. I have long desired to visit my ancestral state, and to know, personally, some of the name who still linger around the homes of my forefathers. That the family re-union will be a delightful occasion, I cannot doubt, and as I cannot be there, I beg you to assure all those who there assemble, that nothing but the most imperative reasons could keep me away."

In 1858 he removed from Cannellton, Ind. to Terre Haute, to spend the remainder of his life. A pulmonary disease soon obliged him to seek relief in another clime. He visited St. Paul, Minnesota, and thence went to Cuba, but finding the climate of Havana too enervating, he returned immediately, much weakened by the voyage. He felt that his days were fast numbering, and he only wished, as he expressed himself in failing breath, to reach home and "die among my people and friends in Illinois, the people whom I love."

Staying a short time at his pleasant home, he yearned for the pure and bracing air of the Upper Minnesota, and taking his two daughters, he again sought temporary relief in St. Paul. But his disease had made too deep inroads upon his strength to be arrested or helped, and he died here on Sunday, Oct. 26, 1862. His remains were taken, as he wished them to be, by his nephew, John H. Rea, of Indianapolis, to Terre Haute for interment.

1452. MARY, born April 6, 1808, married, Jan. 22, 1827, Francis **Walker** of Butternuts, N. Y. She died Oct. 4, 1848, leaving one daughter, Adeline M. now a teacher in Princeton, Ill.

604. JONATHAN. St. Louis, Mo.

1453. NANCY, born in Windham, Sept. 6, 1797, married, in St. Louis, March 13, 1834, John Torode, who died in 1843, leaving no children. She is now living in Galena, Ill.

1454. JULIA ANN, born in Windham, Aug. 4, 1799, married, in St. Louis, May 18, 1837, Isaac Pierson, and has one son, Isaac Huntington. They are now living in Fayette, Mo.

1455. HARRIET, born in Windham, Dec. 4, 1801, married, at Springfield, Ill., Oct. 15, 1840, James Campbell. They reside in Springfield, Ill., and have two children, Archibald and Walter.

1456. EBENEZER, born in Windham, March 17, 1804, and died at three months of age.

1457. DELIA MARY, born in Troy, May 22, 1806, and died, single, in St. Louis, Missouri, Aug. 12, 1853.

1458. MARTHA, born in Northampton, Mass., Nov. 4, 1808, married, March 26, 1845, Benjamin Smith, a merchant, of Fayette, Mo., where they now reside. They have no children.

1459. GEORGE LATHROP, born in Northampton, Mass., Aug. 19, 1811, married, in St. Louis, Mo., April 5, 1838, Hannah F., daughter of Eli Forbes, of Boston, Mass. They reside in Springfield, Ill., where he has been a merchant, and where he is esteemed and honored. He has been twice mayor of the city.

1460. JANE MARIA, born in Roxbury, Mass., Oct. 7, 1811, married, in St. Louis, Mo., Jan. 29, 1835, Nicholas H. Ridgeley, a banker. They reside in Springfield, Ill., and have eight children: Charles, Julia P., William, Anna, Mary, Jane, Henderson, and Octavia.

1461. EMILY PORTER, born in Boston, Mass., Oct. 5, 1818, married, in Springfield, Ill., Nov. 23, 1837, Bela C. Webster, of New York city, where they reside. Their children are: George Huntington, born Aug. 31, 1838; Ellen R., born Feb. 4, 1841; John, born Feb. 15, 1843; Emily, born Aug. 31, 1847; Charles, born July 31, 1845, and died in infancy; Anna L., born Dec. 5, 1850, and died in infancy; Kate Campbell, born Nov. 12, 1855; and Douglas, born Dec 24, 1859.

1462. JOHN GRAHAM, born in Boston, April 28, 1829, and married, in Springfield, Ill., in Oct., 1853, Mary Allen. They have lived in Davenport, Iowa. He volunteered his services to the government of the United States to aid in suppressing the existing rebellion, and was honorably mentioned by his colonel for his bravery in leading his company over the breastworks at Fort Donelson. He was subsequently engaged at the battle of Corinth, as first lieutenant, commanding Co. B., of the Second Iowa volunteers (infantry); and was killed, probably Oct. 4, 1862.

610. ENOCH, Esq. Middletown, Conn.

1462.[1] SARAH MILLER, born May 30, 1793, and died in 1819.

1463. ENOCH, born Feb. 10, 1797, and died July 19, 1799.

1464. MARY GRAY, born Feb. 3, 1799, married, in 1833, William E. Hulbert of Middletown, who is dead. They had two children, William and George.

1465. ENOCH, born Lord's Day, March 15, 1801, graduated at Yale in 1821 and was ordained by bishop Brownell of the Episcopal church, deacon, in 1822, and priest in Philadelphia, St. Andrews Church, in 1825.

He married, May 19, 1828, Charlotte, daughter of John Taylor of New Milford, where he spent about twenty years as minister of St. John's parish. The growth of the parish during his labors is the best evidence of the acceptance with which he served them. In 1847 he went to Bridgeport, Conn., where he engaged in teaching, and at the same time organizing a new parish and building a church at Nichol's Farms, a short distance from the city. He labored also, for some time, in connection with Grace Church, Broad Brook, in the town of East Windsor, Conn.; and is now rector of St. John's Church, North Haven.

618. SAMUEL G., Esq. Troy, N. Y.

1466. SARAH SAYR, born in Waterford, Conn., and married, Nov. 30, 1811, John H. Whitlock of Troy, N. Y. They are now (1862) residing in New London, Conn.

621. HENRY, Esq. Windham, Conn.

This family were all born in Windham.

1467. WALLACE, born Oct. 2, 1824, married, Nov. 8, 1846, Cynthia, daughter of Samuel Ward of Brunswick, Maine. The family still occupy the house which the father left in Windham.

1468. DELIA ADELAIDE, born Feb. 10, 1827, married, Nov. 15, 1852, Salmon C. Gillette of Colchester. They have one child, Walter.

1469. HELEN MARIA, born Feb. 29, 1832, married, Feb. 16, 1852, Elliott P. Cottrell of Hartford. They had one child. She died in Hartford, Sept. 25, 1862, and was buried in Windham.

632. DANIEL. Windham, Conn.

1470. PHILOMELA, born Dec. 30, 1787, married, Sept., 1806, Nathaniel Squier of Ashford, and had ten children.

1471. MERIAL, born June 3, 1789, and died April 23, 1796.

1472. MASON, born Feb. 9, 1791, married, March 19, 1812, Sally Parsons. He died in 1821.

1473. BETSEY, born Sept. 15, 1793, and has lived for many years in the family of Zalmon Storrs of South Mansfield, and has been an exemplary Christian woman.

1474. MARCIA MERINDA, born Oct. 25, 1799, married, Nov., 1829, Thomas Allen of Colchester. They have had two children. Thomas, deceased, and Jestina Marinda.

1475. ELIZA, born April 25, 1804, married, March 24, 1844, Cyrus Palmer of Norwich. They have had two sons, Daniel Huntington, now dead, and Walter.

1476. NANCY, born Aug. 31, 1807, married, March 26, 1842, Zalmon A. Church of Norwich. They have had two children, Merial Tracy and William A.

634. NATHAN. Windham, Conn.

1477. GEORGE WASHINGTON, born in 1800, married, and went with his brother William to Norwich, N. Y., and after his death still further West.

1478. MARVIN, born 1801 and died in 1815.

1479. WILLIAM, born in 1803, married, in 1824, Lucretia Harris, and lived in Norwich, N. Y. He died Aug. 13, 1831.

1480. LUCY ANN, born March 30, 1814, married, Nov., 1831, Stephen Wheeler of Pomfret, where she lived. She died June 30, 1836, leaving two children: Jane, born in 1834, and Charles in 1836.

1481. NATHAN, born in 1811 and died May 13, 1840. He was a sea captain.

1482. EMILY, born May 13, 1816, married, June 3, 1839, David Snow, a flour merchant in New York city, who died in 1850. She married for her second husband, June 15, 1853, V. Van Vleck, a dentist. They are now living in New York city. Her children by her first husband were: Julia Ann, born March 24, 1838; Fielder Huntington, born Jan. 2, 1841; George Hamilton, born Feb. 20, 1843; Charles H. D., born Aug. 30, 1845; and Edward Pye, born Sept. 1, 1849. By her second husband she has Emily Amelia, born July 14, 1854, and died Dec. 13, 1857. Three of the sons are in the Union Army.

1483. LUCIAN, born in 1818. He is a seaman, and in 1858 was first mate of ship Harvest, sailing out of New Bedford.

639. GAMALIEL. Walpole, N. H.

This family, excepting the two oldest, were born in Walpole.

1484. ABIGAIL, born in Windham, Ct., Oct. 11, 1783, and died single in Walpole, May 4, 1849.

1485. EMMA, born Aug. 7, 1785, and died single in Walpole, July 19, 1808.

1486. WILLIAM, born in Leinster, N. H., Dec. 2, 1787, married, Thanksgiving Day, Nov. 1829, Mary Drake Leavey, daughter of Aaron and Sophia Leavey of Chichester, N. H., and died in Keene, N. H., Jan. 30, 1844. He lived awhile in East Windsor, Conn. His wife was born in Chichester, N. H., July 20, 1810, and died at Lake Village, N. H., Dec. 1, 1854.

1487. LUCINDA, born in Walpole, Nov. 20, 1789, married Samuel Hicks of New Hartford, N. Y., a manufacturer, and died Oct. 2, 1820. She had two children, Mary E. and Lucinda Huntington.

1488. LYDIA, born May 2, 1792, and died single in Walpole, Oct. 8, 1812.

1489. OLIVER, born Oct. 25, 1794, married Sophia Lane Abbot, March 31, 1835, and died in Walpole, Jan. 27, 1857. His wife was born in Walpole, July 10, 1808.

1490. LAURA, born Nov. 13, 1796, and died in Walpole, Aug. 26, 1800.

1491. LEVI, born Jan. 1, 1799, and died Aug. 19, 1800.

1492. LAURINDA, born Jan. 27, 1801, married, May 7, 1840, William Conant, and resides at Bellows Falls, Vt. She has one son, William J. Conant.

1493. GEORGE, born Sept. 3, 1803, married, Sept. 5, 1856, Harriet W. Kidder, and lives in Walpole. He has been successful in business, and honored with several official posts which he has filled acceptably. From 1834 to '37 he was in the state legislature; from 1842 to '47, was high sheriff of the county; in 1850 he was a member of the convention for revising the state constitution; and in 1851 he was one of the governor's council.

1494. ELEANORA, born July 23, 1806, married, Oct. 20, 1831, Isaac F. Bellows, and has had three children: George Huntington, Grace E., and Anna F.

640. GURDON. Walpole, N. H.

All but the first of this family were born in Walpole. The dates of this family as reported at different times are very unlike.

1495. MARY BUCKINGHAM, born in Windham, Conn., Aug. 29, 1787, married, Nov. 9, 1806, Ephraim Brown of Westmoreland, N. H., and has since lived in Bloomfield, Ohio, where she died, in Feb., 1862. Their children are: Ephraim Alexander, born Dec. 1, 1807; Geo. W., born May 25, 1810, and died April 12, 1841; Charles, born Aug. 9, 1814; Elizabeth Huntington, born April 12, 1816; James Munroe, born April 2, 1818; Marvin Huntington, born Aug. 12, 1820; Fayette, born Dec. 17, 1823; and Annie Frances, born May 30, 1826.

1496. MARVIN, born in Walpole, N. H., Feb. 11, 1789. He lived with an uncle Williams, in East Windsor, Conn., between the ages of four and twenty-one, and after living five years with his uncle Sherril, in New Hartford, N. Y., he removed to Painesville, Ohio, where he has, since then, lived. He married, first, Feb. 11, 1822, in Bloomfield, Ohio, Mary Goodenow, who died in Painesville, Oct. 30, 1827. He married, second, in Painesville, Sylvia G. Harris of Buffalo, N. Y., May 11, 1828.

1497. EUNICE RIPLEY, born Nov. 10, 1790, married William Palmer of New Hartford, N. Y., in 1809, and died in April, 1810.

1498. RALPH RIPLEY, born in Feb., 1792, and died single in Nov. 1826, in Kendal, Ohio.

1499. ELIZABETH MASON, born Feb. 26, 1794, married, Aug. 29, 1823, Francis Procter of Manchester, Mass., and lives in Bloomfield, Ohio. They had no children.

1500. NANCY AMANDA, born July 15, 1797, married, in Painesville, Ohio, Nov. 18, 1819, Milo Harris of Buffalo, N. Y. Their children are: Eunice Huntington, born Aug. 31, 1820, and Albert Huntington, May 1, 1827. The family live in Painesville, Ohio.

1501. JOSEPH MORGAN, born Dec. 8, 1799, and died, unmarried, Dec. 8, 1833, in New Hartford, N. Y.

1502. GURDON WILLIAMS, born July 6, 1804, married, in New Hartford, Sept. 27, 1832, Bricca Ann Smith, who was born Feb. 6, 1812. He is engaged in a railroad and express agency and resides in Canton. Stark Co., Ohio. He and his wife are members of the Episcopal church.

650. MINOR. Yarmouth, Nova Scotia.

1503. ALTHEA. born Dec. 25, 1786, and died Nov. 16, 1814, in Connecticut.

1504. MINER, born June 28, 1788, graduated at West Point. N. Y., and lived in South Carolina, where he at one time was the editor of a paper. He died in Newbern, N. C. He married, Oct. 28, 1812. Penelope Powell, who died in 1816. He married, again, Jan. 19, 1821, widow Olivia Clementina Clark, daughter of Dr. Robert Dickson of Swansborough. N. C., who had died before 1825, as a letter from her husband written in that year shows.

1505. ABNER WALKER, born Feb. 22, 1790, married, Jan. 3, 1812, Sarah, daughter of Ebenezer Corning, who died without children, Nov. 9, 1849. He married again, Dec. 14, 1854, Ellen, widow of Abner Brown. He died Oct. 21, 1857.

1506. BELA, born May 22, 1792, married, March, 1818, Mary Eleanor, daughter of Richard Fletcher M. D. He died in 1839.

1507. NANCY, born April 11, 1794, married May 19, 1813, James Starr of Yarmouth. N. S. Her children are: William Miner, born April 10, 1814; John Soloman, born Oct. 18, 1815, and died Dec. 1, 1831; James Abner, born March 5, 1817, died Dec. 7, 1857; George Henry, born Sept. 18, 1818; Mary Elizabeth, born Oct. 16, 1824; Harriet Perkins, born Jan. 6, 1826, and died Aug. 19, 1826; Susan Martha, born May 20, 1829; Nancy, born May 15, 1831, and died Oct. 16, 1831; and Annie L., born Nov. 4, 1836.

1508. ASA, born March 6, 1796, was a sailor and is supposed to be dead.

1509. BETSEY, born June 1, 1798, and died in infancy.

1510. HERBERT, born July 27, 1799, married, April 22, 1830, Rebecca, widow of Lieut. Thomas Russel, of H. B. M. Regiment. He early in life interested himself in politics, and to the end showed himself to be a man of the people and for the people. Human rights, even against governmental demands, were sufficient incentives for his earnest and self-sacrificing advocacy. "He became distinguished for his stern devotion to liberal principles, and for incorruptible integrity. Honors and emoluments he spurned and despised, when weighed in the balance of a people's rights." Well was it said of him, "he was in no sense an ordinary man." In a tribute to his memory, found in the Provincial Magazine, and still later, in the Yarmouth Herald, are found most flattering testimonials of his worth. It says of him: "he was the author of no literary work, he threw no new or additional light upon any department of science or philosophy, he was not an orator, nor even a ready and graceful speaker, he led no victorious army, in his manners there was nothing to captivate; and yet, perhaps no man in Nova Scotia ever enjoyed a more deep, general, and hearty popularity. "He was no courtier, no sycophant; and he was too high minded, and had too much self respect to pander to vulgar prejudices. The problem of his popularity is, however, easily solved. With him it was a consequence, not an object. It was the necessary and unsought result of public services ably and faithfully performed.

No public man in Nova Scotia has exhibited more innate sagacity, vigor, and clearness of perception than he. Common sense was a prominent attribute of his intellectual organization. While his views were broad and comprehensive, he had the power of analyzing with great minuteness and accuracy, as well as with facility. He was thoroughly versed in all questions relating to political economy, to commerce, to currency, and to statistics and financial concerns.

In reference to the toiling and industrial classes he occupied a distinguished and anomalous position in the legislature. It was his delight and pride to represent the much neglected claims and interests of those whose labors were adding to the general wealth and improvement of the Province. He desired nothing more ardently than to see the laboring masses of his country intelligent, moral, industrious, and imbued with the spirit of self respect, prosperous and happy.

His patriotism "was a modest, unobtrusive impulse of his nature, which was not proclaimed upon the house-tops; but which was unmistakably exemplified in worthy acts."

The brief eulogy, from which the above extracts are taken, concludes thus: "We have attempted to sketch the lineaments of a clear-headed, strong-minded, and sound-hearted patriot of Nova Scotia. In conclusion, we may, however, say, that a kinder or more affectionate heart never beat towards those who had claims upon its sympathy and love, than that of Herbert Huntington."

That the above sketch is a faithful portraiture of an honored man, is abundantly attested by the unsolicited honors voted him by his fellow citizens. For eighteen years he was a member of the Nova Scotia legislature; in 1839 he was appointed by the House of Assembly, one of two delegates to lay before the colonial secretary in London the provincial grievances. In 1848 he was chosen executive councilor, and in 1849 was appointed financial secretary of the Province. Both of these offices he resigned in 1850 in consequence of declining health. After his death, which occurred in Sept., 1851, the legislature of his native Province unanimously voted to erect to his memory a monument at the public expense.

1511. DENISON, born May 6, 1802, was a seaman and an adventurer, who is supposed to have died somewhere in South America.

1512. ELIZABETH, born Nov. 5, 1805, married, Oct. 1, 1826, George W. Brown, of Newcastle, England. They reside in Yarmouth, N. S., and have had the following children: Jane, born April 23, 1828; Harriet, born Jan. 16, 1832; George Herbert, born Aug. 21, 1834; Henry Huntington, born Jan. 19, 1839; John, born March 29, 1844; and Charles Denison, born Feb. 20, 1846. She died in Yarmouth, Sept. 19, 1850.

1513. LYDIA, born Jan. 13, 1808, and married, Jan. 13, 1831, Thomas Allen, of Newcastle, England. They live in Yarmouth, Nova Scotia.

1514. SOLOMON, born May 1, 1810, and died Oct. 23, 1814.

654. SOLOMON.   Mexico, N. Y.

The first four of this family were born in Connecticut, the rest in Mexico, N. Y.

1515. ELIZA LATHROP, born Sept. 13, 1802, married Avery Skinner, a merchant of Milwaukie, Wis., where they now reside. They have had two children: Warner, who is engaged in the banking business in Mexico, N. Y.; and Eliza, who is married and settled in the same town.

1516. WILLIAM JONES, born Feb. 9, 1804, married, July 4, 1825, Laura Keeler, daughter of David Keeler of Stillwater, N. Y. They reside in Baraboo, Sauk Co., Wis., where he owns and improves a farm. His wife died Aug 9, 1854. He is postmaster and has filled other offices. He has been a successful business man.

1517. HERBERT NELSON, born April 9, 1807, married Amanda M., daughter of Timothy Steele of Plattville, Wis. They reside in Baraboo, where he is a large land holder and merchant, and quite wealthy.

1518. BENJAMIN LATHROP, born Feb. 16, 1810.

1519. SAMUEL PERKINS, born May 20, 1811, married, Sept. 13, 1836, Sarah Ann, daughter of H. Minott of Schuyler, N. Y. She was born March 5, 1813. He has been, for a quarter of a century, a minister of the Methodist denomination; and has resided for six years in Baraboo, Wis. He has been successful, both in worldly and in spiritual things, and is now president of the Conference of that state. His wife died April 15, 1854, and he married again, June 14, 1854, Elizabeth, daughter of James Minot of Schuyler, N. Y. She was born Feb. 28, 1834.

1520. JOHN LATHROP, born March 24, 1817, married, June 14, 1845, Sarah, daughter of Nathaniel Griffith of Delphi, N. Y. She died in 1846, leaving one child. He married again Mary A. Stetson, daughter of John B. Stetson of Wisconsin. They reside in Baraboo, where he is a farmer in good circumstances.

655. JOSEPH DENISON.   Lancaster, Mass.

1521. JOSEPH WELLINGTON, born at Middlebury, Vt., Feb. 20, 1808, married, at Bloomfield, Conn., Sept. 19, 1832, Julia Miller, daughter of William Fowler Miller. He was for many years a merchant and a lawyer in Lancaster, Mass., where he now resides.

1522. GRACIA ANN, born May 1, 1809, married, May 1, 1834, Norman T. Leonard of Westfield, Mass., where they have resided since. Their children are: Gratia Olive, born May 27, 1838, and died April 23, 1846. She is the subject of that beautiful memorial written by Mrs. Richardson and published by the American S. S. Union, under the appropriate title, "The Little Missionary;" Norman Huntington, born Dec. 27, 1841, and died Sept. 15, 1842; and Annie Huntington, born Nov. 29, 1845, and died Feb. 24, 1861. She was a devoted Christian woman, and died in Westfield, June 22, 1858, leaving a large circle of friends to mourn their great loss.

1523. MARGARET, born Oct. 10, 1811, married, first, April, 1831, Alonzo

Booth of Enfield, who died in May, 1838, and second, June, 1844, Chandler Foster, at one time proprietor of City Hotel, Albany, and now (1857) living in that city.

1524. MARY JANE, born Oct. 20, 1820, married, Aug. 11, 1842, Franklin R. Terry of Albany, N. Y., who died Dec. 9, 1857, in St. Paul, Min. His wife now lives in Coeymans, N. Y., having married for her second husband, July 31, 1858, William McGregor of that place.

658. SAMUEL. Middlefield, N. Y.

This family were all born in East Haddam.

1525. SAMUEL, born Jan. 26, 1789, married, Nov. 3, 1814, Jenett Mosely, daughter of Jonah and Esther (Smith) Gates of East Haddam. They moved to Middlefield, N. Y., where she died Dec. 5, 1848. He married, March 31, 1852, Mrs. Eliza (Gillett). widow of William Silliman (657).

1526. MASON COGGSWELL, born Oct. 19, 1790, married, May 14, 1818, Harriet Gates, sister of his brother Samuel's first wife, and who was born in East Haddam, Jan. 31, 1800. He removed to Middlefield, N. Y., where he died Nov. 21, 1857.

1527. ROYAL, born March 18, 1792, and died, unmarried, at Sacketts Harbor, N. Y., in July, 1820.

1528. A SON, died in infancy.

1529. A DAUGHTER, died in infancy.

1530. EDWIN WELLS, born Jan. 16, 1803, married Dimis Abbot. They reside at Minetto, Oswego Co., N. Y., where he is a farmer.

1531. DELIA, born May 19, 1804, and lives with her brother in Minetto, N. Y.

664. LYNDE, REV. Branford, Conn.

1532. SOPHIA, born in Branford, Conn., April 1, 1797, and died in Norwich, Conn., June 9, 1853, unmarried.

1533. LOUISA ALMIRA, born in Branford, Jan. 26, 1802, and died in Norwich, Conn., Aug. 6, 1854, unmarried.

1534. LYNDE ATWATER, born in Branford, Jan. 12, 1804, married Feb. 14, 1833, Margaret Adams Low of Charlestown, Mass., where he now resides. He is an extensive merchant tailor in Boston, Mass.

665. OLIVER. Owego, N. Y.

1535. ABIGAIL, born in Ellington, Conn., Sept. 25, 1796, married, Feb. 10, 1818, Henry Gregory, who was born July 15, 1791, and lived in Ithaca, N. Y. Their children were: Oristus Henry, born Oct. 22, 1818; A. Louisa, born Sept. 21, 1822; and a second son, John Huntington, born Aug. 26, 1824, and has a family in Jersey city.

1536. WAIT TALCOTT, born in Ellington, Conn., May 9, 1798, married, March 11, 1840, Sophronia Carter, daughter of Eliezer and Belinda Carter, Aurora, N. Y. He resides in Ithaca, N. Y., where he has been a merchant, and a prominent man. In 1837 he was elected clerk of the county of Tompkins. Mrs. Huntington died in Ithaca, March 13, 1860, aged fifty-one. He is now (1860) engaged in the manufacture of a calendar, and has an office in New York city.

1537. ORISTUS LYNDE, born in Ellington, Conn., March 22, 1803, married in Ithaca, N. Y., Jan. 3, 1829, Harriet Terrill, a daughter of Job and Keziah (York) Terrill, of New Milford, Conn. She was born in New Milford, Nov. 30, 1803. He was a cabinet maker. He died in Danville, Iowa, Feb. 14, 1858, where his widow still lives.

1538. HORATIO LORD, born at Owego. N. Y.. Dec. 14, 1805, married, in Adams, Ill., May 31, 1839. Ann, daughter of Ebenezer and Mary (Sumner) Turner of Livermore, Me. She was born March 15, 1817. He died in Adams county, Ill., March 28, 1846. His widow married again. March 8, 1853, Jotham D. Bradbury of Prairie Ridge, Ill., where she now lives, having by her second husband two sons.

1539. HARRIET, born in Owego, N. Y., March 3, 1808, married in Ithaca, N. Y., May 5, 1833, William Townley, who was born in Elizabethtown, N. J., March 5, 1803. They have lived in Albany, Ill., and have had three children: Harriet L., born in Quincy, Ill., Sept. 14, 1835, and married, Nov. 22, 1855, Cornelius Knapp of Albany, Ill.; George Huntington, born in Ithaca, N. Y., July 28, 1843; and Charles Q., born in Quincy, Ill., Aug. 9, 1849.

1540. GEORGE OLIVER, born in Owego, N. Y., Oct. 7, 1810, married, in Quincy. Ill., May 21, 1840, Cornelia DeKrafft of Washington, D. C. They lived in Quincy, Ill., where he died of consumption. Feb. 26, 1843. His widow married, in 1851, Daniel Stahl of Quincy, Ill., and died Dec. 17, 1852.

667. ELIPHALET. Lebanon, Conn.

This family were all born in Lebanon.

1541. LYNDE L., born Aug. 15, 1807, is a farmer in his native town. He has filled important offices, and is now deputy sheriff. He married, July 4, 1862, widow Lamb.

1542. CORDELIA LOUISA, born Aug. 20, 1809, and died, Oct. 20, 1812.

1543. JULIETTE, born May 22, 1811, married, in Oct. 1831, William Wattles, M. D., of Sag Harbor, N. Y., and is dead.

1544. CORDELIA ELIZABETH, born Aug. 24, 1813, and lives at home.

1545. HENRY HART, born April 26, 1815, married Eleanor Bristol, and resides in Mount Clemens, Mich.

1546. LUCY ANN, born Aug. 1, 1817, has been a teacher, and is now living in Lebanon.

1547. HARRIET, born Sept. 7, 1819, and died Aug. 15, 1824.

1548. MARY LOUISA, born Aug. 6, 1823, married, Feb. 8, 1852, R. A. Sheldon of Columbus, Ohio, where he died, Feb. 8, 1856.

675. WILLIAM.   Lebanon, Conn.

This family were all born in Lebanon.

1549. SIMEON, born April 26, 1789, married, first, Eliza Jones, who was born April 5, 1795, and died July 24, 1823. He married, for his second wife, May 12, 1824, Achsah Clark, who was born Nov. 20, 1793, and died March 4, 1854. He is a wealthy farmer in Lebanon.

1550. WILLIAM, born April 17, 1791, lives in Lebanon unmarried.

1551. MARY GRAY, born March 31, 1794, married, Nov., 1817, Denison Wattles, a lawyer. Their children are: Alden, James D., Eliza, who married Elkanah Eaton of Plainfield, and Rufus.

1552. EMILY, born Feb. 8, 1796, married, in Lebanon, Horace Strong, a farmer. She died Oct. 1, 1862.

1553. RUFUS, born April 5, 1798, graduated at Yale, in 1817, and died unmarried, in Clinton, Ga., Dec. 10, 1825.

1554. ELIZA, born Nov. 10, 1802, married, April 13, 1835, M. Peabody of Buffalo, N. Y.

1555. DAN, born Dec. 28, 1804, married Emily Wilson, and is a merchant in Norwich city. He was chosen deacon of Dr. Bond's church in 1862.

1556. ELEAZER, born Oct. 8, 1808, married, May 11, 1835, Betsey Throop. He is a farmer, living in Lebanon.

677. DAN.   Hadley, Mass.

1557. CHARLES PHELPS, born May 24, 1802, in Litchfield, Conn., graduated at Harvard, in 1822, and entered the legal profession, residing several years in Northampton, Mass. He married, first, Oct. 28, 1827, Helen S. Mills, who died, March 30, 1844. She was daughter of Elijah Hunt Mills, and was born at Northampton, Mass., Aug. 24, 1806. He married, for his second wife, June 2, 1847, Ellen Greenough, sister of the sculptor of that name. She was born in Boston, Mass., March 28, 1814. He attained an early eminence in his profession, and is now one of the judges of the superior court for Suffolk county, Mass. His family reside in Boston, to which city they removed from Northampton, Mass.

1558. ELIZABETH PORTER, born May 8, 1803, married George Fisher of Oswego, N. Y. He is president of the N. W. Insurance Co. They have six children: Elizabeth Phelps, who married John Sessions, and has three children, Elizabeth Huntington, Clara Fisher, and Addie; Frederic Pitkin; Francis Porter, who married Ann Eliza Crane; George Huntington, who graduated at Harvard College, in 1852; Catherine Whiting, and Edward Thornton.

1559. WILLIAM PITKIN, born July 16, 1804, graduated at Harvard in 1824, and entered the ministry of the Unitarian name. He has been employed as a missionary and teacher, and resides in Waterloo, Wis., on a farm. He married Lucy Edwards of Chesterfield, Oct. 18, 1820.

1560. BETHIA THROOP, born Oct. 7, 1805, and lives with her father in Hadley.

1561. EDWARD PHELPS, born April 25, 1807, married Helen Maria **Williams**, daughter of Prof. Stephen W. Williams of the Berkshire medical institute. **She was born Oct. 4, 1819. He died Oct. 26, 1843.**

1561.[1] JOHN WHITING, born May 28, 1809, went through **the collegiate course at Harvard, and after having** been examined for his bachelor's degree, **died, before commencement, in 1832.**

1562. THEOPHILUS PARSONS, **born July 11, 1811,** married Eliza Fitch Lyon (672) of Pomfret, Conn. **She was born Oct. 14, 1817.** They lived in **Hadley,** where he **died, July 20, 1862.**

1563. THEODORE GREGSON, **born March 18, 1813, married, Feb. 11, 1841, Elizabeth Sumner of Eastford, Conn., who was born Jan. 24, 1816.**

1564. MARY DWIGHT, **born April 18, 1815, and died.**

1565. CATHERINE CAREY, **born May 8, 1817, and died Aug. 15, 1830.**

1566. FREDERIC DAN, **born May 28, 1819, graduated at Amherst College in 1839, with the first** honors **of his class.** He married, Nov. 21, 1842, **Hannah Dana Sargent of** Boston, Mass. Having chosen the ministry as his profession, he was ordained **to this work in the Unitarian denomination, and settled in** Boston, where **he labored with great popularity, until he was called to the** Plummer professorship of Christian **morals in Harvard University.** He was inducted into this responsible **office, Sept. 4, 1855, and his reply to the** discourse of president Walker **on that occasion, contains so distinct a statement of his** theological **position, and of his ministerial aims, that I am happy to quote the following characteristic exposition.**

"I wish to remember, and I beg you, sir, never to suffer me to forget that my special and elect business here is to be a minister of Christ; **not of nature-worship,** which is idolatry, **not of Pantheism, which** is a superstition, **not of a religion** humanly created or developed, which is a self-contradiction, **not of an ethical philosophy, which** has no Jesus for **its embodiment, and no cross for its symbol.** The common need of a renewal, or second birth, **out of the spontaneous life of nature or of sinful estrangement,** into **the life of consecrated choice and principled submission, having the Son of God for its inmost motive, his will for its law, and the prayer which 'asks believing that it shall receive' for its daily breath; reconciliation for offending consciences and forgivenesses to a** repentant faith by **a Redeemer, who is at once** the manifestation of God, **and the example-man;** the ever-living presence of the Comforter, which is the **perpetuation of the** Incarnate Mediatorship in the church; the practical and **universal acting forth of this** religion of love **and grace** thus planted in the **soul, into every form** of noble and beautiful holiness—into integrity, purity, **charity—into the reform of** every social abuse—the **overthrow of every organized wrong—the cleansing of** every secret corruption, and **thus the constructive achievement of** a church of believers, or brotherhood of all nations and tribes and **tongues,** proclaiming **liberty, right, and peace: these are the** messages for the age, and for **all ages, for students and thinkers, for workers and for sufferers."**

The above exposition will show the thoroughly evangelical spirit of Dr.

Huntington. Adopting, literally, the Trinitarian creed, he was admitted successively to the orders of deacon, priest and minister in the Episcopal church, and instituted rector of Emanuel church in Boston, in 1860, where he is now engaged. As preacher, he stands in the front rank of pulpit orators; and he has also won high distinction among our most popular lecturers.

His contributions to our current literature have been very numerous, and it would be difficult to decide whether he excels more as speaker or writer. From the commencement of his college course his pen and voice have been most effectively employed. The fruits of the former have been very numerous on the pages of the Horæ Collegianæ of Amherst College, of which he was one of the editors, the Boston Courier, the Monthly Miscellany, the Christian Examiner, the Christian Register, the Monthly Religious Magazine, of which he was associate editor with Rev. Dr. Gannett, and subsequently sole editor, the Democratic Review, the Boston Post, the Boston Book, Saturday Evening Gazette, American Journal of Education, the Boston Traveler, and the New York Independent. He has also furnished several hymns for festive and religious occasions. Besides these, the following are some of his addresses of a miscellaneous character which were given to the press: " Christ the Pacificator," before the American Peace Society; " Christian Burial," at the consecration of the Mount Hope Cemetery; " The Religion that is natural." before the Young Men's Christian Union; several agricultural addresses; " Unconscious Tuition;" " Hands, Brain, Heart," before the Mass. Mechanic's Charitable Association; address on opening a cemetery in Newton; Bi-Centennial address at Hadley, Mass., June 8, 1859; " Home and College," an address at the Mass. State House, 1860; " The relation of the Sunday School to the Church," an address before the Mass. convention of S. S. Teachers; and " Divine Aspect of Heaven." The following are some the sermons which have been printed: " The Christian Doctrine of Charity," before the Howard Benevolent Society; New Year's Sermon, in South Congregational church, Boston; " Duties and Relations of the Rich to the Poor," at the ninth anniversary of the Warren street Chapel; " Peace the Demand of Christianity;" " The Great Conflict of the Day;" " The Good Samaritan;" " The Famine and the Sword;" "The Simplicity of Christian Duty;" Sermon on the fiftieth anniversary of the Boston Female Asylum; " The Treatment of Poverty," before the society for the prevention of Pauperism; " The Word of Life, a living ministry and a living church," before the graduating class of the Harvard Theological School; a discourse before the Benevolent Fraternity of Churches; " Mercantile Integrity and its securities;" " Learning and Life," to the graduating class of Harvard; " Three Dispensations," in Fisk's " Pulpit Eloquence of the Nineteenth Century;" Election Sermon before Mass. Legislature; " Permanent Realities in Religion;" Sermon at dedication of Appleton Chapel at Harvard University; " The diversified ministry of an unchanging Gospel," preached at the installation of Rev. E. E. Hale over the South Congregational church, Boston; " A Year of Church Work," an anniversary sermon before Emanuel church, Boston. Sept., 1861; and " Two Ways in Religion," a pamphlet in behalf of evangelical truth.

Besides these contributions to our literature. Dr. Huntington issued, in 1856, a volume of " Sermons for the People," containing twenty-six discourses, admirable equally for their charming style, their Christian temper, and their earnestly practical character; a second volume, " The Constitution of Human Society, as illustrating the Goodness. Wisdom and Power of God," containing eight discourses delivered in Brooklyn. N. Y., in 1858 and '9, as the " Graham Lectures;" and the third volume of sermons on " Christian Believing and Living."

He also edited, in 1860, " The Rock of Ages," by Bickersteth, with an Introduction; and in the same year issued the Lyra Domestica. a collection of sacred poetry. In 1861 and 1862 he was editor of the Church Monthly, published in Boston, Mass.

682. JONATHAN, Hon. Haddam, Conn.

1567. JONATHAN E., born Nov. 17, 1809, married, at Littleton. N. Y., in Aug., 1831, Elizabeth A., daughter of Mahlon Johnson. He lived in Newark, N. J., and has a manufactory for moldings.

1568. SARAH, born Nov. 24, 1811, has been a teacher, and now lives in Haddam.

1569. ELIZABETH, born Dec. 30, 1815, married deacon George S. Brainard of Haddam.

1570. CYNTHIA, born May, 3, 1818, married Roger W. Newton of Durham, Conn., where she now lives and has a number of children.

1571. DAVID, born Jan. 22, 1822, and lives in Haddam.

1572. SAMUEL, born Feb. 8, 1824, and lives single in Haddam.

1573. CATHERINE, born June 2, 1826, and lives single in Haddam.

1574. ARISTARCHUS, born Nov. 24, 1834.

686. SELDEN, Col. Haddam, Conn.

1575. JOSEPH, born Nov. 24, 1826, once in business in Hartford, Conn., but now in New York.

1576. EMILY S., born in Higganum, July 31, 1831, a teacher in New York city.

1577. GERTRUDE, born in Liverpool, Eng., Dec. 8, 1832, and died in New York, Aug. 20, 1833.

692. NATHANIEL GILBERT. Bethany, Conn.

1578. MARIA GILBERT, born in Bethany. Conn., Dec. 3, 1817, married, in 1846, J. W. Merwin, of Milford, where she died April 7, 1859.

1579. WILLIAM WARD, born in Bethany, Conn., Nov. 5, 1819, and died in Milford, Conn., April 24, 1848.

1580. REBECCA LOUISA, born in Bethany, Oct. 16, 1821, married, in 1840, J. W. Merwin of Milford, Conn., where she lived until her death, Jan. 23, 1846.

1581. HENRY M., born Aug. 9, 1831, and has lived in Milford. He is now (1862) in the union army.

696. EZRA. Cornwallis, N. S.

1582. EBENEZER, born April 11, 1780, married, Dec. 31, 1806, Elizabeth Strong, and now (1858) lives in Cornwallis, N. S.

1583. SIMON, born Aug. 15, 1786, married Henrietta Lockhart, and lived in Cornwallis, N. S., where he died in 1829.

1584. EZRA, born Dec. 10, 1789, married Charlotte Borden, and lived in Cornwallis, N. S., where he died in 1836.

1585. BETSEY, married John Elliot, and lived in Wilmot, N. S.

1586. RINI.

711. NATHAN. Ashford, Conn.

1587. THOMAS, born in Ashford, Jan. 17, 1799, and died unmarried in Ashford, May 24, 1833.

1588. BETSEY, born in Ashford, March 24, 1801, and married Duty Fitts of Eastford, Conn., where the family now live. He died Dec. 11, 1857.

1589. HARVEY, born in Ashford, Conn., Oct. 1, 1802, and died April 6, 1814.

1590. ALFRED, born in Ashford, Aug. 19, 1804, married Caroline Lilly, and lived in Danielsonville, Conn. He died July 9, 1859.

1591. NANCY, born in Ashford, Sept. 9, 1808, married, in Ashford, Sept. 29, 1837, Lemuel Parkhurst. They lived on a farm in Ashford, and have two daughters, Abby Jane and Julia Ann. She died Feb. 19, 1859.

712. ELIJAH. Ashford, Conn.

This family were all born in Ashford.

1591.[1] CHARLES, born March 19, 1813, and died Aug. 7, 1814.

1592. SOPHRONIA, born May 4, 1815, married Alden B. Whiting, who is a shoe-maker and lives in Providence, R. I. They are members of the Baptist church. They have had six children, only three of whom are living, two daughters and one son.

1593. LOUISA, born Dec. 2, 1817, and died in May, 1859.

1594. ELISHA DANA, born March 21, 1820, married, July 11, 1844, Lucia M., daughter of George Day of Pomfret, Conn. They are living in Eastford, Conn., where he is engaged in farming.

1594.[1] ELIJAH W., born March 17, 1822, and died Feb. 6, 1828.

1595. HARRIET, born Sept. 12, 1825, married Edward Everett Davis, a man of wealth, of Newburyport. They are now living in Davenport, Iowa. They have two sons, Francis Everett and Thomas Huntington.

1596. OLIVE JANE, born Oct. 25, 1830, and is now living in Eastford.

1597. LUCY MARIA, born May 1, 1834, and resides in Orinoco, Min.

SEVENTH GENERATION.

713. DAVID.
Bethel, Vt.

1598. JOHN, born about 1776, and was living with quite a family in Conewango, N. Y.
1599. AMOS.
1600. CYRUS.
1601. ROSWELL.
1602. NANCY.

714. ABNER.

1603. CHARLES, born April 21, 1783, married, in 1811, Philena Mead, of New Haven, Vt., where she died in 1817. He married, for his second wife, in 1820, Betsey Lathrop, and resides in Bethany, N. Y.

1604. SOPHIA, born Aug., 1785, married, in 1805, Calvin Sprague, and lived in New Haven, Vt., where she died in Dec., 1857. Their children were: Charles A. L., born in 1809, married, Harriet Sprague, and lives in Williston, Vt.; Adeline, born in 1811, married, in 1851, J. G. Dickey, and lives in East Constable N. Y.; Lucy, born in 1814, married, in 1811, Elias Hecoks, and lives in New Haven, Vt.; and Fayette, born in 1817, and lives in New Haven, Vt.

1605. LUCRETIA, born July, 1787, married, in 1815, Jeremiah Hotchkiss, and lives in New Haven, Vt. Their children are: Fordyce, born in 1817, and living in Levant, N. Y.; Abner, born in 1819, also living in Levant; Maria, born in 1821, living in Ellington, N. Y.; Charity, born in 1823, married, in 1855, a Gifford, and lived in Levant, where she died in 1857; Jeremiah, born in 1828, married, in 1856, a Miss Gifford, and lives in Levant.

1606. DAN, born March 1, 1790, married, in 1814, Fanny Willey, and lives in Bethany, N. Y.

1607. MARIA, born July, 1792, married, in 1822, Heman Brown, and lived in Bethany, N. Y., where she died in 1841. Their children were: Mary, born in 1823, married, in 1843, Earl Newton, and lives in Palmyra, Wis.; Harriet, born in 1825, married, in 1848, George Varnum; Morgan, born in 1828, married, in 1849, Mary Sweatland, and lives in Kalamazo, Mich.; Munro, born in 1833, and died in Wisconsin in 1855.

1608. ABNER, born Dec. 20, 1791, married, in 1826, Sarah Storing, who died in Batavia, N. Y., in 1842. He married, for his second wife, in 1843, Mary Helmer, and now lives in Batavia, N. Y.

*1608.¹ NABBY, was twin with Abner.

718. JAMES.
Woodstock, Vt.

1609. MARY, born May 24, 1780, married Samuel Hall, by whom she had two children: Hiram, born Oct. 20, 1800; and Harriet, born Nov. 8, 1802. He died, and she married, for her second husband, Silas Adams. Their children were: Lucinda, born June 10, 1809, and died April 9, 1810; Susan B., born Aug 21, 1810; Elvira, born Oct. 11, 1813; and Martha, born Aug. 18, 1817. She died May 17, 1852.

1610. WILLIAM, married Rene Edson, and lived in Randolph, Vt. He died of cholera, in Fort Ann, N. Y.

1611. LURA, born Jan. 11, 1784, married Zebulon Dean, and lived at Bethel, Vt. They had nine children: Rodman, born Oct. 8, 1803; Wyman, born May 29, 1805; Whitman, born April 20, 1807; Hunan, born Oct. 9, 1808; Harry, born May 28, 1810; Rebecca, born June 21, 1812; Abigail, born Sept. 18, 1816; and Phila, born July 20, 1821. She died Feb. 17, 1856.

1612. JAMES, born in 1786, never married.

1613. MARTHA, married Rice Townsend, and had five children; Frederic, Nancy, Rebecca, Mary, and Olive.

1614. DAVID, born in Bethel Vt., Sept. 17, 1790, married, May 3, 1810, Lucretia Plumley of Bethel, and lives in Middlebury, Vt.

1615. SUSAN, born Jan. 8, 1792, in Old Canaan, Conn., married, May 2, 1814, Ira Bartlett, a Methodist preacher, living in Canada East, to which region she went in 1830. Their children are: Amanda, born Feb. 2, 1815, and living in Canada East; Wilder, born Dec. 2, 1816, married, Nov. 17, 1847, Sylvia Parker, and has three children: George, born June 12, 1826, married, Dec. 26, 1854, Flora Parker, and has two children: Ira, born Nov. 29, 1827, and married Oct. 7, 1857, Margaret Shaw.

1616. HENRY HOSFORD, born in Connecticut, Dec. 6, 1794, married, in Granville, Vt., Dec. 6, 1814, Sophia Parker, and died of cholera, in Milwaukie, in Aug., 1849.

1617. REBECCA, married William Alison, a carpenter. They had two children.

1618. JONATHAN M., born in Bethel Vt., in 1799, married Deborah Cleveland, who was born in Pultney, Vt., in 1797. He died in Middlebury, Vt., Dec. 31, 1840, where his widow is still living.

719. WHITMAN. New Haven, Vt.

The first seven of this family were born in Mansfield, Ct., and the last two in New Haven, Vt.

1619. SOPHRONIA, born March 24, 1788, married, in New Haven, Vt., Dec. 25, 1808, Esek Sprague, and died in the same place, July 1, 1841.

1620. CLARISSA, born Aug. 24, 1790, married, in New Haven, Vt., March 4, 1810, Silvester Langdon. They live in Constable, N. Y.

1621. DAMARIS, born Aug. 10, 1792, married, in New Haven, Vt., Dec. 1, 1812, Henry Hendrix, who resided in Highland, Wis., where he died July 11, 1832. He was the son of David Hendrix of Canaan, Conn. Their children were: Lucius H., born Oct. 17, 1814, in New Haven, Vt., married Nancy Spafford, at Cleveland, Ohio; Julian F., born July 14, 1816, and died Oct. 7, 1818, in New Haven, Vt.; Erastus W., born Aug. 22, 1818, and died Sept. 9, 1819; Caroline H., born at Moscow, N. Y., Feb. 12, 1820, married Alexander Coburn, in Cleveland, Ohio; Henry W., born at Moscow, N. Y., Feb. 19, 1822, married Keziah Smith of Burlington Vt.; Anna S., born at Moscow N. Y. Sept. 28, 1824, married Henry B. Morse of Fort Covington, Wis.; Gustavus

SEVENTH GENERATION. 275

S., born in New Haven, Vt., July 19, 1826, married Meribah A. Orton of Cleveland, Ohio; George E., born in New Haven, Vt., March 8, 1828, married Susannah Rowland, at Mineral Point, Wis.; Clara H., born in New Haven, Vt., June 12, 1830, married Edward Dodson of Highland, Wis.

1622. ERASTUS, born Nov. 25, 1794, and died in Mansfield, Conn., Nov. 10, 1795.

1623. SUSAN, born Aug. 28, 1796, married, in New Haven, Vt., May 27, 1818, Joseph Wheeler, and died Feb. 15, 1832.

1624. JOSEPH CLARK, born Oct. 3, 1798, married, in New Haven, Vt., Sept. 28, 1825, Julia A., daughter of Levi Warner, who was born Dec. 24, 1804, and died in Chicago, Ill., Dec. 6, 1852. He is now living with his family in Chicago.

1625. ERASTUS WHITMAN, born Aug. 8, 1802, and died in the city of New York, June 25, 1832, unmarried.

1626. HARRIET, born May 4, 1804, married, at New Haven, Vt., Nov. 4, 1829, John B. Huntley, and lives in Bridport, Vt.

1627. LUCIUS, born Aug. 29, 1806, and died in New Haven, Vt., Jan. 19, 1811.

723. ASA.

1628. HANNAH, born April 1, 1786, married, Dec. 3, 1807, Elisha Parkhurst. Her children were: Hiram, born Sept. 17, 1808, and lives in Minnesota; Laura, born Nov. 23, 1810, and died in 1814; Hannah and Harriet, born Oct. 11, 1812; Phineas, born May 1, 1815, and died in Enfield, N. H., in 1848; Sarah, born Jan. 18, 1817, and died July 11, 1844; Lydia, born Aug. 11, 1820, and died in Sharon, Vt., Sept., 1823; Harvey, born Feb. 20, 1823; and Arannah, born Sept. 13, 1826.

1630. SARAH, born April 4, 1788, married, in Tunbridge, Vt., in 1809, William Clement. Their children have been: Jarvis, Albert, Emily, and Franklin. He died about the year 1820, and about 1825, she married Jacob Davis of Randolph, Vt., by whom she has had, Harriet, Daniel, and Jackson.

1631. MARTHA, born Jan. 15, 1790, married, in Dec. 1808, Saul Downer of Sharon, Vt. Their children are: Worcester; Jason, a lawyer in Wisconsin; Chester; Susan, a teacher; Franklin, Albert, and Alice.

1632. ROSWELL, born Jan. 29, 1792, married, in 1823, Almira Parker. He lived for years in Sharon, Vt., but afterwards went West where he died.

1633. ARANNAH, born Feb. 23, 1794, married in Upper Canada, Mary Hersey. They live in Canada.

1634. ACHSAH, born Nov. 5, 1796, and lives in Enfield, N. H.

1635. LOREN, born Jan. 21, 1799.

724. ZEBULON.

1636. SAMUEL, born April 10, 1805, married, Jan. 14, 1835, Polly Brown of Plattsburg, N. Y. He is now living in Dane, Wisconsin.

1637. LYDIA, born July 24, 1807, married, June 20, 1831, Walter Welch. They are now living in Dane, Wisconsin. They have had several children.

Their oldest son, Daniel, was, when last heard from, in California. Moses, their second son, started for California, to find his brother Daniel, from whom the family had not heard for several months, but at the last news from him, he had not succeeded. Alma, their oldest daughter, married, in 1859, B. F. Chapman; Rhoda, the second, married, Jan. 1, 1861, Hiram Clark; and Maria, the third, married, Jan. 1, 1860, Julius ——. These three daughters had been engaged in teaching. The other children are Alfred and Persis.

1638. THOMAS, born Oct. 6, 1808, and died Oct. 12, 1836.

1639. EUNICE, born April 4, 1810, and now lives unmarried, in the Society of Friends, in Enfield, N. H.

1640. MARY, born June 29, 1813, married, Jan. 16, 1830, Wm. P. Duncan of Canada. They have a numerous family, among whom are Charles, James, Lucretia, Elizabeth, Emily and Almira, the latter two being teachers.

1641. ANNA, born Nov. 20, 1815.

1642. RHODA, born Nov. 26, 1817, and died among the Friends in Enfield, N. H., Aug. 16, 1845.

1643. RUFUS, born Aug. 19, 1822.

725. JONATHAN.

1644. A SON, who died while a member of college.
1645. A SON.
1646. A SON.

726. WILLIAM.   Washington, Vt.

This family were all born in Washington, Vt.

1647. WILLIAM M., born June 2, 1796, and married, April 17, 1821, Nancy Calef. He lives in Washington, Vt.

1648. BENJAMIN, born Nov. 12, 1797, and died single, in Washington, Dec. 30, 1821.

1649. SALLY, born Aug. 10, 1799, and died Sept. 10, of the same year, in Washington.

1650. CYRUS, born Aug. 19, 1800, and died Oct. 3, of the same year, in Washington.

1651. CYNTHIA, born Nov. 10, 1801, and died in Washington, Dec. 20, 1821.

1652. ELIZABETH, born July 25, 1803, and died in Washington, Feb. 11, 1822.

1653. DIANTHA, born June 7, 1805, married, Sept. 25, 1825, Justin Barron of Washington, where they have resided. Their children are: Azro N., born Dec. 5, 1826, and died in Washington, March 6, 1846; Alonzo W., born Jan. 22, 1828, and lives in La Crosse, Wis.; Edwin P., born June 11, 1834, and is in Washington; William Huntington, born April 25, 1838, and lives in La Crosse, Wis.; Cynthia E., born Jan. 24, 1840, and lives in Washington.

1654. NATHANIEL, born May 9, 1807, and died in Washington, Nov. 25, 1825.

1655. LUCY, born Sept. 26, 1810, married, March 18, 1834, Isaac Barron of

Washington, where they live. Their children are: Norman, born Feb. 24, 1835, and lives at St. Mary, M. T.; Harry V., born Dec. 11, 1841, and lives in Washington.

1656. DANA S., born May 2, 1812, and married, Dec. 22, 1836, Abby Austin. They live in Washington.

1657. JOHN P., born Feb. 13, 1814, and married, March 31, 1840, Elizabeth Smith. They live in Washington, where he is a mechanic.

1658. WARREN, born Sept. 1, 1818, married, Feb. 27, 1842, Lydia Smith, and lives in Washington.

1659. HARRY, born April 2, 1820, married, July 22, 1847, Sophia C. Mattoon, and lives in Washington.

727. JOSEPH. Charleston, Vt.

This family were all born in Orange, Vt.

1660. ALMIRA, born in 1808, married, 1832, Lewis Moffat of Charleston, Vt., and has one son, Rinaldo, born in 1834, and married Amelia Hutchinson in 1859, and lives in Charleston, Vt.

1661. JAMES TRUMAN, born Jan. 26, 1811, married, in Jan. 1837, Lucy Fuller, and lives in Lowell, Mass.

1662. EDMUND, born in 1813, and died in Orange, Vt., in 1814.

1663. LAURA ANN, born in 1816, and died in Charleston in 1831.

1664. WILLIAM CARLES, born in 1818, married, in 1841, Eliza Lord, and lives in Richland, Wis.

1665. SYLVANUS CONVERSE, born in 1821, married, in 1845, Hannah M. Warner, and resides in Pulaski, N. Y. He was a member of Dartmouth College in 1842-3.

1666. LEONARD W., born in 1823, marrried, in 1850, Mercy Bear, and lived in Groveland, Mass.

1667. SYLVESTER T., born in 1825, married, in 1850, Adaliza Barnard, and lived in West Charleston, Vt.

738. JOHN. Sunderland, Mass.

1668. ALONZO B., married Lydia A. Mott, and lived in Hartford, Conn. Eight children of this family died in early infancy.

740. ISRAEL. Syracuse, N. Y.

1669. WILLIAM WOODWARD, born in 1808, and died in Geneva, N. Y. in 1832.

1670. JOHN FITCH, born in 1810, and died, unmarried, in New Orleans in 1831.

1671. MARY ANN, born in 1812, married, in 1837, Charles E. Clark, and lives in Buffalo, N. Y.

1672. ISRAEL EDWARDS, born in 1814, and died in infancy.

1673. EUNICE EDWARDS, born in 1817, married, in 1844, E. M. Skinner of Syracuse, where she resides.

1674. LAURA JANE, born in 1819. Has been a teacher, and is still unmarried, in Syracuse, N. Y.
1675. CHARLES BENJAMIN, born in 1821, married, in 1847, Caroline A. daughter of Samuel Barry of New London, Conn.
1676. ISRAEL EDWARDS, born in 1824, and is living in Syracuse unmarried.
1677. SUSAN ARNOLD, born in 1826, married in 1852, Samuel M. Tracy, and lives in St. Anthony, Min.

741. WILLIAM. Wolcottville, Conn.

This family, excepting the last, were born in Harwinton, Conn.
1678. MARY, born Feb. 17, 1810, married, Nov. 4, 1838, Daniel Sammis, and lives in Warsaw, N. Y. Their children are: Collis Huntington, Martha J., Albertus, and Charles. They live in Warsaw. Their father is a farmer.
1679. SOLON, born Jan. 13, 1812, married, June 2, 1840, Harriet Saunders, and resides in Oneonta, N. Y., where he was for years engaged in trade. He has now a carriage manufactory in Oneonta.
1680. RHODA, born Oct. 13, 1814, married, May 10, 1834, Riley Dunbar, and lives in Wolcottville. He was a rake manufacturer. Their children are: George Solon, Adelaide, Adeline, and Edward.
1681. PHEBE, born Sept. 17, 1817, married, Oct. 4, 1840, Henry Pardu, a dealer in shoes, in Oneonta, N. Y. Their children are: Edwin, Edward, Frank, Charles, and Mary H.
1682. ELIZABETH, born Dec. 19, 1819, married, April 5, 1842, Hiram Yager, a farmer, in Kortwright, N. Y. Their children are: Elenora, and Josephine. He died in Oct. 1856.
1683. COLLIS POTTER, born April 16, 1821, married, Sept. 16, 1844, Elizabeth Stoddard, and lives in Sacramento, Cal., where he is a hardware merchant, in the wholesale trade. He has attained quite a prominent rank among the business men of the Pacific coast.
1684. JOSEPH, born March 23, 1823, died single, Feb. 23, 1849.
1685. SUSAN, born Aug. 1826, married, Nov. 16, 1849, Wm. Porter, M. D., a physician, living in New Haven, Conn.
1686. ELLEN M., born in Torrington, Conn., Aug. 12, 1835, and now living in Oneonta. N. Y.

749. DAVID. New York.

1687. DAVID, born Oct. 25, 1808, and died March 19, 1809.
1688. DAVID ISRAEL, born May 10, 1810, married, Aug. 28, 1836, Emily S. Chamberlain of Morristown, N. J. They now live in Jersey City, where he has been several years in business. He formerly lived in New London, where he united with the first Congregational church in 1831.
1689. ISRAEL, born July 1, 1812, and died the 13th of same month.
1690. MARY ANN, born May 13, 1814, and now lives in New York and Hamburg, Conn.
1691. WILLIAM BACKUS, born Oct. 21, 1816, and died unmarried, Nov. 18, 1847.

751. LEVERETT, I. F New Brunswick.

1692. JANE ELIZABETH, born in New Brunswick, N. J., Jan. 23, 1817, married, in Pittsburg, Pa., Dec. 24, 1839, William Potter, son of Rev. John Jones. They reside in Pittsburg, Pa., where Mr. Jones is in the insurance business. They are both members of the Presbyterian church. They have had six children, all born in Pittsburg: William Leverett, born Oct. 29, 1840; Mary Atwood, born March 19, 1842, is a member of the Presbyterian church, now (1861) living in Semukly, Allegany Co., Pa.; Fanny Jones, born Jan. 3, 1844, and died April 10, 1848; Annie Huntington, born Feb. 19, 1846; Harriet Potter, born March 16, 1849; and Jane Elizabeth, born Aug. 4, 1852.

1693. BACKUS WILBUR, born in Brunswick, N. J., Nov. 3, 1818, graduated at Jefferson College, Penn., 1836, and entered the legal profession. He married, at Pine Hills, Dallas County, Ala., Feb. 27, 1845, Anne Eliza, daughter of Daniel M. Riggs, of Tuscaloosa, Ala. He was engaged several years in Tuscaloosa in the practice of law, and afterwards removed to the city of New York, where he now lives.

754. SIMON. Lebanon, Conn.

1694. MARIA, born in Lebanon, Nov. 27, 1796, and married, Sept. 11, 1825, Hezekiah W. Ripley of New York, for many years in the service of the American Bible Society. She died in New York city, Dec. 20, 1850, having had one daughter.

1695. MARIETTA, twin sister with the above, married, Feb. 21, 1824, Henry B. Williams, a farmer in Lebanon. They have children.

1696. SARAH, born Dec. 12, 1799, in Lebanon, and died, Feb. 20, 1801, in Lyme, Conn.

1697. JOHN ROGER, born in Lebanon, Jan. 18, 1802, and lives in Richfield, Ohio.

1698. SIMEON FITCH, born in Lebanon, Dec. 3, 1806, married, May 5, 1835, Antoinette M. Brush of Westport, Conn. He is a physician, residing at Mount Airy, Crawford Co., Wis.

755. AZEL. Spencer, Mass.

The first two of this family were born in Leicester, Mass., the rest in Spencer, Mass.

1699. HARRIET, born Dec. 1, 1798, married, April 13, 1836, Thomas Kingsbury of Spencer, Mass. Their children are: Henry Huntington, born Feb. 15, 1837; Addison, born April 23, 1838; Edwin, born Dec. 24, 1840.

1700. ORIN, born Dec. 19, 1800, married, in Ware, Mass., Oct. 14, 1827, Thankful Mary Ann Paige, and moved to Putnam, Ohio. She died Jan. 24, 1838, and he married, the second time, in Springfield, Ohio, Nov. 7, 1839, Orinda Armstrong. He lived in Zanesville until 1831, when he went to Richmond, Ind., where he now lives.

1701. SELINA, born Sept. 25, 1803, married, June 28, 1827, Lory White of Spencer, Mass., where he died, Nov. 11, 1829, and she married in Leicester, Feb. 1848, Charles Sprague.

1702. ALMA, born July 1, 1805, and died in Spencer, Mass., Sept. 13, 1825.

1703. DULCENA, born June 28, 1807, married, in Spencer, Mass., April 23, 1836, Nathan Craige, Jr., and resides in Spencer. Their children are: George Azel, born Jan. 18, 1837, married, Dec. 22, 1858, Ellen Jones, and has one daughter: Sarah Louisa, born Feb. 2, 1839, married, Sept. 18, 1858, Abraham Capen of Spencer, and has two children: Nathan Huntington, born May 3, 1841, and died Aug. 30, 1846; William Choat, born April 29, 1847, and died Aug. 6, 1847.

1704. AZEL, born May 22, 1809, and died in Union, Mass., Nov. 26, 1811.

1705. JABEZ, born Jan. 19, 1811, married, in Marlboro, June 23, 1836, Mrs. Sarah Parmenter, who died in the same place, Oct. 12, 1852. He now resides in Marlboro, Mass.

1706. OZIAS, born Nov. 10, 1812, married, in Marlboro, Jan. 19, 1844, Mary Rice. They live in Marlboro.

1707. SOPHIA, born March 26, 1816, married, in Spencer, Mass., May 18, 1844, Edward Gershom Rice of Marlboro, Mass. Their children are: Harriet, born April 16, 1845, and died Aug. 1, 1851; Susannah Sophia, born Feb. 13, 1848, and died Aug. 14, 1851; Cornelia Hannah, born Oct. 25, 1849, and died Aug. 17, 1851; Julian Huntington, born Dec. 23, 1851; Cordelia Hyde, born Jan. 25, 1854; Harriet Amelia, born March 17, 1857; and Edward Huntington, born May 16, 1859. The family are now living in Marlboro, Mass.

1708. JULIA ANN, born May 5, 1818, married, in Spencer, Mass., Oct. 12, 1837, Eleazer Bemis.

1709. EMELINE, born March 22, 1821, married, in Spencer, Mass., Nov. 5, 1846, William Allen of Worcester, Mass. Their children are: Charles Huntington, born June 27, 1848, and died Aug. 15, 1850; Harriet Eliza, born Nov. 19, 1851, and died Feb. 1, 1854; Emma Jane, born June 23, 1855, and died July 11, 1855; Nellie Sophia, born Sept. 15, 1860. Mrs. Allen died Nov. 8, 1860.

757. EBENEZER. Becket, Mass.

1710. MEHITABEL, born Oct. 17, 1803, and now lives, unmarried, in Becket, Mass.

1711. SOPHRONIA, born Jan. 28, 1805, and now lives in Becket, Mass.

1712. MELISSA HYDE, born March 15, 1807, married, in New Haven, Conn., May 4, 1847, Amos Townsend, Jr. They reside in New Haven, and are much esteemed for their benevolence and usefulness. They have had one daughter, Sarah Melissa, born May 5, 1849, and died Dec. 9, 1851.

1713. WILLIAM SWIFT, born Nov. 28, 1808, is living single in Becket.

1714. CHARLES, born Jan. 23, 1811, and died Sept. 24, 1812.

1715. FRANCES DIANA, born Jan. 2, 1813, and lived with her sister, Mrs. Townsend, in New Haven. She was an excellent Christian woman, and died in Becket, June 9, 1860.

1716. EMILY CLARK, born Sept. 24, 1815, and died in Becket, Dec. 21, 1836.

SEVENTH GENERATION.

1717. CHARLES THOMAS, born Nov. 17, 1817, married, March 28, 1848, Sarah Huntington White. His wife is daughter of Sophia (1412.) In 1859 he removed to North Brookfield, where he is a farmer. He is deacon of the Congregational church.

1718. GEORGE HENRY, born Oct. 20, 1820, and married, Dec. 31, 1850, Julia Clark, and resides in Becket. He is a farmer.

1719. HARRIET, born Sept. 2, 1822, and died in Becket, Sept. 23, 1824.

1720. SARAH, born Nov. 11, 1826, and died in Becket, Sept. 29, 1829.

762. ROSWELL. Carlisle, N. Y.

1721. EDWIN TRACY, born in Lebanon, Conn., Sept. 27, 1814, married, Sept. 29, 1842, Sarah, daughter of Rev. Charles Wadsworth of Richfield Springs, N. Y. He now resides in Rochester, where he has been for years connected with the Democrat as one of the proprietors. He has been actively engaged in the Sabbath School cause, and for years secretary of the New York state S. S. Union.

1722. HENRY HYDE, born Dec. 25, 1816, married, Sept. 18, 1844, Harriet M. Dow of Carlisle, N. Y., and now lives in Albany, where he has been several years in the office of the Evening Journal of that city.

1723. WILLIAM W., born Sept. 1, 1823, married, May 7, 1848, Susan M. Kirtland of Saybrook. He has been for years a dry goods merchant in New Haven, Conn., where he now lives.

764. ANDREW. Guilford Center, N. Y.

1724. CYRUS, born April 10, 1820, and graduated at Yale in 1843, and studied theology. He married widow Boyd of Baltimore, and has been settled at Ellicott's Mills, Md., engaged both in preaching and teaching. He has furnished several poetic contributions to our current literature. He is now (1862) chaplain to the First regiment of Maryland volunteers in the Union army.

1725. JANE, born Aug. 18, 1821, married, in 1851, Albert S. Case, a broker of New York city, where she has resided. They have four children: Virginia, Albert, Albert and Mary.

1726. MARY, born Feb. 9, 1825, and lives in New York.

1727. ROLLIN, born Sept. 24, 1830, married, Jan. 2, 1854, Anna S. Cox of Saratoga, N. Y., and is living in Baltimore, Md. They have no children.

777. LEVI. Norwich, Conn.

This family were all born in Norwich, Conn.

1728. JOSEPH OTIS, born Aug. 14, 1803, married, Nov. 4, 1843, Elizabeth C. Otis of Pittsfield, Mass. They reside in Norwich town.

1729. CATHERINE ANNA, born Sept. 27, 1806, married, Dec. 9, 1834, William Root of Medina, Ohio. He has been treasurer of the county.

1730. PETER RICHARDS, born Aug. 20, 1809, married, Feb. 21, 1834, Jane Simmons, and is a farmer in Medina, Ohio.

1731. JOHN GRISWOLD, born Feb. 24. 1814, married, Sept. 1, 1836, Mary Isham of Colchester. He was engaged in the lumber business in Norwich city, where he was much esteemed. He died from the small pox, April 17, 1859.

1732. HANNAH Mumford, born Sept. 14, 1816, married William C. Bowers, a merchant of New York city, who died in 1861. Their children are: Margaret Phillips, Catherine Richards, Josephine Otis, Emma Elizabeth, and William Cushing.

790. JAMES. Norwich, Conn.

1733. GEORGE, born Dec. 17, 1809, and died Dec. 18, 1809, in Norwich.

1734. JAMES WILLIAM, born April 5, 1811. He was captain of a vessel and died in New York, Aug. 29, 1851. He was engaged in the cotton trade. He married, in 1842, Eleanor Quidor, who still lives in New York.

1735. ZERVIAH TYLER, born Dec. 15, 1812, and died in Springfield, Mass., at the residence of Mrs. James Dwight, Nov. 18, 1832.

1736. MARIA L., born Feb. 3, 1815, married, Benj. F. (2482).

1737. JULIA ANNA, born March 24, 1817, married, in Norwich city, at the house of Lyman Brewer, Feb. 17, 1857, Amos W. Gay of New York city. They live in Harlem, N. Y.

793 FELIX A. Brooklyn, N. Y.

1738. BENJAMIN SNOW, born in Norwich, Conn., April 23, 1813, graduated at Columbia College, N. Y., in 1834, having been chosen by the Mercantile Library Association in 1830, as the one of their number to be educated. Traveled in Europe in 1836, and married in Paris, Feb. 1, 1838, Frances Seal. Returned to this country and was ordained to the Episcopal ministry by Rt. Rev. Bishop Onderdonk in 1840, and settled as Rector of Christ Church in Middle Haddam, Conn. In 1841 succeeded Rev. Dr. Lee, in Rochdale, Pa., and in 1847 commenced the Institution at Aston Ridge, a seminary for young ladies, of which he had successful control about ten years. He then removed to Brooklyn, N. Y., and was employed as minister of the Church of our Savior for Seamen, in New York. In Nov. 1, 1861, received a call to St. Paul's Church, Flatbush, L. I., where he is now engaged.

1739. ANNE PERKINS, born Sept. 10, 1814, and died single in Brooklyn, N. Y. Oct. 16, 1848.

1740. JOHN FELIX, born April 5, 1825, married, Nov. 16, 1859, Frances Ackerman. He resides in Brooklyn, N. Y., and is now with Morris Ketchum and Co., bankers, in Wall St., N. Y.

807. BENJAMIN N. Rome, N. Y.

1741. BENJAMIN N., born Nov. 16, 1855, and died of scarlet fever at Rome, June 12, 1860.

SEVENTH GENERATION.

813. HENRY S., Rev.   Coldwell, N. Y.

1741.¹ Eliza Rowland, born in May, 1861.
1741.² George, born Aug. 12, 1862.

820. EDWARD.   Rome, N. Y.

1742. Mary Louisa, born June 8, 1845.
1743. George, born July 19, 1847, and died June 7, 1853.
1744. Elizabeth Randall, born Oct. 25, 1850.
1745. William Randall, born Oct. 1, 1854.
1746. Antoinette, born Jan. 7, 1856.

822. DANIEL.   New York City.

1747. Charles Richards, born Jan. 5, 1847, in Brooklyn, N. Y.

823. GURDON, Rev.   Sag Harbor, N. Y.

1747.¹ Channing Moore, born in Sag Harbor, Jan. 4, 1861.

824. JOHN.   Orange, Vt.

1748. Ithamar is said to have gone to Michigan with his sisters.
1749. Marcia.
1750. Mary Ann.
1751. Andrew, died aged eighteen years, at Tunbridge, Vt.
1752. Laura.

826. WILLIAM.   Whiting, Vt.

1753. Delia, born March 3, 1794, married, July 4, 1814, Jesse Cutler, and lived in Highgate, Vt.
1754. Sarah, born Feb. 6, 1796, and lives still at Whiting, Vt.
1755. William P., born Sept. 7, 1801, married, Nov. 19, 1824, Wealthy P. Van Deusen, and resides in Fulton, Jackson county, Iowa.
1756. James, born March 2, 1804, and lives in Whiting, Vt.
1757. Susan C., born June 10, 1807, married, Nov. 13, 1841, Abner C. Rudes, and lives in Coldwater, Mich., where he is a farmer.
1758. Elizabeth W., born April 6, 1811, married, Jan. 8, 1835, David Olmsted, and lives in East Middlebury, Vt.

827. MILLER.   Randolph, Vt

1759. Alvah, married Ann Stevens.
1760. Anna P., married James P. Cleveland.
1761. Jesse, married Minerva Barnes, and lived at Randolph, Vt.
1762. Susan, married Ira Kidder, a merchant of Braintree, Vt.

838. JARED.   Thompson, N. Y.

1763. Eliza, born Dec. 27, 1806, married, Nov. 15, 1826, John S. Marvin. She has six children, and now lives at Howell, Mich.

1764. LYDIA, born July 8, 1808, married, Oct. 1, 1834, David Lownsbury. She has two children, and lives at Fallsburg, N. Y.

1765. LUCIUS W. C. born May 23, 1811, married, Nov. 26, 1834, Elizabeth Gildersleeve of Gardner, Mass. He was killed by a circular saw, in Zenia, Ohio, July 28, 1848.

1766. LORENDA, born July 29, 1813 married, Nov. 10, 1833, Dr. Joseph L. Smith, and has five children. They are living in Liberty, Sullivan Co., N. Y.

1767. WILLIAM, born Jan. 16, 1817, married, May 2, 1844, Rhoda Tibbits. He is a physician, living in Howell, Mich.

1768. NELSON, born March 15, 1819, married, May 10, 1842, Mary Baldwin, and lives near Zenia, Ohio.

1769. JOSEPH GILBERT, born April 14, 1821, married, Oct. 11, 1848, Josephine Colbreth. They live in Thompson, N. Y.

1770. WEALTHY, born Sept. 9, 1824, married, July 4, 1848, Edmund Quinlan. She had three children. They lived at Sheboygan Falls, Wis., where she died in Nov., 1854.

1771. JERUSHA JANE, born Sept. 4, 1827, married, Jan. 1, 1850, William Kellum. She has one child, and lives at Long Eddy, N. Y.

1772. JARED, born Aug. 23, 1830, and died March 18, 1831.

839. JOSEPH. Monticello, N. Y.

This family were all born in Monticello.

1773. SARAH SOPHIA, born Sept. 6, 1810, married, Oct. 8, 1829, Platt Crosby, and lives in Waterloo, N. Y., having had five children.

1774. CHARLOTTE, born Oct. 7, 1814, married, June 5, 1834, Peter B. Webster. They have four children, and live in Monticello.

1775. MARY MINERVA, born May 16, 1818, married, in May, 1844, Henry McKinion, and has two children, living in Ann Arbor, Mich.

1776. HARRIET MARIA, born Dec. 25, 1820, married, Nov. 13, 1839, Shepley Stodder. They had two children. She died April 7, 1848.

1777. JOSEPH GORTON, born Aug. 18, 1822, married, May 6, 1846, Cordelia A. Swift. He died in California, Nov. 2, 1850, and his wife and sons are in New York city.

1778. JOHN GILDERSLEEVE, twin with the above, died July 8, 1830.

1779. CAROLINE, born June 22, 1824, married, Nov. 17, 1841, Rufus B. Wicks. They live in Monticello, and have four children.

1780. HENRY LEWIS, born Sept. 1, 1826, married, Oct. 13, 1852, Emily L. Clark. They live in Waterloo, N. Y.

1781. HENRIETTA AMELIA, born March 20, 1828, married, Oct., 1849, Alfred Quinlan. She died March 5, 1855, leaving three children.

1782. EMMA LOUISA, born Aug. 8, 1830, married, June 2, 1851, George R. Babbitt, and lives in Waterloo, N. Y.

1783. JAMES FERDINAND, born Aug. 3, 1834.

1784. JULIET FRANCES, born Jan. 23, 1838.

1785. CATHERINE SALOME, born Oct. 16, 1841.

1786. CHARLES.
1787. CHAUNCY.

841. JAMES.   Mansfield, Conn.

1788. JAMES PORTER, born Nov. 15, 1821, married, in Mansfield, Nov. 16, 1853, Elizabeth Mory. They live in Mansfield.

1789. SARAH ANN, born Nov. 2, 1823, married, Jan. 20, 1840, Joseph Philips, a merchant of Ashford, and has four children.

1790. EMILY, born Jan. 26, 1827, and died July 11, 1850.

1791. JULIETTE, born Nov. 30, 1830, and lives with her father in Mansfield.

1792. JULIUS CLARK, born Aug. 28, 1834, and died March 19, 1839.

1793. LUCIUS GORTON, born Aug. 28, 1834, and died Nov. 2, 1836.

855. RICHARD.   Utica, N. Y.

1794. SUSAN MARIA, born in Utica, Sept. 17, 1831, married, Jan. 20, 1855 William W. Coffin of Utica. They have two daughters: Grace Mayhew, born Nov. 2, 1855; and Ellen Huntington, born Dec. 20, 1856.

1795. JANE PORTER, born in Utica, April 6, 1833, and died Aug. 4, 1838.

1796. RICHARD HENRY, born in Utica, May 28, 1835. He was instantly killed while in the active discharge of his duties, as fireman, on Sunday evening, May 3, 1857, in New York city. The Southwark Engine Company, to which he belonged, thus testify to his character:

Resolved, That in the death of our lamented companion, Mr. Richard H. Huntington, our department has been bereft of one of its brightest ornaments, and the metropolis of one of its most useful and respected citizens, who, though his sojourn with us was but brief, his promptness and efficiency in the discharge of every duty, his upright and manly bearing, and his frank and generous nature commanded the respect, esteem and love of all who had the honor of his acquaintance.

859. PETER CHESTER.   Lebanon, Conn.

1797. SIMEON C., born in Athens, N. Y., June 21, 1806, married, in 1828, Julia Treadway. He died in Coventry, while on a visit, Feb. 27, 1852, having lived in Norwich, Conn. His widow married Horace Thrall, in Windsor, Conn.

1798. HARRIET FREELOVE, born in Windham, N. Y., Nov. 2, 1811, and now lives in South Coventry, Conn.

1799. CHARLES EDWARD, born in Athens, N. Y., May 4, 1814, and died Nov. 29, 1840, in a furious storm which wrecked the vessel of which he was captain. He had married Sarah Brumham, and was living in New Haven, Connecticut.

1800. ABBY DELIA, born in New London, Conn., March 12, 1815, married, Sept. 21, 1836, Uriah D. Lee of Buffalo, N. Y. She has four children: Edward Ruthven, born Nov. 12, 1837; Charles Huntington, born Jan. 4, 1843, and died in 1845; Charles Williams, born Dec. 8, 1845; and Frank Huntington, born March 19, 1854.

1801. DAVID WARING, born in Montville, Conn., Jan. 3, 1821, was a civil engineer for years, but is now engaged in the manufacture of silk, in South Coventry, Conn.

1802. MARY ELIZABETH, born in Montville, Conn., June 9, 1827, and is living in South Coventry.

1803. WILLIAM WALMSLY, born in Montville, Conn., Jan. 8, 1830, married, Jan. 8, 1854, at Broadbrook, Conn., Maria L. Palmer, daughter of Nelson and Mary Palmer. He lives in New York city, where he has for years been in the dry goods domestic commission business. His wife died Nov. 4, 1856. He married, for his second wife, Sept. 19, 1859, Sarah S., daughter of Dr. Thomas and Almira Cleveland of Providence, R. I. The author is under special obligations to him for timely pecuniary help in completing this work.

867. ELISHA.   Hudson, N. Y.

This family were all born in Hudson.

1804. GEORGE PADDOCK, born Oct. 22, 1809, and died single, in Illinois, March 1, 1840.

1805. THOMAS PADDOCK, born July 26, 1811, is a banker in New York city.

1806. EDWARD CLARK, born Oct. 22, 1815, and is in New York.

1807. ELISHA, born April 4, 1819, and died in Philadelpha, Nov. 1, 1829.

868. ZEPHANIAH.   New London, Conn.

1808. RUTH, born Aug. 30, 1812, married Erastus Saunders of New London. They have one son, Erastus Huntington, who is now (1862) a member of the senior class, Yale College.

1809. LYDIA PADDOCK, born Oct. 19, 1819, married Wm. B. Cunningham. They live in New London, and have had four children.

1809.[1] ANN ELIZABETH, born Jan. 22, 1816, and died Nov. 14, 1825.

875. FREDERICK, CAPT.   Savannah, Ga.

1809.[2] JOHN FREDERICK, died in 1841.

1810. GEORGE WILEY must have been born in 1831, according to his stepmother, Mrs. Richardson. He was lost at sea, with his father.

1810.[1] WILLIAM HENRY, died in 1842.

883. PETER CHESTER.   New York.

1811. LEVI FARR, born in 1823.

1812. ELIZA MATILDA.

1813. MARGARET ANN.

1814. MATHEW ROWE.

1815. EDWARD ST. JOHN W.

1816. JOHN, born in 1827.
1817. CHESTER D.
1818. MARGARET, ANN.
1818.¹ JANE.
1819. ABEL.

898. EBENEZER.

1820. SUSANNAH.
1821. MARIA.
1822. ELIZABETH.
1823. MARGARETT.
1824. CLAYTON.
1825. JEDIDIAH.
1826. HENRY.
1827. CHARLES.

EIGHTH GENERATION.

902. BENJAMIN. Ware, N. H.

1828. HANNAH, born Dec. 13, 1781, married Jonathan Purinton of Lincoln, Vt. Their children were: Benjamin, born Sept. 11, 1803, and died in Ohio, Dec. 16, 1859; John, born Sept. 21, 1807, and died in Ohio, Jan. 10, 1837; Elijah, born Dec. 16, 1809; Jacob, born Dec. 16, 1813, and died in Lincoln, March 11, 1857; Thomas, born Feb. 14, 1816; and Huldah G., born Sept. 3, 1818.

1829. JACOB, born Sept. 3, 1783, married, first, May 4, 1809, Huldah Gove, who died Oct. 20, 1819. He married again, Feb. 1, 1823, Mehetabel Hedding, who died March 4, 1827. He married, the third time, in Oct., 1829, Lavinia B. Breed. He died, July 15, 1857, and his widow, Aug. 13, 1859.

1830. SARAH, born Oct. 9, 1785, married, Oct. 4, 1804, Robert Gove of Deering, N. H. Their children are: Hannah, born Aug. 6, 1826, married Herod Chase, and had two sons: John, born Dec. 21, 1807, is married and has two children; Huldah B., born July 26, 1813, married James N. Estes of South Danvers, and has five children, one of whom, James F., married Margaret E. Stark; Anna H., born Oct. 12, 1818, married Amos Breed, and has three children.

1831. BETSEY, born Feb. 14, 1788, married, in March, 1816, Timothy Matthews, and has no children.

1832. THOMAS, born Feb. 20, 1791, married, Nov. 27, 1816, Anna Johnson. After her death he married, March 24, 1819, Mehetabel Johnson. He lived in Weare, N. H., where he died in 1855.

1833. ANNA, born in 1791, married Daniel Buxton. They live in South Danvers, and have children.

1833.¹ LYDIA, who died young.

1834. JOHN, born Aug. 5, 1797, married, June 20, 1821, Peace Purinton. He was a farmer, and lived in Weare, N. H., where he died in 1822.

1835. BENJAMIN, born in Oct., 1799, married, first, Sally Buxton, and second, Mary A Beard. They live in Danvers. They have had no children.

903. MOSES.   Amesbury, Mass.

This family were all born in Amesbury.

1836. ENOCH, born Dec. 27, 1794, married, Oct., 1821, Rebecca Flanders He is a ship master and farmer. To him the Huntingtons are indebted, mainly, for the list and nearly all the details of the descendants of William Huntington, who settled in Salisbury, Mass., as they appear in this work.

1837. JOHN, born Sept. 7, 1797, married, in 1821, Hannah Jones, who died. He married for his second wife, in 1850, Abigal C. Vining. 'He is a thriving farmer in his native town, occupying a portion of the original homestead.

1838. RUTH, born Sept. 9, 1799, and died in 1800.

1839. JACOB, born Jan. 16, 1801, married, first, Oct. 21, 1831, Elizabeth (2969) who died Sept. 16, 1838. He married again, June 20, 1842, Hannah Peaselee. He is also a successful farmer in his native town. His wife, Hannah, died Nov. 1, 1861.

1840. PHILLIP, born May 22, 1803, married Phurua Sargent, and resides in Haverhill, Mass., where he has a meat market. His wife died in Sept., 1861

1841. DANIEL, born March 17, 1806, married, Dec. 1, 1841, Sarah W. Estes of Amesbury, where they reside.

1842. MOSES, born May 6, 1809; married, July, 1833, Cynthia W. Jepson. He is a farmer and minister of the Friends. He is much esteemed in the community where he has always lived.

1843. LYDIA JONES, born May 14, 1812, married Joel H. Davis of Amesbury, Pleasant Valley. The have three children: Eliza Huntington, born in 1840; Moses Huntington, born in 1843; and Joel Augustus, born in 1849. They live on a part of the original plot of the first William.

1844. EPHRAIM MORREL, born July 16, 1816, married Ruth C. Vining. He is a teacher and farmer, living in New Jersey.

904. JOHN.   Lincoln, Vt.

1845. STEPHEN, born 1794, married Mary Poore, who was born Jan. 1806. They lived in West Newbury, Mass.

1846. MOSES, born July 15, 1797, married Elizabeth Varney of Pontiac, N. Y., where the family have lived.

1847. DANIEL, born Sept. 4, 1799, married Phebe E. Gove, and reside in Pontiac, N. Y.

1848. LYDIA, born Dec. 21, 1801, married Nathan C. Gove, March 31, 1850, in Pontiac, N. Y., where the family have lived.

1849. JOHN, born Feb. 13, 1804, married Lavina Meader, and live in Lincoln, Vt.

1850. HANNAH, born Feb. 28, 1809, and lives in Lincoln, Vt.

1851. SARAH G., born Nov. 26, 1810, married Nathan Green, and has lived in Lincoln, Vt. Their children have been: Louisa Green, born Nov. 17, 1835, and died in 1856; William H., born Feb. 3, 1839; Irvin B., born June 10, 1846, and died March 10, 1847; Mary P., born Nov. 29, 1848; and Nathan L., born Nov. 26, 1850.

1852. MARY, born Aug. 13. 1813, married Elijah Purinton. She died June 25, 1850, in Lincoln, Vt. Their children were: John. born Aug. 29, 1836 Lydia, born Jan. 14. 1838; Horatio N., born Dec. 31, 1839; Lindly H., born May 19, 1844; and Moses H., born June 11. 1847;

908. DAVID. Amesbury, Mass.

This family were all born in Amesbury.

1853. DAVID, born Aug. 23, 1799, and died Oct. 7, 1800.

1854. REBECCA, born Feb. 19, 1801, married, in Oct., 1826, Isaiah Page. She died Jan. 27, 1832, leaving one child, Lydia, who was born Jan. 29, 1829, and died in April, 1844.

1855. ELIZA, born Nov. 10, 1804, married, Oct. 28, 1827, David Goodwin. They reside in Amesbury, where they united with the Congregational church in 1834. They have had nine children: John H., born Oct. 14, 1828, and died April 18, 1834; Sophia A., born Jan. 8, 1830, married, Oct. 28, 1852, John S. Merrill, and has one child; Rebecca, born Oct. 30, 1831; David W., born April 4, 1833; John H., born April 30, 1836, married, Oct. 28, 1860, Eliza G. Brookings of Newburyport; Lydia A., born July 31, 1838, and died March 9, 1843; Hannah J., born Aug. 11, 1840, and died June 18, 1843; Ephraim A; and Eliza A., born April 9, 1843. Eliza A. married, July 29, 1860, William Brookings of Newburyport, and has one son.

1856. LYDIA, born Oct. 28, 1808, and died Feb. 28, 1829.

1857. DAVID, born March 19, 1813, married, Nov. 23, 1834, Clara Osgood, who was born Dec. 8, 1814. They are now living in Lawrence, Mass., where he is employed in the Everett Mills.

910. AMOS. Amesbury, Mass.

1857.[1] WILLIAM, who died young.

1858. PATIENCE, married Ira Buxton and has children.

1859. SARAH, married Stephen Clough.

1860. LYDIA, married, Oliver Bartlett.

1861. MERRIAM, married Eli Beade, and lives in S. Hampton.

1862. NATHAN, born Oct. 8, 1818, married Susan Emery, in Amesbury. He lives on a part of the original Huntington homestead. They are members of the Congregational church.

1863. PHEBE, born March, 1816, died young.

1864. ELIZABETH, born April, 1821, married Eli Beade, (second wife) of S. Hampton.

915. JOHN. Wilmington, N. C.

1865. WILLIAM, born July 3, 1821, married Harriet S. Browne of North Carolina.

916. MOSES. Amesbury, Mass.

1866. CHARLES H., born June 25, 1817, married Mary Jane Latham in 1843, and has no children.
1867. DANIEL H., born April 30, 1820, married Sally B. Horne, in 1844, and lives in Amesbury.
1868. WILLIAM F. M., born April 20, 1827.

921. STEPHEN. Amesbury, Mass.

1869. ELIZABETH R., married Daniel Leonard of Lawrence, Mass.
1870. ABBY.

925. WILLIAM. Amesbury, Mass.

1871. SALLY, born in 1800, married —— Jenkins and David Morill. They live in Salisbury.
1872. EPHRAIM, born in 1801, married Olive McGan. He died, having lived in Amesbury.
1873. WILLIAM H., born in 1811, married Mary Blasdell. They lived in Brentwood, N. H.

928.² TIMOTHY. Litchfield, Me.

This family were all born in Litchfield.
1873.¹ HENRY, is about thirty years old and is in California.
1873.² DANIEL, died in Virginia.
1873.³ ABBY, married a Woodward, and lives in Litchfield.
1873.⁴ SARAH, married a Williams, and lives in Boston, Mass.
1873.ª ALPHEUS, is married and has a drug store in Monmouth, Maine.

928.³ JOSEPH. Atkinson, Me

The names of this family were supplied after the father's record had been printed. His wife was Mary Babb.
1873.ᵇ JOSEPH G., born in 1812.
1873.ᶜ BENJAMIN B., born March 26, 1814, married, June 10, 1841, Aurelia ——, and lives in New Richmond, Wis.
1873.ᶜ URIEL, is in California.
1873.ᵈ MARY, is dead.
1873.ᵉ ELIZABETH, lives in Bradford, Maine.
1873.ᶠ JAMES C., lives in Atkinson, Maine.
1873.ᵍ ANSTIS, is dead.
1873.ʰ GEORGE W., is in Bangor, Maine.
1873.ᵏ WILLIAM, lives in Bradford, Maine.
1873.ˡ HARVEY S., is in California.
1873.ᵐ EMILY, is in Bradford, Maine.
1873.ⁿ DIANTHA, is dead.
1873.ᵒ FRANKLIN, is in California.

EIGHTH GENERATION.

928.[4] WILLIAM. Pittston, Me.

1873.[6] URIEL, is married and lives in California.
1873.[7] SAMUEL, is married and lives in Hallowell, Maine.
1873.[8] ALBERT, is unmarried in California.
1873.[9] DELIA, married Francis M. (1873[17]).
1873.[10] WILLIAM.
1873.[11] EMMA, married a Kimball and lives in Boston, Mass.
1873.[12] ELLEN, married a Moody and lives in East Pittston.
1873.[13] ELIZABETH, is married.

928.[5] BENJAMIN. Litchfield, Me.

This family were all born in Litchfield.
1873.[14] SARAH E., born April 3, 1831, and died Nov. 25, 1843, in Litchfield.
1873.[15] LYDIA ANN, born Dec. 14, 1832, and married, Dec. 3, 1850, Ezra Cobb, and has three children: George, Ellen, and Frank.
1873.[16] LUCY JULIA, born Aug. 19, 1834, and died same day.
1873.[17] FRANCIS MERRIMAN, born March 13, 1836, married, July 7, 1851, Delia, (1873[9]) in Pittston, Maine.
1873.[18] MARY A., born March 13, 1836, married, Oct. 22, 1854, Edward Baker, and has two children: Francis and Emma.
1873.[19] HENRY ALBERT, born June 11, 1838, married, in Bowdoinham, Me., Dec. 4, 1858, Elizabeth Doyle.
1873.[20] GEORGE KINGSBURY, born July 22, 1840, and is now in the Union army, and was disabled at the Oak Swamp fight near Malvern Hill, June 29, 1862.
1873.[21] HIRAM STACY, born Dec. 3, 1842, and died Feb. 11, 1844.
1873.[22] DANIEL TRUE, born Sept. 25, 1847.
1873.[23] REBECCA DAVIS, born Sept. 25, 1847.
1873.[24] FREDERICK S., born Dec. 23, 1849.
1873.[25] BENJAMIN JOSHUA, born Nov. 27, 1851.

928.[8] DANIEL. Litchfield, Me.

1873.[26] ALVIN, married a Jourdan and has a family in Litchfield. He is now (1862) in the Union Army.
1873.[27] REBECCA, died unmarried.
1873.[28] DAVID, died unmarried.

931. GIDEON. Marshfield, Vt.

This list is made from Dr. Joshua's memoranda, made in 1850 at John Huntington's in Thetford, Vt.
1873.[29] JOHN, was a married man with a family, keeping a boarding house for Academy scholars in Thetford, Vt. No number or names of his children are recorded.
1873.[30] AMASA B., also had a family, and was a farmer and run a saw mill at Marshfield, Vt.
1873.[31] BETSEY, was living single at Marshfield.

1873.³² MARY, married Leonard Moons, and lived in Plainfield, Vt.
1873.³³ ROXINA, married Rufus Campbell, and kept tavern at Montpelier, Vt.

932. ABNER. Weare, N. H.

1874. FANNY, born in 1810.
1875. BETTY, born in 1813, married Joseph M. Sargent.
1876. JOHN, born in 1815.
1877. BENJAMIN.

934. JOHN. Bennington, N. H.

1878. RICHARD, born in 1809, married Eliza Chase, and lived in Nashua, N. H.
1879. ELIZABETH, born in 1811, married, —— Burrills, and lived in Weymouth.
1880. JOHN, born in 1813, and has lived in New Orleans.
1881. MOSES, born in 1815, and lives in Nashua.
1882. SHUEA, born in 1817, married John Sumner of Nashua.
1883. OLIVE P., born in 1819.

938. BENJAMIN. Weare, N. H.

1884. ANDREW W., born in 1828.
1885. MARGARET A., born in 1831.

952. GEORGE Bennington, Vt.

A letter from Isaac L., in this family, gives me the only particulars about it which I have been able to collect.

1886. JOSEPH, born about 1802, living (1859) in Dexter, N. Y., having quite a large family of daughters.
1887. MARY, who is dead, was born in 1804.
1888. HUGH CLARK, born 1806, and is without family.
1889. LYDIA, born in 1808, and has a family.
1889.¹ ISAAC L., born in 1810, has had five children, and lives in Theresa, New York.
1889.² SARAH, born in 1812, and has a family of daughters.

953. JOSEPH. Francistown, N. H.

This family were all born in Bennington, Vt.
1890. CATHERINE P., born Dec. 7, 1810.
1891. RODNEY S., born Oct. 20, 1812, married Jan. 7, 1841, in Manchester, N. H., Emeline B. Colley of Bedford, N. H., who was born Feb. 8, 1820. He is a pattern maker, and now resides in Nashua, N. H., where he has been since 1845. They are Congregationalists.
1892. JOHN, born Aug. 12, 1814, married, May 25, 1841, Lucy Boardman, who died in Nashua, N. H., July 22, 1852. He married again, April 6, 1854, Sophronia D. Parker of Merrimac, N. H. He is a machinist and pattern ma-

ker, and has resided in Nashua, N. H., since 1852. They are Congregationalists.

1893. GEORGE, born Oct. 8, 1817, and died Feb. 15, 1827.
1894. HEMAN, born July 16, 1819, and died Oct. 2, 1831.
1895. JOSEPH, born Sept. 12, 1823.

955. JOHN C. Keene, N. Y.

1896. MARGARET ANN FISHER, born Oct. 22, 1809, married, June 13, 1843, Murray Gilman, a shoemaker and farmer. They have four children: John, James, Mary M., and Charlotte. She is a member of the Congregationalist church, and lives in Keene.

1897. JOSEPH, born Jan. 17, 1811, married, June 20, 1839, Sarah Perry. She died Oct. 21, 1856, and he married again, Sept. 22, 1857, Isabella Pringle. They are Presbyterians, and are living at Au Sable Forks, N. Y.

1898. MARY COLBY, born Feb. 17, 1813, married, Feb. 28, 1833, Lincoln Kent, a farmer. She had eight children, and died Aug. 8, 1859: Rhoda C., Clarissa M., Eliza A., George W., Mary A., Lydia A., and Charlotte R.

1899. JOHN C., born June 7, 1814, married Eliza Wissil. He is a farmer, and lives in Scroone, N. Y. They belong to the Methodist denomination.

1900. JAMES FISHER, born Oct. 25, 1815, married Susan Macfarlin. They lived at Au Sable Forks, N. Y., where he died May 1, 1850. They had no children.

1901. GEORGE, born March 12, 1816, and died March 16, 1820.

1902. MOSES BRADFORD, born March 31, 1818, married, Dec. 16, 1847, Sarah Ann Macfarland, who was born Dec. 29, 1815. They are living in North Elba, N. Y., where he is engaged in farming. They are Methodists.

1903. ROXANA DART, born July 9, 1820, married, Feb. 15, 1838, Alonzo Washburn, who is a farmer, living in North Elba, N. Y. She has four children: Charles A., Charlotte B., Daughin C., and Eleanor. The family are Methodists.

1904. CHARLOTTE, born June 26, 1822, and died May 9, 1843.

1905. RHODA CATHERINE STEVENS, born March 5, 1824, and died Aug. 14, 1831.

1906. RUTH R., born Oct. 12, 1826, married, July 4, 1848, Abel Washburn, who is a farmer, living in North Elba, N. Y. The family are Methodists. They have five children: Orra Jane, Clara E., Sarah E. C., Abel E., and George.

958. SAMUEL. Bennington, Vt.

1907. JOSEPH F., born Feb. 6, 1832. He is unmarried.
1908. MARY PERSIS, born Nov. 17, 1833, and died Oct. 21, 1837.
1909. RUTH A., born May 28, 1838, and lives, unmarried, in De Soto, Wis.

961. CHRISTOPHER. Hartford, Conn.

1910. CHARLES, born in Hartford, May 29, 1824, married at Geneva, N. Y., Aug. 24, 1846, Susan Amelia Tomlinson, and lives in Bloomington, Ill. He has been in the shoe business, but is now a railroad engineer. His wife was born June 20, 1827, and died Nov. 18, 1857, and was a daughter of Harvey Tomlinson, of Geneva, N. Y.

1911. GEORGE, born in Hartford. Nov. 29, 1826, and died in Mobile, Ala., Sept. 29, 1853. He was at the time of his death a clerk in a commission house.

1912. HENRY, born in Hartford. Sept. 4, 1829, married, Sept. 9, 1850, Huldah Crow, who was born, Jan. 21, 1819. He is now living in Valparaiso, Ind., and is a farmer.

965. ELISHA HYDE. Penn Yan, N. Y.

The first two of this family were born in Canandaigua, and the rest in Penn Yan.

1913. CHARLES PORTER, born Sept. 11, 1827, and died in Canandaigua, Oct. 18, 1829.

1914. MARY CATHERINE, born Oct. 17, 1829, married, at Penn Yan, Sept. 2, 1850, James Morgan, son of Samuel S. and Sarah (Armstrong) Chapman of Penn Yan. He was born Oct. 10, 1827, and now lives in Cincinnati, Ohio.

1915. EDWARDS WHITE, born Feb. 3, 1832, and died in Penn Yan, Oct. 18, 1833.

1916. EDWARDS CHARLES, born June 10, 1834, married, Oct. 7, 1857, Cornelia Bradley, daughter of Wm. Henry and Mary Ellen (Townsend) Lamport. He was a druggist in his native town, until Nov. 1859, when he removed to Galesburg, Ill., where he is now living.

1917. LUCY SOPHIA, born, June 20, 1836, and lives in Penn Yan.

1918. WILLIAM SPOONER, born Oct. 2, 1839, is engaged as cashier in the banking house established by his father at Beaver Dam, Wis. He married Oct., 1859, Fannie Dearborn, at Springfield, Mass.

968. CHARLES. Franklin, Conn.

1919. CORNELIA RUDD, born April 10, 1811, married Joseph H. Pettis, and has three children. They live in Brooklyn, N. Y.

1920. CARLOS TRACY, born Aug. 6, 1813, married, June 6, 1854, Ellen J. Cobb of Norwich city. He returned from a successful visit to California, and has since been a money broker in Wall street, New York.

1921. NANCY RUDD, born Sept. 22, 1815, married George Howard, and has three children. They live in Tarrytown, N. Y.

971. ASHER. Athens, Pa.

This family, excepting the last, were born in Vernon, Conn.

1922. HARRIET HYDE, born Jan. 12, 1817, and died July 2, 1819.

1923. LYDIA JULIETTA, born Aug. 24, 1818, and died Oct. 19, 1819.

1924. HARRIET HYDE, born July 17, 1820, married, Aug. 25, 1839, Lucius R. Bennet, and died April 21, 1842, leaving one daughter, who is dead.

1925. HEZEKIAH, born Oct. 19, 1822, married, Nov. 18, 1850, Sarah M. Gates. He is a farmer, and lives in East Smithfield, Pa.

1926. LYDIA TRACY, born Oct. 11, 1824, married, July 4, 1848, James M. Gates, and has one daughter, Ednah. They live in Athens, Pa.

EIGHTH GENERATION. 297

1927. NANCY MARIA, born May 14, 1827, married, Sept. 10, 1845, William S. Voorhis, and has two children: Clarence Bingham, and William Fremont, and lives in North Smithfield, Pa.

1928. CHARLES OSCAR, born Dec. 31, 1829, is a harness maker, living in Athens, Pa.

1929. EVELINE HYDE, born June 18, 1830, in Springfield, Pa, and died in Athens, Pa., Dec. 16, 1856.

974. JONATHAN RUDD. Vernon, Conn.

1930. JULIA ANN, born in Vernon, June 28, 1827, and died in the same town, in May, 1853.

975. ZIBA. Franklin, Conn.

1931. ABBY JANE, born Nov. 15, 1825, married, Nov. 4, 1846, Almond Tracy of Franklin, and has three children: Oliver Rudd, William, and Lydia Ellis.

1932. SAMUEL ELLIS, born July 14, 1827, married Caroline Morse, and lives in Franklin.

978. ABEL HALL. Erie County, N. Y.

1933. LUCY ANN JONES, born Sept. 26, 1823, and now lives in Kansas.

1934. ABEL HALL, born May 7, 1825, and is a mechanic, living now (1861) in Galesburg, Ill.

1935. JOSEPH WARREN, died at the age of two years.

1936. JOSEPH WARREN, born Dec. 25, 1828, and is now living.

985. JACOB PERKINS. Londonderry, Vt.

1937. JUDITH SPEAR, born in Chelsea, Vt., in 1830, married, May 19, 1856, Rev. Elliot Merrifield, and is settled in West Wardsboro, Vt. They have two children.

1938. LUCY PERKINS, born in Thetford, Vt. 1832.

1939. MARY JANE, born in Thetford, in 1834.

1940. ARABELLA FISH, born in Ira, Vt., in 1843.

991. ZIBA. Lebanon, N. H.

1941. EMMA, born in Lebanon, N. H., Feb. 14, 1839.

997. EDWIN NEHEMIAH. Lebanon, N. H.

1942. ALICE GERTRUDE, born Sept. 20, 1847, and died in Lebanon, April 13, 1857.

1943. CARRIE MATILDA, born July 8, 1850.

1007. AZARIAH. Franklin, Conn.

1944. JULIETTE LAVINIA, born Oct. 1, 1816, married in March, 1834, Tracy Hastings, of Franklin, where they continue to live. Their children are: Sophia Tracy, who married Rev. Isaac Clark of Elmira, N. Y.; Lucy Ariana, who married Ezra Smith of Franklin, and has one son; and Martha Jane who died.

1945. PARNEL, born March 4, 1819, married, in March. 1835, Western Dickenson of Franklin, where they now live. They have no children.

1946. SARAH ELIZA, born Oct. 17, 1822, married. Feb. 15, 1844, Henry Kingsley of Franklin. Their children are: Henry Huntington, and Silas Hartshorn.

1947. LUCY, born in Nov. 1826, and died in Franklin, in Nov., 1837.

1948. ALITHEA LORD, born in Sept. 1828, married, in Sept., 1845, Amos A. Hall, music teacher of Willimantic, where they now live. Their children are: Althea Adelaide, Ella Gertrude, who is dead, and Anne Wright.

1949. HEZEKIAH, born Feb. 1, 1830, married, Oct. 11, 1853, Frances H. Smith, and lives on the old homestead, in Franklin.

1008. ASAHEL. Utica, N. Y.

1950. HENRY ASAHEL, is married. and living in Boston. Mass., where he is in the wholesale clothing business.

1951. ELIZA SARAH, is living with her brother in Boston.

1012. ELISHA, (M. D.) Lowell, Mass.

1952. JAMES FREEMAN, born Sept. 6, 1826, married, May 30, 1848, Ellen Sophrona Whipple, and was engaged in the hardware business in Marietta, Ohio. He belongs to the Unitarian denomination. He is now (1862) in the Union army, a captain of an artillery company, in which he has done effective service.

1953. FRANCIS CLEAVELAND, born June 3, 1831, and is engaged in the wholesale dry goods business of the firm of Jenkins and Huntington, New York city. The author is much indebted to him for both words and deeds of encouragement in preparing this genealogy.

1954. MARY HINCKLEY, born Sept. 3, 1838, married. Feb. 6, 1861, Josiah Parsons Cooke, jr., professor of chemistry and mineralogy in Harvard College.

1955. ISAAC MANSFIELD, born Dec. 15, 1836, and died Oct. 12, 1837.

1956. WILLIAM REED, born Sept. 20, 1838, graduated at Harvard 1859, studied theology, and was ordained minister of the Episcopal denomination. He is now the office editor of the Church Monthly. His writings indicate a vigorous mind, in active sympathy with all truly human and philanthropic enterprises.

EIGHTH GENERATION.

1013. ASAHEL, Esq.   Salem, Mass.

1957. WILLIAM DEBLOIS, born Aug. 25, 1843, was engaged in fitting for college, when, in 1861, he entered the service of the government. He was on board the U. S. steamship Cambridge.

1958. SARAH LOUISA, born July 23, 1845.

1959. ARTHUR LORD, born June 14, 1848.

1028. WINSLOW TRACY, (M. D.)   Akron, Ohio.

1960. WILLIAM HENRY, born in East Haddam, Conn., June 29, 1832, and married, in March, 1862, Kate Stanley. They are living in Cleveland, Ohio, where he is in business.

1961. FRANCES ELIZABETH, born in Albany, N. Y., July 30, 1834, and has been engaged in teaching in Baton Rouge, La., but is now in Cleveland, Ohio.

1962. CORNELIA WINSLOW, born in Ohio City, Aug. 3, 1837, married William (1145.)

1963. JULIA ALMIRA, born Aug. 6, 1845, and now lives in Cleveland.

1964. EMILY LUCRETIA, born in Akron, Aug. 12, 1849, and now lives in Cleveland.

1034. ELIJAH BALDWIN, REV.   Stamford, Conn.

1965. ABBY SWIFT, born in Windham, Conn., April 7, 1845, and died in same place, Feb. 12, 1846.

1966. JULIA SWIFT, born in Windham, Sept. 1, 1846.

1967. CLARA LOUISA, born in North Killingly, July 27, 1848.

1968. SARAH LEE, born in North Killingly, Sept. 12, 1850, and died in the same place, Dec. 24, of the same year.

1969. EDMUND CLEMENT, born in Meriden, Conn., May 30, 1852, and died in same place, Sept. 9, 1852.

1036. WILLIAM DYER.   Providence, R. I.

1970. WILLIAM TRACY, born in Norwich city, July 16, 1848.

1971. MARY ANNA, born in Providence, R. I., May 28, 1855.

1037. BENJAMIN.   Norwich, Conn.

This family were all born in Norwich.

1972. JOHN W. P., born July 5, 1831, married, in Yoncalla, Oregon, Feb. 18, 1857, Mary Applegate. They are now living in Scottsburg, Oregon.

1973. A SON, born March 24, 1833.

1974. MARGARETTA D., born June 15, 1834.

1975. PELATIAH WEBSTER, born July 2, 1836, married, in Columbus, Ohio, June 3, 1858, Jane N. Beeson, and now resides in Columbus, Ohio.

1976. BENJAMIN NEWTON, born May 21, 1838, married, Sept. 3, 1862, Sarah J. McMahon of Chesterville, Ohio. They live in Columbus, Ohio.

1977. A SON, born Feb. 13, 1840.

1978. SARAH L., born Sept. 8. 1842.
1979. THOMAS DUNLAP, born July 26, 1844, and died in Norwich, Sept. 29, 1861, from a fever taken in camp while in the Union army.
1980. HENRY CLAY, born Jan. 11. 1848, and died Feb. 19th of same year.

1042. GURDON. Rochester, N. Y.

1981. GURDON.

1052. MARVIN. Truxton, N. Y.

1982. J. MONROE, born in Mansfield. Conn., Dec. 6, 1824, married. Nov. 17, 1850, Amelia Sheaver, and lives in Roche acree, Wisconsin. where he is a farmer and joiner.
1983. CHARLES E., born Oct. 9, 1827, married, April 24, 1851, Julia A. Darby, and lives in Truxton, N. Y. He is a farmer.
1984. AURORA F., born Nov. 10. 1831, and now lives with her father in Truxton, N. Y. She is a member of the Baptist church.

1053. DWIGHT. Mansfield Conn.

1985. JOHN, born July 3, 1825. and lives single in Mansfield.
1986. HENRY, born Aug. 6, 1827, married, in 1854, Jane Cadmus, who died in Dec., 1861. He is living (1862) in Eagleville. Conn.
1987. CORNELIA, born July 13. 1829. and lives single in Mansfield.
1988. ANDREW JACKSON, born June 22. 1831, married, March 20, 1856, Eliza Gerrish, and lives in Hartford. Conn.
1989. LOUISA, born May 23, 1833, and lives single in Mansfield.
1990. LUCRETIA, born March 23, 1839.

1056. JOHN. Greensboro, Vt.

1991. ELIZA, born July 29, 1808, married Chauncey Hatch of Belvidere, Ill., in which state they live. She spent some ten years in Florida, and the family are indebted to her for much that appears in this record of her branch of the family.
1992. NATHAN, born Sept. 8. 1810, married Ann Sanders, and lived in Boston, Mass. He died in May. 1842.
1993. MARY, born Feb. 11, 1813, married, Jan. 7, 1835, Benjamin Comings, and lives in Greenboro, Vt.
1994. SAMUEL. born Feb. 22, 1815, and lived in Peru, Ill. He died in Oct., 1838.
1995. JOHN, born Jan. 1, 1818, married Rachel Loring, and lived in Freeport, Ill.
1996. CHARLES B. born Dec. 23, 1820, married Mary Buel, and lived in Perry, N. Y.
1997. ABIGAIL, born Aug. 21, 1823, and died Nov. 12, 1855.
1998. MARTHA, born Aug. 21, 1826, married Charles Smith and lived in East Boston, Mass.

EIGHTH GENERATION.

1057. HENRY.   Greensboro, Vt.

1999. CAROLINE, born Feb. 4, 1808, married, in 1830, Charles Cook, a farmer of Greensboro, where she died Dec. 13, 1857. She had four children: Betsey, Parmalee, John Berry, Charles Henry, and Edward.

2000. ROXANA, born June 14, 1810, married, Jan. 30, 1834, J. N. Stevens of Greensboro, where they are now living on a farm. They have had nine children: Levi Nelson, Henry Huntington, Dan, Caroline, Emily, Helen Esther, Parmalee Augustus, Abby Maria, Josiah, Nelson and Susan Estelle.

2001. BETSEY, born Oct. 6, 1812, married, in June, 1831, Josiah Hall, a farmer, and lives at Cedar Rapids, Iowa. They have five children: Ashbel Huntington, George Weeks, Ellen, Edward C., John P., and Agnes, deceased.

2002. ESTHER BETHIA, born Oct. 20, 1815, married Franklin Blake, a farmer, and went to Mapleton, Kansas. They have had eight children: Sylvia, Bertha Esther, Flora, Henry Franklin, Ellen, Henry, and Esther, the two last, deceased.

2003. HENRY, born June 3, 1818, married, at Craftsbury, Vt., Oct. 5, 1847, Martha Matilda Dustan, who is descended from the Mrs. Dustan of revolutionary fame, and who was born in Craftsbury, Vt., July 10, 1825. He took his medical diploma in Albany, New York, in 1846, and followed the profession of medicine five years, when a bronchial difficulty obliged him to abandon it. He went South in 1851, and now resides in Albany, Ga., where he is a dentist.

2004. ELLEN S., born Dec. 11, 1820, and lives in Greensboro.

2005. PARMALEE F., born July 4, 1825, and lives at Cedar Rapids, Iowa.

2006. EUNICE CARTER, born March 31, 1830, married, July 19, 1855, Edwin Derby, and lives at Cedar Rapids, Iowa. They have had one son, Edwin, now dead.

1081. HARLOW.   Shaftesbury, Vt.

2007. MYRON, born March 20, 1827, married, March 6, 1850, Mary L. Cross, granddaughter of Gen. Samuel Cross. He now owns and improves the old homestead of his grandfather, Amos.

2008. JENETT P., born March 11, 1833, and died in Shaftesbury, Sept. 24, 1839.

2009. HARRET ELLEN, born Aug. 30, 1838, married, Oct. 8, 1856, Horace B. Bottum, and lives in Shaftesbury. They have two children: Harlow Alfred, born July 30, 1857; and a son born Jan. 27, 1862.

1083. GEORGE.   Shaftesbury, Vt.

2010. AMELIA C., born March 16, 1835, and lives (1858) at home. She is a member of the Baptist church.

2011. GEORGE CLARK, born Dec. 20, 1836, and is in a store in Downieville, Cal.

2012. WARD, born Oct. 20, 1838, and is in business with his brother George, in Downieville, Cal.

2013. JULIA ANN, born July 9, 1843, is in Shaftesbury, and a member of the Baptist church. She is fitting herself to teach the ornamental branches of education.

2014. JONAS G., born Nov. 23, 1846, and died Aug. 20, 1848, of scarlet fever.

2015. JENNETT P., born June 19, 1849.

2016. CALVIN GALUSHA, born Aug. 22, 1851.

1081. ELON. Rochester, N. Y.

2017. ALCESTA F., born Oct. 27, 1837, and is living with her father.

2018. ALBERT, born Oct. 16, 1838, is a clerk in Rochester.

2019. SUSAN PAMELA, born Aug. 18, 1841, married, in Dec. 1861, Capt. Horace Hooker, who is now in the Union army.

2020. FRANK, born in July, 1848.

2021. KATE, born in May, 1850.

2022. CARRIE, born Aug. 18, 1852.

2023. WILLIE, born in June, 1854, and died July 28, 1856.

1086. ASA CLARK. Rome, N. Y.

2024. MARY, born Sept. 24, 1816, married, Oct. 31, 1840, Milton Utley, and resides in Westerville, N. Y.

2025. ANSEL, born Aug. 9, 1818, married, Dec. 14, 1848, Caroline Porter, and lives in Rome, N. Y.

2026. ELON, born April 8, 1820, married, Feb. 1, 1843, Mary M. Utley, and lives in Troy, N. Y.

2027. MARTHA, born Feb. 11, 1822, married, Aug. 28, 1856, Rev. S. B. Gregory, and lives in Little Falls, N. Y.

2028. AMANDA, born June 24, 1823, and lives in Rome.

2029. ANN, born March 22, 1825, and died May 2, 1828.

2030. GEORGE, born Jan. 11, 1827, and lives in Rome.

2031. JAY, born March 29, 1829, married, Aug. 27, 1856, Caroline Scott. He fitted for the ministry, at the Hamilton Institute, and was pastor at North Bennington, Vt., which office he resigned April 1, 1860. He has just accepted a call to the Baptist church in Canton, N. Y., where he was settled Oct 1, 1860.

2032. JANE, born April 26, 1831, and lives in Rome.

2033. LAURA, born Feb. 8, 1834, and married, in Rome, Aug. 22, 1860, Rev. J. Tucker, jr., pastor of the church in North Bennington, Vt.

1090. MATTHEW L. Rome, N. Y.

This family were all born in Rome.

2034. HENRY EDWARDS, born April 1, 1827, married, Aug. 10, 1847, Eliza C. Baldwin, daughter of J. S. Baldwin of Pompton, N. J., where she was born Nov. 7, 1829. He is a merchant in Chicago, Ill.

2035. CHARLES RAYMOND, born Jan. 3, 1830, married, Sept. 4, 1849, Julia M., daughter of Charles Hubbard of Troy, N. Y. He was engaged largely in the provision trade in New York city, but is now in business in Chicago, Ill.

EIGHTH GENERATION. 303

2036. CATHERINE MARY. born Feb. 26, 1832, and has been a teacher in the Female Seminary in Troy.

2037. LYNDE CATLIN, born Sept. 17, 1834, and married, Oct. 4, 1859, Clara F., eldest daughter of the late Judge J. B. Thomas of Chicago. She was born Dec. 2. 1847. He is of the firm of Huntington Bros. and Voyell, commission merchants, in Chicago. Ill.

2038. HIRAM LANDON, born Jan. 12, 1838, and died in Rome, N. Y., Aug. 26, 1856.

2039. JAMES ALONZO, born July 4, 1841, and died Jan. 12, 1842.

1091. JAMES. Rome, N. Y.

2040. JOHN HENRY, born Jan. 1, 1830, married, Oct. 15, 1856, Hattie T. Hubbard, and lives in Troy, N. Y.

2041. MATTHEW J., born July 25, 1833, married, April 12, 1855, Hester A. Bigsby, and lives in Utica, N. Y.

2042. POPE CATLIN, born July 30, 1835, and lives in Rome.

2043. MARY ALIDA, born June 13, 1839, and lives in Rome.

2044. WILLIAM M., born July 28, 1841, and died Aug. 26, of the same year.

2045. MARTHA MCKEE, born March 22, 1845, and lives in West Arlington, Vermont.

2046. ALBERT B., born Jan. 25, 1848, and died July 19, 1855.

1095. JACOB GALUSHA. Shaftesbury, Vt.

2047. EDWARD, born July 25, 1832, in Shaftesbury.

2048. ANNA AUGUSTA, born July 9, 1835, in Buffalo city, N. Y., and died Oct. 3, 1855, in Buffalo.

2049. ALGERNON OLIN, born Oct. 26, 1837, in Buffalo city.

2050. CAROLINE MARIA, born July 13, 1843, in Buffalo city.

1098. ALONZO. Chicago, Ill.

2051. SUSANNA MARIA, born in Wallingford, Vt., Nov. 11, 1835, and died in Chicago, Ill., Dec. 22, 1839, of malignant scarlet fever.

2052. STELLA AURELIA, born in Chicago, Dec. 28, 1837, and died in the same place, Dec. 21, 1839, of malignant scarlet fever.

2053. HENRY ALONZO, born in Chicago, March 23, 1840. In 1861 he raised a company of cavalry for the 9th Illinois regiment. In October of that year he was appointed lieutenant in the 4th regiment of U. S. artillery. At the great battle of Shiloh he so signalized his bravery as to be specially mentioned in the report of his battery by his captain.

2054. DANIEL DYER, born in Manchester, Vt., July 25, 1842, and died in Chicago, Jan. 2, 1845, of malignant scarlet fever.

2055. JAY GALUSHA, born in Chicago, Oct. 23, 1844.

2056. FRANCES, born Feb. 2, 1848.

1107. DANIEL GALUSHA. Castile, N. Y.

2057. EDWIN, born Aug. 22, 1823, married March 7, 1844, Jane A. Rathbone, and lives in Rochester, N. Y.

2058. GEORGE B., born Jan. 21, 1827, married, Oct. 3, 1849, Junietta E. Galusha, who died Oct. 29, 1851, in Castile, N. Y., where he is living.

2059. NANCY, born March 15, 1833, married, Sept. 25, 1855, B. B. Higgins, and lives in Perry, N. Y.

2060. MARY, born Aug. 10, 1840.

1108. JONAS. Kalamazoo, Mich.

2061. T. ROMEYN, born Sept. 12, 1829, married first, April 10, 1851, Caroline M. Chapin, who died July 29, 1852. He married second, Nov. 8, 1853, E. M. Fox. He is a physician, and practicing in the same town with his grandfather and father.

2062. CLARISSA A., born March 20, 1836, and died in Perry, N. Y., Sept. 3, 1842.

2063. WILLIAM WESTEL, born Nov. 12, 1840.

1110. MARTIN. Rochester, N. Y.

2064. CLARA, born in New Orleans, Dec. 24, 1845, and lives in Rochester, New York.

2065. MARTIN EDGAR, born in New Orleans, April 23, 1849, and died in Sept., 1849.

2066. JULIA EMMA, born same day and place, and died May 31, 1850.

2067. FLORENCE, born in Rochester, N. Y., May 30, 1853.

1119. SOLOMON THEODORE. Syracuse, N. Y.

2068. LANA ANN, born in Lee, Mass., in March 1833.

2069. WILLIAM, born in Lee, Jan., 1836, and died in 1845.

2070. MARTHA, born in Syracuse, N. Y., in Aug., 1846.

2071. LOUIS THEODORE, born in Syracuse in 1847, and died in 1852.

1121. WILLIAM OZIAS. Milan, Ohio.

The first two of this family were born in Lynn, Mass., the rest in Milan.

2072. HARRIET ELIZABETH, born Aug. 24, 1841.

2073. SARAH MARIA, born April 25, 1844.

2074. CHARLES WILLIAM, born April 19, 1846, and died in April, 1847.

2075. WILLIAM JOSEPH, born Oct. 23, 1848, and died in December of the same year.

2076. MARGARET, born March 9, 1850.

2077. EDWARD THEODORE, born Oct. 17, 1852.

2078. RALPH WALTER, born Jan. 19, 1857.

EIGHTH GENERATION.   305

1132. OZIAS.   Ogdensburg, N.Y.

2079. CHARLES W., born in 1838.
2080. FREEMAN F., born in 1840.
2081. SARAH A., born in 1842.
2082. MINERVA E., born in 1844.
2083. BYRON O., born in 1849.

The above family, and the three following, are as reported to Dr. Joshua, the author being unable to learn anything additional.

1133. CHARLES R.

2084. MARY J., born in 1842.
2085. JAMES J., born in 1844.
2086. CHARLES, born in 1847.

1134. FRANKLIN W.

2087. SOPHIA A., born in 1844.
2088. FLORA, born in 1845.
2089. MARY E., born in 1848.
2090. FRANKLIN, born in 1849.
2091. WILLIAM E., born in 1852.

1137. EDWIN G.   Canton, N.Y.

2092. NELLIE E., born in 1851.

1151. ELISHA.   Mobile, Ala.

2093. JOHN AUGUSTUS, entered Union College, from Mobile, in 1841, and died of yellow fever, in Mobile in 1843, at about nineteen years of age.

2094. CAROLINE ELIZABETH, about three years younger than her brother, married a Mr. Griggs of Mobile.

1156. ENOCH SMITH, REV.   Danbury, Conn.

2095. LUCY, born in Tazewell county, Ill., May 9. 1838, and died of consumption, in Danbury, Dec. 14, 1859. She died in hope of a blessed immortality. She was a member of the Congregational church in Danbury.

2096. FRANCES, born in Tazewell county, Ill., Sept. 5, 1840, and was educated at Mount Holyoke Seminary. She married, in Danbury, Conn., Sept. 9, 1862, Henry T. Hoyt of Danbury.

2097. WILLIAM SMITH, born in Clinton, Conn., March 24, 1843, and died in Danbury, Feb. 13, 1859. This young man was early a subject of grace, and was greatly endeared to his acquaintance for his estimable qualities. He was a member of the Congregational church, and died in the triumphs of Christian faith.

2098. ELIZA MATILDA, born in Danbury, March 5, 1855.
2099. ANDREW BURR, born in Danbury, July 24, 1857.
2099.[1] A SON, born in 1862.

1159. NATHAN BELCHER. Elbridge, N. Y.

2100. JOHN, born Oct 6, 1834, married, in May, 1857, and lives in Sharon, Ill.
  2101. MARIA, born Sept. 4, 1836.
  2102. ANDREW, born Aug. 29, 1838.
  2103. MATILDA, born Sept. 24, 1842.
  2104. THOMAS RIGNEY, born May 9, 1844, died, Nov. 11, 1844.
  2105. ELISHA, born Oct. 18, 1845.
  2106. GILBERT, born March 15, 1848, and died Nov. 27, 1848.

1164. GEORGE. Savannah, Ga.

2107. GEORGIANA, an only child, died Sept. 25, 1842, at her grandfather's in Griswold.

1166. ANDREW. Springfield, Mass.

2108. ANDREW TYLER, born Feb. 26, 1842, is now (1862) in the Union army.
2109. GEORGE BUTLER, born May 9, 1844, and died Aug. 22, 1845.
2110. CHARLES BUTLER, born April 5, 1846, and died May 6, 1846.
2111. HENRY, born Jan 20, 1849, and died April 9, 1850.
2112. WILLIAM FRANCIS, born Feb. 18, 1850.

1168. WILLIAM. Griswold, Conn.

2113. SARAH, born Oct. 4, 1836. She died in Springfield, Mass., Sept. 25, 1862.
2114. HANNAH, born March 21, 1840, is now (1862) teaching in Norwich city.
2115. DANIEL, born July 31, 1844, and is now (1862) in the Union army.
2116. GEORGE, born Sept. 6, 1846, and died Dec. 6, 1846.

1172. FRANCIS. Lysander, N. Y.

2117. DAUGHTER.
2118. DAUGHTER.

1173. JUSTINIAN. South Brookfield, N. Y.

2119. ELIZA, born Dec. 18, 1824, married, Feb. 10, 1851, Dewitt C. Coon, and lives in South Brookfield. They have three children: Ambrosia, Eulalio, and Franklin.
  2120. MARY E., born Jan. 19, 1828, married, Aug. 25, 1847, Rhodes Barker, and lives in South Brookfield. They have three children: Charles, Elizabeth, and George.
  2121. EMELINE E., born Aug. 22, 1829, married, Oct. 12, 1852, Rev. Isaac L. Ogden, and lives in Alleghany, N. Y. They have four children: Walter, Rollo, Florence, and Nelson.
  2122. FRANKLIN C., born Dec. 22, 1832, married, April 12, 1856, Louisa Langworthy, and lives in West Edmeston, N. Y., where he is engaged in the dairy business.

EIGHTH GENERATION. 307

2123. ADELAIDE, born April 4, 1836, married, Feb. 14. 1856, Amos Cheesebrough, M. D., of South Brookfield. They have two children: Clarence, and Carol.

2124. LOUISA, born Aug. 18, 1841. and lives in South Brookfield, N. Y.

1178.² LEMUEL CHENEY. Baldwinsville, N. Y.

2125. LAURA ELIZA, born Dec. 25, 1852.
2126. CHARLES, born Nov. 17, 1855.
2127. ARTHUR, born Feb. 4, 1857.

1182. GEORGE LEE, (M. D.) East Hampton, L. I.

2128. BENJAMIN HOAGLAND, born Sept. 21. 1835, married, in Brooklyn, N. Y., Oct. 13, 1857, Sarah R., eldest daughter of Col. Stephen Haynes. He is in business in New York city.

2129. CHARLES GARDNER, born March 3, 1838, and died Sept. 8, 1848.

2130. ABEL, born Oct 14. 1840, graduated in medicine in 1862, and is now in the practice of his profession in Englishtown, N. J.

2131. GEORGE, born April 9, 1850.
2132. MARY ELIZABETH, born Dec. 19, 1853.

1184. EZRA ABEL, (D. D.) Auburn, N. Y.

2133. CHARLES, born May 28. 1840. and died Dec. 28, 1840.
2134. ANNA MASON, born Oct. 22, 1841, and is a member of the Second Presbyterian church in Auburn.
2135. CHESTER, born Oct. 19, 1843, and is also a member of the above church.
2136. CATHERINE, born Aug. 12, 1845.
2137. SAMUEL VAN VECHTEN, born Nov. 10, 1852.
2138. MARTHA HYDE, born Sept. 9, 1857.

1186. SILAS. Lackawaxen, Pa.

2139. JOEL, born at Lackawaxen.
2140. MARTHA, born at Lackawaxen, Dec. 18, 1849.
2141. ASHER, born at Lackawaxen, July 8, 1851.
2142. MARIA, born in Indiana, Jan. 24. 1853.
2143. CHESTER EZRA, born in Pennsylvania, June 22, 1856.

1187. CHARLES, REV. Hoverleyville, Pa.

2144. ELLEN, born in Pennsylvania, Oct. 23, 1848.
2145. EZRA CHESTER, born in Pennsylvania, May 21, 1850.
2146. CHARLES WARNER, born in Orwell, Pa., Dec. 11, 1852.
2147. JULIUS FOSTER, born in Dushire, Nov. 5, 1855.

1195. ERASTUS.   Brooklyn, N. Y.

2148. THOMAS, born in Brooklyn, N. Y., April 29, 1856.
2148.¹ JAMES.
2148.² MARY.
2148.³ ELIZABETH.

1196. HORACE F.   New York City.

This family were all born in Columbus, Ohio.
2149. MARY ELIZABETH, born July 15, 1835, and is now living in New York.
2150. ELLEN AURELIA, born July 30, 1838, and is now living in New York.
2151. HORACE HOWARD, born Dec. 6, 1839, and died Aug. 25, 1840. There are, also, in this family, three adopted children who will be known only as having the name of Huntington.
2151.¹ OREN WILLIAM, born at Cuyahoga Falls, Ohio, Oct. 22, 1849.
2151.² HATTIE MARIA, born in New York city, May 23, 1856.
2151.³ MINNIE JANETTE.

1198. MILES THOMAS.   Canaan, Conn.

2152. SARAH E., born July 28, 1821, and married, in 1860, William Burton, and lives in Albany.
2153. HORACE, born July 11, 1844, and died Nov. 30, 1845.

1199. JOHN.   Canaan, Conn.

2154. MILES THOMAS, born Aug. 11, 1847.
2155. HORACE, born Aug. 10, 1851.
2156. MARTHA, born April 10, 1853.

1204. BENJAMIN.   Rochester, N. Y.

2157. HELEN, born in 1837.
2158. WILLIAM, born in 1842.
2159. EMMA, born in 1846.

1207. ISAIAH.   Springfield, N. Y.

2160. GEORGIANA, born in 1856.
2161. ISAIAH, born in 1857.

1213. STEPHEN NEWTON.   Hanover, N. H.

2162. ELLEN M., born Aug. 8, 1847.
2163. FANNY C., born July 30, 1853.

1214. WALES MUNRO. (M. D.)   Pittsford, N. Y.

2164. JAMES HOPKINS, born Nov. 20, 1848, in Pittsford.
2165. SARAH ELIZABETH, born Dec. 23, 1853.
2166. CLARISSA M., born Nov. 4, 1859.

EIGHTH GENERATION. 309

1216. HENRY SLADE. Penfield, N. Y.

2167. HORACE LOVETT, born Feb. 3, 1854.

1224. SAMUEL DAVIS. Blue Island, Ill.

2168. WALTER JAMES.
2169. HENRY ROBINSON.

1228. SHUBAEL. Coventry, Pa.

2170. EMMA.
2171. EMILY.
2172. HIRAM.
2173. JANE.
2174. HANNAH.
2175. ALMOND.

1234. ELIJAH. Perrysburg, Ohio.

2176. SARAH, born Feb., 1825, married Edward Olney, professor in Kalamazoo.
2177. CELIA, born Feb. 3, 1827, is a teacher in Sandusky City, Ohio.
2178. CLINTON, born in 1829, and died in 1836.
2179. LAURA, born June 13, 1835, and died in 1856.
2180. MARY, born Sept. 29, 1838, and is a teacher in Perrysburg. Ohio.
2181. HENRY CLAY, born June 20, 1841, is a printer, and lives in Perrysburg, Ohio.
2182. JUDSON, born Nov. 28, 1843.

1235. CHRISTOPHER. West Randolph.

This family were all born in Braintree, Vt.
2183. MARTHA TILSON, born July 19, 1837.
2184. ELIJAH, born Oct. 30, 1839.
2185. EDMUND T., born May 3, 1842.
2186. JOSEPH G., born Feb. 19, 1847, and died May 17, 1847.
2187. SUSAN M., born May 1, 1854.

1243. ADONIRAM JUDSON. Washington City.

2188. ANN JUDSON, born Aug. 2, 1845.

1246. SAMUEL D. Adrian, Mich.

2189. WILLIAM E., born in 1824, and has been in California.
2190. JAMES H., born in 1826, and has been in California.
2191. EDWIN M., born in 1829, and married, in 1851, Lucy E. Reeves. They live in Adrian, Mich.
2192. HIRAM S., born in 1832, married, in 1854, Sarah Gregg, and lives in Adrian, Mich.
2193. SARAH J., born in 1835 and died in Palmyra, N. Y., in 1836.

2194. MARQUIS D. S., born in 1841, and died in Manchester, N. Y., in 1846.
2195. SARAH J., born in 1843, and died in Manchester in 1846.
2196. ALBERT H., born in 1846.
2197. CHARLES H., born in 1850, and died in Palmyra, N. Y., in 1851.

1247. HORACE JEDIDIAH. Rochester, N. Y.

2198. JOHN M., born in 1831, and died in Minden, N. Y., in 1845.
2199. LYDIA A., born in 1834, and died in Rochester, N. Y., in 1854.
2200. SAMUEL M., born in 1838, and is in Rochester.
2201. BENJAMIN M., born in 1840, and has lived in Buffalo, N. Y.
2202. LUCIA, born in 1843, and lives in Rochester.

1248. MARSHAL. Adrian, Mich.

2203. SARAH E., born in 1837, and died in Adrian, in 1844.
2204. WILLIAM J., born in 1842.
2205. MARTHA A., born in 1850.

1250. SETH. Hatley, C. E.

2206. LUCIUS SETH, born May 26, 1827, married, in 1853, Miriam Wood, and lives in Shefford, Canada East, about 35 miles from his father. He is a lawyer.
2207. CAROLINE AMELIA, born May 20, 1829.
2208. CLARISSA ADELIA, born May 20, 1829, married, May 15, 1849, Jesse Hazen, and has three daughters.
2209. THOMAS FREDERIC, born April 5, 1831, and died in March, 1832.
2210. FREDERIC ALEXANDER, born Sept. 29, 1836.
2211. ALMIRA, born June 7, 1838.
2212. MARY EMMA, born April 24, 1842.

1252. JOEL. Miss.

2213. ELIZA, born in 1841, and is in Canada.
2214. OSCAR, born in 1843.

1255. LEVI. Wis.

2215. JOEL THOMAS, born in 1844.

1257. HEMAN. Lowell, Mass.

2216. SYBEL MARIA, born Nov. 25, 1833, and died May 15, 1834.
2217. SOLON HEMAN, born Sept. 7, 1835, and died Dec. 13, 1836.
2218. HARRIET BOYNTON, born July 9, 1837, and died Nov. 4, 1841.
2219. JOHN P., born Nov. 29, 1839.
2220. JAMES HENRY, born Nov. 1, 1841, and was in the Union army.
2221. HANNAH AMELIA, born Feb. 19, 1844, and died April 19, 1847.
2222. ELIJAH BARDWELL, born Sept. 7, 1846, and died April 20, 1847.
2223. MARY ABIGAIL, born Nov. 15, 1848.
2224. MARTHA EMMA, born Sept. 12, 1850.

1258. ANSON. Wauseon, Ohio.

2225. GEORGE ANSON, born in 1829, and died Aug. 8, 1848, in Lowell, Mass

1260. JAMES. Green Lake, Wis.

2226. GEORGE HEMAN, born April 13, 1848.
2227. JAMES HATCH, born Feb. 9, 1850.
2228. ABBY HANNAH, born April 22, 1852.
2229. ALICE C. HATTA, born Aug. 13, 1856.

1261. THOMAS. Canada East.

This family were all born in Compton where they now (1857) reside.
2230. PHILLIP F., born Dec. 8, 1827, and died Oct. 3, 1844.
2231. CAROLINE S. J., born Aug. 9, 1829, and died Nov. 1, 1848.
2232. WILLY JOSIAH, born Feb. 19, 1832.
2233. THOMAS, born Jan. 11, 1834.
2234. LEVI, born Oct. 15, 1835, and died Feb. 26, 1841.
2235. CHARLES, born Nov. 13, 1837, and died of consumption, Dec. 20, 1860.
2236. CHARLOTTE, born Nov. 20, 1839, and died Aug. 11, 1853.
2237. LEANDER, born July 22, 1843.

1264. JOSIAH G. Compton, C. E.

This family were all born in Compton, where they still live.
2238. WALTER, born Oct. 29, 1833.
2239. IRA, born April 3, 1835.
2240. DIMIS, born July 24, 1837.
2241. WILLIE, born April 4, 1850, and died May 30, 1860.
2242. ALVIRA, born Jan. 16, 1852.

1265. BENJAMIN. Compton, C. E.

2242.¹ ESTHER, born April 20, 1833.
2243. MARSHALL, born Aug. 19, 1834.
2244. ACHSA, born Sept. 4, 1837, and died Feb. 7, 1860.
2245. FELICIA, born Aug. 4, 1843.
2246. GILBERT, born Nov. 12, 1845.

1268. SAMUEL BLISS. Newburyport, Mass.

2247. ELIZABETH BARRE, born May 15, 1848.
2248. ISABELLA, born Oct. 10, 1850.

1272. WILLIAM AVERY. Newburyport, Mass.

2249. FRANK W., born June 19, 1847.
2250. EDWARD P., born March 7, 1851.

1281. CHARLES. New Market, Ohio.

2251. JANE, born in 1831, married Dwight W. Keyes, and went to Ogdensburg, N. Y.
2252. CHARLES P., born in 1833, married Sarah Keyes.
2253. GEORGE E., born in 1835, married, in 1854, Juana Ramirez. He went to California, but returned to Willimantic.

1284. ERASTUS. Norwich, Conn.

2254. SARAH ELIZABETH, born April 15, 1845.
2255. WILLIAM FREDERIC, born Feb. 10, 1848.
2256. CHARLES WHITTEMORE, born July 21, 1849.
2257. EDWARD VICTOR, born May 15, 1852, and died Feb. 12, 1853.
2258. HARRIET ROSALIE, born Oct. 10, 1856, and died June 16, 1857.

1285. EDWIN. Osage, Iowa.

2259. JAMES BINGHAM, born in Windham, Conn., March 5, 1840.
2260. JOHN, born in Chaplin, Conn., Feb. 27, 1842.
2261. HARRIET, born in Manchester, Pa., Feb. 12, 1844.
2262. ALICE, born in Manchester, March 26, 1846.
2263. CORA, born March 14, 1848, and died Sept. 27, 1849.
2264. EDWIN, born Dec. 20, 1851.
2265. EVERETT GUILD, born July 28, 1853.
2266. HELEN EDITH, born in Howard County, Iowa, Sept. 6, 1856.
2267. NANCY URANIA, born in Osage, Iowa, Feb. 13, 1859.

1286. HORATIO. Osage, Iowa.

2268. OLIVER PALMER, born Nov. 13, 1841, and died Aug. 3, 1846.
2269. EUGENE LESLIE, born April 18, 1844.
2270. ELIZA ADELLE, born Sept 23, 1846.
2271. MARY ELIZABETH, born Feb. 12, 1849.
2272. OLIVER PALMER, born June 11, 1851.
2273. HORATIO ELEAZER, born Sept. 24, 1853.
2274. WILLIAM H. STEWART, born June 12, 1857.
2275. JULIA.
2275.¹ A SON.

1290. ABNER. Worcester, Mass.

2276. CLARISSA, born Jan., 1836.
2277. MARY E., born in May, 1837, and died in April, 1840.
2278. BETSEY W., born in Feb., 1839, and died in April, 1840.
2279. WALDO, born in April, 1842, and died in the following September.
2280. MARY ANN, born in April, 1845.
2281. CHARLES, born in Aug., 1849.

EIGHTH GENERATION. 313

1294. ALBERT. Auburn, Mass.

2282. ELLA M., born in May, 1841.
2283. ALBERT W., born in April, 1843.
2284. ELIZABETH, born in Jan., 1852.

1297. EBENEZER HARTSHORN. Madison, Wis.

2285. LUCRETIA MINERVA, born in Independence, N. Y., Jan. 21, 1845.
2286. MARY M., born in Independence, June 26, 1849.
2287. ELLEN E., born in Independence, Oct. 3, 1851, and died Oct. 9, 1851.
2288. FRANK REYNOLDS, born in Madison, Wis., Jan. 23, 1858.
2289. HATTIE, born in Madison, March 19, 1860.

1298. ELEAZER PECK. Bingham, Pa.

2290. FREDERIC PORTER, born July 11, 1843.
2291. JULIA MARIA, born Jan. 4, 1846.
2292. CHARLOTTE SOPHIA, born Dec. 24, 1848.
2293. OLIVE PECK, born Sept. 15, 1850.
2294. LEWIS KOSSUTH, born Sept. 23, 1851.
2295. EBENEZER, born Sept. 27, 1853.
2295.¹ SON.

1299. JARED HYDE. Townshend, Vt.

2296. MARGARET, born Jan. 12, 1843.

1302. DEWITT CLINTON. Rochester, N. Y.

2297. CHARLES FINNEY, born June 18, 1855.

1306. JOHN. New London, Conn.

2298. LE ROY SUNDERLAND, born July 19, 1827, and is living in New London, and still unmarried. He is organist and teacher of Music.
2299. CHARLES WESTLEY, born March 13, 1829. He has been successful as a teacher of vocal and instrumental music. He has been for years organist in the South Congregational church in Hartford. He married, July 6, 1858, Martha E. Eddy. In addition to his connection with the South church in Hartford, he is professor of music in the state normal school in New Britain.
2300. MARY JANE, born Dec. 20, 1831, married Oct. 9, 1856, Theodore Beach, and lives in South Bergen, N. J. They have two sons, Charles Huntington, born Oct. 2, 1857, and Melvin, born Nov. 24, 1859.
2301. ELIZA, born May 18, 1834, married, July 2, 1854, Henry Osborne of New London, and lives in that city. They have two children: Jenny, born June 25, 1855, and died Jan 22, 1857; and Frederick, born Dec. 3, 1857.
2302. JOHN, born May 16, 1836, and lives in New London, single. He is a machinist, but now (1862) is in the Union army.
2303. ANNA, born Dec. 20, 1839, married, Feb. 5, 1861, Lewis Wilkinson,

40

a manufacturer of fire arms. He is now in Boston. Mass., where he is inspector of arms, and a contractor.

2304. BENJAMIN FRANKLIN, born July 6, 1840, and is living at home in New London.

1307. FREDERIC A.   Mexico, N. Y.

2305. JAMES S., born Sept. 8, 1823, and died July 16, 1825.

2306. JAMES, born Nov. 8, 1826, and died on the 23d of same month.

2307. LAURELIA A., born Dec. 12, 1827, married, June 5, 1853, Jonas Smedley. Their children are: Florence A., born June 26, 1854, and died Oct. 11, 1856; and Frederick A., born Oct. 1, 1857.

2308. MARY E., born Sept. 12, 1830, married, Nov. 19, 1848, Ellery C. Gillette. Their children are: Adelaide L., born Sept. 27, 1851; and Dora A., born Aug. 26, 1856.

2309. LAURA A., born June 23, 1833, married, Nov. 14, 1850, Lester Seeley.

2310. FRANCES L., born Oct. 31, 1835, and died March 16, 1837.

2311. FREDERICK A., born Jan. 26, 1839, and died Feb. 13, 1841.

1312. R. G. H.   New York City.

2312. RANDOLPH, born Dec. 8, 1829, married, Sept. 6, 1854, Louisa Elizabeth Hayes, only daughter of Gad Hayes of Bloomfield, N. Y., who was born June 30, 1833. He is in the drug business, in New York city.

2313. SAMUEL HENRY, born Dec. 22, 1831, married, in Richmond, Va., Jan. 5, 1856, Susan Denin, the actress. He died in Elmira, N. Y., July 16, 1861.

2314. FRANCES BALDWIN, born July 22, 1833, and still lives with her father in New York city.

2315. ROBERT GOODLOW, born May 3, 1836, and died of dysentery, at Whampoa, China, Dec. 7, 1855.

2316. ALBERT, born July 18, 1839, and died in New York, June 10, 1858.

2317. ISABELLA GRAHAM, born July 30, 1844, and died in New Haven, Sept. 2, 1858. "This beautiful child for months has been wasting away by consumption. Although her sufferings were severe at times, yet not a murmur escaped her lips. She often spoke of her trust in Christ. In the morning, after a very painful night, she said to a friend who had sometimes prayed with her, 'I wanted you to pray with me last night. I could not pray aloud —I could only just think my prayers!' During the day she was more comfortable, and talked of Heaven with delight, saying to the friends about her, 'Meet me there.'"

1316. AMBROSE W.   Union Square, N. Y.

2318. ESTHER, born April 24, 1819, and died March 24, 1821.

2319. JANE, born Sept. 12, 1821.

2320. BENJAMIN F., born Aug. 2, 1823, is living in California.

2321. CHARLES GERALDI, born May 31, 1826, married, Sept. 14, 1854, A.

EIGHTH GENERATION. 315

Brown, who was born in Platteville, Wis., in 1838. They are living (1862) in Galena, Ill.

2322. ALFRED, born May 9, 1829, is now (1862) in the Union army.

2323. ADELIA ANN, born Jan. 6, 1835, married, Feb. 2, 1860, Chauncey H. Booth, who is now (1862) in the Union army. They have one son, Clarence Huntington, born April 23, 1862.

2324. ELIZABETH, born March 10, 1837, and died Sept. 27, 1838.

2325. BRUCE M., born Oct. 31, 1843.

2326. EMMET W., born April 3, 1848.

2327. HENRY J., born July 17, 1850.

1318. ELISHA. Wauseon, Ohio.

2328. WILLIAM RUFUS, born Aug. 26, 1823, married Mary H. Butler of Delta, Ohio.

2329. EVALINE PARTHENA, born Aug. 2, 1826, and died July 13, 1828.

2330. LUCIA, born July 1, 1829, married Charles N. Clark, and had one son, Edward, who died Dec. 2, 1860, aged seven years. They live in Clinton, Ohio.

2331. ELIZABETH STEVENS, born Nov. 28, 1832, married Lowell W. Taft, has one son, and lives in Michigan.

2332. CHARLES GUSTAVUS, born July 4, 1835.

2333. MARY HILLS, born Sept. 9, 1838, married James F. Hunt of Wauseon, and has one son, Alfred Clement.

2334. EDWARD WADE, born Dec. 1, 1841, and died March 30, 1845.

2335. ALBERT WALES, born Sept. 4, 1846.

1319. APOLLOS. Sandusky City, Ohio.

2336. MARY LOUISA, born June 24, 1826, and died Jan. 21, 1834.

2337. EVALINE CORNELIA, born Jan. 29, 1828, married Henry H. Smith, and lives in Rodman, Jefferson county, N. Y. Their only child, a son, is dead.

2338. LAURA BUCKLEY, born Sept. 20, 1829, and died March 30, 1852.

2339. GEORGE W., born Aug. 24, 1831, and died Aug. 24, 1832.

2340. ELIZABETH S., born July 4, 1833, and died Sept., 1847.

2341. JANE ROWLAND, born Aug. 8, 1837, married, in Sandusky city, June 28, 1861, John McKelvey. They have one daughter, Janet Huntington, born April 2, 1862.

2342. HENRY CLAY, born Nov. 21, 1841.

1323. WILLIAM. Pisgah Grove, Iowa.

2343. CHAUNCEY DYER, born Oct. 20, 1806, married, Nov. 28, 1825, Clarissa Bull, who was born April 6, 1806.

2344. NANCY, born Oct. 20, 1806, and died March, 1807.

2345. DIMICK BAKER, born May 26, 1808, and is a sort of military chieftain among the Mormons, as occasional reports disclose.

2346. PRECENDIA LATHROP, born Sept. 10, 1810.

2347. ADALINE ELIZABETH, born Aug. 3, 1815, and died Nov. 26, 1826.

2348. WILLIAM D., born Feb. 8, 1818.
2349. ZINA DIANTHA. born Jan. 31, 1821.
2350. OLIVER BOARDMAN, born Oct. 14, 1823.
2351. JOHN DICKENSON, born Feb. 11, 1827, married, March 8, 1851, Adelaide L. Danks, who was born at Manneville, N. Y., March 15, 1831. He is engaged in the telegraph office; and is a teacher of penmanship and drawing in Watertown, N. Y.

1324. DYER. Watertown, N. Y.

This family were all born in Watertown.

2352. ANN ELIZA, born July 16, 1821, married, May 15, 1854, Solon D. Hungerford, of Watertown, and has one child, Robert Bradnor, born July 8, 1857.

2353. MARY SUSAN, born Aug. 12, 1824, married, Oct. 14, 1851, Joseph Addison, lawyer, and has one child, Mary Ann, born June 7, 1856.

2354. GEORGE CLARK, born Sept. 13, 1828.

2355. RICHARD HENRY, born Nov. 14, 1834, in New York city.

1325. JOHN LATHROP. Watertown, N. Y.

This family were all born in Watertown, N. Y.

2356. JOHN JAY, born Sept. 9, 1816, married, April 15, 1850, Mary Ann Harbottle. He died in Watertown, Oct. 30, 1856.

2357. CYNTHIA PRECENDIA, born April 11, 1818, and died July 13, 1841.

2358. ALDEN, born June 5, 1820, and died July 1, 1820.

2359. VICTORINE ROSALIA, born July 23, 1821, married, Oct. 3, 1841, John Guy Harbottle of Watertown. She had one son, George V., born Sept. 1, 1842, who died Nov. 29, 1856. She died June 9, 1843.

2360. WILLIAM LATHROP, born Aug. 25, 1823, married, Nov. 25, 1847, at Depauville, N. Y., Mary Jane Johnson, who died early in 1862. He is a merchant now residing at Depauville, N. Y.

2361. HIRAM LORD, born Nov. 17, 1825, married, in Scarboro, Me., Oct. 4, 1848, Elizabeth S. Milliken, who died in New York city, Jan. 16, 1854. He married again, in Brooklyn, N. Y., Oct. 4, 1858, Anna, daughter of W. W. Powell of Brooklyn. He resides in Brooklyn where he is engaged in manufacturing gentlemen's furnishing goods.

2362. MORRISON, born April 1, 1828, and died April 11, 1828.

1326. HIRAM.

2363. KIMBALL COLUMBUS, now living at South Danvers, Mass.

1327. AMBROSE WOODWARD.

2364. JULIA, born Sept. 4, 1819, married, Oct. 9, 1845, William Adams Sigourney of Adams, N. Y., where they reside.

2365. AMBROSE PERLEY, born Jan. 17, 1823.

2366. HORACE CHERRY, born Nov. 7, 1831, married, July 10, 1855, Mary A. Dake, who was born April 2, 1832. They live in Watertown.

EIGHTH GENERATION.   317

2367. EVELINE ANN, born July 7, 1835, married, in Watertown. May 15, 1855, Robert Hitchcock.

1329. CYRUS THOMPSON. Watertown, N. Y.

2368. HENRY, born Sept. 10, 1825, and married, March 26, 1851.
2369. CHARLES, born Feb. 15, 1827, married, Dec. 26, 1856, Helen M. Oakes.
2370. ELIZA P., born Nov. 3, 1829, married, Feb. 20, 1855, a Goulding.
2371. HIRAM C., born July 29, 1836.
2372. JOHN W., born Jan. 22, 1844.

1330. HENRY WILLIAM. Catahoula, La.

2373. JULIA, born Aug. 8, 1818, married Henry D. Mandeville, a lawyer and planter in Louisiana. She died July 8, 1851, leaving three children.
2374. HENRY, born July 25, 1820, and lives in Louisiana.
2375. ARCHIBALD, born Sept. 5, 1822, and died April 2, 1841.
2376. MARY, born Nov. 14, 1824, and married W. Haug, a physician. They are living in Catahoula, La.
2377. FLORENCE, born Dec. 12, 1826, married, May 16, 1850, H. H. Emerson, M. D., of Louisiana. She died Feb. 12, 1853, having one son.
2378. SAMUEL, born Feb. 25, 1829, and is now living in Louisiana.
2379. A DAUGHTER, born Oct. 31, 1832, and died Nov. 14th of the same year.
2380. HORACE, born Jan. 31, 1834, and died Jan. 25, 1838.
2381. HELEN DUNBAR, born Aug. 6, 1836, is married, and lives in New Orleans.
2382. EDITH, born June 7, 1838, and is dead.

1333. SAMUEL HOWARD, HON. Hartford, Conn.

2383. CATHERINE BRINLEY, born Jan. 1, 1837.
2384. MARIA CHAMPION, born Dec. 27, 1838.
2385. ROBERT WATKINSON, born Dec. 3, 1840, and is now (1862) a lieutenant in the U. S. N.
2386. SAMUEL, born Dec. 17, 1842, is a member of the senior class in Yale College.
2387. HENRY KENT, born March 27, 1844, entered Yale College in 1862.
2388. SARAH BLAIR, born Nov. 30, 1847.
2389. ELIZABETH ADAMS, born Nov. 30, 1847.

1334. HEZEKIAH. Hartford, Conn.

This family were all born in Hartford.
2389.[1] ELIZABETH SUMNER, born March 3, 1858, and died May 12, 1858.
2389.[2] CATHERINE SUMNER, born April 19, 1859.
2389.[3] GEORGE SUMNER, born March 20, 1861.

1336. FRANCIS JUNIUS. Hartford, Conn.

2390. HELEN, born Jan. 3, 1836, and died Feb. 18, 1839.
2391. FRANCIS, born Nov. 2, 1837, and died Sept. 3, 1838.
2392. FRANCIS, born Sept. 1, 1839, and died April 28, 1842.
3293. WILLIAM WHETTEN, born Dec. 9, 1841.
2394. EDWARD BOUVERIE, born Feb. 5, 1844.
2395. MARGARET KENT, born Jan. 5, 1846.
2396. ARCHIBALD DUNBAR, born Nov. 26, 1851.

1337. ROGER, HON. Norwich, Conn.

2397. HARRIET DENISON, born Jan. 9, 1815, and died May 22, 1816, in Norwich.
2398. JAMES DENISON, born Jan. 25, 1817, served an apprenticeship at the tin business in Meriden, where he he still lives single.
2399. MARY ANN, born March 30, 1819, and lives with her mother in Norwich, unmarried.
2400. LYDIA LAMBERT, born Nov. 6, 1821, and died Feb. 22, 1824.
2401. LOUIS CHARLES LAMBERT, born April 26, 1824, married, Dec. 20, 1848, Mary L. Tuite of St. Martins, W. I., where he lives and is engaged in the manufacture of salt.
2402. JOHN HOSDICK, born July 7, 1827, and died Oct. 23, 1828.
2403. AMELIA MATILDA, born Nov. 15, 1829, married, in Norwich, Dec. 9, 1857, C. C. Thomas, M. D., of Augusta, Ga., who was a surgeon with Cols. Calhoun and Gadsden in Mexico, and is now (1862) a surgeon in the Southern army.
2404. GILBERT CLEMENT, born April 9, 1841, and is now (1862) with his mother in Norwich.

1343. SIMON, REV.. Walsingham, C. W.

2405. WILLIAM EDWARD, born in 1834, and is married.
2406. JAMES EDGERTON, born in 1839.
2407. A TWIN with the above.

1344. DANIEL LATHROP. Yantic, Norwich.

2408. MARY EDGERTON, born Oct. 3, 1830, married, Oct 9, 1854, Lewis A., son of Lewis Hyde of Norwich. They have four children : Mary Anna, Lewis Huntington, Susan Huntington, and William Trumbull.
2409. WILLIAM TRUMBULL, born July 21, 1832, entered Yale College in 1855, but left in the Junior year, from ill health. He is now (1861) in Toledo.
2410. HENRY GREEN, born Oct. 26, 1834, married, June 20, 1861, Sarah Ruggles, daughter of Samuel Gladding of Providence. He is in business in Norwich city.
2411. SUSAN CLEVELAND, born March 12, 1837.

EIGHTH GENERATION. 319

2112. ANNA A. L., born Aug. 15, 1839, and died Nov. 20, 1846.
2113. DANIEL LATHROP, born April 28, 1841, and died Sept. 8, 1843.
2114. DANIEL LATHROP, born May 26, 1845, and died Oct. 25, 1845.

1347. EDWARD A., DEA.   Norwich, Conn.

2115. HARRIET E., born June 27, 1851.
2116. MARY ELDRIDGE, born Dec. 29, 1854.

1350. GEORGE CABOT.   Kelley's Island, Ohio.

2117. GEORGE, born Aug. 12, 1834, died Aug. 29, 1834.
2118. SARAH W., born June 19, 1836, died June 30, 1836.
2119. ERASTUS, born Aug. 15, 1838.
2120. SIMON, born Dec. 15, 1839, and is now (1862) in the Union army.
2121. DAVID KELLEY, born March 28, 1845.
2122. JOSEPH ALFRED, born Feb. 10, 1850.

1352. JOSEPH HYDE.   Norwich City, Conn.

2123. SARAH WILLIAMS, born in Brunswick, Ohio, June 27, 1837.
2124. GEORGE FREDERIC, born in Brunswick, Ohio, Feb. 27, 1839, and died April 30, 1855.
2125. CHARLES LYMAN FOSTER, born in West Boxford, Mass., Aug. 3, 1841, and is now in the Union Army.

1354. HENRY DWIGHT.   Cincinnati, Ohio.

This family were all born in Cincinnati.
2126. MARGARETTA, born March 5, 1847, and died March 29, 1849.
2127. EDWARD HALLAM, born July 12, 1849.
2128. FRANK, born Aug. 4, 1851.
2129. HENRY WILLIAMS, born Jan. 26, 1855.

1355. JOHN CALDWELL.   Cincinnati, Ohio.

2430. ELIZABETH MITCHELL, born July 5, 1849.
2431. DWIGHT WILLIAMS, born Aug. 9, 1851.
2432. KATE TALLMAN, born Nov. 5, 1853.
2433. MITCHELL, born May 2, 1856, and died Oct. 19, 1861.

1356. WILLIAM COIT.   Cincinnati, Ohio.

2434. SAMUEL JOHNSTON, born July 20, 1852.
2435. SARAH WILLIAMS, born Aug. 2, 1854.
2435.¹ MARY ELIZABETH, born Jan. 17, 1857, and died of diptheria, Sept., 1860.

1357. FREDERIC GILBERT.   Cincinnati, Ohio.

2436. MARY, born in Cincinnati, April, 1862.

1359. JABEZ, Dea. Norwich City.

2437. JEDIDIAH, born Sept. 15, 1794, graduated at Yale College in 1814. He married, July 2, 1834, Rebecca M. Snow, who died Sept. 3, 1835, aged 33 years. He married, for his second wife, Feb. 24, 1841, Happy Kinney of Norwich, where he now lives.

2438. FAITH TRUMBULL, born Sept. 20, 1796, married, Oct. 10, 1821, Rev. Edward W. Hooker, D. D., late professor of theology in the East Windsor Theological Seminary. She died May 5, 1850. Their children were: Mary Lanman, born Oct. 8, 1822, married. Rev. Porsen Clark of Hartford, Wis., and has had three children; Faith Huntington, born Nov. 16, 1824, married, May 11, 1846, Rev. E. I. Montague of Summit, Wis., and has had two children: Elizabeth Peck, born Feb. 10, 1827, and died Dec. 31, 1849; Elias Cornelius, born July 9, 1832; Sarah Huntington, born April 6, 1835; and Edward, born Oct. 31, 1837.

2439. PETER LANMAN, born Oct. 13, 1798, and died May 19, 1802.

2440. SARAH LANMAN, born June 18, 1802, married, July 21, 1833, Rev. Eli Smith, D. D., the eminent American missionary at Beyrout, Syria.

The memoir of this gifted and truly christian member of the family has been worthily compiled and written by her brother-in-law, the Rev. Dr. Edward Hooker. The memorial is a just tribute to her great excellence and usefulness; its careful study could but be grateful and profitable to every one who bears her name.

Doing good to others, would, I think, most exactly express her life-work from early childhood to its close. She early acquired a mastery over every form of self-seeking, that she might live for others. At the age of eighteen, with a consideration unusual with one of her years, she deliberately consecrated herself to the service of Christ. "I am anxious," her correspondence testifies, "to fill up life with usefulness, that God may be honored." In the sabbath school of her own church, among the poor and unfortunate in her own neighborhood, with the remnant of the neglected Mohegan Indians, for whose spiritual and temporal good she unweariedly toiled, in her sympathy and cheerful labors for the unfortunate Greeks during their struggles, and for the perishing heathen of a foreign land, she equally exhibited this leading aim of her life. And she was anxious that her kindred might possess the same spirit. She says of them all. "If the numerous Huntingtons are useful in their generation, it is of little consequence whether they are conspicuous."

In fulfilment of this most earnest desire of her heart she engaged, as early as the year 1827, in an effort to secure the secular and religious instruction of the Mohegan Indians—a small remnant of that tribe still left, upon the West bank of the Thames, some five miles below Norwich. Here, with much praying and toil, she established a missionary school, both for the week day and the sabbath; and with the aid of two such kindred spirits as Miss Breed of Norwich, and Miss Raymond of Montville, she accomplished a good work. The nature and method of this work are best exhibited in her own words.

"Seated in my little missionary apartment, which serves for parlor, bed-

Very affectionately
your Sister
Sarah L. Sm...

room, kitchen, school-room, and chapel, I have composed myself to the sweet employment of answering your good and long letter. I have a school of eighteen or twenty, including four adults, one man, two married women, and a 'Squasisse.' They come at half-past nine and stay until four, having half an hour's intermission; and we carry on arithmetic, millinery, tailoring, &c., besides the ordinary avocations of a school. All these, with the government of untutored, untamed beings, nearly exhaust my powers, during the day; and at evening I have work to fit and my 'profession' to study. But I am quite satisfied. I came here for their benefit and not to please myself. Our sabbath school is nearly twice as large, embracing whites, and is kept up four hours of the sabbath, besides an intermission. I leave home Sunday morning and return the next Sunday evening, and Miss Raymond does the same, so we are both here on the Sabbath."

Nor were her labors here unrewarded. She persevered in enlisting her friends in the measure, until she had secured a chapel and an appropriation from Congress of five hundred dollars towards a house for a permanent teacher, and an annuity of four hundred for his support.

But more than this. She had won the confidence and affectionate regard of the neglected children for whom she labored, nor have the years which have since passed, effaced her loved form and her holy teachings from the memory of their still grateful hearts. The writer, many years after she had left them, heard from the lips of more than one of them the simple story of their gratitude. Well and truthfully did her early friend, Mrs. Sigourney, thus embalm in her sweet verse these labors.

> Hear I the murmured echo of thy name,
> From yon poor forest-race? 'Tis meet for them
> To hoard thy memory, as a blessed star,
> For thou didst seek their lowly homes, and tell
> Their sad-browed children of a Savior's love,
> And of that clime where no oppressor comes.
> Cold winter found thee there, and summer's heat,
> With zeal unblenching. Though, perchance, the sneer
> Might curl some worldling's lip, 'twas not for thee
> To note its language, or to scorn the soul
> Of the neglected Indian, or to tread
> Upon the ashes of his buried kings
> As on a loathsome weed. Thy own fair halls
> Lured thee in vain, until the hallowed church
> Reared its light dome among them, and the voice
> Of a devoted shepherd, day by day,
> Called back these wanderers to the sheltering fold
> Of a Redeemer's righteousness.

Nor less truthfully, or with less grace, did the Rt. Rev. Bishop Lee of Delaware, allude to these labors for the Indians, in the address which he delivered at the great bi-centennial celebration, in Norwich, in 1859. I quote from memory, yet am sure I report the spirit of the touching record. "With an angel's alacrity she entered on this work. Where strong men would have shrunk back, this fair and delicate woman never hesitated."

But another field of labor was prepared for her, when she was no longer needed here. Just two months after her marriage she embarked at Boston for Malta, on her way to Syria, the missionary field to which she had cheerfully consecrated the remainder of her days. The same prayerfulness, the same affectionate consideration toward her parents and friends, and the same intelligent preparation for her work, which had previously made her so useful and acceptable, were in this most important and trying decision no less apparent. She had prepared both herself and friends, and now that she had started on the final mission of her life, she went as one who has lost all sense of a duty calling for self-denial, in the conscious enjoyment of a privilege of which she deemed herself unworthy. On the 28th Jan. 1834, she reached Beyroot, her future home. In sight of Lebanon, she felt herself to be on sacred ground; and though in the midst of an ignorance and heathenism that touched her deepest sympathies, she was now satisfied to find herself in the very spot to which her heavenly Father had led her. She had no will but to work henceforth in this heaven-appointed field. Here, for about two years and a half, she was permitted to enjoy the labors of the successful missionary. Early and late, each day, in season and out of season, wherever she might be, she was ever at the work which she loved. She came to feel each half hour sacred to some special and useful service. While in Beyroot, she was, at the same time, engaged in learning the language, in teaching a school, in aiding her husband in preparing manuscript for the press, and in superintending the needed domestic arrangements of her large household.

But she was not destined to a long service in this heathen land. Her health having given out, she left Beyroot in June, 1836, with her husband, to visit Smyrna. On the passage occurred an event which, while it illustrated the simplicity and strength of her faith, aggravated the symptoms of her disease. Off to the north of Cyprus their vessel struck upon a reef, and they were obliged to trust themselves to the long-boat, by which they were length safely landed on the uninhabited coast of Asia Minor. From this sandy beach, they were next morning removed, by a lumber boat from Damietta, in Egypt, to the deserted harbor of Selefkeh. Here, for about five days, she was exposed to burning sun and the chill air of night alike, with scarcely the defenses of ordinary clothing, this having been much of it lost by the wreck. One sabbath and one birth-day she thus spent. Yet this dying woman found, even then, occasions for gratitude. She had, it is true, none of those comforts which had before blessed her natal days—the presence of her dear friends, and the bountiful tokens of their love; she had not even a sufficiency of food, or the comfort of a place for rest; but she had sources of joy which sustained her; even there, angels, no doubt, ministered to her. That lone, and we should say, desolate sabbath, brought, as she herself testified, to her, "a feast of fat things." From his pulpit of stones, the Rev. Mr. Wynne, who had also shared their fate in the shipwreck, read from the English liturgy. "Never," she said, "did I so realize the beauty of that formulary, and its value under such circumstances."

At length, on the sixth day after they had been wrecked, they were taken off; and on the 13th of July they were landed at Smyrna. But her disease had now assumed a positive form. It was rendered certain that her lungs were too much diseased to admit of her recovery; and the succeeding weeks only the more confirmed the fears of her husband, as they gradually carried her down toward her end. On the 7th of August she was removed to Boojah, a village some five miles from Smyrna. Here, in resignation and in Christian joy, she awaited her end. In communion with her Savior, in pleasant memories of dear friends in other lands, and in spirit-longings for the communion of sainted friends, who had already gone above, she had great delight; until she was called, herself, to all the glory and joy of a Christian's final triumph. She had finished her life-work: she had given up all she had clung to on earth; she had nobly resigned her earthly interest in her devoted and loved husband, and she was ready to go. Too weak to utter words for human ears, she spoke her last benediction in the sweet smile which lighted up her face, as with the radiance of her new home, in Heaven.

An appropriate monument marks the place of her interment, in a quiet spot in the village where she died, on which this record may be read:

"To benevolent efforts for the youth and the ignorant of her native city; for the neglected remnant of its aboriginal inhabitants, and for the benighted females of Syria, she devoted all her ardent, expansive, and untiring energies, as a servant of Christ, until, sinking under missionary labors at Beyroot, she was brought hither, and died in triumphant faith, Sept. 30, 1836, aged 34."

2441. EDWARD BOYLSTON, born June 18, 1806, married, June 6, 1832, Sarah Anna (2445). He has been engaged in business for years, in Boston, Mass., and his family reside in Roxbury.

2442. PETER LANMAN, born Sept. 16, 1809, and graduated at Yale College, in 1828. During his junior year he became the subject of a revival which then occurred in college, and with all the earnestness of his ardent nature devoted himself to the life of a Christian, and to the work of preparation for the ministry. The memoir of his sister Sarah L., states, that "for the purpose of obtaining means to prosecute his professional studies, and also for the benefit to be derived to his own character, he went to Natchez, Miss., to engage in the labors of a private tutor in a family." But he was not to succeed in this leading aim of his heart. A fall which he had received before going South, had seriously affected his spine, and soon began to show its results upon his entire nervous system. He was forced to abandon his professional studies, and return home again, to linger awhile in great suffering, until death should come to his relief. He died, solaced with all the most precious ministries of his beloved home, and of his unwavering faith, Dec. 24, 1832.

The following tribute from the pen of his classmate and friend, the Rev.

Dr. Tryon Edwards, is so appropriate, that I am happy to be allowed to let it complete this estimate of one so gifted and so promising. He says:

"I knew him well. He was active and earnest in temperament; impulsive, warm-hearted, and generous; strong in all his statements and prejudices; good in all departments of study, but excelling as a belles-lettres scholar; cultivated in taste; refined in feeling; cordial in manner, and a true gentleman in address, and in all his intercourse, and evidently one to make his mark in the world, in whatever sphere he might be placed. In his junior year in college he became deeply impressed with the subject of religion, and united himself to the College church. From this time, all his strong traits were turned into a new channel, and his earnest ambition was directed to the true ends of living. Had he been spared, he would have made a man of prominence and usefulness."

1364. JOSHUA, REV.   Boston, Mass.

This family were all born in Boston.

2113. SUSAN MANSFIELD, born Sept. 10, 1810, married, first, Charles H. Strong of New York city, who died. She married the second time, Wolcott Richards, M. D., of Cincinnati, Ohio.

2114. JOSEPH ECKLEY, born Feb. 11, 1812, graduated at Yale, in 1832, his name having, after his youngest brother's death, been changed to Joshua. He has pursued a professional course of study, both in medicine and theology. He graduated in medicine at Yale College, in 1837, and from 1838 to 1845 he was in the United States naval service as assistant surgeon. He has been for several years engaged in teaching a private school for boys in the city of Brooklyn, N. Y.

He spent much time during his leisure for several years in gathering materials for a genealogical list of the Huntington family, and very kindly allowed the writer of this the use of his manuscript. The collection embraced about two thousand of the descendants of the two Huntingtons who were pioneers in the settlement of Norwich, and was of very great value in the construction of this genealogical memoir of the family.

2115. SARAH ANN, born June 23, 1813, married Edward B. (2411).
2116. ELIZABETH MOORE, born March 6, 1815, and died Sept. 25, 1821.
2117. MARY, born Sept. 23, 1816, married Jedidiah (821).
2118. JOSHUA, born Dec. 2, 1819, and died Aug. 25, 1821.

1365. DANIEL, REV.   New London, Conn.

2119. MARY HALLAM, born June 20, 1813, and died Feb. 20, 1820. This little girl gave pleasing evidence of early piety. Her memoir, written by her father, was published by the American Tract Society.

2120. ANNE MOORE, born Dec. 28, 1814, married, April 20, 1841, Alfred Hebard of Windham, Conn., who graduated at Yale in 1832. They now live in Carondelet, Missouri, and have had four children, two of whom are now

(1857) living: Augustus Huntington, born June 21, 1842; and Mary Saltonstall, born June 3, 1847.

2451. HANNAH SAGE, born Aug. 26, 1816, married, Nov. 10, 1841, Franklin Chappell, a merchant of New London, Conn., who died Feb. 19, 1849, leaving three children: Frank Huntington, born Feb. 4, 1843; William Saltonstall, born April 15, 1847; and Alfred Hebard, born May 12, 1849.

2452. CHARLES FRENCH, born Dec. 15, 1824, married, June 30, 1846, Abby M. Burrell of Portland, who is dead. He does business in Boston and lives in Brookline, Mass.

2453. WILLIAM SALTONSTALL, born Sept. 25, 1828, married Lucy Erskine of Abington, and lives in North Bridgewater, Mass. He is now (1862) in the Union army, and his family in Abington, Mass.

2454. MARY HALLAM, born Sept. 25, 1828, and died Nov. 21, 1831.

2455. MARY ALMA, born Sept. 13, 1834, and lives in New London.

2456. ALMA LOUISA, born Dec. 23, 1830, and died Dec. 21, 1834.

1366. THOMAS, (M. D.)   Brooklyn, Conn.

2457. ANN ELIZABETH, born Dec. 19, 1819, married, Oct. 22, 1838, Dea. Charles Clark, then of Norwich city, and now of Brooklyn Conn. They have five children: Charles, Edward, Anna, Mary, and George Huntington, born 1859. Two of the sons have been in the Union army.

2458. MARY WHITING, born July 2, 1821, and died Jan. 2, 1824.

2459. HARRIET, born June 10, 1823, married, March 10, 1846, William A. Coggshall. They live in Providence, R. I. and have four children: Anna, born in Jan., 1847; William, Arabella, and Ada.

2460. CHARLOTTE S., born May 19, 1825, married, April 16, 1846, John H. Clark of Providence, R. I., where they live. They have three children: John, born Jan. 26, 1847; Elizabeth Huntington, born July 4, 1853; and Frederick Arthur, born Feb. 22, 1856. Mr. Clark is one of the Coney Steam Engine Co. of Providence.

2461. HENRY, born Feb. 14, 1827, married, May 17, 1854, Anna D. Pond of Providence, R. I. He lives in Geneva, Ill.

2462. LOUISA, born Feb. 5, 1832, and died July 7, 1839.

2463. EMILY CLARK, born Oct. 22, 1833, married, Sept. 3, 1860, John E. Miller of Plainfield, Ill. They have one son, Henry Huntington.

2464. GEORGE, born Nov. 5, 1835.

2465. THOMAS, born May 25, 1838, is now (1862) in the Union army

2466. JOHN CLARK, born Aug. 22, 1842. He is now (1862) in the Union army.

1367. JOSEPH.   Norwich, Conn.

2467. JOSEPH CAREW, born Saturday, Jan. 23, 1792, married, Sunday, Oct. 1, 1816, Julia Stewart Dodge of New York city, who was born March 28, 1799. She was daughter of David Dow Dodge and Sarah Cleveland, and died in New York, Dec. 23, 1859, aged sixty years. He was several years in business in his native town, and removed to New York city in 1834. He was a man very active in religion, and was ordained deacon of the Tenth Presbyterian church, New York. He died in that city April 30, 1852.

2468. LUCY COIT, born Saturday, Nov. 22, 1794, married, May 25, 1817, Stephen B. Cleveland, a merchant of Bloomfield, N. J., where she died March 24, 1818, leaving one son, Joseph Huntington, born Feb. 22, 1818.

2469. EUNICE EDGERTON, born Wednesday, Sept. 13, 1797, married, July 7, 1825, Henry Strong, LL. D. (563) of Norwich, for many years one of the first lawyers of the state. They had one daughter, Mary Eunice, born Oct. 27, 1827, now Mrs. Gulliver of Norwich Town; and one son, Henry Ellsworth, born March 15, 1829, and died the 31st of the same month. Judge Strong died Nov. 12, 1852.

2470. BENJAMIN FRANKLIN, born Thursday, Jan. 2, 1800, and died May 3, 1801.

2471. OLIVER ELLSWORTH, born Friday, Sept. 3, 1802, married, June 10, 1830, Mary Ann, daughter of Joseph Strong, of Norwich, who died Nov. 23, 1840, aged thirty-three years. He graduated at Yale college in 1825, but engaged in commercial pursuits. He went in 1837 to Cleveland, Ohio, where he now lives.

2472. ANDREW BACKUS, born Dec. 16, 1805, married, in Baltimore, Dec. 17, 1829, Jane Eliza Norris. He was a merchant, and died in Baltimore, Jan. 10, 1851. His wife died in Norwich, Sept. 20, 1861, aged fifty-seven years.

2473. HANNAH PHELPS, born April 29, 1808, married, Dec. 20, 1826, John T. Adams, son of Richard Adams of Norwich city. She died in Michigan, leaving one son, John Richard, born Nov. 24, 1828; and Hannah Lydia, born June 9, 1838, who married James E. Learned, and lives in Owego.

2474. LYDIA COIT, born April 29, 1808, and died Nov. 28, 1829.

2475. SALLY ANN, born May 18, 1811, married, Hon. Jabez W. (1383). She died in Norwich at her sister's, Mrs. Strong's, June 26, 1861.

2476. GEORGE FREDERIC, born Dec. 27, 1813, and died Sept. 3, 1819.

1370. CHARLES P., HON.   Norwich City, Conn.

2477. ABBY LATHROP, born Sept. 7, 1803, and died Feb. 14, 1804.

2478. JOHN PERITT, born Feb. 14, 1807, married, April 26, 1830, Sarah Coit, daughter of Deacon Asher Perkins, who was born July 6, 1808, and died in Brooklyn, N. Y., Oct. 20, 1843. He was a merchant in New York city. He died at the Merchant's Hotel in Norwich city, Jan. 4, 1849.

2479. CHARLES WEBSTER, born July 16, 1808, married, Nov. 10, 1834, Sarah F. Spear, who was born Feb. 5, 1817. He lived in New York, and died in June, 1853. His widow is still living in New York.

2480. RUTH LEFFINGWELL, born March 10, 1810, married, June 2, 1830, James S. Ripley, a merchant of New York city, and son of Major Dwight Ripley of Norwich city. He was born March 18, 1806. Their children are: Charles P. H., born Nov. 26, 1832; Martha, born July 23, 1834; Mary Perit, born Oct. 7, 1836; Grace, born in New York, June 18, 1838, and died in Norwich, Aug. 9. 1839; William Coit, born May 29, 1840; and Samuel Huntington, born in Brooklyn, N. Y., June 9, 1842, and died Aug. 5, 1843.

2481. SAMUEL ANDREWS, born Feb. 5, 1812, and died of varioloid in New York, April 28, 1834, unmarried.

2482. BENJAMIN FRANKLIN, born Oct. 24, 1813, married, April 17, 1837, Maria L. (1736). He is a farmer and lives in Franklin, Conn.

2483. JAMES MUNROE, born Aug. 8, 1817, married, Oct. 11, 1841, Emily Brewster, daughter of Appleton Meech, of Norwich city. She died in Norwich, Dec. 14, 1843. He married, for his second wife, Nov. 24, 1846, Sarah E., daughter of Dr. Morey Burgess of Plainfield, Conn. He has been successfully engaged in the iron trade, and now (1862) in extensive shipping and importing business in Norwich city, where he resides. The family are greatly indebted to him for the Family Meeting, held so pleasantly in Norwich in 1857, as the Genealogist of the family is for his words and deeds of encouragement.

2484. WILLIAM HENRY, born Aug. 31, 1820, has spent several years abroad and is now living in Paris, France. He is the writer of the article on Paris in the new encyclopedia, published by the Appletons. He is a vigorous writer and a successful European correspondent for the New York press.

1372. ALFRED ISHAM.

2485. ALFRED SIMS, born in October, 1819, married, in 1851, Emily Shearer, and has been a commission merchant in Mobile, Ala.

2486. CAROLINE LOUISA, died young.

2487. BENJAMIN WOLCOTT, born July 16, 1832, married Elizabeth Wade, and has been a commission merchant in New Orleans, La.

2488. JULIA, died young.

2489. HENRY CHESTER, is a merchant in New Orleans.

2490. EDWARD, is a lawyer in New Orleans.

2491. LLOYD, is in business in New Orleans.

1382. THOMAS MUMFORD. Norwich, Conn.

2492. THOMAS Z. BOWERS, born Nov. 6, 1819, and died July 4, 1827.

2493. JOHN MYERS, born in New York city, April 3, 1821, graduated at Yale, 1843, and entered the legal profession. He married, in Boston, Mass., Sept. 2, 1856, Mary A., daughter of Elisha Parks, who was born in Boston, March 11, 1825. He is a lawyer in Chicago, and now (1862) engaged in the commissariat of the Union army.

2494. HENRY BOWERS, born Feb. 16, 1823, married, Oct. 18, 1853, Lucinda Willis, and lives on a farm in Lebanon, Conn.

2495. GEORGE WOLCOTT, born April 6, 1825, married, in Pittsfield, Mass., June 23, 1848, Catherine L., daughter of the Hon. Henry H. Childs. She died in Pittsfield, June 20, 1852. He married, for his second wife, in New York city, June 15, 1854, Alice, daughter of Henry and Delia Alden Henderson of Baltimore, Md. He is a physician, having graduated at the Berkshire

Medical College, in 1847, and was settled in Rock Island, Ill., in the practice of medicine. He died in 1859.

2496. MARY ELIZABETH, born Sept. 16, 1829, married Timothy Childs, M. D., late of the Pittsfield Medical College, and now professor in the New York city Medical school.

1387. RUFUS.   Windham, Conn.

2497. MARY, born in Windham, May 11, 1859, and died Oct. 7, 1861.
2497.¹ ELIZABETH SMITH, born Nov. 3, 1861.

1393. JAMES.   Cleveland, Ohio.

2498. MATILDA ERMINA, born Jan. 12, 1848, in Cleveland.
2499. EDWARD AUGUSTUS, born July 20, 1849, in Cleveland.
2500. MARY ANTOINETTE, born Aug. 10, 1851, in Cleveland.
2501. CORNELIA, born May 30, 1856, in Cleveland, and died Aug. 20, 1857.
2502. ALICE AUGUSTA, born in Newburg, Ohio, Nov. 18, 1859.
2502.¹ JAMES, born Oct. 23, 1861.

1407. RALPH.   Boston, Mass.

2503. JULIA, born Dec. 3, 1810, married, April 14, 1836, John Warren James, a lawyer in Boston, of eminence, both in his profession and in politics. She is a woman of great excellence of character, and has shown talent in occasional contributions to the poetry of the day. Mr. James died in Boston, Feb. 7, 1861. He was a man who has been considerably in public life. His talents were of a high order; and he had diligently and successfully improved them. His biographer speaks of him as "a moving encyclopædia, for he seemed to know the contents of every volume on the shelves of the Boston Athenæum." The main features of his character and life are sketched among the Hundred Boston Orators, by Loring.

1408. SAMUEL.   St. Domingo.

2504. FANNY.
2505. MARY.
2506. RALPH EDWARD.
2507. SAMUEL, died young, while in Mr. Powell's school, in West Farms, New York.

1409. BENJAMIN.

2508. AMELIA DOLBEAR, born July 29, 1820.
2509. CHARLES SANDERS, born Nov. 4, 1821. He was early devoted to the sea, and his whole career was filled with testimonials to the unselfish, exuberant generosity of his heart. In his first voyage from Salem, Mass., to Sumatra, visiting several Eastern ports and returning, from Oct., 1835, to Jan., 1838, commencing as light hand before the mast, and closing it as clerk, he won

the esteem **and confidence of the captain and officers of the ship, "for his fidelity and zeal in perfecting himself in his profession."** In a second voyage in the same **vessel, the captain leaving his post at Genoa, he was made first supercargo, and with the mate completed the voyage.** The third voyage he commenced, in 1841, as master of the ship, and returned in April 1842, having spent six and a half years upon the water, with only some ten weeks at home. During his next voyage an incident occurred, which both tested his seamanship and proved him to be a humane and generous man. After crossing the equator off the coast of South America, he fell in with a Portuguese vessel, which had been disabled, and which was in a sinking condition. At great peril, both to himself personally, and to his crew, he rescued fourteen of the Portuguese, and carried them into Rio Janeiro. This voyage was succeeded by seven others, in the "Borneo," and all of them successful, "without any accident whatever." In Oct., 1848, he sailed in the ship "Augustine Hurd," for Australia and Van Dieman's Land, and returned in 1850. He was about starting on another voyage, when he was taken with a sickness which ended, prematurely, his useful and promising life.

2510. FRANCES, died young.

2511. CAROLINE ELIZABETH, married William D., son of Rev. Dr. Flint of Medford, Mass.

2512. FRANCES SOPHIA, married, April 23, 1850, William A. Wright, a merchant of Boston, where they live.

1416. FORDYCE, JUDGE.   Vergennes, Vt.

2513. SARAH JANE, born Aug. 9, 1819, married, Sept. 5, 1843, John H. BOWMAN.

2514. ANN ELIZA, born Feb. 20, 1826, and lives in Vergennes, Vt.

1419. JOSEPH LYMAN.   Mason, Mich.

2515. CYRUS BURR, born June 17, 1826, died in 1848.
2516. DYTHA ANN, born May 25, 1828.
2517. COLLINS DWIGHT, born Feb. 25, 1831.
2518. RALPH BENNETT, born Jan. 2, 1833, is now (1862) in the Union army.
2519. LYMAN BARTO, born July 10, 1835.
2520. GEORGE MILO, born March 20, 1838.
2521. WILLIAM JULIUS, born Aug. 19, 1840.
2522. CHARLES GILBERT, born Jan. 1, 1843.
2523. ELLEN MARIA, born Aug. 5, 1845.

1420. ALFRED HENRY.   St. Albans, Vt.

2524. MINERVA HILL, born Jan. 4, 1831, married Frederick, son of deacon Luther L. and Almira (Brainard) Dutcher **of St. Albans.**
2525. JANE, born June 24, 1834.
2526. ELIHU HILL, born Jan. 22, **1840.**

1421. COLLINS HICKOX. St. Albans, Vt.

2527. ELIZABETH SARAH, born July 6, 1837.
2528. FRANCIS, born Aug. 16, 1840.
2529. COLLINS FRELIGH, born Oct. 5, 1854.
2530. CAROLINE MARIA, born March 1. 1856.

1423. CHARLES ANDREW. Rockford, Ill.

2531. EMILY WATERMAN, born at Perry, N. Y., May 1, 1844, and died in Rockford, Ill., June 23, 1848.
  2532. CHARLES JONATHAN, born at Rockford, Ill., Dec. 9, 1846.
  2533. THOMAS WATERMAN, born at Rockford. Ill. Jan. 16, 1848.
  2534. JOHN BURNHAM, born at Rockford, Ill., Sept. 28, 1850.
  2535. SARAH ELINOR, born at Rockford. Ill., Aug. 25, 1853.
  2536. JAMES MARSH, born at Rockford, Ill., March 8, 1855.
  2537. ALFRED HENRY, born at Rockford, Ill., Sept. 1, 1856.
2537.[1] BELA SHAW.
2537[2] LUCRETIA.

1424. SAMUEL. Burlington, Vt.

2537.[3] SAMUEL, born Oct. 16, 1842.
2538. SARAH ANN ELIZA, born Feb. 22, 1846.
2539. LUCY ABBEY, born Aug. 20, 1849.

1427. JAMES. Cambridge, Mass.

2540. JONATHAN G., born Jan. 11, 1854, and died Oct. 14, 1856.
2541. CHARLES ASA, born March 25, 1856, and died Oct. 5, 1856.
2542. ELIZA PRENTISS, born Oct. 31, 1857.

1428. SIMEON. Farmersburg, Iowa.

2543. EBENEZER CUTLER, born Feb. 7, 1850, and baptized in St. Albans, Vermont.
  2544. ELIZA CAROLINE, born March 21, 1852, and baptized in St. Albans, Vermont.
  2545. SARAH LOUISA, born March 1, 1856, in Burritt, Ill., where she died, March 24, 1856.
  2546. CHARLES KELLOGG, born in Farmersburg, Iowa, Dec. 15, 1859.

1429. FLAVIUS JOSEPHUS. Painesville, Ohio.

This family were all born in Painesville.
  2547. COLBERT CARTHON, born Aug. 25, 1820, and went to California in 1849.
  2548. MIRZA LODOISKA, born May 29, 1822, married, June 30, 1842, Joseph C. Sedgebeer of New York. He is the inventor and extensive manufacturer of an improved French burr-stone for mills. He carries on his manufacturing

in Cincinnati, Ohio, though his residence is in Painesville. Their children are: Charles Huntington, born July 27, 1844, and died Aug. 1, 1847; Adela Gertrude, born in Rochester, N. Y., June 11, 1848; Charles Mortimer, born May 19, 1853, in Geneva, Ohio; and Eugene Huntington, born in Cincinnati, Ohio, April 9, 1859.

2549. LAURA JOSEPHINE, born March 10, 1828, and died June 20, 1845.

1430. EDWARD G. South Coventry, Conn.

This family were all born in South Coventry.

2550. JOSEPH, born Jan. 9, 1818, and died Sept. 12, 1818.

2551. LOUISA P., born July 12, 1821, and died Dec. 13, 1828.

2552. SAMUEL, born March 6, 1824, married, June 15, 1851, Mary Ruggles of Bolton, and settled in Coventry. He died Jan. 29, 1854.

2553. JAMES, born in 1832, studied law in Poughkeepsie, N. Y., and is now a practicing attorney in Woodbury, Conn.

2554. EDWARD GRIFFIN, born Sept. 17, 1837, and died Oct. 10, 1838.

2555. MARIA, born Oct. 22, 1843, and still resides in Coventry.

1431. FRANCIS. Painesville, Ohio.

2556. FRANCIS, born after the death of his father, and died early.

1433. JULIAN CLAUDE. Painesville, Ohio.

2557. SAMUEL P., born Sept. 4, 1824, married, for his first wife, Sept. 4, 1847, Mary Ann Cole, who died May 4, 1859. He married again, Feb. 28, 1861, Lucy Anne Morgan. He is a dentist and lives in Painesville.

2558. ROBERT, born July 7, 1826, and died July 15, 1827.

2559. LUCY, born Oct. 7, 1827, married, Jan. 1, 1847, Henry C. Tombes, and lived in Ashtabula, Ohio.

2560. EDWIN, born Nov. 6, 1830, married, Sept. 24, 1856, Rougene Carpender, and lived in Webster City, Iowa, where he was in the legal profession. He is now living in Painesville, Ohio.

2561. HENRY, born Oct. 30, 1833, and lives in Painesville, Ohio, where he is a farmer.

1436. ROBERT GILES, (M. D.) Ellsworth, Ohio.

2562. ELLEN L., born June 6, 1837.

2563. MARY D., born April 22, 1839.

2564, 2565 and 2566. died in infancy.

1439. HENRY AUGUSTUS. Sugar Creek, Ind.

2567. KATE, born July 5, 1851, and died Oct. 30, 1853.

2568. ELIZA, born Jan. 20, 1853.

2569. THOMAS H., born Sept. 6, 1854.

2570. MARY A., born May 14, 1856.

1440. JULIUS. Sugar Creek, Ind.

2571. MARY E., born Aug. 5, 1847, and died Nov. 4, 1853.
2572. MARTHA FRANCES, born Dec. 24, 1848.
2573. SAMUEL, born Oct. 26, 1852.
2574. JOSEPH, born Feb. 12, 1855.

1441. SEPTIMUS GEORGE. Sugar Creek, Ind.

2575. A SON, born and died Aug. 9, 1852.
2576. DARWIN, born Oct. 30, 1853, and died Feb. 19, 1856.
2577. ELLEN, born Aug. 30, 1855, and died March 3, 1856.
2578. A SON, born June 23, 1857.

1446. NATHANIEL. Terre Haute, Ind.

2579. EUGENE, born in 1823, married Emeline (2586) and is now (1863) living in Winnebago City, Minn.
2580. NATHANIEL, born in 1825, and has lived for years in New York city.

1448. JAMES, HON. Starkey, N. Y.

2581. GEORGE PITKIN, born Nov. 30, 1826, and is a merchant in Attica, Ind. He has not married.
2582. HENRY M. born April 2, 1835, and is a farmer in Iowa.
2583. MARY P., born March 20, 1841.
2584. CYNTHIA, born Sept. 2, 1843.

1449. HALLAM, COL. Hudson, Ind.

2585. ADALINE, married Asher White.
2586. EMELINE, married Eugene (2579.)
2587. NATHANIEL, is a lawyer in California.
2588. JAMES, born in 1831, and is not married.
2588.[1] HENRY CLAY, died Nov. 1, 1838.
2589. JOSEPH, died June 18, 1852.

1451. ELISHA M., JUDGE. Terre Haute, Ind.

2590. ROBERT PALMER, born Sept. 7, 1842, appointed midshipman in the U. S. Navy in 1853, and now (1862) ensign on board a U. S. ship bound for the Pacific.
2591. MARY ST. CLAIR, born Aug 13, 1844, and died Oct. 13, 1845.
2592. MARY LOUISE, born Dec. 24, 1846.
2593. GERTRUDE, born Sept. 8, 1848.
2594. CHRISTOPHER, born July 11, 1850.
2595. HETTIE KEY, born March 21, 1852, and died in Dec. of the same year.

1459. GEORGE LATHROP. Springfield, Ill.

The first of this family was born in St. Louis, the rest in Springfield, Ill.
2596. MARY FORBES, born March 12, 1839, and died March 30, 1840.
2597. CHARLES LATHROP, born Jan. 2, 1841, appointed midshipman in the U. S. Navy in 1858, and now (1858) is acting master on board the U. S. steamer Cambridge.
2598. ALICE MORGAN, born July 6, 1843.
2599. EMILY WEBSTER, born Sept. 18, 1845.
2600. GEORGE LATHROP, born Sept. 20, 1847.
2601. CLARA SOPHIA FORBES, born Nov. 28, 1849.
2602. ELLEN JOSEPHINE, born April 20, 1852.
2603. ARTHUR, born June 23, 1855.
2604. A DAUGHTER, born Dec. 28, 1857.

1462. JOHN G. Davenport, Iowa.

2604.¹ MINNIE.
2604.² MARY.

1465. ENOCH. REV. North Haven, Conn.

2605. CHARLOTTE TAYLOR, born Feb. 3, 1829, and died April 23, 1831.
2606. JOHN TAYLOR, born Jan. 30, 1830, graduated at Trinity College, Hartford, with honor, and ordained minister of the Episcopal church in 1853. He married, in Norwich, Conn., Nov. 25, 1856, Elizabeth Tracy, daughter of Erastus Williams (1369) of Norwich. He was rector of St. John's church, New Haven, a few years, and is now (1862) rector of St. James' church in Great Barrington, Mass.
2607. SAMUEL GRAY, born Aug. 19, 1831, and is in business in New York.
2608. SOPHIA DEMING, born Oct. 7, 1833.
2609. MARY GRAY, born Feb 22, 1836, married, in June, 1860, Rev. James Edward Coley, rector of St. James', Westville, New Haven.
2610. GEORGE BOARDMAN, born Oct. 4, 1838, and died April 6, 1839.
2611. SARAH WARD, born Jan, 19, 1841.

1467. WALLACE. Windham, Conn.

2612. JOSEPHINE, born Jan. 6, 1848.
2613. SAMUEL TRIPP, born Aug. 10, 1854.

1472. MASON.

2614. MARY ANN, born in 1813, married Gilbert Patton of Columbia, Conn.
2615. HARRIET NEWELL, married a Mr. Elliott, a missionary, and went to Illinois.

1479. WILLIAM. Norwich, N. Y.

2616. MARVIN W., born in 1824, and is married.
2617. KATE, born in 1826, and lived in Oswego, N. Y.

1486. WILLIAM. Keene, N. H.

2618. ELEANORA BELLOWS, born in Andover, N. H., Dec. 13, 1831, married, Sept. 23, 1849, Horatio N. Burrel, a carpenter at Lake Village, N. H. Their children are: William Huntington, born July 3, 1850; Frederic, born Sept. 2, 1854; and Eugene, born Nov. 16, 1857. They are living now (1858) in Oronoco, Olmstead county, Minn.

2619. GEORGE HOWARD, born at Andover, N. H., July 4, 1833, and is living in Madison, Wis.

2620. ELIZABETH ARMSTRONG, born at Walpole, N. H., Oct. 20, 1836, married, Nov. 30, 1854, Andrew J. Prescott, an engineer at Lake Village, N. H.

2621. MARY GRACE, born in Walpole, N. H., April 6, 1838.

1489. OLIVER. Walpole, N. H.

This family were all born in Walpole.

2622. EDWARD LANE, born Oct. 23, 1838. He was in the Union army, and has just been (Nov. 1, 1862) reported dead.

2623. SOPHIA MARY, born March 17, 1842, and is now (1857) in the Deaf and Dumb Asylum at Hartford, Conn.

2624. ALMIRA SUSAN, born Dec. 28, 1844, with her sister in the Deaf and Dumb Asylum at Hartford, Conn.

2625. ABBY REBECCA, born April 7, 1850, also with her sisters in the Deaf and Dumb Asylum at Hartford, Conn.

1493. GEORGE. Walpole, N. H.

2626. MARY KIDDER, born Feb. 20, 1856.

1496. MARVIN. Painesville, Ohio.

All but the first two of this family were born in Painesville.

2627. EDWARD FREDERIC, born in Bloomfield, Ohio, Nov. 7, 1823, married, in Racine, Wis., in 1846, Sarah Brownell, and lives in Salem, Wis.

2628. OREGON EDGAR, born in Bloomfield, Jan. 27, 1825, married Jane Foster, in 1848 and lives in Painesville.

2629. HENRY, born Sept. 3, 1826, is living unmarried in Warren, Ill.

2630. GURDON HARRIS, born Dec. 21, 1828, married Selina Cowden of Green, Ohio, and lives in Painesville.

2631. FRANCIS HEZEKIAH, born May 2, 1831, and died July 19, 1834.

2632. SYLVIA ELIZABETH, born April 16, 1833, and lives in Bloomfield, Ohio.

2633. MARY ANN, born May 21, 1834, and lives with her father in Painesville.

EIGHTH GENERATION. 335

2634. CAROLINE ROGERS, born April 1, 1836, married a Mr. Green, and lives in Painesville.
2635. HARRIET MARIA, born July 24, 1837.
2636. SARAH BOND, born March 25, 1839.
2637. MARVIN, born Nov. 20, 1842.
2638. ELLEN PAINE, born Nov. 8, 1851.
2639. LOUISA PETERSON, born April 23, 1854.

1502. GURDON WILLIAMS. Canton, Ohio.

2640. ALFRED SMITH, born Sept. 27, 1833, is now (1862) in the quartermaster's department of the Union army.
2641. SARAH LOUISA, born Oct. 9, 1835.
2642. MARY ELIZABETH, born Aug. 16, 1837.
2643. MORGAN GURDON, born Jan. 30, 1840.
2644. JULIA ANN, born April 30, 1842, and died March 9, 1847.

1504. MINER. South Carolina.

From a letter dated June 11, 1821, and a second one dated 1825, written by the father of this family, and copied for the author by Annie L. Starr (1507) of Yarmouth, N. S., the following facts have been gathered.

2615. A SON, that died in infancy.
2615.[1] A DAUGHTER, that died in infancy.
2615.[2] FABIUS PATRICK BROWN, born April 10, 1817.
2615.[3] MARY ALATHEA.
2615.[4] ROBERT, who died in infancy.

1505. ABNER WALKER. Nova Scotia.

2646. MARTHA JANE, born Jan. 18, 1856.

1506. BELA. Nova Scotia.

2647. RICHARD, born Feb. 13, 1819, married, at Sydney, Cape Breton, Sept. 1, 1847, Isabella M. Armsworthy. He has been considerably in public life, and is now editor of the Yarmouth Tribune. He wields a ready and strong pen in defense of protestantism and of education.
2648. MARTHA, born Nov., 1820, married, April 19, 1852, John Burrill. She died in Jan., 1854. Her only child, Mary Fletcher, was born and died in 1853.

1510. HERBERT. HON. Yarmouth, N. S.

2649. JAMES, born Jan. 23, 1831.
2650. CHARLES, born Aug. 27, 1833, is in California.
2651. JOHN, born Feb. 14, 1835.
2652. HERBERT, born April 16, 1838.
2653. AGNES, born March 30, 1841.

1516. WILLIAM JONES. Baraboo, Wis.

The first four of this family were born in Mexico, N. Y., the last in Baraboo.

2654. ELIZA, born Nov. 9, 1827, married, Aug. 31, 1846, Seneca Lamberton, and lives in Baraboo. Their children are: Adelbert L., born May 27, 1848; William A., born July 7, 1851; and Frank W., born Dec. 24, 1853.

2655. WILLIAM, born June 25, 1830, married Mary Ann Talmon, and lives in Baraboo.

2656. ANN, born June 29, 1832, married, Jan. 1, 1849, Summer J. Lamberton of Baraboo, where they reside. Their children are: Kate Adell, born July 25, 1850; Albert G., born March 17, 1852, and died Dec. 19, 1852; Clarabel, born Oct. 7, 1854; and Charles W., born Aug. 28, 1857.

2657. CHARLES H., born March 2, 1846, and is in Baraboo.

2658. GEORGE W., born Aug. 23, 1836, and lives in Baraboo. He is in the Union army, and for his meritorious conduct in the battle of Corinth, has been promoted.

1517. HERBERT N. Baraboo, Wis.

These children were born in Scribon, N. Y.

2659. LOUISA A., born Sept. 16, 1839, married, Jan. 15, 1859, William Stanley.

2660. SUSAN C., born June 29, 1842, and died Oct. 16, 1842.

1519. SAMUEL PERKINS. Baraboo, Wis.

The first six of this family were born in Mexico, N. Y., the rest in Baraboo.

2661. MARY ANN, born Sept. 15, 1839. She married, in April, 1860, Seth McGilvia, a successful farmer of Baraboo. They have one child, Zervia S., born April 5, 1862.

2662. HOWARD, J., born July 27, 1841. He is now (1863) in the Union army, having left his studies while fitting for college in 1861. He is sergeant major of the regiment which he first joined.

2663. ROSELLE, born July 22, 1843.

2664. ROSANTHE, born July 22, 1843, and died, Sept. 10, 1843.

2665. EMOGINE, born July 18, 1844.

2666. SAMUEL D., born May 29, 1846.

2667. NELLIE EUDORA, born July 1, 1855.

2668. ARMILLA J., born Dec. 22, 1857.

1520. JOHN LATHROP. Baraboo, Wis.

2669. LYDIA ANN, born Feb. 1846, in Mexico, N. Y.

2670. HARRIET A., born Oct. 15, 1854, in Baraboo, Wis.

2671. ARTHUR W., born Sept. 22, 1856, in Baraboo.

1521. JOSEPH WELLINGTON, ESQ. Lancaster, Mass.

This family were all born in Lancaster, Mass.

2672. GEORGE MILLER, born Aug. 25, 1833, and resides in Charleston, S. C., where he is engaged in mercantile transactions.

EIGHTH GENERATION. 337

2673. JULIA MARIA, born Aug 25, 1833, and died Sept. 23, 1833.
2674. HORATIO MILLER, born June 26, 1836, and died Sept. 17, 1836.
2675. JOSEPH MILLER, born June 20, 1838, and died July 2, 1841.
2676. HORATIO HARRISON, born July 24, 1840, and died July 8, 1841.
2677. JULIA MILLER, born June 11, 1845, and now lives in Rhinebeck, N. Y.
2678. JOSEPH MILLER, born Aug. 28, 1847, and is now in Lancaster, Mass.

1525. SAMUEL. Middlefield, N. Y.

2679. MARTHA ADELINE, born in East Haddam, Conn., Oct. 23, 1815, and died single in Middlefield, N. Y., Dec. 12, 1842.

2680. MARY AMELIA, born in Middlefield, N. Y., May 14, 1818, married, May 1, 1844, Waldo Skinner, who was born in Woodstock, Conn. He is a merchant and manufacturer, and lives in Madison, Wis. They have five children: Ella Eureka, born Aug. 2, 1845, and died in Hudson, Ohio, in July, 1848; Julius Huntington, born in Hudson, Ohio, in July, 1848, and died the next month; Beulah Huntington, born in Middlefield, N. Y., in Feb., 1850; Waldo Huntington, born in Madison, Wis., in March, 1852; and Mary Huntington, born in Madison, Jan., 1855, and died in July of the same year.

2681. SAMUEL, twin with Mary A., died May 17, 1818.

2682. SAMUEL GATES, born in Middlefield, N. Y., May 28, 1820, married, Sept. 21, 1848, Jane Hannah Church, who died in Middlefield, N. Y., June 5, 1851. He married again, July 20, 1852, Adeline Julia Parmale, and resides at Middlefield Centre, N. Y. She was daughter of Rev. Alvin and Viletto Parmale.

2683. DOROTHY JENNETT, born in Middlefield, May 28, 1820, married, Dr. Aborn T. Bigelow of Worcester, N Y., Jan. 8, 1850. Their children are: Polly Josephine, born in Worcester, Feb. 6, 1851; Uriah Huntington, born in Worcester, Aug. 1, 1852; and Martha Irene, born in Worcester, Sept., 1854.

2684. WILLIAM SILLIMAN, born in Middlefield, Sept. 22, 1822, married, Aug. 1, 1850, Mary Ann Walker, daughter of Dea. William and Sarah Ingalls Walker. They live at Middlefield, N. Y., where he is a last manufacturer.

2685. LAURA ALMIRA, born in Middlefield, Aug. 11, 1826, married William Orrin, son of William and Lucy (Day) Brainard of East Haddam, Conn., Oct. 9, 1851, where they now live. They have one daughter, Mary Almira, born in E. Haddam, Jan. 17, 1853.

2686. ESTHER ELVIRA, born Aug. 4, 1826, in Middlefield, where she died, Jan. 17, 1827.

1526. MASON COGGSWELL. Middlefield, N. Y.

This family were all born in Middlefield.

2687. JONAS GATES, born March 2, 1819, and died Jan. 17, 1820.
2688. ROYAL, born March 19, 1821, and died March 4, 1849.
2689. HARRIET, born May 20, 1824, married, Feb. 3, 1846, George Clyde Allen of Albany, N. Y., where they reside, having had two children: Lorena, born Jan. 20, 1850; and Ella, born May 25, 1857.

43

2690. EDMUND, born Oct. 3, 1826, and died March 19, 1827.
2691. EDWIN, born Oct. 3, 1826, and died April 14, 1828.
2692. MASON, born July 21, 1829, and died Jan. 22, 1830.
2693. LOUISA, born Dec. 3, 1833, married, Jan. 4, 1854, Erastus Green Blair of Middlefield, N. Y., where they now reside.
2694. JANE, born Jan. 30, 1841, married, Oct. 1, 1858, Norman L. Mason.

1530. EDWIN WELLS. Minetto, N. Y.

2695. MARY E., born May 29, 1836, and died May 22, 1856.
2696. SARAH B., born Feb. 14, 1838. She is a teacher in Virginia, and is a member of the Presbyterian church.
2697. HARRIET N., born Feb. 5, 1840. She is a member of the Presbyterian church.
2698. FRANCES H., born Aug. 27, 1842. She is a member of the Presbyterian church.

1534. LYNDE ATWATER. Charlestown, Mass.

2699. DAVID LOW, born April 10, 1834. He graduated at Yale in 1855. Abandoning the wish and purpose of his heart, a preparation for the work of the gospel ministry, he entered upon medical studies and graduated at the Philadelphia medical school. He is now a practicing physician in Philadelphia, where he married, May 9, 1860, Annie Martha, daughter of William H. Allen, LL. D., President of Girard College. She died Nov. 8, 1861, aged 24 years. He is now (1862) a surgeon in the Union army.
2700. LOUISA, born June 4, 1836, and died Dec. 3, 1836.
2701. GEORGE LYNDE, born June 14, 1838.
2702. LYDIA LOUISA, born April 20, 1840, and died Aug. 14, 1845.
2703. SAMUEL EAMES, born July 11, 1842.
2704. CHARLES, born Dec. 15, 1844, and died Jan. 30, 1845.
2705. ANNA WILLIAMS, born Dec. 20, 1845.
2706. MARGARET, born March 18, 1848.

1536. WAIT TALCOTT. Ithaca, N. Y.

2707. LOUISA, born in Ithaca, Aug. 9, 1841.
2708. MARY CORNELIA, born in Ithaca, May 2, 1845.
2709. WILLIAM THEODORE, born in Ithaca, June 17, 1850, and died July 20, 1850.

1537. ORISTUS LYNDE. Danville, Iowa.

2710. SOPHIA, born in Ithaca, N. Y., June 22, 1833, and died July 8, 1834.
2711. SABETH, born in Ithaca, Oct. 10, 1834, married, in Danville, Iowa, Sept. 30, 1857, George H. Mix of West Hartford, Conn.
2712. OLIVER LYNDE, born in Danville, Iowa, May 3, 1847, and died Aug. 26, 1854.

1538. HORATIO LORD. Adams county, Ill.

2713. CORNELIA ANN, born in Ellington, Ill., March 19, 1841.

2714. EMILY ELIZABETH, born in Ellington, Ill., Sept. 2, 1843, and died in Quincy, Ill.

1540. GEORGE OLIVER. Quincy, Ill.

2715. GEORGE OLIVER, born in Quincy, Ill., Feb. 23, 1841, and died Sept. 24, 1842.

1545. HENRY HART. Mount Clemens, Mich.

2716. ARTHUR DWIGHT.

1549. SIMEON. Lebanon, Conn.

2717. ELIZABETH, born April 30, 1819, married, June 7, 1854, Rev. Walter Long, pastor of the Mystic Bridge Congregational church.

2718. SARAH, born Aug. 28, 1821, married Isaac Johnson, merchant of Norwich city, where she died Aug. 26, 1851.

2719. A son, who died July 24, 1823.

2720. IRA CLARK, born July 28, 1827, married Adelaide Stebbins, daughter of William Stebbins of Brooklyn. He was in the book trade, and one of the firm of Edwards & Huntington, New York city. He died of consumption, in Brooklyn, N. Y., Feb. 9, 1858.

2721. CLARISSA WILLIAMS, born Feb. 26, 1831, married, Dec. 24, 1856, George W. Standish, a teacher of Lebanon, Conn., where they now live. They have one son, Clark Huntington, born in Sept. 1862.

2722. WILLIAM LYMAN, born Aug. 23, 1843, and lives in Lebanon, Conn., where he has a family.

1555. DAN. Norwich, Conn.

2723. GEORGE WILSON, born Jan. 15, 1839, and is engaged in business with his father.

2724. EMILY, born Jan. 3, 1841, and is living with her father.

2725. JANE GRAY, died Sept. 9, 1843, aged about one year.

2726. EDWARD WEBSTER, born Jan. 2, 1848.

1556. ELEAZER. Lebanon, Conn.

This family were all born in Lebanon.

2727. MARY GRAY, born Aug. 11, 1836, married, in Nov. 1862, Hart, son of Moses Talcott of Glastenbury, Conn.

2728. WILLIAM, born May 18, 1839, married a Miss Perry, and lives in Lebanon.

2729. ELLEN BLISS, born Jan. 1, 1843.

1557. CHARLES PHELPS, Hon. Boston, Mass.

This family were all born in Northampton, Mass.

2730. HELEN FRANCES, born July 7, 1831, and married in Boston, Mass., Dec. 23, 1858, Josiah P. Quincy, son of Hon. Josiah Quincy of Boston. Their children are: Josiah Huntington, born Oct. 15, 1859; and Helen, born Sept. 6, 1861.

2731. CHARLES WHITING, born Sept. 22, 1834, graduated at Harvard, in 1854, and is engaged in the law profession in Ware, Mass.

2732. ELIJAH HUNT MILLS, born July 22, 1836.

2732.¹ HELEN BETHIA, born July 12, 1838, and died July 25, 1839.

2733. MARY ELIZABETH, born March 19, 1840.

2734. EDWARD STANTON, born April 3, 1841.

2735. HARRIETTE MILLS, born May 18, 1843, and died July 8, 1844.

2736. HENRY GREENOUGH, born March 24, 1848.

2737. LAURA CURTIS, born Sept. 15, 1849.

1559. WILLIAM PITKIN. Milwaukie, Wis.

2738. LUCY BETHIA, married Prof. S. Fellows of Galesville.

2739. WILLIAM EDWARDS.

2740. HELEN MARIA.

2741. CATHERINE FRANCES.

2742. FREDERIC SARGENT.

2743. FLORA.

1562. THEOPHILUS PARSONS. Hadley, Mass.

2744. WALTER ELLIOT, born in Hadley, March 27, 1842.

2745. MARIA WHITING, born in Hadley, March 9, 1845.

2746. EDWARD DWIGHT, born in Hadley, June 1, 1857.

1566. FREDERIC DAN, (D. D.) Boston, Mass.

2747. GEORGE PUTNAM, born in Boston, Mass., July 3, 1844.

2748. ARRIA SARGENT, born in Roxbury, Mass., June 22, 1848.

2749. CHARLES EDWARD, born in Roxbury, Oct. 2, 1852, and died Oct. 19, 1852.

2750. JAMES OTIS SARGENT, born in Roxbury, July 23, 1854.

2751. WILLIAM, born in Hadley, Mass., July, 1856.

2752. RUTH GREGSON, born in Cambridge, Nov. 3, 1859.

2752.¹ MARY LINCOLN, born in Boston, Nov. 15, 1861.

1567. JONATHAN E. Newark, N. J.

2753. EDWARD PAYSON, born July 7, 1832, and died Nov. 15, 1833.

2754. EDWARD BAXTER, born Dec. 26, 1833, and died Dec. 28, 1837.

2755. HARRIET WINSLOW, born July 14, 1835, and died Jan. 4, 1836.

2756. JONATHAN HENRY, born Dec. 14, 1836, and married, June 23, 1858.

EIGHTH GENERATION. 341

Eunice, daughter of Stephen B. Alling of Newark, N. J., where they are living.

2757. SARAH JOHNSON, born Jan. 4, 1839, and died Dec. 11, 1843.
2758. JACOB SELDEN, born Oct. 11, 1840, and died Dec. 9, 1843.
2759. ANN ELIZA, born July 26, 1842, and died Dec. 18, 1843.
2760. CYNTHIA SELDEN, born Sept. 21, 1844, and died Aug. 12, 1845.
2761. SAMUEL COMSTOCK, born Feb. 25, 1846.
2762. CATHARINE ELIZABETH, born Feb. 16, 1849.

1582. EBENEZER. Cornwallis, N. S.

2763. DAVID, born May 14, 1809, married Jane Dill of Lewiston Falls, and lived in Roxbury, Mass., where he was a carpenter.
2764. EBENEZER, born Jan. 16, 1811, married, in 1834, Jemima A. Alline, and lives in Cornwallis, N. S.
2765. BATHSHEBA, married Reuben Loomis of Cornwallis, a farmer.
2766. SOPHIA, married Israel Daniels, a farmer of Annapolis, N. S.
2767. HANNAH, married Foster Williams of Wilmot, N. S.
2768. RENE, lived in Bridgetown, N. S.
2769. SARAH ELLIS.
2770. HARRIET, married a Wood.
2771. REBECCA ANNIE, was living single.

1583. SIMON. Cornwallis, N. S.

2772. DAVID, born in 1824, married Ann Miller, and lives in Cornwallis.
2773. JOHN, born in 1826, married Sophia Miller, and lives in Cornwallis.
2774. JAMES, born 1828, and has lived in Cornwallis.

1584. EZRA. Cornwallis, N. S.

2775. BENJAMIN, born in 1827, married Ann Duncan, and lives in Cornwallis, N. S.
2776. JOSEPH, born in 1829, and is living, unmarried, in Cornwallis, N. S.

1590. ALFRED. Danielsonville, Conn.

2777. SARAH ANN LILLIE, born Dec. 20, 1831.
2778. SUSAN ELIZABETH, born March 28, 1837, and died Jan. 10, 1843.
2779. JOSEPH.

1594. ELISHA D. Eastford, Conn.

2780. HENRY EUGENE, born in Eastford, Feb. 29, 1845.
2781. LUCIA MARILLA, born in Eastford, Nov. 12, 1848.
2782. HARRIET BROWN, born in Eastford, June 5, 1852.
2783. ALBERT DAY, born in Eastford, Sept. 3, 1859, and died Jan. 8, 1860.

1603. CHARLES. Bethany, N. Y.

2784. BETSEY MEAD, born 1812, married, in 1857, Orlando Miller, and lives in Middlebury, Vt.

2785. CHARLES A., born Feb. 9, 1824, married, in 1854, Margaret L. Post, and lives in Bethany, N. Y.

1606. DAN. Bethany, N. Y.

2786. EMELINE, born in 1814, married, in 1838, Royal Clement, and lives at Alexander, N. Y.

2787. CHRISTINA, born in 1817, married, in 1841, Danford Newton, and lives in Alexander, N. Y.

2788. SOPHIA, born in 1819, married, in 1840, Orrin Putnam, and lives in Bethany, N. Y.

2789. NELSON W., born in 1822, married, in 1849, Mary Conklin, and lives in Middlebury, N. Y.

2790. FRANCES, born in 1831, and lives in Bethany, N. Y.

1608. ABNER. Batavia, N. Y.

2791. MARY, born 1828, married, in 1854, Daniel Sprague, and lives in Batavia.

2792. WALTER, born in 1834, and lives in Michigan.

2793. HENRY, born in 1845, and lives in Batavia.

1610. WILLIAM. Wisconsin.

2794. EDSON, who has a family somewhere in the West.

2795. ALONZO.

2796. HENRY.

2797. HULDA.

1614. DAVID. Bethel, Vt.

2798. DENSMORE, born Aug. 19, 1811, married, June 14, 1833, Louis Carey.

2799. POLLY, born Sept. 27, 1813, and died Feb. 27, 1832.

2800. ELIZA J., born Oct. 28, 1818, married, Jan. 10, 1831, Delos Rose of New York, who died Jan. 30, 1837, leaving one son, William H., born Oct. 28, 1836. She married, for her second husband, July 4, 1840, N. P. Sherman, by whom she has four children: Osceola, born May 25, 1842; Martha, born May 27, 1844, and died July 15, 1847; Teram M., born Nov. 15, 1847; and Emily, born Oct. 23, 1849.

2801. LAREY, born Nov. 20, 1820, and died Sept. 21, 1822.

2802. LOYAL, born Nov. 27, 1822, married, March 5, 1846, Arabell Deloss. They are living in Middlebury, Vt.

2803. CLARILLA, born Oct. 15, 1829, and died July 15, 1831.

2804. DELIA, born Jan. 12, 1833, married E. S. Eggleston, and has four children: an infant that died, Edwin H., Flora E., and Guy E.

EIGHTH GENERATION.

1616. HENRY HOSFORD. Milwaukie.

2805. CARR NOBLE, born Sept. 29, 1815, married, in 1846, Sarah Gibbon, and lives in Portage City, Wis.

2806. ABRAM A., born Dec. 18, 1818, married, Jan. 28, 1844, E. J. Ward of Kentucky, and now lives in Columbus, Wis.

2807. LORENZO, born Dec. 6, 1820, and died April 7, 1821.

2808. LORINDA, born Dec. 6, 1820, and died Sept. 27, 1822.

2809. JAMES H., born June 24, 1825, married, Aug. 9, 1849, Cynthia P. Robinson. They live in Fountain Prairie, Wis.

2810. THOMAS B., born June 28, 1827, and has lived in New York City. He is at present, (Feb., 1860,) mate of the ship Universe, between Liverpool and New York.

2811. ISAAC A., born Jan. 28, 1830, and died at Kalamazoo, Mich., April 7, 1848.

1618. JONATHAN M. Middlebury, Vt.

2812. WARREN W., born in Burlington, Vt., Oct. 10, 1820, married, in Buffalo, N. Y., in 1842, Eliza A., daughter of Henry and Sarah (Hosford) Jeudivine. She was born in Geneva, N. Y., in 1823. They are now living in Galena, Ill.

2813. JAMES P., born in 1822, and married Eugenia Heath of Middlebury, Vt., where they now live.

2814. CHARLES C., born in 1824, married Sarah Ransom, and is a machinist living in Middlebury, Vt.

2815. LAURA A., born in 1826, married Horatio N. Upson, and lives in Middlebury, Vt.

2816. GEORGE E., born in 1828, married Malvina Post of Canada East, and lives in Middlebury, Vt.

2817. LYMAN W., born in 1831, married Mary Hathron of Weybridge, Vt., and lives in Middlebury, Vt.

2818. ALBERT C., born in 1834, is a machinist living in Burlington, Vt.

1624. JOSEPH CLARK. Chicago, Ill.

This family, excepting the second and last, were born in New Haven, Vt.

2819. SOPHRONIA, born June 19, 1826, and now lives in Chicago.

2820. DEWITT CLINTON, born in Middlebury Vt., Jan. 10, 1828, and now lives in Chicago.

2821. ERASTUS DARWIN, born March 23, and lives in Chicago, Ill.

2822. JOSEPH CLARK, born Feb. 27, 1832, and lives in Chicago, Ill.

2823. LAVINIA CHAPMAN, born April 16, 1834, and lives in Chicago, Ill.

2824. CHARLES WARNER, born in Middlebury, Vt., April 27, 1842, and died in Chicago, Ill., Sept. 12, 1856.

1632. ROSWELL.
Sharon, Vt.

This family, seven in number, were born in Sharon, and all but two died in childhood. The names of the survivors are:

2825. EMELINE. 2826. ELBERT.

1633. ARANNAH.
Canada.

2827. HENRY. 2828. CHARLES. 2829. MARGARET. 2830. MARTHA.

1636. SAMUEL.
Wisconsin.

2831. JAMES. 2832. ORPHA. 2833. MARY. 2834. KEZIA. 2835. MARIA. 2836. ELIZABETH.

1647. WILLIAM M.
Washington, Vt.

2837. CYNTHIA, born in Boston, Mass., Aug. 7, 1822.

2838. BENJAMIN L., born in Montpelier, Vt., Dec. 16, 1826. He is a grocer in his native town and has a family.

2839. ALMEDIA, born Nov. 30, 1829, and died in Washington, Jan. 19, 1830.

2840. WILLIAM L., born in Washington, Nov. 30, 1831. He is a mechanic. He is married.

2841. ORRIN P., born in Washington, March 1, 1833. He is an ironsmith.

2842. DELIA G., born in Washington, Oct. 16, 1835.

2843. LESTER, born in Washington, Dec. 24, 1838.

1656. DANA S.
Washington, Vt.

2844. GEORGE, born in Holland, N. Y., May 6, 1838.

2845. CHAUNCEY, born in Corinth, Vt., Sept. 1, 1840, and died March 24, 1858.

2846. HENRY C., born in Corinth, Vt., April 22, 1844.

2847. AUSTIN B., born in Corinth, Vt., Sept. 24, 1846.

1657. JOHN P.
Washington, Vt.

2848. REBECCA, born in Washington, Dec. 29, 1840, and died March 29, 1841.

2849. JULIA A., born in Washington, Sept. 6, 1842.

2850. ETHAN ALLEN, born in Washington, March 16, 1847, and died Dec. 17, 1855.

1658. WARREN.
Washington, Vt.

2851. CHARLES W., born in Washington, Dec. 26, 1842.

2852. GEORGE E., born Dec. 29, 1844, in Washington.

2853. FRANK A., born in Washington, March 11, 1851.

EIGHTH GENERATION.

1659. HARVEY. Washington, Vt.

2854. CLARA E., born in Washington, April 22, 1849, and died May 26, of the same year.
2855. FLORA, born Aug. 6, 1853, in Washington.

1661. JAMES S. Lowell, Mass.

2856. LUCIUS W., born Aug. 14, 1838, and is living in Lowell.
2857. ALMA ESTELLE, born Feb. 13, 1855, and is with her parents in Lowell.

1664. WILLIAM C. Richland, Wis.

There are eight children in this family but their names I have been unable to get.

1665. SYLVANUS C. Pulaski, N.Y.

2858. HANNAH, born in 1853, and is in Pulaski, N. Y.
2859. CONVERSE, born in 1857, and is in Pulaski, N. Y.

1666. LEONARD. Groveland, Mass.

2860. CHARLES.
2861. FREDERICK.

1667. SYLVESTER T. West Charleston, Vt.

2862. ALLIE, born in 1855.

1668. ALONZO B. Hartford, Conn.

2863. JOHN HENRY, born in 1831.
2864. WILLIAM WILBERFORCE.
2865. MARY FRANCES.
2866. SOPHIA F.

1675. CHARLES B. New York.

2867. CHARLES BARRY, born in 1848.

1679. SOLON. Oneouta, N.Y.

2868. LEONORA, born Aug. 7, 1841.
2869. HOWARD, born Dec. 13, 1843.
2870. GEORGE, born Sept. 26, 1847, and died Jan. 6, 1852.
2871. EDWARD, born Feb. 27, 1850.
2872. HARRIET, born Oct. 20, 1852, and died Aug. 1, 1855.
2873. WILLARD, born July 21, 1856.

1688. DAVID ISRAEL. Jersey City, N. J.

The first four of this family were born in New York city and the rest in Jersey City.

2874. DAVID, born June 30, 1837, and died in Sept. of the same year.
2875. LOUISA, born Oct. 31, 1838, and died Aug. 5, 1851.
2876. MARTHA, born May 26, 1840.
2877. EMILY SOPHIA, born Aug, 7, 1841.
2878. DAVID I., born Sept. 14, 1843.
2879. MARY E., born June 15, 1845.
2880. MARIA born Dec. 7. 1846.
2881. MARCUS WILBUR, born May 5, 1848.
2882. WILLIAM BACKUS, born Feb. 10, 1850.
2883. HENRY. born Aug. 22, 1852.
2884. GEORGE, born March 30, 1855, and died Nov. 30, of the same year

1693. BACKUS WILBUR, New York City.

2885. MARY, born in Tuscaloosa, Ala., April 27, 1846.
2886. JOHN, born near Selma, Ala.. April 4, 1848.
2887. MADELEINE, born at Livingston, Ala., Nov. 1, 1850.
2888. GRACE, born at Selma, Ala., Aug. 25, 1853.
2889. WILBUR, born in New York city, Nov. 10, 1855.
2890. ANNIE, born in New York city. Feb. 19. 1858.
2890.[1] GERTRUDE, born in New York city, Jan. 5, 1861.

1698. SIMEON FITCH. Rising Sun, Wis.

2891. SARAH D., born at Akron, Ohio, March 5, 1836, married, at Freeman, Wis., Parsons D. Miner of Mass.
2892. HENRY B., born at Akron. Ohio. Dec. 27, 1838.
2893. EDMUND F., born at Catskill, N. Y., April 23, 1840.
2894. SAMUEL S., born at Oswego, N. Y., March 9. 1842.
2895. HEZEKIAH R., born at Oswego. N. Y.. Jan. 28. 1844.
2896. MARY C., born in Oswego, N. Y., Jan. 19, 1846.
2897. EMMA, born at Oswego, N. Y.. Jan. 19, 1846.
2898. JULIA D., died at Oswego. March 16, 1848.

1700. OREN. Richmond, Ind.

2899. ELIZA JANE, born in Putnam, Ohio, Sept. 13, 1828, and died July 26, 1829.
2900. MARTHAM, born in Zanesville, May 27, 1830.
2901. JULIUS AZEL, born July 26, 1840.
2902. GARRY ARMSTRONG, born June 4, 1843, and died Feb. 28, 1852
2903. GEORGE, born Nov. 6, 1854.

EIGHTH GENERATION. 347

1705. JABEZ. Marlboro, Mass.

This family were all born in Marlboro.
2904. JOHN GOODHUE, born April 19, 1837.
2905. SARAH HOWE, born Jan. 5, 1839, married, Oct. 11, 1860, Theodore Maham of Marlboro.
2906. AZEL, born Aug. 10, 1841, and died Aug. 11, 1841.
2907. GEORGE DAY, born April 23, 1843.

1706. OZIAS. Marlboro, Mass.

2908. MARY ANN, born May 20, 1845.
2909. WILLIAM BRADFORD, born Feb. 3, 1847.
2910. EMMA SUSANNAH, born Oct. 4, 1851.

1717. CHARLES THOMAS. Stockbridge, Mass.

2911. CHARLES WHITE, born May 22, 1854.

1718. GEORGE HENRY. Becket, Mass.

2913. EMILY CLARK, born Jan. 31, 1852, and died July 21, 1853.
2914. GEORGE EBENEZER, born in Becket, March 5, 1859.

1721. EDWIN TRACY. Rochester, N. Y.

2915. HENRY FITCH, born Jan. 22, 1844.
2916. CHARLES WADSWORTH, born July 24, 1848.
2917. EDWARD TRACY, born Aug. 27, 1850.
2918. ELLEN MARY, born Jan. 18, 1858.

1722. HENRY HYDE. Albany, N. Y.

2919. LOUISA CLINTON, born Nov. 2, 1845.
2920. FLORENCE WILLIAMS, born June 5, 1852.

1723. WILLIAM W. New Haven, Conn.

2921. WILLIAM ROSWELL, born March 8, 1849.
2922. ARTHUR TRACY, born Aug. 4, 1850.
2923. ALICE SHIPMAN, born July 2, 1853.
2924. FREDERICK KIRTLAND, born April 7, 1857.
2925. GEORGE PRATT, born July 12, 1860.

1728. JOSEPH OTIS. Norwich, Conn.

2926. ANN OTIS, born June 29, 1844.
2927. JOSEPH OTIS, born April 29, 1846.

1730. PETER RICHARDS. Medina, Ohio.

2928. JANE and others whose names I have not obtained.

1731. JOHN GRISWOLD. Norwich City, Conn.

2929. JEDEDIAH, born Aug. 7, 1837, married, June 6, 1860, Annie E. Hazzard of Kingston, R. I. They have one child, born Jan. 2, 1863.
2930. JOHN RICHARDS, born May 25, 1846.
2931. CHARLES ISHAM, born Nov. 16, 1856, and died Sept. 7, 1860.

1738. BENJAMIN SNOW. Flatbush, L. I.

2932. ALBERT, born in Feb., 1840, and died same month.

1740. JOHN FELIX. Brooklyn, N. Y.

2933. LOUISA, born Oct. 29, 1853.
2934. WILLIAM S., born Feb. 15, 1855.
2935. JAMES MILNOR.
2935.[1] CHARLOTTE, born Dec. 25, 1860.

1755. WILLIAM P. Fulton, Iowa.

2936. LORAIN W., born June 17, 1825, and lives in Ogdensburg. N. Y.
2937. DELIA A., born April 7, 1827, married, Oct. 10, 1847, E. W. Sessions, and lives in Fulton, Iowa.
2938. WILLIAM H., born Oct. 8, 1828, married, Aug. 29, 1852, Agnes Powell, and resides in Fulton, Iowa.
2939. HORACE, born Nov. 30, 1830, still single in Fulton.
2940. SUSAN E., born Aug. 16, 1833, and lives unmarried in Fulton.
2941. HANNAH M. J., born June 13, 1841, and lives in Fulton.

1765. LUCIUS W. C. Zenia, Ohio.

2942. CAROLINE E., born Oct. 3, 1835, died at Zenia, July 20, 1849, of cholera.
2943. ANN MARIA, born Sept. 4, 1837, married, Sept. 4, 1855, D. J. Mozart, and has one child: Sarah F., born Jan. 26, 1839, and died at Zenia, July 20, 1849, of cholera.
2944. JULIETTA, born Nov. 22, 1844.

1767. WILLIAM. Howell, Mich.

2945. THERINA C., born Oct. 14, 1845.
2946. MARIETTE E., born Aug. 10, 1847, and died Oct. 11, 1849.
2947. WILLIAM C., born June 4, 1850.
2948. EMMA L., born Nov. 11, 1854.

1768. NELSON. Zenia, Ohio.

2949. EDWIN M., born in Chelsea, Mass., Aug. 7, 1845, and died at Zenia, Ohio, Sept. 27, 1846.
2950. LUCIUS W. C., born at Zenia, July 7, 1849.
2951. MARY C., born at Zenia, May 20, 1853.
2952. SARAH A., was a twin sister of the above.
2953. LAURA EVA, born at Zenia, Nov. 16, 1854.

EIGHTH GENERATION. 349

1769. JOSEPH GILBERT. Thompson, N. Y.

2954. ALICE JANSEN, born Aug. 22, 1849.
2955. MARY ESTHER, born Dec. 8, 1851.
2956. EDWARD LEE, born Sept. 12. 1853.

1777. JOSEPH GORTON. California.

2957. WILLIAM SWIFT, born in Monticello, N. Y., Sept. 27, 1847, and is in New York.
2958. JOSEPH GORTON, born in Monticello. N. Y., Sept. 19, 1849.

1780. HENRY LEWIS. Waterloo, N. Y.

2959. GILBERT CLARK, born at Bunker Hill, Ill., Oct. 18, 1854.
2960. GLEN WOOD, born at Bunker Hill, Ill., Aug. 19, 1856.

1788. JAMES PORTER. Mansfield, Conn.

2961. HERBERT OTHELLO.

1797. SIMEON. Norwich, Conn.

2962. JULIETTE AUGUSTA, born Nov. 28, 1829, married James M. Bonner, and lived in Windsor, Conn., where he died. They had two children. She married, after his death, Benjamin Middleton of Muscatine, Iowa, where they now live.
2963. FREDERIC MORTIMER, born April 7, 1830, married Nancy Lee of Meriden, where they now (1860) live.
2964. CHARLES TREADWAY, born Feb., 1840, and died 1847, in Norwich, Connecticut.
2965. ALONZO C., born Oct. 27, 1835, and is in Hartford, Conn. He is now in the Union army.

1773. CHARLES C. New Haven, Conn.

2966. ANNA, died aged 17 years.

1803. WILLIAM W. New York.

2967. NELSON PALMER, born July 11, 1856.

NINTH GENERATION.

1829. JACOB. Henniker, N. H.

2968. ELIJAH BROWN, born June 15, 1811, married, Oct. 24, 1838, Mary P. Breed. They live in Henniker, N. H., where he is a farmer. He is, in religion, a Friend, as are the rest of this family.

2969. ELIZABETH, born March 29, 1813, married, Oct. 21, 1834, Jacob (1839), and died Sept. 16, 1838.

2970. SARAH, born May 31, 1815, and died June 15, 1834.

2971. ROBERT G., born May 21, 1817, and died Oct. 22, 1819.

2972. FRANKLIN THEOPHILUS, born Aug. 21, 1830, married, June 15, 1853, Lavina Gove. He is a farmer, and lives in Henniker.

2973. HULDAH G., born March 23, 1834, married, in May, 1857, Joshua Buxton of Danvers, Mass. They have one son, Horace F., born March 1, 1858.

2974. A SON, born July 25, 1838, and died Sept. 27, 1858.

2975. JOSEPH JOHN, born March 16, 1840.

1832. THOMAS. Weare, N. H.

2976. ANNA J., born April 26, 1820, married Dow Chase. Their children were: Benjamin H., born Sept. 18, 1839; Sarah J., born May 21, 1841, and died March 10, 1842; Nathaniel J., born April 28, 1843; George D., born Jan. 3, 1847, and died May 11, 1851; Asa P., born March 7, 1850; and Sarah M., born June 6, 1854. Mrs. Chase died June 2, 1859.

2977. SARAH G., born May 10, 1822, and died May 11, 1841.

2978. MARY J., born July 15, 1824, and died Oct. 18, 1826.

1834. JOHN. Weare, N. H.

2979. JAMES HARVEY, born May 10, 1822, and died Sept. 19, 1831.

2980. SALLY MARIA, born Aug. 17, 1825, married, Nov. 9, 1847, George Emerson, and resides in Lynn, Mass. They have one child: Mary B., born May 16, 1851.

2981. EZRA, born March 20, 1829, married, Sept 4, 1851, Mehetabel G. Bodge. He is a member of the Society of Friends, a machinist, and lives in Manchester, N. H.

2982. WILLIAM C., born March 29, 1831, married, Oct. 2, 1857, Sarah Ann Chadwick, and lives in Newark, N. J., where he is one of the proprietors of the Huntington Machine Company.

1836. ENOCH. *Amesbury, Mass.*

2983. HANNAH LOUISA, born July 9, 1822, is a teacher.

2984. MOSES, born March 15, 1824, died Aug. 9, 1825.

2985. ALEXANDER McRAE, born May 15, 1825, is a teacher. He was at one time in California, but is now in Amesbury, Mass.

2986. MOSES PAGE, born Aug. 30, 1827, married Rhoda Bartlett and is a mechanic.

2987. JACOB RANDALL, born July 31, 1829, married, Aug. 13, 1857, Harriet N. Janvrin. He is a carriage maker and lives in Amesbury, Mass.

1837. JOHN. *Amesbury, Mass.*

2988. PHILIP J., born in Nov., 1822, and died in 1825.

2989. JOHN DEAN, born in 1826, married Sept. 28, 1856, Mary J. Page. They now live on a part of the original Huntington houselot. He is in the Union army and has been in thirteen engagements.

2990. RUTH ANN, born March 28, 1827, and is a teacher.

2991. PHILIP JONES, born May 23, 1831, and died in November of the same year.

2992. MOSES NEWELL, born Dec. 20, 1834.

1839. JACOB. *Amesbury, Mass.*

2993. BENJAMIN FRANKLIN, born Sept. 7, 1838.

2994. ELIZABETH H., born May 17, 1844.

2995. JOHN WARREN, born Aug. 10, 1853.

1840. PHILIP. *Haverhill, Mass.*

2996. CHARLES OTIS, born in 1831, married, in 1857, Mary Merril.

2997. CAROLINE A., born 1829, married Walter Dale and died in May, 1850, leaving one child.

2998. JAMES ALBERT, born June 29, 1834, married Harriet Evans.

2999. ELLEN F., born June 8, 1836, and married Gilman Sleeper. They have one daughter, born in 1861.

3000. FREDERIC E., born April 18, 1838.

3001. SUSAN L., born March 18, 1840.

1841. DANIEL. *Amesbury Mass.*

3002. GEORGE F., born Aug. 24, 1846.

3003. SARAH A., born May 29, 1850.

3004. DANIEL E., born May 3, 1852.

1842. MOSES. Amesbury, Mass.

3005. ABRAHAM J., born in Amesbury, June 20, 1831.

1841. EPHRAIM M. New Jersey.

3006. CHARLES E., born in Nov., 1850.
3007. NELLIE, born Nov. 4, 1855.

1845. STEPHEN. West Newbury, Mass.

This family were all born in West Newbury, Mass.

3008. JOHN LEWIS, born Dec. 30, 1825, married, Oct. 23, 1849, Elizabeth Ann Bailey of Newbury, who was born May 2, 1828. They now reside in Georgetown, Mass.

3009. MICAJAH POORE, born April 15, 1828, married Mary Smith, who was born in Newburyport, Mass., in June, 1828. He is in the Union army, and was wounded at the Antietam battle.

3010. MARY ELIZABETH, born July 1, 1833, married Kendrick Winter Pickett, of Georgetown, Mass., where they now live.

3011. WILLIAM HENRY, born March 4, 1841, and lives still in West Newbury, Mass.

3012. MOSES POORE, born Jan. 22, 1846.

1846. MOSES. West Newbury, Mass.

3013. LEWIS V., born Aug. 18, 1825, and died June 7, 1832.
3014. GEORGE, born June 23, 1827, and died in 1857.
3015. NATHAN G., born Nov. 16, 1830, married Lydia Dillingham and has lived in Granville, N. Y.
3016. LYDIA, born Dec. 24, 1833.

1847. DANIEL. Pontiac, N. Y.

3017. ANNA B., born May 20, 1824, married Cyrus Morrison of Granville, N. Y. They have two children: Harriet Adelia, born May 25, 1845; and Helen Eliza, born Feb. 1, 1849.

3018. ELVIRA, born March 13, 1830, married Selden Waite.
3019. WILLIAM D., born May 13, 1836.

1849. JOHN. Lincoln, Vt.

3020. SARAH JANE, born June 24, 1830, married Robert Elliot. Their children are: Cynthia S., born Sept. 19, 1851; and Irving, born Aug. 31, 1853. They live in Lincoln, Vt.

3021. ACHSAH M., born Sept. 10, 1833, and married William Taber.
3022. ELIZA M., born Jan. 25, 1837.
3023. CLARK S., born Oct. 11, 1842.

1857. DAVID. Lawrence, Mass.

3024. CLARA A., born July 2, 1836.
3025. CHARLES S., born Feb. 12, 1838, and died in Sept., 1847.
3026. SARAH B., born May 15, 1840.
3027. JAMES N., born Oct. 16, 1841, married, Dec. 10, 1860, **Betsey Ann Maguire**, and lives in Lawrence, Mass.
3028. ELLEN O., born March 30, 1843, and died in July, 1855.
3029. LAURA A., born Oct. 26, 1844, and died Aug. 7, 1845.
3030. THOMAS A., born July 25, 1846, and died in Aug., 1850.
3031. CHARLES T., born Nov. 8, 1849.
3032. FRANK D., born April 21, 1851.
3033. ELLEN A., born Aug. 21, 1855.

1862. NATHAN. Amesbury, Mass.

3034. LOUISA, born July 10, 1847.
3035. SUSAN, born Nov. 23, 1848.
3036. SARAH, born July 5, 1850.
3037. NATHAN, born Dec. 16, 1853.
3038. ELLA J., born March 9, 1855.
3039. EMERY OSBOURN, born May 26, 1860.

1865. WILLIAM.

3040. MARY D., born Jan. 31, 1848.
3041. HOMER A., born Jan. 6, 1857.
3042. THOMAS MARSHALL, born Feb. 23, 1859.

1867. DANIEL H. Amesbury, Mass.

3043. WILLIAM A., born June 20, 1848, and died in the same year.
3044. WILLIAM A., born Nov. 30, 1849.
3045. HENRY L., born Aug. 4, 1852.
3045.[1] ELIZABETH, born in 1857.

1872. EPHRAIM. Amesbury, Mass.

3046. WILLIAM H., born in 1826, married Philene Brake.

1873. WILLIAM H. Brentwood, N. H.

3047. MARY, born in 1835, married Oliver Carter, and has one child.
3048. EMELINE, born in 1838.
3049. SARAH, born in 1842.
3050. HANNAH H., born in 1844.
3051. CHARLES, born in 1849.

1873.⁷ SAMUEL. Hallowell, Me

3051.⁵ SAMUEL.

1873.⁷ FRANCIS M. Litchfield, Me.

3051.⁶ A DAUGHTER.

1891. RODNEY S. Nashua, N. H.

3052. JOSEPHINE A., born in Manchester, N. H., Dec. 6, 1841.
3053. ELMER C., born in Manchester, N. H., Dec. 11, 1844.
3054. QUINCY M., born in Nashua, N. H., April 12, 1851.
3055. KATE MARIA, born in Nashua, N. H., Aug. 12, 1852, and died Dec. 15, 1860, of diptheria.

1897. JOSEPH. Au Sable Forks, N. Y.

3056. GEORGE, born March 23, 1840, fell in the battle of Antietam, near Sharpsburg, Md., Sept. 17, 1862.
3057. JOSEPH, born April 9, 1845.
3058. HELEN LOUISA, born Nov. 15, 1848.
3059. IDA JANE, born May 2, 1851.
3060. SARAH EVA, born Aug. 31, 1853.
3061. JOHN CHARLES FREMONT, born June 20, 1858.
3062. JAMES FRANKLIN, born July 15, 1860.
3062.¹ HENRY, born Aug. 30, 1862.

1899. JOHN C. Scroon, N. Y.

3062.² JULIA. 3062.³ SAMUEL. 3062.⁴ GEORGE. 3062.⁵ JANE. 3062.⁶ SARAH ANN. 3062.⁷ ALBERT.

The above list of names (from 955) reached me as the work was going through the press.

1902. MOSES B. North Elba, N. Y.

3063. ANN MARIA, born Oct. 26, 1848.
3064. JAMES WALLACE, born Nov. 13, 1851.
3065. ADA ISABELL, born May 13, 1854.

1910. CHARLES. Bloomington, Ill.

3066. GEORGE WILLIAM, born June 22, 1850, and died March 13, 1854.
3067. MARY ISABELLA, born July 30, 1847.
3068. EDWARD HARVEY, born Nov. 27, 1853, and died April 24, 1854.

1912. HENRY. Valparaiso, Ind.

This family were all born in Valparaiso.
3069. CHRISTOPHER H., born April 6, 1851, and died Nov. 26, 1853.
3070. AMELIA FRANCES, born March 12, 1853.
3071. GEORGE WILLIAM, born Aug. 11, 1855.

1916. EDWARDS CHARLES. Galesburg, Ill.

3072. CARA LOUISE, born in Penn Yan, N. Y., Feb. 22, 1859.

1925. HEZEKIAH.

3072.¹ FLORENCE CAROLINE, born in July, 1851.
3072.² CHARLES ASHER, born in Jan. 1855.
3072³ A SON.

1932. SAMUEL ELLIS. Franklin, Conn.

3072.⁴ ZIBA JEDIDIAH, born in 1856.

1949. HEZEKIAH. Franklin, Conn.

3073. HEZEKIAH, born June 4, 1855, and died March 26, 1856.
3074. HENRY LESLEY, born Jan. 29, 1857.
3075. ASAHEL ADELBERT, born July 1, 1860.

1950. HENRY ASAHEL. Boston, Mass.

3076. SARAH E., born Feb. 5, 1851.
3077. EMMA L., born May 26, 1852.
3078. CORNELIA D., born Aug. 29, 1856.

1952. JAMES F. Marietta, Ohio.

3079. KATE WHIPPLE, born Dec. 3, 1849, in Exeter, N. H.
3080. FRANK HENRY, born June 22, 1851, in Lowell, Mass., and died Aug. 15, 1852.
3081. EDWARD WELLS, born in Marietta, Ohio, April 14, 1856.
3082. OLIVER MAYHEW, born in Marietta, June 9, 1858.
3083. ALICE, born in Marietta, Aug. 8, 1860.

1972. JOHN W. P. Yoncalla, Oregon.

3084. BENJAMIN, born in Yoncalla. Oregon, Sept. 9, 1859.
3084.¹ THOMAS DUNLAP, born in Aug., 1861.

1975. PELETIAH WEBSTER. Columbus, Ohio.

3085. BENJAMIN, born in Columbus, Ohio, Aug. 27, 1859.
3085.¹ THOMAS DUNLAP, born Sept. 4, 1861.

NINTH GENERATION.

1982. J. MUNROE.   Roche a Cree, Wis.

3086. DWIGHT, born Sept. 26, 1853.
3087. CLARISSA, born April, 1854.
3088. CELESTIA, born July 31, 1857.

1983. CHARLES E.   McGrawville, N. Y.

3089. CHARLES HERBERT, born April 5, 1853.
3090. HELEN, born Dec. 1, 1858.

1986. HENRY.   Eagleville, Conn.

3091. DWIGHT CADMUS, born Nov. 2, 1855, and died April 25, 1856.
3091.¹ GEORGE A., born in March, 1857.

1988. ANDREW JACKSON.   Hartford, Conn.

3092. CHARLES GERRISH, born Oct. 20, 1856.
3092.¹ MARY LOUISA, born May 18, 1858.
3092.² JENNIE, born Aug. 6, 1860, and died Sept. 7, 1862.

1992. NATHAN.   Boston, Mass.

3093. ANNETTE.

1995. JOHN.   East Wareham, Mass.

3094. SAMUEL AVERILL, born in 1847.
3095. ISABEL, born in 1849.

1996. CHARLES B.   Perry, N. Y.

3096. JANE ELIZABETH, born in 1850.

2003. HENRY (M. D.)   Albany, Ga.

3097. CHARLES DUSTUN, born Aug. 9, 1848, and died Aug. 16, 1849.
3098. HENRY D., born July 16, 1850.
3099. LAURA CORBIN, born April 9, 1853, and died July 12, 1857.
3100. FREDERIC WALTER, born Nov. 27, 1858.

2007. MYRON.   Shaftesbury, Vt.

3102. FRANKLIN AMOS, born Dec. 5, 1850.
3103. CHARLES HYDE, born Dec. 17, 1853.
3104. WILLIAM, born Dec. 5, 1856.
3105. HELEN JANE, born June 23, 1859.
3105.¹ HENRY, born May 11, 1861.

2026. ELON.   Troy, N. Y.

3106. MARY, born in 1844.
3107. CHARLES, born in 1847.
3108. JANE, born in 1849.

2031. JAY, Rev. — Canton, N. Y.
3109. WILLIAM S., born June 10, 1858.

2034. HENRY EDWARDS. — Chicago, Ill.
3110. MARY E., born in Troy, N. Y., Sept. 10, 1849.
3111. KATE, born in Troy, June 21, 1862, and died in Troy, Aug., 1853.
3112. ALICE, born in Troy, Dec. 21, 1853.

2035. CHARLES RAYMOND. — New York City.
3113. JULIA, born June 10, 1851.
3114. EVA, born Nov. 13, 1852.
3115. KATE, born Jan. 24, 1856.
3116. CHARLES RAYMOND, born July 15, 1857.

2037. LYNDE C. — Chicago, Ill.
3117. CHARLES GRISWOLD, born in Chicago, Oct. 16, 1860.

2057. EDWIN. — Rochester, N. Y.
3118. ELLA, born Aug. 29, 1847.

2058. GEORGE B. — Castile, N. Y.
3119. JUNIETTA E., born Oct. 20, 1850.

2061. T. ROMEYN, (M. D.) — Perry, N. Y.
3120. ABBY A., born May 9, 1852.
3121. FREDERIC WILLIAM, born Oct. 25, 1854.
3121.¹ HARRY H., born in Dec., 1859.

2122. FRANKLIN C. — South Brookfield, N. Y.
3122. SHIRLEY L., born in South Brookfield, Aug. 6, 1859.
3123. IVA LORD, born Oct. 10, 1860.

2128. BENJAMIN HOAGLAND. — Brooklyn, N. Y.
3124. STEPHEN WALLACE, born Oct. 14, 1858.
3125. MARY ELMIRA, born Nov. 25, 1860.

2206. LUCIUS SETH. — Shefford, C. E.
3126. RUSS WOOD, born Feb. 14, 1855.

2299. CHARLES W. — Hartford, Conn.
3126.¹ ALICE born Oct. 6, 1861.

NINTH GENERATION. 359

2312. RANDOLPH. New York City.

3127. ROBBIE GUY, born in New York, April 10, 1856, and died June 27, 1858.

3128. RANDOLPH HOWARD, born in New York City, July 22, 1858, and died April 2, 1861, of hydrocephalus.

3128.¹ A DAUGHTER.

2321. G. GERALDI. Galena, Ill.

3128.² AN INFANT.

2328. WILLIAM RUFUS. Wauseon, Ohio.

3129. CARRIE.

2343. CHAUNCY D.

3130. ADELAIDE ELIZABETH, born Dec. 28, 1831.
3131. SARAH IMOGENE, born Dec. 6, 1846.

2351. JOHN D. Watertown, N. Y.

3132. WILLIAM H., born in Watertown, Aug. 1, 1854.

2356. JOHN JAY. Watertown, N. Y.

3133. CHARLES JAY, born Feb. 27, 1851, and died Aug. 29, of same year.

2360. WILLIAM LATHROP. Depauville, N. Y.

3134. EMMA JANE, born May 31, 1849.
3135. MARY JOSEPHINE, born Oct. 27, 1850, and died Dec. 9, 1857.
3136. WILLIAM HENRY, born Jan. 23, 1856.

2361. HIRAM LORD. Brooklyn, N. Y.

3137. JOHN LORD, born Sept. 24, 1849.
3138. LIZZIE S., born Jan. 16, 1854, and died Aug. 13, 1854.
3138.¹ FRED POWELL, born Oct. 4, 1860.
3138.² ELLA EDWINA, born June 13, 1862.

2366. HORACE C. Watertown, N. Y.

3139. HARRISON S., born July 25, 1857.

2401. LOUIS C. LAMBERT. Phillpsburg, St. Martins.

3140. ELIZA MATILDA, born Sept. 13, 1850.
3141. CAROLINE MARIA, born June 10, 1852.
3142. LOUIS CHARLES LAMBERT, born May 28, 1854.
3143. JAMES CLEMENT, born April 17, 1857.
3144. EDWARD CARROL, born June 22, 1859, and died Oct. 26, 1860.

2437. JEDIDIAH. Norwich, Conn.

3145. SARAH LANMAN, born April 23, 1835.
3146. MARY HAMPTON, born July 8, 1836, and died in Norwich, June 7, 1861.
3147. JOSEPH OTIS, born in 1838, and died Nov. 15, 1841.

2441. EDWARD BOYLSTON. Roxbury, Mass.

3148. PETER LANMAN, born June 8, 1833.
3149. SUSAN MANSFIELD, born June 22, 1835, in New York city, and married in Roxbury, Jan. 4, 1860, Rev. Francis B. Perkins of Montague, Mass.
3150. EDWARD TRUMBULL, born Feb. 22, 1837, and died in New York city, May 23, 1837.
3151. EDWARD NORTON, born Sept. 14, 1835, at Poughkeepsie, N. Y., and died Oct. 27, 1861, in Roxbury, Mass.
3152. MARY LANMAN, born March 23, 1842, in Brooklyn, N. Y.
3153. FREDERICK JABEZ, born Dec. 6, 1844, in Boonton, N. J.
3154. ELIZABETH MORE, born July 14, 1851, in Dorchester, Mass., and died same day.

2452. CHARLES F. Brookline, Mass.

3155. ALMA FRENCH, born May 14, 1847.

2453. WILLIAM SALSTONSTAL.

3155.[1] ADELAIDE HEBARD.
3155.[2] MARY ALMA.
3155.[3] WILLIAM.

2467. JOSEPH C. New York.

3156. DAVID L. DODGE, born in Norwich, April 30, 1818, married, Feb. 3, 1847, Martha Van Dresar. He was a merchant, for years, in New York city. He is now living in Scranton, Pa.
3157. GEORGE FREDERIC, born in Norwich, Jan. 5, 1820, graduated in medicine at the Albany Medical College, and is now living, in the practice of his profession, in Portage City, Wis. He married, Dec. 11, 1844, Flora, daughter of James Cleland of New York city. He is now (1862) surgeon in the Union army.
3158. LUCIA COIT, born in Norwich, April 11, 1822, married Sept. 5, 1840, George Hale White, M. D., of Hudson, N. Y., who died April 11, 1857. She married again, Oct. 23, 1861, Stephen L. Magoun. They live in Hudson, N. Y.
3159. MARY STRONG, born in Norwich, Feb. 14, 1824, and died April 12, 1826.
3160. WILLIAM STUART, born in Norwich, April 2, 1827, and died March 24, 1831.
3161. JULIA PORTER, born in Norwich, Feb. 16, 1829, married, July 1,

1848, William H. Grenelle of New York city, where she still resides. Their children are: Julia Stewart, born Dec. 27, 1849; William Earl, born June 1, 1852; Charles Frederick, born Oct. 13, 1855, and died June 11, 1861; and Joseph Huntington, born July 8, 1861.

3162. LYDIA COIT, born in Norwich, Jan. 25, 1831, and died Sept. 20, 1832.

3163. JOSEPH ELLSWORTH, born in Norwich, May 28, 1833, and died Sept. 7, 1834.

3164. CHARLES STUART, born in New York city, March 20, 1835, and died Aug. 31, 1835.

3165. CHARLES STUART, born in Waterford, N. Y., June 17, 1838, and is living in New York city. He has been in the U. S. service, during the present war.

3166. SARAH CLEVELAND, born in Hudson, N. Y., Feb. 15, 1840, married, April 12, 1859, William Lewis, son of William North Seymour, of New York city. They have one son, William N., born at Yonkers, N. Y., Feb. 20, 1861, and died Feb. 26, 1861; and a daughter, Julia Huntington, born in New York, March 1, 1862.

2471. OLIVER ELLSWORTH. Cleveland, Ohio.

3167. HENRY STRONG, born July 15, 1836, in New York city. He graduated at Yale College in 1857, and was engaged in teaching, for some months, in Norwalk, Conn. He pursued his theological studies in Andover, Mass., and was licensed to preach, by the Essex South Association, Tuesday, Jan. 14, 1862.

3168. HARRIET LUCRETIA, born in Norwich, March 2, 1832, and died in New York, June 2, 1834.

3169. LYDIA COIT, born in New York, Nov. 26, 1834, and died in Norwich, Sept. 7, 1835.

3170. CHARLES ELLSWORTH, born April 18, 1837, and died in Ohio City, May 9, 1841.

2472. ANDREW BACKUS. Baltimore, Md.

3171. JOSEPH WILLIAMS NORRIS, born Nov. 26, 1830, and died April 24, 1831.

3172. JOSEPH WILLIAMS NORRIS, born Jan. 27, 1832, married, July 8, 1855, the youngest daughter of William and Sybilla Pippitt, who was born Oct. 10, 1825. In 1858, he was preparing himself for the ministry of the Episcopal church, to go into some missionary field.

3173. EUNICE SARAH NORRIS, born Nov. 20, 1833, and married, June 28, 1859, Samuel Barrington of Philadelphia. They have one child, Eveline.

3174. ANDREW BACKUS, born in Norwich, Jan. 1, 1835, married Sarah Annie, daughter of John McGinley of Philadelphia. She was born Oct. 5, 1832.

3175. CHARLES SNOWDEN, born March 1, 1837.

3176. JANE ELIZA, born June 17, 1839.

3177. JOHN BUCKLER, born Jan. 21, 1841, and died Aug. 3, 1841.

3178. ROSALIE LETITIA NORRIS, born March 17, 1842, and died July 12, 1842.
3179. EDWARD SHAEFFER NORRIS, born July 7, 1843, and died March 9, 1844.
3180. GEORGE FREDERICK, born April 28, 1845, and is now (1862) in the Union army.
3181. RICHARD THOMAS, born May 24, 1847.

2478. JOHN P. New York City.

3182. MARY P., born Feb. 12, 1831, is with her grandfather Perkins, in Norwich.
3183. FRANCIS PERKINS, born July 24, 1832, and died Aug. 25, 1832.
3184. FRANCIS P., born July 4, 1833, and died July 3, 1835.
3185. FRANCIS PERKINS, born June 3, 1835, and died May 2, 1846, in Roxbury, Mass.
3186. CHARLES P., born Aug. 9, 1836, is living in Milwaukie, Wis.
3187. JOHN P., born April 12, 1838, and died Dec. 6, 1838, in New York.
3188. ABBY PERKINS, born Oct. 8, 1839, and died Jan. 2, 1842.
3189. SAMUEL HENRY, born Dec. 12, 1841, and died Sept. 11, 1843, in Brooklyn, N. Y.
3190. EDWARD P., born July 12, 1843, and died April 14, 1844, in Franklin, Conn.

2479. CHARLES WEBSTER. New York.

3191. JULIA HOWELL, born Sept. 15, 1837, married Proctor Hutchinson, and lived in New York city, where he died. They had two children, Henry Clay and Julia, who is the adopted child of James M. (2483.)
3192. CHARLES PHELPS, born Sept. 16, 1839, and is living in New York, and is a clerk in the firm of Porter and Spencer,

2482. BENJAMIN F. Franklin, Conn.

3193. BENJAMIN F., born Aug. 28, 1839, in Brooklyn Ohio.
3194. EMILY LEE, born April 14, 1841.
3195. JOSEPH LAWSON.
3196. WEATHERLY, born Aug. 28, 1843.
3197. HANNAH PHELPS, born Nov. 1, 1845.
3197.[1] MARIA PERIT, died in infancy.
3197.[2] MARIA PERIT.

2483. JAMES M. Norwich City, Conn.

3198. ROSCOE, born Nov. 30, 1843.
3198.[1] JULIA, born in New York City, March 27, 1859.

2493. JOHN M. Chicago, Ill.

3199. AUSTIN PARKS, born in Chicago, Dec. 7, 1857.

NINTH GENERATION.

2494. HENRY BOWERS. Lebanon, Conn.

3200. THOMAS M.

2495. GEORGE WOLCOTT, (M. D.) Rock Island, Ill.

3201. ANNIE CHILDS, born in Reading, Mass., May 25, 1849, and died in Pittsfield. Feb. 18, 1852.
3202. THOMAS MYERS, born in Pittsfield, May 6, 1852.
3203. KATE MARY, born in Pittsfield, May 6, 1852, and died in Pittsfield, Aug. 12, 1853.
3204. TIMOTHY CAMPBELL, born May 6, 1855, in St. Louis, Mo.
3205. ALICE HENDERSON, born in Rock Island, Sept. 17, 1856.

2557. SAMUEL P. Painesville, Ohio.

3206. CHARLES E., born June 10, 1852.
3207. JULIAN C., born Sept. 1, 1855, and died Sept. 18, 1856.
3207.¹ FREDERICK RUSSEL, born Jan. 18, 1862.

2569. EDWIN. Painesville, Ohio.

3208. FRANK C., born Jan 28, 1858.
3209. JULIAN JACKSON, born Aug. 6, 1860.

2579. EUGENE. Winnebago City, Wis.

The two oldest children, a son and daughter, died in Indiana in 1850 and 1851.
3209.¹ JOSEPH N. born May 4, 1852.
3209.² FLORA A., born Dec. 23, 1854.
3209.³ CYNTHIA A. born Dec. 25, 1857.
3209.⁴ PENINA JANE, born July 29, 1861.

2606. JOHN S., REV. New Haven, Conn.

3210. WINSLOW WILLIAMS, born in New Haven, Oct., 1857, and died March 1, 1858.
3211. JOHN WILLIAMS, born July 28, 1859.
3211.¹ HARWOOD, born in 1862.

2627. EDWARD FREDERIC. Salem, Wis.

3212. EMMA.
3213. OMAR.
3214. A DAUGHTER.

2628. OREGON EDGAR. Painesville, Ohio.

3215. MARVIN.
3216. GEORGE EDGAR.

2747. RICHARD. Yarmouth, N. S.

3217. FRANKLIN, born at Halifax, N. S., July 26, 1849.
3218. LILLIAN FLETCHER, born at Chelsea, Mass., March 12, 1851.
3219. GERTRUDE WELTON, born at same time, died in Chelsea, Sept., 1852.
3220. HERBERT ALLEN, born at North Chelsea, Mass., July 5, 1844, and died at Yarmouth, N. S., April, 1855.
3221. WILFRID, born in Yarmouth, Oct. 5, 1856.

2632. SAMUEL GATES. Middlefield, N. Y.

3222. HELEN WILSON, born in Middlefield, N. Y., Nov. 27, 1849.
3223. AGNES CHURCH, born in Middlefield, N. Y., Jan. 4, 1851.
3224. GEORGE MANN, born in Middlefield, N. Y., Aug. 2, 1853.
3225. ALICE PARMELEE, born in Middlefield, N. Y., Jan. 25, 1857.

2664. WILLIAM SILLIMAN. Middlefield, N. Y.

3226. SAMUEL SILLIMAN, born Sept. 12, 1853, and died next day.
3227. WILLIAM WALKER, born Sept. 12, 1853.
3228. SARAH JOSEPHINE, born Dec. 25, 1860.

2722. WILLIAM L. Lebanon, Conn.

3228.¹ FREDERIC CLARK, born Sept. 25, 1862.

2763. DAVID. Roxbury, Mass.

3229. MARIA, born in 1850.

2798. DENSMORE.

3230. LOYAL, born Sept. 9, 1835.
3231. LUCRETIA, born Jan. 6, 1840, married, Sept. 12, 1860, Cronlius Buman.
3232. HENRY, born June, 14, 1843.
3233. MARTHA, born July 12, 1853.

2802. LOYAL. Middlebury, Vt.

3234. ARABELLA, born March 9, 1847.
3235. DELOSS, born Feb. 3, 1856, and died in infancy.

2806. ABRAM A. Columbus, Wis.

3236. HENRY M., born Dec. 20, 1846.
3237. MARY AMANDA, born Dec. 15, 1848, and died in March, 1853.
3238. SARAH SOPHIA, born June 2, 1852, and died in March, 1853.
3239. FREDDY, born Oct. 22, 1854, and died in Sept., 1856.
3240. JAMES, born Oct. 21, 1857.
3241. JENNY, born Oct. 21, 1857.

NINTH GENERATION.

2809. JAMES H. — Fountain Prairie, Wis.

3242. ALBINA H., born Dec. 4, 1851.
3243. MARY S., born Nov. 11, 1853.
3244. JAMES B., born Oct. 8, 1856.

2812. WARREN W. — Galena, Ill.

3245. HENRY J., born in Buffalo, N. Y., in 1844, and died in Galena, Ill. Sept. 4, 1854.

2831. BENJAMIN L. — Montpelier, Vt.

3246. WILDER P., born May 7, 1852, in Montpelier.
3247. FLORENCE E., born March 27, 1855.
3248. CHARLES F., born June 8, 1857.

2840. WILLIAM L. — Washington, Vt.

3249. EVA BELL, born Aug. 22, 1857.

2938. WILLIAM H. — Fulton, Iowa.

3250. WILLIAM FRED, born July 4, 1853.
3251. CHARLOTTE J., born Dec. 23, 1855.

2963. FREDERIC M. — Meriden, Conn.

3252. ELLEN.
3253. ORAMEL.
3254. INFANT.

TENTH GENERATION.

2968. ELIJAH B.   Henniker, N. H.
3255. SEWELL C., born May 5, 1856.

2972. THEOPHILUS FRANKLIN.   Henniker, N. H.
3256. LAURETTE, born May 22, 1854.
3257. DANA E., born Dec. 13, 1857.

2981. EZRA.   Manchester, N. H.
3258. ELLEN, born July 8, 1853.
3159. OLIVE C., born Nov. 18, 1856.

2982. WILLIAM.   Newark, N. J.
3260. CLARENCE WILLIAM, born May 31, 1857.
3261. EMILY PENNINGTON, Aug. 17, 1859.

2987. JACOB RANDALL.   Amesbury, Mass.
3262. FANNIE JANVRIN, born Aug. 1, 1858.
3263. MARY JOANNAH, born Aug. 3, 1859.

2989. JOHN DEAN.   Amesbury, Mass.
3264. HANNAH MARIA, born Aug. 21, 1858.
3265. ALFRED LEWIS, born Aug. 5, 1860.
3265. A SON, born in 1862.

2998. JAMES ALBERT.   Haverhill, Mass.
3265.[1] WALTER EVANS, born in 1861.

3008. JOHN L.   Georgetown, Mass.
3266. MYRA ELLEN, born June 17, 1852.
3267. JOSEPH BAILEY, born April 15, 1854, and died Aug. 25, 1854.

3009. MICAJAH P. *Newburyport, Mass.*

3268. STEPHEN ARTHUR, born in Oct., 1859.

3156. DAVID L. D. *Elvira, Iowa.*

3269. JULIA WHITE, born in Fon du Lac, Wis., Nov. 14, 1847, and died April 13, 1852, in New York city.
3270. LUCIE COIT, born in New York city, June 16, 1850.
3271. JOSEPH CAREW, born in Waupun, Wis., March 6, 1854.
3272. STEPHEN VAN DUSAR, born in Fon du Lac, Wis., April 25, 1855.

3157. GEORGE F. (M. D.) *Portage City, Wis.*

3273. ELIDA, born in New York city, Oct. 19, 1845.
3274. FREDERICK GRENELLE, born in New York city, May 4, 1848.
3275. CHARLES CLEVELAND, born in Portage City, Wis., June 5, 1855.
3276. NELLIE, born in Portage City, Wis., Nov. 10, 1859.

3172. JOSEPH W. N. *Philadelphia.*

3277. A SON, born May 12, 1856, and died of dysentery, July 22, 1858.

NOTE.

The Author will be greatly obliged to those who detect omissions or errors in the preceding record, if they will indicate them to him, for correction in a future edition of the work.

APPENDIX A.

A list of such supposed descendants of Simon as the author has been unable to assign to their proper places in the family record. A still longer list had been made, which, by some unaccountable process was misplaced, and hence cannot appear with the rest.

The first on this list, David, with his two brothers, is claimed by the descendants to have removed from some part of Connecticut to Newport and Dighton, R. I.

1. DAVID, married, Feb. 17, 1763, Comfort Bowers, who died Sept. 17, 1779. He married the second time, Feb. 28, 1788, Elizabeth Barker, at Tiverton, R. I. He died Nov. 26, 1813, aged 76, and his second wife died May 11, 1829, aged 80. He settled in Newport, R. I., where he died.

The list which follows was mainly furnished by Mrs. Baldwin, wife of No. 20. The family went from Connecticut to Newport, R. I.

2. WILLIAM, brother of the above David, who was never married.

3. JOHN, brother to the two above, never married.

3.¹ REBECCA, half sister of the above brothers, is said to have **married a Casey**, and is remembered by David (11), as living in her widowhood with his grandfather.

1. DAVID.

4. NANCY, born May 8, 1764, died Sept. 16, 1786.

5. REBECCA, born Nov. 12, 1765, died Sept. 16, 1770.

6. JOSEPH, born Nov. 20, 1767, married Sarah Wanton, Sept. 9, 1792, died Dec., 1815.

7. DAVID, born Nov. 18, 1769, died Nov. 22, 1771.

8. PHILIP, born Dec. 31, 1771, died Aug. 1798 unmarried.

9. REBECCA, born Oct. 4, 1776, died Oct., 1857, unmarried.

6. JOSEPH.

10. STEPHEN A., born Aug. 29, 1793, died Sept. 25, 1817.

11. DAVID, born April 6, 1795, married Sarah Bunker, Oct. 8, 1818, in Nantucket, where they live.

12. EDWARD W., born June 20, 1796, married Mary E. Culbert, Dec. 5, 1829, and lived in Nantucket, died Dec. 18, 1844.

13. JOSEPH, born Sept. 17, 1797, died Oct. 4, 1818.

14. ELIZABETH, born March 12, 1799, married, July 4, 1826, Benjamin Barnard of New York city.

15. JOHN P., born Aug. 16, 1800, died in infancy.

16. FRANCES P., born Oct. 16, 1802, married Ammiel Paddock, Oct. 28, 1825, at Nantucket. He died, and she married a Mr. Compton of New York city.

17. SAMUEL A., born Oct. 30, 1805, died in infancy.
18. GEORGE R., born Dec. 19, 1812, died January, 1815, unmarried.

11. DAVID. Nantucket Island.

19. HARRIET B., born Aug. 11. 1819, married George S. Cleveland, Feb. 2, 1841, and has three children: George S., Sarah H., and Henry Francis.
20. STEPHEN A., born April 27. 1822, married Clarissa Lovejoy Baldwin, June 20, 1848. They live in Nantucket.
21. EDWARD R., born Oct. 6, 1824, died April 3, 1851.
22. LYDIA E., born Oct 10, 1827, died Nov. 20, 1833.
23. SARAH B., born March 10, 1830, died Nov. 23, 1833.
24. JOSEPH W., born May 13, 1833.
25. DAVID, born April 8, 1836, died August 26, 1838.

20. STEPHEN A. Nantucket Island.

26. SAMUEL B., born April 1, 1849, died Sept. 17, 1850.
27. STEPHEN, born Oct. 24, 1850.
28. GEORGE S., born June 21, 1852.
29. DAVID A., born March 12, 1854.
30. SARAH B., born Feb. 8, 1857, died Aug. 20, 1858.
31. HARRIET ANN, born Feb. 10, 1859.

32. THOMAS S., born June 20, 1820, graduated at Yale, 1849. Went South, where, for a few years, he was occupied as a teacher and in the study of belles-lettres. Thence he went to Cincinnati, where his father had removed. In 1844 he was living as a farmer in Wisconsin; but since 1850 has resided principally in Cincinnati, as a land surveyor, until the present year (1860), when he removed, with his family, to a new settlement on Lake Pepin. (College Class record). Though one year in college with this member of the Huntington family, the author has been unable, after many enquiries and much correspondence, to ascertain anything of his parentage.

The following are taken from the gravestones of the old Norwich City burying ground in East Chelsea.

33. HARRIET, died Sept. 29, 1815, aged thirty-nine.
34. ABIGAIL, daughter of John Huntington, died in New York, Aug., 1804.
35. DANIEL, died at Wawekus Hill, Dec., 1805.
36. ELIPHALET, died in Norwich, Oct., 1815, aged thirty-eight.
37. JOHN, died in Norwich, Oct. 1815, aged seventy.
38. MRS. PHEBE, died at Acton, Vt., Aug. 17, 1816, aged eighty.
39. E. HUNGTINGTON, whose wife and three daughters died at Charlotte, on the Genesee river, in August, September, and October, 1819. The daughters were:
40. MARTHA, aged twenty-seven.
41. PHEBE, aged twenty-one.
42. HARRIOT, aged seventeen.

APPENDIX A. 371

The following are from the South Mansfield church records.
43. ELIJAH, married, Eleanor Arnold. Dec. 15, 1774.
44. ABNER, married Abigail Leavens. Oct. 18, 1781.
45. ELIZABETH, married John Butts, May 5, 1795.

The following two are from "Hinman's first Puritan settlers of Connecticut."
46. RACHEL, of Norwich, married Jos. Bingham of Windham, Nov. 30, 1742, as his second wife.
47. ABNER, married Mary Wightman, Nov. 14, 1749.

The following are from Lebanon records.
48. ELEAZER, married Jemima Right, July 15, 1725.
49. JOHN, married Mary, widow of Jos. Hutchinson, July 2, 1721.
50. ROSWELL, died July 2, 1809.

51. HIRAM "of Norwich," married, Ann E. Mason, March 3, 1847. (Norwich paper).
52. SARAH AMANDA of Mexico, N. Y., married Giles Kilbourn. (Kilbourn Genealogy). He was born in Plainfield, N. Y., and lives in Antrim, Mich. Birth. Dec. 12, 1820.
53. SARAH, married, Ralph Abbot, merchant, of Hudson, N. Y. (Abbot Genealogy).
54. WILLIAM, son of William and Sarah, born in Amesbury, July 6, 1780.

The following is communicated by F. J. Huntington of Hartford, from a business letter received by him from Rev. Silas Huntington, Aylwin, Canada East.
55. SILAS, a medical doctor, born in the city of Hartford, Conn., went into Canada, when a young man, and married a daughter of Major Adams, an officer in the revolution. He had one brother and several sisters, all of whom are dead. His father's name was Silas, probably. He had four sons and three daughters who are all married and hold respectable positions in society. One of the sons is the Rev. Silas, above.

Though I have written twice for additional information I have heard nothing further from this family.

APPENDIX B.

A list of such recent immigrants into the country as have been found.

I.

WILLIAM, a son of John, who was born in Liverpool, he having been born in Cornwall, where his mother lived. His father was a seaman. He has one sister, Mrs. Elizabeth Peabody, living in Frederickton, N. B. He has one daughter, Elizabeth Ann, in Chelsea, and two sons: Joseph and Thomas, the latter having one son, Thomas, in Wisconsin. He is living in Boston.

The above came to Boston in 1829, where he is now (1858) a maker of nautical instruments.

II.

1. THOMAS, a native of Wells, England. Came about the middle of the revolutionary war. An only son, having but two sisters, one of whom married a Broadbier. He died in 1799.

1. THOMAS. *New Rochelle, N. Y.*

2. JAMES P., born in 1786, married Mary A. Constant of New Rochelle, and lived there until his death in 1855.
3. GRACE, born in 1792, married Lanman Davenport, and lives in New Rochelle. She has three children.
4. ANN, born 1795, married H. Edson of Troy, and had four children. She died in 1840.

2. JAS. P. *New Rochelle, N. Y.*

5. CHARLOTTE, who married Wm. Baber of New Rochelle.
6. GRACE, who married T. W. Thorne, Jr., of New Rochelle.
7. MARY, who married Geo. Daniels of New Rochelle.
8. JANE, who died March 6, 1858, in New Rochelle.
9. ANN.
10. THOMAS, Captain of steamer San Francisco, married, in St. Louis, Mo., Sept. 4, 1860, Mary, daughter of Robert Baker of St. Louis.
11. JAMES.
12. ISAAC.
13. LAWRENCE D., who resides in New Rochelle, and is a banker in New York city.

III.

1. THOMAS, married Elizabeth Cotton, daughter of Lorette and James (Lewis) Cotton. Left Manchester, England, in the Fall of 1829, for New York. The family came May 1, 1830, reaching New York June 11. The mother died on the 22d of same month, and he, in Rahway, N. J., in 1834.

APPENDIX B.

1. THOMAS.

2. THOMAS, born Jan. 7, 1803, died Nov., 1831, unmarried, in New York.
3. HENRY, born in 1805, and died in 1830.
4. JOHN, born June 1, 1807, came to New York in 1831, with his sister Jane.
5. CHARLES, born July 14, 1809, married, in Manchester, Eng., April 22, 1830, Frances Pearce. He lives in New Haven, Conn.
6. ELIZABETH, born in 1811, married Raterey. They had no children. He is dead and she is living with Jane.
7. MARY, born in 1814, died in New York, 1835.
8. JANE, born in 1818, married John Eareslight. Has several children in Cincinnati, Ohio.

5. CHARLES.   New Haven, Conn.

9. FRANCES ELIZABETH, born July 7, 1832, married, 1850, William Duane.
10. MARY JANE, born March 29, 1835, married, May 5, 1855.
11. CHARLES EDWARD, born April 28, 1837.
12. WILLIAM HENRY, born July 5, 1840, died aged three years six and one half months.
13. PENELOPE, born Feb. 28, 1844.
14. ADELIA, died young.

IV.

1. ———, came to Jersey with a large property, and invested it in the manufacture of iron. He had fourteen children, most of whom died young. I have obtained the names only of the following three. This account, and the list which follows, was furnished by John G. (11).
2. ABRAHAM, went to Moorsbury, Northumberland county, Pa., and thence to White Deer Creek, Union county. 3. SIMON. 4. A DAUGHTER, who married a Nickle.

2. ABRAHAM.

5. WILLIAM, born at White Deer Creek, married a Kinman, and went to Hartley, Union county, where he died in 1852, and where his widow still (1857) lives. He had nine children.
6. SARAH, who married David Hannah, and lived in Center county, Pa., where she died about ten years ago.
7. BETSEY, died when a young woman.
8. JOHN, who lives in Kelley township.
9. SAMUEL. 10. GABRIEL.

5. WILLIAM.

11. JOHN G., living at Montgomery Station, where he is engaged on the railroad, and as a farmer.

V.

GEORGE, who came to this country in the year 1834, and who lives, unmarried, in Providence, R. I.

VI.

John, who was the only son of Thomas and Elizabeth (Robinson), grandson of John and Jane (Dean), and great grandson of Joseph Huntington, a stone mason and farmer of Cheshire, England. He married, Mary Graham, and came to this country in 1817. He lives at Black Earth, Wis., and has five children living. His eldest daughter is Mrs. Orval Hubbard of Rockland Co., Wis. He has also two sisters, Mrs. Williams and Darlington, living in Wisconsin. The above account is from a letter addressed by John, above, to Gurdon. (No. 1401).

VII.

————. An Episcopal clergyman of Huntington, L. I. He came previously to the revolutionary war. He had a family, one of his daughters marrying a Saxton, a second a Hackstaff, and a third, William Hallock. Mrs. George Abbe of Windham, Conn., is a descendant of his, being a daughter of the above Capt. Hackstaff. For this information I am indebted to the late Mrs. Hyar, a sister of Mrs. Abbe. It has recently been fully corroborated by the independent statements of Rev. William A. Hallock, D. D., of the Tract House, New York city.

APPENDIX C.

DR. JOSEPH HUNTINGTON'S GENEALOGICAL LETTER.

I have thought it best to preserve this letter with such facts respecting it as have been learned, since it seems to have been the source of all our mistaken family tradition. The letter, I think, has never been published in full. The Genealogical Register has an extract from it and gives it as having been addressed to Eliphalet (235) a younger brother of the author. Having met the letter, or parts of it (in different forms,) I am inclined to think that the main part of it was kept by Dr. Huntington, as embodying the result of his inquiries, and sent out by him to such members of the family as were likely to be interested in it, or to such as might add to its correctness. And the introduction may have been such as the particular case seemed to call for. Some of the copies could not have been addressed to a brother of the author, and others were evidently directed to persons not connected with the family. To whom the original was written I think cannot be ascertained. The following copy exhibits the letter, as begun and ended, but to whom addressed does not appear from the letter itself. The copy was handed to Dr. Joshua Huntington of Brooklyn, by Francis J. Huntington.

COVENTRY, March 26, 1793.

DEAR SIR—Your letter of the 23d inst. gave me great delight, as I thereby find you have an affection to our family and wish to be acquainted with our descent and pedigree. Near thirty years ago I made the most careful inquiry I was able, and from various persons and means I obtained the intelligence I now send you.

Near the close of the reign and tragical death of Charles the 1st, who was then the King of Great Britain, i. e. near the year 1640, (for in 1648 the king was behead-d) the original stock of our family in America, who was a citizen of Norwich, in England, and a religious puritan under persecution, (with many others in those days,) with his wife and three sons, embarked for America. His name was Simon Huntington. This good man was grandfather to your grandfather and mine. He was more than fifty years of age, and his wife some years younger. Their three sons were in the bloom of youth. Their names were Christopher, Simon and Samuel. They made their course for the mouth of the Connecticut river; but our progenitor being seized with a violent fever and dysentery, died within sight of the shore, whither he was brought and now lies buried either in Saybrook or Lyme, as both towns were but one at first.

His widow, our grandfather's grandmother, was a lady of good family, piety and virtue, and had a valuable fortune left her in money, and not long after she was married to a gentleman in Windsor, which town was settled almost as early as any in Connecticut. His name was Stoughton. There the good lady finished her life in affluence and comfort.

The three sons settled first at Saybrook: but soon after the younger, viz: Samuel, removed into New Jersey and settled at **Newark, where there is a respectable family of our name and kindred, though not very numerous in the branches of it.**

Not long after the settlement of our ancestors at Saybrook the venerable Mr. Fitch came over to take the pastoral charge of them. Soon after this, they made the discovery of the township we call Norwich, and which they so named in regard to the city of Norwich, in England, from which the most respectable part of them came.

The people began to emigrate from Saybrook to Norwich in considerable numbers, and all dearly loved their minister. A warm contention arose between the emigrants and those that remained at Saybrook, with regard to their minister, which Mr. Fitch decided very wisely. He told them that he had a dear love for them all, but he could do no other than cleave to the major part, wheresoever their residence might be. Accordingly, as the greater part of the charge soon removed to Norwich, he also settled there; was the first minister of that town, a faithful and worthy servant of Christ, and a friend to the souls of men. Laboring many years in the sacred work there, until old age deprived him of further usefulness, he then removd to Lebanon and there died. This good man was the progenitor of all who bore the name in Norwich and the towns adjacent.

But to return to our family. About the time that Samuel, before mentioned, removed to Newark, the other two brothers came to Norwich, viz: Christopher and Simon, and there lived in honor, piety and prosperity to a good old age.

The sons of Christopher were Christopher, Thomas and John. The sons of this last mentioned Christopher were, Christopher, Isaac, Jabez, Matthew, Hezekiah, John and Jeremiah. The sons of Thomas were Thomas, Jedidiah, Christopher, Eliezer, William and Simon. John left but one son, bearing his own name.

This, you will note, brings the pedigree of our family down, in one branch of it, to a collateral line with your father and mine, i. e. in the branch of Christopher, the son of Simon, who was the original stock of all who bear the name in this country.

I next acquaint you with another branch, i. e. the branch of Simon, son of the original Simon, from whence you and I have our descent direct. His sons were Simon, Joseph, Samuel, Daniel and James. The sons of the last mentioned Simon, were Simon, Ebenezer and Joshua. The sons of Joseph were Joseph, Nathaniel, Jonathan, David and Solomon. The sons of Samuel were Samuel, Caleb, John and Simon. The sons of Daniel were Daniel, Jonathan and Benjamin. The sons of James were James, Peter and Nathaniel.

With regard to that branch in New Jersey, descended from Samuel, son of the original Simon, he left one son, Samuel by name, on a collateral line with our grandfather Joseph. This Samuel had three sons, Thomas, Simon and Samuel, which were on a collateral line with you father and mine.

This is an account of all the male issue of our family, from the original Simon down to our own immediate parents, and contains a series of about a century and a half. We have kindred of the same name now in England, and among them some very respectable, as the family was at the time of the emigration of our progenitors. A brother of the original Simon, whose name was Samuel, was captain of the King's Life Guard, and much in his favor. With regard to the succeeding branches of our family in this country, they are somewhat numerous, though not so much dispersed as some other families. We can with great facility at any time collect an account of them, as they are on a collateral line with us of lower descent, and are all with us in open view, whenever we wish to visit them or inquire after them. The whole difficulty is over in bringing the pedigree down as far as I have brought it. If my life should be spared, however, I had thought of adding an account of two or three generations more, which may be easily done, only by writing to those who are of equal descent with ourselves, each one will readily send in **an account of his own posterity."**

Of the letter copied above, the first and last paragraphs have never been printed—all the rest may be found, with but very slight verbal difference, in the Genealogical Register.

One sentence of the letter supposes it to have been addressed to the author's own cousin. "Our grandfather Joseph," could have been used only to a son of one of Joseph's sons. I find among the memoranda collected by Dr. Joshua (2444) this very timely minute: "March 25, 1847. I have to-day seen another copy of this letter addressed to Mr. Roger Huntington." The inference is very direct that that letter must have been directed to Roger (245) the son of Dr. Jonathan of Windham, there being no other grandson of Joseph of this name.

That another copy of a part of this letter was sent to Eliphalet, the author's brother, is also quite probable; and it is likely that that was the particular one from which the printed copy was made. Another copy still I have seen, addressed to Minor Huntington (650) though it contained but a part of the letter as printed.

But what is most perplexing about the letter is, that it should embody so much error, with such apparent unconsciousness. It would seem that living so near the generations of which the letter treats, after an apparent investigation extending through a period of thirty years, the author could not have accepted so much that a later day proves utterly without foundation. And the only solution of the difficulty is found in the supposition that that the Dr. consulted tradition only, without attempting its correction or verification by actual records.

It is also unaccountable, that such an omission as that of the Salisbury Huntingtons, could have, at that time, been made by one so intelligent as the author of that letter. He seems not to have been aware of the existence of that branch of the family at all.

The examination of the Newark records would have shown him that Samuel was a nephew, and not a brother of the two pioneers in the settlement of Norwich.

The circumstantial account of the death of Simon off the mouth of the Connecticut river, would also be inexplicable but for the recorded testimony of the Roxbury church. The fact of his death on the passage, even though it were by the small pox, and on mid ocean, might very easily have been changed through the influence of the intervening years and generations, into a death by dysentery, and on the waters of Long Island Sound. And the only natural inference would be that the body must have been buried on the banks of the Connecticut. Thus, or in some such way, arose the tradition on which we so long relied.

INDEX.

I

[This Index contains the Christian names of the Huntingtons, enrolled in this work, as descended from SIMON (No. 1), excepting such as died in childhood. The birthplace, or some other place of residence is indicated, and also the surnames of the husbands of the daughters.]

No.	Name	Place		No.	Name	Place
1181.	Abby L.	East Hampton, N. Y.		907.	Abigail, (Currier).	Amesbury, Mass.
1800.	Abby D., (Lee).	Buffalo, N. Y.		917.	Abigail.	Amesbury, Mass.
1870.	Abby,	Amesbury, Mass.		951.	Abigail.	Francistown, N. H.
1873.[3]	Abby, (Woodward).	Litchfield, Me.		956.	Abigail, (Burtts)	Francistown, N. H.
1931.	Abby J., (Tracy).	Franklin, Conn.		1165.	Abigail.	Griswold, Conn.
2228.	Abby H.	Green Lake, Wis.		1484.	Abigail.	Walpole, N. H.
2625.	Abby R.	Walpole, N. H.		1535.	Abigail, (Gregory).	Ithaca, N. Y.
3120.	Abby A.	Perry, N. Y.		1997.	Abigail.	Greensboro, Vt.
388.	Abel.	Norwich, Conn.		276.	Abner.	New Haven, Vt.
427.	Abel.	Willington, Conn.		714.	Abner.	Perry, N. Y.
468.	Abel, (Hon.).	East Hampton, L. I.		932.	Abner.	Weare, N. H.
977.	Abel H.	Michigan.		1290.	Abner.	Worcester, Mass.
1819.	Abel.	Courtland, N. Y.		1505.	Abner W.	Nova Scotia.
1934.	Abel H.	Galesburg, Ill.		1608.	Abner.	Batavia, N. Y.
2130.	Abel, (M. D.).	Englishtown, N. J.		2806.	Abram A.	Columbus, Wis.
62.	Abigail, (Calkins).	Lebanon, Conn.		3005.	Abraham J.	Amesbury, Mass.
87.	Abigail, (Carew).	Norwich, Conn.		3021.	Achsa H., (Taber).	Lincoln, Vt.
144.	Abigail, (Lathrop).	Franklin, Conn.		1634.	Achsah.	Enfield, N. H.
169.	Abigail, (Conant).	Norwich, Conn.		2244.	Achsah.	Canada East.
211.	Abigail, (Steele).	Tolland, Conn.		2123.	Adelaide, (Cheesebrough).	
230.	Abigail, (Kimball).	Windham, Conn.				S. Brookfield N. Y.,
309.	Abigail, (Pearce).	Norwich, Conn.		2323.	Adelaide A., (Booth).	Mexico, N. Y.
327.	Abigail, (Hough).	Lebanon, N. H.		3130.	Adelaide E.	
378.	Abigail, (Talcott).	Bolton, Conn.		3155.[1]	Adelaide H.	
546.	Abigail, (Dr. Farnsworth).			1142.	Adaline E., (Platt).	Owego, N. Y.
		Windsor, Ohio.		2585.	Adaline, (White).	Hudson, Ind.
606.	Abigail, (Mills).	Canandaigua, N. Y.		992.	Adnah.	Ohio.
691.	Abigail.	Rocky Hill, Conn.		3065.	Ada I.	North Elba, N. Y.
710.	Abigail, (Lilly).	Ashford, Conn.		1243.	Adoniram J., (Rev.).	Augusta, Ga.
739.	Abigail, (Keese).	Keeseville, N. H.		3223.	Agnes C.	Middlefield, N. Y.
766.	Abigail.	Woodbury, Conn.		651.	Alathea, (Taylor).	Windham, Conn.
796.	Abigail.	Norwich, Conn.		1011.	Alathea.	Topsfield, Mass.

INDEX.

1948.	Alathea L.,(Hall).Willimantic,Conn.	1873.[26]	Alvin	Litchfield, Me.
1388.	Alathea C	Windham, Conn.	2242.	Alvira	Compton, C. E.
1503.	Alathea	Yarmouth, N. S.	994.	Alvan	Strongsville, Ohio.
2985.	Alexander McR	Amesbury, Mass.	1873.[40]	Alpheus	Monmouth, Me.
2017.	Alcesta F	Rochester, N. Y.	1759.	Alvah	
1702.	Alma	Spencer, Mass.	773.	Alza, (Proctor)	Woodbury, Conn.
3155.	Alma F	Brookline, Mass.	415.	Amanda S., (Chaplin)	
2857.	Alma E	Lowell, Mass.			Windham, Conn.
3242.	Albina H	Fountain Prairie, Wis.	416.	Amanda A., (Backus)	
1031.	Albert E	Bozrah, Conn.			Windham, Conn.
1294.	Albert	Auburn, Mass.	1092.	Amanda, (Burrows)	Rome, N. Y.
1353.	Albert W	Cincinnati, Ohio.	2028.	Amanda	Rome, N. Y.
1873.[9]	Albert	California.	1873.[30]	Amasa	Marshfield, Vt.
2018.	Albert	Rochester, N. Y.	1316.	Ambrose W	Union Square, N Y.
2196.	Albert H	Adrian, Mich.	2365.	Ambrose P	Watertown, N. Y.
2283.	Albert W	Auburn, Mass.	1327.	Ambrose P	Watertown, N. Y.
2316.	Albert	New York City.	1160.	Amelia	Ashford, Conn.
2335.	Albert W	Wauseon, Ohio.	2010.	Amelia C	Shaftesbury, Vt.
2818.	Albert C	Burlington, Vt.	2403.	Amelia M., (Thomas)	Augusta, Ga.
413.	Alice, (Baldwin)	Norwich, Conn.	2508.	Amelia D	Boston, Mass.
729.	Alice, (Wadham)	Boston, Mass.	3070.	Amelia F	Valparaiso, Ind.
1219.	Alice S., (Ingals)	Hanover, N. H.	161.	Amos	Shaftesbury, Vt.
1251.	Alice, (Crosby)	Roxbury, Vt.	438.	Amos	Shaftesbury, Vt.
1942.	Alice G	Lebanon, N. H.	910.	Amos	Amesbury, Mass.
2229.	Alice C. H	Green Lake, Wis.	1078.	Amos C	Shaftesbury, Vt.
2262.	Alice	Osage, Iowa.	1599.	Amos	
2502.	Alice A	Cleveland, Ohio.	162.	Ame	Preston, Conn.
2598.	Alice M	Springfield, Ill.	343.	Amy, (Robertson)	Norwich, Conn.
2923.	Alice S.	New Haven, Conn.	836.	Amy, (Clark)	Ashford, Conn.
2954.	Alice J	Thompson, N. Y.	1068.	Amy	
3083.	Alice	Marietta, Ohio.	3093.	Annette	Boston, Mass.
3112.	Alice	Chicago, Ill.	1746.	Antoinette	Rome, N. Y.
3126.[1]	Alice	Hartford, Conn.	1519.	Apollos	Sandusky City, Ohio.
3205.	Alice	Rock Island, Ill.	5.[1]	Ann	Saybrook, Conn.
3225.	Alice P	Middlefield, N. Y.	19.	Ann, (Bingham)	Norwich, Conn.
2862.	Allie	West Charleston, Vt.	877.	Ann M., (Chapman)	
1266.	Almira	Canada East.			Claverack, N. Y.
1313.	Almira, (Holden).S. Dansville, N Y.	1861.	Ann C.,(Richards) N. London, Conn.
1169.	Almira, (Moffat)	Charleston, Vt.	2188.	Ann J	Washington, D. C.
2624.	Almira S	Walpole, N. H.	2352.	Ann E., (Hungerford)	
3242.	Almira H	Fountain Prairie, Wis.			Watertown, N. Y.
1702.	Alma	Spencer, Mass.	2457.	Ann E, (Clark)	Brooklyn, Conn.
3155.	Alma F	Brookline, Mass.	2514.	Ann E	Vergennes, Vt.
2857.	Alma E	Lowell, Mass.	2656.	Ann, (Lamberton)	Baraboo, Wis.
1032.	Alfred J	Bozrah, Conn.	2926.	Ann O	Norwich, Conn.
1372.	Alfred I	New Orleans, La.	2945.	Ann M., (Mozart)	Zenia, Ohio.
1420.	Alfred H	St. Albans, Vt	3063.	Ann M	North Elba, N Y.
1590.	Alfred	Danielsonville, Conn.	90.	Anna, (Adgate)	Norwich, Conn.
2332.	Alfred	Mexico, N. Y.	281.	Anna, (Collins)	Litchfield, Conn.
2485.	Alfred S	Mobile, Ala.	393.	Anna, (Hartshorn).Franklin, Conn.
2537.	Alfred H	Rockford, Ill.	403.	Anna, (Fitch)	Norwich, Conn.
2640.	Alfred S	Canton, Ohio.	556.	Anna, (Ripley)	Windham. Conn.
3265.	Alfred L	Amesbury, Mass.	613.	Anna, (Edgerton).Windham, Conn.
487.	Alisthena	Hampton, Conn.	653.	Anna, (Perkins)	Windham, Conn.
2049.	Algernon O	Shaftesbury, Vt.	661.	Anna, (Huntington) Norwich, Conn.
2175.	Almond		750.	Anna	Lyme, Conn.
1122.	Almond F	Syracuse, N. Y.	830.	Anna P., (Barnes)	Chelsea, Vt.
1668.	Alonzo B	Hartford, Conn.	851.	Anna	Norwich, Conn.
1938.	Alonzo, (Esq.)	Chicago, Ill.	969.	Anna, (Cook)	Albany, N. Y.
2795.	Alonzo	Wisconsin	1016.	Anna, (Robinson)	
2905.	Alonzo, C	Hartford, Conn.			Attleborough, Mass.

1017.	Anna M., (Brewster).Oswego, N. Y.	1127.	Angeline	
1641.	Anna	1275.[1]	Ariel	
1760.	Anna P., (Cleveland) Randolph, Vt.	186.	Asa	Canaan, Conn.
1801.[1]	Anna	342.	Asa	New Haven, Conn.
1833.	Anna, (Buxton)....South Danvers.	425.	Asa	Mansfie d, Conn.
2048.	Anna A	Buffalo, N. Y.	497.	Asa	Rochester, N. Y.
2134.	Anna M	Auburn, N. Y.	504.	Asa, (Hon.)	Hanover, N. H.
2303.	Anna, (Wilkinson)...Boston, Mass.	723.	Asa	Lebanon, N. H.
2412.	Anna A	Norwich, Conn.	1046.	Asa	Mansfield Conn.
2454.	Anna M., (Jebard) Carondelet, Mo.	1086.	Asa C	Rome, N. H.
2705.	Anna W	Charlestown, Mass.	1287.	Asa H	
2963.	Anna	New Haven, Conn.	1508.	Asa	Nova Scotia.
2976.	Anna J., (Chase)....Weare, N. H.	397.	Asahel, (Rev.)	Torfield, Mass.
3017.	Anna B., (Morrison) Granville, N. Y.	1013.	Asahel, (Esq.)	Salem, Mass.
111.	Anne, (Ordway)...Amesbury, Mass.	3075.	Asahel A	Franklin. Conn.
151.	Anne,(Huntington).Norwich, Conn.	530.	Asenath, (Tracy)..Windham, Conn.
165.	Anne, (Wetmore)..Norwich, Conn.	978.	Asenath, (Andius)..Tunbridge, Vt.
194.	Anne, (Hovey)....Mansfield, Conn.	464.	Asher, (Dr.)	Chenango, N. Y.
248.	Anne, (Roundy)..Windham, Conn.	778.	Asher	Norwich, Conn.
471.	Anne	Franklin, Conn.	781.	Asher P	Norwich, Conn.
897.	Anne	Rome, N. Y.	971.	Asher	Athens, Pa.
800.	Anne	Rome, N. Y.	2141.	Asher	Laxawaxen, Pa.
1739.	Anne	Brooklyn, N. Y.	1161.	Aurelia M., (Cole)....Danville, Ill.
1262.	Annie S	New York City.	1160.	Aurelia	
2890.	Annie	New York City.	1211.	Aurelia	
178.	Andrew, (Dea.)....Griswold, Conn.	3070.	Aurelia F	Valparaiso, Ind.
190.	Andrew	Pittsford, N. Y.	1984.	Aurora F	Truxton, N. Y.
219.	Andrew	Norwich, Conn	2817.	Austin B	Washington, Vt.
295.	Andrew	Lebanon, Conn.	3199.	Austin P	Chicago, Ill.
456.	Andrew, (Dr.)....Ashford, Conn.	126.	Azariah	Norwich, Conn.
503.	Andrew, (Dr.)....Pittsford, N. Y.	395.	Azariah, (Dea.)....Franklin, Conn.
558.	Andrew	Norwich, Conn.	1007.	Azariah	Franklin, Conn.
705.	Andrew	Mansfield, Conn.	755.	Azel	Spencer, Mass.
764.	Andrew, (Rev.)....Guilford, N. Y.	1704.	Azel	Union, Mo.
829.	An rew	Middlebury, Vt.	959.	Backus	Bozrah, Conn.
1166.	Andrew	Springfield, Mass.	1693.	Backus W., (Esq.).New York City.
1310.	Andrew, (Rev.)....Mexico, N. Y.	129.	Barnabas, (Dea.)...Franklin, Conn.
1751.	Andrew	Tunbridge, Vt.	894.	Barnabas, (Dea.)....Lisbon, Conn.
1884.	Andrew W	Weare, N. H.	1005.	Barnabas	Lisbon, Conn.
1988.	Andrew J	Hartford, Conn.	697.	Bathsheba	Lebanon, Conn.
2099.	Andrew B	Danbury, Conn.	2765.	Bathsheba, (Loomis)..Nova Scotia.
2102.	Andrew	Elbridge, N. Y.	1506.	Bela	Nova Scotia.
2472.	Andrew B	Baltimore, Md.	2537.[1]	Bela S	Rockford, Ill.
2108.	Andrew S	Springfield, Mass.	92.	Benjamin, LL. D..Norwich, Conn.
3174.	Andrew B	Baltimore, Md.	143.	Benjamin	Norwich, Conn.
2025.	Ansel	Rome, N. Y.	318.	Benjamin	New York City.
1258.	Anson	Wauseon, Ohio.	365.	Benjamin	Kennebunk, Me.
1574.	Aristarchus	Haddam, Conn.	495.	Benjamin	Springfield, N. Y.
1940.	Arabella F	Londonderry, Vt.	515.	Benjamin	Canada East.
3231.	Arabella	Middlebury, Vt.	817.	Benjamin N., (Hon.)..Rome, N. Y.
1959.	Arthur L	Salem, Mass.	840.	Benjamin	Thompson, N. Y.
2127.	Arthur	Baldwinsville, N. Y.	962.	Benjamin	Weare, N. H.
2603.	Arthur	Springfield, Ill.	928.7	Benjamin	Litchfield, Me.
2671.	Arthur W	Baraboo, Wis.	938.	Benjamin	Weare, N. H.
2716.	Arthur D	Mt. Clemens, Mich.	1037.	Benjamin	Norwich, Conn.
2922.	Arthur T	New Haven, Conn.	1204.	Benjamin	Rochester, N. Y.
2375.	Archibald	Catahoula, La.	1265.	Benjamin	Canada East.
2396.	Archibald D	Hartford, Conn.	1409.	Benjamin	Boston, Mass.
2668.	Armilla J	Baraboo, Wis.	1518.	Benjamin L	Mexico, N. Y.
2748.	Arria S	Boston, Mass.	1648.	Benjamin	Washington, Vt.
1633.	Araunah	Canada.	1738.	Benjamin S., (Rev.).Flatbush, N. Y.

1741.	Benjamin N..........Rome, N. Y.	2231.	Caroline S. J.........Canada East.
1835.	Benjamin..........Danvers, N. H.	2486.	Caroline L........................
1873.[5]	Benjamin B...New Richmond, Wis.	2511.	Caroline E. (Flint)..Medford, Mass.
1873.[25]	Benjamin J........Litchfield, Me.	2530.	Caroline M.......St. Albans, Vt.
1877.	Benjamin ....Weare, N. H.	2634.	Caroline R. (Green)..............
1976.	Benjamin N.....Columbus, Ohio.	.....	..............Painesville, Ohio.
2128.	Benjamin H......New York City.	2942.	Caroline E..........Zenia, Ohio.
2201.	Benjamin M........Buffalo, N. Y.	2997.	Caroline A., (Dale) Haverhill, Mass.
2304.	Benjamin F....New London, Conn	3051[2]	Caroline M. H., New Richmond, Wis.
2320.	Benjamin ....Mexico, N. Y.	3141.	Caroline M..........St. Martins.
2482.	Benjamin F......Franklin, Conn.	1943.	Carrie M.........Lebanon, N. H.
2487.	Benjamin W....New Orleans, La.	2322.	Carrie...........Rochester, N. Y.
2773.	Benjamin..........Nova Scotia.	3129.	Carrie...........Wauseon, Ohio.
2838.	Benjamin L....Washington, Vt.	3072.	Cara L............Galesburg, Ill.
2993.	Benjamin F.....Amesbury, Mass.	1920.	Carlos T ....New York City
3084.	Benjamin.........Yoncalla, Ohio.	798.	Catherine (Williams)...Utica N. Y.
3085.	Benjamin.........Columbus, Ohio.	1263.	Catherine..........Canada East.
3193.	Benjamin F......Franklin, Conn.	1565.	Catherine C........Hadley, Mass.
1055.	Bethia, (James).Lansingburg, N. Y.	1573.	Catherine.......Haddam, Conn.
1560.	Bethia T........Hadley, Mass.	1729.	Catherine A. (Root).Medina, Ohio.
461.	Betsey (Prentice)....Gilead, Conn.	1785.	Catherine S......Monticello, N. Y.
470.	Betsey, (Bingham). Norwich, Conn.	1890.	Catherine P .....Bennington, Vt.
636.	Betsey. ....Windham, Conn.	2036.	Catherine............Troy, N. Y.
707.	Betsey, (Bowditch) Providence, R. I.	2136.	Catherine............Auburn, N. Y.
732.	Betsey............Nova Scotia.	2383.	Catherine B......Hartford, Conn.
746.	Betsey K. (Bunce)................	2389.[2]	Catherine S......Hartford, Conn.
775.	Betsey, (Young)..................	2741.	Catherine F......Milwaukie, Wis.
936.	Betsey, (Fifield).....Weare, N. H.	2762.	Catherine E........Newark, N. J.
944.	Betsey, (Cochran)....New Boston.	1085.	Calvin..........New Orleans, La.
1038.	Betsey M. (Cheeseborough)......	2016.	Calvin G ....Shaftesbury, Vt.
	..................Lisbon, Conn.	2805.	Carr N ....Portage City, Wis.
1044.	Betsey, (Denham)..Lebanon, Ohio.	3088.	Celestia......Roche a Cree, Wis.
1288.	Betsey, (Carpenter).Ashford, Ohio.	1597.	Celia ....Windham, Conn.
1340.	Betsey, (Bennet)...Norwich, Ohio.	2177.	Celia....... Sandusky City, Ohio.
1473.	Betsey..........Mansfield, Ohio.	848.	Chandler...............Vermont.
1509.	Betsey ....Nova Scotia.	1747.[1]	Channing M.....Sag Harbor, N. Y.
1585.	Betsey, (Elliot) .....Nova Scotia.	469.	Charles........Chittenango, N. Y.
1588.	Betsey, (Fitts).....Eastford, Conn.	858.	Charles..............New York.
1831.	Betsey, (Matthews)............	889.	Charles M.........Montpelier, Vt.
1873.[31]	Betsey..........Marshfield, Vt.	968.	Charles..........Franklin, Conn.
1875.	Betsey, (Sargent)	1020.	Charles M........Bozrah, Conn.
2001.	Betsey, (Hall)....Cedar Rapids, Ia.	1123.	Charles R.....................
2784.	Betsey M., (Miller). Middlebury, Vt.	1118.	Charles F.........Owego, N. Y.
706.	Beulah ....Ashford, Conn.	1187.	Charles, (Rev.)..Hoverleyville, Pa.
2083.	Byron O. .....Ogdensburg, N. Y.	1209.	Charles..................Georgia.
2325.	Bruce M..........Mexico, N. Y.	1281.	Charles ....New Market, Ohio.
81.	Caleb..........Lebanon, Conn.	1351.	Charles L........Norwich, Conn.
182.	Caleb (Dea.)......Norwich, Conn.	1370.	Charles P. (Hon.)..Norwich, Conn.
272.	Caleb ....Ashford, Conn.	1423.	Charles A........Rockford, Ill.
486.	Caleb ....Hampton, Conn.	1557.	Charles P. (Hon.)....Boston, Mass.
699.	Caleb ....Cape Breton.	1603.	Charles B.........Bethany, N. Y.
899.	Careline, (Woodward).	1675.	Charles B..........New York.
	......New Haven, Conn.	1717.	Charles T..North Brookfield, Mass.
1029.	Caroline M., (Hamlin)...........	1747.	Charles R........New York City.
	...........Buffalo, N. Y.	1786.	Charles...........Liberty, N. Y.
1131.	Caroline M., (Mitchell) Morris, N. Y	1799.	Charles E......New Haven, Conn.
1779.	Caroline, (Wicks) Monticello, N. Y	1827.	Charles.......................
1999.	Caroline, (Cook) .Greensboro, Vt.	1866.	Charles H......Amesbury, Mass.
2050.	Caroline M..... Shaftesbury, Vt.	1910.	Charles........Bloomington, Ill.
2094.	Caroline E., (Griggs)..Mobile, Ala.	1928.	Charles O...........Athens, Pa.
2207.	Caroline A.........Canada East.	1983.	Charles E.........Truxton, N. Y.

INDEX. 383

No.	Name	Location	No.	Name	Location
1996.	Charles B.	Perry, N. Y.	1422.	Charlotte B., (Kellogg)	
2035.	Charles R.	Chicago, Ill.			Farmersburg, Iowa.
2079.	Charles W.	Ogdensburg, N. Y.	1774.	Charlotte, (Webster)	
2086.	Charles				Monticello, N. Y.
2126.	Charles	Baldwinsville, N. Y.	2236.	Charlotte	Compton, C. E.
2146.	Charles W.	Hoverleyville, Pa.	2292.	Charlotte S.	Bingham, Pa.
2235.	Charles	Compton, C. E.	2460.	Charlotte S. (Clark)	Providence, R.I.
2252.	Charles P.	New Market, Ohio.	2935.	Charlotte	Brooklyn, N. Y.
2256.	Charles W.	Norwich, Conn.	3251.	Charlotte J.	Fulton, Iowa.
2281.	Charles	Worcester, Mass.	1787.	Chauncy	Liberty, N. Y.
2297.	Charles F.	Rochester, N. Y.	2343.	Chauncy D.	
2299.	Charles W.	Hartford, Conn.	2845.	Chauncy	Washington, Vt.
2321.	Charles G.		1050.	Charissa, (Reynolds)	
2332.	Charles G.	Wauseon, Ohio.			Mansfield, Conn.
2369.	Charles	Watertown, N. Y.	1072.	Chloe, (Douglass)	Shaftesbury, Vt.
2425.	Charles L. F.	West Boxford, Mass.	445.	Civil, (Gillet)	Colchester, Conn.
2452.	Charles F.	Brookline, Mass.	1817.	Chester D.	
2479.	Charles W.	New York City.	2135.	Chester	Auburn, N. Y.
2509.	Charles S.	Salem, Mass.	2143.	Chester E.	Laxawaxen, Pa.
2522.	Charles G.	Mason, Mich.	477.	Clarissa	Charlotte, Vt.
2532.	Charles J.	Rockford, Ill.	1003.	Clarissa, (Bottom)	Lisbon, Conn.
2546.	Charles K.	Farmersburg, Iowa.	1050.	Clarissa, (Reynolds)	Mansfield, Conn.
2597.	Charles L.	Springfield, Ill.	1201.	Clarissa D., (Hubbell)	
2650.	Charles	Yarmouth, N. S.			Birmingham, Conn.
2657.	Charles H.	Baraboo, Wis.	1113.	Clarissa, (Andrus)	
2731.	Charles W.	Ware, Mass.	1589.	Clarissa, P.	Windham, Conn.
2785.	Charles A.	Bethany, N. Y.	1620.	Clarissa, (Langdon)	Constable, N. Y.
2814.	Charles C.	Middlebury, Vt.	2166.	Clarissa M.	Pittsford, N. Y.
2824.	Charles W.	Chicago, Ill.	2208.	Clarissa A., (Hazen)	Canada.
2828.	Charles S.	Sharon, Vt.	2276.	Clarissa	Worcester, Mass.
2851.	Charles W.	Washington, Vt.	2721.	Clarissa W. (Standish)	
2860.	Charles	Groveland, Mass.			Lebanon, Conn.
2867.	Charles B.	New York City.	3087.	Clarissa	Roche a Cree, Wis.
2911.	Charles W.	Stockbridge, Mass.	477.	Clarissa	Charlotte, Vt.
2916.	Charles W.	Rochester, N. Y.	1967.	Clara L.	Stanford, Conn.
2931.	Charles J.	Norwich, Conn.	2964.	Clara	Rochester, N. Y.
2996.	Charles O.	Haverhill, Mass.	2601.	Clara S. F.	Springfield, Ill.
3006.	Charles E.	New Jersey.	3024.	Clara A.	Lawrence, Mass.
3031.	Charles T.	Lawrence, Mass.	3260.	Clarence W.	Newark, N. J.
3051.	Charles	Brentwood, N. H.	3023.	Clark S.	Lincoln, Vt.
3089.	Charles H.	McGrawville, N. Y.	4.	Christopher	Norwich, Conn.
3072.[2]	Charles A.		14.	Christopher, (Dea.)	Norwich, Conn.
3092.	Charles G.	Hartford, Conn.	42.	Christopher	Franklin, Conn.
3103.	Charles H.	Shaftesbury, Vt.	123.	Christopher	Bozrah, Conn.
3107.	Charles	Troy, N. Y.	189.	Christopher	Norwich, Conn.
3116.	Charles R.	New York City.	197.	Christopher, (Rev.)	Norwich, Vt.
3117.	Charles G.	Chicago, Ill.	381.	Christopher, (Dr.)	Bozrah, Conn.
3165.	Charles S.	New York City.	510.	Christopher	Covington, Pa.
3175.	Charles S.	Baltimore, Md.	964.	Christopher	Hartford, Conn.
3186.	Charles P.	Milwaukie, Wis.	1235.	Christopher	Randolph, Vt.
3192.	Charles P.	New York City.	2594.	Christopher	Terre Haute, Ind.
3206.	Charles E.	Painesville, Ohio.	2787.	Christiana, (Newton)	
3248.	Charles F.	Montpelier, Vt.			Alexander, N. Y.
3375.	Charles C.	Portage City Wis.	1434.	Colbert	Painesville, Ohio.
583.	Charlotte, (Marsh)	Worthington, Me.	2547.	Colbert C.	California.
792.	Charlotte	Norwich, Conn.	1421.	Collins H.	St. Albans, Vt.
819.	Charlotte, (Young)	New York City.	2517.	Collins D.	Mason, Mich.
842.	Charlotte, (Landphere)		2529.	Collins F.	St. Albans, Vt.
		Ashford, Conn.	1683.	Collis P.	Sacramento, Cal.
867.	Charlotte	Bloomfield, N. Y.	2263.	Cora	

384 INDEX.

1180. Cornelia......East Hampton, L. I.	App. A.	Daniel E........Wawekus Hill.
1346. Cornelia E........Norwich, Conn.	74.	David.......Windham, Conn.
1919. Cornelia R., (Pettis) Brooklyn, N. Y.	113.	David........Amesbury, Mass.
1962. Cornelia W......Cleveland, Ohio.	252.	David.........Columbia, Conn.
1987. Cornelia.........Mansfield, Conn.	289.	David, (Rev.)..North Lyme, Conn.
2501. Cornelia........Cleveland, Ohio.	472.	David, (Rev.)..Harpersville, N. Y.
2713. Cornelia A.........Ellington, Ill.	713.	David..............Bethel, Vt.
3078. Cornelia D.........Boston, Mass.	749.	David.........New York City.
1544. Cordelia E.......Lebanon, Conn.	908.	David.........Amesbury, Mass.
2859. Converse,.........Pulaski, N. Y.	947.	David..........Marshfield, Vt.
1824. Clayton..........................	1571.	David..........Haddam, Conn.
683. Cynthia, (Sayre)....Canton, N. Y.	1614.	David..........Middlebury, Vt.
1262. Cynthia, (Parker).....Canada East.	1688.	David I......Jersey City, N. J.
1651. Cynthia..........Washington, Vt.	1801.	David W...South Coventry, Conn.
2357. Cynthia P........Watertown, N. Y.	1857.	David.........Lawrence, Mass.
2837. Cynthia.........Washington, Vt.	1873.22	David..........Lawrence, Mass.
768. Cynthia, (Bunnel) Woodbury, Conn.	2421.	David K....Kelley's Island, Ohio.
1232. Cynthia, (Loundsbury)..........	2699.	David L., (Dr.)...Philadelphia, Pa.
1370. Cynthia, (Newton)..Durham, Conn.	2763.	David............Roxbury Mass.
2585. Cynthia,.........Starkey, N. Y.	2772.	David..............Nova Scotia.
3209.3 Cynthia A..Winnebago City, Wis.	2878.	David I......Jersey City, N. J.
1329. Cyrus T........................	3156.	David, L. D........Scranton, Pa.
1600. Cyrus...........................	37.	Deborah, (Elliot)..Amesbury, Mass.
1650. Cyrus...........................	104.	Deborah, (Homan) Amesbury, Mass.
1721. Cyrus, (Rev.)...Ellicott's Mills, Md.	212.	Deborah,........Tolland, Conn.
2515. Cyrus B.........Mason, Mich.	528.	Deborah, (Balcam) Windham, Conn.
1621. Damaris, (Hendrix).Highland, Wis.	544.	Deborah (Kent)....Tolland, Conn.
677. Dan, (Rev.).........Hadley, Mass.	908.	Delia..............................
1157. Dan................Mississippi.	1457.	Delia M..........St. Louis, Mo.
1355. Dan, (Dea.)........Norwich, Conn.	1468.	Delia A., (Gillette) Colchester, Conn.
1606. Dan.............Bethany, N. Y.	1531.	Delia............Minetto, N. Y.
3257. Dana..........Henniken, N. Y.	1752.	Delia, (Cutler).......Highgate, Vt.
1656. Dana S........Washington, Vt.	1873.9	Delia, (1873.7)...................
28. Daniel...........Norwich, Conn.	2804.	Delia, (Eggleston)................
89. Daniel............Norwich, Conn.	2842.	Delia G.........Washington, Vt.
280. Daniel..........Lebanon, Conn.	2937.	Delia A., (Sessions)..Fulton, Iowa.
288. Daniel..........Lebanon, Conn.	1507.	Denison.........South America.
299. Daniel, (Dr.)....Woodbury, Conn.	1102.	Delos.............Minnesota.
306. Daniel..........Norwich, Conn.	1302.	De Witt C., (Rev.).Rochester, N. Y.
414. Daniel..........Norwich, Conn.	2820.	De Witt C..........Chicago, Ill.
442. Daniel, (Dr.).........Perry, N. Y.	2798.	Densmore, (Carey).....Bethel, Vt.
460. Daniel, (Dea.).....Griswold, Conn.	1116.	Dimis F..............Milan, Ohio.
554. Daniel..........Norwich, Conn.	446.	Dimis, (658)...East Haddam, Conn.
632. Daniel..........Windham, Conn.	2240.	Dimis............Canada East.
721. Daniel..........Constable, N. Y.	383.	Dinah, (Judd)....Franklin, Conn.
735. Daniel..........Lebanon, Conn.	1295.	Dianna, (Cobb)..Spring Mills, N. Y.
767. Daniel..........Onondaga, N. Y.	1652.	Diantha, (Barron).Washington, Vt.
822. Daniel..........New York City.	2345.	Dimmick B.............Utah.
928.8 Daniel..........Litchfield, Maine.	136.	Dorcas, (Lathrop)..Norwich, Conn.
917. Daniel..........Marshfield, Vt.	201.	Dorcas..........Windham, Conn.
1107. Daniel G..........Carlisle, N. Y.	172.	Dorothy, (Leonard)................
1344. Daniel L..........Norwich, Conn.		.............Woodstock, Conn.
1365. Daniel, (Rev.)..New London, Conn.	657.	Dorothy, (Silliman)...............
1841. Daniel..........Amesbury, Mass.		...........East Haddam, Conn.
1847. Daniel..........Pontiac, N. Y.	2683.	Dorothy G., (Bigelow)............
1867. Daniel H..........Amesbury, Mass.		..........Worcester, N. Y.
1873.2 Daniel..............Virginia.	1053.	Dwight.........Mansfield, Conn.
1873.22 Daniel T....Litchfield, Maine.	2431.	Dwight W........Cincinnati, Ohio.
2015. Daniel...........Bozrah, Conn.	3086.	Dwight.......Roche a Cree, Wis.
2421. Daniel K....Kelley's Island, Ohio.	3091.	Dwight C.........................
2004. Daniel E.........Amesbury, Mass.	1824.	Dyer...........Watertown, N. Y.

2516.	Dytha A............Mason, Mich.	2191. Edwin M...........Adrian, Mich.
1703.	Dulcena, (Crary)....Spencer, Mass	2264. Edwin.............Osage, Iowa.
69.	Ebenezer, (Dea.)...Norwich, Conn.	2560. Edwin..........Painesville, Ohio.
282.	Ebenezer............West Indies.	163. Elias............Preston, Conn.
535.	Ebenezer, (Hon.)...Townshend, Vt.	188. Elias............Lebanon, N. H.
555.	Ebenezer.........Norwich, Conn.	441. Elias..........Shaftesbury, Vt.
561.	Ebenezer, (Gen.)...Norwich, Conn.	501. Elias...........Lebanon, N. H.
579.	Ebenezer, (Dr.)....Vergennes, Vt.	56. Eleazer..........Mansfield, Conn.
757.	Ebenezer..........Becket, Mass.	199. Eleazer..........Mansfield, Conn.
898.	Ebenezer...................West.	270. Eleazer...........Lebanon, Conn.
1297.	Ebenezer H........Madison, Wis.	527. Eleazer..........Mansfield, Conn.
1456.	Ebenezer.........Windham, Conn.	529. Eleazer..........Windham, Conn.
1582.	Ebenezer............Nova Scotia.	694. Eleazer..........Hartford, Conn.
2295.	Ebenezer..........Bingham, Pa.	1045. Eleazer..........Mansfield, Conn.
2543.	Ebenezer C.....Farmersburg, Iowa.	1274. Eleazer..........................
2764.	Ebenezer............Nova Scotia.	1298. Eleazer P.........Bingham, Pa.
2185.	Edmund T....West Randolph, Vt.	1556. Eleazer...........Lebanon, Conn.
2893.	Edmund F........Rising Sun, Wis.	App A. Eleazer.........................
630.	Edney, (Edgerton).Franklin, Conn.	1123. Eleanor..........Syracuse, N. Y.
896.	Edna L............................	1494. Eleanora, (Bellows).Walpole, N. H.
2794.	Edson.............................	142. Elijah (Hon.)......Bozrah, Conn.
808.	Edward...............Rome, N. Y.	170. Elijah............Norwich, Conn.
820.	Edward...............Rome, N. Y.	275. Elijah............Ashford, Conn.
873.	Edward..........Middletown, N. J.	355. Elijah..........Amesbury, Mass.
1222.	Edward.............Hanover, N. H.	408. Elijah............Bozrah, Conn.
1347.	Edward A., (Dea.)..Norwich, Conn.	511. Elijah, (Rev.).....Braintree, Vt.
1390.	Edward.........Windham, Conn.	600. Elijah...........Scotland, Conn.
1430.	Edward G., (Dea.).................	712. Elijah...........Ashford, Conn.
	........South Coventry, Conn.	756. Elijah............Carlisle, N. Y.
1561.	Edward P..........Hadley, Mass.	922. Elijah..........Salisbury, Mass.
1806.	Edward C..........New York.	1054. Elijah B., (Rev.)...Stamford, Conn.
1815.	Edward St. J.......New York.	1284. Elijah.........Perrysburg, Ohio.
2047.	Edward...........Shaftesbury, Vt.	184. Elijah......West Randolph, Vt.
2077.	Edward T...........Milan, Ohio.	2732. Elijah H. M........Boston, Mass.
2250.	Edward P.....Newburyport, Mass.	2968. Elijah B........Henniker, N. H.
2334.	Edward W.........Wauseon, Ohio.	App. A. Elijah.........................
2394.	Edward B.........Hartford, Conn.	2526. Elihu H...........St. Albans, Vt.
2427.	Edward H.........Cincinnati, Ohio.	235. Eliphalet........Scotland, Conn.
2441.	Edward B.........Boston, Mass.	268. Eliphalet, (Rev.) Killingworth Conn.
2490.	Edward.........New Orleans, La.	312. Eliphalet........Norwich, Conn.
2499.	Edward A........Cleveland, Ohio.	340. Eliphalet.........Plainfield, Vt.
2622.	Edward L..........Walpole, N. H.	520. Eliphalet.......Mansfield, Conn.
2627.	Edward F...........Salem, Wis.	569. Eliphalet........Windham, Conn.
2726.	Edward W.........Norwich, Conn.	667. Eliphalet........Lebanon, Conn.
2734.	Edward S.........Boston, Mass.	1386. Eliphalet, (Dr.)...Windham, Conn.
2746.	Edward D..........Hadley, Mass.	App. A. Eliphalet.......Norwich, Conn.
2871.	Edward...........Oneonta, N. Y.	124. Elisha...........Norwich, Conn.
2917.	Edward T........Rochester, N. Y.	274. Elisha..........Windham, Conn.
2956.	Edward L........Thompson, N. Y.	336. Elisha..........Norwich, Conn.
3081.	Edward W.........Marietta, Ohio.	382. Elisha...........Franklin, Conn.
3144.	Edward C............St. Martins.	541. Elisha..........Rotterdam, N. Y.
3051.4	Edward P. H., New Richmond, Wis.	760. Elisha...........Mansfield, Conn.
3151.	Edward N..........Roxbury, Mass.	867. Elisha............Hudson, N. Y.
1916.	Edwards C.........Galesburg, Ill.	965. Elisha H..........Penn Yan, N. Y.
997.	Edwin N.........Lebanon, N. H.	1012. Elisha, (Dr.).......Lowell, Mass.
1111.	Edwin..........Shaftesbury, Vt.	1035. Elisha T.........Norwich, Conn.
1137.	Edwin G..........Canton, N. Y.	1151. Elisha............Mobile, Ala.
1285.	Edwin..............Osage, Iowa.	1318. Elisha..........Wauseon, Ohio.
1530.	Edwin W.........Minetto, N. Y.	1451. Elisha M., (Hon.)..Terre Haute, Ill.
1721.	Edwin T.........Rochester, N. Y.	1594. Elisha D.........Eastford, Conn.
2057.	Edwin..........Rochester, N. Y.	1807. Elisha.........Philadelphia, Pa.

49

2105.	Elisha............Elbridge, N. Y.	1682. Elizabeth, (Yager)..............
2526.	Elisha........................	............Cortwright, N. Y.
26.	Elizabeth, (Backus)............	1744. Elizabeth R........ Rome, N. Y.
	..........Norwich, Conn.	1758. Elizabeth, (Olmsted)..........
31.	Elizabeth, (Hoyt). Amesbury, Mass.	............East Middlebury, Vt.
51.	Elizabeth, (Hyde,). Franklin, Conn.	1822. Elizabeth................
55.	Elizabeth (Chappel)............	1864. Elizabeth, (Beade)..........
	............Mansfield, Conn.	..........S. Hampton, Mass.
79.	Elizabeth, (Clark). Lebanon, Conn.	1869. Elizabeth R., (Leonard)..........
98.	Elizabeth, (Hyde). Franklin, Conn.	............Lawrence, Mass.
103.	Elizabeth, (Whittier)...........	1873.e Elizabeth........Bradford, Me.
	..........Amesbury, Mass.	1873.13 Elizabeth..............
109.	Elizabeth........Amesbury, Mass.	1879. Elizabeth, (Burrill)..........
131.	Elizabeth........Franklin, Conn.	............Weymouth, Mass.
120.	Elizabeth P........Newark, N. J.	2148.3 Elizabeth........Brooklyn, N. Y.
145.	Elizabeth, (Davenport)..........	2247. Elizabeth B....Newburyport, Mass.
	............Stamford, Conn.	2284. Elizabeth..........Auburn, Mass.
159.	Elizabeth........Norwich, Conn.	2331. Elizabeth S., (Taft.)........Mich.
206.	Elizabeth........Norwich, Conn.	2340. Elizabeth S...Sandusky City, Ohio.
225.	Elizabeth........Windham, Conn.	2370. Elizabeth, (Goulding)..........
326.	Elizabeth, (179)....Norwich, Conn.	..........Watertown, N. Y.
345.	Elizabeth, (Hendricks)..........	2389. Elizabeth A......Hartford, Conn.
	..........Plainfield, Vt.	2430. Elizabeth M......Cincinnati, Ohio.
371.	Elizabeth........Amesbury, Mass.	2416. Elizabeth A..............
398.	Elizabeth, (Tracy)......New York.	2497.1 Elizabeth S......Windham, Conn.
436.	Elizabeth, (Bottum)............	2527. Elizabeth S......St. Albans, Vt.
	..........Shaftesbury, Vt.	2620. Elizabeth A., (Prescott)..........
534.	Elizabeth........Mansfield, Conn.	............Lake Village, N. H.
562.	Elizabeth (Chester)............	2717. Elizabeth (Long).....Mystic, Conn.
	..........Wethersfield, Conn.	2836. Elizabeth............Wisconsin.
584.	Elizabeth, (Porter)............	2969. Elizabeth, (1859)..Henniker, N. H.
	..........Worthington, Mass.	2991. Elizabeth H......Amesbury, Mass.
591.	Elizabeth, (Jones). Wilkesbarre, Pa.	3045. Elizabeth ....Amesbury, Mass.
625.	Elizabeth, (Johnson)............	App. A. Elizabeth (Barnard)............
	..........Brunswick, Me.	............New York City.
652.	Elizabeth, (Brewster)............	App. A. Elizabeth (Butts)..........
	..........Windham, Conn.	1172.1 Eliza, (Babcock).....Preston, Wis.
701.	Elizabeth ......Mansfield, Conn.	1223. Eliza, (Nye)......Pittsford, N. Y.
805.	Elizabeth, (Young)...Rome, N. Y.	1280. Eliza, (Davison)..............
828.	Elizabeth, (Wilson)............	1450. Eliza, (Rea)................
	..........Sacketts Harbor, N. Y.	1475. Eliza, (Palmer)....Norwich, Conn.
913.	Elizabeth, (Osborne)............	1515. Eliza, (Skinner)...Milwaukie, Wis.
	..........Amesbury, Mass.	1554. Eliza, (Peabody).....Buffalo, N. Y.
1064.	Elizabeth...................	1741.1 Eliza R..........Caldwell, N. Y.
1117.	Elizabeth ...New Haven, Conn.	1763. Eliza, (Marvin)......Howell, Mich.
1136.	Elizabeth B., (McLean)..........	1812. Eliza M..................
1193.	Elizabeth, (Sherman)...California.	1855. Eliza, (Goodwin)..Amesbury, Mass.
1269.	Elizabeth, (Larned)........Ark.	1951. Eliza............Boston, Mass.
1360.	Elizabeth M......Norwich, Conn.	1991. Eliza, (Hatch)....Belvidere, N. Y.
1370.	Elizabeth, (Wolcott)............	2098. Eliza M..........Danbury, Conn.
	..........Litchfield, Conn.	2119. Eliza, (Coon)..............
1380.	Elizabeth, (Denton)............	..........South Brookfield, Mass.
	..........New Orleans, La.	2213. Eliza..................
1384.	Elizabeth M., (Griswold)........	2270. Eliza A..........Osage, Iowa.
	..........New York City.	2301. Eliza, (Osborn). New London, Conn.
1499.	Elizabeth, (Proctor)............	2370. Eliza P., (Goulding)............
	..........Bloomfield, Ohio.	............Watertown, N. Y.
1512.	Elizabeth (Brown)....Nova Scotia.	2541. Eliza C........St. Albans, Vt.
1558.	Elizabeth, (Fisher)..Oswego, N. Y.	2542. Eliza P........Cambridge, Mass.
1569.	Elizabeth, (Brainard)............	2568. Eliza........Sugar Creek, Ind.
	..........East Haddam, Conn.	2654. Eliza, (Lamberton) .Baraboo, Wis.

INDEX. 387

2860.	Eliza J., (Rose)................	2826.	Elbert ....Sharon, Vt.		
3022.	Eliza M............Lincoln, Vt.	3053.	Elmer C..........Nashua, N. H.		
3140.	Eliza M............St. Martins.	2618.	Eleanora, (Burrel)...Orinoco, Min.		
1076.	Emily, (Spencer).....Shaftesbury.	3273.	Elida..........Portage City, Wis.		
1405.	Emily B., (Williams)............	1190.	Elizur.....................		
	.........Tecumseh, Mich.	1709.	Emeline, (Allen)..Worcester, Mass.		
1143.	Emily C., (Phelps).Syracuse, N. Y.	2121.	Emeline E., (Ogden) Allegany, N. Y.		
1444.	Emily, (Danielson).Butternuts, N. Y.	2586.	Emeline (2579)..........		
1376.	Emily.............Norwich, Conn.		.........Winnebago City, Min.		
1461.	Emily, (Webster)..New York City.	3048.	Emeline........Brentwood, N. H.		
1482.	Emily, (V. Vleck).....New York.	2786.	Emeline, (Clement)............		
1552.	Emily, (Strong)...Lebanon, Conn.		............Alexander, N. Y.		
1576.	Emily S.............New York.	2326.	Emmet W..........Mexico, N. Y.		
1716.	Emily C.....Becket, Mass.	3039.	Emery O........Amesbury, Mass.		
1790.	Emily........Mansfield, Conn.	2665.	Emogene............		
1873.m	Emily..........Bradford, M.	236.	Enoch, (Rev.)...Middletown, N. Y.		
2171.	Emily.....................	610.	Enoch, (Esq.)...Middletown, N. Y.		
1964.	Emily L......Cleveland, Ohio.	1156.	Enoch S., (Rev.)...Danbury, Conn.		
2463.	Emily C., (Miller)....Plainfield, Ill.	1465.	Enoch, (Rev.)..North Haven, Conn.		
2531.	Emily W.......Rockford, Ill.	1836.	Enoch........Amesbury, Mass.		
2599.	Emily W.......Springfield, Ill.	771.	Elvira, (Manville).Woodbury, Conn.		
2714.	Emily E........Ellington, Ill.	1141.	Elvira M., (Swift)..Brooklyn, N. Y.		
2724.	Emily.........Norwich, Conn.	3018.	Elvira, (Waite)...........		
2877.	Emily S........Jersey City, N. J.	118.	Eunice O..........Newark, N. J.		
3194.	Emily L.......Franklin, Conn.	166.	Eunice.........Norwich, Conn.		
3261.	Emily P.......Newark, N. J.	171.	Eunice, (Williams)..Norwich, Conn.		
2282.	Ella M.........Auburn, Mass.	242.	Eunice, (Devotion) Windham, Conn.		
3038.	Ella J..........Amesbury, Mass.	283.	Eunice.........Lebanon, Conn.		
3118.	Ella..........Rochester, N. Y.	294.	Eunice, (Willes)..Franklin, Conn.		
3138.2	Ella E..........Brooklyn, N. Y.	303.	Eunice, (Carew)...Norwich, Conn.		
1686.	Ellen M..........Oneonta, N. Y.	351.	Eunice, (Avery....Norwich, Conn.		
1873.12	Ellen, (Moody)..East Pittston, Me.	406.	Eunice........Bozrah, Conn.		
2004.	Ellen S..........Greensboro, Vt.	437.	Eunice, (Stanley)..Greensboro, Vt.		
2144.	Ellen........Hoverleyville, Pa.	483.	Eunice, (Leonard)..Ashford, Conn.		
2150.	Ellen A..........New York.	522.	Eunice, (Hebard).Windham, Conn.		
2162.	Ellen M.........Hanover, N. H.	603.	Eunice, (Mather)..Scotland, Conn.		
2523.	Ellen M..........Mason, Mich.	622.	Eunice, (Abbe)...Windham, Conn.		
2562.	Ellen L..........Ellsworth, Ohio.	657.	Eunice, (Ripley)..Windham, Conn.		
2602.	Ellen J..........Springfield, Ill.	676.	Eunice, (Mason)....Lebanon, Conn.		
2638.	Ellen P..........Painesville, Ohio.	742.	Eunice.........Lebanon, Conn.		
2729.	Ellen B..........Lebanon, Conn.	759.	Eunice, (555)......Norwich, Conn.		
2918.	Ellen M..........Rochester, N. Y.	883.	Eunice, (Wainwright)............		
2999.	Ellen F., (Sleeper).Haverhill, Mass.		............Salisbury, Mass.		
3033.	Ellen A........Lawrence, Mass.	1024.	Eunice.........Bozrah, Conn.		
3252.	Ellen ....Meriden, Conn.	1071.	Eunice........Shaftesbury, Vt.		
3258.	Ellen........Manchester, N. H.	1229.	Eunice, (Clinton)..............		
1084.	Elon..........Rochester, N. Y.	1291.	Eunice...............		
1112.	Elon..........Kalamazoo, Mich.	1498.	Eunice, (Palmer)............		
2026.	Elon..........Troy, N. Y.		........New Hartford, N. Y.		
1941.	Emma..........Lebanon, N. H.	1639.	Eunice.........Enfield, N. H.		
2159.	Emma..........Rochester, N. H.	1673.	Eunice E., (Skinner) Syracuse, N. Y.		
3077.	Emma L..........Boston, Mass.	2006.	Eunice C., (Derby)............		
3134.	Emma J........Depauville, N. Y.		........Cedar Rapids, Iowa.		
1485.	Emma..........Walpole, N. H.	2170.	Eunice..................		
3212.	Emma..........Salem, Mass.	2469.	Eunice E., (Strong).Norwich, Conn.		
1782.	Emma L., (Babbit).Waterloo, N. Y.	3173.	Eunice S. N........Baltimore, Md.		
1873.11	Emma, (Kimball)....Boston, Mass.	348.	Ephraim J.........Norwich, Conn.		
2170.	Emma..........Coventry, Pa.	1844.	Ephraim M.........Newark, N. J.		
2897.	Emma..........Rising Sun, Wis.	360.	Ephraim.........Amesbury Mass.		
2910.	Emma S........Marlboro, Mass.	1872.	Ephraim.........Amesbury, Mass.		
2948.	Emma L..........Howell, Mich.	475.	Erastus.............Havana.		

388 INDEX.

556.	Erastus	Norwich, Conn.	2377.	Florence, (Emerson)	La.
961.	Erastus	Bozrah, Conn.	2920.	Florence W	Albany, N. Y.
1195.	Erastus	New York.	3247.	Florence E	Montpelier, Vt.
1284.	Erastus	Greenville, Conn.	3072.[1]	Florence C	
1625.	Erastus W	New York.	1416.	Fordyce, (Hon.)	Vergennes, Vt.
2119.	Erastus	Kelley's Island, Ohio.	589.	Frances, (Rev. Dr. Griffin)	
2821.	Erastus D	Chicago, Ill.			Boston, Mass.
279.	Ezekiel	Lebanon, Conn.	736.	Frances	Lebanon, Conn.
734.	Ezekiel	Lebanon, Conn	799.	Frances, (Deering)	New York City.
508.	Esther, (Niles)	Haverhill, N. H.	1413.	Frances, (Buel)	Troy, N. Y.
617.	Esther, (Rosekrantz)		1715.	Frances D	New Haven, Conn.
		Waterford, N. Y.	1961.	Frances E.,(1145)	
733.	Esther				Cleveland, Ohio.
1317.	Esther	Mexico, N. Y.	2056.	Frances	Chicago, Ill.
2002.	Esther B.,(Blake)	Mapleton, Kansas.	2514.	Frances B	New York City.
2242.[1]	Esther	Canada East.	2512.	Frances F., (Wright)	Boston Mass.
2265.	Everett G	Osage, Iowa.	2698.	Frances H	Minetto, N. Y.
1103.	Eveline	Buffalo, N. Y.	2790.	Frances	Bethany, N. Y.
2337.	Eveline C., (Smith)	Rodman, N. Y.	App. A.	Frances P., (Paddock)	
2367.	Eveline A., (Hitchcock)				New York City.
		Watertown, N. Y.	1172.	Francis	Lysander, N. Y.
1929.	Eveline H	Athens, Pa.	1336.	Francis J	Hartford, Conn.
2269.	Eugene L	Osage, Iowa.	1431.	Francis	Painesville, Ohio.
2579.	Eugene	Terre Haute, Ind.	1873.[17]	Francis M	Pittston, Me.
3114.	Eva	New York City.	1953.	Francis C	New York City.
3249.	Eva B	Washington, Vt.	2096.	Francis, (Hoyt)	Danbury, Conn.
179.	Ezra	Norwich, Conn.	2392.	Francis	
696.	Ezra	Nova Scotia.	2528.	Francis	St. Albans, Vt.
1184.	Ezra A., (D. D.)	Auburn, N. Y.	3185.	Francis P	
1191.	Ezra	New York.	2920.	Frank	Rochester, N. Y.
1584.	Ezra	Nova Scotia.	2249.	Frank W	Newburyport, Mass.
2115.	Ezra C	Hoverleyville, Pa.	2288.	Frank R	Madison, Wis.
2981.	Ezra	Manchester, N. H.	2428.	Frank	Cincinnati, Ohio.
2615.[2]	Fabius P. B	South Carolina.	2853.	Frank A	Washington, Vt.
1362.	Faith T., (318)	New York City.	3052.	Frank D	Lawrence, Mass.
2438.	Faith T., (Hooker)	Vt.	3208.	Frank C	Painesville, Ohio.
498.	Fanny	Thornton, Vt.	1134.	Franklin W	
507.	Fanny, (Baker)	Haverhill, N. Y.	1873.	Franklin	California.
647.	Fanny	Columbia, Conn.	3102.	Franklin A	Shaftesbury, Vt.
688.	Fanny, (Bull)	Wethersfield, Conn.	5117.	Franklin	Nova Scotia.
831.	Fanny, (Bicknell)	Lebanon, N. H.	2090.	Franklin	
990.	Fanny, (Peck)	Lebanon, N. H.	2122.	Franklin C	South Brookfield, N. Y.
1070.	Fanny (Barton)	Shaftesbury, Vt.	2972.	Franklin T	Henniker, N. H.
1212.	Fanny M	Hanover, N. H.	3102.	Franklin A	Shaftesbury, Vt.
1220.	Fanny, (Spencer)	Laconia, N. H.	5217.	Franklin	Nova Scotia.
1277.	Fanny, (Dodge)	Berlin, Pa.	358.	Frederick	Hudson, N. Y.
1399.	Fanny, (Carter)	Delavan, Wis.	875.	Frederick	Savannah, Geo.
1415.	Fanny (Danielson)	Butternuts, N. Y.	1307.	Frederick A	Mexico, N. Y.
1874.	Fanny	Weare, N. H.	2210.	Frederick A	
2163.	Fanny C	Hanover, N. H.	1557.	Frederick G	Cincinnati, Ohio.
2504.	Fanny	St. Domingo.	2712.	Frederick S	Milwaukie, Wis.
3262.	Fanny J	Amesbury, Mass.	1566.	Frederick D., (D. D.)	Boston, Mass.
2245.	Felicia	Canada East.	2801.	Frederick	Groveland, Mass.
301.	Felix	Norwich, Conn.	2290.	Frederick P	Bingham, Pa.
793.	Felix A	Brooklyn, N. Y.	2924.	Frederick K	New Haven, Conn.
1429.	Flavius J	Painesville, Ohio.	2861.	Frederick	Groveland, Mass.
2088.	Flora		2963.	Frederick M	Meriden, Conn.
3209.[2]	Flora A	Winnebago, Wis.	5000.	Frederick E	Haverhill, Mass.
2743.	Flora	Milwaukie, Wis.	3160.	Frederick W	Albany, Ga.
2855.	Flora	Washington, Vt.	3121.	Frederick W	Perry, N. Y.
2067.	Florence	Rochester, N. Y.	3153.	Frederick J	Roxbury, Mass.

INDEX. 389

3228.¹ Frederick C......Lebanon, Conn	2914.	George E.........Becket, Mass.
3274. Frederick G....Portage City, Wis.	2825.	George P......New Haven, Conn.
3207.¹ Frederick R......Painesville, Ohio.	3002.	George F...... Amesbury, Mass.
1873.²¹ Frederick S.........Litchfield, Me.	3014.	George.....West Newbury, Mass.
3138.¹ Frederick P......Brooklyn, N. Y.	3056.	George......Au Sable Forks, N. Y.
864. Freelove, (Lathrop).New York City.	3071.	George W......Valparaiso, Ind.
2080. Freeman F.....Ogdensburg, N. Y.	3091.¹	George A .. ....Eagleville, Conn.
639. Gamaliel.........Walpole, N. H.	3157.	George F., (Dr.).Portage City, Wis.
2902. Garry A.........Richmond, Ind.	3180.	George F........Baltimore, Md.
315. George, (Hon.)......Rome, N. Y.	3224.	George M......Middlefield, N. Y.
817. George............Rome, N. Y.	3216.	George E...... Painesville, Ohio.
865. George..........West Indies.	3224.	George M................
952. George.........Bennington, Vt.	App. A.	George R................
1051. George, (Hon.).......Bath, N. Y.	App. A.	George S......Nantucket Island.
1083. George........Shaftesbury, Vt.	2107.	Georgiana.........Savannah Ga.
1147. George M........Oswego, N. Y.	2160.	Georgiana......Springfield, N. Y.
1164. George.........Savannah, Ga.	2593.	Gertrude.....Terre Haute, Ind.
1182. George L., (Dr.) East Hampton, L. I.	2800.¹	Gertrude........New York City.
1350. George C....Kelley's Island, Ohio.	518.	Gideon........Pompanoosuc, Vt.
1375. George W......New Orleans, La.	931.	Gideon........Marshfield, Vt.
1447. George P.........Canada East.	1339.	Gilbert.........Norwich, Conn.
1459. George L.......Springfield, Ill.	2246.	Gilbert.........Canada East.
1477. George W.............West.	2404.	Gilbert C.......Norwich, Conn.
1493. George.......Walpole, N. H.	2559.	Gilbert C......Waterloo, N. Y.
1540. George O.........Quincy, Ill.	2960.	Glen W........Waterloo, N. Y.
1718. George H......Becket, Mass.	804.	Gloriana.........Rome, N. Y.
1741.² George.......Caldwell, N. Y.	2880.	Grace......New York City.
1801. George P.............Ill.	1522.	Gracia A., (Leonard).........
1873.⁵ George..............		........Westfield, Mass.
1875. George...............	173.	Gurdon.......Norwich, Conn.
1873.⁶ George.........Bangor, Me.	314.	Gurdon........Rome, N. Y.
1873.²⁹ George K.......Litchfield, Me.	400.	Gurdon, (Dr.)......Cairo, N. Y.
1883. George..............	570.	Gurdon.......Tecumseh, Mich.
1911. George.........Mobile, Ala.	643.	Gurdon .....Walpole, N. H.
2011. George C.......Downieville, Cal.	823.	Gurdon, (Rev.)...Sag Harbor, L. I.
2030. George..........Rome, N. Y.	1042.	Gurdon.........Batavia, N. Y.
2058. George B.........Castile, N. Y.	1404.	Gurdon..........Chicago, Ill.
2131. George.....East Hampton, L. I.	1502.	Gurdon W.......Canton, Ohio.
2225. George A.........Lowell, Mass.	1981.	Gurdon........Rochester, N. Y.
2226. George H......Green Lake, Wis.	2630.	Gurdon H.....Painesville, Ohio.
2153. George E.........California.	1449.	Hallam.........Hudson, Ind.
2354. George C......Watertown, N. Y.	18.	Hannah.........Newark, N. J.
2389.³ George S.......Hartford, Conn.	32.	Hannah, (Chandler).........
2424. George F.......Brunswick, Ohio.		........Amesbury, Mass.
2464. George.........Brooklyn, Conn.	40.¹	Hannah.........Newark, N. J.
2476. George F............	65.	Hannah, (Huit)....Lebanon, Conn.
2495. George W., (Dr.)...Rock Island, Ill.	149.	Hannah, (Tomlinson)..........
2520. George M........Macon, Mich.		........Stratford, Conn.
2581. George P.........Attica, Ind.	164.	Hannah.......Norwich, Conn.
2600. George L.......Springfield, Ill.	175.	Hannah (559)...Norwich, Conn.
2619. George H......Madison, Wis.	191.	Hannah, (Worcester).Thornton, Vt.
2658. George W.......Baraboo, Wis.	296.	Hannah, (Lyman)..Hatfield, Mass.
2672. George M....Charleston, S. C.	311.	Hannah, (Turner)..Norwich, Conn.
2701. George L......Charlestown, Mass.	346.	Hannah, (Culver)..........
2723. George W.......Norwich, Conn.	357.	Hannah, (Hoyt)..Amesbury, Mass.
2747. George P........Boston, Mass.	417.	Hannah, (Waldo)...Bingham, Vt.
2816. George E......Middlebury, Vt.	552.	Hannah, (Lyman).Woodstock,Conn.
2844. George.......Washington, Vt.	663.	Hannah........Lebanon, Conn.
2852. George E......Washington, Vt.	708.	Hannah, (Lilley)..Ashford, Conn.
2903. George........Richmond, Ind.	813.	Hannah T., (Smith).Camden, N. Y.
2907. George D.....Marlborough, Mass.	843.	Hannah, (Cleveland).....Vermont.

No.	Name	Location		No.	Name	Location
901.	Hannah M., (Beecher)		2770.	Harriet, (Wood)	Nova Scotia.
		New Haven, Conn.	2782.	Harriet B.	Eastford, Conn.
905.	Hannah	Amesbury, Mass.	App. A.	Harriet B., (Cleveland)	
914.	Hannah, (Herbert), Amesbury, Mass.				Nantucket Island.
924.	Hannah	New Hampshire.	App. A.	Harriet A	Nantucket Island.
937.	Hannah, (Holt)	Groton, Mass.	App. A.	Harriot	
949.	Hannah	Francistown, N. H.	3139.	Harrison S	Watertown, N. Y.
999.	Hannah	Bowdoinham, Me.	993.	Harry	Lebanon, N. H.
1016.	Hannah, (Balis)	Oswego, N. Y.	1659.	Harry	Washington, Vt.
1022.	Hannah D., (Hough). Putnam, Conn.		3121.1	Harry H	Perry, N. Y.
1218.	Hannah W., (Ingalls)		2289.	Hattie	Madison, Wis.
		Hanover, N. H.	2151.2	Hattie	New York.
1227.	Hannah, (Putnam)	Roxbury, Vt.	3211.1	Harwood..Great Barrington, Mass.	
1338.	Hannah T., (Dickinson)		1589.	Harvey	Ashford, Conn.
		Hatfield, Mass.	1873.1	Harvey	California.
1368.	Hannah (588)	Painesville, Ohio.	1469.	Helen M., (Cottrel). Hartford, Conn.	
1628.	Hannah, (Parkhurst)..Enfield, N. H.		2157.	Helen	Rochester, N. Y.
1732.	Hannah M., (Bowers)		2266.	Helen E	Osage, Iowa.
		New York City.	2381.	Helen D	New Orleans, La.
1828.	Hannah, (Purinton)	Lincoln, Vt.	2396.	Helen	
1850.	Hannah	Lincoln, Vt.	2730.	He'en F., (Quincy)	Boston, Mass.
2114.	Hannah	Griswold, Conn.	2740.	Helen M	Milwaukie, Wis.
2174.	Hannah		3051.3	Helen A. H..New Richmond, Wis.	
2451.	Hannah S., (Chappell)		3058.	Helen L	Au Sable Forks, N. Y.
		New London, Conn.	3099.	Helen	McCrawville, N. Y.
2473.	Hannah P., (Adams).Norwich, Conn.		3195.	Helen J	Shaftesbury, Vt.
2767.	Hannah, (Williams)	Nova Scotia.	3222.	Helen W	Middlefield, N. Y.
2858.	Hannah	Pulaski, N. Y.	1257.	Heman	Lowell, Mass.
2941.	Hannah M. J	Fulton, Io.	801.	Henrietta, (Wright)	Rome, N. Y.
2983.	Hannah L	Amesbury, Mass.	313.	Henry, (Hon.)	Rome, N. Y.
3050.	Hannah H	Brentwood, N. H.	435.	Henry	Shaftesbury, Vt.
3197.	Hannah P	Franklin, Conn.	595.	Henry	Coventry, Conn.
3264.	Hannah M	Amesbury, Mass.	624.	Henry	Windham, Conn.
1081.	Harlow, (Dea.)	Shaftesbury, Vt.	806.	Henry	Rome, N. Y.
900.	Harriet, (Trowbridge).Oswego, N.Y.		878.	Henry	Hudson, N. Y.
940.	Harriet, (Lull)	Warner, N. H.	1000.	Henry	
1097.	Harriet A., (Steadman).Rome, N.Y.		1057.	Henry	Greensboro, Vt.
1146.	Harriet L., (Swift)		1162.	Henry	Griswold, Conn.
1171.	Harriet, (Babcock)..North East, Pa.		1216.	Henry S., (Dr.)	Penfield, N. Y.
1226.	Harriet A., (Gibson).Rochester,N.Y.		1330.	Henry W	Cataboula, La.
1279.	Harriet	Norwich, Conn.	1354.	Henry D	Cincinnati, Ohio.
1363.	Harriet S., (DeWitt). Norwich,Conn.		1439.	Henry A	Sugar Creek, Ind.
1406.	Harriet, (Gray)	Dublin, Ireland	1545.	Henry H	Mt. Clemens, Mich.
1455.	Harriet, (Campbell).Springfield, Ill.		1581.	Henry M	Milford, Conn.
1539.	Harriet, (Townley)	Albany, Ill.	1616.	Henry H	Milwaukie, Wis.
1595.	Harriet, (Davis)	Davenport, Io.	1722.	Henry H	Albany, N. Y.
1626.	Harriet, (Huntley)	Bridport, Vt.	1780.	Henry L	Waterloo, N. Y.
1699.	Harriet, (Kingsbury). Spencer, Mass.		1826.	Henry	
1776.	Harriet M., (Stodder)		1873.12	Henry	California
1798.	Harriet F..South Coventry, Conn.		1873.12	Henry A	
1924.	Harriet H., (Bennet)	Athens, Pa.	1942.	Henry	Valparaiso, Ind.
2009.	Harriet E.,(Bottum).Shaftesbury,Vt.		1950.	Henry A	Boston, Mass.
2072.	Harriet E	Milan, Ohio.	1986.	Henry	Eagleville, Conn.
2261.	Harriet	Osage, Iowa.	2005.	Henry, (Dr.)	Albany, Ga.
2415.	Harriet E	Norwich, Conn.	2034.	Henry E	Chicago, Ill.
2459.	Harriet,(Coggshall).Providence, R.I.		2053.	Henry A	Chicago, Ill.
2615.	Harriet N., (Elliot)	Illinois.	2109.	Henry R	Blue Island, Ill.
2635.	Harriet M	Painesville, Ohio.	2181.	Henry C	Perrysburg, Ohio.
2670.	Harriet A	Baraboo, Wis.	2327.	Henry J	Mexico, N. Y.
2689.	Harriet, (Allen)	Albany, N. Y.	2542.	Henry C	Sandusky City, Ohio.
2697.	Harriet N	Minetto, N. Y.	2568.	Henry	Watertown, N. Y.

INDEX. 391

No.	Name	Location		No.	Name	Location
2374.	Henry	Louisiana.	2167.	Horace L	Penfield, N. Y.
2387.	Henry K	Hartford, Conn.	2366.	Horace C	Watertown, N. Y.
2410.	Henry G	Norwich City, Conn.	2939.	Horace	Fulton, Iowa.
2429.	Henry W	Cincinnati, Ohio.	1286.	Horatio	Osage, Iowa.
2461.	Henry	Geneva, Ill.	1538.	Horatio L	Adams, Ill.
2489.	Henry C	New Orleans, La.	2273.	Horatio E	Osage, Ill.
3494.	Henry B	Lebanon, Conn.	2562.	Howard J	Baraboo, Wis.
2571.	Henry	Painesville, Ohio.	2869.	Howard	Oneonta, N. Y.
2582.	Henry M	Iowa.	621.	Huldah, (Johnson)	Brunswick, Me.
2629.	Henry	Warren, Ill.	1254.	Huldah, (Harvey)	Canada East.
2736.	Henry G	Boston, Mass.	2797.	Huldah	Wisconsin.
2780.	Henry E	Eastford, Conn.	2973.	Huldah, (Buxton)	Danvers, Mass.
2793.	Henry	Batavia, N. Y.	1888.	Hugh C	
2796.	Henry	Wisconsin.	3059.	Ida J	Au Sable Forks, N. Y.
2827.	Henry	Sharon, Vt.	3005.	Ida I	North Elba, N. Y.
2846.	Henry C	Washington, Vt.	2239.	Ira	Canada East.
2883.	Henry	Jersey City, N. J.	2729.	Ira C	New York City.
2892.	Henry B	Rising Sun, Wis.	3123.	Ira L	South Brookfield, N. Y.
2915.	Henry F	Rochester, N. Y.	43.	Isaac	Norwich, Conn.
3045.	Henry L	Amesbury, Mass.	135.	Isaac	Bozrah, Conn.
3062.¹	Henry	Au Sable Forks, N. Y.	358.	Isaac	Amesbury, Mass.
3074.	Henry L	Franklin, Conn.	407.	Isaac	Bozrah, Conn.
3098.	Henry D	Albany, Ga.	769.	Isaac	Woodbury, Conn.
3105.¹	Henry	Shaftesbury, Vt.	928.	Isaac	Amesbury, Mass.
3167.	Henry S	Norwich, Conn.	1023.	Isaac	Bozrah, Conn.
3232.	Henry		1889.¹	Isaac L	Theresa, N. Y.
3236.	Henry M	Columbus, Wis.	2811.	Isaac A	Kalamazoo, Mich.
3245.	Henry J	Galena, Ill.	2248.	Isabella	Newburyport, Mass.
1510.	Herbert, (Hon.)	Yarmouth, N. S.	2317.	Isabella G	New York City.
1517.	Herbert N	Baraboo, Wis.	3095.	Isabel	East Wareham, Mass.
2652.	Herbert	Nova Scotia.	1207.	Isaiah	Springfield, N. Y.
2961.	Herbert O	Mansfield, Conn.	2164.	Isaiah	Springfield, N. Y.
3220.	Herbert A	Nova Scotia.	287.	Israel	Lebanon, Conn.
1894.	Herman		740.	Israel, (Hon.)	Syracuse, N. Y.
46.	Hezekiah, (Hon.)	Norwich, Conn.	1676.	Israel E	Syracuse, N. Y.
167.	Hezekiah	Norwich, Conn.	1748.	Ithamar	
192.	Hezekiah	Haverhill, N. H.	3123.	Iva L	South Brookfield, N. Y.
247.	Hezekiah	Windham, Conn.	44.	Jabez, (Col.)	Windham, Conn.
402.	Hezekiah	Franklin, Conn.	150.	Jabez, (Hon.)	Windham, Conn.
420.	Hezekiah	Windham, Conn.	217.	Jabez, (Gen.)	Norwich, Conn.
543.	Hezekiah, (Judge)	Hartford, Conn.	418.	Jabez	Windham, Conn.
1014.	Hezekiah	Topsfield, Mass.	761.	Jabez	Lebanon, Conn.
1334.	Hezekiah	Hartford, Conn.	1359.	Jabez, (Dea.)	Norwich, Conn.
1925.	Hezekiah	East Smithfield, Pa.	1705.	Jabez	Marlboro, Mass.
1949.	Hezekiah	Franklin, Pa.	1383.	Jabez W., (Hon.)	Norwich, Conn.
2895.	Hezekiah R	Rising Sun, Wis.	96.	Jacob	Norwich, Conn.
386.	Hiram	Chelsea, Vt.	114.	Jacob	Amesbury, Mass.
1326.	Hiram	Watertown, N. Y.	366.	Jacob	Amesbury, Mass.
2038.	Hiram L	Rome, N. Y.	901.¹	Jacob	Amesbury, Mass.
2172.	Hiram		985.	Jacob P., (Rev.)	
2192.	Hiram S	Adrian, Mich.			Guilford Centre, Vt.
2361.	Hiram L	Brooklyn, N. Y.	1095.	Jacob G	Shaftesbury, Vt.
2371.	Hiram C		1829.	Jacob	Henniker, N. H.
App. A.	Hiram		1839.	Jacob	Amesbury, Mass.
3041.	Homer A	Amesbury, Mass.	2987.	Jacob R	Amesbury, Mass.
478.	Horace	Canaan, Conn.	29.	James	Norwich, Conn.
1196.	Horace F	New York City.	94.	James	Norwich, Conn.
1247.	Horace J	Rochester, N. Y.	277.	James	Lebanon, Conn.
1332.	Horace A	Natchez, Miss.	324.	James	Royalton, Vt.
1358.	Horace	Cincinnati, Ohio.	509.	James	
2155.	Horace	Canaan, Conn.	602.	James	Windham, Conn.

INDEX.

718.	James............Woodstock, Vt.	2694.	Jane, (Mason)...................
790.	James............Norwich, Conn.	2928.	Jane............Medina, Ohio.
841.	James............Mansfield, Conn.	3096.	Jane E.... ....Perry, N. Y.
845.	James....................	3108.	Jane............Troy, N. Y.
1091.	James.... ....Rome, N. Y.	3176.	Jane E............Baltimore, Md.
1260.	James......Green Lake, Wis.	323.	Jared............Mansfield, Conn.
1393.	James........Cleveland, Ohio.	456.	Jared............Owego, N. Y.
1427.	James ....Cambridge, Mass.	838.	Jared............Howell, Mich.
1448.	James, (Hon.)......Dundee, N. Y.	1140.	Jared B........Syracuse, N. Y.
1612.	James....................	1299.	Jared H........Townshend, Vt.
1661.	James T............Lowell, Mass.	1772.	Jared........................
1734.	James W., (Capt.)...New York City.	341.	Jasper............Norwich, Conn.
1756.	James............Whiting, Vt.	2031.	Jay............Canton, N. Y.
1783.	James F........Monticello, N. Y.	2055.	Jay G............Chicago, Ill.
1788.	James P........Mansfield, Conn	784.	Jedediah......Norwich City, Conn.
1873.f	James C........Atkinson, Maine.	2929.	Jedediah......Norwich City, Conn.
1900.	James F....Au Sable Forks, N. Y.	54.	Jedidiah........Mansfield, Conn.
1952.	James F., (Capt.)...Marietta, Ohio.	119.	Jedidiah........Windham, Conn.
1982.	James M..........Wisconsin.	512.	Jedidiah......Brighton, N. Y.
2085.	James J....................	557.	Jedidiah, (Gen.)...Norwich, Conn.
2148.1	James............Brooklyn, N. Y.	821.	Jedidiah V., (Rev.).New York City.
2164.	James H..........Pittsford, N. Y.	1270.	Jedidiah P....Pompanoosuc, Vt.
2190.	James H..........Adrian, Mich.	1825.	Jedidiah................
2220.	James H..........Lowell, Mass.	2437.	Jedidiah........Norwich, Conn.
2227.	James H......Green Lake, Wis.	1237.	Jehiel............Braintree, Vt.
2259.	James B..........Osage, Iowa.	2008.	Jennette P......Shaftesbury, Vt.
2398.	James D......Meriden, Conn.	2015.	Jennette........Shaftesbury, Vt.
2406.	James E......Walsingham, C. W.	3241.	Jenny............Columbus, Wis.
2483.	James M......Norwich City, Conn.	52.	Jeremiah........Lebanon, N. H.
2502.1	James........Cleveland, Ohio.	185.	Jeremiah........Shaftesbury, Vt.
2536.	James M..........Rockford, Ill.	403.	Jeremiah........Onondaga, N. Y.
2553.	James, (Esq.)...Woodbury, Conn.	93.	Jerusha, (Hyde)....Franklin, Conn.
2588.	James............Hudson, Ind.	118.	Jerusha, (Clark)...Lebanon, Conn.
2649.	James............Yarmouth, N. S.	333.	Jerusha............Norwich, Conn.
2750.	James O. S........Boston, Mass.	644.	Jerusha, (Sherrill)................
2774.	James............Nova Scotia.		............New Hartford, N. Y.
2809.	James H....Fountain Prairie, Wis.	574.	Jerusha ....Ellington, Conn.
2813.	James P........Middlebury, Vt.	861.	Jerusha, (Tilley)....Hudson, N. Y.
2831.	James....................	1771.	Jerusha J., (Kellum)............
2935.	James M..........Brooklyn, N. Y.		............Long Eddy, N. Y.
2998.	James A........Haverhill, Mass.	850.	Jesse............Norwich, Conn.
3027.	James N........Lawrence, Mass.	1761.	Jesse ....Randolph, Vt.
3062.	James F....Au Sable Forks, N. Y.	370.	Joanna, (Colby)....Weare, N. H.
3064.	James W........North Elba, N. Y.	465	Joel............Manlius, N. Y.
3143.	James C............St. Martins.	1188.	Joel, (Rev.)......Albany, N. Y.
3240.	James............Columbus, Wis.	1252.	Joel............Mississippi.
3244.	James B....Fountain Prairie, Wis.	2139.	Joel....................
942.	Jane, (Sleeper)................	2215.	Joel T............Wisconsin.
1100.	Jane, (Harpending)Shaftesbury, Vt.	6.	John............Amesbury, Mass.
1460.	Jane M., (Ridgley)..Springfield, Ill.	16.	John............Norwich, Conn.
1580.	Jane............Eastford, Conn.	50.	John............Norwich, Conn.
1692.	Jane E., (Jones).....Pittsburg, Pa.	64.	John............Tolland, Conn.
1725.	Jane, (Case)......New York City.	85.	John............Lebanon, Conn.
1818.1	Jane....................	99.	John............Amesbury, Mass.
2032.	Jane............Rome, N. Y.	110.	John............Amesbury, Mass.
2173.	Jane....................	176.	John, (Rev.) ......Salem, Mass.
2251.	Jane, (Keyes)...Ogdensburg, N. Y.	207.	John............Tolland, Conn.
2319.	Jane......Union Square, N. Y.	226.	John............Windham, Conn.
2341.	Jane R., (McKelvey)............	285.	John........East Haddam, Conn.
	............Sandusky City, Ohio.	325.	John............Norwich, Conn.
2525.	Jane............St. Albans, Vt.	349.	John... ......Amesbury, Mass.

INDEX. 393

365.[1]	John	Amesbury, Mass.	2493.	John M	Chicago, Ill.
367.	John	Weare, N. H.	2534.	John B	Rockford, Ill.
434.	John	Middlebury, Vt.	2605.	John T., (Rev.)	
449.	John	Syracuse, N. Y.			Great Barrington, Mass.
459.	John	Griswold, Conn.	2651.	John	Nova Scotia.
523.	John	Mansfield, Conn.	2773.	John	Nova Scotia.
536.	John	Mexico, N. Y.	2863.	John H	Hartford, Conn.
567.	John	Windham, Conn.	2886.	John	New York City.
738.	John	Sunderland, Mass.	2904.	John G	Marlboro, Mass.
824.	John	Orange, Vt.	2930.	John R	Norwich, Conn.
856.	John	Zanesville, Ohio.	2975.	John J	Henniker, N. H.
872.	John B	New Orleans, La.	2989.	John D	Amesbury, Mass.
882.	John F	Norwich, Conn.	2995.	John W	Amesbury, Mass.
904.	John	Lincoln, Vt.	3008.	John L	Georgetown, Mass.
915.	John	Wilmington, N. C.	3061.	John C. F	Au Sable Forks, N. Y.
934.	John	Bennington, Vt.	3137.	John L	Brooklyn, N. Y.
945.	John	Francistown, N. H.	3211.	John W	New Haven, Conn.
955.	John	Keene, N. Y.	App. A. 3.	John	
960.	John	Bozrah, Conn.	App. 37.	John	Norwich, Conn.
1049.	John	Bath, N. Y.	App. 49.	John	
1056.	John	Greensboro, Vt.	429.	Jonas	Mansfield, Conn.
1129.	John	Peterboro, N. Y.	439.	Jonas	Chelsea, Vt.
1199.	John	Canaan, Conn.	1108.	Jonas, (Dr.)	Kalamazoo, Mich.
1306.	John	New London, Conn.	73.	Jonathan, (Hon.)	Windham, Conn.
1325.	John L	Watertown, N. Y.	91.	Jonathan	Norwich, Conn.
1355.	John C	Cincinnati, Ohio.	112.	Jonathan	Amesbury, Mass.
1403.	John	Hampton, Conn.	253.	Jonathan, (Rev.)	Worthington, Mass.
1462.	John G	Davenport, Iowa.	269.	Jonathan	East Haddam, Conn.
1520.	John L	Baraboo, Wis.	505.	Jonathan	Norwich, Conn.
1561.[1]	John W	Hadley, Mass.	586.	Jonathan, (Dea.)	St. Albans, Vt.
1598.	John	Conewango, N. Y.	601.	Jonathan	St. Louis, Mo.
1650.	John P	Washington, Vt.	682.	Jonathan, (Hon.)	Haddam, Conn.
1670.	John F	New Orleans, La.	725.	Jonathan	Lebanon, Conn.
1697.	John R	Richfield, Ohio.	974.	Jonathan R	Vernon, Conn.
1731.	John G	Norwich, Conn.	1415.	Jonathan, (Rev.)	Nashville, Tenn.
1740.	John F	Brooklyn, N. Y.	1597.	Jonathan E	Newark, N. J.
1778.	John G		1618.	Jonathan M	Middlebury, Vt.
1809.[2]	John F		2756.	Jonathan H	Newark, N. J.
1816.	John		23.	Joseph, (Dea.)	Windham, Conn.
1834.	John	Weare, N. H.	71.	Joseph, (Dea.)	Windham, Conn.
1837.	John	Amesbury, Mass.	141.	Joseph	Norwich, Conn.
1849.	John	Lincoln, Vt.	228.	Joseph	Windham, Conn.
1873.[29]	John	Thetford, Vt.	234.	Joseph, (D. D.)	Coventry, Conn.
1876.	John	Weare, N. H.	286.	Joseph	Harwinton, Conn.
1880.	John	New Orleans, La.	369.	Joseph	Francistown, N. H.
1892.	John	Nashua, N. H.	422.	Joseph S	Newburg, N. Y.
1899.	John C	Scroone, N. Y.	568.	Joseph	Windham, Conn.
1972.	John W. P	Scottsburg, Oregon.	587.	Joseph	Coventry, Conn.
1985.	John	Mansfield, N. Y.	646.	Joseph B	Norwich, Conn.
1995.	John	Freeport, Ill.	655.	Joseph D	Westfield, Mass.
2040.	John H	Troy, N. Y.	680.	Joseph	Killingworth, Conn.
2093.	John A	Mobile, Ala.	727.	Joseph	Orange, Vt.
2100.	John	Sharon, Ill.	731.	Joseph	Lebanon, Conn.
2219.	John P	Lowell, Mass.	743.	Joseph	Canada West.
2260.	John	Osage, Iowa.	889.	Joseph	Monticello, N. Y.
2302.	John	New London, Conn.	928.[3]	Joseph	Atkinson, Me.
2351.	John D	Watertown, N. Y.	953.	Joseph	Francistown, N. H.
2356.	John J	Watertown, N. Y.	1115.	Joseph F	Milan, Ohio.
2372.	John W	Watertown, N. Y.	1192.	Joseph V. K	New York City.
2466.	John C	Brooklyn, Conn.	1246.	Joseph, (Rev.)	Williamstown, Vt.
2478.	John P	Brooklyn, N. Y.	1352.	Joseph H	Norwich, Conn.

50

INDEX.

1367.	Joseph..........Norwich, Conn.	1208. Julia, (Payne) ....Mohawk, N. Y.
1419.	Joseph L...........Mason, Mich.	1331. Julia A., (King)..Bloomfield, Ohio.
1501.	Joseph M.....New Hartford, N. Y.	1454. Julia A., (Pierson)....Fayette, Mo.
1521.	Joseph W......Lancaster, Mass.	1708. Julia A., (Benus)....Spencer, Mass.
1575.	Joseph...............New York.	1737. Julia A., (Gay)....New York City.
1624.	Joseph C...........Chicago, Ill.	1930. Julia A..........Vernon, Conn.
1684.	Joseph.........................	1963. Julia A..........Cleveland, Ohio.
1727.	Joseph O.........Norwich, Conn.	1966. Julia S..........Stamford, Conn.
1769.	Joseph G.........Thompson, N. Y.	2013. Julia A..........Shaftesbury, Vt.
1777.	Joseph G...........California.	2275. Julia...........Osage, Iowa.
1886.	Joseph..........Dexter, N. Y.	2364. Julia, (Sigourney)....Adams, N. Y.
1895.	Joseph.........................	2291. Julia M..........Bingham, Pa.
1897.	Joseph......Au Sable Forks, N. Y.	2373. Julia, (Mandeville)..Catahoula, La.
1907.	Joseph F........................	2503. Julia, (James)......Boston, Mass.
1936.	Joseph W........................	2677. Julia M..........Rhinebeck, N. Y.
2422.	Joseph A....Kelley's Island, Ohio.	2819. Julia A..........Washington, Vt.
2444.	Joseph E.........Brooklyn, N. Y.	2898. Julia D..........Rising Sun, Wis.
2467.	Joseph C.........New York City.	3113. Julia..........New York City.
2574.	Joseph........Sugar Creek, Ind.	3161. Julia P., (Grenelle).New York City.
2589.	Joseph.........................	3198.[1] Julia..........Norwich City.
2678.	Joseph M........Lancaster, Mass.	3191. Julia H.........New York City.
2776.	Joseph..........Nova Scotia.	2941. Julietta........Zenia, Ohio.
2779.	Joseph......Danielsonville, Conn.	1543. Juliette, (Wattles).Sag Harbor, N.Y.
2822.	Joseph C........... Chicago, Ill.	1784. Juliette F......Monticello, N. Y.
2927.	Joseph O... .....Norwich, Conn.	1792. Juliette........Mansfield, Conn.
2958.	Joseph G...........California.	1944. Juliette L., (Hastings)..........
2975.	Joseph J........Henniker, N. H.	........Franklin, Conn.
3057.	Joseph......Au Sable Forks, N. Y.	2962. Juliette A., (Middleton)..........
3172.	Joseph W. N. ....Baltimore, Md.	........Muscatine, Iowa.
3195.	Joseph L.........Franklin, Conn.	1440. Julius, (Dr.) ....Sugar Creek, Ind.
3209.[1]	Joseph N....Winnebago City, Wis.	2147. Julius F......Hoverleyville, Pa.
3271.	Joseph C...........Elvira, Iowa.	2901. Julius A........Richmond, Ind.
App. A. 13.	Joseph.....................	995. Julian..........Boston, Mass.
App. A. 24.	Joseph W..Nantucket Island.	1433. Julian C......Painesville, Ohio.
2612.	Josephine.......Windham, Conn.	3209. Julian A......Painesville, Ohio.
3052.	Josephine A......Nashua, N. H.	3119. Junietta E........Castile, N. Y.
70.	Joshua..........Norwich, Conn.	1173. Justinian........Brookfield, N. Y.
368.	Joshua.........Francistown, N. H.	2021. Kate..........Rochester, N. Y.
559.	Joshua, (Col.).....Norwich, Conn.	2432. Kate T........Cincinnati, Ohio.
626.	Joshua..........Windham, Conn.	2617. Kate..........Oswego, N. Y.
849.	Joshua...........................	3035. Kate M........ ...Nashua, N. H.
948.	Joshua............Nashua, N. H.	3079. Kate W........Marietta, Ohio.
1026.	Joshua H............Mississippi.	3115. Kate..........New York City.
1364.	Joshua (Rev.).......Boston, Mass.	2854. Kezia..........Wisconsin.
2444.	Joshua, (M. D.)...Brooklyn, N. Y.	2863. Kimball C....South Danvers, Mass.
271.	Josiah, (Dea.)...Rocky Hill, Conn.	454. Laura,(Silliman) East Haddam,Conn.
693.	Josiah............LeRoy, N. Y.	984. Laura (Blodgett).....Boston, Mass.
1264.	Josiah G...........Canada East.	1069. Laura, (Bottum)....Oxford, C. W.
2232.	Josiah...........................	1120. Laura H........ Milan, Ohio.
49.	Judith, (Leffingwell).Norwich,Conn.	1126. Laura (Henderson)..............
107.	Judith ....Amesbury, Mass.	1158. Laura H., (Flint).Brockville, C. W.
356.	Judith, (Brown)...Salisbury, Mass.	1177. Laura P., (Robinson).Pulaski, N. Y.
909.[1]	Judith.........Amesbury, Mass.	1321. Laura (Buckley)...............
923.	Judith, (Follensbee)..............	........Sacketts Harbor, N. Y.
	.............Amesbury, Mass.	1391. Laura..........Windham, Conn.
928.[9]	Judith, (Wilson)..Amesbury, Mass.	1418. Laura J., (Hoyt)....Hinesburg, Vt.
1937.	Judith S., (Merrifield)..........	1663. Laura A......Charleston, Vt.
	.........West Wardsboro, Vt.	1674. Laura J......Syracuse, N. Y.
2182.	Judson.........Perrysburg, Ohio.	1752. Laura......................
1074.	Julia ....Shaftesbury, Vt.	2063. Laura, (Tucker)................
1178.	Julia M., (Smith)....Manlius, N. Y.	.... North Bennington, Vt.

INDEX. 395

#	Name	Location	#	Name	Location
2068.	Laura A.	Lee, Mass.	2802.	Loyal.	Middlebury, Vt.
2125.	Laura E.	Baldwinsville, N. Y.	3230.	Loyal.	
2179.	Laura.	Perrysburg, Ohio.	153.	Lucy, (Storrs).	Mansfield, Conn.
2309.	Laura A., (Seeley).	Mexico, N. Y.	171.	Lucy, (Williams).	Norwich, Conn.
2336.	Laura B.	Sandusky City, Ohio.	215.	Lucy, (Dr. Tracy).	Norwich, Conn.
2549.	Laura J.	Painesville, Ohio.	307.	Lucy, (Hyde).	Lebanon, Conn.
2685.	Laura A., (Brainard).		316.	Lucy, (Dr. Brown).	Rochester, N. Y.
		East Haddam, Conn.	430.	Lucy, (Burnham).	Bennington, Vt.
2737.	Laura C.	Boston, Mass.	455.	Lucy.	Griswold, Conn.
2815.	Laura A., (Upson).	Middlebury, Vt.	577.	Lucy, Greene.	Vergennes, Vt.
2953.	Laura E.	Zenia, Ohio.	613.	Lucy, (House).	Hebron, Conn.
2823.	Lavinia C.	Chicago, Ill.	737.	Lucy.	
2307.	Laurelia A., (Smedley).		745.	Lucy, (Blazo).	Vermont.
		Mexico, N. Y.	786.	Lucy, (Perkins).	Norwich, Conn.
3256.	Laurette.	Henniker, N. H.	803.	Lucy.	Rome, N. Y.
1492.	Laurinda (Conant) Bellows Falls, Vt		995.	Lucy, (Spooner).	Boston, Mass.
2237.	Leander.	Compton, C. E.	1004.	Lucy, (Bishop).	Lisbon, Conn.
1178.²	Lemuel C.	Baldwinsville, N. Y.	1163.	Lucy.	Griswold, Conn.
892.	Leonard.		1173.¹	Lucy A., (Babcock).	Milton, Wis.
1666.	Leonard W.	Groveland, Mass.	1342.	Lucy T., (Miner).	Norwich, Conn.
2868.	Leonora.	Oneonta, N. Y.	1369.	Lucy, (Col. Tracy).	Norwich, Conn.
2298.	Le Roy S.	New London, Conn.	1400.	Lucy, (Blanchard).	Tecumseh, Mich.
2845.	Lester.	Washington, Vt.	1414.	Lucy.	Worthington, Mass.
300.	Levi.	Norwich, Conn.	1426.	Lucy, (Benedict).	Cambridge, Mass.
494.	Levi.	Onondaga, N. Y.	1480.	Lucy A. (Wheeler).	Pomfret, Conn.
777.	Levi.	Norwich, Conn.	1516.	Lucy A.	Lebanon, Conn.
1255.	Levi.	Wisconsin.	1597.	Lucy M.	Orinoco, Min.
1811.	Levi F.	New York City.	1655.	Lucy (Barrow).	Washington, Vt.
751.	Leverett J., (Rev.).		1917.	Lucy S.	Penn Yan, N. Y.
		New Brunswick, N. J.	1933.	Lucy A. J.	Kansas.
1130.	Lewis.	Canton, N. Y.	1958.	Lucy P.	Londonderry, Vt.
2294.	Lewis K.	Bingham, Pa.	1947.	Lucy.	Franklin, Conn.
3013.	Lewis V.	West Newbury, Mass.	2095.	Lucy.	Danbury Conn.
2491.	Lloyd.	New Orleans, La.	2468.	Lucy C., (Cleveland).	
389.	Lois, (Lathrop).	Lebanon, N. H.			Bloomfield, N. J.
832.	Lois, (Martin).	Plainfield, N. H.	2539.	Lucy A.	Burlington, Vt.
980.	Lois G., (Parker).		2559.	Lucy (Tombes).	Ashtabula, Ohio.
1635.	Loren.		2738.	Lucy B., (Fallows).	Galesville, Wis.
2936.	Lorain.	Ogdensburg, N. Y.	986.	Lucia.	Boston, Mass.
1766.	Lorinda, (Smith).	Liberty, N. Y.	1314.	Lucia.	Watertown, N. Y.
635.	Louisa, (Butler).	Hampton, Conn.	1520.¹	Lucia, (Clapp).	Watertown, N. Y.
662.	Louisa, (Collins).	Wyoming, Pa.	2202.	Lucia.	
752.	Louisa.	North Lyme, Conn.	2330.	Lucia, (Clark).	Clinton, Ohio.
1374.	Louisa M.	Norwich, Conn.	2781.	Lucia L.	Eastford, Conn.
1438.	Louisa A., (Ritchey).	Franklin, Ind.	3158.	Lucia C., (White).	Hudson, N. Y.
1533.	Louisa A.	Norwich, Conn.	3270.	Lucie C.	Elvira, Iowa.
1593.	Louisa.	Ashford, Conn.	1483.	Lucian.	New Bedford, Mass.
1989.	Louisa.	Mansfield, Conn.	1457.	Lucinda, (Hicks).	
2124.	Louisa.	South Brookfield, N. Y.			New Hartford, N. Y.
2707.	Louisa.	Ithaca, N. Y.	1627.	Lucius.	New Haven, Vt.
2639.	Louis P.	Painesville, Ohio.	1765.	Lucius W. C.	Zenia, Ohio.
2659.	Louisa A., (Stanley).	Baraboo, Wis.	2950.	Lucius W. C.	Zenia, Ohio.
2693.	Louisa, (Green).	Middlefield, N. Y.	2206.	Lucius S., (Esq.).	Shefford, C. E.
2875.	Louisa.	Jersey City, N. J.	2856.	Lucius W.	Lowell, Mass.
2919.	Louisa C.	Albany, N. Y.	304.	Lucretia.	Norwich, Conn.
2933.	Louisa.	Brooklyn, N. Y.	589.	Lucretia, (Norton).	Buffalo, N. Y.
3034.	Louisa.	Amesbury, Mass.	854.	Lucretia, (Porter).	Norwich, Conn.
3218.	Lillian F.	Yarmouth, N. S.	1030.	Lucretia L. (Stark).	Granville, Ohio.
2401.	Louis C. L.	St. Martins, W. I.	1301.	Lucretia, (Powers).	Hebron, Wis.
3142.	Louis C. L.	St. Martins, W. I.	1394.	Lucretia.	Windham, Conn.
1889.	Lovejoy.		1605.	Lucretia, (Hotchkiss)	New Haven, Vt.

1990.	Lucretia........Mansfield, Conn.	2519.
3231.	Lucretia, (Buman)..........	2817.
2285.	Lucretia M........Madison, Wis.	2887.
2537.[2]	Lucretia...........Rockford, Ill.	1282.
835.	Lura, (Freeman)..Mansfield, Conn.	1474.
1611.	Lura, (Dean).........Bethel, Vt.	1749.
18.	Lydia...........Norwich, Conn.	2881.
58.	Lydia, (Wales)....Franklin, Conn.	127.
160.	Lydia...........Amesbury, Mass.	254.
156.	Lydia, (Galusha)..Shaftesbury, Vt.	390.
216.	Lydia, (Fitch)...Canterbury, Conn.	886.
220.	Lydia, (Bill).......Norwich, Conn.	1118.
260.	Lydia, (Tinker).Worthington, Mass.	1183.
273.	Lydia ....Lebanon, Conn.	
347.	Lydia, (Lovegrove).Lebanon, Conn.	1523.
439.	Lydia, (Loomis)..Shaftesbury, Vt.	1813.
506.	Lydia, (Bush)....Brockport, N. Y.	1818.
517.	Lydia............Roxbury, Vt.	1823.
532.	Lydia............Vermont.	1885.
612.	Lydia, (North).............	1896.
645.	Lydia, (Houston)...Middlebury, Vt.	
698.	Lydia.........Lebanon, Conn.	1974.
730.	Lydia..................	2076.
776.	Lydia.........Norwich, Conn.	2296.
876.	Lydia...........Hudson, N. Y.	2395.
884.	Lydia, (Jerome)...........	27 6.
920.	Lydia, (Evans)...Amesbury, Mass.	2820.
973.	Lydia, (Peek).....Franklin, Conn.	1974.
1021.	Lydia B........Bozrah, Conn.	1695.
1093.	Lydia, (Wright)......Rome, N. Y.	
1105.	Lydia.........Shaftesbury, Vt.	1179.
1114.	Lydia M., (Galusha)...........	1381.
	...San Francisco, Cal.	1578.
1206.	Lydia, (Hardy)...Springfield, N. Y.	1607.
1215.	Lydia, (Rowley)..Rochester, N. Y.	1694.
1225.	Lydia, (Slade).....Hanover, N. H.	1736.
1341.	Lydia, (Tilson)......Braintree, Vt.	1821.
1245.	Lydia ....Canada East.	2101.
1256.	Lydia, (Fuller)......Canada East.	2142.
1341.	Lydia, (Bailey)......Bozrah, Conn.	2384.
1488.	Lydia..........Walpole, N. H.	2555.
1513.	Lydia, (Allen) ...New Castle, Eng.	2715.
1637.	Lydia, (Welch).......Dane, Wis.	2835.
1764.	Lydia, (Lownsbury) Fallsburg, N. Y.	2880.
1809.	Lydia P., (Cuningham).......	3197.[2]
	...New London, Conn.	3229.
1843.	Lydia J., (Davis)..Amesbury, Mass.	66.
1848.	Lydia, (Gove)......Pontiac, N Y.	608.
1856.	Lydia..........Amesbury, Mass.	616.
1860.	Lydia, (Bartlett)..Amesbury, Mass.	893.
1873.[15]	Lydia A., (Cobb).............	1114.
1889.	Lydia	
1926.	Lydia T., (Gates)......Athens, Pa.	1260.
2476.	Lydia C........Norwich, Conn.	1432.
2668.	Lydia A..........Mexico, N. Y.	
2702.	Lydia L....................	1458.
3016.	Lydia......West Newbury, Mass.	1615.
664.	Lynde, (Rev.).....Branford, Conn.	1651.
1534.	Lynde A.,..........Boston, Mass.	1998.
1541.	Lynde L........Lebanon, Conn.	2027.
2037.	Lynde C..........Chicago, Ill.	2045.

Lyman B	.........Mason, Mich.	
Lyman W	......Middlebury, Vt.	
Madeleine	.......New York City.	
Marcia, (Bingham).Norwich, Conn.		
Marcia M., (Allen).Colchester, Conn.		
Marcia	....	
Marcus W	.....Jersey City, N. J.	
Margaret, (Tracy)..Norwich, Conn.		
Margaret, (Tracy).Windham, Conn.		
Margaret, (Lathrop)...Chelsea, Vt.		
Margaret, (Snyder)...............		
Margaret H	...........Milan, Ohio.	
Margaret E., (West)..............		
..............Columbus, N. Y.		
Margaret, (Foster)...Albany, N. Y.		
Margaret: A.......................		
Margaret A.......................		
Margaret......................		
Margaret A........ Weare, N. H.		
Margaret A. F., (Gilmore)......		
..................Keene, N. Y.		
Margaret D.......Norwich, Conn.		
Margaret..........Milan, Ohio.		
Margaret.......Townshend, Vt.		
Margaret K......Hartford, Conn.		
Margaret......Charlestown, Mass.		
Margaret......... Sharon, Vt.		
Margaretta D.....Norwich, Conn.		
Marietta, (Williams)............		
...............Lebanon, Conn.		
Mariette, (Gardner).Brooklyn, N. Y.		
Maria H., (Perkins).Norwich, Conn.		
Maria G., (Merwin)..Milford, Conn.		
Maria, (Brown).....Bethany, N. Y.		
Maria, (Ripley).........New York.		
Maria, (2482)......Franklin, Conn.		
Maria...........................		
Maria..........Elbridge, N. Y.		
Maria..........Laxawaxen, Pa.		
Maria C..........Hartford, Conn.		
Maria..........Coventry, Conn.		
Maria W..........Hadley, Mass.		
Maria...........................		
Maria.........Jersey City, N. J.		
Maria P.......Franklin, Conn.		
Maria..........Roxbury, Mass.		
Martha........Norwich, Conn.		
Martha, (Pier)..Cooperstown, N. Y.		
Martha, (Hulburt) Middletown, Conn.		
Martha..........Rochester, N. Y.		
Martha A., (Hanchett)..........		
..................Syracuse, N. Y.		
Martha, (Rood)....Canaan, Conn.		
Martha D., (Mathews)		
............Painesville, Ohio.		
Martha, (Smith).....Fayette, Mo.		
Martha, (Townsend)............		
Martha, (Downer).....Sharon, Vt.		
Martha, (Smith).East Boston, Mass.		
Martha, (Gregory).Little Falls, N. Y.		
Martha M.....West Arlington, Vt.		

INDEX. 397

No.	Name	Location	No.	Name	Location
2070.	Martha	Syracuse, N. Y.	797.	Mary A., (Grace)	Norwich, Conn.
2138.	Martha H.	Auburn, N. Y.	812.	Mary, P.	Rome, N. Y.
2140.	Martha	Laxawaxen, Pa.	814.	Mary, M.	Rome, N. Y.
2156.	Martha	Canaan, Conn.	854.	Mary	
2183.	Martha T.	West Randolph.	906.	Mary	Amesbury, Mass.
2205.	Martha A.	Adrian, Mich.	918.	Mary	
2224.	Martha E.	Lowell, Mass.	951.	Mary, (Osgood)	Keene, N. Y.
2572.	Martha F.	Sugar Creek, Ind.	1015.	Mary A.	Topsfield, Mass.
2646.	Martha J.	Nova Scotia.	1025.	Mary, (Yerrington)	Norwich, Conn.
2648.	Martha, (Burrill)	Nova Scotia.	1059.	Mary	Greensboro, Vt.
2679.	Martha A.	Middlefield, N. Y.	1075.	Mary, (Whipple)	Shaftesbury, Vt.
2830.	Martha	Sharon, Vt.	1087.	Mary, (Steadman)	Rome, N. Y.
2876.	Martha	Jersey City, N. J.	1109.	Mary M.	Shaftesbury, Vt
3233.	Martha		1125.	Mary	Syracuse, N. Y.
App. A.	Martha		1189.	Mary S., (Williams)	
2900.	Markham	Richmond, Ind.			Chittenango, N. Y.
1052.	Marvin	Truxton, N. Y.	1197.	Mary, (King)	Bridgeport, Conn.
1496.	Marvin	Painesville, Ohio.	1205.	Mary, (Antisdell)	
2616.	Marvin W.	Norwich, N. Y.			Cooperstown, N. Y.
2637.	Marvin	Painesville, Ohio.	1311.	Mary, (Richardson)	Salem, N.H.
3215.	Marvin	Painesville, Ohio.	1345.	Mary A.	Norwich, Conn.
1110.	Martin	Rochester, N. Y.	1395.	Mary J.	Windham, Conn.
1248.	Marshall	Adrian, Mich.	1398.	Mary, (Wells)	Delevan, Wis.
2243.	Marshall	Canada East.	1402	Mary	Windham, Conn.
8.	Mary, (Goldsmith)	Amesbury, Mass.	1437.	Mary E., (Bright)	Franklin, Ind.
21.	Mary, (Forbes)	Preston, Conn.	1443.	Mary	
30.	Mary, (Davis)	Amesbury, Mass.	1452.	Mary, (Walker)	Butternuts, N.Y.
78.	Mary, (Fitch)	Canterbury, Conn.	1464.	Mary G., (Hulbert)	
82.	Mary	Lebanon, Conn.			Middletown, Conn.
88.	Mary, (Carew)	Norwich, Conn.	1495.	Mary B., (Brown)	Bloomfield, Ohio.
101.	Mary	Amesbury, Mass.	1524.	Mary J., (Terry)	Coeymans, N. Y.
139.	Mary, (Fitch)	Norwich, Conn.	1548.	Mary L., (Sheldon)	Columbus, Ohio.
155.	Mary	Mansfield, Conn.	1551.	Mary G., (Wattles)	Lebanon, Conn.
200.	Mary	Windham, Conn.	1564.	Mary D.	Hadley, Mass.
227.	Mary, (Fitch)	Windham, Conn.	1609.	Mary, (Hall)	Woodstock, Vt.
250.	Mary, (Abbe)	Windham, Conn.	1640.	Mary, (Duncan)	Canada.
259.	Mary, (Tinker)	Windham, Conn.	1671.	Mary A., (Clark)	Buffalo, N. Y.
262.	Mary, (Porter)	Bridgewater, Mass.	1678.	Mary, (Sammis)	Warsaw, N. Y.
322.	Mary, (Carew)	Norwich, Conn.	1690.	Mary	Hamburg, Conn.
350.	Mary, (Peasely)	Newtown, N. H.	1726.	Mary	New York.
364.	Mary, (Elliot)	Concord, N. H.	1742.	Mary L.	Rome, N. Y.
374.	Mary S.		1750.	Mary A.	
396.	Mary, (Rudd)	Franklin, Conn.	1775.	Mary M., (McKinion)	
411.	Mary, (Carpenter)	Norwich, Conn.			Ann Arbor, Mich.
428.	Mary	Mansfield, Conn.	1802.	Mary E.	South Coventry, Conn.
447.	Mary, (Bissel)	St. Johnsbury, Vt.	1852.	Mary, (Purinton)	Lincoln, Vt.
474.	Mary, (Rose)	Geneva, N. Y.	1873.[18]	Mary, (Buker)	
482.	Mary, (Fuller)	Hampton, Conn.	1873.[22]	Mary, (Moons)	Plainfield, Vt.
500.	Mary, (Worcester)	Thornton, Vt.	1887.	Mary	
502.	Mary, (Richardson)	Lebanon, N. H.	1898.	Mary C., (Kent)	Keene, N. Y.
516.	Mary, (Le Baron)	Canada East.	1914.	Mary C., (Chapman)	
563.	Mary, (Strong)	Norwich, Conn.			Cincinnati, Ohio.
611.	Mary, (Russel)	Middletown, Conn.	1939.	Mary J.	Londonderry, Vt.
633.	Mary, (Symonds)	Windham, Conn.	1954.	Mary H., (Cooke)	Cambridge, Mass.
656.	Mary, (Baldwin)	Windham, Conn.	1971.	Mary A.	Providence, R. I.
659.	Mary	East Haddam, Conn.	1993.	Mary, (Comings)	Greensboro, Vt.
672.	Mary, (Lyon)	Abington, Conn.	2024.	Mary, (Utley)	Westerville, N. Y.
679.	Mary, (Ratty)	Killingworth, Conn.	2043.	Mary A.	Rome, N. Y.
720.	Mary, (Chapman)		2060.	Mary	Castile, N. Y.
772.	Mary, A.	Woodbury, Conn.	2084.	Mary J.	
789.	Mary, B.	Norwich, Conn.	2089.	Mary E.	

2120. Mary E., (Barker).............. 3106. Mary................Troy, N. Y.
      ....South Brookfield, N. Y. 3110. Mary E.............Chicago, Ill.
2132. Mary E.......East Hampton, L. I. 3125. Mary E.........Brooklyn, N. Y.
2148.² Mary.............Brooklyn, N. Y. 3135. Mary J.........Depauville, N. Y.
2149. Mary E...............New York. 3146. Mary H.........Norwich, Conn.
2180. Mary...........Perrysburg, Ohio. 3152. Mary L.........Roxbury, Mass.
2212. Mary E............Hatley, C. E. 3155.² Mary A.........Abington, Mass.
2223. Mary A...........Lowell, Mass. 3182. Mary P....Norwich City, Conn.
2271. Mary E............Osage, Iowa. 3243. Mary S....Fountain Prairie, Wis.
2280. Mary A........Worcester, Mass. 3263. Mary J........Amesbury, Mass.
2286. Mary M..........Madison, Wis. 645. Mason............Columbia, Conn.
2300. Mary J., (Beach)............... 1472. Mason..........Windham, Conn.
      ....South Bergen, N. J. 1526. Mason C.......Middlefield, N. Y.
2308. Mary E., (Gillette)............. 476. Matilda, (Pease)....Charlotte, Vt.
2333. Mary H., (Hunt)...Wauseon, Ohio. 996. Matilda C., (Pushee)..Boston, Mass.
2336. Mary L.....Sandusky City, Ohio. 1158. Matilda, C., (Clark)..Chaplin, Conn.
2353. Mary S., (Lawyer).Watertown, N. Y. 2103. Matilda..........Elbridge, N Y.
2376. Mary.............Catahoula, La. 2498. Matilda E........Cleveland, Ohio.
2399. Mary A............Norwich, Conn. 45. Matthew...........Preston, Conn.
2408. Mary E., (Hyde)...Norwich, Conn. 154. Matthew.........Mansfield, Conn.
2416. Mary E.............Norwich, Conn. 440. Matthew...........Rome, N. Y.
2430. Mary............Cincinnati, Ohio. 1041. Matthew......................
2447. Mary, (821).................... 1600. Matthew L..........Rome, N. Y.
2449. Mary H...North Bridgewater, Mass. 2041. Matthew J..........Utica, N. Y.
2455. Mary A........New London, Conn. 1814. Matthew R...........New York.
2496. Mary E., (Childs)..New York City. 193. Mehetabel, (Basset).Mansfield,Conn.
2500. Mary A.........Cleveland, Ohio. 231. Mehetabel,(Webb).Windham, Conn.
2505. Mary............St. Domingo. 519. Mehetabel............Canada East.
2563. Mary D.......... Ellsworth, Ohio. 538. Mehetabel, (Betts)...Canada West.
2570. Mary A........Sugar Creek, Ind. 612. Mehetabel......Middletown, Conn.
2583. Mary P........Starkey, N. Y. 1710. Mehetabel........Becket, Mass.
2592. Mary L........Terre Haute, Ind. 1278. Melany, (Lincoln).Windham, Conn.
2614.² Mary..........Davenport, Iowa. 1712. Melissa H., (Townsend)..........
2609. Mary G., (Coley).New Haven, Conn.   ....New Haven, Conn.
2614. Mary A., (Patten)..Columbia, Conn. 912. Merriam, (Peasely)..............
2621. Mary G...........Walpole, N. H. 351. Merriam, (Brown).Amesbury, Mass.
2626. Mary K..........Walpole, N H. 1861. Merriam, (Beade)................
2633. Mary A........Painesville, Ohio.   ....South Hampton, L. I.
2645.³ Mary A.........South Carolina. 970. Merana,(Bennet).Canterbury, Conn.
2642. Mary E...........Canton, Ohio. 3000. Micajah P... West Newbury, Mass.
2661. Mary A...........Baraboo, Wis. 1198. Miles T..........Canaan, Conn.
2680. Mary A., (Skinner)..Madison, Wis. 2154. Miles T..........Canaan, Conn.
2695. Mary E...........Minetto, N. Y. 827. Miller.........................
2708. Mary C.........Ithaca, N. Y. 650. Miner............Nova Scotia.
2727. Mary G., (Talcott)..Lebanon, Conn. 1504. Miner...........Newbern, N. C.
2733. Mary E............Boston, Mass. 961.² Minerva........................
2752.¹ Mary L............Boston, Mass. 1080. Minerva......Bowdoinham, Mass.
2791. Mary, (Sprague).....Batavia, N. Y. 1303. Minerva, (Osgood)..Townshend, Vt.
2808. Mary............Wisconsin. 1121. Minerva............Syracuse, N. Y.
2865. Mary F.........Hartford, Conn. 1280. Minerva, (Justin)..Manchester, Pa.
2879. Mary E.........Jersey City, N. J. 2082. Minerva E......Ogdenburg, Pa.
2885. Mary..........New York City. 2524. Minerva H., (Dutcher)...........
2896. Mary C.........Rising Sun, Wis.   ....St. Albans, Vt.
2908. Mary A........Marlboro, Mass. 2154.³ Minnie J...........New York.
2951. Mary C..........Zenia, Ohio. 2604.¹ Minnie D......Davenport, Iowa.
2955. Mary E........Thompson, N. Y. 2548. Mirza L., (Sedgebier)..........
3010. Mary E.......Georgetown, Mass.   ....Painesville, Ohio.
3040. Mary D.........Amesbury, Mass. 702. Molley.........Windham, Conn.
3047. Mary, (Carter)...Brentwood, N. H. 2643. Morgan G........Canton, Ohio.
3067. Mary L........Bloomington, Ill. 1846. Moses...........Pontiac, N. Y.
3092.¹ Mary L...........Hartford, Conn. 1842. Moses.........Amesbury, Mass.

INDEX. 399

903.	Moses...........Amesbury, Mass.	392.	Nebemiah, (Esq.).............	
1902.	Moses B........North Elba, N. Y.		..........Peterborough, N. Y.	
916.	Moses..........North Elba, N. Y.	410.	Nehemiah, (Dea.)....Bozrah, Conn.	
1881.	Moses............Nashua, N. H.	1768.	Nelson............Zenia, Ohio.	
935.	Moses.............Weare, N. H.	2789.	Nelson W.....Middlebury, N. Y.	
2986.	Moses P........Amesbury, Mass.	2967.	Nelson P..........New York City.	
2992.	Moses N........Amesbury, Mass.	2992.	Nellie...........Canton, N. Y.	
3012.	Moses P....West Newbury, Mass.	2667.	Nellie E.........Baraboo, Wis.	
3266.	Myra E......Georgetown, Mass.	3067.	Nellie............New Jersey.	
1079.	Myron...........Shaftesbury, Vt.	3376.	Nellie..........Portage City, Wis.	
2007.	Myron..........Shaftesbury, Vt.	1213.	Newton S.........Hanover, N. H.	
963.	Nabby, (Bidwell)............	961.3	Noel........Middletown, Vt.	
	........South Manchester, Conn.	1099.	Norman S................Illinois.	
853.	Nabbe..........Norwich, Conn.	524.	Olive.........Mansfield, Conn.	
961.	Nabby...........Bozrah, Conn.	629.	Olive, (Robinson)..Hampton, Conn.	
317.	Nancy............Rome, N. Y.	1048.	Olive, (Johnson)..Mansfield, Conn.	
328.	Nancy, (Calkins)......Chelsea, Vt.	1057.	Olive, (Wadsworth).Middlebury, Vt.	
774.	Nancy, (Otis).....Norwich, Conn.	1169.	Olive, (Avery).....Griswold, Conn.	
1033.	Nancy L., (Thompson)...........	1253.	Olive, (Richardson)............	
	..........Norwich, Conn.	1300.	Olive, (Lewis). Independence, N. Y.	
1040.	Nancy E., (Ward)..Norwich, Conn.	1596.	Olive J..........Eastford, Conn.	
1106.	Nancy, (Clark)....Shaftesbury, Vt.	1883.	Olive P.............	
1244.	Nancy J..........Braintree, Vt.	2293.	Olive P..........Bingham, Pa.	
1320.	Nancy, (Whitney)....Mexico, N. Y.	3259.	Olive C.......Manchester, N. H.	
1377.	Nancy L........Norwich, Conn.	264.	Oliver........Lebanon, Conn	
1453.	Nancy, (Torode)......Galena, Ill.	665.	Oliver, (Gen.)......Oswego, N. Y.	
1476.	Nancy, (Church)...Norwich, Conn.	1489.	Oliver..........Walpole, N. H.	
1500.	Nancy A., (Harris).Painesville, Ohio.	2272.	Oliver P..........Osage, Iowa.	
1507.	Nancy, (Starr).......Nova Scotia.	2350.	Oliver B..................	
1591.	Nancy, (Parkhurst).Ashford, Conn.	2471.	Oliver E.........Cleveland, Ohio.	
1602.	Nancy.....................	3082.	Oliver M........Marietta, Ohio.	
1921.	Nancy R., (Howard).............	3213.	Omar..........Salem, Wis.	
	......Tarrytown, N. Y.	3253.	Oramel........Meriden, Conn.	
1927.	Nancy M., (Voorhis)...Athens Pa.	2628.	Oregon E......Painesville, Ohio.	
2059.	Nancy, (Higgins).....Perry, N. Y.	1700.	Orin..........Richmond, Ind.	
2267.	Nancy U.........Osage, Iowa.	2151.1	Orin W............New York.	
App. A.	Nancy....................	2840.	Orin P.........Washington, Vt.	
157.	Nathan........Shaftesbury, Vt.	1537.	Oristus L........Danville, Iowa.	
246.	Nathan........Windham, Conn.	2832.	Orpha....................	
634.	Nathan........Windham, Conn.	2214.	Oscar.............Mississippi.	
711.	Nathan.........Ashford, Conn.	480.	Owen..........Canaan, Conn.	
1062.	Nathan........Shaftesbury, Vt.	450.	Ozias..........Norwich, Conn.	
1080.	Nathan.......Rochester, N. Y.	712s.	Ozias...................	
1159.	Nathan B........Elbridge, N. Y.	1132.	Ozies........Ogdensburg, N. Y.	
1481.	Nathan.................	1706.	Ozias..........Marlboro, Mass.	
1862.	Nathan.......Amesbury, Mass.	1080.	Pamela.........Rochester, Vt.	
1992.	Nathan........Boston, Mass.	1945.	Parnell,(Dickinson) Franklin, Conn.	
3015.	Nathan G......Granville, N. Y.	2005.	Parmalee F....Cedar Rapids, Iowa.	
3037.	Nathan......Amesbury, Mass.	685.	Parthenia, (Mather).Haddam, Conn.	
27.	Nathaniel.......Norwich, Conn.	1858.	Patience, (Buxton) Amesbury, Mass.	
72.	Nathaniel.....Windham, Conn.	1077.	Peace, (Bottum)..Shaftesbury, Vt.	
97.	Nathaniel......Norwich, Conn.	1975.	Pelatiah W......Columbus, Ohio.	
229.	Nathaniel........Ellington, Conn.	3209.4	Penina J....Winnebago City, Wis.	
573.	Nathaniel........Ellington, Conn.	95.	Peter..........Norwich, Conn.	
599.	Nathaniel......Butternuts, N. Y.	850.	Peter C.........Lebanon, Conn.	
692.	Nathaniel G., (Rev.).Bethany, Conn.	883.	Peter C............New York.	
1446.	Nathaniel, (Hon.).Terre Haute, Ind.	1730.	Peter R.........Medina, Ohio.	
1654.	Nathaniel......Washington, Vt.	2442.	Peter L........Norwich, Conn.	
2580.	Nathaniel......New York City.	3148.	Peter L.........Roxbury, Mass.	
2587.	Nathaniel..........California.	514.	Perez.............Canada East.	
135.	Nehemiah........Bozrah, Conn.	119.	Phebe G............Whipanong.	

400   INDEX.

337.	Phebe, (Hyde)	Norwich, Conn.	1586.	Rene	Nova Scotia.
372.	Phebe, (Lee)	Newark, N. J.	339.	Reuben	Norwich, Conn.
526.	Phebe	Vermont.	879.	Reuben C	Nippenau, N. Y.
1293.	Phebe		885.	Reuben	Courtland, N. Y.
1681.	Phebe, (Pardee)	Oneonta, N. Y.	1273.	Reuben	
App. A.	Phebe	Acton, Vt.	855.	Richard	Utica, N. Y.
412.	Philip	Norwich, Conn.	1796.	Richard H	New York City.
1840.	Philip	Haverhill, Mass.	1878.	Richard	Nashua, N. H.
2230.	Philip F	Compton, C. E.	2355.	Richard H	New York City.
App. A.	Philip		2647.	Richard	Nova Scotia.
421.	Philena,(Boardman)	Windham,Conn.	3181.	Richard T	Baltimore, Md.
703.	Philena		704.	Robert D	Windham, Conn.
1470.	Philomela,(Squier)	Windham, Conn.	895.	Robert	
452.	Philoxena, (Phelps)	Syracuse, N. Y.	1060.	Robert	Greensboro, Vt.
703.	Philura	Windham, Conn.	1312.	Robert G. H	New York City.
983.	Philura		1436.	Robert, (Dr.)	Ellsworth, Ohio.
1027.	Philura L., (Lathrop)		2315.	Robert G	Whampoa, China.
		Cleveland, Ohio.	2385.	Robert W	Hartford, Conn.
897.	Polly, (Brainard)	Verona, N. Y.	2590.	Robert P	Terre Haute, Ind.
953.	Polly		245.	Roger	Windham, Conn.
981.	Polly		329.	Roger	Hartford, Vt.
1047.	Polly, (Brigham)	Mansfield, Conn.	553.	Roger, (Dr.)	Norwich, Conn.
2042.	Pope C	Rome, N. Y.	1337.	Roger, (Hon.)	Norwich, Conn.
1328.	Precendia, (Kimball)		1891.	Rodney S	N. H.
		Watertown, N. Y.	1727.	Rollin	Baltimore, Md.
2346.	Precendia L		2061.	Romeyn, (Dr.)	Kalamazoo, Mich.
344.	Priscilla, (Billings)		3198.	Roscoe	Norwich, Conn.
3054.	Quincy M	Nashua, N. H.	2663.	Roselle	Baraboo, Wis.
319.	Rachel, (Tracy)	Whitestown, N. Y.	521.	Roswell	Windham, Conn.
746.	Rachel, (Frank)	Starkboro, Vt.	753.	Roswell	N. C.
App. A.	Rachel		762.	Roswell	Woodbury, Conn.
451.	Ralph,(Dr.)	Memphis, Mich.	1275.	Roswell	
1174.	Ralph B		1601.	Roswell	
1407.	Ralph	Boston, Mass.	1632.	Roswell	Sharon, Vt.
1498.	Ralph R	Kendall, Ohio.	App. A.	Roswell	
2078.	Ralph W	Milan, Ohio.	1061.	Roxana	Greensboro, Vt.
2506.	Ralph E	St. Domingo.	1903.	Roxana D., (Washburn)	
2518.	Ralph B	Mason, Mich.			North Elba, N. Y.
2312.	Randolph	New York City.	2000.	Roxana, (Stevens)	Greensboro, Vt.
3128.	Randolph H	New York City.	1873.²³	Roxina	Montpelier, Vt.
76.	Rebecca, (Crane)	Windham, Conn.	1527.	Royal	Sacketts Harbor, N. Y.
83.	Rebecca, (Clark)	Lebanon, Conn.	2688.	Royal	Middlefield, N. Y.
138.	Rebecca, (89)	Bozrah, Conn.	671.	Rhoda	Lebanon, Conn.
256.	Bebecca, (Holbrook)		674.	Rhoda, (Lyman)	
		Columbia, Conn.			East Haddam, Conn.
399.	Rebecca, (El is)	New York.	747.	Rhoda, (Tryon)	
405.	Rebecca, (Lathrop)	Bozrah, Conn.			New Hartford, N. Y.
684.	Rebecca, (Mather)	Windsor, Conn.	929.	Rhoda	Amesbury, Mass.
787.	Rebecca, (Perkins)	Norwich, Conn.	1642.	Rhoda	
834.	Rebecca, (Lewis)	Brandon, Vt.	1689.	Rhoda, (Dunbar)	
1505.	Rebecca				Wolcottville, Conn.
1509.	Rebecca, (Prentice)		3126.	Russ W	Shefford, C. E.
		Waterford, Conn.	12.	Ruth	Saybrook, Conn.
1580.	Rebecca L., (Merwin)		13.	Ruth, (Pratt)	Norwich, Conn.
		Milford, Conn.	41.	Ruth, (Wheelock)	Windham, Conn.
1854.	Rebecca, (Page)	Amesbury, Mass.	57.	Ruth, (Lincoln)	Mansfield, Conn.
1617.	Rebecca, (Alison)		125.	Ruth, (Sherman)	Franklin, Conn.
1873.²³	Rebecca D	Litchfield, Me.	204.	Ruth, (Trumbull)	Mansfield, Conn.
2771	Rebecca A	Nova Scotia.	352.	Ruth, (Butler)	Norwich, Conn.
App. A.	Rebecca		379.	Ruth, (Baldwin)	Boston, Mass.
2768.	Rene	Nova Scotia.	547.	Ruth, (Malvesey)	Enfield, Conn.

INDEX. 401

865.	Ruth............Hudson, N. Y.	958.	Samuel.........Bennington, Vt.
881.	Ruth, (Hasbrouck).Norwich, Conn.	982.	Samuel.............................
957.	Ruth S............Nashua, N. H.	1210.	Samuel.......Springfield, N. Y.
962.	Ruth B., (Boutelle)..Boston, Mass.	1224.	Samuel D.......Blue Island, Ill.
976.	Ruth, (Ainsworth)...Medina, Ohio.	1242.	Samuel P..........Brainton, Vt.
1073.	Ruth............Shaftesbury, Vt.	1246.	Samuel D.........Adrian, Mich.
1322.	Ruth M............................	1268.	Samuel B....Newburyport, Mass.
1808.	Ruth, (Saunders)...................	1315.	Samuel....Prairie City, Kansas.
	..........New London, Conn.	1333.	Samuel H., (Hon.)..Hartford, Conn.
1906.	Ruth R., (Washburn)............	1401.	Samuel B..........Huron, Ohio.
	..........North Elba, N. Y.	1424.	Samuel..........Burlington, Vt.
1909.	Ruth A..........De Soto, Wis.	1468.	Samuel..........St. Domingo, W. I.
2078.	Ruth W............Milan, Ohio.	1485.	Samuel..............................
2480.	Ruth L., (Ripley)..Norwich, Conn.	1509.	Samuel P., (Rev.)....Baraboo, Wis.
2752.	Ruth G..........Boston, Mass.	1525.	Samuel.......Middlefield, N. Y.
2980.	Ruth A.........Amesbury, Mass.	1572.	Samuel.........Haddam, Conn.
310.	Rufus...........Norwich, Conn.	1636.	Samuel.............Dane, Wis.
1387.	Rufus.........Windham, Conn.	1873.5	Samuel...........Hallowell, Me.
1553.	Rufus............Clinton, Geo.	1932.	Samuel E............Franklin.
1643.	Rufus............................	1994.	Samuel..............Peru, Ill.
770.	Russel........Woodbury, Conn.	2136.	Samuel Van V.....Auburn, N. Y.
1259.	Ruby.............................	2260.	Samuel M.......Rochester, N. Y.
668.	Sabeth........Norwich, Conn.	2313.	Samuel H.......New York City.
2711.	Sabeth, (Mix).West Hartford, Conn.	2378.	Samuel...........Louisiana.
722.	Sabry, (Fuller).....New York.	2380.	Samuel........Hartford, Conn.
846.	Sally............Vermont.	2434.	Samuel J......Cincinnati, Ohio.
871.	Sally B., (Utley)...Hudson, N. Y.	2480.	Samuel A.......New York City.
950.	Sally.......Francistown, N. H.	2507.	Samuel.......West Farms, N. Y.
1233.	Sally, (Graves)...................	2537.3	Samuel.......Burlington, Vt.
1259.	Sally.........Braintree, Vt.	2552.	Samuel.......Coventry, Conn.
1871.	Sally, (Morill)..Salisbury, Mass.	2557.	Samuel P....Painesville, Ohio.
2475.	Sally A........Norwich, Conn.	2573.	Samuel......Sugar Creek, Ind.
2980.	Sally M., (Emerson)..Lynn, Mass.	2607.	Samuel G.......New York City.
9.	Samuel..........Newark, N. J.	2613.	Samuel T.....Windham, Conn.
25.	Samuel, (Lieut.)..Lebanon, Conn.	2666.	Samuel D.........Baraboo, Wis.
36.	Samuel......Amesbury, Mass.	2682.	Samuel G....Middlefield, N. Y.
40.	Samuel..........Newark, N. J.	2703.	Samuel E....Charlestown, Mass.
80.	Samuel, (Dea.)...Lebanon, Conn.	2761.	Samuel C..........Newark, N. J.
108.	Samuel.......Salisbury, Mass.	2894.	Samuel S.......Rising Sun, Wis.
115.	Samuel..........Newark, N. J.	3051.5	Samuel..........Hallowell, Me.
117.	Samuel..........Newark, N. J.	3094.	Samuel A....East Wareham, Me.
160.	Samuel.........Norwich, Conn.	App. A.	Samuel B..........................
187.	Samuel............Virginia.	20.	Sarah, (Tracy)....Norwich, Conn.
198.	Samuel..........Mansfield.	33.	Sarah.......Amesbury, Mass.
209.	Samuel.........Tolland, Conn.	47.	Sarah, (Bingham).Windham, Conn.
232.	Samuel, (LL. D)..Norwich, Conn.	68.	Sarah, (Lathrop)..Norwich, Conn.
261.	Samuel, (Rev.).East Haddam, Conn.	77.	Sarah, (Wright)..Windham, Conn.
385.	Samuel..........Buffalo, N. Y.	84.	Sarah........Lebanon, Conn.
432.	Samuel, (Dr.)....Greensboro, Vt.	102.	Sarah........Amesbury, Mass.
505.	Samuel.........Hanover, N. H.	121.	Sarah W........Newark, N. J.
525.	Samuel........Mansbury, Conn.	130.	Sarah, (Kingsbury).Norwich, Conn.
545.	Samuel...........................	134.	Sarah, (Bliss).....Norwich, Conn.
551.	Samuel........Norwich, Conn.	146.	Sarah, (Wetmore).Stratford, Conn.
588.	Samuel, (Gov.)..Painesville, Ohio.	184.	Sarah, (Freeman)..Hanover, N. H.
618.	Samuel G., (Hon.).....Troy, N. Y.	213.	Sarah (s6).......Lebanon, Conn.
658.	Samuel......Middlefield, N. Y.	291.	Sarah (233)....Worthington, Mass.
666.	Samuel.........Lebanon, Conn.	354.	Sarah, (Sawyer)...Newbury, Mass.
880.	Samuel.........Norwich, Conn.	373.	Sarah, (Crane).....Newark, N. J.
933.	Samuel...........................	375.	Sarah............New Jersey.
939.	Samuel.........Concord, N.H.	484.	Sarah..........Hampton, Conn.
946.	Samuel.........Marshfield, Vt.	496.	Sarah, (Niles)....Cambridge, N. Y.

51

582.	Sarah, (Brewster)..............	2777.	Sarah A. L...Danielsonville, Conn.
	........Worthington, Mass.	2891.	Sarah D., (Miner)...Freeman, Wis.
678.	Sarah, (Wilcox)..Branford, Conn.	2905.	Sarah H..........Marlboro, Mass.
709.	Sarah.............Ashford, Conn.	2952.	Sarah A..........Zenia, Ohio.
758.	Sarah, (Rockwell)..Lebanon, Conn.	2977.	Sarah G..........Weare, N. H.
788.	Sarah, (Williams) Stockbridge, Mass.	3003.	Sarah A..........Amesbury, Mass.
909.	Sarah, (Page).......Berwick, Me.	3020.	Sarah J., (Elliot).......Lincoln, Vt.
911.	Sarah, (Baxton)..Amesbury, Mass.	3026.	Sarah B.........Lawrence, Mass.
928.[1]	Sarah.............................	3026.	Sarah..........Amesbury, Mass.
967.	Sarah, (Marble).Manchester, Conn.	3049.	Sarah..........Brentwood, N. H.
1043.	Sarah, (Hanks).......Bath, N. Y.	3060.	Sarah E.....Au Sable Forks, N. Y.
1135.	Sarah A., (White)............	3076.	Sarah E..........Boston, Mass.
	........Ogdensburg, N. Y.	3131.	Sarah I.............................
1185.	Sarah A......Schenectady, N. Y.	3145.	Sarah L..........Norwich, Conn.
1194.	Sarah M........Harpersville, N.Y.	3166.	Sarah C., (Seymour) New York City.
1217.	Sarah.............Hanover, N. H.	3228.	Sarah J........Middlefield, N. Y.
1231.	Sarah, (Clark)................	App.	A. Sarah B........................
1276.	Sarah (634)......Windham, Conn.	App.	A. Sarah A........................
1379.	Sarah I......Norwich, Conn.	686.	Selden..........Higganum, Conn.
1411.	Sarah, (Clapp)..Worthington, Mass.	1704.	Selina, (White).....Spencer, Mass.
1417.	Sarah W..........Vergennes, Vt.	593.	Septimius G..........Indiana.
1425.	Sarah ....St. Albans, Vt.	1441.	Septimius G.......................
1462.[1]	Sarah M......Middletown, Conn.	1250.	Seth..........Canada East.
1466.	Sarah S., (Whitlock)..........	3255.	Sewell C..........Henniker, N. Y.
	........New London, Conn.	3122.	Shirley L..South Brookfield, N. Y.
1568.	Sarah............Haddam, Conn.	531.	Shubael..........Woodstock, Conn.
1630.	Sarah, (Davis)......Randolph, Vt.	1228.	Shubael..........Coventry, Pa.
1754.	Sarah.............Whiting, Vt.	1882.	Shuea, (Sumner)....Nashua, N. H.
1773.	Sarah S., (Crosby).Waterloo, N. Y.	888.	Sidney............Ohio.
1779.	Sarah A., (Philips)..Ashford, Conn.	681.	Silence..........East Haddam.
1830.	Sarah, (Gove)......Deering, N. Y.	466.	Silas..........Norwich, Conn.
1851.	Sarah G., (Green)....Lincoln, Vt.	715.	Silas..........New Haven, Vt.
1859.[11]	Sarah, (Clough)...Amesbury, Mass.	1186.	Silas H..........Lackawaxen, Pa.
1873.	Sarah, (Williams)...Boston, Mass.	334.	Simeon, (Capt.)..........Norwich.
1889.[2]	Sarah..........Francistown, N. H.	1549.	Simeon..........Lebanon.
1946.	Sarah E., (Kingsley)............	1698.	Simeon F., (Dr.)..Mount Airy, Wis.
1958.	Sarah L............Salem, Mass.	1797.	Simeon C..........Norwich.
1978.	Sarah L..............Norwich.	1.	Simon..........England.
2073.	Sarah M............Milan, Ohio.	5.	Simon, (Dea.).....Norwich, Conn.
2081.	Sarah A........Ogdensburg, N. Y.	22.	Simon, (Dea.).....Norwich, Conn.
2113.	Sarah...........Griswold, Conn.	39.	Simon..........Newark, N. J.
2152.	Sarah E................Canaan.	61.	Simon..........Mansfield.
2165.	Sarah E............Pittsford, N. Y.	67.	Simon..........Norwich.
2176.	Sarah, (Olney)...Kalamazoo, Mich.	86.	Simon..........Lebanon, Conn.
2254.	Sarah E..........Norwich City.	122.	Simon..........Newark.
2388.	Sarah B..............Hartford.	205.	Simon..........Mansfield.
2423.	Sarah W..........Brunswick, Ohio.	214.	Simon, (Rev.).....Norwich, Conn.
2435.	Sarah W..........Cincinnati, Ohio.	578.	Simon, (Hon.)....Hinsdale, Mass.
2440.	Sarah L., (Smith, D. D.)...Beyrout.	754.	Simon..........Lebanon, Conn.
2445.	Sarah A., (2411)....Boston, Mass.	1543.	Simon, (Rev.)..Walsingham, C. W.
2513.	Sarah J., (Bowman).Vergennes, Vt.	1428.	Simon J......Farmersburg, Iowa.
2535.	Sarah E............Rockford, Ill.	1583.	Simon..........Cornwallis, N. S.
2538.	Sarah A. E........Burlington, Vt.	1698.	Simon F., (M. D.)....Mt. Airy, Wis.
2545.	Sarah L.............................	2420.	Simon..........Kelly's Island, Ohio.
2611.	Sarah W......North Haven, Conn.	75.	Solomon..........Windham, Conn.
2636.	Sarah B........Painesville, Ohio.	177.	Solomon..........Hebron, Conn.
2641.	Sarah L............Canton, Ohio.	257.	Solomon..........Windham, Conn.
2696.	Sarah B................Virginia.	448.	Solomon..........Milan, Ohio.
2718.	Sarah, (Johnson)....Norwich City.	654.	Solomon..........Mexico, N. Y.
2757.	Sarah J..........Newark, N. J.	1119.	Solomon T........Syracuse, N. Y.
2769.	Sarah E..........Cornwallis, N. S.	1001.	Solon..........West Indies.

1679.	Solon............Oneonta, N. Y.	1820.	Susannah.................	
1063.	Sophia, (Wright, M. D.),.........	2051.	Susannah M. ......Chicago, Ill.	
	............Cincinnati, Ohio.	237.	Sybil, (Eells)...Glastenbury, Conn.	
1149.	Sophia, (Byles)....Ashford, Conn.	267.	Sybil, (May)..East Haddam, Conn.	
1412.	Sophia, (White)....Hinsdale, Mass.	298.	Sybil............Stratford, Conn.	
1694.	Sophia, (Sprague)..New Haven, Vt.	330.	Sybil, (Hammond),Chemung, N. Y.	
1532.	Sophia,........Norwich, Conn.	601.	Sybil, (Morgan).........Vermont.	
1707.	Sophia, (Rice).....Marlboro, Mass.	642.	Sybil, (Ripley)....Middlebury, Vt.	
2087.	Sophia A.................	1170.	Sybil............Griswold, Conn.	
2608.	Sophia D....North Haven, Conn.	1410.	Sybil, (Eager)..Worthington, Mass.	
2623.	Sophia M........Walpole, N. H.	765.	Sybilla, (Curtis), Woodbury, Conn.	
2766.	Sophia, (Daniels)..Annapolis, N. S.	1203.	Sylvia. (Keeler)......Minden, N. Y.	
2788.	Sophia, (Putnam)..Bethany, N. Y.	2632.	Sylvia E..........Bloomfield, Ohio.	
2866.	Sophia F..........Hartford, Conn.	1665.	Sylvanus C........Pulaski, N. Y.	
1592.	Sophronia, (Whiting)..Prov'ce. R. I.	1667.	Sylvester T......Charleston, Vt.	
1619.	Sophronia, (Sprague)..........	930.	Tabitha........Amesbury, Mass.	
	............New Haven, Vt.	972.	Talitha, (Lathrop)..Vernon, Conn.	
1711.	Sophronia........Becket, Mass.	258.	Temperance, (Edwards).........	
2819.	Sophronia. ....Chicago, Ill.		................Guilford, Vt.	
1213.	Stephen N.......Hanover, N. H.	268.	Thankful....... Tolland, Conn.	
1230.	Stephen...........Roxbury, Vt.	548.	Thankful, (Hartshorn).........	
921.	Stephen................		...............Hartford, Conn.	
1271.	Stephen D.....Pompanoosuc, Vt.	979.	Theoda, (Leech).............	
1845.	Stephen.....West Newbury, Mass.	1563.	Theodore G........Hadley, Mass.	
3124.	Stephen W......Brooklyn, N. Y.	128.	Theophilus, (Dea.)...Bozrah, Conn.	
3268.	Stephen A....Newburyport, Mass.	384.	Theophilus........Clarence, N. Y.	
3272.	Stephen Van D......Elvira, Iowa.	1562.	Theophilus P......Hadley, Mass.	
App. A. Stephen...............		2936.	Theophilus F.............	
App. A. Stephen A.....Nantucket Island.		2945.	Thevina C.........Howell, Mich.	
641.	Submit, (Smith)..Windham, Conn.	3.	Thomas.........Newark, N. J.	
723.	Submit (513).............	15.	Thomas, (Dea.)....Mansfield, Conn.	
943.	Susan........Francistown, N.H.	38.	Thomas........Newark, N. J.	
1129.	Susan J................	53.	Thomas.......Mansfield, Conn.	
1335.	Susan L., (Cook)..Rochester, N. Y.	180.	Thomas, (Dr.)....Ashford, Conn.	
1615.	Susan, (Bartlett)....Canada East.	196.	Thomas........Mansfield, Conn.	
1623.	Susan, (Wheeler)..New Haven, Vt.	363.	Thomas........Boston, Mass.	
1677.	Susan A., (Tracy).St. Anthony, Min.	380.	Thomas, (Dea.)....Middletown, Vt.	
1685.	Susan, (Porter)..New Haven, Conn.	473.	Thomas, (Esq.)....Hartford, Conn.	
1757.	Susan C., (Rudes).Coldwater, Mich.	513.	Thomas..........Canada East.	
1762.	Susan, (Kidder)......Braintree, Vt.	926.	Thomas........Amesbury, Mass.	
1794.	Susan M., (Coffin)....Utica, N. Y.	941.	Thomas.......Francistown, N. H.	
2019.	Susan P., (Hooker).Rochester, N.Y.	1639.	Thomas J........Norwich, Conn.	
2187.[1]	Susan M..............	1261.	Thomas..........Canada East.	
2411.	Susan C......Yantic, Norwich.	1366.	Thomas, (Rev.)....Brooklyn, Conn.	
2443.	Susan M., (Richards)........	1382.	Thomas M........Norwich, Conn.	
	............Cincinnati, Ohio.	1587.	Thomas........Ashford, Conn.	
2940.	Susan E ....Fulton, Iowa.	1638.	Thomas.	
3001.	Susan L........Amesbury, Mass.	1805.	Thomas P......New York City.	
3035.	Susan... ...Amesbury, Mass.	1832.	Thomas..........Weare, N. H.	
3149.	Susan M., (Perkins)............	1979.	Thomas D......Norwich, Conn.	
	..........Montague, Mass.	2148.	Thomas ....Brooklyn, N. Y.	
17.	Susannah, (Griswold)............	2233.	Thomas...........Compton, C. E.	
	.............Norwich, Conn.	2465.	Thomas.........Brooklyn, Conn.	
34.	Susannah, (Downer)...........	2533.	Thomas W........Rockford, Ill.	
278.	Susannah, (Dann)!...........	2569.	Thomas H.....Sugar Creek, Ind.	
	.......Wyoming Valley, Pa.	2810.	Thomas B......New York City.	
352.	Susannah, (Peaseley).Weare, N. H.	2990.	Thomas........Lawrence, Mass.	
716.	Susannah....Cincinnati, Ohio.	3042.	Thomas M................	
809.	Susannah, (Dalliba)...Rome, N. Y.	3084.[1]	Thomas D......Yoncalla, Oregon.	
825.	Susannah, (Whitney)............	3200.	Thomas M........Lebanon, Conn.	
	............Tunbridge, Vt.	3085.[1]	Thomas D.......Columbus, Ohio.	

404   INDEX.

#	Name	Location	#	Name	Location
3202.	Thomas M	Rock Island, Ill.	741.	William	Alabama.
App.A.	Thomas S		744.	William	Wolcottville, Conn.
106.	Timothy	Amesbury, Mass.	794.	William	Charlotte C. H., Vt.
362.	Timothy	Amesbury, Mass.	826.	William	Whiting, Vt.
927.	Timothy	Amesbury, Mass.	857.	William H	Sidney, Ohio.
928.[1]	Timothy	Litchfield Me.	919.	William	Amesbury, Mass.
3204.	Timothy C	Rock Island, Ill.	925.	William	Amesbury, Mass.
1096.	Truman C	Shaftesbury, Vt.	928.[4]	William	Pittston, Me.
147.	Tryphena	East Windsor, Conn.	1056.	William D	Providence, R. I.
648.	Tryphoza	Columbia, Conn.	1121.	William O	Milan, Ohio.
2515.	Tyrus B	Mason, Mich.	1145.	William S	Cleveland, Ohio.
391.	Uriel, (Dr.)	Bowdoinham, Me.	1168.	William	Griswold, Conn.
1002.	Uriel	Bowdoinham, Me.	1176.	William E	Baldwinsville, N. Y.
1873.[c]	Uriel	California.	1221.	William	Hanover, N. H.
1873.[d]	Uriel	California.	1272.	William A	Lawrence, Mass.
2359.	Victorine R., (Harbottle)		1323.	William	Pisgah Grove, Iowa.
		Watertown, N. Y.	1356.	William C	Cincinnati, Ohio.
1536.	Wait T	Ithica, N. Y.	1412.	William C	De Soto, La.
1292.	Waldo	Auburn, Mass.	1479.	William	Norwich, N. Y.
1214.	Wales M., (Dr.)	Pittsfield, N. Y.	1486.	William	Keene, N. H.
1467.	Wallace	Windham.	1516.	William J	Baraboo, Wis.
2012.	Ward	Downieville, Ca.	1550.	William	Lebanon, Conn.
1658.	Warren	Washington, Vt.	1559.	William P., (Rev.)	Waterloo, Wis.
2812.	Warren W	Galena, Ill.	1579.	William W	Milford, Conn.
565.	Wealthan (245)	Windham, Conn.	1610.	William	Randolph, Vt.
409.	Wealthy, (Tracy)	Norwich, Conn.	1647.	William M	Washington, Vt.
565.	Wealthy (285)	Windham, Conn.	1664.	William C	Richland, Wis.
673.	Wealthy, (Fitch)	Lebanon, Conn.	1669.	William W	Geneva, N. Y.
690.	Wealthy	Rocky Hill, Conn.	1691.	William B	New York.
837.	Wealthy, (Hatch)	Monticello, N. Y.	1713.	William S	Becket, Mass.
1019.	Wealthy A., (Gager)	Bozrah, Conn.	1723.	William W	New Haven, Conn.
1770.	Wealthy, (Quinlan)	Sheboygan, Wis.	1745.	William R	Rome, N. Y.
3196.	Weatherly	Franklin, Conn.	1755.	William P	Fulton, Iowa.
2889.	Wilbur	New York City.	1767.	William, (Dr.)	Howell, Mich.
3246.	Wilder P	Montpelier, Vt.	1803.	William W	New York.
3121.	Wilfred	Nova Scotia.	1810.[1]	William H	Wilmington, N. C.
2873.	Willard	Oneonta, N. Y.	1868.	William F. M	Amesbury, Mass.
1028.	Winslow T., (Dr)	Ackron, Ohio.	1873.[k]	Willia	Bradford, Me.
891.	Walter	Barre, Vt.	1873.	William H	Brentwood, N. H.
1378.	Walter	New Orleans, La.	1873.[10]	William	Pittston, Me.
2168.	Walter J	Blue Island, Ill.	1918.	William S	Beaver Dam, Wis.
2238.	Walter	Canada East.	1956.	William R., (Rev.)	Lowell, Mass.
2744.	Walter E	Hadley, Mass.	1957.	William D	Salem, Mass.
2792.	Walter	Michigan.	1960.	William H	Cleveland, Ohio.
3265.[1]	Walter E	Haverhill, Mass.	1970.	William T	Providence, R. I.
719.	Whitman	New Haven, Vt.	2063.	William	Kalamazoo, Mich.
2.	William	Salisbury, Mass.	2091.	William E	
35.	William	Amesbury, Mass.	2097.	William S	Danbury, Conn.
59.	William	Mansfield, Conn.	2112.	William F	Springfield, Mass.
105.	William	Amesbury, Mass.	2158.	William	Rochester, N. Y.
181.	William	Hampton, Conn.	2189.	William E	California.
266.	William, (Capt.)	Lebanon, Conn.	2204.	William J	Adrian, Mich.
321.	William	Middlebury, Vt.	2255.	William F	Norwich, Conn.
353.	William	Amesbury, Mass.	2274.	William H. S	Osage, Iowa.
359.	William	Amesbury, Mass.	2328.	William R	Clinton, Ohio.
361.	William	Amesbury, Mass.	2348.	William D	
424.	William	Windham, Conn.	2360.	William L	Depauville, N. Y.
481.	William	Windham, Conn.	2393.	William W	Hartford, Conn.
542.	William	Watertown, N. Y.	2405.	William E	Walsingham, C. W.
675.	William	Lebanon, Conn.	2409.	William T	Toledo, Ohio.
726.	William	Washington, Vt.	2452.	William S.	North Bridgewater, Mass.

2484.	William H	Paris, France.	3136.	William H	Depauville, N. Y.
2521.	William J	Mason, Mich.	3155.³	William	Abington, Mass.
2635.	William	Baraboo, Wis.	3227.	William W	Middlefield, N. Y.
2684.	William S	Middlefield, N. Y.	3250.	William F	Fulton, Iowa.
2722.	William L	Lebanon, Conn.	App.	A., William	
2728.	William	Lebanon, Conn.	2232.	Willy J	Canada East.
2739.	William E	Milwaukie, Wis.	1373.	Wolcott	Norwich, Conn.
2751.	William	Boston, Mass.	221.	Zachariah	Norwich, Conn.
2840.	William L	Washington, Vt.	564.	Zachariah, (Gen.)	Norwich, Conn.
2864.	William W	Hartford, Conn.	724.	Zebulon	
2882.	William B	Jersey City, N. J.	335.	Zephaniah	Norwich, Conn.
2909.	William B	Marlboro, Mass.	868.	Zephaniah	New London, Conn.
2921.	William R	New Haven, Conn.	431.	Zeruiah, (Cole)	Kingsbury, N. Y.
2934.	William S	Brooklyn, N. Y.	988.	Zeruah, (Ford)	Lebanon, N. H.
2938.	William H	Fulton, Iowa.	255.	Zerviah, (Youngs)	Windham, Conn.
2947.	William C	Howell, Mich.	263.	Zerviah, (Harvey)	
2957.	William S	New York.			East Haddam, Conn.
2982.	William C	Newark, N. J.	533.	Zerviah, (Jones)	
3011.	William H	West Newbury, Mass.	1735.	Zerviah T	Springfield, Mass.
3019.	William D	Pontiac, N. Y.	387.	Ziba, (Hon.)	Lebanon, N. H.
3044.	William A	Amesbury, Mass.	975.	Ziba	Franklin, Conn.
3046.	William H	Amesbury, Mass.	991.	Ziba	Lebanon, N. H.
3104.	William	Shaftesbury, Vt.	3072.⁴	Ziba, J	Franklin, Conn.
3109.	William S	Canton, N. Y.	2340.	Zina D	
3132.	William H	Watertown, N. Y.			

II.

INDEX TO THE DESCENDANTS OF HUNTINGTON DAUGHTERS WHO ARE RECORDED IN THIS WORK, EMBRACING BOTH CHILDREN AND GRANDCHILDREN.

90. ADGATE, Thomas, Jonathan.
98. ADGATE, Thomas.
250. ABBEY, Mexari.
1169. AVERY, William, Elizabeth.
1474. ALLEN, Thomas, Justina M.
1609. ADAMS, Lucinda, Susan B., Elvira, Martha.
1709. ALLEN Harriet E., Nellie S.
2473. ADAMS, John R., Hannah L.
2689. ALLEN, Lorena, Ella.
26. BACKUS, Joseph, Samuel, Ann, Simon, James, Elizabeth, Sarah, Ebenezer.
41. BINGHAM, Jerusha.
47. BINGHAM, Sarah, Thomas, Tryphena.
134. BLISS, John, Elizabeth, Zephaniah, Sarah, William.
146. BEERS, Lucy, Sarah A., Lucy P.
220. BILL, Sylvester, Lynde, Lydia, Hannah, Gordon, Ephraim, Abigail, Zachariah H., William, Hannah.
259. BUCKINGHAM, Joseph T.
316. BROWN, Benjamin H., Matthew, George H., Henry H., Mary A., Elizabeth R.

416. BACKUS, Gurdon H.
430. BURNHAM, Eleazer, Rebecca, Julia A., Polly, Asa N., Lucy, Sophia A., Charlotte M.
436. BOTTUM, Lemuel, Nathan H.
582. BREWSTER, Theodosia, Sarah, Zipporah, Eliza, Lucy, Elisha.
656. BALDWIN, John, Julia A.
562. BACKUS, Jonathan T., John,
748. BUSCE, Timothy D., Susan.
897. BRAINARD, Israel H., Mary, Harriet, Cornelia, Elizabeth, David L.
901. BEECHER, George H., Jane M., Fanny H.
956. BURTT, Ebenezer, Lydia, Elbridge, Samuel, George, Orandel, Mary, Francis.
984. BLODGETT, Zeruah H., Lucia C., Hiram W. H., Mary L.
1003. BOTTUM, Martin H., Rufus, Mary, John B.
1004. BISHOP, Barzillai, Nathan B., Roger A., Lucy, Mary, Elizabeth, Abigail.
1016. BALIS, Gurdon H., Henrietta E.
1017. BREWSTER, Lucius H., Anna H., William B.

INDEX.

1079. BARTON, Jane E., Edwin H., Lorenzo M., Caroline A., Fanny, Mary Ann, Mary A., Gardner.
1149. BYLES, Josiah, Abigail, Lucy, Andrew H., Zerviah.
1282. BINGHAM, Eliza A., Antoinette, Mary.
1341. BAILEY, Julia, Mary, Maria.
1413. BUEL, Lucy.
1426. BENEDICT, Sarah, Charlotte F., Kate F.
1494. BELLOWS, George H., Grace E., Anna T.
1495. BROWN, Ephraim A., George W., Charles, Elizabeth H., James M., Marvin H., Fayette, Annie F.
1512. BROWN, Jane, Harriet, George H., Henry H., John, Charles D.
970. BENNET, Charles T., Pardon H., Martha, Merare, Jos. B., Asahel E., Palmer.
1732. BOWERS, Margaret P., Catherine B., Josephine O., Emma E., William C.
1607. BROWN, Mary, Harriet, Morgan, Munroe.
1615. BARTLETT, Amanda, Wilder, George, Ira.
1653. BARRON, Arno N., Alonzo W., Edwin P., William H., Cynthia E.
1655. BARRON, Norman, Harry V.
1873. BUKER, Francis, Emma.
2002. BLAKE, Sylvia, Bertha E., Flora, Henry, Franklin, Ellen.
2009. BOTTUM, Harlow A.
2120. BARKER, Charles, Elizabeth, George.
2300. BEACH, Charles H., Melvin.
2618. BURREL, William H., Frederic, Eugene.
2683. BIGELOW, Polly J., Uriah H., Martha I.
2685. BRAINARD, Mary A.
2973. BAXTER, Horace F.
3173. BARRINGTON, Eveline.
2323. BOOTH, Clarence H.
79. CLARK, Mary, Moses, Anna, Elizabeth, John, James.
83. CLARK, Mary, Abigail, Joseph, Lydia, Rebecca, Asahel.
87. CAREW, Daniel, Abigail, and Eliphalet.
88. CAREW Simeon, Mary, Joseph, Benjamin, Anne, Ebenezer, Daniel.
148. CLARK, John, Jabez, Jerusha, Hezekiah, Tryphena, Deodatus, Hannah, Henry, Erastus, Thaddeus, Elizabeth, Elizabeth, Anna, Jerusha, Charlotte, Edwards, Sarah J.
216. COGGSWELL, Mason F., James, Samuel.
281. COLLINS, Lewis, Elizabeth, Lois, Eunice, Anna, Charles, Rhoda, Lorain, Darius, David.
303. CAREW, Anne, Charles, Simon, Ebenezer, Elizabeth.
322. CAREW, Eliphalet, Azor, Molly, Betsey, Nabby.
346. CULVER, Roswel.
373. CRANE, John S., Joseph, William.
411. CARPENTER, George, Mary E., Gardner, Henry, John, Charles.
562. CHESTER, Elizabeth, Mary, Hannah, Sarah, John, Charlotte, Henry, Julia, William, George.
589. CRAWFORD, Frances H., James D., Lyndon S., Ellen M.
662. COLLINS, Oristus, Lorenzo, Abner, Alonzo, Philura, Lucius, Decius, Huntington L., Aretas, Theron, Charles J.
765. CURTISS, Sybilla C., David H., Sarah, Nathan, Daniel, Elvira, Mary A. N., William.
877. CHAPMAN, Maria H., Emily A., Edward H., John G., Ann J., Juliette.
969. COOK, Ruth A., Sarah H., Lucy L., Lydia T.
1251. CROSBY, Eliza, Abigail, Mary A., Susan, Thomas H., Alonzo, Edwin, Charles, Olive, Levi, Albert, Joel.
1295. COBB, Lucy M., Daniel H., Henry H., Aurelius H., Lydia P., Lyman H., George H.
1335. COOK, Susan K.
1399. CARTER, France L., Mary.
1399. CORMAN, Josephine, Mary E., Frankey.
1411. CLAPP, Lewis, Alexander H., William T.
1455. CAMPBELL, Archibald, Walter.
1476. CHURCH, Merial T., William A.
1192. CONANT, William J.
1630. CLEMENT, Jarvis, Albert, Emily, Franklin.
1703. CRAIGE, George A., Sarah L.
1725. CASE, Virginia, Albert, Mary.
1791. COFFIN, Grace M., Ellen H.
1809. CUNNINGHAM.
1999. COOK, Betsey P., John B., Charles H., Edward.
1873. COBB, George, Ellen, Frank.
2350. CLARK, Edward.
2451. CHAPPEL, Frank H., William E., Alfred H.
2457. CLARK, Charles, Edward, Anna, Mary, George H.
2459. COGGSHALL, Anna, William, Arabella, Ada.
2460. CLARK, John, Elizabeth H., Frederic A.
2119. COON, Ambrosia, Eulaloo, Franklin.
2123. CHEESEBROUGH, Clarence, Carol.
2468. CLEVELAND, Joseph H.
2976. CHASE, Benjamin H., Nathaniel J., Asa P., Sarah M.

INDEX. 407

19. App. A. CLEVELAND, George S., Sarah H., Henry F.
1038. CHEESEBROUGH, Nancy, Sarah, Elam P. A., Eunice P., Diah L.
145. DAVENPORT, John, Elizabeth, James, Huntington, Elizabeth H., John A., Mary W., Theodosia, Theodore, Rebecca A., Matilda, Betsey C., Abigail F., Mary A., Frances L.
242. DEVOTION, Ebenezer, John, Jonathan, Eunice, Martha, Lewis.
278. DANA, Evais, Daniel, Susannah, Anderson, Ariel, Sylvester, Eleazer.
809. DALLIBA, Anne H., Susan, James E., Sarah P., Mary H., Susan E., Katherine.
1043. DENHAM, Cordelia.
1072. DOUGLASS, Henry H., Norman R., Thomas, Chloe L., Margaret A., George S., Charles.
1338. DICKERSON, Abby H., Samuel H., Philura T., Harriet M.
1444. DANIELSON, Lucius, Fanny.
1445. DANIELSON, Aborene, Ashley G., Mary H., Fanny R., Emily A., Amelia A., Jenette S., Susan A.
1595. DAVIS, Francis E., Thomas H.
1611. DEAN, Rodman, Wyman, Whitman, Human, Harry, Rebecca, Abigail, Philo.
1630. DAVIS, Harriet, Daniel, Jackson.
1631. DOWNER, Worcester, Jason, Chester, Susan, Franklin, Albert, Alice.
1640. DUNCAN, Charles, Lucretia, Elizabeth, James, Emily, Almira.
1680. DUNBAR, George S., Adelaide, Adeline, Edward.
1843. DAVIS, Eliza H., Moses H., Joel A.
1263. DEWITT, Harriet R., Henry, Martha, Mary, Ann, Joshua, Susan, Harriet.
98. EDGERTON.
237. EELLS, Roger, Mercy, Sybil, John.
399. ELLIS, Urania, Mary.
1410. EAGER, Samuel H., Jennison, James, Joseph, Jonathan H., Mary, Lucy, Julia.
2980. EMERSON, Mary B.
2804. EGGLESTON, Edwin H., Flora E., Guy E.
3020. ELLIOT, Cynthia S., Irving.
403. FITCH, Edward G., Charles.
673. FITCH, Wealthy, Elizabeth, Thomas, Marietta, Eleazer.
835. FREEMAN, Azariah, Philura, Lorenzo, Enoch, H., Truman, Jared G.
1256. FULLER, Albert, Malvina.
1371. FREEMAN, Huntington W.
1358. FISHER, Elizabeth P., Frederic P., Francis P., George H., Catherine W., Edward T.
139. FITCH, Gerard, Eunice, Nabby, Ebenezer, Roger, Mary, Oliver, Elizabeth, Sarah, Charles.
169. FRINK, Hannah.
184. FREEMAN, Peyton R., Jonathan, Christopher, Edward, Sarah, Asa, Francis A., Sarah H., Abigail A., Samuel, Peyton R., Sarah H., Hunlock W., Anna E., Charlotte W.
216. FITCH, Ebenezer, Lydia, Jabez G., Sarah, Anna, Chauncey, Samuel, Lucy, Alice.
227. FITCH, Roswell, Anna, Jabez, Joseph, Betsey, James G.
156. GALUSHA, Mary, David, Jacob, Jonah, Amos, Elijah, Olive, Lydia, Anna.
17. GRISWOLD, Francis, Samuel, Lydia, Hannah, Sarah, John, Joseph, Daniel.
577. GREENE, Wealthy, Polly, John, Job, Sarah, Lucy H., William E.
589. GRIFFIN, Frances L., Ellen Maria.
1049. GAGER, John, Charles, Maria, Eliza.
1179. GARDNER, John L., Charles H., Frances L.
1406. GRAY, Wilson H.
1468. GILLETTE, Walter.
1535. GREGORY, Oristus H. A., Louisa, John.
850. GOVE, Hannah, John, Huldah B., Anna H.
1851. GREEN, Louisa G., William H., Mary P., Nathan L.
1855. GOODWIN, John H., Sophia A., David W., John H., Lydia A., Hannah J., Ephraim A., Eliza A.
2308. GILLETTE, Adelaide L., Dora A.
2161. GRESELLE, Julia S., William E., Charles F., Joseph H.
1976. GATES, Ednah.
1896. GILMORE, John, James, Mary M., Charlotte.
31. HOYT, John, Jacob, Mary, David, Sarah, Timothy, Elizabeth, Thomas, Micah, Daniel, David.
51. HYDE, Ely, Matthew, Christopher, James, Lorissa, Deborah, Azraih, Uri, Elizabeth.
93. HYDE, Phebe, Jerusha.
98. HYDE, Thomas, Vaniah, Jerusha, Elizabeth, Priscilla, Zerviah, Mary, Jane.
115. HEDDEN, David, Job, Simon.
127. HYDE, Andrew, Jude, George, Amasa, Rodney, Lewis, Lydia, Mary.
307. HYDE, Elizabeth, Eunice.
337. HYDE, Chloe.
256. HOLBROOK, Rebecca, Abel.
263. HARVEY, Elisha, Asabel, Huntington, Samuel, Sybil, Olive.

613.	Horse, Simon, Lucy.	49.	Leffingwell, Hannah, Judith, Joanna, Samuel, Cyrus, Jeremiah, Eunice, Sarah, Asa, Rufus.
643.	Horston, Henry A., Jerusha L., Mary A.		
1029.	Hamlin, Charles W., Harriet C.	57.	Lincoln, Samuel, John, Nathaniel, Eleazer.
1043.	Hanks, Eveline, Rosilla, Mary.		
1100.	Harpending, Ogden G.	68.	Lathrop, William, Joshua, Ezra, Jeremiah, Andrew.
1201.	Hummell, Rose H.		
1464.	Hulbert, William, George.	114.	Lathrop, Charles, Nabby, Burrel, Gerard, Charlotte, Augustus.
1487.	Hicks, Mary E., Lucinda H.		
1560.	Harris, Eunice H., Albert H.	206.	Lyman, Jonathan.
1605.	Hotchkiss, Fordyce, Abner, Maria, Charity, Jeremiah.	372.	Lee, Mrs. Rozenkrantz.
		405.	Lathrop, Mary, Eunice, Rebecca J.
1609.	Hall, Hiram, Harriet.	439.	Loomis, Lydia, Asa, Julia, Daniel, Russel, Warren, Alfred.
1631.	Hendrix, Lucius H., Caroline H., Henry W., Anna S., Gustavus S., George E., Clara H.	516.	LeBaron, Elijah H., Japhet.
		672.	Lyon, Samuel H., Samuel, Eliza F.
1944.	Hastings, Sophia Tracy, Lucy Ariana, Martha Jane.	972.	Lathrop, A. Willis, E. Huntington, Philena M., Eliza L., Nancy H.
2001.	Hall, Ashbel H., George W., Ellen, Edward C., John B.	1027.	Lathrop, Elizabeth H.
		1278.	Lincoln, John, Lucy, Emily, Steadman, Giles.
2359.	Harbottle, George V.		
2438.	Hooker, Mary L., Faith H., Elizabeth P., Elias C., Sarah H., Edward.	1300.	Lewis, Clinton H.
		1522.	Leonard, Gratia O., Norman H., Annie H.
2450.	Henard, Augustus H., Mary S.		
2408.	Hyde, Mary A., Lewis H., Susan H., William T.	1800.	Lee, Edward R., Charles W., Frank H.
1948.	Hall, Althea A., Ellor G., Anna W.	2654.	Lamberton, Adelbert L., William A., Frank W.
3191.	Hutchinson, Henry C., Julius, James M.	2656.	Lamberton, Cate A., Clarabell, Charles W.
1218.	Ingalls, Asa H.	552.	Lyman, Eliphalet, Daniel, Asa, Joseph, Hannah, Mary.
1219.	Ingalls, Mary A., Orville H.		
591.	Jones, Joel, Joseph H., Fanny H., Margaret E., Maria, Eliza, Samuel, Mary J., Matthew H.	267.	May, Huntington.
		583.	Marsh, Aurora, Aurilla, Rufus, Ruby, Sophia.
1371.	Jackson, Laura W., Mary E., Julia H., Frederic W., Joseph C., John P., Hannah W., Huntington W., Schuyler B.	601.	Morgan, Sybil, Samuel, Harriet, Hezekiah R., William, Alice.
		663.	Mather, Alathea, Harriet, Charles.
		676.	Mason, Bethia H., Emma E., Mary L., Rhoda L., Julia A., Wealthy F., John G. H., Abby J.
1018.	Johnson, Semantha, John.		
1692.	Jones, William L., Mary A., Annie H., Harriet P., Jane E.	685.	Mather, Edward H., Mary, Samuel, Julia, Harriet, Sarah.
41.	Kirtland, Dr. John.		
129.	Kingsbury, Asa, Sarah, Eunice, Lucy.	967.	Marble, Charles, Henry, George.
		1432.	Matthews, Samuel, Alfred, Rodney.
230.	Kimball, Mary, Elijah, Eunice, Jesse, Abigail, Lydia, Enoch, Richard, Ebenezer.	1437.	Mitchell, Emerson.
		1855.	Merrill, Rebecca.
		2463.	Miller, Henry H.
405.	Kelley, Henry.	1660.	Moffat, Rinaldo.
1197.	King, Mrs Rodgers.	2661.	McGilvia, Zervia.
1328.	Kimball, George W., Cornelia E., Mary P., Joseph C., Josephine C.	2913.	Mozart, Sarah F.
		3017.	Morrison, Harriet A., Helen E.
1699.	Kingsbury, Henry H., Addison, Edwin J.	596.	Norton, Abiel A., Elizabeth H., Fanny R., Mary L., Charles D., Porter.
1946.	Kingsley, Henry H., Silas H.		
1352.	King, Henry W., Julia A., Susan H., Leicester, David, Helen D., Hezekiah H., Catherine B.	612.	North, Lydia H.
		1223.	Nye, Minerva E., Samuel H., Ida S., Silas.
1898.	Kent, Rhoda C., Clarissa M., Eliza A., George W., Mary A., Lydia A., Charlotte R.	2301.	Osborne, Frederic.
		2121.	Ogden, Walter, Rollo, Florence, Nelson.

INDEX.

13. PRATT, Samuel.
41. PATTEN, Rev. Dr. William.
281. PIERPONT, John.
461. PRENTICE, Andrew.
476. PEASE, Frederick S., Calvin, Erastus H., Aaron G., Calvin, Thomas H., Peter E., Mary M., Reuben O., Roscius M.
584. PORTER, Elizabeth, Mary, Ruth, Huntington, Jonathan, Enos, Nahum, Sarah.
608. PIER, Jonathan H.
653. PERKINS, Anna H., Samuel H., Horatio N., Harriet.
773. PROCTOR, Nathaniel L., William H.
854. PORTER, Frances O., Charles H., George E., Abby H., Jane S., Susan L., Cornelia M., Charles H., George S., Jane S., Ellen H.
990. PECK, Eli, Alonzo, John M., Parthenia W.
1301. POWERS, Edward C., Ellen M.
1381. PERKINS, Sarah H., Elizabeth D.
1451. PIERSON, Isaac H.
1475. PALMER, Daniel, Walter.
1591. PARKHURST, Abby J., Julia A.
1628. PARKHURST, Hiram, Hannah, Harriet, Phinehas, Sarah, Lydia, Harvey, Avannah.
1681. PARDEE, Edwin, Edward, Frank, Charles, Mary H.
1692. POTTER, William L., Mary A., Fanny J., Annie H., Harriet P., Jane E.
1828. PURINTON, Benjamin, John, Elijah, Jacob, Thomas, Huldah G.
1852. PURINTON, John, Lydia, Horatio N., Lindly H., Moses H.
1854. PAGE, Lydia.
973. PECK, Lydia S., Maria, Samuel R., Thomas S., George W., Henry M.
786. PERKINS, John A., George A., Mary B., Rebecca H., Isaac H., Edward H., Simeon A.
2730. QUINCY, Josiah H., Helen.
248. ROUNDY, Azael, Amey, Ede, Alvin, Samuel, Anne.
396. RUDD, John C., Ricardo, Charles, Edward H., Mrs. Mathews.
502. RICHARDSON, Daniel, A., Mary H., Elias H.
566. RIPLEY, John H., William, Elizabeth, A., Elbridge, Harriet, Justin.
611. RUSSEL, Mary H., Harriet, Julia A., Charles H., William H., Abigail T., Frances H., Sarah E., Frances H., Henrietta L., Talcott H., Thomas H., Philip G., Edward H.
611. ROACH, Jane T., Talcott R., Fanny H., Samuel G. S., Mary R.
617. ROZENKRANTZ, Sally H., Enoch H., Mary J., Sarah H., Ann E.

629. ROBINSON, Thomas, Whitney, Oliver, Olive, Lewis, Betsey, Nathan, Mary.
637. RIPLEY, Bradford, Elizabeth, Christopher, Elipha et, Eunice, Ralph H., Laura, James.
642. RIPLEY, Samuel P., Julia, William Y., Erastus, Laura, Elizabeth, George H.
679. RATTY, Mary.
758. ROCKWELL, Azel, Philura, Emily, Eunice H., Elijah F., Andrew H., Sarah A.,
1215. ROWLEY, Andrew, H, Sarah, E., Helen, Eliza V.
1253. RICHARDSON, Chauncey, Frederic D., Emma, Louisa.
1361. RICHARDS, Henry A., Wolcott, Channing, Anne H., Eliza, Peter, Hannah D., George, Jedidiah H.
1371. RANKIN, Frederic R., Anne, Laura, Charles, Robert, Fanny, Frank, Mary, Cornelia.
1438. RITCHIE, Emily, Angeline E., Mary E., Clarinda.
1450. REA, John H., William, Wallace.
1460. RIDGELEY, Charles, Julia P., William, Anna, Mary, Jane, Henderson, Octavia.
1707. RICE, Julian H., Cordelia H., Harriet A., Edward H.
2800. ROSE, William H.
1050. REYNOLDS, Adeline, Melissa, Elizabeth, Sarah, Julia, Glenn W., Jane, John, George, Edwin, Benjamin F., Albert N.
2480. RIPLEY, Charles P. H., Martha, Mary P., Grace, William C., Samuel H.
127. STORRS, Lathrop, Huchings, Margaret, Olive.
211. STEELE, Aaron, James, Samuel, Andrew, Deborah.
437. STANLEY, Mary.
563. STRONG, Joseph H., Mary Huntington, Henry.
589. SMITH, Edward D. G., Lyndon A., Sanford H., Frances L.
633. SYMONDS, Jeduthan, Jerusha, Mary.
641. SMITH, Alathea, Parthena, Lucy, Henry, Lucretia, Hezekiah H., Edmund, Edwin, Julia, Sophia.
657. SILLIMAN, William, Dorothy, Joseph, Eliphalet, Huntington, Oliver, Olive.
679. STREET.
813. SMITH, Hannah H., Henry H.,
854. STEDMAN, Charles, Frank, George, Thomas.
1030. STARK, Olive.
1225. SLADE, William, Lydia.
1482. SNOW, Julia A., Fielder H., George H., Charles D., Edward P.

52

1507. STARR, William M., John S., James, A., Mary E., Harriet P., Susan M., Anne L.
1515. SKINNER, Warner, Eliza.
1558. SESSIONS, Elizabeth H., Clara F., Addie.
1604. SPRAGUE, Charles A. L., Adeline, Lucy, Fayette.
1678. SAMMIS, Collis H., Martha J., Albertus, Charles.
1808. SAUNDERS, Erastus Huntington.
2000. STEVENS, Levi N., Henry H., Dan, Caroline, Emily, Helen E., Parmelee A., Abby M., Josiah, Nelson, Susan E.
2307. SMEDLEY, Frederic A., Florence.
2469. STRONG, Mary E., Henry E.
2548. SEDGEBIER, Adela G., Charles M., Eugene H.
2680. SKINNER, Ella, E., Beulah H., Waldo H., Mary H.
2800. SHERMAN, Osceola, Teram M., Emily.
5166. SEYMOUR, Julia H.
20. TRACY, Lydia, Simon.
90. TURNER, Philip, Bela, John, Anne.
127. TRACY, John, Mary, Margaret, Lydia, John, Zebadiah L., Bela, Ulysses, Rachel, Harriet, Esther, Emily.
149. TOMLINSON, Jabez H., Gideon.
215. TRACY, Lucy, Alice, Lucretia, Lydia, Philura.
409. TRACY, Jared W., James J., Edward H., Sarah G., Cornelia M., Lydia H.
311. TURNER, Julia F. M., George F., Betsey H., Charles.
530. TRACY, John.
124. TILSON, Dwight, Nancy J., Joseph M., Jonathan E.
254. TRACY, Solomon.
259. TINKER, Sarah, John, Nehemiah, Almarina, Lawson, Alexander, Joel, Polly, Bela, Joseph B., Lydia.
250. TINKER, Abigail G., Elisha, John, James, Ralph.
319. TRACY, Susannah, Margaret, William, Ann H., Charles, Catherine, Henry, Edward H., Frances.
398. TRACY, Anne H., Calvin, Chester, Elizabeth, Irene, Gurdon H., Mary.
854. THOMAS, Edward S., William, Martha.
900. TROWBRIDGE, Lewis B., Alfred C., Frederic E.
1033. THOMPSON, Elizabeth H., Malvina H., Arne, Caroline H.
1369. TRACY, William S., Winslow, Elizabeth D., Lucy, Hannah P., Elisha D., Stephen D

1539. TOWNLY, Harriet L., George H., Charles Q.
1613. TOWNSEND, Frederic, Nancy, Rebecca, Mary, Olive.
1713. TOWNSEND, Sarah M.
1931. TRACY, Oliver R., William, Lydia E.
1927. VOORHIS, Clarence B., William F.
254. WILLIAMS, Temperance.
294. WILLES, Jabez, Temperance, Martha, Joseph H.
729. WADHAMS, Jerusha L.
893. WOODWARD, Elizabeth, Sarah, Harriet, Maria.
1189. WILLIAMS, Helen B., Frances A.
1320. WHITNEY, Byron, Franklin.
1371. WOLCOTT, Mary A. G., Hannah H., Joshua H., Elizabeth, Frederic H., Laura M., Elizabeth H., Alice, Frederick H., Gardner H.
1371. WHITEHEAD, Frederic W.
1405. WILLIAMS, Mary H., John L., Charles G., Gurdon H.
1412. WHITE, Sarah H., Joseph H., Sophia M., James, Jonathan H., Simon H., Ralph H.
1452. WALKER, Adeline M.
1461. WEBSTER, Ellen R., George H., John, Emily, Kate C., Douglas.
1637. WELCH, Daniel, Moses, Alma, Rhoda, Maria, Alfred, Persis.
1480. WHEELER, Jane, Charles.
1551. WATTLES, Alden, James D., Eliza, Rufus.
1903. WASHBURN, Charles A., Charlotte B., Daughin C., Elenore.
1906. WASHBURN, Orra J., Clara E., Sarah E. C., Abel E., George.
41. WHEELOCK, Elizabeth, Eleazer, Ruth, Abigail, John, Sarah, Ruth, Mary, Abigail, John, Eleazer, James.
77. WRIGHT, Eliphalet, Elizabeth, Sarah, Elisha, Mary, Amariah.
146. WETMORE, Tryphena, Hezekiah.
148. WELD, Lewis.
165. WETMORE, Andrew.
678. WILCOX, E. H.
1010. WARD, Henry H., Thomas S., Ann E., Kneeland H., Henry, George W., Elizabeth, H., Emma V., Nancy B.
255. YOUNGS, William, Mrs. Manning, Mrs. Bingham, William.
775. YOUNG, Levi H., Guilford D., Cornelia A., Jane G., Marcus B., C. Cassius.
1682. YAGER, Elenora, Josephine.
1925. YERRINGTON, Marietta T., Theodore W., Arthur M., Charles A.

INDEX. 411

III.

INDEX TO INTERMARRIAGES AND DESCENDANTS NOT BELONGING TO THE TWO PRECEDING INDEXES.

ALLEN, W., (D. D.)	41	CLARK, Hiram	1637
ABEL, Thomas	98	CULVER, Jona. E., Asa L.	346
APHTHORP, Charles W.	145	COLE, Abel	430
ATKINSON, Frances	184	CLEVELAND, Aaron P.	563
ALVORD, Melinda	259	CLEMSHIRE,	969
AVERY, Mary W.	439	CHOSE, Mrs. Sarah	1371
BACKUS, Rev. Simon	26	COBURN, Alexander	1621
BACKUS, Eleazer F.	562	COGGSWELL, James, (M. D.)	145
BACKUS, Rev. Dr. Jonathan	562	COGGSWELL, Rev. Dr.	216
BACKUS, Rev. John	562	COGGSWELL, Mason F., (M. D.)	216
BOGG, Moses	319	COGGSWELL,	1363
BRAINARD, Clarissa	267	CHERRY, Rev.	465
BRAINARD, Horace	657	CONVERSE, Sherman	653
BUSHNELL, Jonathan	98	CONVERSE,	1363
BUSHNELL, Ebenezer	148	CROSS, Clarissa	439
BRUEN, Rev. Matthias	145	CHASE, Herod	1830
BAKER, Deborah	148	CAMPBELL, Jane	641
BROOKINGS, Eliza G.	1855	CLIFFORD, Samuel A.	984
BROOKINGS William	1855	CORMAN, Dudley	1399
BALDWIN, John	637	CHAPMAN, B. F.	1637
BRADLEY, Edward	899	COGGSHALL, Mehetabel	145
BUCK, William H.	969	COATS, HARRIET	641
BARSTOW, John	1341	COIT, Daniel L.	220
BARSTOW, Horatio	1363	CHAUNCY, Charles	562
BARTLETT, Joseph	31	CRAWFORD, Rev. Robert	589
BEERS, David	146	CRAWFORD, Francis H., James D., Lyndon	
BRINSMADE, Mary	41	S., Ellen M.	
BINGHAM, Joseph	41	COLLAGHER, Charles H.	984
BINGHAM, Alfred	255	CRANE, Anne E.	1558
BOORMAN, James	145	CAPEN, Abraham	1763
BUSH, Rev. J. S.	184	DAVENPORT, Rev. J. S.	145
BURNETT, Clark	641	DAVENPORT, Rev. J. R.	145
BUCKINGHAM,		DOUTHILL, William P.	1438
BANCROFT, De W. C.	809	DUNCAN, Elizabeth	184
BUTLER,	1363	DOOLITTLE, Jesse W.	148
BROWN, Asa R.	984	DRAPER, ALLEN	430
BROWN, Abby E.	1050	DABOLL, Dr.	662
BROWN, Lucius	1341	DUNHAM, Nancy	148
BARNARD, Ruth	31	DODSON, Ed.	164
BLISS, Lucy	148	DUTTON, William H.	809
BLISS, Hon. Geo. C.	148	DICKEY, J. G.	1604
BURLEIGH, Ednah	98	EDWARDS, Hannah	26
BARKER, Rebecca	98	EDWARDS, Eunice	26
BARKER, Eliphalet	98	EATON, Jacob S.	1050
BECKWITH, (Dea.)	98	EDGERTON, Joshua	98
BEACH, Eliza	439	ESTES, James N.	1830
BABCOCK, Nelson	642	ESTES, James F.	1830
BOLLES, Asa M.	679	ELDERKIN, Jedidiah	148
BURLEY, Augustus H.	809	ELDERKIN, Mary A.	148
BARON, Maria P.	1017	FROTHINGHAM, Cornelia	1371
BARROWS, Fayette	1050	FITCH, Abigail	145
CHALLIS, Sarah	31	FRY, Lydia B.	476
CHEESEBROUGH, Harriet G.	145	FRENCH, Capt.	307
CLARK, Rev. Porson	2438	FREEMAN, Fred	1371
CLARK, Isaac	1944	FISHER, Samuel, (D. D.)	145
CLARK, Edwards	653	FISHER, Rev. Samuel W.	145
CLARK, Annie B.	897	FOSTER, Hon. L. F. S.	296

INDEX.

Fowler, Oliver	1341	Lewis, Rebecca	149
Flint, Sophia	148	Lyman, Martha	296
Frink, Amanda	611	Lyman, Rev. Ephraim	1361
Fosdick, Alvan	215	Larabee, Julia	637
Fuller, Harry	641	Leach, Luther D.	641
Fuller, Nancy B.	657	Lockwood, Rev. Peter	145
Galusha, Gov. Jonas	156	Lyon, Dr. Philip	211
Galusha, George	430	Loomis, Sarah	398
Galusha, Truman	439	Lester, Mary	657
Garfield, Rev.	901	Learned, James E.	2473
Gifford,	1605	Lathrop, Elizabeth	211
Green, Rev. Dr.	216	Lathrop, Thomas	220
Goodell, J. F.	643	Lathrop, Horace	637
Goff, Job	1043	Leffingwell, Elisha	215
Gulliver, Dr.	2469	Lawrence, Julia	475
Goodrich, Rev. Chauncy	319	Maltby, Sarah	41
Gillet, Eliza	657	Morsley, Abigail	148
Gilman, W. C.	220	Morris, Eleanor	854
Goodale, Levi	899	Manning, Fred	255
Hyde, Rev. John	98	Merrill, John S.	1855
Hyde, Andrew, Jude	127	Merriam, Wm.	1027
Hyde, George, Amasa, Rodney	127	McGiven, Mary M.	1328
Hyde, Lewis, Lydia, Mary	127	Morse, Henry B.	1621
Hyde, Joseph	641	Marble, Rev. Dr.	184
Hunt, Rev. N. S.	676	Mosher, Aaron	230
Haughton, Julia A.	1361	Mattoon, Charles, Rev. Charles N.	430
Haughton, James	1361	McNiell, M. K.	758
Hawkins, Amanda	1050	Maples, Rev. C. P.	1179
Hough, Philura	184	McLane, Rev. Dr.	1361
Hough, Dr. Alanson	405	Montague, Rev. E. J.	2438
Hebard, Henry	230	Nott, Lucretia	98
Harrington, George	405	Noyes, William Curtis	319
Hammond, Martha S.	430	Norton, Porter	596
Hale, Diantha	641	Newton, Earl	1607
Hubbard, George W.	1338	Ostrander, John	1043
Howland, Joseph	220	Orton, Meribah A.	1621
Howland, Abby	1371	Patten, William, (D. D.)	41
Hococks, James	281	Porter, Sophia	148
Hutchins,	1363	Porter, Caroline R.	758
Harris, Rev. O.	591	Pierrepont, James	281
Hecocks, Elias	1604	Pierpont, Dr. John, Robert, Evelyn	281
Hubbard, Mary E.	611	Pomeroy, Rev., (D. D.)	41
Hubbard, Francis H	611	Pike, Dr. A. W.	184
Hubbard, Asahel	643	Parker, Milton D.	319
Ives, Charles T.	1328	Parker, Sylvia, Flora	1615
Judd, Daniel	98	Phelps, Hon. Oliver	596
Jackson, J. P.	1371	Perkins, Samuel H., Hannah	148
Jones, Ellen	1703	Perkins, Dr. Elisha	216
Knight, Joseph	98	Perkins, Rev. George	311
Knapp, Cornelius	1539	Perkins, Lucy	319
Kirkland, Rev. Samuel	41	Perit, Peletiah	220
Kirkland, John, (D. D.)	41	Page, Anna	439
Kellogg, Henry K	1328	Post, John K	901
Kirtland, Louisa	319	Quinlan, Mary	31
King, Walter	148	Ring, Joanna	31
Kingsley, J. L.	220	Ripley, Prof.	41
Kelley, John, Henry	405	Runyon, Rebecca	1050
Kelley, Jabez	307	Rankin, Robert G.	1371
Kelsey, Lorenzo A.	641	Radcliff, Peter W.	145
Lancaster, John	31	Roach, P. R.	611
Larned, George	611	Rodgers, Mrs.	1197

INDEX. 413

RALSTON, Rebecca	562	SLATER, Martha ... 1050
RALSTON, Matthew C.	562	SPENCER, Mary J. ... 1050
RICE, Jonas	642	SPAFFORD, Nancy ... 1621
ROWLAND, Susannah	1621	TRACY, Lucy ... 90
STORRS, Benjamin, Lathrop	127	THOMAS, Louisa H. ... 409
STORRS, Huchings, Margaret, Oliver	127	THOMAS, Edward Y. ... 775
STEDMAN, George T.	854	THOMAS, David S. ... 775
SHURTLEFF, Harriet	211	THOMAS, William O. ... 854
STILES, Roderick	765	TOMLINSON, Gov. Gideon ... 119
STILES, Rufus	765	TALCOTT, Arad ... 390
STARK, Margaret E.	1850	TURNER, Dr. Philip ... 215
STREET, Rev. Owen	679	THOMPSON, Theo. W. ... 809
SAYRE, Jonathan	1013	THOMPSON, Geo. W. ... 897
SESSIONS, John	1558	VERNA, Edward ... 148
SPRAGUE, Harriet	1604	VARNUM, George ... 1607
SKINNER, Thomas, (D. D.)	145	WELLS, David F. ... 1338
SKINNER, Gov.	281	WOODWARD, Prof. ... 41
STURGIS, Anna	146	WHELPLEY, Rev. P. M. ... 145
SAUNDERS, Rev. Dr. D. C.		WOODRUFF, Helen V. R. ... 184
SAUNDERS, Asa	1050	WHITEHEAD, Asa ... 1371
SUMMERS, Maria	765	WEBB, Samuel ... 337
SEWARD, Rev. Dwight H.	612	WRIGHT, Joseph J. ... 591
SOUTHMAYD, Samuel Gray	611	WILD, ... 1363
STOCKER, John	642	WELLS, Mary S. ... 145
SHUMWAY, Charles	1050	WELLS, William H. ... 319
STARKWEATHER, Charles	1410	WELLS, Ebenezer ... 562
SWEATLAND, Mary	1605	WELLS, George ... 1444
SMITH, George	146	WELD, Elizabeth ... 148
SMITH, Urania	430	WELD, Lewis ... 148
SMITH, Sherman	430	WOLCOTT, Jemima ... 211
SMITH, Dr. Lyndon A.	589	WOOD, Caroline M. ... 430
SMITH, Dr. Edward D., Lyndon A., Rev.		WOOD, Seneca ... 430
Sanford, Frances Louisa	589	WILLIAMS, Erastus ... 1369
SMITH, Ezra	1944	WILCOX, Stephen J. ... 1412
SMITH, Albert	1369	WHEELER, Eliza M. ... 145
SMITH, Keziah	1621	WHITEHOUSE, Mary ... 184
STRONG, Julia F.	765	WENTWORTH, N. S. ... 969
SWIFT, Earl	637	WADSWORTH, Daniel ... e ... 237
SWIFT, Achsah D.	809	WARNER, Maria ... 672
SWIFT, Josephine	1361	WHITNEY, Eli ... 809
STODDARD, Elizabeth	765	

IV.

AN INDEX TO THE NAMES OF THE HUSBANDS OF THE HUNTINGTON DAUGHTERS.

90.	Adgate, Capt. Thomas.... Norwich	1513.	Allen, Thomas..... Newcastle, Eng.
90.	Abel, Capt. Joshua...... Norwich	1609.	Adams, Silas...... Woodstock, Vt.
250.	Abbe, Richard........ Windham	1617.	Alison, William.... Woodstock, Vt.
331.	Avery, Jabez......... Norwich	1709.	Allen, William... Worcester, Mass.
622.	Abbe, George W...... Windham	2353.	Addison, Jos., Esq. Watertown, N. Y.
976.	Ainsworth, Dr...... Medina, Ohio	2473.	Adams, John T., Esq..... Norwich.
977.	Andrus, Richard...... Chelsea, Vt	2689.	Allen, George C.... Albany, N. Y.
1113.	Andrus, Martin..............	19.	Bingham, Jonathan..... Windham.
1169.	Avery, Rev. William. P... Griswold	26.	Backus, Joseph......... Norwich.
1205.	Antisdell, Hosea F............	47.	Bingham, Thomas...... Windham.
	......Cooperstown, N. Y.	134.	Bliss, John............. Norwich.
1474.	Allen, Thomas....... Colchester	146.	Beers, Samuel......... Stratford.

INDEX.

193.	Basset, Nathan..........Windham.	1426. Benedict, Herman.............
220.	Bill, Capt. Ephraim.....Norwich.	..........West Vernon, Ohio.
316.	Brown, Dr. Matthew....Rochester.	1437. Bright, Jabez G.....Franklin, Ind.
332.	Butler, Benjamin.......Norwich.	1494. Bellows, Isaac F....Walpole,N. H.
344.	Billings, Benjamin............	1495. Brown, Ephraim..Bloomfield, Ohio.
351.	Brown, Stephen...Newbury, Mass.	1512. Brown, George W. Yarmouth, N. S.
356.	Brown, William...Salisbury, Mass.	1523. Booth, Alonzo......Enfield, Conn.
379.	Baldwin, Dr. Thomas. Boston, Mass.	1569. Brainard, George S. Haddam, Conn.
413.	Baldwin, William........Norwich.	1538. Bradbury, J. P...Prairie Ridge, Ill.
416.	Backus, Gurdon.......Windham.	1607. Brown, Heman....Bethany, N. Y.
421.	Boardman............Windham.	1615. Bartlett, Ira Rev.....Canada West.
430.	Burnham, Hon. Asa.Bennington,Vt.	1653. Barron, Justin....Washington, Vt.
436.	Bottom, Simon....Shaftesbury, Vt.	1655. Barron, Isaac.....Washington, Vt.
447.	Bissel, Benj....St. Johnsbury, Vt.	1708. Bemis, Eleazer.....Spencer, Mass.
479.	Bingham, Wheelock....Windham	1732. Bowers, Wm. C........New York.
506.	Bush, Dr.........Brockport, N. Y.	1782. Babbitt, George R. Waterloo, N. Y.
507.	Baker, H. S........Haverhill, N. H.	1833. Buxton,Daniel.South Danvers,Mass.
528.	Balcam, Azariah......Windham.	1858. Buxton Ira......Amesbury, Mass.
538.	Betts, Hezekiah....Upper Canada.	1860. Bartlett, Oliver....Amesbury, Mass.
582.	Brewster, Elisha..............	1861 & 4. Beade.........South Hampton.
	........Worthington, Mass.	1879. Burrills............Weymouth.
635.	Butler, William.........Hampton.	1873.15 Baker, Edward.............
652.	Brewster, Benjamin.....Windham.	2002. Blake, Franklin..Mapleton, Kanzas.
656.	Baldwin, Hon. John....Windham.	2009. Bottum, Horace B.Shaftesbury, Vt.
688.	Bull............Wethersfield.	2120. Barker, Rhodes...............
707.	Bowditch, Nathan.....Providence.	.........South Brookfield, Mass.
739.	Bird, John............Vermont.	2152. Burton, Wm........Albany, N. Y.
745.	Blazo, Paul...........Vermont.	2300. Beach, Theodore.....New London.
748.	Bunce, Allen K..........Lyme.	2513. Bowman, John H..Vergennes, Vt.
768.	Brunell, Zethun......Woodbury.	2618. Burrel, Horatio N...Oronoco, Min.
831.	Bicknell, Nathan..Lebanon, N. H.	2648. Burrill, John.......Nova Scotia.
830.	Barrus, Comfort......Chelsea, Vt.	2683. Bigelow, Dr. Aborn T.........
897.	Brainard, Rev. Israel.Verona, N. Y.	............Worcester, N. Y.
901.	Beecher, John........New Haven.	2685. Brainard, William O. East Haddam.
911.	Buxton, James.............	2693. Blair, Erastus G. Middlefield, N. Y.
956.	Burt, Ebenezer............	2962. Bonner, James M......Windsor
962.	Boutelle, David......Boston, Mass.	2973. Buxton, Joshua....Danvers, Mass.
963.	Bidwell, Horace.South Manchester.	2981. Bodge, M. G.................
970.	Bennet, Jonathan B...Canterbury.	3231. Burman, Crodius..Middlebury, Vt.
984.	Blodgett, Bela......Boston, Mass.	2523. Booth, Chauncey H..Mexico, N. Y.
1003.	Bottom, Martin........Lisbon.	1924. Bennet, Lucius R....Athens, Penn.
1004.	Bishop, Barzillai..........Lisbon.	3172. Barrington, Samuel...Philadelphia.
1016.	Balis, Calvin....Oswego, N.Y.	App.A. 14. Barnard Benj..New York City.
1017.	Brewster, Hon. David P.........	App.A. 46. Bingham....Windham, Conn.
	......Oswego, N. Y.	32. Chandler................
1047.	Brigham, Stephen.....Mansfield.	62. Calkins, James.........Lebanon.
1069.	Bottum, William H..Oxford, C. W.	76. Crane, John..........Windham.
1070.	Barton, Gardner,,,Shaftesbury, Vt.	55. Chappel, Caleb........Lebanon.
1077.	Bottum, N. H.....Shaftesbury, Vt.	79. Clark, Moses..........Lebanon.
1092.	Burrows, David......Rome, N. Y.	83. Clark, Joseph.........Lebanon.
1149.	Byles, Dea. Elisha......Ashford.	87. Carew, Thomas........Norwich.
1171.	Babcock, P....North East, Penn.	88. Carew Joseph.........Norwich.
1173.[1]	Babcock, John....Preston, Wis.	148. Clark, Dr. John........Lebanon.
1173.[2]	Babcock, A......Milton, Wis.	169. Conant, Rev.............
1282.	Bingham, James......Norwich.	281. Collins, Charles......Litchfield.
1321.	Buckley, Samuel.............	303. Carew, Ebenezer.....Norwich.
	.....Sacketts Harbor, N. Y.	322. Carew, Eliphalet......Norwich.
1340.	Bennet, Asher..........Norwich.	328. Calkins, Frederick...Chelsea, Vt.
1341.	Bailey, Joseph..........Bozrah.	346. Culver, Jonathan............
1409.	Blanchard, Stillman..Rutland, Vt.	351. Challis, Thomas........Newbury.
1413.	Buel, Judge Elam....Troy, N. Y.	370. Colby, Joseph......Weare, N. H.

INDEX. 415

373.	Crane, Daniel......Newark, N. J.	2798.	Carey, **Lewis**........Bethel, Vt.
411.	Carpenter, Gardner...Norwich.	2976.	Chase, **Dow**.......Weare, N. H.
415.	Chaplin, Benjamin......Windham.	3047.	Carter, Oliver....Brentwood, N.Y.
431.	Cole, David....Kingsbury, N.Y.	2609.	Coley, Rev. Jas. E..Westville, Conn.
562.	Chester, Col. **John**...........	3.	App. A. Casey...............
	......Wethersfield, Conn.	19.	App.A. Cleveland,Geo. S........
662.	Collins, Dr. Lewis.Wilkesbarre, Pa.	30.	Davis, Jeremiah......Amesbury.
720.	Chapman, Erastus,........	34.	Downer..........Amesbury.
765.	Curtiss, David S..Woodbury,Conn.	145.	Davenport, Abraham Hon........
836.	Clark, John..........Ashford.		...........Stamford.
843.	Cleveland..........Royalton.	242.	Devotion, Ebenezer....Windham.
877.	Chapman, John..Claverack, N. Y.	278.	Dana, Anderson........Wyoming.
907.	Currier........Amesbury, Mass.	344.	Dolph, Mark A...........
944.	Cochran, David.New Boston,Conn.	799.	Deering, Dr. N. H.....New York.
969.	Cook, John......Albany, N. Y.	809.	Dalliba, Maj. Jas. S....Rome, N. Y.
1038.	Cheesborough, Elam......Lisbon.	1044.	Denham, Josephus..Lebanon, Ohio.
1101.	Cole, John M.........Danville, Ill.	1072.	Douglas, Geo......Shaftesbury, Vt.
1106.	Clark, Jeremiah...Shaftesbury,Vt.	1277.	Dodge, Samuel K......Berlin, Pa.
1158.	Clark, Francis........Chaplin.	1280.	Davison, Andrew...........
1229.	Clint n, Simon...........	1330.	Dunbar................
1234.	Clark, Loren............	1338.	Dickenson, Solomon.Hatfield, Mass.
1251.	Crosby, Ebenezer.........	1365.	DeWitt, John..........Norwich.
1288.	Carpenter, Alfred.......Ashford.	1380.	Denton, Gabriel W...New Orleans.
1295.	Cobb, **Horace**...Spring Mills, N. Y.	1444.	Danielson, Eli.....Butternuts, N. Y.
1329.[1]	Clapp........Watertown, N. Y.	1445.	Danielson, Fred..Butternuts, N. Y.
1335.	Cook, Rev. J. B.Binghampton,N.Y.	1595.	Davis, Edward E..Davenport, Iowa.
1399.	Carter, William C...Delavan,Wis.	1611.	Dean, Zebulon........Bethel, Vt.
1411.	Clapp, Levi...Worthington, Mass.	1630.	Davis, Jacob.......Randolph, Vt.
1455.	Campbell, James...Springfield, Ill.	1631.	Downer, Saul........Sharon, Vt.
1469.	Cottrel, Elliot P....Hartford.	1640.	Duncan, Wm. P.........Canada.
1476.	Church, Zalmon A.....Norwich.	1680.	Dunbar, Riley......Wolcottville.
1492.	Conant, William, Bellows Falls,Vt.	1843.	Davis, Joel H....Amesbury, Mass.
1671.	Clark Charles E....Buffalo, N. Y.	1745.	Dickenson, Western.....Franklin.
1630.	Clement, William..Tunbridge, Vt.	2006.	Derby, Edwin..Cedar Rapids, Iowa.
1703.	Craige, Nathan.....Spencer, Mass.	2524.	Dutcher, Fred.....St. Albans, Vt.
1725.	Case, Albert S......New York.	2997.	Dale, Walter..........Haverhill.
1753.	Catier, Jesse........Highgate, Vt	2766.	Daniels........Annapolis, N. S.
1760.	Cleveland, James P............	37.	Elliot..............Amesbury.
1773.	Crosby, Platt.....Waterloo, N.Y.	237.	Eells, Rev. John.Glastenbury,Conn.
1794.	Coffin, William W....Utica, N. Y.	258.	Edwards, Wm......Guilford, Vt.
1809.	Cunningham......New London.	364.	Elliot..........Concord, N. H.
1859.	Clough, Stephen..Amesbury, Mass.	399.	Ellis, Stephen........New York.
1873.[33]	Campbell, Rufus...Montpelier, Vt.	630.	Edgerton, Uriel........Franklin.
1914.	Chapman, Jas. M.Cincinnati, Ohio.	631.	Edgerton, David....Munson, Mass.
1954.	Cooke, Prof. Josiah P..........	920.	Evans, Reuben..Amesbury, Mass.
	........Cambridge, Mass.	1410.	Eager, Nath...Worthington, Mass.
1993.	Comings, Benj....Greensboro, Vt.	1585.	Elliot, John........Wilmot, N. S.
1873.[15]	Cobb, Ezra..............	2377.	Emerson, H. H., (M. D.).Louisiana.
1999.	Cook, Charles....Greensboro, Vt.	2613.	Elliot, Rev..............Illinois.
2119.	Coon, D...South Brookfield, N. Y.	2804.	Eggleston, E. S........Bethel, Vt.
2123.	Cheesborough, Amos (Dr.)......	2980.	Emerson, Geo........Lynn, Mass.
	.........South Brookfield, N. Y.	3020.	Elliot, Robert........Lincoln, Vt.
2330.	Clark, Charles N....Clinton, Ohio.	21.	Forbes............Preston.
2451.	Chappell, Franklin..New London.	78.	Fitch, **Theo**........Canterbury.
2457.	Clark, Dea. Charles.Brooklyn,Conn.	139.	Fitch, **Eb**..........Norwich.
2459.	Coggshall,Wm. A.Providence, R. I.	169.	Frink, **Thos**........Norwich.
2460.	Clark, John H..Providence, R. I.	184.	Freeman, **Jona**........Hanover.
2468.	Cleveland Stephen B.....	216.	Fitch, Dr. **Jabez**.....Canterbury.
	......Bloomfield, N. J.	227.	Fitch, Jabez........Windham.
2496.	Childs, Timothy, (M. D.).NewYork.	403.	Fitch, Capt. **Oliver**......Norwich.
2786.	Clement Royal...Alexander, N. Y.	482.	Fuller, Samuel........Hampton.

416 INDEX.

No.	Name	Place	No.	Name	Place
546.	Farnsworth, Dr. H.	Windsor, Ohio.	291.	Huntington (233)	Worthington.
673.	Fitch, Simon	Lebanon.	307.	Hyde, Ebenezer	Lebanon.
722.	Fuller, Erastus	New York.	326.	Huntington (179)	
746.	Frank, Andrew	Starkboro, Vt.	327.	Hough, Hon. David	Lebanon, N. H.
835.	Freeman, Enoch	Mansfield.	330.	Hammond, Dudley	Chemung, N.Y.
923.	Follensbee, Joseph	Amesbury, Mass.	337.	Hyde, Ebenezer	
			345.	Hendricks, Benj.	
936.	Fifield	Weare, N. H.	357.	Hoyt, Moses	Amesbury.
988.	Ford, Hezekiah	Lebanon, N. H.	393.	Hartshorn, Silas	Franklin.
1138.	Flint, Samuel	Brockville, C. W.	446.	Huntington (658)	East Haddam.
1256.	Fuller, Samuel	Compton, C. E.	522.	Hebard	Windham.
1523.	Foster, Chandler	Albany, N. Y.	548.	Hartshorne, Jona.	Hartford.
1558.	Fisher, Geo.	Oswego, N. Y.	565.	Huntington (245)	
1588.	Fitts, Duty	Eastford, Conn.	613.	House, Simon	Hebron.
2511.	Flint, Wm. D.		616.	Hulbert, Edward	Middletown.
2738.	Fallows, Prof. S.	Galesville.	643.	Houston, James L.	Middlebury, Vt.
8.	Goldsmith, Joshua		661.	Huntington (182)	Norwich.
17.	Griswold, Capt. Samuel		728.	Huntington (513)	
156.	Galusha, Jacob	Shaftesbury.	759.	Huntington (555)	
345.	Graham, Dr.		827	Hatch, Zephaniah	Monticello, N. Y.
445.	Gillet, Caleb	Colchester.	881.	Hasbrouck, Abel	
577.	Green, Benj. E.	Worthington, Mass.	914.	Herbert, Jas.	
589.	Griffin, Edwin Dorr, (D. D.)	Boston, Mass.	937.	Hoit, Sol.	Groton, Mass.
			1022.	Hough, Dr. Henry W	Putnam
797.	Grace, John H	Norwich.	1029.	Hamlin, Daniel R.	Buffalo, N.Y.
1019.	Gager, David A	Bozrah.	1043.	Hanks, Elisha	Bath, N. Y.
1114.	Galusha, E. B.	San Francisco, Cal.	1100.	Harpending, Smith	Shaftesbury, Vt.
1179.	Gardner, David	Brooklyn, N.Y.	1126.	Henderson	
1226.	Gibson	Dundas, C. W.	1144.	Hanchett, Milton W.	Syracuse, N.Y.
1233.	Graves, Josiah		1201.	Hubbel, John R.	Birmingham.
1384.	Griswold, John	New York.	1206.	Hardy, Peter	Springfield, N. Y.
1406.	Gray, Moses Esq.	Dublin, Ireland.	1254.	Harvey, Alanson	Eaton, C. E.
1468.	Gillette, Salmon C.	Colchester.	1276.	Huntington (634)	
1535.	Gregory, Henry	Ithaca, N. Y.	1313.	Holden, Jas.	So. Dansville, N.Y.
1737.	Gay, Amos W	New York.	1362.	Huntington (318)	
1830.	Gove, Robert	Deering, N. H.	1368.	Huntington (588)	
1848.	Gove, Nathan C.	Pontiac, N. Y.	1418.	Hoyt, Rev. Otto S.	Hinesbury, Vt.
1854.	Green, Nathan	Lincoln, Vt.	1450.	Hoag, Henry	Butternuts, N. Y.
1855.	Goodwin, David	Amesbury, Mass.	1464.	Hulbert, Wm. E.	Middletown.
1896.	Gilmore, Murry	Keene, N. Y.	1487.	Hicks, Samuel	New Hartford, N.Y.
2027.	Gregory, Rev. S. B.	Little Falls, N Y.	1500.	Harris, Milo	Buffalo, N. Y.
2094.	Griggs	Mobile, Ala.	1605.	Hotchkiss, Jer.	New Haven, Vt.
2308.	Gillette, Ellery C.	Mexico, N. Y.	1609.	Hall, Samuel	
2370.	Goulding	Watertown, N. Y.	1624.	Hendrix, Henry	Highland, Wis.
2634.	Greer	Painesville, Ohio.	1627.	Huntley, John B.	Bridport, Vt.
3161.	Grenelle, Wm. H.	New York.	1736.	Huntington (2482)	Franklin.
1926.	Gates, James M	Athens, Pa.	1921.	Howard, Geo.	Tarrytown, N. Y.
31.	Hoyt, Lieut. Thos.	Amesbury.	1873.9	Huntington (1873½)	
51.	Hyde, Capt. Mat.	Norwich.	1948.	Hall, Amos A	Willimantic.
65.	Huit	Lebanon.	1911.	Hastings, Tracy	Franklin.
93.	Hyde, Abner	Norwich.	1962.	Huntington (1145)	Cleveland, Ohio.
98.	Hyde, Thos.	Franklin.	1991.	Hatch, Chauncy	Belvidere, Ill.
104.	Homan, Thos.	Danvers.	2001.	Hall, Josiah	Cedar Rapids, Iowa.
117.	Hedden	Newark, N. J.	2019.	Hooker, Horace	
138.	Huntington (89)		2059.	Higgins, B. B.	Perry, N. Y.
151.	Huntington (92)		2096.	Hoyt, Henry T	Danbury, Conn.
175.	Huntington (559)		2208.	Hazen, Jesse	Canada East.
194.	Hovey, Edmund	Mansfield.	2333.	Hunt, James F.	Wauseon, Ohio.
213.	Huntington (86)		2352.	Hungerford, Solon D.	Watertown, N. Y.
256.	Holbrook	Columbia.			
263.	Harvey, Elisha	East Haddam.	2359.	Harbottle, John G.	Watertown, N.Y.

INDEX. 417

2367.	Hitchcock, Robert............... ....Watertown, N. Y.	552. 672.	Lyman, Rev. Eliph....Woodstock. Lyon, Rev. Walter......Pomfret.
2408.	Hyde, Lewis A....Norwich, Conn.	674.	Lyman, Wm. (D. D.)...Millington.
2438.	Hooker, Edward W., (D. D.)..... ....East Windsor.	708. 710.	Liley, Nathan............Ashford. Lilley, Emmaus........Mansfield.
2445.	Huntington (2441)...Boston, Mass.	834.	Lewis, Samuel........Brandon, Vt.
2447.	Huntington (821)...St. Louis, Mo.	842.	Landphere, Solomon,......Ashford.
2450.	Hebard, Alfred....Carondelet, Mo.	864.	Lathrop, Jas..........New York.
2475.	Huntington (1383)......Norwich.	940.	Lull, Lewis........Warner, N. H.
2586.	Huntington (2579).Winnebago, Min.	972.	Lathrop, Azariah.........Vernon.
2969.	Huntington (1839).Henniker, N. H.	979.	Leech............................
3191.	Hutchinson......New York City.	1027	Lathrop, C. L.....Cleveland, Ohio.
1218.	Ingalls, O. S......Hanover, N. H.	1232.	Lounsbury, Letsome............
1219.	Ingalls, O. S......Hanover, N. H.	1269.	Larned, Chas. H........Arkansas.
30.	Joyce, Abraham......Amesbury.	1288.	Lincoln, John......Lebanon, Pa.
383.	Judd, Samuel..........Franklin.	1300.	Lewis, Paul B..Independence, N.Y.
533.	Jones, Benj................	1522.	Leonard, Norman T............
591.	Jones, Amasa...Wilkesbarre, Pa.		...............Westfield, Mass.
621.	Johnson, Anson....Brunswick, Me.	1620.	Langden, Silvester.Constable, N.Y.
625.	Johnson, Ebenezer.Brunswick, Me.	1755.	Lounsbury, David..Fallsbury, N.Y.
884.	Jerome, John............Norwich.	1800.	Lee, Uriah D.......Buffalo, N. Y.
1048.	Johnson, Hazard......Mansfield.	1869.	Leonard, Daniel....Lawrence, Mass.
1055.	James, Elisha..Lansingburgh, N. Y.	2654.	Lamberton, Seneca..Baraboo, Wis.
1283.	Justin, Nathan....Manchester, Pa.	2656.	Lamberton, Sumner J..........
1692.	Jones, Wm. P......Pittsburg, Pa.		..............Baraboo, Wis.
1871.	Jenkins........................	2717.	Long, Rev. Walter...Mystic, Conn.
2503.	James, John W. Esq.Boston, Mass.	2765.	Loomis, Reuben..Cornwallis, C. E.
2718.	Johnson, Isaac..........Norwich.	2353.	Lawyer, J. A....Watertown, N. Y.
130.	Kingsbury, Asa....Franklin, Conn.	267.	May, Rev. Eleazer......Haddam.
230.	Kimball, Richard..Scotland, Conn.	547.	Malvesey, Abraham..Enfield, Conn.
544.	Kent, Gamaliel.....Tolland, Conn.	583.	Marsh, Thomas.Worthington, Mass.
739.	Keese, Benj......Keeseville, N. Y.	601.	Morgan, Col. Samuel........Vt.
1194.	Keyes, Henry P...Conneaut, Ohio.	603.	Mather, Increase........Scotland.
1197.	King, Lorenzo W......Bridgeport.	606.	Mills, Elisha....Canandaigua, N.Y.
1203.	Keller, J. P.....Minden, N. Y.	676.	Mason, Daniel..........Lebanon.
1328.	Kimball, Jos....Watertown, N. Y.	684.	Mather, Allen M.........Windsor.
1332.	King, Leicester..Bloomfield, Ohio.	685.	Mather, Allen M.........Windsor.
1422.	Kellogg, Simon H..St. Albans, Vt.	771.	Manville, James.......Woodbury.
1699.	Kingsbury, Thos....Spencer, Mass.	832.	Martin, Dr. Sylvanus...........
1762.	Kidder, Ira........Braintree, Vt.		............Plainfield, N. H.
1771.	Kellam, Wm....Long Eddy, N. Y.	967.	Marble, Henry...North Manchester.
1898.	Kent, Lincoln......Keene, N. Y.	1131.	Mitchell, E. M......Morris, N. Y.
1946.	Kingsley, Henry.......Franklin.	1136.	McLean, Rev...................
2251.	Keyes, Dwight W.Ogdensburg,N.Y.	1342.	Miner, Cyrus...........Norwich.
1873[11]	Kimball............Boston, Mass.	1432.	Mathews, Dr. John H...........
App. A. 52.	Kilbourn.....Antrim, Mich.		............Painesville, Ohio.
49.	Leffingwell, Samuel......Norwich.	1437.	Seth T. Mitchel.....Franklin, Ind.
57.	Lincoln, Samuel........Windham.	1524.	McGregor......Coeymans, N. Y.
68.	Lathrop, Wm...........Norwich.	1578.	Merwin, J. W............Milford.
136.	Lathrop, William........Norwich.	1580.	Merwin, J. W............Milford.
144.	Lathrop, Azariah........Franklin.	1660.	Moffat, Lewis......Charleston, Vt.
172.	Leonard, Dr............Norwich.	1763.	Marvin, John S......Howell, Mich.
296.	Lyman, Joseph (D. D.)....Hatfield.	1775.	McKinion, Henry..Ann Arbor,Wis.
347.	Lovegrove, Edward.............	1831.	Matthews, Timothy............
372.	Lee, Wm........Newark, N. J.	1873.[12]	Moody,........East Pittston, Me.
389.	Lathrop, Samuel...Lebanon, N. H.	1871.	Merill..........................
390.	Lathrop, Rufus......Chelsea, Vt.	1873.[32]	Moons, Leonard.......Plainfield,Vt.
405.	Lathrop, Ezra....Bozrah, Conn.	1937.	Merrifield, Rev. Elliot.........
439.	Loomis, Russel...Litchfield, Conn.		..........W. Wardsboro, Vt.
483.	Leonard, Dr......Ashford, Conn.	2373.	Mandeville, Henry D..Catahoula, La
516.	Le Baron, Japhet......Hatly, C. E.	2463.	Miller, John E......Plainfield, Ill.

53

2784.	Miller, Orlando.....Middlebury,Vt.	1475.	Palmer, Cyrus...........Norwich.
2711.	Mix, Geo. H......Danville, Iowa.	1197.	Palmer, Wm...New Hartford, N.Y.
2891.	Miner, Parsons D...Freeman, Wis.	1199.	Proctor, Francis..Bloomfield, Ohio.
2905.	Mahan, Theodore..Marlboro, Mass.	1554.	Peabody, M........Buffalo, N. Y.
2943.	Mozart, D. I........Zenia, Ohio.	1591.	Parkhurst, Lemuel.......Ashford.
2962.	Middleton, Benj...Muscatine, Iowa.	1628.	Parkhurst, Elisha...Enfield, N. H.
3017.	Morrison, Cyrus....Granville, N. Y.	1681.	Pardee, Henry.....Oneonta, N. Y.
2694.	Mason, Norman L............	1685.	Porter, Dr. William...New Haven.
3158.	Magown, Stephen L..Hudson, N Y.	1789.	Philips, Joseph........Ashford.
2661.	McGilvia, Seth......Baraboo, Wis.	1828.	Puranton, Jonathan.Lincoln, N. H.
496.	Niles, Stephen....Cambridge, N.Y.	1852.	Puranton, Elijah.....Lincoln, N: H.
508.	Ezra............Haverhill, N. H.	1854.	Page, Isaiah.......Amesbury, Mass.
596.	Norton, Joseph G...Buffalo, N. Y.	1919.	Pettis, Joseph H...Brooklyn, N. Y.
612.	North, Col. Simeon........Berlin.	2614.	Patton, Gilbert......Columbia.
1223.	Nye, Loren......Pittsford, N.Y.	2620.	Prescott, Andrew J...........
1570.	Newton, Roger W..Durham, Conn.		............Lake Village, N. H.
2787.	Newton, Danford..Alexander, N. Y.	2788.	Putnam, Orrin.....Bethany, N. Y.
111.	Ordway, Moses........Amesbury.	3119.	Perkins, Rev. F. B. Montague, Mass.
550.	Olmsted .....East Hartford, Conn.	3010.	Pickett, Kendrick W............
774.	Otis, Joseph......Norwich, Conn.		............Georgetown, Mass.
913.	Osbourn, Samuel.............	16.App.A. Paddock, Ammiel.Nantucket.
954.	Osgood, Iddo......Keene, N. Y.	1770.	Quinlan, Edmund.Sheboygan, Wis.
1303.	Osgood, Miles....Townshend, Vt.	1781.	Quinlan, Alfred............
1758.	Olmsted, David............	2730.	Quincy, Josiah P...Boston, Mass.
	............East Middlebury,Vt.	248.	Roundy, Samuel......Windham.
2121.	Ogden, Rev. Isaac..Allegany, N.Y.	343.	Robertson, James........Norwich.
2176.	Olney, Professor...........	396.	Rudd, Jonathan......Franklin.
	.......Kalamazoo, Mich.	471.	Rose, Alvan........Geneva, N. Y.
2301.	Osborne, Henry.....New London.	502.	Richardson, Daniel.Lebanon, N. H.
13.	Pratt............Saybrook.	566.	Ripley, Eleazer......Windham.
262.	Porter, Rev. John....Bridgewater.	611.	Russel, Matthew T....Middletown.
309.	Pierce, John........Norwich.	617.	Rosekrants, Benj....Middletown.
350.	Peasely, John....Newtown, N. H.	629.	Robinson, Asa.........Hampton.
352.	Peasely John......Weare, N. H.	637.	Ripley, Capt. Ralph.....Windham.
452.	Phelps, Heman....Syracuse, N. Y.	642.	Ripley, Nathaniel......Windham.
461.	Prentice, John.....Gilead, Conn.	679.	Ratty, Jonah......Killingworth.
476.	Pease, Salmon.........Canaan.	689.	Robbins............
584.	Porter, Asa....Worthington, Mass.	758.	Rockwell, Joseph.......Lebanon
608.	Pier, Thomas..Cooperstown, N. Y.	956.	Rust, Ebenezer........Hancock.
653.	Perkins, Rev. Samuel...Windham.	1006.	Robinson, Stephen ....
773.	Proctor, Nath........Woodbury.		........Attleborough, Mass.
786.	Perkins, Augustus......Norwich.	1050.	Reynolds, Christopher..Mansfield.
787.	Perkins, Augustus......Norwich.	1177.	Robinson, Edward M........
854.	Porter, Epaphras.......Norwich.		........Pulaski, N. Y.
909.	Page..........Berwick, Maine.	1200.	Rood, Willis C........Canaan.
912.	Peasely, Jedediah...........	1215.	Rowley, Wm. C..Rochester, N. Y.
973.	Peck, Asa.......Franklin, Conn.	1253.	Richardson, D. C...........
980.	Parker................	1311.	Richardson, Roswell..Salem, N. H.
990.	Peck, John W....Lebanon, N. H.	1361.	Richards, Peter....New London.
995.	Pierce, John S....Boston, Mass.	1438.	Ritchie, Dr. James..Franklin, Ind.
996.	Pushee, James H...Boston, Mass.	1450.	Rea, John............
1142.	Platt, Frederick E..Oswego, N. Y.	1460.	Ridgeley, Nicholas H........
1143.	Phelps, Jared F....Syracuse, N. Y.		........Springfield, Ill.
1208.	Payne, Seth B.....Mohawk, N. Y.	1694.	Ripley, Hezekiah W....New York.
1227.	Putnam, Gen. Thomas........	1707.	Rice, Edward G...Marlboro, Mass.
	............Roxbury, Vt.	1729.	Root, William......Medina, Ohio.
1262.	Parker, Daniel....Compton, C. E.	1757.	Rudes, Abner C...Coldwater, Mich.
1301.	Powers, Joseph.....Hebron, Wis.	1782.	Rabbitt, George R..Waterloo, N.Y.
1309.	Prentice, Thomas.Waterford, Conn.	1861.	Reade, Eli...South Hampton, Mass.
1381.	Perkins, George......Norwich.	1864.	Reade, Eli...South Hampton, Mass.
1554.	Pierson, Isaac....Fayette, Mo.	2480.	Ripley, James S...Norwich,Conn.

INDEX. 419

2800.	Rose, Delos............New York.	2689.	Skinner, Waldo.....Madison, Wis.
2443.	Richard, Wolcott.Cincinnati, Ohio.	2721.	Staudish, George W....Lebanon.
125.	Sherman, Joshua..Franklin, Conn.	2791.	Sprague, Daniel....Batavia, N. Y.
153.	Storrs, Experience.....Mansfield.	2800.	Sherman, N. P.......New York.
211.	Steele, James..........Tolland.	2937.	Sessions, E. W......Fulton, Iowa.
354.	Lawyer, Micah....Newbury, Mass.	3166.	Seymour, Wm. Lewis...New York.
437.	Stanley, Hon. Timothy...........	2939.	Sleeper, Gilman......Haverhill.
	.............Greensboro,Vt.	20.	Tracy, Dr. Solomon......Norwich.
454.	Silliman, William....East Haddam.	70.	Turner, Capt. Philip....Norwich.
563.	Strong, Joseph, D. D.....Norwich.	127.	Tracy, John.............Norwich.
577.	Strong Asa........Vergennes, Vt.	149.	Tomlinson, Gideon.....Stratford.
633.	Symonds, Jeduthun....Windham.	201.	Trumbull, Walter......Mansfield.
641.	Smith, Miner............Windham.	213.	Throop, Capt. Daniel....Lebanon.
644.	Sherrill, Jacob.New Hartford, N. Y.	215.	Tracy, Dr. Elisha......Norwich.
657.	Silliman, William... East Haddam.	254.	Tracy,................Groton.
683.	Sayre, Daniel.....Canton, N. Y.	259.	Tinker, Capt. Nehemiah.Windham.
813.	Smith, Rev. Henry..Camden, N. Y.	260.	Tinker, Elihu..........Windham.
886.	Snyder, Maurice.................	311.	Turner, Dr. John.......Norwich.
942.	Sleeper, Nathan................	319.	Tracy, William G........Rome.
966.	Spooner, William B..Boston, Mass.	378.	Talcott, Job............Bolton.
1003.	Smith, Rufus....,...Griswold, Conn.	398.	Tracy, Calvin.........Coventry.
1030.	Stark, Lemuel.....Granville, Ohio.	409.	Tracy, Joseph W........Norwich.
1075.	Spencer, Charles....Shaftesbury,Vt.	530.	Tracy, Zebediah.......Windham.
1087.	Steadman, George....Rome, N. Y.	651.	Taylor, Midad..........Windham.
1097.	Steadman, George....Rome, N. Y.	747.	Tryon, William..................
1141.	Swift, James M.......New York.		.........New Hartford, N. Y.
1146.	Swift, James M.......New York.	861.	Tilley, William........Norwich.
1178.	Smith, Charles......Manlius, N. Y.	900.	Trowbridge, Capt. Elias.........
1195.	Sherman, H. V. S......California.		............Oswego, N. Y.
1220.	Spencer, Dr. George E...........	1033.	Thompson, Alba C......Norwich.
	.............Laconia, N. H.	1241.	Tilson, Jarvis.......Braintree, Vt.
1225.	Slade, Thompson...Hanover, N. H.	1369.	Tracy, Col. Elisha......Norwich.
1458.	Smith, Benjamin.....Fayette, Mo.	1453.	Toroole, John........Galena, Ill.
1470.	Squier, Nathaniel......Windham.	1524.	Terry, Franklin K...Albany, N. Y.
1482.	Snow, David...........New York.	1539.	Townley, William.....Albany, Ill.
1507.	Starr, James.......Yarmouth, N. S.	1613.	Townsend, Rice.................
1515.	Skinner, Avery.....Milwaukie, Wis.	1677.	Tracy, Samuel M.St. Anthony, Min.
1548.	Sheldon, R. A....Columbus, Ohio.	1712.	Townsend, Amos.....New Haven.
1552.	Strong, Horace ....Lebanon.	1931.	Tracy, Almond.........Franklin.
1604.	Sprague, Calvin...New Haven, Vt.	2033.	Tucker, Rev. J.................
1619.	Sprague, Esek...New Haven, Vt.		.........North Bennington, Vt.
1673.	Skinner, E. M.....Syracuse, N. Y.	2331.	Taft, Lowell W.........Michigan.
1678.	Sammis, David.....Warsaw, N. Y.	2403.	Thomas, C. C .....Augusta, Ga.
1701.	Sprague, Charles....Spencer, Mass.	3021.	Taber, William......Lincoln, Vt.
1766.	Smith, Dr. Joseph L. Liberty, N. Y.	2559.	Tombes, Henry C.Ashtabula, Ohio.
1776.	Stodder, Shepley...............	2727.	Talcott, Hart...Glastenbury, Conn.
1808.	Sanders, Erastus.....New London.	871.	Utley,............Hudson, N. Y.
1875.	Sargent, Joseph M..............	2024.	Utley, Milton....Westerville, N. Y.
1882.	Sumner, John......Nashua, N. H.	2815.	Upson, Horatio N..Middlebury, Vt.
1998.	Smith, Charles..East Boston, Mass.	1482.	Van Vleck, V......New York City.
2000.	Stevens, J. N......Greensboro, Vt.	1927.	Voorhis, Wm. S.................
2307.	Smedley, Jones......Mexico, N. Y.		.........North Smithfield, Pa.
2309.	Seeley, Lester ......Mexico, N. Y.	41.	Wheelock, Dea. Ralph...Windham.
2336.	Smith, Henry H....Rodman, N. Y.	58.	Wales, Dea, Nath......Windham.
2364.	Sigourney, Wm. A...Adams, N. Y.	77.	Wright, Ebenezer.....Windham.
2440.	Smith, Eli, (D. D.)....Smyrna, Asia.	103.	Whittier, Andrew......Amesbury.
2443.	Strong, Charles H......New York.	146.	Wetmore, Hezekiah..Middletown.
2469.	Strong, Henry, (LL. D.)...Norwich.	165.	Wetmore, Prosper.....New York.
2548.	Sedgebier, Joseph C............	171.	Williams, John ......Norwich.
	..........Painesville, Ohio.	174.	Williams, Samuel......Norwich.
2659.	Stanley, William....Baraboo, Wis.	191.	Worcester, Rev. Noah ...Brighton.

420 INDEX.

231.	Webb, Zebulon........Windsor.	1466.	Whitlock, J. H........Troy, N. Y.
254.	Williams,.............Windsor.	1480.	Wheeler, Stephen..Pomfret, Conn.
294.	Willes, Dea. Joshua......Franklin.	1543.	Wattles, Dr. Wm.Sag Harbor, N.Y.
417.	Waldo, Horatio......Bingham, Vt.	1551.	Wattles, Denison, Esq....Lebanon.
566.	Worcester, David..Thornton, N. H.	1592.	Whiting, Alden B.Providence, R. I.
678.	Wilcox, John..........Branford.	1597.	Weeks,.................Ashford.
729.	Wadhaus, Solomon....Boston, Vt.	1623.	Wheeler, Joseph..New Haven, Vt.
788.	Williams, Cyrus.Stockbridge, Mass.	1637.	Welch, Walter...........Canada.
798.	Williams, Col. William.Utica, N. Y.	1695.	Williams, Henry B.......Lebanon.
801.	Wright, Benjamin H..Rome, N. Y.	1701.	White, Lory......Spencer, Mass.
825.	Whitney, David....Tunbridge, Vt.	1774.	Webster, Peter B..Monticello, N. Y.
828.	Wilson, Rev. James..............	1779.	Wicks, Rufus B..Monticello, N. Y.
	........Sacketts Harbor, N. Y.	2303.	Wilkinson, Lewis...Boston, Mass.
833.	Wainwright, William.Salisbury, Vt.	2425.	Wolcott, Richard, (M. D.)........
899.	Woodward, Samuel B..New Haven.		............Cincinnati, Ohio.
928.²	Wilson........................	2512.	Wright, William A..Boston, Mass.
1040.	Ward, Henry..........Norwich.	2767.	Williams, Foster......Nova Scotia.
1063.	Wright, Dr. Thos..Cincinnati, Ohio.	2770.	Wood,.............Nova Scotia.
1067.	Wadsworth,......Middlebury, Vt.	3018.	Waite, Selden.................
1075.	Whipple, Asa H..Shaftesbury, Vt.	3158.	White, Dr. Geo. H..Hudson, N. Y.
1093.	Wright, Thomas G....Rome, N. Y.	1903.	Washburn, Alonzo...Keene, N. Y.
1135.	White, Ayres...Ogdensburg, N. Y.	1906.	Washburn, Abel....Keene, N. Y.
1183.	West, Charles C...Columbus, N. Y.	1873.²	Woodward......Litchfield, Maine.
1189.	Williams, Isaiah L..............	1873.⁴	Williams...........Boston, Mass.
	....Chittenango, N. Y.	2385.	White, Asher........Hudson, Ind.
1320.	Whitney, John......Mexico, N. Y.	3048.	Waite, Selden......Pontiac, N. Y.
1371.	Wolcott, Hon. Fred....Litchfield.	255.	Youngs, John........Windham.
1398.	Wells, Hezekiah....Delavan, Wis.	775.	Young, Guilford.................
1405.	Williams, Daniel..Tecumseh, Mich.	805.	Young, Charles C.....Rome, N. Y.
1412.	White, Joseph.....Hinsdale, Mass.	819.	Young, Charles C ...Rome, N. Y.
1452.	Walker, Francis..Butternutts, N. Y.	1025.	Yerrington, E. W........Norwich.
1461.	Webster, Bela C......New York.	1682.	Yager, Hiram....Kortwright, N. Y.

V.

INDEX TO THE SURNAMES OF THE WIVES OF THE HUNTINGTONS.

Adgate, 14, 23.
Arnold, 53.
Abel, 325.
Andrus, 338, 464, 1107.
Allen, 472, 667, 1462, 2699.
Avery, 646, 1168.
Armstrong, 639, 1760.
Atwater, 664.
Austin, 955, 1656.
Adams, 154, 1199.
Alling, 2756.
Abbot, 1489, 1530.
Applegate, 1972.
Ackerman, 1740.
Alline, 2764.
Armsworthy, 2647.
Bayley, 2, 1056.
Brewster, 14, 42.
Backus, 15, 198, 217, 380.
Bingham, 28, 123, 252, 465.
Basset, 59.

Buckingham, 75, 89.
Bull, 89, 1336, 2343.
Brown, 97, 157, 435, 570, 1505, **1636**.
Bates, 185.
Barley, 246.
Bliss, 338, 453, 518.
Buxton, 353, 902, 1835.
Bennet, 385, 586, 1924.
Baldwin, 142, 429, 1768, 2034, 20 App. A.
Blakesley, 472.
Burbridge, 473.
Blodget, 499.
Bugbee, 520.
Benjamin, 578.
Bibbins, 624.
Butler, 711.
Burbank, 824, 1260.
Bunker, 904, 11 App.
Badger, 928.
Boynton, 932, 1257.
Babb, 928.³

INDEX. 421

Baker, 974, 1323.
Babcock, 1028, 1268, 1171, 1172,[1] 1173.[1]
Boswell, 1035.
Blydenburg, 1110.
Bridgman, 1213.
Bartlet, 1290, 2986.
Blanchard, 1326.
Brinley, 1333.
Burnham, 1387.
Bradford, 1407.
Bartow, 1419.
Beckwith, 1429.
Bennight, 1449.
Breed, 1829, 2968.
Butler, 23, 28.
Beeson, 1975.
Boardman, 1892.
Bristol, 1515.
Borden, 1584.
Bear, 1666.
Barnard, 1667, 14 App.
Barry, 1675.
Brush, 1698.
Boyd, 1724.
Barnes, 1761.
Brumham, 1799.
Beard, 1835.
Browne, 1865.
Blasdell, 1873.
Buel, 1996.
Brake, 3046.
Bigsby, 2041.
Burrel, 2452.
Brownell, 2627.
Burgess, 2483.
Bailey, 3008.
Bowers, 1 App.
Barker, 1 App.
Bodge, 2981.
Crane, 3.
Clark, 5, 25, 161, 434, 667, 719, 838, 952, 1086, 1324, 1366, 1430, 1718, 1780.
Chapman, 124, 1916.
Carew, 142, 143, 1367.
Cutler, 181.
Case, 272.
Curtiss, 324.
Chester, 334.
Carey, 339.
Clement, 340, 1339.
Colby, 35, 369, 370.
Culver, 381.
Champion, 395.
Champlin, 418.
Catlin, 440.
Cheeney, 465-
Callegan, 472.
Chadwick, 510, 2982.
Coit, 558.
Corning, 599, 1505.
Cheever, 618.
Comstock, 682.
Colburn, 712.
Converse, 727.
Carly, 749.
Chipman, 764.
Cleveland, 826, 1618, 1803.
Cobb, 829, 1920.
Currier, 908.
Cunningham, 928.[4]
Conant, 992.
Chick, 928.[7]
Carson, 1028.
Cole, 1084, 2557.
Cowles, 1156.
Charevoy, 1159.
Crandall, 1173.
Cahill, 1186.
Christian, 1243.
Caer, 1248.
Cherry, 1327.
Colfax, 1366.
Campbell, 1382.
Chanlatte, 1408.
Carter, 1536.
Colley, 1891.
Crow, 1912.
Calef, 1647.
Chamberlain, 1688.
Cox, 1727.
Colbreth, 1769.
Chase, 1878.
Cadmus, 1986.
Cross, 2007.
Chapin, 2061.
Carpenter, 2560.
Childs, 2495.
Conklin, 2789.
Church, 2682.
Clelland, 3157.
Culbert, 12 App.
Cowden, 2630.
Darby, 94, 1983.
Dean, 179.
Davis, 190, 529.
Dimock, 197.
Devotion, 232, 234.
Denison, 257, 274, 1337.
Dana, 275.
Daniels, 312.
Durkee, 321.
Dyer, 329, 1098.
Dogget, 432.
Draper, 453.
Dows, 472.
Day, 480, 518, 1594.
Dresser, 542.
Dow, 587, 1722.
Densman, 718.
Derby, 726.
Drowne, 915.
Downing, 1166.

Downer, 994.
Deblois, 1013.
Denton, 1147.
Dunbar, 1330.
Dolliver, 1409.
Dickson, 1504.
DeKrafft, 1540.
Dearborn, 1918.
Doyle, 1873,19
Dustan, 2603.
Duncan, 2775.
Dill, 2763.
Danks, 2351.
Dake, 2366.
Dodge, 2467.
Deloss, 2802.
Denin, 2313.
Dillingham, 3015.
Ensworth, 12.
Edwards, 44, 1439, 1559.
Edgerton, 95, 133, 292, 554.
Elderkin, 150, 245.
Ellsworth, 229.
Elliot, 268.
Ellis, 975.
Evans, 1332.
Edson, 1610.
Estes, 1841.
Emery, 1862.
Erskine, 2453.
Evans, 2998.
Eddy, 2299.
Frink, 46, 756.
Fuller, 177, 1312, 1661.
Flint, 226.
Fairbanks, 261.
Foote, 289.
Frasier, 339.
Freeman, 425.
Fowler, 448.
Franklin, 478.
Field, 511.
Fitch, 696, 740, 754, 1318, 1436.
Foster, 738, 1352, 2628.
French, 1365.
Forbes, 1459.
Fletcher, 1357, 1506.
Freligh, 1421.
Flanders, 1836.
Fox, 2061.
Gager, 22.
Goodwin, 35, 361.
Gaylord, 42, 1008.
Griswold, 81, 380, 1247.
Gifford, 128.
Gray, 236, 675.
Gates, 261, 1172, 1525, 1526, 1925.
Gilbert, 271.
Gorton, 323.
Gould, 358.
Green, 387, 868, 1207.

Grist, 412.
Galusha, 441, 412, 1083, 1108, 1112, 2058.
Goddard, 442, 1108.
Gustin, 515.
Graham, 604.
Goetschius, 883.
Greenslit, 1007.
Givens, 1151.
Gorden, 1234.
Graves, 1327, 1329.
Gainey, 1410.
Goodenow, 1496.
Gore, 1829, 2972, 1817.
Griffith, 1520.
Gillet, 1525.
Greenough, 1557.
Gildersleeve, 1765.
Grow, 1912.
Gerrish, 1988.
Gibbon, 2805.
Gregg, 2192.
Gladding, 2410.
Hunt, 6.
Hovey, 56, 1250.
Huntington, 86, 89, 92, 179, 182, 233, 245, 318, 513, 555, 559, 588, 634. 658, 821, 1145, 1383, 1839, 1873,17 2441, 2482, 2579, 2969.
Hinckley, 135, 1012.
Hedden, 116.
Heath, 154, 1264, 1265, 2813.
Hartshorn, 199.
Hale, 234.
Hyde, 295, 469, 556, 971, 1081, 1132.
Havens, 313.
Hine, 342.
Hoyt, 367, 916, 925, 971.
Hall, 384, 928,² 1119.
Hunton, 387.
Hough, 394, 410.
Hurd, 438.
Horr, 451.
Hatch, 511, 1312, 1991.
Howard, 545.
Hickox, 586.
Hibbard, 723.
Hendrick, 885.
Horne, 921, 1867.
Hoag, 939.
Henry, 1090, 1091.
Hollister, 1130.
Hoagland, 1182.
Hopkins, 1214.
Holman, 1237.
Howell, 1246.
Hicks, 1261.
Horton, 1286.
Hamilton, 1415.
Hills, 1318.
Hill, 1420.
Harris, 1479, 1496.

INDEX.

Holden, 1448.
Hedding, 1829.
Hazzard, 2929.
Hubbard, 2035, 2040.
Haynes, 2128.
Helmer, 1608.
Hersey, 1633.
Henderson, 2495.
Harbottle, 2356.
Hathron, 2817.
Hayes, 2312.
Hutchinson, App. A., 49.
Isham, 561, 1731.
Ingraham, 1292.
Jones 97, 99, 978, 654, 1133, 1549, 1837.
Johnston, 618, 978, 1854, 1356.
Johnson, 53, 686, 1255, 1567, 1832, 2360.
Jepson, 1842.
Jendivine, 2812.
Janvin, 2987.
Jourdan, 1873.28
Kempton, 318.
Keeney, 334.
Kent, 543.
Kelley, 1020, 1350.
Kinney, 1036, 2437.
Kingsbury, 1134.
Ketts, 1228.
Kinner, 1306.
Keeler, 1316, 1173, 1516.
Kellogg, 1428.
Kidder, 1493.
Kirtland, 1723.
Keyes, 2252.
Lathrop, 16, 42, 43, 91, 173, 179, 214, 392, 542, 604, 1344, 1370.
Leffingwell, 69, 408, 410.
Landphere, 178.
Leonard, 45.
Loomis, 271, 1430.
Lovejoy, 369.
Lord, 397, 460, 1325, 1664.
Lee, 468, 2963.
Ladd, 541.
Leavens, 714.
Livingston, 1090.
Lyon, 1156, 1562.
Lovett, 1216.
Loring, 1166, 1995.
Lyman, 1347.
Lambert, 1837.
Lanman, 1359.
Lindsley, 1356.
Low, 1534.
Lamb, 1541.
Lockhart, 1583.
Lamport, 1916.
Lilly, 1590.
Latham, 1866.
Langworthy, 2122.
Lynde, 264.

Miller, 29, 826, 827, 992, 1298, 1521, 2772, 2773.
Martin, 36, 400.
Morgan, 45, 422, 1005, 1334, 2557.
Mason, 74, 274. App. A, 51.
Metcalf, 80, 85, 285.
Maxfield, 108.
Marsh, 186, 277.
Murdock, 247.
Moore, 306, 557, 569, 1302, 1442.
Maples, 407.
Mosher, 494.
Munroe, 503, 1096.
Maine, 504.
McClellan, 561.
Marsden, 541.
Mumford, 564.
Mills, 579, 1557.
Morse, 593, 1932.
Marvin, 751.
Moulton, 1002.
Maxwell, 875.
McKee, 1091.
McCymon, 1316.
Mitchell, 1355.
Mansfield, 1364.
Markle, 1446.
Minott, 1519.
Macfarlan, 1900, 1902.
Mead, 1603.
Maguire, 3027.
Mattoon, 1659.
Mott, 1668.
Mory, 1788.
Meader, 1849.
McGan, 1872.
McMahon, 1976.
Milliken, 2361.
Meech, 2483.
McGinley, 3174.
Merril, 2996.
Norton, 105.
Newton, 497.
Newell, 536.
Nichols, 724.
Neally, 1051.
Norris, 2472.
Owens, 855.
Osborne, 910.
Olin, 1095.
Oliver, 1121.
Otis, 1728.
Osgood, 1857.
Oakes, 2369.
Pembroke, 97.
Perkins, 70, 300, 301, 314, 386, 394, 2478.
Pitkin, 270.
Preston, 286.
Pride, 321.
Prevost, 339.
Prudden, 400.

INDEX.

Potter, 414.
Putnam, 501.
Parmilee, 511, 1057, 2682.
Palmer, 529, 1803.
Peck, 535.
Phelps, 558, 677, 1140.
Post, 840, 2785, 2816.
Paddock, 867.
Page, 903, 2989.
Philbrick, 934.
Peterson, 935.
Pettee, 953.
Pierce, 997, 1198.
Perritt, 1037, 1370.
Partet, 1137.
Patterson, 1258.
Price, 1285.
Porter, 1350, 2025.
Parkman, 1433.
Paine, 1434.
Pherson, 1441.
Parsons, 1472.
Plumley, 1614.
Parker, 1632 1892, 1616.
Perry, 1897, 2728.
Pringle, 1897.
Paige, 1700.
Parmenter, 1705.
Purinton, 1834.
Peaseley, 1839,
Poore, 1845.
Powell, 2361, 2938, 1594.
Pond, 2461.
Parks, 2493.
Pippitt, 3172.
Paddock, 16, App. A.
Quigley, 386.
Quidor, 1734.
Rockwell, 4, 73.
Reynolds, 52, 1297.
Ripley, 71, 566.
Rudd, 179, 235, 382, 1451.
Ryan, 336.
Rowell, 355.
Reddington, 504.
Richardson, 512, 1252.
Read, 521.
Robinson, 569, 755, 1224, 2809.
Richards, 777, 822.
Randal, 820.
Royce, 839.
Reed, 1036.
Reeves, 1246.
Ridgeway, 1187.
Ross, 1204.
Rodgers, 1272, 1306.
Raymond, 1297.
Rowland, 1319.
Ranney, 1365.
Russell, 1510.
Riggs, 1693.

Rice, 1706.
Rathbone, 2057.
Ramirez, 2253.
Ransom, 2814.
Ruggles, 2552.
Right, App. A., 48.
Swain, 3.
Standish, 61.
Slade, 192, 504, 505.
Steele, 207, 1517.
Selden, 269,
Scott, 407, 2031.
Stark, 408.
Stanley, 435, 1960.
Smith, 456, 495, 567, 568, 839, 3009, 1343, 1658, 1949, 1416, 1502, 1657.
Slade, 504, 505.
Sears, 658.
Stewart, 686.
Swift, 757, 1028, 1777.
Snow, 793, 2437.
Sill, 823.
Storrs, 841.
Stuart, 857.
Stickney, 958.
Sprague, 991.
Spear, 985.
Stevens, 985.
Starkweather, 1053.
Strong, 1099, 1281, 1582, 2471.
Safford, 1176.
Sharp, 1178.?
Sly, 1284.
Stone, 1294.
Sumner, 1334, 1563.
Saltonstall, 1365.
Sims, 1372.
Streit, 1421.
Stevens, 14, 1427, 1759.
Seavey, 1486.
Stetson, 1520.
Silliman, 1525.
Sargent, 1566, 1840.
Storing, 1608.
Saunders, 1679.
Stoddard, 1683.
Simmons, 1730.
Seal, 1738.
Shearer, 1982, 2485.
Sanders, 1992.
Spear, 2479.
Stebbins, 2720.
Sessions, 2937.
Tracy, 50, 214, 314, 551, 632, 762, 968, 1931.
Thurston, 72.
Throop, 266, 1556.
Tomlinson, 299, 1910.
Thomas, 315, 839, 2018, 2037.
Talcott, 384, 665, 1156.
Tuttle, 427, 1319, 1446.

INDEX. 425

Townsend, 449, 1393.
Tooker, 503.
Thatcher, 531.
Trumbull, 557.
Tucker, 692, 1018.
Tyler, 790, 1168.
Thompson, 1052.
Tillson, 1235.
Taylor, 1465.
Terrill, 1537.
Turner, 1538.
Tibbitts, 1767.
Treadway, 1797.
Talmon, 2655.
Utley, 807, 2026.
Upjohn, 503.
Vincent, 744.
VanVechten, 1184.
Vanderhoff, 1195.
Van Deusen, 1755.
Vining, 1837, 1844.
Varney, 1846.
Van Dresar, 3156.
Wolcott, 28, 1371.
Wetmore, 44.
Williams, 46, 217, 556, 640, 1561, 2606.
Wheeler, 45.
Warner, 64, 1624, 1665.
Watrous, 52.
Wright, 129, 226.
Ward, 180, 579, 610, 1467, 2806.

West, 188.
Whitman, 276, App. A., 47.
Wales, 318.
Watermah, 321.
Weed, 345.
Wait, 439, 784, 1299.
Wells, 541, 658.
Walker, 654, 1424, 2684.
Weller, 655.
Waring, 859.
Wilson, 928.³
Wilkins, 938.
Webb, 964, 1196.
White, 905, 1431, 1717.
Welch, 226, 1034.
Whiton, 1159.
Willard, 1159.
Worthington, 1167.
Witter, 1307.
Winter, 1310.
Watkinson, 1333, 1373.
Waterman, 1423.
Wissell, 1899.
Willey, 1606.
Wadsworth, 1721.
Whipple, 1952.
Wade, 2487.
Willis, 2494.
Wood, 2206.
Wanton, 6, App.
Yogun, 1401.

VI.

A LIST OF THE HUNTINGTONS, WHOSE LETTERS TO THE AUTHOR HAVE AIDED IN ARRANGING THIS GENEALOGICAL MEMOIR.

Abel, (Hon.).........468
Asa, (Hon.)..........504
Andrew, (Rev.).......764
Asenath..............977
Azariah.............1007
Asahel, (Esq.)......1013
Asa C...............1086
Alonzo..............1095
Andrew..............1160
Adoniram J., (Rev.).1243
Ambrose W...........1316
Apollos.............1319
Aurelia M...........2403
Ann Eliza...........2514
Abraham A...........2806
Benjamin............ 495
Betsey.............. 692
Benjamin N.,(Hon.).. 807
Benjamin............1037
Bethia T............1560
Backus W., (Esq.)...1693

Benjamin S., (Rev.)....1738
Caroline M............1029
Cornelia..............1180
Christopher...........1235
Collins H.............1421
Charles T.............1717
Cyrus, (Rev.).........1724
Carlos T..............1920
Charles O.............1928
Charles R.............2035
Charles G.............2321
Charles P.............1557
Colbert...............1434
Charles A.............1423
Charles...............1603
Charles T.............1717
Charles...............1910
Charles E.............1983
Charles B.............2650
Charles P.............3186
Charles W.............2299

Charles F.............2452
Clara A...............3024
Daniel, (Dea.)........ 460
Dan, (Rev.)........... 677
D. Grace..............2842
Dwight................1053
DeWitt C..............1302
Daniel, (Rev.)........1365
David I...............1688
David.................1857
Elijah................ 408
Ebenezer, (Hon.)...... 535
Eliphalet............. 667
Edward, (Hon.)........ 820
Edwin N............... 997
Elisha, (M. D.).......1012
Elizabeth.............1117
Enoch S., (Rev.)......1156
Ezra A., (D. D.)......1184
Erastus...............1195
Edwin.................1285

54

INDEX.

Ebenezer H........1297	Israel........... 740	Marshall...........1248
Elisha........1318	Isaac L........1889	Mary A...........1344
Edward A........1347	Jared........ 453	Marvin...........1496
Elipalet, (M. D.)........1386	Jedediah........ 784	Marietta...........1695
Eugene........2579	James........ 841	Moses B...........1902
Edward G........1430	Joseph........ 953	Mirza L...........2548
Elisha M., (Hon.)........1451	John C........ 955	Mary A...........2633
Enoch, (Rev.)........1465	Jabob P., (Rev.)........ 985	Maria W...........2745
Elizabeth........1473	Julian........ 995	Nathan...........1080
Emily........1482	Joshua H........1026	Nathan B...........1159
Edwin W........1530	Julia........1074	Nancy...........1507
Eunice........1639	Jacob G........1695	Oren...........1700
Edwin T........1721	Jane........1100	Pelatiah W...........1975
Ephraim M........1843	Jonas, (Dr.)........1108	Randolph G. H...........1312
Edward B........2441	Justinian........1173	Rufus...........1387
Elijah B........2968	John........ 119	Ralph...........1407
Enoch........1836	James........1260	Rollin...........1727
Edwards C........1916	John L........1325	Rodney S...........1891
Eliza........1991	James........1393	Randolph...........2312
Elijah B........2968	James........1427	Richard...........2647
Felix A........ 793	Julian C........1433	Sarah M...........1194
Fanny........ 990	James, (Hon.)........1448	Stephen N...........1213
Francis J........1336	Jonathan E........1567	Seth...........1251
Fred. D., (D. D.)........1566	Joseph C........1624	Samuel H...........1383
Francis C........1953	Jane E........1692	Simon...........1428
Frances S........2512	Jabez........1705	Samuel...........1424
Gideon........ 518	John G........1731	Samuel P., (Rev.)...........1519
Gurdon, (Rev.)........ 823	Julia Anna........1737	Samuel...........1572
George, (Hon.)........1051	John F........1740	Solon...........1679
George........1983	John........1849	Simeon F...........1698
George L., (M. D.)........1182	John........1892	Sylvester T...........1667
George C........1350	James F........1952	Thomas........... 513
Gurdon........1404	John W. P........1972	Talitha........ 972
George L........1459	Jedidiah V........ 821	Thomas...........1261
George........1493	John D........2351	Thomas, (Rev.)...........1366
Gurdon W........1502	Jedidiah........2437	Thomas P...........1805
George H........1718	Joshua, (M. D.)........2444	T. Romeyn, (M. D.)...........2061
George........2030	James M........2483	Thomas B...........2810
George W., (M. D.)........2495	John M........2493	William........... 726
George H........2619	Julia........2503	William D...........1036
George M........2672	James........2553	William O...........1121
Henry S., (Rev.)........ 813	Jedediah........2929	William A...........1272
Hannah A........1016	John L........3008	Wales M., (M. D.)...........1214
Harlow........1081	Joseph W. N........3172	William C...........1442
Horace F........1196	John T., (Rev.)........2606	Wallace...........1467
Henry S........1216	Kimball C........2565	Walt T...........1536
Heman........1257	Louisa........ 752	William S...........1713
Horatio........1286	Lucia........ 986	William W...........1723
Henry D........1354	Lucretia........1301	William P...........1755
Harriet........1537	Lynde A........1534	William, (Dr.)...........1767
Hannah........1628	Lucy Ann........1546	William S...........1918
Henry L........1780	Lucia M........1534	William H...........1960
Harriet F........1798	Lynde C........2037	William T...........2409
Henry........1912	Louis C. L........2401	William S...........2684
Henry A........1950	Loyal........2802	Warren W...........2812
Henry, (M. D.)........2003	Marvin........1052	Zerviah T........... 790
Harriet........2459	Mary S........1189	Ziba........... 991
Henry S........3167		

INDEX.

The following list embraces those of other names than Huntington, whose correspondence has aided in this work. The number appended to the most of the names will show the member of the family with whom they are connected by descent or marriage.

Name	No.	Name	No.	Name	No.
Andrus, Sena	997	Gilman, W. C.	220	Potter, Rev. D. F.	
Bancroft, Geo.		Gray, Judge Thomas		Rea, J. H.	1450
Bushnell, Rev. Horace		Goodwin, David	1855	Rice, Julia R.	642
Buckingham, Hon. J. T.	259	Grenelle, Wm. H.	3161	Rockwell, Prof. E. F.	758
Buckingham, Rev. J. A.	259	Gay, A. W.	1737	Rockwell, Andrew H.	758
Bartlett, Amanda	1615	Hulbert, S. G.	1464	Rockwell, Emily	758
Burley, A. H.	809	Hulbert, G. H.	1464	Robinson, A. C.	1006
Beecher, Geo. H.	901	Hendrix, Henry	1621	Russel, Wm. H.	611
Bradbury, Ann T.	1538	Hooker, E. W., (D. D.)	2438	Russel, Julia A.	611
Balis, H. A.	1016	Hoyt, Rev. Otto S.	418	Ritchie, Jas., (M. D.)	1436
Brewster, Hon. D. P.	1017	Hoadley, C. J.		Richards, Rev. Geo.	1361
Brown, Geo. H.	1512	Harvey, Asahel	263	Ross, James W.	1234
Bidwell, Horace	963	Jackson, John P.	1371	Silliman, Joseph	657
Bishop, N. P.	1094	Jackson, Mrs. E. W.	1371	Savage, James	
Brewster, Rev. Cyrus		Jones, J. H., (D. D.)	591	Sigourney, Mrs. Lydia H.	
Clark, J. T., Esq.		Jones, Joel, (Hon.)	591	Silsbee, Capt. B. H.	2509
Cothren, Wm.		Judd, Sylvester		Stevens, J. N.	2000
Caulkins, Miss F. M.		Jones, Wm. P.	1692	Stoughton, Wm.	
Chapman, Rev. F. W.		Kilbourn, P. K.		Stahl, Daniel	1540
Coffin, Wm. W.	1794	Knapp, Cornelius	1539	Starr, Geo. H.	1507
Chapman, John	877	Leonard, Rev. R. C.		Starr, Anne L.	1507
Clark, Mrs. M. B.	897	Leonard, N. T., Esq.	1522	Tracy, Wm., (LL. D.)	319
Clapp, A. H.	1411	Leffingwell, Frances		Tracy, John	127
Clark, Judge Edwards	653	Marble, Henry	967	Tracy, John	530
Carter, Wm. C.	1399	McEwen, Abel, (D. D.)		Thompson, Mrs. G. W.	897
Collins, Rev. Chas. J.	662	Noyes, Wm. C.	319	Van Buren, Martin	
Cook, Susan K.	1335	North, Pres. Simeon	612	Walworth, Reuben H.	
Crawford, Robert	589	Norton, Chas. D., Esq.	596	Whitlock, J. H.	1466
Burnham, Eleazer	430	Perkins, Samuel H.	653	Woodward, Dr. Ashbel	
Barton	1070	Pearson, Prof. Jonathan		Wentworth, N. S.	969
Dwight, Wm. T., (D. D.)		Porter, Geo, E.	854	White, Joseph	1412
Dickenson, A. H.	1338	Post, J. M.	901	Wolcott, J. Huntington	1371
Danielson, A. G.	1445	Pease, Thomas H.	476	Whitney, F. H.	1320
Edwards, Tryon, (D. D.)		Pease, Fred. S.	476	Waldo, Rev. Daniel	
Freeman, Asa	184	Patterson, D. W.		Williams, Judge Thos. S.	
Gilman, D. C.	220				

CORRECTIONS AND ADDITIONS.

The inability of the author to read proof without delaying too much the printing of this Memoir, will explain several typographical errors in it; and his hearty thanks are due, both to the extra care of the printer and to the faithful proof reading of his eldest daughter, Julia, (No. 1966), that no more such errors have occurred. The following list contains, mainly, those errors which affect the sense of the text.

Page 9, line 19, for "their," read other.
Page 55, line 10, for "thicken," read thicker.
Page 64, No. 3, line 5, for "1651," read 1657.
Page 86, No. 86, line 2, for "204," read 213.
Page 110, No. 229. Add to the record the following two names, Elizabeth, born May 14, 1767, and Sylvester, born Aug. 2, 1771, and died in 1862. Elizabeth married in 1786, Daniel L. Coit, of Norwich, and died March 8, 1846. She had the following children: Daniel W., Lydia, who married J. L. Kingsley, Henry H., Maria, who married Pelatiah Perit, of New York, Eliza, who married William C. Gilman, of New York, and Joshua.
Page 149, No. 430. This record is unintelligibly punctuated. The children of Lucy are: Eleazer, Rebecca, Julia Ann, Polly, Asa N., Lucy, Sophia, Adeline, and Charlotte Maria. They should have been preceded by the semi-colon.
Page 174, No. 611. This record is unintelligibly punctuated. The children of Mary are: Mary H., Harriet, Julia A., Charles, William H., Abigail T., Frances H., and Sarah E.; and they should be preceded by the semi-colon.
Page 193, No. 784, for "Jedidiah," read Jedediah.
Page 195, No. 813. Add to this record: He married at Caldwell, New York, June 30, 1859, Geneva, youngest daughter of David and Eliza Crosby, of New York. The daughter, Hannah, married, Nov. 10, 1858, and has one child, Henry Huntington.
Page 206, line 19, for "351," read 561.
Page 211, No. 996, for "Parker," read Pushee.
Page 219, No. 1055, for "Jones," read Janes.
Page 233, No. 1248, for "Case," read Caer.
Page 242, No. 1356. Add: She died in January, 1863.
Page 242, line 13, for "457" read 557.
Page 247, No. 1371, line 1, for Ferdinand read Frederic.
Page 260, No. 1466, line 1, for "Sayr," read Sage.
Page 261, No. 1486, line 2, for "Leavey," read Seavey.
Page 270, line 5, for "deacon, priest and minister," read deacon and priest.
Page 286, No. 1803, line 2, for "1854," read 1855.
Page 298, No. 1953, line 1, for June, read Jan.
Page 283, No. 1741, for "in May," read at Lake George, April 21, 1861.
Page 316, No. 2353, for "Addison, lawyer," read Addison Lawyer.
Page 318, No. 2398, for "still lives single," read has recently married.
Page 327, No. 2483, line 4, for "Dr. Morey," read Capt. Nathan.
Page 349, for No. "1773, Charles C., read 1799, Charles E.
Page 363, line 16, for "2569," read 2566.
Page 364, line 2, for "2747," read 2647; line 9, for "2632," read 2682; and in line 14, for "2664," read 2684.
Page 365, line 9, for "2831," read 2838.
Page 362, for "3195" and "Joseph Lawson and 3196, Weatherly," read 3196 Joseph Lawson Weatherly.

NOTE.—The Author is under obligations to the Rev. Frederic A. Starr for permission to use the excellent plate from which our engravings for No. 1184 were printed. He is also indebted for a similar favor to the American Tract Society, New York City, for the engravings which accompany No. 2240.

For any detected omission to make due acknowledgements for any assistance given the Author in the progress of this work, he trusts the fault will be laid not to his lack of grateful appreciation, but to the multitude and pressure of his engagements.

www.ingramcontent.com/pod-product-compliance
Lightning Source LLC
Chambersburg PA
CBHW022136300426
44115CB00006B/206